ISRAEL AND THE BOMB

ISRAEL AND THE BOMB

Avner Cohen

Columbia University Press

NEW YORK

Columbia University Press

Publishers Since 1893

New York   Chichester, West Sussex

Copyright © 1998 Columbia University Press

All rights reserved

Library of Congress Cataloging-in-Publication Data

Cohen, Avner, 1951–

  Israel and the bomb / Avner Cohen.

    p.   cm.

  Includes bibliographical references and index.

  ISBN 0–231–10482–0 — ISBN 0-231–10483–9 (pbk.)

  1. Israel—Military policy. 2. Nuclear weapons—Israel.
I. Title.

  UA853.I8C62   1998

  355.02'17'095694—dc21   98–3402

Casebound editions of Columbia University Press books
are printed on permanent and durable acid-free paper.

Printed in the United States of America

c 10 9 8 7 6 5 4 3 2

p 10 9 8 7 6 5 4 3 2 1

In memory of my father, Tuvia Cohen,
whose concern has become my own

Contents

Preface

The seeds of this study were planted about a decade ago in a long theoretical article I wrote with Benjamin Frankel. In that article we elaborated on the term "nuclear opacity" as an explanatory ideal-type concept to account for the conduct of second-generation nuclear proliferators.[1] By "nuclear opacity" we meant a situation in which the existence of a state's nuclear weapons has not been acknowledged by the state's leaders, but in which the evidence for the weapons' existence is strong enough to influence other nations' perceptions and actions. We argued that the term "nuclear opacity" captured more accurately the political reality of second-generation nuclear proliferators than other terms, such as "nuclear ambiguity," "covert proliferation," or "latent proliferation," then in use to describe the phenomenon.

In 1989 I was awarded a Research and Writing Grant from the John D. and Catherine T. MacArthur Foundation, entitled "Israel's Invisible Bomb: Culture, Politics, and the Non-Proliferation Norm," to study domestic (that is, political, social, and cultural) dimensions, as well as regional and global policy aspects, of Israel's nuclear opacity. My initial research design did not provide a historical background, since I did not believe then that the pertinent documents would be available.

I joined the Center of International Studies at MIT as a visiting scholar in May 1990 and was preparing to begin the research when my plans changed as a result of the Iraqi invasion of Kuwait, the ensuing crisis and Gulf War, the establishment of the UN Special Commission on Iraq, and the renewed Middle East peace process. These developments, because of their bearing on the nuclear question in the Middle East, changed the direction of my research. In 1991–92, while I codirected the MIT Project on Arms Control in the Middle East, I wrote and published numerous policy-oriented working papers and op-ed articles. I also began to write a book, with Marvin Miller of MIT, on nuclear weapons proliferation in the Middle East.

By 1992–93 I came to two realizations about my research. First, I became convinced of the importance of understanding the evolution of Israel's nuclear opacity. I concluded that Israel's nuclear past was not only fascinating for historians, but that it also constrained the possibility of future arms control in the Middle East in ways that are not often appreciated by analysts and policy makers. Second, I discovered that archival material was becoming available to reconstruct the political history of Israel's nuclear weapons program.

These realizations changed the project's focus and methodology. It became primarily historical, focusing on the origins and evolution of Israel's nuclear opacity. The method is historical reconstruction and interpretation. The materials are mainly primary sources: declassified archival materials, oral testimonies, memoirs, and press clippings. Much of the archival material I discovered in Israel, the United States, and Norway is presented here for the first time.

On the Israeli side, the Israel State Archives (ISA) in Jerusalem, in accord with its thirty-year declassification policy, has opened almost all the Foreign Ministry's documents (cataloged under Foreign Ministry Record Groups, or FMRG) for the period before 1966. There I also discovered most of the correspondence on nuclear issues between President John F. Kennedy and Israeli Prime Ministers David Ben Gurion and Levi Eshkol.

Other Israeli archives were also useful. Many of Ben Gurion's personal diaries and letters have been declassified and are now available at the David Ben Gurion Archive (DBGA) at the Ben Gurion Research Center at Sdeh Boker. In the Weizmann Institute's archives in Rehovot I found documents on the birth of the nuclear physics department at the Institute and the break, in the early 1950s, of several Israeli nuclear physicists with the Ministry of Defense. In the nearby Yad Chaim Weizmann Archive I found documents referring to Ben Gurion's scientific adviser and the founder of the Israel Atomic Energy Commission (IAEC), Ernst David Bergmann.

The remaining portion of this research was conducted in the United States, since Israel's nuclear opacity was a result of a symbiotic American-Israeli effort to respond to their respective concerns about nuclear weapons and proliferation. In the last few years most of the American documents relevant to the evolution of Israel's nuclear opacity have been declassified, covering the period until 1970. Until then most of the relevant archival material was either sanitized or unavailable. In 1992 Virginia Foran of the Carnegie Endowment for

International Peace and I submitted a series of Freedom of Information Act (FOIA) requests for the correspondence between Kennedy and Ben Gurion, and between Kennedy and Eshkol. By November 1995 we had received most of the requested documents. Now much of that correspondence is declassified and presented here for the first time.

Since March 1994 the Lyndon B. Johnson Library (LBJL) in Austin, Texas, has kept me informed on newly declassified material. In 1995 I obtained declassified documents regarding the Eisenhower administration's reaction to Dimona from the Dwight D. Eisenhower Library (DDEL) in Abilene, Kansas. During my visits in 1996–97 to the United States National Archives (USNA) in College Park, Maryland, I found new information about the American visits to Dimona in the 1960s.

In addition to accessing recently declassified documents, I trace Israel's nuclear history through an interpretation of veiled references to the nuclear projects contained in published materials. Thus Munya Mardor's little-known book, *RAFAEL*, published in Hebrew by the Ministry of Defense, contains authoritative testimony on how Israel moved toward what he calls "the age of the Big Projects." Much of Mardor's story can be read as a firsthand account of the early history of Israel's nuclear program.[2]

Over the years Shimon Peres has written and spoken much, if only elliptically, about his role in Israel's nuclear project. In his 1995 memoirs Peres discusses the subject more openly, elaborating on his role as the project's chief executive ("it became my responsibility to decide what could be done and what could not"). His account is self-serving and selective, but it provides an eyewitness account of the man who ran the project in its formative period.

Without access to the files of the Israeli Atomic Energy Commission (IAEC), Ministry of Defense, the Prime Minister's papers on nuclear issues, the minutes of cabinet meetings, and the like, critical evidence on the Israeli decision-making process is still missing.[3] This is a serious limitation on this study. I tried to compensate by conducting more than 150 interviews with key individuals in Israel, the United States, and France. Several of these interviews were quite extensive; spanning the course of several days.

These interviews yielded important results, but I am aware of the limitations of oral histories. Human memory is fragile and selective, especially when speaking of events that took place three or four decades ago. Individuals may vividly recall an episode in which they were involved but forget much of the context in which the episode was embedded. Dates, numbers, and names were frequently forgotten or confused. These problems, common to oral histories, were accentuated in the case of recalling details related to Israel's nuclear program. Secrecy and compartmentalization hindered memories even more. Recognizing the limits of oral history, I treated the interviews as supplementary evidence on matters for which I had independent documentation. One exception, however, were the interviews with the leaders of the American Atomic Energy Commission (AEC) teams, who visited the Dimona reactor in the 1960s. I used their recollections as the primary source of information about the visits.

Much of the information obtained in these interviews was not used in this study but did enrich my own understanding of the period under investigation. Talking with these individuals, most of them in their seventies and eighties, and listening to their stories, were among the most gratifying aspects of this enterprise.

Some of the interviewees insisted that all or portions of their interviews be off the record. Others insisted on anonymity, allowing me to use their words without attribution. I have honored these requests.

Washington, D.C.
April 1998

ACKNOWLEDGMENTS

An eight-year research and writing project could not have been brought to a successful conclusion without the generous support, encouragement, and care of many individuals and institutions. It is a pleasure to express my thanks to them.

The nature of my research, and the scarcity of archival material on key aspects, forced me to rely on the memories and recollections of many of the participants. Throughout 1992–97 I interviewed more than 150 individuals. Most agreed to be acknowledged, but some asked to remain anonymous. I am deeply indebted to all of them. They gave me much of their time, often hosting me in their homes. Without their help this book would have been poorer.

Some deserve special thanks. First and foremost among them is Marvin Miller. Marvin brought me to the Defense and Arms Control Studies program at MIT and was a close collaborator and friend during my five years there. Few equal Marvin's endearing combination of knowledge, wisdom, and humor. I have benefited from all three. Marvin constantly reminded me of the merits of this project, followed my research closely, read almost every draft, corrected substantive and stylistic errors, and always stood by me. This book is as much his as it is mine.

There were others who helped beyond the call of duty. These people, many of whom played a significant role in the making of the history of which I write, generously gave me of their time and attention, reading and rereading many drafts and versions of this work as it evolved. They provided me with insightful and sage advice, on matters ranging from substantive historical commentary to copyediting. Among these people—I am honored to consider them friends—are, on the Israeli side, Arnan (Sini) Azaryahu, Uri Haber-Schaim, Avraham Hermoni, Zvi Lipkin, Yuval Ne'eman, and Uri Rechav; on the American side, George Bunn, Floyd Culler, John Hadden, Spurgeon Keeny, James Leonard, and Paul Warnke.

Others who were exceedingly helpful in commenting on different versions of this work are: Granville Austin, Aluf Benn, Tom Blanton, the late McGeorge Bundy, William Crawford, Hermann Eilts, Myer (Mike) Feldman, Andrei Finkelstein, David Fischer, Virginia Foran, Karen Gold, Culver Glysteen, Victor Gilinsky, Richard Helms, David Holloway, Carl Kaysen, Steven Lee, Peter Lavoy, Robert Komer, Myron Kratzer, Paul Leventhal, Andrea Livingston, Avishai Margalit, Olav Njólstad, Richard Parker, William Quandt, George Rathjens, Jack Ruina, Ben Sanders, Leonard Spector, Michael Sterner, Brad Thayer, Mark Trachtenberg, Michael Wheeler, Jim Walsh, and Idith Zertal.

For my research I received generous financial support from many institutions. Special thanks are owed to the W. Alton Jones Foundation, and particularly to George Perkovich, the Foundation's Secure World Program director, for their faith in this project. The project came into being as a result of a research and writing grant from the John D. and Catherine T. MacArthur Foundation. Other foundations supported the project during its MIT phase (1991–95): The Carnegie Corporation of New York, the Ploughshares Fund, the Prospect Hill Foundation, the Merck Fund, the Rockefeller Brothers Fund, the Rockefeller Foundation, and the Winston Foundation.

During the last few months of preparing and editing the manuscript for print, I was a Jennings Randolph Senior Fellow at the United States Institute of Peace in Washington, D.C. I am grateful to the program director, Joseph Klaits, and program officer Sally Blair, for allowing me the time to complete the project and for their gentle and wise encouragement.

I spent many lonely days in pursuit of documents in the United States and Israel in the following institutions: the Dwight D. Eisenhower Library in Abilene, Kansas; the John F. Kennedy Library in Dorchester, Massachusetts; the Lyndon B. Johnson Library in Austin, Texas; the United States National Archives (site II) in College Park, Maryland; the National Security Archives at George Washington University, Washington, D.C.; the David Ben Gurion Archive in Sdeh Boker; Israel State Archives in Jerusalem; the Yad Chaim Weizmann Archive in Rehovot; the Weizmann Institute Archives; and Yad Tabenkin Archive in Efal. I have benefited from the assistance of the knowledgeable and professional staffs of these institutions. A few archivists went far beyond the call of duty: Suzanne Forbes of the John F. Kennedy Library, John Wilson, the Lyndon B. Johnson Library foreign policy archivist; Yehosua

Fruendlich of the Israel State Archives; and Nili Gat of the Weizmann Institute Archives. I especially thank Harriet Schwar, chief of the Middle East and Africa Division in the State Department's Office of the Historian, for her care in tutoring me in using and finding materials in the U.S. National Archives.

Several individuals made their personal archives available to me. I am especially grateful to the Norwegian foreign correspondent and author Odd Karsten Tveit for giving me access to his impressive archival collection. Tveit's assistance was especially important for my discussion of Norwegian-Israeli relations in the nuclear domain. Ya'acov Sharett allowed me to consult the complete handwritten diaries of his father, Moshe Sharett. Uri Haber-Schaim invested time and effort to search his files for documents from the early 1950s which probably do not have copies anywhere else.

No one could have tackled the original manuscript—much too long, at times cumbersome, often repetitive—other than my friend of many years, Ben Frankel. I know no one with comparable knowledge of Israeli politics, culture, and history, nuclear proliferation issues, and a deeper love and respect for the English language. This combination made him the most qualified editor for this book. I also know, and appreciate, that no editor would have given me the time and patience Ben did so graciously.

I am thankful to the staff at Columbia University Press for their generous help in bringing this manuscript to publication. I especially want to thank the Press's editor-in-chief, Kate Wittenberg, for her critical editorial suggestions. Additional thanks go to the copy editor, Rita Bernhard, for her attentive and meticulous work.

I wish to acknowledge the help of my literary agent, David Hendin, who stepped in to provide professional and unselfish support for the project.

My friend Karen Gold knows how much I owe her; her love, support, and encouragement were invaluable.

Finally, a word of wholehearted thanks to my research assistant at the United States Institute of Peace (USIP), Joseph Kupsky, who untiringly gave hours of meticulous attention and care to correct the many flaws and imperfections in the manuscript. Joe also compiled the bibliography and index.

ABBREVIATIONS

ENGLISH LANGUAGE ACRONYMS

ACDA	United States Arms Control and Disarmament Agency
ACRS	Arms Control and Regional Security
AEC	Atomic Energy Commission
AEE	Egypt's Atomic Energy Establishment
CD	Conference on Disarmament
CIA/CS	Clandestine Service of the Central Intelligence Agency
CIA/OSI	Office of Scientific Intelligence at the Central Intelligence Agency
CIA/PIC	Photographic Intelligence Center of the Central Intelligence Agency
DCI	Director of Central Intelligence
FMCT	Fissile Material Cut-off Treaty
IAEA	International Atomic Energy Agency
IAEC	Israel Atomic Energy Commission
IAF	Israeli Air Force
IDF	Israel Defense Forces (*Tzva Haganah Le'Israel*)
IL	Israeli Lira
INFCIRC	IAEA Information Circular
JAEIC	Joint Atomic Energy Intelligence Committee
LANL	Los Alamos National Laboratory
LLNL	Lawrence Livermore National Laboratory
MLF	Multilateral Nuclear Forces
NATO	North Atlantic Treaty Organization
NIE	National Intelligence Estimate
NPT	Nuclear Non-Proliferation Treaty
NRP	National Religious Party of Israel
NSAM	National Security Action Memorandum
NSC	National Security Council
NWFZ	Nuclear-Weapon-Free Zone
NWS	Nuclear-Weapon State
ORNL	Oak Ridge National Laboratory

PTBT	Partial Test Ban Treaty
PWR	Pressurized Water Reactor
SNIE	Special National Intelligence Estimate
SSM	Surface-to-Surface Missile
UAR	United Arab Republic (the name of the short-lived federation between Egypt and Syria [1958–61]. After the breakup of the federation, Egypt retained the name UAR, now used interchangably with "Egypt")
UNEF	United Nations Emergency Forces
USIB	United States Intelligence Board

Foreign Language Acronyms

AMAN	Agaf Modi'in (Israeli Military Intelligence)
CEA	Commissariat a l'Energie Atomique (French Atomic Energy Commission)
EMET	Agaf Mechkar Ve'Tichun (Research and Planning Division, a division of the Ministry of Defense)
ETH	Eidgenosse Technische Hochschule (Federal Technical University, Switzerland)
HEMED	Ha'il Mada (Science Corps, a department of the IDF)
KAMAG	Kirya Le'Mechkar Gariini (Israeli nuclear research center at Dimona)
MAPAI	Mifleget Poalei Eretz Israel (Israel Workers' Party)
MAPAM	Mifleget Ha'poalim Ha'Meuchedet (United Workers Party)
PALMACH	Plugut Machatz (Assault Units)
RAFAEL	Rashut Le'Pituach Emtzaei Lechima (Armaments Development Authority)
RAFI	Reshimat Poalei Israel (Israel Workers' List)
SIECC	Société Industrielle d'Etudes et de Constructions Chimiques

ISRAEL AND THE BOMB

Introduction

Since about 1970 it has been commonly assumed that Israel has been a nuclear-weapon state. The Israeli nuclear program, however, has remained opaque—shrouded in secrecy, officially unacknowledged, and insulated from domestic Israeli politics. How did Israel's nuclear opacity evolve? What made it possible?

Israel began its nuclear program in earnest about four decades ago, when it constructed the core of its nuclear infrastructure in Dimona. In 1966–67 Israel completed the development stage of its first nuclear weapon, and on the eve of the Six-Day War it already had a rudimentary, but operational, nuclear weapons capability.[1] By 1970 Israel's status as a nuclear-weapon state became an accepted convention.[2]

Israel was the sixth nation in the world and the first in the Middle East to acquire nuclear weapons. Its nuclear behavior, however, has been distinct from that of the first five states. To this day, Israel has not acknowledged possessing nuclear weapons. Israel's nuclear weapons development notwithstanding, Prime Minister Levi Eshkol announced more than three decades ago that Israel would not be the first nation to introduce nuclear weapons into the Middle East, and the six Israeli prime ministers who followed him have adhered to this declaratory policy. Israel's nuclear posture has remained opaque.

It is important to distinguish between opaque and ambiguous nuclear postures. In an article Benjamin Frankel and I wrote in 1988 we characterize the difference:[3]

"Ambiguity" is probably still the most often used term in reference to proliferator states. It has been invoked to refer to almost any kind of suspect proliferation behavior. The trouble is that the term itself is ambiguous. The dic-
tionary provides two definitions for the word: one, "doubtful or uncertain";
the other, "capable of being understood in two or more possible senses." The
term may thus be used in the nuclear proliferation context to denote two distinct situations of ambiguity, which may or may not overlap.

In the former there is a genuine uncertainty, that is, lack of sufficient
knowledge as to the technical nuclear status of the country under study. In
this case, ambiguity is the result of a lack of clarity as to the degree of [tech-
nical advancement] of the nuclear program in question. Argentina and Brazil
can be said to be such ambiguous nuclear states.

The other sense of nuclear ambiguity refers to an ambivalence—political,
military or even cultural in origin—on the part of the suspect country's leadership concerning nuclear weapons. Such ambivalence can be found even
among states with undisputed weaponized nuclear programs.[4]

Israel is an ideal type of nuclear opacity. Nuclear opacity has been Israel's
way of coping with the tensions and problems attending the possession of
nuclear weapons. It has also been Israel's contribution to the nuclear age (in
addition to pioneering certain weapon designs). Nuclear opacity is a situation
in which a state's nuclear capability has not been acknowledged, but is recognized in a way that influences other nations' perceptions and actions, encom-
passing the second sense of nuclear ambiguity.

This book is a political history of Israel's nuclear program in its formative
years, documenting the origins and evolution of Israel's policy of nuclear
opacity. It focuses on a two-decade period, from about 1950 until 1970, during which David Ben Gurion's vision of Israel as a nuclear-weapon state was
realized.

There is, however, an appearance of paradox in writing a history of Israel's
nuclear program: How can one write a history whose central characteristic is
opacity? Can opacity be studied?

Some who were involved in the events discussed in the book have suggested
that writing the history of Israel's nuclear program was, for the time being, an
"impossible task." The archives of the Israel Atomic Energy Commission
(IAEC), for example, are still sealed and are likely to remain so for many years.
Without the IAEC archival material it is impossible to write a comprehensive
history of Israel's nuclear project. Recognizing that much of the technological
and organizational sources were unavailable, I have chosen to focus on the
political dimensions.[5] This study is thus primarily an effort to reconstruct the
domestic and international politics, and understand the culture, which gave rise

to Israel's posture of nuclear opacity. Within the limits of the available material and considerations of national security, it is possible to reconstruct the political history of Israel's nuclear quest.[6]

Over the last three decades, Israel's nuclear opacity has evolved into a national security strategy. It is considered by most Israelis to have been a successful policy, consonant with the complexity of Israel's security situation. Nuclear opacity, however, has not been the product of a well-thought-out strategy. It grew in fits and starts in response to emerging needs and shifting pressures on different levels. Like much else in Israeli history, opacity is a product of a series of improvisations. It evolved in four stages from the mid-1950s to 1970: secrecy, denial, ambiguity, and opacity; and it had four sources: domestic, international, regional, and conceptual-technical.

The domestic sources of opacity are found in the dispositions of individuals, elite groups, and societal and cultural attitudes toward nuclear weapons. Though Ben Gurion did not think in terms of nuclear opacity, his attitudes were essential in shaping Israel's nuclear stance. When the critical decisions concerning Dimona and related issues were made in 1957–58, Ben Gurion shared with his senior colleagues only the minimum amount of information necessary; it was only discussed on a "need to know" basis. Secrecy, concealment, and vagueness were Ben Gurion's traits in dealing with nuclear matters, at home and abroad.

All Zionist parties, on the Left and Right alike, felt inhibited in voicing reservations in public regarding the nuclear project. Owing to the secrecy and technological complexity of the subject, few were competent and informed enough to debate the issue. Even those who understood Ben Gurion's interest in a nuclear option were reluctant to discuss the issue in public. Notwithstanding some reservations, Zionist parties were committed to the imperative of *kdushat ha-bitachon*—the sanctity of security. For those few who did insist on debating the issue in public, the efforts of the military censor made it difficult to state their case properly. The taboo, however, was more self-imposed than imposed by law. It is among the most powerful societal sources of opacity, and it has endured to the present.

The drift toward opacity accelerated under Eshkol. The nuclear issue remained insulated from the rest of the domestic political agenda. Eshkol never brought the nuclear issue to the cabinet, except to get approval of his reorganization of the IAEC in 1966. Eshkol shifted Ben Gurion's denial policy to a policy of ambiguity. In line with his promise to President Johnson not to introduce nuclear weapons into the Middle East, Eshkol strengthened his commitment to conventional deterrence through arms purchases from the United States.

After the 1967 war Israel moved toward a "bomb-in-the-basement" posture.

As domestic politics became less relevant to the nation's nuclear policy, bureaucratic politics became more of a factor. It was the appointed guardians, not the politicians, who made the real decisions. The Nuclear Non-Proliferation Treaty (NPT), for example, was hardly discussed in the cabinet. By 1970 a tradition had been established which held that the political arena was not the appropriate forum in which to decide the nation's nuclear policy. This pattern, too, was an important tenet of opacity. Chapters 1–4, 8, 12, and 15 focus on these domestic sources of opacity.

Opacity was also shaped by Israel's interactions with outside powers. In the early stages of the project, Israel's relationship with France was essential to its embarking on the nuclear weapons path. France's contribution to the Israeli project went beyond supplying materials and know-how. In Paris in the mid-1950s Shimon Peres and his associates learned how a democratic nation can become a nuclear state without making an explicit decision to do so. There were, as a result, many similarities between the French and Israeli treatment of nuclear issues. The French contribution to Israel's nuclear project is described in chapters 3 and 4.

If France was the nation from which Israel learned how a democracy can go nuclear opaquely, then the United States was the superpower whose response to Israel's nuclear program greatly shaped the way Israel stumbled into opacity. The record indicates that Israel's manner of acquiring a nuclear capability, and the mode of nuclear proliferation it developed, were strongly influenced by the evolution of American nonproliferation policy in the 1960s.

The United States was not in a position to stop the Israeli nuclear program, but the American-Israeli security dialogue determined how Israel became a nuclear-weapon state. Israel did so opaquely, not overtly, in a way that was considerate of American policies and that avoided defying American nonproliferation policy. During the 1960s the United States and Israel groped for answers that would satisfy their strategic needs, national goals, and political requirements. The search continued for nearly a decade, marked by three pairs of leaders: Kennedy-Ben Gurion, Johnson-Eshkol, and Nixon-Meir. In a Hegelian dialectical path, the search progressed through three political phases: confrontation, ambiguity, and reconciliation. Israel's nuclear opacity was the answer to this decade-long search.

The Israeli nuclear case was an important factor in the shaping and evolution of American nonproliferation policy throughout the 1960s. Israel was the first case of nuclear weapons proliferation with which the United States had to contend, outside Russia, Britain, France, and China, and at a time when the United States had not yet developed a coherent nonproliferation policy. Israel was a small, friendly state surrounded by larger enemies, and, unlike Germany

—about whose nuclear ambitions the United States also worried—it was outside the sphere of superpower containment. Moreover, unlike the Soviet Union, the United Kingdom, and France (and, later, China and India), Israel did not aspire to the status of a great power. Israel also enjoyed strong domestic support in the United States. The challenge of how to apply the American opposition to the spread of nuclear weapons to the complexity of the Israeli case had lasting effects, and was an important learning experience for three American administrations in their search for a coherent nonproliferation policy.

The American-Israeli security dialogue in the 1960s evolved around three issues: the supply of American conventional weapons to Israel; American assurances for Israeli security; and inhibitions on Israel's nuclear program. On a few occasions the two parties were on the verge of collision, but a public showdown was avoided because neither wanted it. Through these episodes of confrontation and near-confrontation, the United States and Israel learned how to cope with the Israeli nuclear program. The nuclear relationship between the United States and Israel is covered in eight chapters, 5–7, 9–11, and 16–17.

The Israeli nuclear posture was also influenced by the Arab world, particularly Egypt. Israel had to be careful not to provoke the Arabs to develop their own nuclear weapons. Secrecy and ambiguity were essential to keep the Arabs at bay. It was also believed that if the Arabs became convinced that Israel was developing nuclear weapons, they would launch a preemptive attack on Dimona to prevent it. This concern was featured in American-Israeli discussions at the time. The United States was also concerned that Israeli nuclearization would lead to Soviet involvement in the nuclear escalation in the region, either by providing Egypt with nuclear weapons or by including it under the Soviet nuclear umbrella.

Apart from seemingly contributing to the escalation of the crisis that preceded the Six-Day War, the Israeli nuclear program did not become a major issue in the Arab world. As long as Israel kept a low profile, Arab governments and leaders tended to marginalize the issue. The Egyptian defeat in the 1967 war created circumstances that eased the Israeli drift from ambiguity to opacity. However, the Arab pattern of using Israeli opacity to maintain a low profile on the nuclear issue continued. In a peculiar way, the Arabs were also a partner, albeit a junior one, in the making of opacity. Chapter 13 discusses the reactions of the Arab world to Israel's nuclear program.

Finally, an important aspect of the makeup of Israel's nuclear opacity involved a cluster of conceptual-epistemic-technical issues concerning the definition of nuclear weapons: What constitutes a nation's nuclear-weapon status? When is the nuclear-weapon threshold crossed? What is the meaning of Israel's "nonintroduction" pledge?

In the case of all five declared nuclear states—the United States, the Soviet Union, Britain, France, and China—crossing the nuclear threshold was symbolized by a full-yield nuclear test. For years a nuclear test was taken as a necessary step in the nuclear proliferation ladder, both for technical and political reasons. Technically, the testing of a weapons system—any weapons system—was considered the last stage in the development process.[7] Politically, the first full-yield nuclear test signifies the transition from secrecy to the public phase. A test provided a clear-cut and visible criterion for recognizing when and how the nuclear threshold had been crossed.

Nuclear proliferation was thus perceived as an either/or process: as long as a country did not conduct a full-yield test it was still given the benefit of the doubt concerning its nuclear status. Israel made its nuclear pursuit piecemeal and by taking advantage of this conceptualization of the proliferation process. It became a nuclear-weapon state, while avowing not to be the first to introduce nuclear weapons into the region.

The issue of Israel's nuclear status became more subtle after the 1967 war. At that time Israel was interested in changing the perception of its nuclear program without breaking its earlier pledges. During the battle over the NPT in October 1968, Prime Minister Levi Eshkol and Foreign Minister Abba Eban stated that Israel "has now acquired the technical know-how" to produce nuclear weapons, even though both emphasized, "it was a long way from this to producing nuclear weapons."[8] These statements, while leaving unclear the question of what Israel was doing in the nuclear field, conveyed the notion that Israel should be regarded as having a nuclear weapons capability or option.

These ambiguities became a matter of contention between the United States and Israel in late 1968, during the negotiations on the sale of the American F-4 Phantom jets. During the early period of the Nixon administration, questions were raised again about Israel's commitment not to introduce nuclear weapons into the region, but not for long. By 1970 it was accepted that Israel was a nuclear-weapon state. I discuss these issues in chapters 16 and 17.

Israel chose a road less traveled to reach an independent nuclear deterrence capability. It was not a lonely road, however. This book is about that journey and Israel's travel companions. The history I offer is incomplete and interpretative. Because of opacity, some aspects of the story can be traced only indirectly and circumstantially. Like black holes in cosmology or elementary particles in subatomic physics, opaque nuclear programs leave traces through their effects.

This work is not the last word on the subject, but rather an opening of a historical dialogue. Future historians, with access to more archival documentation, should be able to fill the gaps and correct the unavoidable mistakes. Even historians with access to all the archival material, however, will have difficulties reconstructing Israel's nuclear history. In the early years many of the important decisions were made in secret and in oral discussions, leaving no paper trail.[9] Such a secret history dies with those who made it or knew of it. Since opacity evolved through disinformation and subterfuge, often subtle, even insiders face difficulty in later years in distinguishing truth from fiction. The final word, therefore, is a call for skepticism.

In the end I am of two philosophical minds about the book. I believe that the history I offer is about what "actually" happened. I also recognize that it is ultimately a "story," and all stories are mere interpretations. In the end, we are always within the hermeneutic circle. I stress the interpretative quality of this narrative not merely because of my own antipositivistic, skeptical outlook. It is derived primarily from the fact that Israel's nuclear past remains fundamentally opaque, perhaps even to its own makers. It is a story about opacity.

The idea that Israel should acquire a nuclear-weapon capability is as old as the state itself. In the early days it took more than a little *chuzpa* to believe that tiny Israel could launch a nuclear program, but for a state born out of the Holocaust and surrounded by the hostile Arab world, not to do so would have been irresponsible. David Ben Gurion, Israel's first prime minister, entertained the vision early on, but until the mid-1950s it was no more than a hope for the future. In 1955–58, however, following his return to power and the establishment of special relations with France, sufficient resources became available to initiate a national nuclear project.

Three men set the nuclear project in motion: the nation's political leader, his chief scientist, and his chief executive officer.[1] Ben Gurion believed that Israeli scientists could provide the ultimate answer to Israel's security problem. Ernst David Bergmann, an organic chemist, tutored Ben Gurion in nuclear matters for many years. Shimon Peres exploited the international opportunity to make the dream into a reality. Without these men the Israeli program would not have been launched.

DAVID BEN GURION

David Ben Gurion arrived in Palestine in 1906 as a twenty-year-old pioneer from Plonsk, Poland, committed to socialist Zionism. Four decades later, on 15 May 1948, he declared the creation of the State of Israel and became its first prime minister. He served as prime minister for fourteen years, longer than any other Israeli prime minister.

From 1935 until 1948, as chairman of the Jewish Agency Executive, the governing body of the Yishuv (the Jewish community in Palestine), he led the campaign which ended in the creation of Israel. The backdrop for his tireless campaign was the rise of Nazism, the Second World War, and the Holocaust.

Israel's nuclear project was conceived in the shadow of the Holocaust, and the lessons of the Holocaust provided the justification and motivation for the project. Without the Holocaust we cannot understand either the depth of Ben Gurion's commitment to acquiring nuclear weapons or his inhibitions about nuclear-weapon policy. Over the years Ben Gurion's fears and anxieties became national policy.

"The story of the Yishuv leaders during the Holocaust was essentially one of helplessness," writes Tom Segev.[2] The determination not to be helpless again, a commitment to the idea that Jews should control their own fate, characterized Ben Gurion's determined campaign for Jewish statehood after the Second World War. It also inspired his pursuit of nuclear weapons.

Imbued with the lessons of the Holocaust, Ben Gurion was consumed by fears for Israel's security.[3] His preoccupation with security stemmed from his understanding of the geopolitical realities of the Arab-Israeli conflict. As the War of Independence concluded in 1949 with an impressive Israeli victory, Ben Gurion became convinced that the cessation of hostilities would not lead to a lasting peace, but would be only a temporary pause before the next round of Arab-Israeli military conflict.[4] Ben Gurion saw Arab hostility toward Israel as deep and long-lasting. In his view, peace could not come until the Arabs reconciled themselves to the losses of the 1948 war and until they became convinced that the defeat of 1948 was not merely a reversible error caused by the ineptitude and division of their corrupt leadership. To have peace with Israel required that they accept their losses as final.[5] Ben Gurion's pessimism about the inevitability of the next round influenced Israel's foreign and defense policy for years.

Ben Gurion's worldview and his decisive governing style shaped his critical role in initiating Israel's nuclear program. Ben Gurion was fascinated by twentieth-century science and technology and energetically promoted scientific research in Israel.[6] Scientific achievements were, for him, the hallmarks of the Zionist state, a secular manifestation of the idea of Israel as the "chosen people." "We are inferior to other peoples in our numbers, dispersion, and the characteristics of our political life," he remarked, "but no other people is superior to us in its intellectual prowess. Until now we have disseminated our intellectual capital in foreign lands, and helped many nations in the great scientific achievements of the nineteenth and twentieth centuries . . . There is no reason why the genius of science would not blossom and flourish in his native land."[7]

Ben Gurion believed that science and technology had two roles in the realization of Zionism: to advance the State of Israel spiritually and materially, and to provide for a better defense against its external enemies. As Peres would put it, "Ben Gurion believed that Science could compensate us for what Nature has denied us."[8] Ben Gurion's romantic, even mystical, faith in science and technology sustained his utopian vision of a blossoming Negev desert and the use of nuclear power to desalinate sea water.[9]

Since the late 1940s Ben Gurion had a special fascination with nuclear energy. In a pamphlet Ben Gurion wrote in November 1948 for distribution among new recruits to the Israel Defense Forces (IDF), he wrote, "We are living in an age of scientific revolutions, an era that discloses the atom, its miraculous composition and the tremendous power hidden in it."[10] This theme is repeated in speeches, diary notes, and conversations in which Ben Gurion referred to the atomic revolution as an unprecedented transformation of the history of civilization.[11]

Ben Gurion insisted from the beginning that Israel must base its security on science and technology, the only areas where it could have a significant advantage over its more numerous Arab enemies. In mid-1947, as chairman of the Jewish Agency, the governing body of the Jewish community in Palestine, Ben Gurion set the priority of scientific defense research. He created a scientific department at the headquarters of the Haganah, the semi-official Jewish defense organization, and allocated it an annual budget of 10,000 mandatory pounds. This budget was so large that the heads of the department did not know at first what to do with it.[12] In March 1948 the General Staff of Haganah (soon to become the Israel Defense Force, or IDF) formally recognized the scientific department as a staff unit in the operations branch. The new department was responsible for coordinating and assigning tasks to the newly created Ha'il Mada (Science Corps, known by the Hebrew acronym HEMED).[13] The first commanding officer of HEMED, Shlomo Gur, recalls that HEMED was Ben-Gurion's favorite military organization.[14]

Ben Gurion had no qualms about Israel's need for weapons of mass destruction. In an April 1948 letter to one of his operatives in Europe, Ben Gurion issued instructions to seek out East European Jewish scientists who could "either increase the capacity to kill masses or to cure masses; both things are important."[15] At that time such capacity meant chemical and biological weaponry. Because Israel's survival was at stake, it could not afford not to develop such capabilities. It did not follow, however, that Ben Gurion was sanguine about the use of such weapons. He never admitted that Israel was in possession of weapons of mass destruction, and he did not suggest their use.

Israel's geopolitical circumstances were central to Ben Gurion's strategic pessimism. The Arabs found it difficult to accept the military defeat in 1948 because of their strategic advantages. Israel was too small to achieve a decisive, final defeat of the Arab nations, and its military victories were only temporary and limited. The size of the Arab population and resources made it unlikely that they could be persuaded to accept Israel. After each defeat the Arabs could regroup and hope for victory in another military round.

Ben Gurion was especially anxious about an Arab coalition led by a charismatic leader carrying the banner of Arab unity. During his last years in office, his anxiety intensified. He told one of his aides: "I could not sleep all night, not even for one second. I had one fear in my heart: a combined attack by all Arab armies."[16] He expressed these fears to foreign leaders, including Dwight D. Eisenhower, John F. Kennedy, and Charles de Gaulle.[17]

The only solution to Israel's security problem was a robust deterrent force. Since the mid-1950s Ben Gurion had sought this goal in two ways. First, through an alliance with one or more Western powers, which would formally guarantee Israel's territorial integrity; second, by building a nuclear weapons option. Until his last day in office Ben Gurion expressed an interest in a military pact with, or formal security guarantees from, the United States, but from the mid-1950s on he came to doubt the feasibility and credibility of the idea, and whether it was in Israel's interest.[18]

Without access to the pertinent classified archival materials, it is difficult to say when exactly Ben Gurion began to think about nuclear weapons as a practical option. He was fascinated with the idea from the first days of the State, but it was only after he returned to the Ministry of Defense in 1955, and after Eisenhower's Atoms for Peace program, that he became convinced the time had come to pursue the effort in earnest. "What Einstein, Oppenheimer and Teller, the three of them are Jews, made for the United States," wrote Ben Gurion in 1956, "could also be done by scientists in Israel for their own people."[19] Ben Gurion's determination to launch the nuclear project was the result of strategic intuition and obsessive fears, not of a well-thought-out plan. He believed Israel needed nuclear weapons as insurance if it could no longer compete with the Arabs in an arms race, and as a weapon of last resort in case of an extreme military emergency. Nuclear weapons might also persuade the Arabs to accept Israel's existence, leading to peace in the region.[20]

He never spelled out these reasons publicly. His only public reference to the nuclear program was in a speech to the Knesset in December 1960, in which he talked of the nuclear project's "peaceful purposes." Away from the public eye, however, he was less reticent, even if his comments were veiled. On 27 June 1963, eleven days after he announced his resignation, Ben Gurion delivered a farewell address to the employees of the Armaments Development Authority (RAFAEL) in which, without referring to nuclear weapons, he provided the justification for the nuclear project:

> I do not know of any other nation whose neighbors declare that they wish to terminate it, and not only declare, but prepare for it by all means available to them. We must have no illusions that what is declared every day in Cairo, Damascus, Iraq are just words. This is the thought that guides the Arab leaders. . . .
>
> Our numbers are small, and there is no chance that we could compare ourselves with America's 180 million, or with any Arab neighboring state. There is one thing, however, in which we are not inferior to any other people in the world—this is the Jewish brain. And science, if a lay person like myself could say, starts from the brain. And the Jewish brain does not disappoint; Jewish science does not disappoint. . . . I am confident, based not only on what I heard today, that our science can provide us with the weapons that are needed to deter our enemies from waging war against us. I am confident that science is able to provide us with the weapon that will secure the peace, and deter our enemies.[21]

Ben Gurion knew that the birth of the State of Israel was the result of Hitler's atrocities—the need to find a home for Jewish survivors—rather than as a triumph of Zionism. Even after the 1948 war Ben Gurion continued to believe that the survival of the State of Israel was not assured, surrounded as it was with larger and richer neighbors vowing to destroy it.

When, in the early 1950s, Ben Gurion decided, against strong opposition from both the Right and Left, that the State of Israel should accept financial reparations from Germany, he justified it by saying that Jews will never again be helpless: "They [the Arabs] could slaughter us tomorrow in this country . . . We don't want to reach again the situation that you were in. We do not want the Arab Nazis to come and slaughter us."[22] The reparations from Germany would make Israel strong so that potential perpetrators, contemplating inflicting another catastrophe on the Jewish people, would know that they would pay a steep price if they tried.

In his public speeches and writings as prime minister Ben Gurion rarely discussed the Holocaust. In private conversations and communications with foreign leaders, however, he returned to the lessons of the Holocaust time and again. In his correspondence with President John F. Kennedy in 1963, he linked Arab enmity to Israel with Hitler's hatred of the Jews, and wrote:

I know that it is difficult for civilized people to visualize such a thing—even after they have witnessed what had happened to us during the Second World War. I do not assume that could happen today or tomorrow. I am not so young anymore, and it may not happen in my lifetime. But I cannot dismiss the possibility that this may occur, if the situation in the Middle East remains as it is, and the Arab leaders continue to insist on and pursue their policy of belligerency against Israel. And it does not matter whether it will or will not happen during my lifetime. As a Jew I know the history of my people, and carry with me the memories of all it has endured over a period of three thousand years, and the effort it has cost to accomplish what has been achieved in this country in recent generations. . . . Mr. President, my people have the right to exist, both in Israel and wherever they may live, and this existence is in danger.[23]

Anxiety about the Holocaust reached beyond Ben Gurion to infuse Israeli military thinking. The destruction of Israel defined the ultimate horizon of the threat against Israel. Israeli military planners have always considered a scenario in which a united Arab military coalition launched a war against Israel with the aim of liberating Palestine and destroying the Jewish state. This was referred to in the early 1950s as *mikre ha'kol*, or the "everything scenario."[24] This kind of planning was unique to Israel, as few nations have military contingency plans aimed at preventing apocalypse.

ERNST DAVID BERGMANN

For a small and technologically dependent nation in the mid-1950s to embark on a nuclear project, more than the leadership's political commitment was required. There was also a need for scientific and organizational leadership to set goals, devise strategies, assign tasks, allocate funds, recruit scientists and managers, and oversee operations. These make the difference between a leader's vision and a credible nuclear-weapon project.

From the beginning Ben Gurion had two faithful and committed lieutenants: Ernst David Bergmann and Shimon Peres. Ben Gurion provided the political authority and commitment, while Bergmann and Peres delivered the energy and enthusiasm required to make the project a reality.

Israel Dostrovsky, who replaced Bergmann at the helm of the IAEC in 1966, characterized Bergmann's role in this way:

The role of Professor David Bergmann, Ben Gurion's advisor on these issues, was vital. In my view Ben Gurion accepted the judgment of Bergmann without question. Hence, all suggestions that were brought for discussion must have been endorsed by Bergmann first, and if Bergmann had been persuaded, Ben Gurion would have been as well.[25]

For fifteen years before working for Ben Gurion, Bergmann was the protégé of Chaim Weizmann, an eminent chemist and Ben Gurion's rival in the Zionist movement. When Bergmann, a young organic chemistry lecturer, was expelled by the Nazis in 1933 from the University of Berlin, Weizmann hired him to head the newly established Daniel Sieff Research Institute in Rehovot (in 1949 it was incorporated into the new Weizmann Institute of Science).[26] On his return to Palestine after the Second World War, he resumed his position as scientific director of the Sieff Institute and was expected to be its director after Weizmann. The close relationship between the two, however, came to a bitter end in the late 1940s for personal reasons and differences over the way Bergmann ran the Institute[27] (see chapter 3).

Bergmann was drawn to Ben Gurion in the late 1940s because of Ben Gurion's conviction that Israel's future depended on harnessing science and technology. In August 1948 Ben Gurion appointed Bergmann head of the scientific department of the IDF.[28] On 15 July 1951 Bergmann was made scientific adviser to the minister of defense, and in early 1952 was appointed director of research of the newly created Division of Research and Infrastructure (*Agaf Mechkar Ve'tichun*, or EMET) of the Ministry of Defense. Even with this increased responsibility he continued to teach organic chemistry at the Hebrew University. In June 1952 the Israel Atomic Energy Commission (IAEC) was quietly established, with Bergmann as its head. He held these three posts until his final resignation in April 1966.[29]

In his eulogy for Bergmann, Shimon Peres described the extraordinary alliance between Ben Gurion and Bergmann: "Bergmann's scientific vision was attracted to Ben Gurion's statesmanlike vision, and the plowman met the sower. From the start a visionary alliance was forged between them, over science, defense and politics, that marked some of the most fateful moves of the State of Israel."[30] Bergmann, a German Jew, was attracted to Ben Gurion's statesmanship and to the opportunity to shape Israel's scientific future. Ben Gurion was attracted to Bergmann's scientific vision and optimism.[31] Bergmann, with his conviction that science can provide solutions to every problem, was Ben Gurion's ideal Zionist scientist: one who subjects science to the service of the Zionist revolution.[32]

Bergmann also shared Ben Gurion's conviction that the Holocaust justified Israel in taking any steps to ensure its survival. "I am convinced," Peres cited him as saying, "that the State of Israel needs a defense research program of its own, so that we shall never again be as lambs led to the slaughter."[33] Bergmann elaborated on this theme in a 1966 letter to Meir Ya'ari, the leader of the left-wing MAPAM, who opposed nuclear weapons. After writing that the spread of nuclear weapons was unavoidable and that many countries, including Arabs, would achieve nuclear capability, he said:

> I was surprised that a man like you . . . is prepared to close his eyes and assume that reality is how we would all like to see it. There is no person in this country who does not fear a nuclear war and there is no man in this country who does not hope that, despite it all, logic will rule in the world of tomorrow. But we are not permitted to exchange precise knowledge and realistic evaluations for hopes and illusions. I cannot forget that the Holocaust came on the Jewish people as a surprise. The Jewish people cannot allow themselves such an illusion for a second time.[34]

Bergmann's "overabundance of zeal," as Peres referred to it, were regarded as a flaw by other scientists, who questioned his scientific judgment.[35] His tendency to exaggerate on scientific matters that he little understood, for example, was evident in his report on the Atoms for Peace Conference in 1955. Commenting on the notion of "nuclear fusion," he wrote, "The prevailing view is that one of the possibilities to obtain the high temperatures required for thermonuclear reactions is by putting together a few hollow charges," and added that "for the last two years our people too have been playing with this idea." The three scientists who were members of the Israeli delegation to the conference were embarrassed by the comments and asked him to delete them. Amos de Shalit noted that he was "concerned that those who are not informed about the subject would get a very misleading idea about our activities in this field by reading such statements"; Dostrovsky suggested removing the entire reference to fusion, and taking out the reference to "hollow charges"; and Giulio (Yoel) Racah noted that "this is the first time I hear that we are playing with the idea for two years, and I would like to know who are those 'we'. "[36]

Bergmann's zeal, however, was important in his relationship with Ben Gurion. He educated Ben Gurion on the nuclear revolution, persuading him that nuclear energy might be the key for the survival and prosperity of Israel. In his view, nuclear energy would enable Israel to compensate for its disadvantages in natural resources and military manpower. Nuclear technology would open options for civilian and military applications, because, "by developing atomic energy for peaceful uses, you reach the nuclear option. There are no two atomic energies."[37]

Bergmann steered the direction of Israel's nuclear activities from 1948 to 1955. He founded the IAEC in 1952 and shaped its early activities. His autocratic conduct within the IAEC, however, drove its physicists to the Weizmann Institute, and they soon formed the main opposition to his plans. His role diminished further as Israel's nuclear project began to take shape. He was not a good administrator, and appeared oblivious to economic considerations.

In 1956–58, when the important decisions were made, Bergmann was still the chairman of the IAEC, but he was no longer the man in charge. Shimon Peres, who made the decisions on behalf of Ben Gurion, consulted many experts, often without Bergmann's presence. On the critical issue of the reactor, Peres overruled Bergmann's idea that Israel should build the reactor on its own, forming instead a partnership with France to supply the reactor and other facilities.

Under Prime Minister Levi Eshkol, his role dwindled further. Bergmann no longer enjoyed the trust and authority he had under Ben Gurion, and in June 1964 he offered his resignation to Eshkol.[38] Eshkol did not accept the resignation, and Bergmann was persuaded to stay on. In 1965 Ben Gurion and Peres left MAPAI to form a new party, RAFI. Bergmann's involvement in RAFI ended whatever rapport he may have had with Eshkol. When, on 1 April 1966, he submitted his resignation from his three posts at the Ministry of Defense, his resignation was welcomed. Eshkol decorated him with Israel's highest award for contribution to the security of the State, and nominated himself, in his capacity as prime minister, to be the new chairman of the IAEC.

Shimon Peres

Bergmann inspired Ben Gurion to believe that Israel could have a nuclear weapons option, but it was Shimon Peres who persuaded Ben Gurion in 1956–57 that the time was right to initiate the nuclear project. From the beginning Peres was entrusted by Ben Gurion to lead Israel's pursuit of a nuclear capability. Dostrovsky writes:

> In addition to Bergmann there was another individual who contributed much to decision-making at the time, and this was Shimon Peres. He personally took it upon himself to promote the issues involved with atomic energy, particularly the relationship with France that started then. There is no doubt that because of the great push that he gave to this effort, it was advanced.[39]

This is an understatement. Although Peres never served in uniform, he was the *wunderkind* of Israel's defense establishment. In 1947, at only twenty-three years of age, he was recruited by Levi Eshkol to join the Haganah headquarters staff in Tel Aviv, located in the Red House. Within months Peres took charge of arms procurement deals, something he continued to pursue in higher positions for years to come. After a brief period as the administrator of the Israeli navy, Peres was sent in 1949 to the Ministry of Defense's mission in New York, first as deputy and later as head of mission.[40]

In 1952, on returning from New York, Peres was appointed deputy director-general of the Ministry of Defense. A year later, at age twenty-nine, he was appointed director-general, the highest civil servant at the ministry. Running the daily operations of the ministry, he became acquainted with Bergmann's nuclear vision. "I was as intrigued as Ben Gurion and as enthusiastic as Bergmann," Peres would write (134). Peres's boundless energy and political skills became the necessary ingredient in realizing Israel's nuclear hopes.

After Ben Gurion returned to power in 1955, Peres supervised the regrouping of the national nuclear program and led the search for ways to make it a reality. Until his resignation from the Ministry of Defense a decade later, Peres was the man in charge of Israel's nuclear project. Peres later wrote:

> From the outset, I resolved to keep my role entirely out of the public lime-light. . . . For this reason, my name was never included in any formal com-mittee created in the area of atomic energy. That did not, however, prevent me from effectively running the entire program on behalf of Ben Gurion, nor did it impair in any way my authority. Ben Gurion trusted me. Professor Bergmann worked with me with no reservations. In time, I was able to win the trust and confidence of the other scientists, engineers and senior person-nel engaged in the project. (135)

Some would question the accuracy of the last sentence, but it is indisputable that Peres played a pivotal role in making the early decisions that determined the character and direction of the project. In his 1995 memoirs Peres cites some of the principles that guided him in leading the program, writing that, at the outset, he knew what the project's limits were. He took issue with both Bergmann's optimistic view that Israel could take the nuclear path on its own, and with "almost the entire scientific community's" opposition "to any effort on Israel's part to enter upon the nuclear age" (133–35). One principle that guided him through "what could be done and what could not," was,

> to insist that we need not invent things that had already been invented by oth-ers elsewhere. Originality was necessary, of course, but it was not an end in itself. This outlook brought me into headlong collision with Bergmann. He believed that Israel had the potential and the ability to build its own nuclear

reactors; I maintained that, if it were at all possible, we would be better to buy one abroad. (135)

This dispute between Peres and Bergmann was linked to the question of the role of foreign supplier. By 1955 it was doubtful whether Israel could receive meaningful nuclear assistance from a Western power that would help Israel achieve its goal. As part of the Atoms for Peace program, the United States indicated its readiness to sell Israel a small experimental reactor under U.S. safeguards, but apart from training and basic research, it was recognized that this would not allow Israel to realize a nuclear weapons option. The help would have to come from another place. From the late 1940s Bergmann and others saw France as Israel's best hope for nuclear assistance. Bergmann cultivated scientific exchanges between the French atomic energy commission (CEA) and the IAEC, but in 1955 it became clear that without a political breakthrough, these friendly relations would fall short of Israel's needs.

Peres changed that. Of Peres's many indispensable contributions to making Israel a nuclear power, none is more important than his forming and cementing the nuclear relationship between France and Israel. More than any other Israeli decision maker, Peres grasped that a unique opportunity emerged for such cooperation. In the face of stiff opposition and bitter criticism, he proceeded, indefatigably and single-mindedly, to exploit this opportunity. Peres was the architect of the Franco-Israeli alliance that made the Dimona deal possible. Peres would later say that, as early as 1953, he was looking for opportunities to forge closer relations with France. These efforts yielded few results during the tenure of Pinhas Lavon, who was skeptical of Peres's French orientation, but the return of Ben Gurion to power in 1955 provided the necessary political backing for Peres's efforts (117–19). The relationship with France was another principle of Peres's leadership of Israel's nuclear program.

[It] was that, of all the countries engaged in nuclear research and development, only France might be prepared to help us. I believed, therefore, that all our diplomatic efforts should be focused on France—on the French government and on the French scientific and industrial community. (135)

Whether these tenets were undergirding the Israeli program "at the outset," and to what extent they were a matter of forethought, is open to question. It is the case, however, that evolving circumstances between the summer of 1956 and the fall of 1957 created a unique opportunity for Israel to launch its nuclear weapons program, and that it was Shimon Peres who, more than any other individual, was responsible for shaping this opportunity.

Peres was also instrumental in selecting the project's scientists and managers. Unlike the Manhattan Project, to which many distinguished American physicists were asked to contribute, many Israeli scientists were left out. The Manhattan Project needed as many of the best physicists to prove that a nuclear bomb could be developed, a fact on which subsequent nuclear programs were able to build. In Israel participation was limited also because top Israeli scientists had reservations about Bergmann's and Peres's nuclear vision. As a result, it was decided to bypass the scientific establishment. In Peres's words:

> I concluded early on that Israel's own nuclear physics "establishment," in the main, would not be a source of support. Most of the top men simply did not believe that Israel had the ability to build its own nuclear option, and they gave frank voice to their opinion. My decision, therefore, was to approach the younger generation, men just recently graduated from the Technion in Haifa, who had an initial grounding in the discipline and had not yet been infected by the doubts and reservations of their more senior colleagues. In any event, most of the Israeli scientists who worked on building and operating our nuclear reactor were drawn from the ranks of these younger graduates. (135)

Decades later Peres explained the philosophy that had guided him in the following way: "Between existing and investing for the long-run I thought that my role was to represent the future. The Chief of Staff is on the job for three, four, years. I thought in terms of ten years ahead."[41] There is no doubt that such a long-term outlook led Peres, with the support of Ben Gurion and the inspiration of Bergmann, to initiate, set up, and promote the nuclear project and other long-term projects that the senior officers of the IDF at the time had often opposed. But this is not the whole story.

For the young and politically ambitious Peres, there were political and bureaucratic reasons that attracted him to the nuclear project, beyond his belief in the project's contribution to Israel's security. Peres's rise in the Ministry of Defense was meteoric, and he enjoyed Ben Gurion's support; but he also faced resentment and criticism, even scorn, from experienced senior IDF officers, especially PALMACH veterans. In the eyes of these senior officers, Peres's lack of military experience undermined his credibility on national security issues. These officers also had reservations about investing the nation's limited defense resources in the nuclear project, which many regarded as a fantasy.

For Peres, establishing a secret nuclear project under his own supervision meant also creating a new political and bureaucratic power base. It added to his special relationship with Ben Gurion and allowed Peres to promote a new strategy for Israeli national security, a strategy that made traditional military strategy less relevant. The nuclear project also led Peres, an avid reader who has always been interested in ideas and who sought the company of intellectuals, to form an alliance with experts and professionals, primarily scientists and technocrats. This alliance with the new "knowledge elite" became over the years one of Peres's distinguishing characteristics as a politician and a leader.[42]

OTHERS

The success of a scientific-technological project of the magnitude of the Israeli nuclear project cannot be explained by appealing to the "great men" theory of history. Ben Gurion, Bergmann, and Peres could not have succeeded on their own without the help of others. The contributions of a number of individuals are just as important, as is the ethos that emphasizes the importance and feasibility of the nuclear project.

Israel Dostrovsky was born in Russia in 1918 and moved with his family to Palestine a year later. Dostrovsky was among the first Israeli natives ("Sabras") to become scientists. He studied physical chemistry at University College in London, receiving his doctorate in 1943. He taught and researched for five years in the United Kingdom, becoming an authority on isotope research. He returned to Palestine in 1948 and founded the Department of Isotope Research at the Weizmann Institute. At the same time, as a major in the IDF Science Corps, he created HEMED GIMMEL, the unit that led the way to the nuclear project. This combination of government service and academic work would mark Dostrovsky's career. It was difficult at times to distinguish Dostrovsky's involvement in science from his involvement in defense projects. Thus the technical methods that Dostrovsky and his colleagues developed in the early 1950s in the areas of isotope separation and uranium extraction were claimed by both the Weizmann Institute and the IAEC as their own inventions.

In 1965, after Dostrovsky completed four years of research at Brookhaven National Laboratory in New York, Deputy Minister of Defense Zvi Dinstein asked him to reorganize the IAEC to ensure the prime minister's control over nuclear matters. Against the backdrop of the bitter rift between Ben Gurion and Eshkol, this was a complex and sensitive assignment. When Bergmann departed in mid-1966, Eshkol became the chairman of the IAEC, and Dostrovsky became the commission's director-general until 1971.

The Katchalsky-Katzir brothers of the Weizmann Institute—the late Aharon (born 1913) and Ephraim (born 1916)—were among HEMED founders (Aharon was the secretary of the scientific department while Ephraim was HEMED commander for a brief period in 1948). They were among the first to receive doctorates from the Hebrew University, doing interdisciplinary work in organic chemistry and biology. In the mid-1940s, before Bergmann returned to Palestine, Aharon Katzir was the scientist closest to Ben Gurion. He was the first to discuss the bombing of Hiroshima and Nagasaki with Ben Gurion.[43] As a young lecturer at the Hebrew University in 1946–47, Aharon Katzir recruited science students to form the first units dedicated to experimenting with weaponry and explosives for the Haganah. These recruits became the core of HEMED in early 1948.[44]

Though the Katzir brothers did not devote their full time to defense research, they had a lifelong involvement in RAFAEL projects and were occasionally drafted for help on matters relating to lead projects (in 1968 Ephraim Katzir agreed to serve as a chief scientist at the Ministry of Defense for a limited period).[45] Their role in making the nuclear project possible was more political than technical or scientific.

Shalheveth Freier was also among the individuals who greatly contributed to the nuclear project. He was one of those mysterious individuals who became a legend in their own time. In the pre-state period he played a role in organizing an intelligence network in Jerusalem for the Haganah; he was also involved in the activities of *Aliyah Bet* (smuggling Jewish refugees from Europe to Palestine in defiance of British restrictions) and *Rechesh* (armaments procurement). In 1954 he was the acting administrator of EMET, replacing Munya Mardor. In the summer of 1956, when the Israeli-French deal was put together, Peres and Bergmann asked Freier to be the Israeli science attaché at the embassy in Paris, taking charge of putting together the secret deal. Peres commented that Freier was the kind of person the project needed in France. The Israeli-French agreement was so extraordinary in its scope and implementation that there was a need for an extraordinary person to manage its political subtleties in the context of France's Fourth Republic.[46] Years later, in the capacity of director-general of the IAEC (he replaced Dostrovsky in 1971), Freier was involved in securing opacity as Israel's nuclear doctrine.[47]

Another constituency that contributed to the initiation of the nuclear project in 1956–57 was the small group of scientists and engineers concentrated around Machon (Institute) 4. When Peres and Bergmann began to draw the master plan for the project, based on obtaining a large production reactor and other assistance from France and a smaller research reactor from the United States, they were helped by the small group of nuclear enthusiasts waiting impatiently for the age of reactors (Israel Pelah, Ze'ev [Venia] Hadari-Pomerantz, and others). Peres and Bergmann were also given advice, at times critical, by the nuclear physicists of the Weizmann Institute (Amos de Shalit, Zvi Lipkin, Igal Talmi, Gideon Yekutielli, and others).

Then there were those who played an important role in implementing the project once the political decision was made. Colonel Manes Pratt, the legendary Ordinance Corps commander, an engineer by profession, was the most significant figure among the executors. In his memoirs Peres describes how he selected Pratt to run Dimona's construction:

> I realized that much would depend on the character and ability of the project manager. I looked for a "pedant," a man who would not compromise over detail, whether vital or ostensibly marginal. . . . At the same time, the candidate had to be a man with an "open mind," that is, a capacity to learn on the job; after all, he would not have any prior experience in building nuclear reactors. My choice fell on Manes Pratt. . . . Pratt had three university degrees and a finely developed aesthetic sense, which stood in incongruous contrast to his tough, no-nonsense approach to work. . . . I knew when I appointed him that he would give me a hard time, and indeed he did: he was never prepared to accept any product of our own Military Industries unless it met the most stringent international standards.[48]

Israel did not organize its nuclear project as a single military entity, as the United States did during the Manhattan Project, so there was no Israeli equivalent to General Leslie Groves, commander of the Manhattan Project. In terms of his leadership style and management approach, however, Pratt was the closest Israeli replica of Groves. Much of the credit for building the Dimona complex belongs to Pratt.

Munya Mardor had an important role in promoting the idea of the project before and after it was launched in 1955–58. In the pre-state period he was a key figure in the effort to procure arms in Europe, and later was briefly in charge of the navy. In 1951 Ben Gurion asked him to reorganize and transform HEMED into a postwar, civilian organization named EMET. Afterward, Mardor administered EMET and was committed to make the nuclear dream a reality. In early 1958, after the initial commitment was made, Mardor was asked by Ben Gurion and Peres to ready EMET for the age of the "new projects." EMET was again reorganized and expanded under the new name of Armaments Development Authority (RAFAEL).[49]

Mardor had hoped to be placed in charge of all aspects of Israel's nuclear activity, but this did not happen. Pratt's insistence that he should report only to Peres and Ben Gurion, Peres's own divide-and-rule style of management, and security considerations created from the start a fragmented project. There emerged two prime contractors—Pratt and Mardor—and a few subcontractors, all reporting directly to Peres.

Other key individuals played important roles in Israel's nuclear vision. The late Jenka (Yevgeni) Ratner, an engineer with an artist's touch who was legendary at HEMED for his knowledge of explosives, was in charge of several aspects of the nuclear project since the mid-1950s. The late Eliezer Gon was Ratner's deputy for a number of years and contributed his technical ingenuity to the project. Avraham Hermoni, a chemist who became a professional technical manager, played an important role in developing and monitoring policies for the project in the 1960s. There was also a group of academics who were the theoreticians of the project.

Although the contributions of all these people were invaluable, they pale in comparison to those of Ben Gurion, Bergmann, and Peres. It was Ben Gurion who made the decisions and took the political responsibility to set the project in motion. The judgment to launch the program was a daring political decision, and the credit belongs solely to Ben Gurion. Ben Gurion did not know what the odds for success were, and he could not tell whether the French would assist Israel and for how long, but he was convinced that Israel must try it and that Israeli ingenuity would accomplish it. Ben Gurion, the charismatic leader, was supported by Bergmann, a visionary scientist, and by Peres, an indefatigable, resourceful, and creative politician and executive.

The presence of these three individuals at that particular time and place made the Israeli nuclear project possible. To the extent that one can make such historical judgments, it can be said that, in the absence of any one of these three men and without their unique collaboration, there would not have been an Israeli nuclear project. Other people helped and made important contributions, but the primary credit belongs to these three.

It was during Israel's War of Independence, almost a
decade before Israel launched its nuclear program,
that Ben Gurion was persuaded by Bergmann, the
Katzir (Katchalsky) brothers, Dostrovsky, and others
that a national nuclear project was within Israel's scientific abilities.[1] The distance between that belief and
its realization would not be easy to cover.

Early Days

In his diary in late 1948 Ben Gurion mentions twice
that he was told about a Jewish, Palestinian-born
physicist named Moshe Sordin, who was working on
the construction of the first French reactor. A few
weeks later Sordin was brought to Israel to discuss the
future of nuclear reactors; among the people he met
was Ben Gurion.[2]

This anecdote reveals an important tenet of Israel's
early pursuit of nuclear energy: no opportunity to
enhance Israel's access to the nuclear field, however
remote, should be ignored. In late 1948 Israel did not
have a single nuclear physicist, and it was years away
from initiating a dedicated nuclear project, but the
vision and commitment were already there. The question was how to translate that vision into reality.

In a 1969 interview Bergmann claimed that as early
as 1949–50 it was thought "at the highest political level"
that France would be the logical place for Israel to look
for nuclear assistance.

We felt that Israel could not develop such a program on its own, but needed to collaborate with a country close to its technical level. First it was important to train Israeli experts. Then we would decide exactly what sort of collaboration to seek and what kind of contribution could be made in a joint endeavor, considering Israel's capacities and resources. Every effort was to be made to keep cooperation from being entirely one-directional.[3]

This statement, perhaps more of an after-the-fact rationalization than a reflection of thinking at the time, highlights another tenet of the Israeli approach to nuclear issues in the early 1950s: Israel made a commitment to nuclear energy at the highest national level before it had specific ideas about how and when it could pursue it. In order to ask other powers for scientific and technical assistance, however, Israel had to be in a position to reciprocate, and to do that, Israel had to create a national cadre of accomplished nuclear scientists.[4]

On Bergmann's recommendation, in 1949 Ben Gurion authorized HEMED to fund the postgraduate study of six promising physics graduate students, who served in HEMED during the war. The postgraduate work would take place at the world's best overseas universities and laboratories of nuclear physics. Professor Giulio Racah of the Hebrew University, then the only professor of theoretical physics in Israel and the mentor of the six young physicists, used his contacts to select the appropriate research site for each. Amos de-Shalit and Igal Talmi were sent to the *Eidgenosse Technische Hochschule* (ETH) in Zurich, the first to study with Scherrer, the second with Wolfgang Pauli; Uri Haber-Schaim was sent to the University of Chicago to study under Enrico Fermi; Gideon Yekutieli worked on experimental physics with Professor Powell in Bristol; Gvirol (Gabi) Goldring worked on experimental nuclear physics at Imperial College in London; Israel Pelah studied at Amsterdam University in Holland.[5]

The geological survey of the Negev desert in 1949–51 was another early activity aimed to increase Israel's access to the necessary nuclear materials. It was prompted by rumors that the British might have discovered oil fields and uranium ore deposits in the northern Negev, and was conducted by a special branch of the Science Corps, HEMED GIMMEL, headed by Daniel Sieff Institute's physical chemist Dr. (Major) Israel Dostrovsky, shortly after the Israel Defense Forces (IDF) seized the Negev during the 1948 war. A preliminary survey found no oil, but led to the decision to carry out a more extensive geological mapping of the area. This survey took two years, as new scientific instrumentation was purchased and new laboratories built for the unit in an adjunct to the Weizmann Institute.[6] The results of the survey were disappointing—no significant sources of uranium were found, except for small quantities in phosphate deposits. Following the survey, a new government-owned organization was created in 1951 to explore Israel's natural resources, and the nonnuclear energy aspects of HEMED GIMMEL were transferred to this new civilian body.[7]

Bergmann's Ascent

In the spring and summer of 1951 the growing tension between Chaim Weizmann, Israel's first president and the founder of the Weizmann Institute of Science, and his long time protégé Ernst David Bergmann, the scientific director of the institute, reached a final showdown. Questions involving political loyalties, disagreements over the role of the Weizmann Institute, and personal affairs combined to sour the father-son relationship between the two.

Some of these issues related to Bergmann's commitment to HEMED. As a scientific director of the Daniel Sieff Institute in 1947–50, Bergmann changed the character of the institute against Weizmann's wishes. He converted its facilities into a HEMED base, committing the institute to meet the needs of the scientific department of the Haganah (and later the Ministry of Defense), of which Bergmann was a board member and, since 1949, chairman.[8] Bergmann even proposed "to convert the Weizmann Institute into Israel's national scientific center, dedicated to both civilian and military tasks."[9]

This new reality and the idea of national science were unacceptable to the ailing Weizmann, who had returned to his institute in 1949 while serving as Israel's first president. Weizmann did not oppose investment in military technology, but he was against using the institute for such purposes. He thought that transforming the institute's resources and personnel into a HEMED base, as Bergmann did, undermined the ideas on which he had founded the institute and ruined its scientific credibility. Such activities, he believed, should be appropriately conducted within the government's own research center.[10] There were personal aspects to his opposition. He did not want the institute to be dependent on funds obtained from Ben Gurion's Ministry of Defense. From Weizmann's perspective, Bergmann, his would-be scientific heir, had betrayed him twice—once by putting his calling as a scientist aside in favor of full-time military research, and, second, by shifting his allegiance and becoming the scientific adviser of Ben Gurion, Weizmann's arch political rival. Personal issues concerning Mrs. Weizmann, Bergmann, and his future wife, Ms. Hani Itin, who then worked as Weizmann's secretary, only intensified the drama of the mentor and his erstwhile protégé. After eighteen years of intimate association it became impossible for the two men to talk with each other.[11]

On 8 July 1951 Meyer Weisgal, the chairman of the Executive Council of the institute (and Weizmann's closest confidant) wrote the following about the Bergmann affair to the American members of the council, Dewey Stone and Harry Levine:

> The situation with regard to Bergmann, and his relationship with the Chief [Weizmann], the concomitant results of the morale of the Institute had deteriorated beyond any possibility of repair. . . . The atmosphere in the [Weizmann's] "House" can be better imagined than described. The Chief has reached the end of his tether; was absolutely determined to liquidate the matter once and for all. The position of the inmates of the Household (perhaps a Freudian slip) was indeed unenviable . . . All of them were assailed with this question morning, noon and evening, and very often even during the middle of the night. It was beyond human endurance.[12]

At the end, out of concern for both the institute's future and for Bergmann's own life (there was a concern that he could commit suicide), certain terms of arrangement were agreed to in an exchange of letters between the two. On 2 July Weizmann wrote a letter to Bergmann in which he notified him that "after due considerations" he "relieved" him of his duties and responsibilities as scientific director of the Weizmann Institute, but Bergmann would continue his functions as the head of the Department of Organic Chemistry. "It is understood," the letter continued, "that you will take your sabbatical leave as from [the] 15th [of] July 1951." The next day Bergmann wrote to Weizmann, acknowledging his letter of the previous day, and taking note of Weizmann's decision. Bergmann added, "in accordance to your wish, I shall continue in my capacity as the Head of the Department of Organic Chemistry; I shall begin my Sabbatical leave on or about the 15th [of] July 1951." As part of that arrangement Bergmann wrote to Weisgal that he accepted Weisgal's suggestion to resign as a governor of the Weizmann Institute, even though he saw "no logical reason" for this suggestion.[13]

This exchange of letters meant the end of the Bergmann era at the Weizmann Institute. Bergmann never returned to be the head the organic chemistry department of the institute; he left the institute for good. Meanwhile, 15 July 1951 also marked the beginning of an era at the Ministry of Defense. In another exchange of letters that day, Ben Gurion appointed Bergmann as his scientific adviser and asked the army's chief of staff to appoint him as HEMED commander. The second appointment never materialized. Bergmann did not want to be HEMED commander, nor could he see himself functioning in uniform. But he wholeheartedly accepted his new appointment as Ben Gurion's scientific adviser.

His idea of creating a national, defense-oriented science center, an idea

Weizmann did not permit him to pursue at the Weizmann Institute, hereafter became his motto at the Ministry of Defense. Bergmann lobbied Ben Gurion to make the ministry the home for all nationally relevant scientific-technological projects. He proposed to extend and strengthen the small science department at the ministry—in 1949–51 a weak body whose function was to coordinate the scientific research conducted by HEMED—into a new division at the ministry and to transform HEMED into a civilian body directly under the new division. In a letter to Ben Gurion dated 1 July, Bergmann wrote the following:

> If my concern is justified that the Weizmann Institute would follow very quickly the [Hebrew] University's path, there would not be in the country an institute for any research. The establishment of an authorized organ for research, especially when the research is military, as a division at the Ministry of Defense under your sponsorship would be like a declaration that the government and the state consider science one of the pillars of the nation's building. Hence, I see in your consent to my proposal a significant political move.[14]

Bergmann's criticism of the Hebrew University and the Weizmann Institute was biased and ultimately self-serving, but he had a point. The Hebrew University reflected the German model of scientific research as practiced in the first half of the century. It promoted the notion that the purpose of research was pure, theoretical knowledge. Applied science was taken as a kind of engineering knowledge that is inferior to, and derivative of, pure science. Development-oriented research of the kind Bergmann had in mind was more appropriately pursued by industry.[15]

Bergmann was himself a product of this German academic tradition, but he believed that this tradition would be an obstacle to Israel's transformation into an advanced technological society. His own unsuccessful experience at the Weizmann Institute, prior to his dismissal, forced him to recognize that the only solution was for the government to build a research and development infrastructure of its own, outside the normal academic channels. Bergmann, with little knowledge of American post–Second World War science, sought to imitate the French model of government-sponsored national research centers. He recognized, as his letter indicates, that only the Ministry of Defense, under Ben Gurion's leadership, could promote the development of nationally sponsored science and technology.

FROM HEMED TO EMET

Bergmann's firing from the Weizmann Institute and his appointment as Ben Gurion's scientific adviser came at a period of major reorganizations at the IDF and the Ministry of Defense. The ninety-thousand-strong wartime IDF was reduced to about thirty-five thousand recruits, and there was a need to refashion Israel's military doctrine—to build a new military based on a small regular army and a large, quick-to-be-mobilized reserve force.

The role of HEMED was also under review. HEMED was still part of the IDF—although its military role was not clear to the supreme command—but the majority of its employees were civilians. The board of the Scientific Department at the Ministry of Defense was supposed to guide HEMED activities, but members of the board, all with full-time positions elsewhere, were hardly involved in the activities of HEMED centers. Each of the five HEMED centers—with some 560 employees—acted as an autonomous research unit, only loosely administrated by HEMED command. As the military budget shrunk in 1950–51, the IDF was determined to rid itself of the burden of supporting HEMED. The army was interested in acquiring complete, off-the-shelf weapon systems, not in investing scarce money in uncertain long-term research.[16]

Against this background, Bergmann proposed to Ben Gurion the expansion of the small Scientific Department in the Ministry of Defense into a new division that would control all the HEMED research units. This new division, in Bergmann's vision, would be in charge of all the national research sponsored by the Ministry of Defense, possibly even all governmental research.[17] In late 1951 a new civilian research branch at the Ministry was established, but with less research authority than Bergmann had proposed.

For the task of administering the new division Bergmann selected Munya Mardor, an experienced Haganah operator with a penchant for secrecy. Mardor, sensing the differences in vision between Bergmann and the heads of the Ministry about the role of the new division, was initially reluctant to take the job, but Ben Gurion persuaded him to do so. In early 1952 Ben Gurion appointed Bergmann and Mardor to lead the new R&D division. Bergmann, already Ben Gurion's scientific adviser, was also appointed chief of research—in effect, the chief scientist at the Ministry—and Mardor was appointed the director of the new division. Ben Gurion also chose the name of the new division—*Agaf Mechkar Ve'Tichun* (Research and Infrastructure Division, or EMET in its Hebrew acronym). The word "emet" means "truth" in Hebrew, which pleased Ben Gurion. All HEMED research centers were transferred to the control of EMET.[18]

The transfer of authority over HEMED from the IDF to the Ministry also signaled a shift in military research from short-term needs to long-term planning. In 1948–49 HEMED tasks consisted primarily of quick technological responses to the challenges arising from the war, with most solutions amounting to not much more than improvised fixes restricted by the scarcity of resources. Most of the recruits were students and young faculty from the Hebrew University and the Technion, the research was simple and practical, and there was no clear boundary between development and production. The creation of HEMED GIMMEL indicated a commitment to long-term research, but it, too, operated as an autonomous unit.

Under EMET, the HEMED centers were reorganized as civilian *Machons* (institutes, in Hebrew). Bergmann was determined to assert central control over HEMED GIMMEL, now renamed Machon 4, and to develop it as the center for nuclear research of EMET. After completing the geological survey of the Negev, HEMED GIMMEL continued to operate as an autonomous center, funded by governmental and academic budgets, including the Weizmann Institute. Some of the activities and individuals of HEMED GIMMEL, including its commander, Dostrovsky, were closely associated with the Department of Isotope Research at the Weizmann Institute. Given Bergmann's relations with the institute, the question of who was to control HEMED GIMMEL was especially sensitive.[19]

THE CREATION OF THE IAEC

In early spring 1952, at Bergmann's urging, Ben Gurion created the Israel Atomic Energy Commission (IAEC) (CEA, or *Commissariat à l'energie atomique*, as was printed then on its official letterhead)—it took two more years for the IAEC existence to become public—and installed Bergmann as its chair.[20] The IAEC was the vehicle for the implementation of Bergmann's notion of nationally sponsored science. Five of the six original members of the IAEC were well-known scientists: Shmuel Sambursky (the Hebrew University; the head of Israel's Scientific Council), Giulio (Yoel) Racah (the Hebrew University), Saul C. Cohen (the Hebrew University), Franz Ollendorff (Technion), Israel Dostrovsky (Weizmann Institute), and former chief of staff Ya'acov Dori, the only nonscientist member of the committee.[21] This distinguished board gave the new body an appearance of scientific and political independence, but it was only a veneer. Under Bergmann, the IAEC functioned as a subsidiary of the Ministry of Defense. Bergmann turned Machon 4 into the central laboratory of the IAEC.

For Bergmann, the IAEC, like the French CEA, was a project-oriented executive body dedicated to planning and building the nation's nuclear energy infrastructure. He wanted to launch such a national project as soon as possible. Other members of the IAEC, particularly Racah and Sambursky, saw the role of the IAEC differently. For them, the IAEC was a coordinating research agency, a national body whose objectives were to coordinate the training and research of scientists in the field of nuclear energy, mostly through academic research institutions, and to represent the nation in international forums on nuclear issues. This put Chairman Bergmann at odds with most of the academic members of the IAEC. In 1954 the debate centered on the issues of production or research.

Here is the background. In the early 1950s the working presumption within the IAEC/EMET leadership was that in order for Israel to launch a national nuclear project—building power and production reactors—it must be able to produce heavy water and extract natural uranium, the raw materials necessary to operate nuclear reactors. Because it was believed that these materials were rare, Israel could leverage access to them to get assistance in building its reactor. If Israel wanted to enter the nuclear energy field, it had to develop an indigenous capacity to produce heavy water and to extract uranium from its phosphates ore. These objectives determined the focus of Machon 4.

In 1952–53 a research team from Machon 4, led by Dostrovsky, developed a new and cheaper process to produce water enriched with heavy oxygen (O^{18}) based on distillation rather than electrolysis.[22] The idea was that a similar process could be utilized to produce water enriched with deuterium (H^2)— "heavy water," a material used in reactors. In addition, a chemical method of separating uranium from phosphate deposits was being developed. Both processes yielded results in experiments, and it was thought that they could be viable in commercial production. On 15 March 1954 Bergmann briefed Prime Minister Moshe Sharett that with these two new inventions, Israel could gain access to the basic nuclear materials—uranium and heavy water. Once Israel had access to these materials, Bergmann added, "this will enable us to build a nuclear reactor and to produce nuclear power. For the time being we are concentrating our efforts in extracting uranium."[23]

Bergmann's report to the prime minister, however, was too optimistic, even misleading. Other members of the IAEC disagreed with Bergmann's assessment. Sambursky, a member of the IAEC and the head of the scientific council, maintained that Bergmann's claim that Israel could develop the capacity to produce nuclear energy was a pipe dream, and that Israel should leave the production of nuclear materials to established nuclear powers.

Bergmann, on the other hand, thought that the two processes might have the potential for commercial production and would gain Israel respect and access to the nuclear technological know-how of others, particularly France and, to a lesser degree, Norway. These were the only countries in Europe (except the United Kingdom) with operating nuclear reactors; both countries were also interested in the technology for the separation of plutonium.[24] Given that in 1953–54 Israel had no experts in nuclear reactor physics and also that transferring nuclear engineering and reactor technology from the United States,

Britain, and Canada to foreign governments was still prohibited, Bergmann made special efforts to cultivate scientific and commercial relations with the nuclear establishments of France and Norway.

For Bergmann to achieve his long-term objective—obtaining a nuclear reactor and more—nuclear cooperation with France was the key. Using his connections in France, Bergmann successfully negotiated with his French counterpart in the CEA the sale of the two patents for possible commercial production.[25] Since France did not have access to raw materials nor to American nuclear technology, the Israeli inventions seemed important to France's nuclear program. The CEA was interested in Bergmann's reports that Israel had found an efficient method of extracting uranium from low-grade ores and a possibly cheaper alternative to Norway's heavy water. Bertrand Goldschmidt, one of France's leading nuclear scientists and the director of chemistry at the CEA, remembers the positive response of the administrator-general of the CEA, Pierre Guillaumat—"They are serious people"—to Bergmann's proposed sale. According to Goldschmidt, Bergmann asked the sum of 100 million (old) francs for the rights to the processes, and, after bargaining, "we agreed on 60 million. Within days we got five or six books explaining those methods."[26] In August 1954 Minister of Defense Pinhas Lavon briefed Sharett about the successful conclusion of these negotiation with both France and the United Kingdom.[27]

For Israel the real reward was the formation of a working relationship with the CEA. This opened the French Nuclear Research Center at Saclay and Chatillon to Israeli scientists. In late 1953 the first two Israeli physicists, Zvi Lipkin and Israel Pelah, were sent to these centers to study reactor physics ("pile physics," in the language of the time) and engineering. Amos de Shalit, soon on his way back to Israel from MIT, stayed in Saclay for a four-month course in reactor physics.[28]

Norway was the other country Bergmann looked to for nuclear cooperation. In the late 1940s and early 1950s, under the leadership of a young physicist named Gunnar Randers, Norway developed an extensive nuclear infrastructure, with an eye to both defense and energy.[29] As early as 1947 Norway decided to construct an experimental nuclear reactor funded by the Ministry of Defense from funds intended initially for the purchase of long-range artillery. The reactor was built with French assistance and went critical in 1951.[30] Norway was producing heavy water, but it lacked natural uranium. This was the context of Bergmann's initiative to get Norway interested in a joint venture to extract uranium from phosphate.

On 10 May 1954 Bergmann wrote Randers that "we have now completed the development of our processes for extraction of uranium from phosphates rocks; it appears that the method is commercially attractive, although the initial concentration of uranium is low. We are now considering putting up a factory which . . . will produce in the first years 5–10 tons of uranium per year." The problem was, Bergmann added, that "in the present situation of the State of Israel, we are lacking both engineering experience and money." Given both countries' interest in uranium, Bergmann raised the question, "in an informal manner," whether "the Norwegian Atomic Energy Commission would be interested to participate in an uranium factory to be erected in Israel."[31]

The two inventions turned out to be less significant than had been claimed at the time, and they were not put to commercial use anywhere. France and the United Kingdom, which bought the Israeli patents, did not use them;[32] Norway turned down Bergmann's "informal offer."[33] Eisenhower's Atoms for Peace program made these inventions obsolete by making American nuclear technology and expertise available. Nevertheless, these inventions contributed greatly to Israel's nuclear development by leading to nuclear cooperation with France and Norway.[34]

These efforts, however, shed light on the internal struggle within the IAEC in 1954. Bergmann was not interested in setting up a modest research and training program at the IAEC, as some of the academic members of the IAEC suggested. Instead, he was busy, at home and abroad, lobbying and marketing the chemical processes as Israel's path to the nuclear age. The tensions between Bergmann and the opposing academic school, represented primarily by Sambursky, intensified in the summer of 1954, when the United States offered Israel a nuclear research reactor as part of the Atoms for Peace program.[35]

In late June there was a discussion in Prime Minister Sharett's office on the question of a national nuclear master plan. The immediate issue was Israel's response to the American offer. Bergmann and Dostrovsky argued that Israel needed not only uranium but also technical knowledge, and that this could be acquired within a few years, rather than a generation.[36] Bergmann wanted the IAEC to concentrate on producing nuclear materials. Sambursky continued to advocate a more cautious view, arguing that the IAEC should focus on promoting theoretical research, not industrial production.

The dispute within the IAEC, and the need to respond to the U.S. offer, made it more urgent to clarify who had jurisdiction over nuclear affairs—the prime minister or the minister of defense. This issue was less pressing when Ben Gurion held both portfolios, but now the posts were held by two cabinet members. Sharett may have asked Ben Gurion for clarifications, because ten days later Ben Gurion wrote back that "it is difficult for me to answer your question because at the time I did not ask myself if I was acting in my capacity as prime minister or as minister of defense. It makes more sense to me now that I did it on behalf of the prime minister office."[37]

THE NUCLEAR PHYSICISTS' REVOLT

At issue in the early 1950s was the question of how to pursue nationally sponsored science programs like nuclear research. This question arose in other countries as well. In the United States most of the Manhattan Project's nuclear physicists went back to their universities after the war. The new nuclear laboratories at Los Alamos, Livermore, Oak Ridge, and Argonne were associated with academic research, and universities such as Berkeley, Harvard, MIT, Princeton, Chicago, Cornell, and Caltech provided training in nuclear physics that enabled their graduates to move into positions in national laboratories. In the 1950s French universities were not in the forefront of nuclear physics research, and physics graduate students had to learn their nuclear physics and quantum mechanics abroad. When young French nuclear physicists returned home, they were taken by the CEA and given the freedom to do nuclear physics research in France's national laboratories. They revolutionized French science by teaching nuclear physics and quantum mechanics then unavailable at the Sorbonne.

The Israeli case in the early 1950s was similar to the French. At the Hebrew University, the only Israeli institute of higher learning then offering physics, there was only one full professor of theoretical physics (Giulio Racah) and one lecturer in nuclear physics (Solly Cohen). Bergmann, who had just been expelled from the Weizmann Institute, hoped to follow the French example. He wanted the IAEC to be, like the French CEA, a national center for nuclear energy activities, not merely an administrative organ coordinating research among universities and research centers.

The group of six physicists, which had been sent abroad in late 1949, was central to Bergmann's vision of state-sponsored science. He recognized that it was essential to maintain the integrity of the group in order to create the core of nuclear physics research in Israel, and he believed that the IAEC lab, Machon 4, was a more suitable place from which to run national science than the Hebrew University.

By late 1951 the six Israeli physicists were completing their doctoral studies and planning their return to Israel. Four of them met in Zurich early that year to discuss how the group could set up a national nuclear physics program. After the meeting they wrote a letter to Bergmann, suggesting that while they should not be separated from the planning for the reactor, it would be essential to maintain a training and research program, with some affiliation with the Hebrew University.[38] For them, the most urgent priority was to train a new cadre of Israeli nuclear physicists at home. In the absence of indigenous nuclear physics training, and without a new cadre of professionals, they believed that the talk about long-term nuclear projects—a reactor and subsequent military applications—was empty.

EARLY FRICTION

Uri Haber-Schaim returned to Israel in October 1951 to launch the physics program at HEMED GIMMEL. De Shalit and Talmi also arrived at about that time, but then left to continue their postgraduate work at MIT and Princeton University, respectively. In late 1951 Zvi Lipkin, a veteran of the MIT Radiation Lab in the Second World War and a recent Princeton Ph.D. who had immigrated to Israel a year earlier, was recruited by the physics group at HEMED GIMMEL. In March 1952 Gideon Yekutieli arrived from England and joined the group. They were committed to setting up a national nuclear physics program, but soon discovered that there was a gap between their hopes and the reality they found in HEMED GIMMEL. Moreover, Bergmann himself was seen as the problem.[39]

On at least two occasions in 1951–52 there was an effort by the physicists to establish an academic program at a HEMED base in Jerusalem, in coordination with members of the Hebrew University faculty (Racah and Cohen), but bureaucratic opposition derailed the plan. Dostrovsky, their immediate boss in HEMED GIMMEL, opposed the division of the project between the physicists in Jerusalem and the chemists in Rehovot. Bergmann supported Dostrovsky and argued that "we cannot leave Dostrovsky without physicists." Another effort to set up a summer seminar in Rehovot for five or six advanced students from Jerusalem also failed.[40]

In a 1952 meeting with the nuclear physicists, Bergmann made clear the reasons behind his opposition, setting the project's priorities as follows: "First, the reactor, then nothing, then education, and at last your research."[41] Bergmann's attitude bred little confidence among the nuclear physicists. He considered the IAEC as a project-driven administration, but at the time there was no project-oriented activity taking place in HEMED GIMMEL. The reactor was Bergmann's priority, but in 1952 there were no reactor physicists in Israel. Haber-Schaim began to look into the physics involved in a reactor project, and in the spring of 1952, together with Yekutieli, proposed a series of experiments that could be used to train new physicists in the field. They proposed building a small, subcritical, reactor for basic training and research, but the uranium needed to start the program was not available.

With no opportunity to set up a training program or to start physics reactor experiments, Haber-Schaim and Yekutieli returned, in mid-1952, to their earlier work in high-energy (cosmic radiation) physics. Bergmann, who was fond of flowery titles, insisted that the two physicists' institutional affiliation should be the "Cosmic Ray Section, IAEC."[42] This research was not related to the nuclear project and was unclassified, but when Haber-Schaim and Yekutieli published a paper in September without obtaining a security clearance from Bergmann, and with the Weizmann Institute as their institutional affiliation, Bergmann reprimanded them.

In late November 1952 Haber-Schaim and Yekutieli wrote a letter of resignation to the IAEC.[43] Dostrovsky promised to protect them and urged them to stay on, and they agreed.[44] It was not long, however, before Bergmann and Haber-Schaim clashed again,[45] and Haber-Schaim left Israel for a physics position in Switzerland and, later, in the United States. The incident typified the deterioration in relations between Bergmann and the nuclear physicists who resented Bergmann's and Mardor's management style and view of the project's purpose.[46]

The Haber-Schaim affair, and the way he was fired by Bergmann, taught the physicists a lesson and strengthened their determination to end their formal relations with the IAEC under Bergmann. In December 1952 de Shalit wrote to Haber-Schaim that he was eager to leave the IAEC for the Weizmann Institute: "I do not want any contact with Bergmann or dependence on him," he wrote. "[Bergmann] knows exactly what I think of him and my views about how the way things should be managed. I do not see any reason why the [IAEC] should have labs of its own, and in my opinion it would fulfill its mandate if it would take care to meet the needs of the existing labs."[47]

AMOS DE SHALIT'S REVOLT

De Shalit, an internationally known physicist, formed an alliance with Meyer Weisgal, the chancellor of the Weizmann Institute, to establish a home there for the whole nuclear physics group. Weisgal found de Shalit a natural ally in his campaign to build the Weizmann Institute as the nation's preeminent science center. Weisgal was eager to expand the Weizmann Institute by adding a Department of Nuclear Physics, with the de Shalit group as its core; de Shalit and his colleagues, who wanted to build a national nuclear physics program, preferred to do so at the Weizmann Institute, rather than as Bergmann's pawns at the Ministry of Defense.[48]

The political timing of the de Shalit-Weisgal alliance was excellent. In the summer of 1953 Ben Gurion announced his retirement from his posts of prime minister and minister of defense, and appointed Pinhas Lavon acting minister of defense. On 7 December 1953 Ben Gurion formally resigned and moved to kibbutz Sdeh Boker in the Negev desert.[49] Lavon became minister of defense, and Foreign Minister Moshe Sharett became prime minister. The hawkish and inexperienced Lavon and the experienced dovish diplomat Sharett survived in power for barely a year, leaving the Israeli leadership in disarray.[50]

Nuclear research, too, was affected by the changes in the Ministry of Defense. Lavon's interest in organizational changes and budgetary cuts allowed de Shalit and Weisgal to pursue their own plans. Lavon was known to entertain all kinds of wild ideas, including the use of unconventional weapons against the Arabs,[51] but he had little faith in Bergmann's nuclear vision. Lavon agreed with de Shalit that Israel was not yet ready to build its own reactor, and decided to postpone the reactor project. He was persuaded that the national focus should be on setting up a training and research program in nuclear physics, and that the natural setting for such training was in academia, not in the Ministry of Defense. With the Weizmann Institute's interest in setting up a modern national nuclear physics program, it made sense to move the entire physics department of Machon 4 to the Weizmann Institute. De Shalit made it clear that the physicists would remain committed to contributing to national needs in nuclear energy, but that their work would be done for the IAEC on a contractual basis.[52]

On 20 January 1954 Lavon made the decision to transfer the physics department of Machon 4 to the Weizmann Institute. Mardor met with the physicists in a last-minute effort to change their minds, but to no avail.[53] In late April the nuclear physics department of Machon 4, its personnel and its scientific equipment, was moved to the Weizmann Institute at the cost of half a million Israeli pounds. On 1 May 1954 the Department of Nuclear Physics of the Weizmann Institute came into being, with Amos de Shalit, the architect of the deal, as its first head.

TWO VIEWS ON THE BREAKUP

Lavon's decisions to terminate the reactor project and move the IAEC nuclear physicists shattered the ambitious vision of Bergmann and Mardor. Their anger was directed at Lavon, Weisgal, and de Shalit and his colleagues.[54] In his book *Rafael*, Mardor explained that the transition from HEMED to EMET meant a move toward "long-term" planning. EMET was committed to "the establishment of infrastructure in the areas of science and technology [that] will allow independent research and development of weapons systems that will be in the future vital to the security of the state and its existence."[55] Lavon's decision was a retreat from this vision, bringing to an end an era that had hardly begun.[56]

For the leaders of EMET, the de Shalit-Weisgal deal was a betrayal and a theft. The nuclear physicists were sent overseas by Bergmann to fulfill a national mission; now they appeared to have abandoned that mission.[57] For Bergmann the affair must have been reminiscent of the past. In 1951 Weisgal was at the center of the rift between Bergmann and Weizmann, and was the architect of Bergmann's removal from the institution he had helped to build. In the three years since he had left the Weizmann Institute, Bergmann devoted himself to building a national science institution within the Ministry of Defense, especially in the area of nuclear energy. He founded the IAEC in 1952 with the hope of creating an alternative to the Hebrew University and the Weizmann Institute. The nuclear physics group was his greatest hope. Now Weisgal had again intervened and taken the physicists away.

The physicists, as we saw, perceived things differently. As Lipkin recalls:

> In 1954, it was clear that the future development of nuclear physics and nuclear energy in Israel depended on having a facility with a machine, either reactor or accelerator, which could enable physicists, chemists, students and technicians to work with their hands locally on devices that produced nuclear reactions and radioactive isotopes.... The IAEC was not interested in developing nuclear physics at that time.... The Hebrew University was also not ready to do this. But Meyer Weisgal was ready to find the funding for obtaining an accelerator, hiring the whole physics group at the IAEC ... and establishing a group of critical size as a beginning of Israel's national research nuclear center.[58]

In Retrospect

Was Lavon right to cut the budget for nuclear research? Lavon made the right decision, regardless of his motives. The fact was that without substantial foreign assistance, Israel was not capable of launching the reactor project. Bergmann's vision was, to the physicists, an "expression of ignorance and arrogance."[59] Lavon accepted the judgment of de Shalit and his colleagues that Israel was not yet in a position to build a reactor without foreign assistance. In 1952–54 such assistance (from France or elsewhere) did not appear to be forthcoming. Lavon also accepted de Shalit's argument that a training and research program was what Israel needed most, and that the Weizmann Institute was the right setting for that. Instead, the IAEC should contract out jobs for the nuclear physicists at the Weizmann Institute when the time was right, but it should not employ them.

De Shalit and Weisgal thus reversed Bergmann's effort to follow the French model of science, preferring the American model instead. De Shalit and his group also did not believe that the IAEC, under Bergmann's leadership, was qualified to develop the foundations for nuclear energy in Israel.

Most of the EMET chiefs who opposed the move of the nuclear physicists— among them Shalheveth Freier, then the acting director of EMET—eventually concluded that the move was inevitable, good for Israeli nuclear physics, and even beneficial for the national nuclear project. The negative reaction of the leaders of EMET to the departure of the nuclear physicists was unwarranted.[60]

Within a year the situation changed. In early 1955 Ben Gurion returned to power, first to the Ministry of Defense and later to the prime minister's office. The nuclear pursuit was first priority again. Abroad, Eisenhower's Atoms for Peace program made possible the first Geneva Conference on the Peaceful Uses of Atomic Energy. Nuclear technology and know-how, classified since the days of the Manhattan Project, was being declassified and released. Most significant, during the next two years unique political circumstances arose in France. A nuclear project was ready to be born.

With the return of Ben Gurion to power in 1955, nuclear energy became a matter of national priority. Ben Gurion gave political backing and financial support to those in the Ministry of Defense who were committed to promoting nuclear energy—Peres, Bergmann, Mardor, and the nuclear enthusiasts at Machon 4. There was also a change in the international climate concerning nuclear energy, in the wake of Eisenhower's December 1953 Atoms-for-Peace initiative. Until then, nuclear energy in the United States, Canada, and Britain, the three major countries dealing with nuclear energy, was largely closed to other countries. The Atoms for Peace initiative made nuclear energy technology available to the rest of the world.

In Israel in 1955 policy makers and scientists agreed that the country must take advantage of the new opportunities posed by the American program to initiate a national nuclear energy project. There was no agreement, however, over what the objectives, priorities, and timetable of the project should be, and how to pursue them. The debate revolved around how ambitious the project should be, and particularly to what extent the interest in military applications should drive the effort. In 1955–56 it was not clear how far Israel could advance its nuclear ambitions. The debates took place behind closed doors, among policy makers and scientists, establishing the pattern of secrecy and opacity that would characterize the Israeli nuclear program.

BEN GURION'S RETURN

At the end of 1954, while Ben Gurion was on leave in the Negev kibbutz of Sdeh Boker, Israel's political and defense leadership was embroiled in scandals and intrigues; much of it came to be known as the Lavon Affair (see chapter 8). In early 1955 Ben Gurion was asked by the MAPAI leadership to return to his old post as minister of defense. Soon thereafter Ben Gurion determined that the time had come for Israel to launch a national nuclear energy project, with the objective of developing nuclear weapons.

Little is known on how Ben Gurion had reached this conclusion. What is known, however, is that during 1954, the year Ben Gurion was in Sdeh Boker, his close group of loyalists at the Ministry of Defense—Peres, Dayan, and Bergmann—briefed him regularly on the important issues of state, especially matters of security.[1] He received reports on the frustrations of his loyalists with Lavon's reckless policies, including Bergmann's anger over Lavon's decision to dismantle the nuclear physics section of Machon 4 and sell it to the Weizmann Institute.

It appears that Ben Gurion shared Bergmann's anger. There is evidence to suggest that, in late 1954, Ben Gurion was preoccupied with the nuclear project. On 16 December 1954, in a closed-door session with MAPAI leaders, including Prime Minister Sharett and Minister of Defense Lavon, Ben Gurion raised the issue.[2] He warned of the consequences of polarization at home, and cautioned that the seven Arab nations that fought Israel in its War of Independence were to form a united Arab nation, most likely under Egyptian hegemony. The more the Arabs became united, the less they would accept Israel. Ben Gurion also saw Israel itself as weakening and losing its pioneering spirit, with its electoral system allowing, even encouraging, ethnic division and instability. The mass immigration into Israel was creating national divisions, not unity. Toward the end of his address Ben Gurion said the following: "And another issue that must be given more resources by the state is the development of science. It might be that our ultimate security would rest on that. But I will not talk about it any further. This could be the last thing that may save us."[3]

Ben Gurion's subsequent expressions make clear what he had in mind. On 24 April 1955, in a special cabinet session dedicated to security briefing, Ben Gurion presented his colleagues with a bleak picture of the state of the Arab-Israeli conflict and its consequences for Israel's long-term security. He depicted Egyptian president Nasser as Israel's most dangerous enemy, determined to destroy Israel once the right opportunity presented itself. He focused on the increasingly negative balance of military power between Israel and its neighbors, concluding that Israel's long-term security must be based on its own strength, not on external guarantees. According to the Sharett diaries, Ben Gurion explicitly alluded to "the future of atomic research" as one of his primary objectives.[4]

Three days later Ben Gurion publicly expressed his philosophy of self-reliance. In an Independence Day address, Ben Gurion told the country that "the future of Israel was not dependent on what the gentiles would say, but on what the Jews would do." This attitude became the motto of the nuclear program.

The cabinet discussion was followed by a meeting at the Ministry of Defense on 5 May 1955, about the need to invest more in scientific research. Mardor, in quoting Ben Gurion, noted the latter's elliptical, yet unmistakable, remarks in the meeting:

> "We are in a situation in which it is worthwhile for us to spend sums of money, even if there is only a hope to reach such a thing," Ben Gurion said. "I am certainly in favor of it. . . . Our security problem could have two answers: if possible, political guarantees, but this is not up to us. But on what depends on us, we must invest all our power, because we must have superiority in weapons, because we will never achieve superiority in manpower. All those things that have to do with science, we must do them."[5]

For the leaders of EMET these words meant an endorsement of their philosophy, and a promise of resources to implement that philosophy.[6] In 1955 EMET began to recruit advanced students in science, mathematics, and engineering for the project. The first recruits were selected by Bergmann and Jenka Ratner, the head of Machon 3 of EMET and the future chief of the bomb project. A few of the recruits were sent for postgraduate work at the Institute of Nuclear Science and Techniques at Saclay, near Paris, and the Chatillon Nuclear Establishment, the home of France's first nuclear reactor.[7] This time the recruits were told more explicitly about their EMET mission. After being granted their security clearances and sworn to secrecy, the recruits were told by Ratner in unequivocal language that they were chosen for Israel's most secret national project—a project that would result in the building of an Israeli nuclear device.[8] Arrangements were made so that the new recruits would stay with EMET for some time after they finished their postgraduate studies. The leaders of EMET were determined not to repeat the mistakes of the past in selecting the new scientists. Unlike Racah's selection of de Shalit's group in 1949 on the basis of science alone, in 1955–56 Ratner and Bergmann selected people who were ready to commit themselves to the top-secret project.

ATOMS FOR PEACE: OPPORTUNITIES AND DEBATES

The year 1955 was also a year of great international excitement over the use and spread of nuclear energy. On 8 December 1953, in a speech at the UN, President Eisenhower unveiled his Atoms for Peace program which reversed the American policy of nuclear denial and brought an end to a decade of nuclear secrecy.[9] The speech symbolized the age of unlimited faith in nuclear energy. It manifested the expectation that nuclear energy would be the third wave of the industrial revolution, and that American technology should lead the march. The distinction between peaceful and destructive uses of atomic energy, and the belief that it was possible to promote the one and to control the other, was the ethos of this program.

Soon thereafter Eisenhower asked Congress to amend the Atomic Energy Act of 1946 to allow the United States to declassify nuclear scientific information and theoretical and experimental research data, and to allow distribution of nuclear materials. Research reactors, previously prohibited for export by law, were promoted as a necessary step toward the future; techniques for uranium enrichment and plutonium separation were declassified. Atoms for Peace was successful in promoting American nuclear technology, but it was less successful in maintaining safeguards and control. The Eisenhower administration released so much information that later administrations saw fit to reclassify some of it.

Israel took full advantage of the new developments. In 1954 the United States offered Israel a small experimental reactor as part of the negotiations on the regional water issue, and both Sharett and Ben Gurion supported the IAEC recommendation that Israel should sign on to the American offer. Israel was the second nation, after Turkey, to join the Atoms for Peace initiative. According to Sharett's diary, on 18 May 1955, the draft of the contract reached the prime minister's office. "I called Ben Gurion and he stepped immediately into my office. We read the contract and we found no fault in it," Sharett wrote in his diary. "It does not prohibit us from contacting other powers, nor even the use of nuclear power to be produced in our own means. On the other hand, it promises us a reactor for experiments and also research, and requires only one limitation: not to use this reactor for any other purpose."[10] Two months later, on 12 July 1955, Israel and the United States signed a general agreement for peaceful nuclear cooperation, including an agreement for the purchase of a small research nuclear reactor.[11] While in July 1955 Israel had nothing like a nuclear master plan, it was clear to Israeli decision makers that the agreement with the United States should not foreclose other options.

The first Geneva Conference on the Peaceful Use of Atomic Energy was convened in August 1955. The presumption underlying the conference was that, within fifty years, nuclear and solar energy would replace fossil fuels. Some twenty-five thousand delegates and observers attended the meetings, with private industry sending hundreds of its own people. Israel sent its entire nuclear elite to the Geneva conference. Bergmann was the delegation's deputy head, and Dostrovsky, de Shalit, Racah, Cohen, Lipkin, and Pelah came as delegates, advisers, or observers.

During the Geneva conference the Israeli delegation discussed its nuclear energy plans with the American delegation. Most of these discussions were about reactors, specifically the original ideas Israeli scientists had come up with to increase the capabilities of the reactor the United States had previously offered Israel. The purpose of this special design was to use the reactor to produce small quantities of plutonium from Israel's stock of natural uranium. Bergmann told American officials that the IAEC physicists had devised "what they thought was an original concept," utilizing a core of enriched uranium and a blanket of natural uranium, plus heavy water as a neutron moderator and coolant.

Bergmann mentioned this point in his meeting with the chair of the AEC, Admiral Lewis Strauss. Bergmann explained that Israel wanted something more powerful than the original research reactor the United States had offered Israel, "something like a real reactor," a reactor that would allow Israel to train engineers and chemists in working with the "new elements, such as plutonium." Bergmann compared the reactor design concept to the pressurized-water reactor (PWR).[12] Strauss's response, according to Bergmann's report, was categorical: "You could not do anything that would provide you even the slightest quantities of plutonium."[13] In a response to Bergmann's comment that the Israeli ideas would not violate the framework agreement—in any case the few grams of plutonium that it would produce "could not endanger the security of the United States"—Strauss said that although it was not clear yet how the safeguards system would be put together, "there would be control." To relieve the tension that was created, writes Bergmann, Strauss asked them when Rosh Hashana and Yom Kippur took place and suggested that the Israeli proposals be submitted to the AEC via the embassy by the end of September.[14]

Another meeting took place between Bergmann, Dostrovsky, and de Shalit, and Ambassador Morehead Patterson, President Eisenhower's special ambassador on nuclear energy. At the outset Bergmann declared that "Israel wanted to go forward immediately towards the development of atomic power," citing Israel's difficulties in securing oil. Bergmann also told the Americans that Israel was producing uranium from phosphates and heavy water, "both in small quantities."[15] In this meeting, too, Bergmann discussed the Israeli ideas to upgrade the design of the reactor, comparing those ideas to the U.S. design of its Shipping-port power reactor.[16] Referring to the fact that such a reactor would produce small quantities of plutonium, Bergmann asked whether the American-Israeli agreement would permit Israel to construct such a reactor, and what would be the fate of the plutonium.

As to the American response, there is some difference between the American and Israeli reports. According to the American memorandum, "Ambassador Patterson stated that he had no idea what the answer would be to these questions," noting that "the research reactor program was intended merely to start the process of education which would ultimately lead to power." According to Bergmann's report, Patterson praised the Israeli initiative and expressed his opinion that Israel would have no problem with the United States on this. Patterson stressed, however, that the final decision laid with the AEC, not the president. Patterson was also said to suggest that in order to avoid difficulties the Israelis should propose initially something that would not stir objection, with the intention of adding to the proposal later. "In any case, there was no chance of effective control."[17]

Bergmann's final report (classified "top secret") on the conference, which was circulated in two versions among governmental agencies and individuals, reveals something about the long-term hopes of the IAEC and the gap between those hopes and its present poverty. Bergmann urged the government "to make all efforts to get as much assistance as possible from the United States, in both information and material; this effort needs to be made as early as possible, for political considerations may influence the American response to our request."[18] Specifically, Bergmann proposed that Israel immediately purchase from the United States the small swimming-pool reactor, "with those improvements that our scientists propose and are accepted by the Americans," under the Atoms for Peace program. "Such a reactor can be obtained in a relatively short time; it would allow us to educate our people." He also recommended buying in the United States twenty tons of heavy water, "conditional on no U.S. control." These two purchases were to be carried out immediately. In addition, he recommended accumulating the quantities of thorium and uranium that "will be needed for our future plans." All this and more was based on the assumption "that in the future we will have to rely on ourselves."[19]

An even more revealing letter, dated 28 August 1955, involving Israel's hidden agenda and the lessons of the Geneva conference, was written by de Shalit to Mardor. The letter contains sharp criticism of the approach Bergmann proposed, providing a window to what Bergmann and Mardor had in mind, including what the "improvements that our scientists propose" were. De Shalit cautioned Mardor against imprudence in the nuclear field. It is worth citing the letter at length:

One of the main purposes of our trip to Geneva was to find out to what extent the United States would be ready to provide us with the enriched uranium in a form suitable for use in the special reactor which we were contemplating. This special reactor, as you may recall, was designed in such a way that in addition to the enriched uranium which we would receive from the United States, we would use some of our own natural uranium in such a way that we would produce about 8 grams of plutonium a month with our uranium. This quantity of uranium was required by Dr. Dostrovsky to facilitate experiments at a higher level than the preliminary lab stage of separating plutonium.

Following talks that we had with various people in Geneva, the summary of which was submitted to you in the above mentioned report, I think it is possible to reach the following conclusions:

A. We should forget about submitting a plan which does not indicate the real purposes. Practically all the people with whom we talked were fully aware of the problem of plutonium, and it is evident that the issue cannot be snuck in through talk about fissile products, power plants, etc. I do not think that there is anyone among the responsible individuals in the United States who would believe that a state which was in possession of a large scale plutonium separation capacity, and which would have the objective capabilities of doing so, would not exploit its knowledge for military purposes or at least conduct experiments in that direction. For this reason it should be clear that to the extent that we would be allowed or helped in research involving plutonium separation it would mean that we were being actively helped in nuclear weapons research. I leave it to individuals wiser and better than me to decide whether our chances are good or bad, but . . . if we were to be allowed to proceed in the direction of plutonium separation it would better to ask directly for plutonium rather than to try to outsmart everyone and build a complicated reactor for that purpose.[20]

De Shalit thus opposed the idea that Israel could secretly use its Atoms for Peace reactor for extracting plutonium, taking it upon himself to balance Bergmann's optimism and remind the leadership of the political risks and technological limits of the enterprise. From that time on, the nuclear physicists at the Weizmann Institute, under the leadership of de Shalit, would be the sharpest critics of the Bergmann-Mardor alliance.

POLITICAL DEVELOPMENTS

Within weeks after the Geneva conference, the situation in Israel and the region changed in ways that influenced the future of the nuclear project. In Israel, following the general elections in late July, Ben Gurion formed the cabinet and assumed his old posts of prime minister and minister of defense. Sharett agreed to serve as his foreign minister. This was a victory for Ben Gurion's activist defense policy. Sharett offered an alternative policy toward a resolution of the Arab-Israeli conflict. He believed that a dialogue with Nasser was possible, and that a security understanding, preferably in the form of a guarantee of Israel's territorial integrity, should be reached with the United States. Sharett urged a policy that would limit the use by Israel of military force in order to facilitate a political solution.[21]

Ben Gurion rejected Sharett's objectives and his choice of means. He saw Arab hostility to Israel as fundamental and enduring. Nasser's pan-Arabic rhetoric made him Israel's most dangerous enemy. An activist Israeli policy of military reprisals was necessary to keep Nasser in check, perhaps even leading to his fall. Only ten days after coming back to the Ministry of Defense, Ben Gurion approved a major reprisal raid against the Egyptian army in the Gaza strip.[22]

Ben Gurion was also skeptical about the availability of U.S. security guarantees to Israel. In the early 1950s Ben Gurion entertained the idea of a defense pact between the United States and Israel, which would guarantee Israel's 1949 cease-fire borders, as the best solution for Israel's predicament.[23] When he returned to power, however, he no longer thought such a pact was feasible and stressed the reasons why both sides would avoid such a formal alliance.[24] The response to Israel's security problems did not lie in diplomacy, but in an activist defense policy based on a deterrence posture Israel would develop on its own. A nuclear option would be central to this posture.

A second development was the large Czech-Egyptian arms deal, which was announced by Nasser in late September 1955. The deal would double or even triple Egypt's military strength, especially in artillery, armor, and in the air, threatening the Egyptian-Israeli military balance.[25] A month later Nasser announced the closing of the Straits of Tiran to Israeli shipping, an action Israel considered an act of war. In December 1955 Ben Gurion submitted to the cabinet a military plan to occupy and reopen the straits, but the cabinet, under Sharett's influence, rejected it. Another Egyptian-Israeli war appeared likely.[26] It was calculated that the Egyptians needed eight months to deploy their new weapons, so that the Egyptian army would be capable of attacking Israel by the following summer.[27] Israel had to choose between waiting until Egypt was ready to fight or initiating a preventive war. Ben Gurion responded to the deteriorating situation by launching an urgent campaign to purchase military hardware abroad, and by accelerating research and production of weapons at home.

Among his initiatives, Ben Gurion ordered rush development of a cheap unconventional deterrence capability—chemical munitions—to be produced at EMET facilities. Ben Gurion considered it vital for Israel to maintain a capability "which could set up another line of defense for Israel, beyond the conventional means of the IDF, in case the enemy would use non-conventional weapons in the battlefield or against civilian population." He ordered that this capability be made operational before war could break out. This was the "project that preceded the nuclear option."[28]

PERES AND THE FRENCH ADVENTURE

In late 1955 the Foreign Ministry and the Defense Ministry were competing with each other for securing sources of armaments. Sharett's effort focused on obtaining American weapons, while Peres concentrated on French material. Peres had started advocating a French orientation in areas of armaments and military technology as early as 1953.[29] These early efforts yielded little, though, because Lavon did not back his efforts in France.[30]

With Ben Gurion back in power, especially after the Czech-Egyptian arms deal in September, the dealings with France were given a boost. Within months France became Israel's primary arms supplier, with major deals for jet fighters, tanks, and other military equipment.[31] By the spring of 1956 Peres reached a comprehensive security understanding with the government of Guy Mollet. The details of that understanding were formalized in a secret conference in Vermars on 22 June 1956 between the senior military representatives of the two countries.[32]

The circumstances contributing to the development of the relationship were both geopolitical and domestic. By 1955–56 the situation in France's North African colonies was deteriorating, and the French military establishment viewed Nasser as the force behind the Algerian rebellion, which was becoming uncontrollable.[33] A militarily strong Israel, capable of threatening Nasser, was now in France's interest.

The warming of the French-Israeli relationship after September 1955 was not only the result of geopolitics, but was also driven by domestic, economic, and even personal forces. With the help of the French ambassador in Israel, Pierre Gilbert, Peres formed a pro-Israeli coalition combining pro-Jewish and socialist sentiments with nationalistic interests in the expansion of the French aerospace and nuclear industries. Peres also took advantage of the structural weaknesses of the Fourth Republic. Recognizing the fragmentation of France's policy-making organs, Peres developed a close relationship with the French defense and interior (intelligence) ministers, bypassing the pro-Arab Quai d'Orsay bureaucracy.[34] As Sylvia Crosbie puts it:

With the executive paralyzed by a domineering legislature, which was in turn immobilized by its own failings, there was widespread freedom of action at various levels of the bureaucracy. This enabled a relatively small group of individuals in the defense establishment and related ministries to cooperate intimately with Israel without any formal arrangement, sometimes in opposition to official government policy. Acting independently and often autonomously, they were in essence conducting their own foreign relations directly with the Israel Defense Ministry.[35]

Peres arranged to obtain French weapons through unconventional channels, using these channels to explore whether France would assist Israel in pursuing nuclear weapons. That France itself was still undecided about the acquisition of its own nuclear weapons, and that the pronuclear camp advanced its cause stealthily and incrementally, made it easier for Peres to advance Israel's nuclear objective. Defense Minister Maurice Bourges-Maunoury, a supporter of French nuclear weapons, understood Peres's vision just as he understood the need to keep the two countries' nuclear plans opaque.

THE BERGMANN—DE SHALIT DISPUTE

During the year following the Geneva conference, the IAEC debated ideas and proposals about how to initiate a national nuclear energy project. Until the early summer of 1956 the focus of those debates was the nuclear assistance that the United States had offered Israel. There was a national consensus that Israel should take advantage of the 1955 bilateral nuclear cooperation agreement and build a reactor with American technological and financial assistance, but it was less clear what type of reactor it should be and, even more fundamentally, what kind of a national program Israel should pursue. There were two reasons for the lack of clarity: (1) uncertainty as to the scope and nature of assistance that the United States would offer, for example, what kind of reactor the United States would be willing to help Israel construct under the conditions of the 1955 bilateral agreement, which firm should be the project's contractor, the terms of the financial assistance from the U.S. government, and issues concerning the fuel (lease or purchase); and (2) fundamental disagreements as to what should be the appropriate scope and objectives of the Israeli project at this initial stage.

Given those uncertainties and debates, a large IAEC delegation—headed by Bergmann and including Dostrovsky, de Shalit, Pelah, and Lipkin—was sent in the spring of 1956 to the United States and Canada for an educational tour. The objective was to visit nuclear energy research centers (national laboratories, universities, and industry) to garner advice on which reactors were available and the firms that could supply them. On 11 April Bergmann and his team paid a visit to the AEC headquarters to discuss Israeli plans. Bergmann informed his hosts that Israel was planning to construct a 10-MW research reactor fueled by natural uranium and moderated by heavy water (the uranium to be produced in Israel itself). Bergmann explained the rationale for this kind of reactor by saying that "Israel enjoyed a fairly advanced technological position in the atomic field" and decided, therefore, to "skip over the experimental phase of operating a swimming pool type" of research reactor. He also stated that the specifications of the reactor had already been given to a number of American firms and that the IAEC expected to receive bids in a few weeks. Bergmann indicated that Israel would like to obtain from the AEC "research quantities" of enriched uranium and the heavy water required for the reactor as part of the agreement, and asked whether such requests would pose any particular difficulties. The Americans replied that, in principle, a purchase of heavy water posed no special problems as long as it was used for peaceful purposes. It was agreed that Israel would submit an official request for heavy water as well as the specifications of the reactor necessary to qualify for American financial assistance at a later date, once a formal decision had been made.[36]

In reality, however, no immediate decision was made. The visit only intensified the internal debate in the IAEA. Once again, the primary antagonists were Bergmann and de Shalit. Bergmann advocated an ambitious dual-purpose nuclear energy program, that is, one with both peaceful and military applications. In a memorandum to Peres, written in July 1956, Bergmann urged that Israel build two reactors at the same time—a small research reactor near the Weizmann Institute in Rehovot or in Nachal Soreq, and a larger one in the Negev, as well as explore other possibilities. Bergmann concluded: "If we pursue all these paths, we may be confident that some of them at least will lead to our goal."[37] Even without foreign assistance, Israel should go ahead and build a nuclear reactor on its own.[38]

De Shalit (as well as Lipkin) considered Bergmann's ideas "dangerous and fantastic."[39] Instead, de Shalit advocated a modest program directed at research and training by way of building a small swimming pool research reactor. De Shalit opposed Bergmann's idea of the 10-MW natural uranium, heavy-water reactor for technological-scientific, financial, and—not the least—political reasons. It appears that de Shalit thought that Bergmann's ideas would compromise Israel's "peaceful use" pledge under the 1955 agreement. As to Bergmann's interest to start a nuclear power program immediately, De Shalit did not think that Israel was ready for that. Israel did not have adequate manpower to start such a program. All the major decisions regarding power and military applications should be postponed.

This was the state of affairs in the spring of 1956. Israel seemed unable to make up its mind what type of nuclear program it should pursue. Ben Gurion and Peres sympathized with Bergmann's visionary ideas, but they also carefully considered de Shalit's view that Bergmann's grand vision was ungrounded in reality and therefore dangerous. Peres recognized that Bergmann's concept was unfeasible the way he conceived it, but he looked for other ways to make it politically and technologically feasible. Peres focused his efforts on France, not the United States, but for the time being, in mid-1956, the IAEC pursued its plans without making a decision.

In early summer the IAEC submitted the information needed for its request for a $350,000 American grant toward a small, pool-type research reactor.[40] At the same time (17 July 1956), however, Bergmann wrote to the AEC chairman, Lewis Strauss, that Israel was interested in purchasing from the AEC 10 tons of heavy water to use in a 10-MW natural uranium, heavy-water reactor it was about to build. The Americans interpreted Bergmann's letter to imply that the Israelis were contemplating "the construction of a second reactor of a type that will not permit them to obtain U.S. nuclear fuel under the existing research agreement."[41]

Ironically the author of this memo had no idea how this assessment was accurate in September 1956, but for reasons he could not be aware of. By the summer of 1956 Shimon Peres's French connection bore fruit: the geopolitical situation created a unique window of opportunity to bypass the need to choose between Bergmann's and de Shalit's options. As noted earlier, efforts to acquire French nuclear assistance began in the late 1940s, but nobody could predict, even by late 1955, that France would be ready to supply Israel with a comprehensive nuclear package, including both a large reactor that could produce significant quantities of plutonium and the technology to separate it from the irradiated reactor fuel, a so-called reprocessing plant.

THE SUEZ OPPORTUNITY

By early 1956, as French-Israeli military relations intensified, Peres became convinced that France could be the primary source of nuclear assistance. He looked for the political opening that would allow the extension of the Franco-Israeli alliance to the nuclear field. If this could happen, then the whole debate between Bergmann and de Shalit would be rendered irrelevant. Peres agreed with de Shalit that Bergmann's optimism was unwarranted, but he, like Bergmann, was not ready to postpone the big project. With this in mind, Peres focused much of his activities in Paris from early 1956 in developing a strategy to persuade France to be Israel's foreign nuclear supplier, that is, to provide Israel with the kind of assistance that would allow it to initiate a nuclear program aimed ultimately at producing nuclear explosives.

In parallel with the negotiations with the United States, Peres and Bergmann approached their colleagues at the French Ministry of Defense and the CEA about Israel's interest in buying a nuclear reactor from France as part of a closer French-Israeli nuclear relationship. At the time France was debating its own nuclear future, both in the area of civil power and military applications. The small and young French nuclear industry was interested in finding a major international client that would allow France to establish its credentials as a nuclear player. On the other side of the Atlantic, both the United States and Canada had already been engaged in major deals of exporting nuclear know-how, technology, and material to new nations, such as India.[42]

Yet, the French hesitated.[43] By spring, Peres concluded that this hesitation might be overcome if Israel offered them something of value in return, for example, intelligence cooperation concerning the relations between Egypt and the Algerian rebels.[44] Ben Gurion therefore authorized the creation of a special intelligence relationship between *Agaf Modi'in* (AMAN, Israeli military intelligence) and its French counterpart, suggesting that a tacit exchange of intelligence for nuclear help, among other things, could be fashioned.[45] Whether the intelligence cooperation would have been enough to bring about French nuclear assistance to Israel was never tested, since the situation changed almost overnight.

On 26 July 1956 Nasser announced the nationalization of the Suez Canal.[46] The Egyptian challenge to the Mollet government provided Peres the opportunity to push the French-Israeli alliance a step further. The opportunity presented itself the next day, when French defense minister Bourges-Maunoury asked Peres for an urgent meeting. According to Peres, Bourges-Maunoury wasted little time in asking how long it would take the IDF to cross the Sinai Peninsula and reach the canal. When Peres replied that, in his assessment, it could be done in less than two weeks, Bourges-Maunoury then asked if Israel would be prepared to participate in a tripartite military operation, in which Israel's specific role would be to cross the Sinai. Peres responded: "Under certain circumstances I assume that we would be so prepared." To the admonition of an aide, who told Peres that he—Peres—had no authority to promise Israel's participation and that he might be punished, Peres responded that he would "rather risk his neck than risk missing a unique opportunity like this."[47] Peres's biographer writes that Peres readily replied in the affirmative because he calculated that this could be the opportunity that would give Israel the reactor.[48]

The results came quickly. In August Shalheveth Freier, the first Israeli science liaison associated with the evolving nuclear project, arrived in Paris,[49] and on 17 September 1956 (or 21 September, according to Peres's biographer) the CEA and the IAEC reached an agreement in principle on the sale to Israel of a "small" research reactor, one like the EL-3 reactor at Saclay.[50] The physicist Bertrand Goldschmidt, who was in charge of external relations at the CEA and who attended that meeting, recalled that Peres and Bergmann "explained to us that they wanted our help to create . . . something like 'nuclear capacity'."[51] The agreement still needed political approval, but there is little doubt that the French understood what the deal was about. For the French commissariat, selling the reactor to Israel meant the export of French nuclear technology, a way to advertise France's young nuclear industry and to establish its credentials in the field.[52]

In his 1995 *Memoirs* Peres acknowledged that the nuclear issue was discussed briefly at the end of the secret Sèvres conference (22–24 October), when the British-French-Israeli collaboration was cemented. According to Peres, "Before the final signing, I asked Ben Gurion for a brief adjournment, during which I met Mollet and Bourges-Maunoury alone. It was here that I finalized with these two leaders an agreement for the building of a nuclear reactor at Dimona, in southern Israel, and the supply of natural uranium to fuel it."[53]

It was not the case that the nuclear reactor was the price for Israel's involvement in the French operation in the Suez. Although the nuclear issue was an important element in the Israeli calculation for cooperation with the French in the Suez campaign—and that cooperation played a role in facilitating the September reactor deal—it was not a simple bargain. It was an implicit incentive for both nations, not a condition.[54] This point is seen in the record of the Sèvres conference, in which Ben Gurion negotiated the terms of the Israeli participation in the Suez campaign. The nuclear issue was not raised during the substantive negotiations about the Israeli role. It was only after the understandings of the Sèvres conference were reached that Peres briefly mentioned the reactor deal, which had already been concluded at the technical level, and thanked the French.[55] Had Ben Gurion been unsatisfied with the political or military terms of the Israeli participation in the Suez operation, the nuclear deal, in itself, would have been insufficient to persuade him to allow Israel to participate in the French-inspired operation.[56]

The nuclear reactor deal that Peres initiated with the CEA in September, and which was affirmed at Sèvres, was not the Dimona reactor as we know it. The agreement was about a smaller reactor. Pierre Péan makes it clear that the September agreement did not cover a Dimona-type reactor. Rather, he states that the "small" reactor was located at Rishon Le-Zion, near the Weizmann Institute, and that early construction work had already begun at that site.[57] In the discussions preceding the Suez campaign, "the plutonium-producing nature of the reactor" was not emphasized, and certainly the sale did not include a plutonium separation plant.[58]

As the Suez crisis deepened, the original plan changed. On 6 November the Soviets issued an ultimatum to the three states involved in the campaign to stop the operation, but their most dire threat was directed at Israel, accusing it of "criminally and irresponsibly playing with the fate of its own people . . . which puts in jeopardy the very existence of Israel as a State."[59] In a separate letter to Ben Gurion, Prime Minister Nikolai Bulganin warned that the Soviets were able to attack Israel with missiles. Eisenhower, who had just been elected to a second term, also demanded an immediate cease-fire and withdrawal. By the early morning hours of 8 November Ben Gurion had secretly sent Shimon Peres and Golda Meir to Paris, to "find out what the French stand would be in the event of specific Soviet intervention."[60] He wanted to know what France could do for Israel before making a decision on withdrawal from the Sinai.[61]

French foreign minister Christian Pineau, Defense Minister Maurice Bourges-Maunoury, and Maunoury's close aide, Abel Thomas, could offer no words of encouragement. They pledged that France would stand at Israel's side, but it was evident that France had nothing concrete to offer Israel in the face of the Soviet nuclear threat. Pineau told the Israelis that he took the Soviet threats very seriously, and urged Israel to comply with the ultimatum.[62]

Israeli sources are silent on what happened at this point, but according to Péan, who cites French sources, it was in these talks that the idea of substantial French nuclear assistance to Israel was conceived.[63] According to Thomas, Peres raised the issue of French nuclear assistance to Israel as a security guarantee if Israel withdrew from the Sinai. This timely nuclear assistance would constitute the ultimate guarantee of Israel's existence. Péan quotes Peres: "I don't trust the guarantees of others. . . . What would you think if we prepared our own retaliation force?"[64] Bourges-Maunoury and Thomas, two advocates of French nuclear weapons, responded positively. Now they had to convince the high commissioner of the CEA, Francis Perrin, and Guy Mollet, who had not approved the French nuclear weapons program before Suez, to support the nuclear ambitions of both countries. With the Suez crisis as the backdrop, and a pledge in hand, Peres began to put together the Dimona package.

The French-Israeli deal that made the Dimona project possible was the outcome of a unique historical moment when France and Israel found themselves in an unorthodox alliance. The situation in the Middle East and North Africa, domestic forces in both countries, and the Suez crisis undergirded the extraordinary alliance. The Soviet threats at the height of the Suez campaign ignited the nuclear ambitions of both nations.

The road to Dimona was a bumpy one. Dimona was a gigantic construction and engineering project for the Israel of 1958. It required materials, technical expertise, and financing unavailable in Israel. These needs and uncertainties were the sources of Israel's nuclear opacity.

THE DIMONA DEAL

The Suez crisis had important consequences for the French nuclear program. It demonstrated France's vulnerability to American and Soviet pressure. Only by developing its own nuclear weapons would the humiliation France had suffered in the Suez be avoided in the future.[1] Guy Mollet's initial hesitation about nuclear weapons "was transformed overnight into a determined and positive interest in national nuclear armament."[2] In late November 1956, only ten months after Mollet had declared his support of EURATOM and his opposition to French atomic weapons,[3] his government agreed to establish an interministerial atomic program for national defense. The *Commissariat l'Energie Atomique* (CEA) was authorized to carry out research on atomic explosions, produce design prototypes of nuclear devices, and prepare for nuclear testing. It was responsible for providing the plutonium required for the new program and to perform the research that would produce highly enriched uranium. The decision meant, in effect, that France was establishing a military nuclear program.

Shimon Peres could now be more straightforward about his intentions in revising the Israeli request for French nuclear assistance. The small EL-102 reactor—similar to the experimental EL-3 18-MW research reactor at Saclay[4]—that the CEA planned for Israel in the fall of 1956, before the Suez operation, was upgraded in early 1957 to a large plutonium-producing reactor of generally the same order as the G-1 reactor at Marcoule (40-MW thermal power) which became critical in 1956.[5] The new reactor was capable of producing ten to fifteen kilograms of plutonium a year.[6] Israel also asked France for the technology needed to extract plutonium from the spent reactor fuel, requesting that Saint Gobain, the company building the Marcoule G-1 plutonium extraction plant, build an underground chemical plant attached to the reactor.[7] The underground facility would be composed of four parts: (1) a preparation workshop for spent fuel; (2) hot laboratories for analysis of irradiated spent fuel; (3) a storage facility for waste materials from the reactor; and (4) a reprocessing plant for extracting plutonium.[8] The last part was the key to a dedicated program with military applications. It would take another year of negotiations before an agreement was reached.

In May 1957 the window of opportunity appeared to open wider when Peres's closest ally, Maurice Bourges-Maunoury, replaced Mollet as prime minister. Bourges-Maunoury, however, conditioned his agreement on Mollet's consent, and the latter kept changing his mind about it. Mollet was agreeable to the idea in a meeting with Peres, but later, in a meeting with Golda Meir on 10 July, he told her that he "opposed this matter."[9] Francis Perrin, the scientific head (high commissioner) of the CEA, also kept changing his mind.[10]

In late September, with Bourges-Maunoury's government on the verge of collapse, Foreign Minister Christian Pineau expressed his concern about the deal, saying that there was no precedent for the kind of nuclear assistance Israel was requesting, and that it could damage France's interests if it became known.[11] To accommodate Pineau's objections, Peres pledged that the reactor would be utilized merely for "scientific research."[12] Pineau, with Peres at his side, signed on to the political part of the agreement, which Peres personally carried to Bourges-Maunoury's office. At Peres's request, Bourges-Maunoury obtained from his cabinet a formal decision to confirm the agreement. This formal act was critical, because that night the Bourges-Maunoury government was voted out of office by the French National Assembly.[13]

On 3 October 1957 the Dimona agreement was signed as two sets of formal documents. The documents are still classified, and they are likely to remain so for a while. Enough is known about the agreement, however (through Péan's book), and about the developments it engendered, to know that it was an important landmark in Israel's path toward its posture of nuclear opacity. "The Dimona operation was so secret that nobody knew the entire truth," said Pierre Guillaumat, the chairman of the CEA. "What happened is all the more difficult to discern because it happened at several levels: that of the State (presidency of the cabinet, ministers, CEA) and that of the industrialists."[14]

The agreement was divided into two sets of documents, one political and the other technical.[15] The political agreement was vague and dealt with the legal obligations of the parties. Peres pledged to Pineau that Israel's objective was peaceful, and that Israel would consult with France on any international action concerning Dimona.[16] The technical agreement, signed by the heads of the CEA and the Israel Atomic Energy Commission (IAEC), apparently left several essential issues unstated.[17] According to Péan, key understandings about the Dimona project were not put in writing but remained oral understandings between individuals.[18] On a few occasions the written documents did not reflect reality. The power of the EL-102, for example, was stated in the documents to be 24 megawatts, but Péan's sources claim that the reactor was twice to three times more powerful than what the documents indicated.[19]

For security reasons, the EL-102 operation of the *Société Alsacienne*, the chief industrial architect of the Dimona project which dealt with both the "client" (the unspecified name the CEA and the industrialists used to refer to the IAEC) and the subcontractors, was conducted through a front financial entity created for this purpose.[20] The most sensitive and secret aspect of the agreement was the reprocessing plant, to which there was no reference in the official documents. The contract for this aspect of the project was signed directly with the manufacturer, Saint Gobain, whose dealings with the Israeli client were concealed through another entity, known as *Société Industrielle d'Etudes et de Constructions Chimiques* (SIECC), leaving no mention of Israeli involvement in the paper trail.[21]

Because of the scope of the project and the unconventional manner in which it was created and managed, Israeli officials had an interest in concealing the magnitude of the projects even from insiders. The French-Israeli bargain was struck when France was still undecided about its own military nuclear program; when some of Israel's best friends in France were hesitant about the consequences of the requested assistance; when French political actors needed a measure of deniability if the pact became known; when governments of the Fourth Republic came and went and administrators were concerned about what might happen next; and when supporters of the French-Israeli alliance on both sides had a sense that this alliance was unnatural and would be short-lived because of France's historical interests in the Arab world. Keeping the agreement opaque was the answer to these concerns.

The Dimona project was vulnerable from the start. The deal was complex, containing controversial and sensitive aspects, extending over years, making it vulnerable to domestic political changes in France. Particularly the Israelis were afraid that a new government in France could reverse the understandings. Secrecy and concealment were designed to minimize the vulnerability of the project, which they did. In time, they became habitual.

French officials who were involved in making the Dimona deal understood it for what it was. The French Foreign Ministry, however, aware of the unprecedented nature of the deal, still insisted that Israel sign an agreement that the cooperation was only for scientific research. Israel was compelled to sign it. This was not the first time Israel found itself with no choice but to make a commitment it could not keep. Norway, Israel's second nuclear supplier, was next in line.

NORWAY'S HEAVY WATER

The Dimona reactor required significant quantities of natural uranium and heavy water. By 1956–57 Israel already knew that it was unable to turn its scientific inventions into commercial production. France, which had purchased the chemical processes from Israel in 1954, could not supply Israel with heavy water of its own. Israel had to find heavy water elsewhere.

Since 1955 Bergmann pressed the Israeli government to obtain twenty tons of heavy water from the United States, cheaply and he hoped without safeguards.[22] In the spring of 1956 Bergmann told AEC officials that Israel decided to construct a 10-MW research reactor, moderated by heavy water and fueled by natural uranium, and inquired whether it would be possible to purchase ten tons of heavy water from the AEC. He was told that this could be arranged, in principle (meaning, under peaceful use safeguards), and was urged to submit a formal request once Israel was ready.[23] Bergmann made such a request in a formal letter to Chairman Strauss in July. In September the AEC notified Israel that it was willing to sell the requested amount, but it would have to take place under the aegis of a new bilateral nuclear power agreement which provided a more rigorous safeguards procedures than the current bilateral research agreement.[24] In response to a subsequent Israeli query as to why there was a need for stronger safeguards than those of the existing agreement, Israel was told that "certain types of research reactors, such as that planned by Israel, had excessive plutonium production capabilities which necessitated the controls of the power reactor type."[25] The reactor to which the AEC referred was the 10-MW reactor that Bergmann had spoken about in his earlier discussions with the AEC in 1956. After this answer Israel lost interest in the American heavy water and no longer raised the issue with the AEC; nor did the AEC ask Israel questions about what happened to the plan to construct that 10-MW reactor and Israel's urgent need for ten tons of heavy water.

Enter Norway. By 1956–57 the Norwegian company Norsk Hydro was the only European commercial producer of heavy water. In early 1956, in parallel to the American route, Israel also approached Norway about buying twenty tons of Norwegian heavy water. The first contact was informal and quiet. It took place in Zurich in March 1956, during the second conference of the world labor movement. Haakon Lie, the influential secretary general of the Norwegian ruling Labor Party (*Arbeiderpartiet*) and a close ally of Israel, along with Finn Moe, a former ambassador to the UN and chairman of the parliamentary committee in charge of foreign relations, were approached on the matter by Reuven Barkat, the head of the international department of the *Histadrut* (Israel's Labor Federation). The Norwegians were asked to explore whether and how soon Norwegian heavy water could be available for Israel. The initial reply was that, owing to its current orders, it would be impossible for Norsk Hydro to deliver the required amount before the end of 1960.

Israel did not give up. As the sale of American heavy water got complicated with the safeguards issue, Israel became more interested in Norwegian heavy water. In August 1956 Bergmann wrote Gunnar Randers, the director of the Norwegian Institute for Atomic Energy, about Israel's interest to purchase ten tons of heavy water from Norsk Hydro. Randers responded that the firm was still unwilling to make any commitment beyond its present line of orders, but his personal view was that there was "a good chance" for a deal later on, when new contracts would be written.[26]

The negotiations with the Norwegians intensified in 1957–58, when it became clear that Israel had no chance to obtain American heavy water without safeguards. We do not know exactly how Israel explained its need for the large amount of heavy water, but it is inconceivable that Randers and his associates did not understand Dimona's purpose. In a letter dated 9 August 1957, Randers wrote Fredrik Moller, the director of NORATOM, a newly established company created to promote the Norwegian nuclear industry, that Israel needed the heavy water for a 40-MW production reactor fueled by natural uranium and moderated by heavy water. The reactor was to be used for "technical training and production of plutonium for Israel's future nuclear energy needs."[27] This sentence reveals it all.[28]

Still, Randers had difficulties closing the deal. For one thing, Norsk Hydro had commercial interests in the Arab world and was reluctant to sell heavy water to Israel, so the sale had to be made through NORATOM. To make the deal more attractive to the Norwegians, it was presented as part of a broader agreement of nuclear cooperation between NORATOM and the IAEC. For another thing, to overcome issues of availability and politics the sale was in fact a three-party transaction: Israel purchased heavy water from NORATOM that had been sold two years earlier to Britain. It suited the British, as their immediate demand for heavy water declined, and it suited the Norwegian who wanted to sell it to Israel. Britain, which had received its twenty-five tons of heavy water without safeguards, agreed to leave the issue of safeguards to the Norwegian government.

The Norwegian Foreign Ministry, however, insisted on Norwegian control of the water. Bergmann protested and wrote Randers that "as long as the controls of which one speaks so much today in the field of atomic energy are only applied by the big countries to the smaller ones, they are unwarranted, unjust and represent an infringement of the sovereignty of the smaller countries."[29] Randers agreed that if the United States did not oppose the sale, Norway should sell Israel the heavy water with no strings attached.[30]

After long discussions during the second part of 1958, Israel gave in on the matter of control.[31] On 12 December 1958 Randers wrote Bergmann that "our foreign office appears to become more and more jittery about discussing" the "ascertainment paragraph," which detailed the procedures Norway would undertake to ascertain the peaceful purpose of the deal.[32]

On 25 February 1959 Chaim Yahil, the Israeli minister in Oslo, and Harlvard Lange, the Norwegian minister of foreign affairs, exchanged documents that set the terms of the Norwegian control of the heavy water. Israel guaranteed that any heavy water sold to it by Norway "will be employed solely for the promotion and development of the peaceful use of atomic energy and not for any military purpose," and that "the Norwegian Government shall be given the opportunity to ascertain to its satisfaction that the use of the heavy waters [is] in accordance with these guarantees."[33]

A few months later the Norwegian Foreign Ministry informed the AEC about the agreement between Norway and Israel, assuring the United States that the agreement provided for safeguards and inspection rights.[34] In August 1959, in a conversation with an officer of the American Embassy in Oslo, Randers was asked about Israel's nuclear activities. Randers was vague, even misleading, noting that "the Israelis were very slow in making decisions concerning the design of their reactor and that consultations would probably continue over a three or four year period."[35] In 1959 nothing was farther from the truth.

DISSENSION AT HOME

Doubts about the Dimona project persisted in Israel even as Peres was negotiating an agreement in Paris. The questions did not touch on issues of strategy or politics. The project's ultimate objectives, though well understood, were rarely discussed.

A primary issue in those discussions in 1957 was the political credibility of France's pledge. Many questioned Peres's optimistic view that France could be trusted to provide Israel with the long-term technological assistance for acquiring the production reactor and reprocessing plant needed to complete the project. Without such assistance Israel could not start the project on its own. Given the lack of explicitness and the secrecy, which characterized the French-Israeli dealings, how could Israel be sure that French assistance would be sustained over the long run? The professional view, presented to decision makers primarily by de Shalit and Dostrovsky, was that Israel would be unable to finish the job on its own.[36]

Prominent scientists also argued that the cost of building the big Dimona reactor, in addition to the small Soreq reactor, was prohibitive for Israel. Others worried about the difficulties of keeping the project secret for an extended period. It would not be easy to provide a scientific rationale for having a second, larger reactor under construction while the first research reactor, under American safeguards, was still incomplete. Aware of these considerations, Israel Dostrovsky continued to advocate a different approach to the problem, a cheaper and safer alternative that did not require such an extreme degree of dependence on a foreign power.[37]

There were personal clashes as well. The small scientific community involved in the deliberations was not confident in the competence of EMET leaders to carry out a project of such magnitude. De Shalit argued that both Ernst Bergmann and Munya Mardor were unqualified for the mission. Instead, Peres was urged to find an Israeli General Groves, that is, a competent military man with a technical and engineering background and eye for detail who could run the Dimona project. It was even argued that EMET as an organization should be kept out of the Dimona project.[38]

Ben Gurion was aware of these reservations. He kept in touch with de Shalit—in part through his daughter, Renana Leshem, a biologist—and had followed his scientific career since the late 1940s. In 1956–59 de Shalit was among the small coterie with which Ben Gurion consulted on how best to set up Israel's nuclear program, including nuclear energy. De Shalit explained to Ben Gurion why he thought a national nuclear project of the kind Bergmann had been advocating would be too big for Israel, and could result in financial and political loss and a setback in basic scientific research.[39]

The IDF was hardly involved in the early consultations.[40] Chief of Staff Dayan, whose views Ben Gurion regarded highly, had been informed of Peres's activities in France regarding the nuclear program, and of the objections within the scientific community. Sometime in the spring of 1957 he called a meeting in his office, soliciting the opinions of leading scientists such as de Shalit and Dostrovsky (but not Bergmann's, who was not invited). Dayan had doubts regarding the technological-scientific feasibility of the undertaking, as well as the reliability of the French. Ne'eman, who attended the meeting as a senior intelligence officer, recalls that both de Shalit and Dostrovsky stressed the difficulties and uncertainties involved in the Dimona route, though neither argued that the project was infeasible. Ne'eman's own view was that despite the major uncertainties involving the French, the risk was worth taking.

Dayan remained a skeptic, but apparently he did not raise formal objections on behalf of the IDF.[41] Ben Gurion was personally interested in Dayan's views, but he decided not to solicit the views of the military as an organization. He wanted to avoid a budgetary competition between the IDF modernization plans in conventional weapons systems and the nuclear project. In doing so Ben Gurion established that decisions about the nuclear issue was a civilian matter. The responsibility for the project ultimately belonged with the civilian leadership. This pattern persisted for years.

Another objection in 1957 came from Foreign Minister Golda Meir. She urged Ben Gurion not to trust Peres's optimism about French nuclear assistance. As Peres was negotiating the nuclear deal in Paris, Meir and, though to a lesser extent, Mossad chief Isser Harel, argued that reliance on a tacit French commitment was too politically risky. After Meir's meeting with Mollet in July, in which he expressed his opposition to the deal, she almost convinced Ben Gurion that Peres's idea was unrealistic.[42] She was concerned that Peres's "unorthodox diplomacy" could backfire, and she worried that secret agreements reached in this fashion would not withstand domestic political changes in France.

Much of her opposition to Dimona, however, derived from her opposition to Peres himself. According to Peres, his "rocky relationship" with Golda had started in the early 1950s and deteriorated after she replaced Moshe Sharett as foreign minister in the summer of 1956.[43] The full wrath of the combative Meir, and that of her less combative predecessor Sharett, was aimed at Peres and the way he built relations with the French defense and nuclear establishments since the mid-1950s, as well as his taking advantage of the structural political weaknesses of the Fourth Republic. The representatives of the Ministry of Defense in Paris reported directly to Peres, bypassing the Foreign Ministry.[44] Meir complained tirelessly to Ben Gurion about Peres's conducting of an independent foreign policy by the Defense Ministry, but to no avail.[45]

BEN GURION'S CONCERNS

Despite many objections, Ben Gurion adopted Peres's and Bergmann's vision of pursuing two nuclear paths simultaneously—one public, the other secret. In a public ceremony on 20 March 1957 Israel had finally signed a contract with the United States to build a small swimming-pool research reactor in Nachal Soreq as part of the Atoms for Peace program. In the meantime, Peres continued to push for the other French reactor. On 27 September, hours before Peres's departure for Paris to put the deal together with Bourges-Maunoury's government, Ben Gurion sent him a note wishing him well in the important mission.[46] A week later, after the agreement was signed, Ben Gurion's military aide cabled Peres: "You could not have given the Old Man a better present for this Yom Kippur."[47]

Despite scientists' criticism, Ben Gurion chose to keep Bergmann at the IAEC.[48] Ben Gurion was aware of the risks that de Shalit, Dostrovsky, and others had been warning about, but he was convinced that Israel must take those risks. The military success of the Sinai operation did not assuage his fears for Israel's security.[49] While the Israeli public enjoyed a sense of confidence following the success of the Suez campaign, Ben Gurion's political and military outlook grew gloomier.[50] He was especially concerned with the establishment of a grand Arab coalition against Israel. These fears were not without justification. The Suez campaign had reinforced Nasser's position within the Arab world, and calls for Arab unification stirred up the Arab masses. In 1958 Egypt and Syria merged into a political-military federation known as the United Arab Republic (UAR).

Ben Gurion was especially concerned about a surprise attack by an Arab coalition, starting with aerial bombardment of Israeli cities. He feared that Israel might fail to deter an Arab coalition from launching such a war, and that Israel would be unable to mobilize its reserves in time. Even a security guarantee from a Western power might be irrelevant because of the time it would take to rush aid to Israel.[51] In his meeting with de Gaulle in June 1960, Ben Gurion responded to de Gaulle's commitment to Israel's security by elaborating on his concerns about Israel's vulnerability to an Arab surprise attack. He argued, as he had with Eisenhower in March, that if Egypt launched a surprise attack on Israel, Israel would suffer catastrophically—even if outside help were extended to Israel. The point was clear, if unstated: Israel must not depend on the help of an outside power in a time of emergency.[52] "If Nasser should break Israel's air force," American ambassador Walworth Barbour quoted Ben Gurion, "the war would be over in two days." Any American or French military assistance would come too late.[53] Ben Gurion voiced similar concerns in almost every communication he had with foreign leaders.[54]

Ben Gurion's foreign and defense policy were driven by this pessimistic outlook. They followed two tracks—diplomacy and deterrence. One diplomatic initiative, known as the "periphery strategy," sought alliances with non-Arab minorities on the periphery of the Middle East in order to contain pan-Arab Nasserism.[55] Ben Gurion also sought a security guarantee for Israel from a Western state. This search intensified after the Suez campaign, but in the late 1950s Ben Gurion concluded that the United States, France, or NATO would not agree to give such a guarantee. Ben Gurion, however, continued this quest until he left office in 1963.[56]

In the late 1950s, as he gave up trying to obtain a guarantee from an external power, deterrence became Ben Gurion's major goal. He sought to strengthen Israel's conventional forces, especially its air force, by acquiring sophisticated weapon systems to balance those that the Soviets were supplying to Nasser. The second pillar of Israel's deterrence capability was an independent nuclear program, which would serve as "an option for a rainy day" (this phrase was one more code term used by politicians and journalists to refer to the program). Ben Gurion pursued both paths, while keeping the two as separate as possible.

The two approaches to bolstering Israel's deterrence posture were not easy to pursue simultaneously. In 1958 the IDF was still a small army equipped with antiquated weapons. On 1 April 1958 the IDF regular order of battle was thirty-seven thousand troops, including a navy of sixteen hundred men and women and an air force of thirty-one hundred men and women. The combat force structure of the IDF was made of one regular infantry brigade, twelve reserve brigades, one regular paratroops brigade, one regular armored brigade, and two reserve armored brigades; the Israeli Air Force (IAF) had 118 jets. Facing the thirteen Israeli infantry brigades were forty-five to forty-eight Arab infantry brigades.[57]

In the late 1950s the IDF embarked on an expansion and modernization program. In the 1957–60 period IAF purchased from France thirty supersonic Super Mystéres and twenty-eight Vautour light bombers, and signed contracts for sixty Mirages (soon to become seventy-two). The Armored Corps initiated a program to purchase dozens of British Centurion medium tanks (later increasing the number to hundreds), and the navy purchased its first submarines. Ben Gurion also approved a plan to build a new modern air base in Hatzerim in the Negev, as well as other training bases.

These were costly programs, but they were in keeping with Ben Gurion's commitment to the idea that the IDF must be able to defeat any combination of Arab armies in a conventional war. According to figures listed in Ben Gurion's diaries, the 1958–59 defense procurement budget was about $35 million, and its main purchases were new airplanes for the air force.[58] According to other official figures, in 1957 the entire defense budget of Israel was IL286 million, of which IL83 million (33.7 percent) went for procurement; in 1960 the defense budget was IL342 million, of which IL97 million (28.4 percent) went for procurement.[59] These figures do not include the real cost of the nuclear project.

It is difficult to assess the exact cost of developing the infrastructure needed for the nuclear project in 1958–65. This is primarily because the funding of the project was conducted in those days in a "nonorthodox" fashion, and a significant portion of it—especially the funds that were raised by special donations overseas—did not appear in the regular defense budget. The issue was not merely security. There was a deliberate interest on the part of Ben Gurion and Peres to keep the senior officers of the IDF out of the financial picture, leaving them with the impression that the special project did not compete with the regular IDF needs.

This notwithstanding, the official figures of the defense budget indicate that in the late 1950s, and more so in the early 1960s, the science and R&D components of the defense budget grew significantly. The R&D budget of the defense budget was IL7 million (2.8 percent of the budget) in 1957, IL12 million (4.2 percent of the budget) in 1958, IL25 million (7.3 percent of the budget) in 1960, IL44 million (11.2 percent of the budget) in 1961, and IL99 million (14.4 percent of the budget) in 1963. By the mid-1960s the R&D component stabilized at the level of 11 percent.[60] In his diaries Ben Gurion mentioned authorization of U.S.$5 million in 1958—around 15 percent of the defense budget, and more than twice that in 1959—for *Mifalei Pituach* (Development Projects), the bureaucratic name for the Dimona project.[61] According to official data presented by Israel privately to the United States in early 1961, "the reactor and ancillary facilities are expected to cost $34 million, of which $17.8 million would be foreign exchange. The reactor itself is expected to cost $15.4 million, of which $10 million would be foreign exchange."[62] Even these figures, certainly not the complete numbers, highlight how heavy the Dimona cost was in relation to the rest of the defense budget.[63]

In his 1995 memoires Shimon Peres writes that the Dimona reactor alone cost about $80 million (in 1960 dollars).[64] Other estimates made by critics of Peres referred to a cost of about $300 million.[65] It is likely that the real numbers concerning the initiation of the Dimona project would never be fully known.[66]

A PROJECT DIVIDED

Much of the scientific criticism of the Dimona project centered on the ability of the EMET/IAEC team under Bergmann and Mardor to meet the engineering challenge. Peres appointed a three-man planning committee (*va'adat tichnun*), headed by de Shalit with Ze'ev (Venia) Hadari Pomerantz and Zvi Lipkin as members, bypassing both Bergmann and Mardor. The fate of the project depended on whether the right person would lead it. Lipkin recalls that they "were impressed by the French engineers who had come to visit Israel during this period. Those engineers were really top grade engineers who knew how to handle large scale projects." The EMET/IAEC team was not qualified for the job.

Peres, who accepted the recommendation, could think of only one man with the required qualities. He was Colonel Manes Pratt, an engineer by training who had been an Ordnance Corps chief, and who served in 1956 as Israel's military attaché in Burma. Though Pratt had no scientific background or knowledge of nuclear issues, he seemed to have the prerequisite temperament. With de Shalit, Hadari, and Lipkin with him, Peres called Pratt in Burma and offered him the opportunity to be Dimona's builder. "I looked for a 'pedant,' a man who would not compromise over detail, whether vital or ostensibly marginal," Peres wrote. "I knew that in the nuclear realm the most minor relaxation of standards could lead to national disaster. . . . At the same time, the candidate had to be a man with an 'open mind,' that is, a capacity to learn on the job; . . . I knew when I appointed him that he would give me a hard time, and indeed he did."[67]

Pratt asked for time to learn the subject. "Within a few months," Peres wrote, "he became Israel's foremost expert in nuclear engineering."[68] In those few months Lipkin became Pratt's tutor in everything that had to do with reactor physics and engineering. Lipkin became Pratt's "constant companion, teaching him everything he needed to know about nuclear physics and nuclear engineering, and being available to answer and explain any questions . . . that might arise."[69] The massive excavation work at the Dimona site began sometime in late 1957 or early 1958.[70]

Selecting Pratt to be czar of Dimona, reporting only to Ben Gurion and Peres, was decisive for the nuclear project. It also had bureaucratic repercussions. In early 1957 Mardor decided to take a leave of absence from EMET,[71] perhaps in protest over the decision to build and operate Dimona outside EMET. Mardor's leave, however, did not last long. In the spring of 1958 Peres asked him to return to the ministry. "New programs emerged," Mardor wrote, "big projects of development and manufacturing of sophisticated weapons systems."[72] On 5 June 1958 Ben Gurion reorganized EMET as a new research and development authority within the Ministry of Defense.[73] The new authority was renamed RAFAEL, the Hebrew acronym for the Armaments Development Authority.

RAFAEL was a continuation of EMET, but the change was more than in its name. The new organization had a new mission, new approach, and new management style. EMET was a research-oriented organization; it was organized according to fields of research (that is, electronics, mechanics, chemistry, physics). RAFAEL was more development oriented, and, in addition to the fields of research, it was organized by specific projects.[74] The organizational changes were designed to achieve an integrative work aimed at producing complete weapon systems. RAFAEL was to bring Israel, in Mardor's oblique words, into the age of "large and long-term projects, aiming at weapon systems, integrated technologies, and a knowledge base that the great powers had."[75] RAFAEL's mission was "the development of powerful and sophisticated deterrent weapons systems that Israel could not purchase elsewhere."[76] "We were convinced," wrote Mardor, "of the vital need for those new powerful weapons systems that would assure the state of Israel against those who are against its existence."[77]

The founding of Dimona and RAFAEL were landmarks in Israel's nuclear pursuit. Dimona and RAFAEL were different types of organizations. RAFAEL was devoted to research and development of large military projects, while Dimona was a gigantic construction project which required materials, technical expertise, and financing that were unavailable in Israel and had to be obtained abroad. Dimona did not require special research and development. This difference, in addition to Pratt's insistence on autonomy, led to the decision to build Dimona outside the jurisdiction of EMET or RAFAEL. The problems resulting from this division would haunt the project from the start.

The problem of managing the program was more complicated than the problem which, in the United States, is called interservice rivalry. The Israeli project, unlike the Manhattan Project, was dependent on outside assistance. Israel thus did not need a General Groves or Robert Oppenheimer as the project's leaders. Instead, an improvising politician like Peres, with the gift of finding and exploiting opportunities, became the project's leader. He was able to get the materials, technical experts, and funding needed for the project. Everything depended on him.

Peres's management style, and the initial separation among the different units working on different aspects of the project, determined the project's organizational structure. It was divided among administrations, outside organizations, contractors, and managers, with an inherent redundancy and duplication. In the area of theoretical physics calculations, for example, the effort was initially divided among three quasi-academic research groups, each focusing on essentially the same problems but working separately and independently. The *Milchamot Ha'yehudim* (Wars of the Jews) over budgets and authority among these organizations took much of Peres's attention, requiring him to employ "delicate inter-personal and inter-departmental diplomacy."[78] Peres himself became the chief administrator of the entire project.

Because of the project's dependence on outside assistance in materials, technical expertise, and financing, there was no multiyear master plan for the program in its first years. There were no guidelines that demarcated areas of responsibilities, missions, and budgets among the administrations and organizations involved. One reason for this was the uncertainty about the project's budget as a whole, as well as its individual components. There was no multiyear budget for the project; in fact, even the annual budget was continually changing. Another reason was the political tentativeness associated with the French assistance over many years, an uncertainty that rippled through the program. Another reason was the Israeli lack of experience. For some years, for example, the project lacked a progress evaluation system. This was only corrected later, when PERT (Progress Evaluation Report Technique) was introduced.[79]

Financing was an important aspect of the nuclear project. Its funding was as unorthodox as any of its other aspects. Dimona was built largely through a special fund-raising effort that Ben Gurion and Peres conducted outside the official state budget. "We set up a discreet fund-raising operation, which raised contributions totaling more than $40 million—half of the cost of the reactor, and a very considerable sum in those days," Peres wrote. "Most of this money came from direct personal appeals, by Ben Gurion and myself, to friends of Israel around the world."[80]

In his diary Ben Gurion noted laconically that, on 2 June 1958, he discussed with Finance Minister Eshkol the "benediction [*kiddush*] of the atomic power station."[81] A later entry, written in his diary on 31 October 1958, Ben Gurion summarized a conversation he had with Abe Feinberg, a wealthy Jewish businessman and major Democratic fund-raiser. "We have talked about the Weizmann Institute," Ben Gurion wrote, "and I told him about Lord Rothschild's two proposals. With regard to the second proposal—benedictions—he told me that there is already a beginning. It appears that [Issac] Wolfson has given $5 million dollars. There is a need for $25 million, because the annual budget deficit is about a million and a half. Benedictions will provide 5 percent and a sum of twenty-five million will be sufficient. He believes that it would be possible to find 'benedictors' among American Jews."[82] The idea of keeping a separate financing system for the nuclear program was important not only for secrecy but also to avoid a debate with the army over budgets and doctrine. This feature of the project lasted many years.

DIVISION AT HOME

Ben Gurion's decisions in 1957–58, and the groundbreaking excavation at Dimona, did not bring an end to the opposition to the project. In the first three

years of the project, despite the secrecy, there remained a few pockets of opposition and criticism. Some of it reflected anger about the lack of due process and
procedure; some of it stemmed from financial concerns; and some of it involved
domestic party politics.

In February 1958 all seven members of the IAEC signed a collective letter of
resignation to Ben Gurion, leaving Bergmann a chairman without a committee.[83] The resignation, orchestrated by Racah, Sambursky, and Ollendorff, was
over procedure, not substance. The letter stated that even though the IAEC had
not been convened once since 1956, "things were allegedly done in the name of
the IAEC, which in fact did not exist, without the Israeli scientists who were
close to the profession participating in the planning, if such planning existed."[84]
Still, some of the critical decisions on Dimona were made outside Bergmann's
IAEC. The IAEC had become no more than a rubber stamp. Most of its commissioners had little sense of how and for what purpose their chair, Bergmann,
was using it. Subsequently Ben Gurion met Racah and Ollendorff in an effort
to form two separate committees—the scientific and administrative committees—which would allow the scientists a role in research while keeping them
out of defense projects. Ben Gurion told them that under the new arrangement,
they should seek out Peres if they needed information, but that all principal
issues would come to him.[85] This effort to reorganize the IAEC failed, and it
remained an empty shell at the Ministry of Defense for many years.

There were indications of a broader opposition to the nuclear project in the
scientific community. Mardor writes of an "aggressive, well-focused and continuous" campaign by "distinguished scientists and representatives of academic
institutions against the intents of the defense establishment and its research and
development apparatus."[86] RAFAEL found it difficult to recruit senior scientists
to take part in its projects.

In the late 1950s, however, the real opposition to the project came from Ben
Gurion's colleagues in MAPAI. Ben Gurion did not obtain a cabinet decision on
the secret project he had initiated, and he did not allow the issue to be debated
in the military. Only the senior cabinet members who had to know about the
project—Meir, Eshkol, and Minister of Commerce Pinhas Sapir—were told
about it,[87] and even they knew only the aspects relevant to them, not much
more.

By 1958–60 the fact that a huge project was in the making could no longer be
concealed from the other members of the leadership. The excavation and building of Dimona were unprecedented in its scope and in security requirements.
Some aspects of the project were more visible: the shortage in some raw materials for construction, the hundreds of French employees, the sizable manpower
needed to guard the new excavation and construction site. Senior military offi-

cers were also aware of Ben Gurion's interest in a nuclear option. Ben Gurion was also concerned about the reactions of the scientific and political communities to the project. Both groups could claim to have a say on a decision of such magnitude. The cost of the project, even more than its political and strategic aspects, was the most susceptible to debate.

Yet Ben Gurion was determined to avoid a debate, even behind closed doors. He feared that even the most secret debate about the project in the cabinet or military would compromise it. Any leak could destroy the feeble connection with the French. Such a debate would also force him to declare his strategic objectives, something with which he was uncomfortable. To maintain secrecy and minimize the risk of opposition, Ben Gurion and Peres decided to run the nuclear project underground, outside the normal state budget.

The secrecy was not sufficient to eliminate all opposition. At about 1959–60 some of Ben Gurion's senior political colleagues in MAPAI had reservations about the project, and skepticism about the project became enmeshed with criticism of Ben Gurion's direction on issues of technology and politics. Peres's credibility and motives also came under criticism, and Golda Meir led the charge.[88] Meir and Peres had feuded over many issues for many years. Meir was concerned about two aspects of the project: the reliability of the French, and the repercussions of an American discovery of the Dimona secret.[89] She thought that Israel should inform the United States of the Dimona reactor, stating that the project was for peaceful purposes and leaving room for a future weapons option.

In 1959–60 Meir's opposition to Peres and the nuclear issue became entangled with the generational struggle for leadership in MAPAI. It became increasingly difficult to separate the policy issues from the political and personal issues. Peres was perceived by his older political opponents as a man of technological fantasies and a political threat; they believed he was building a secret state within a state, accountable to no one but Ben Gurion and himself, under the cover of secrecy and security. They feared he would bring down Ben Gurion and the party, damaging Israel's foreign relations.

Still, in the late 1950s, before the Lavon Affair erupted, no one could dispute Ben Gurion's political and moral authority in MAPAI and the cabinet. Ben Gurion made clear to dissenting ministers that the Dimona project was his project, and that Peres was acting under his authority. In early 1960 Dimona's opponents in the cabinet, headed by Eshkol, proposed bringing the issue to a debate before the leadership forum of MAPAI (*Haverenu*), hoping that a wider discussion would solidify the opposition. Ben Gurion refused, insisting that the issue would be discussed only among himself, Eshkol, Meir, and Peres.[90] Because of his unquestioned authority on defense issues, and the sensitivity of the project, the critics reluctantly accepted that the project was too close to Ben

Gurion's heart, and gave up the effort to pursue a broader discussion of the subject.

THE BREAK WITH DE GAULLE

A year and a half after the excavation of the Dimona site had begun, the fears of the project's critics materialized. At the end of May 1958 Charles de Gaulle was named France's new prime minister, and in December he became the first president—for a term of seven years—of the new Fifth Republic. He was brought back from a self-imposed political exile, entrusted with the task of curing the ills that had plagued the Fourth Republic. By June de Gaulle had become aware of what he later termed "the improper military collaboration established between Tel Aviv and Paris after the Suez Expedition, which permanently placed Israelis at all levels of French services," and he was determined to end it.[91] De Gaulle was taken aback when he learned of the unorthodox manner in which the relations were conducted.[92] According to Péan, the excavation for the reactor began a few months before de Gaulle took power, but the massive work under the supervision of the CEA began after the change of government.[93] It took almost two years to translate de Gaulle's determination into a new French nuclear policy vis-à-vis Israel.[94]

These two years, mostly during the term of Jacques Soustelle, minister of atomic energy and a staunch supporter of Israel, were critical and made the future of the Dimona project possible, as the construction of much of the Dimona reactor under the supervision of the CEA continued as planned.[95] By the second part of 1959 Saint Gobain Nucleaire began supervising the excavation work for the reprocessing plant, "which took place next to and below the building site of the reactor."[96] By that time dozens of Israeli scientists and technicians were doing research and training at Saclay, Marcoule, and other CEA sites.

Things changed with the resignation of Soustelle. After Soustelle's departure, Perrin asked for a meeting with de Gaulle in which he informed him that, throughout 1959, the construction of the reprocessing plant had continued despite de Gaulle's instructions. De Gaulle again demanded an end to this cooperation. When Perrin returned to the CEA he ordered all cooperation to cease.[97] On 13 May 1960 Foreign Minister Maurice Couve de Murville formally notified the Israeli ambassador, Walter Eitan, that France had decided to sever its nuclear ties with Israel. France made three demands on Israel, indicating that the objective of the new French policy was to prohibit the production and reprocessing of weapon-quality plutonium in Dimona. The French asked Israel to lift the secrecy over Dimona and to declare the reactor's peaceful nature. France also wanted the reactor to be subjected to international inspection, probably by the IAEA. Finally, until Israel accepted these conditions, France would not supply it with natural uranium fuel for the reactor.[98]

The French decision caused consternation in Ben Gurion's inner circle. The end of French assistance would put the entire Dimona project at risk. De Gaulle's decision was a sharp reversal from the written and unwritten obligations of his predecessors. Mollet and Bourges-Maunoury understood what the Dimona commitment was all about, which made the French assistance so unique and sensitive. De Gaulle recognized how unprecedented the deal was, and for this reason refused to go along with it, reluctant to provide Israel with a nuclear option. France was trying to regain its position in the Arab world, and nuclear cooperation with Israel would not be helpful in that effort.

In reaction to the French decision, Ben Gurion asked to see de Gaulle, and a meeting between the two was hastily arranged for 14 June 1960. Peres, who had been sent a few days earlier to prepare the meeting, heard from Couve de Murville the reason for the French decision: France had never given such assistance to another country, and it could not afford to do so now.[99] The French were flexible on the timing of making Dimona public. The concern of the French was not the reactor or its secrecy as such, but the essence of the project—the reprocessing plant. Peres responded that "Israel is now in the middle of the lake, to return is just as complicated as to go ahead."[100] Couve de Murville repeated his arguments, but he left the issue open. A cable from Eitan to Jerusalem indicated that both he and Peres felt that some progress had been made.[101] The issue was left to the leaders.

De Gaulle met Ben Gurion on 14 June. Most of their conversation was a general exchange on world affairs and ideas between two elderly statesmen. The real issue—Dimona—was hardly mentioned. When the meeting ended without reference to nuclear and military cooperation between the two countries, de Gaulle suggested that they schedule a working meeting three days later.[102] In the meantime, Ben Gurion met with Prime Minister Michel Debré and discussed the nuclear issue, but no progress was made. Eitan noted in his cable that "Debré talked from the mouth of Couve. The matter has not yet been discussed with de Gaulle."[103]

On 17 June Ben Gurion and de Gaulle met again privately. This time the talks focused on nuclear cooperation. Both sides wanted to avoid confrontation, but they found no immediate solution. Ben Gurion pledged that Israel would not build a nuclear weapon, and said he understood de Gaulle's need to change France's assistance to Israel, but he suggested deferring the decision for further talks between Peres and Guillaumat.[104] De Gaulle was not convinced, but promised to "reconsider" the French position.[105] Despite de Gaulle's expressions of friendship, the trip produced no resolution of the nuclear impasse.

On 1 August 1960 Couve de Murville summoned Eitan and notified him that France was determined to end its nuclear assistance if Israel continued to oppose publicity and an inspection of the Dimona reactor site. In exchange, France would be ready to compensate Israel financially for abrogating the agreement.[106] Ben Gurion saw two alternatives—accepting the money and ending French assistance or refusing to accept the French decision as final and insisting on finding another solution. The second avenue would be a difficult one, but Israel had little to lose at that point. Ben Gurion rejected the French offer and sent Peres to Paris to negotiate a compromise. In the meantime, Pratt and his advisers studied what would be the minimum requirements under which the completion of the project would be possible, even if slowed down significantly.

It took three months before Peres was ready to negotiate the matter with Couve de Murville. Peres's argument was that the French proposal "meant both reneging on previous French government decisions and robbing Israel of its eventual reactor and of five years of Herculean effort. No amount of money could compensate us for the wasted work."[107] Peres also said that revealing the details of the agreement between France and Israel would lead to an Arab boycott of the French companies that had cooperated with Israel.[108]

A compromise was reached: while the government of France would end its own direct involvement through the CEA in the Dimona project, it would allow French companies with existing contracts to continue their work on the reactor. This would allow Israel to continue the project on its own. Israel, for its part, would soon make a public statement about the peaceful purposes of the Dimona project, and in return France would drop its demand for outside inspection.[109]

This was the second major delay in two and a half years of translating de Gaulle's orders into policy. The nine-month delay, and Peres's compromise, were critical to the project. The firm responsible for building the reactor received no instructions to stop, and its work continued until the reactor was handed over to the Israelis after the start-up stage, sometime in 1963 or 1964.[110] As to the reprocessing plant, Israel "went on the hunt to find French industrialists" who could replace Saint Gobain in furnishing the equipment and carrying out the assembly of the chemical plant.[111] By that time, having acquired the plans and specifications from Saint Gobain, Israel had taken over construction of the reprocessing plant.[112] In 1963 SIECC returned to spend two more years completing the three less sensitive elements of the chemical plant, leaving Dimona in June 1965.[113]

Israel's Model: A Comparative Note

Does Israel show a unique decision-making pattern or model for initiating a nuclear-weapon project? To reflect on this question we should compare the Israeli case with the other three cases of Western democracies that decided to develop nuclear arsenals—the United States, Britain, and France.

The Manhattan Project provided the first model. On 9 October 1941, at the conclusion of a meeting in the White House in which the president's science adviser, Vannevar Bush, and Vice President Henry Wallace participated, President Franklin Delano Roosevelt made the decision to initiate a research and development program aimed at producing an atomic bomb. Bush briefed Roosevelt about the British study—the Maud Report—which explored the feasibility of building a uranium bomb. The report concluded that such a bomb was practicable, and likely to lead to decisive results in the war," and it urged the British government to make this project "the highest priority" in order "to obtain the weapons in the shortest possible time."[114] Bush told Roosevelt that such a project would require building expensive production plants and stressed the vast uncertainties involved. He asked Roosevelt to authorize an immediate action on a research project which, if successful, would lead to the development and production of the atom bomb. Roosevelt authorized it on the spot. He told Bush, however, not to proceed beyond research without further instructions from him. He also instructed Bush that funds would be available from a special source, and emphasized the need for secrecy.

Roosevelt's decision set in motion the biggest and most secretive American project of the Second World War. The initiating decision was a lonely decision, a decision not backed up by a policy debate. For the sake of secrecy Roosevelt authorized bypassing normal procedures of government. The project's expenditures were buried in the Department of War's budget, and it was exempted from congressional oversight. The Manhattan Project set up the precedent of a secret project operating like a state within a state whose leaders reported directly to the president and to the secretary of war. Despite the secrecy, however, the initial decision was a dedicated, top-to-bottom decision. This, too, was a precedent: the project's decisions could be traced and timed. They were secret but explicit decisions.

The British nuclear project followed a similar pattern. The British initiating decision was made in January 1947 by Prime Minister Clement Attlee and a small cabinet subcommittee. Most members of his cabinet knew nothing about it. The decision was made without parliamentary or public debate. Secrecy was deemed essential until the project became an accomplished fact. As in the American case, it was a top-bottom decision by the national leadership. Here, too, the objectives of the project were defined explicitly at the highest level.[115]

France followed a different path. "If the Fourth Republic had lasted beyond the spring of 1958," writes McGeorge Bundy, "we might have a full case history of a country that acquired nuclear weapons mainly because the government never decided not to."[116] The French "invented" nuclear opacity. Bureaucrats, supported by cabinet ministers, advanced the nuclear project while premiers publicly insisted that no final decision had been made. Instead of one decision, like in the American and British cases, there were many small decisions.

The fragmentation of the decision into many smaller decisions allowed French bureaucrats to continue in their weapons work, while also allowing room for political deniability at the top. As a result, no political decision to move forward to produce nuclear weapons was made. This ambivalence ended when Prime Minister Guy Mollet became convinced, in the wake of the 1956 Suez campaign, that France needed an independent nuclear deterrent. When, in April 1958, Prime Minister Félix Gaillard announced that France would conduct a nuclear test, it was after all the critical decisions had already been made.

French nuclear opacity, not the result of a deliberate and well-planned strategy of ambiguity but of a manifestation of the weak Fourth Republic, was short-lived. By 1960 French nuclear conduct came to resemble the American and British. In France, as in the United States and Britain, less than five years elapsed between a commitment to acquiring nuclear weapons and becoming a nuclear-weapon state. In each of the cases the incubation period was short. Public declaration became the last stage of the process of acquiring nuclear weapons.

The Israeli case combines features of the American-British and French models. Without archival material, it is impossible to reconstruct how exactly the Israeli project was initiated in 1955–58, but there are hints to draw the general picture. For example, Munya Mardor noted that certain veiled comments by Ben Gurion were understood to mean "a positive attitude and confirmation for the existence of the long-term and big projects, and an intention to act to implement them."[117] It appears that in 1955 EMET executives were waiting for the go-ahead signal, and they took Ben Gurion's comments to be that signal. Ben Gurion did not have to spell out his wishes or issue written directives. In his eulogy to Shalheveth Freier, Peres noted that Ben Gurion was reluctant to "nail down" the specifics of his nuclear vision, "for nailing down would have meant to identify specific objectives too early, and too fast, and that would have been too complicated."[118] Those objectives were left unspelled, somewhat ambiguous. Ben Gurion was thus able to maintain maximum flexibility, and also maximum deniability.

Peres and other project executives behaved similarly. Peres said that the word "bomb" was never used; it was a taboo word. Mardor used to present the issue in terms of a research of various "subcomponents," emphasizing that no decision was made about producing a complete weapon system. Freier said that the most important decisions in the early days of the project were never written down. The paper trail was often designed to conceal or mislead.

This modus operandi was thus remarkably similar to the way France started its nuclear project, with which Ben Gurion's executives became intimately acquainted. Long-term objectives were kept not only secret but also opaque. Like the French, Ben Gurion presented the project in terms of building "options" for the future—civil energy or security—in order to escape a debate at home and avoid confrontations with foreign powers.

At the same time, Israel's nuclear path also exhibits elements of the Anglo-American model. The nuclear project was conceived by the highest political authority, David Ben Gurion, who, since 1955, made it a national priority. Like Roosevelt and Attlee, Ben Gurion, on his own, made the early decisions that made the project possible. Like them, he recognized the need for secrecy and was apprehensive about the consequences of a policy debate, even among top ministers and governmental officials, fearing that such debate would endanger the future of the project. Like them, Ben Gurion, at the beginning, sought funds for the nuclear project outside the normal government channels, and exempted the project from democratic accountability.

In the end, all the nuclear-weapon projects that preceded the Israeli program emerged into the open. They led to nuclear testing, followed by a political declaration. The presence and role of nuclear weapons were acknowledged. In this respect, perhaps more than in others, the Israeli project is unique: opacity has become its permanent feature.

Since the Baruch Plan, the United States had opposed the spread of nuclear weapons. In the 1950s, however, it still lacked a coherent nuclear non-proliferation policy.[1] The United States dealt with proliferation risks through legislation, through bilateral safeguards agreements on nuclear cooperation, and by supporting the creation of international organizations such as the International Atomic Energy Agency (IAEA) and EURATOM. Promoting the peaceful use of nuclear energy became a tool of American foreign policy.[2] The United States was also committed to safeguarding its atomic assistance to foreign governments. Safeguarding, however, did not mean outlawing nuclear proliferation.

The Eisenhower administration opposed the spread of nuclear weapons, but it recognized that sovereign nations had the right to pursue such an objective on their own. The objective of the IAEA was to promote the peaceful use of nuclear energy and to set in place a safeguards system to ensure that nuclear cooperation would not be bent to military purposes. At the same time, its statute did not forbid member states from acquiring nuclear weapons, or require IAEA safeguards on nuclear materials and facilities acquired without IAEA assistance. The idea of a no-weapons pledge was considered by American policy makers but was rejected by the Eisenhower administration as infeasible.[3] Secretary of State John Foster Dulles was convinced that it would be difficult for the United States to persuade other nations to forgo the right to build nuclear weapons as long as the Big Three continued to do so.

By the late 1950s it became clear that technologically advanced nations would be able to acquire nuclear weapons on their own. The Soviets acquired the bomb in 1949, the British in 1952, and it was only a matter of time until France did the same. Other West European nations—Sweden, Italy, and Switzerland—also considered acquiring nuclear weapons. The question for America was whether to provide NATO with nuclear weapons, making it unnecessary for NATO members to build their own independent nuclear arsenals, or, instead, limit its security commitment to Europe. The Eisenhower administration chose to introduce nuclear weapons into NATO, allowing for greater nuclear sharing with its members.[4] Recognizing the growing American nuclear deployment in NATO, the Atomic Energy Act was amended to accommodate the new reality. In 1958 the Act was amended to allow the transfer of weapon-grade fissionable material and weapons design information to nations that had "made substantial progress in the development of nuclear weapons" (the reference was to Great Britain). The Eisenhower administration thus gave priority to nuclear weapons cooperation with allies over efforts to stem nuclear weapons proliferation.

When, in 1958, the idea of an international agreement to prevent the further spread of nuclear weapons was introduced by Ireland, the Soviets supported it while the United States and its NATO allies opposed it. This called for the nuclear nations not to transfer nuclear weapons to nonnuclear states and for the nonnuclear states not to manufacture them. The Eisenhower administration opposition had to do with concerns about allied nuclear deployments.[5] A year later, when Ireland modified its resolution by introducing a weaker language,[6] the United States supported it while the French and Soviets abstained. In 1960, when the Irish proposal was amended further, calling on the nuclear states not only to refrain from relinquishing their control over nuclear weapons but also from transmitting "information needed for their manufacture," the Soviet Union voted in favor of the proposal and the United States abstained, citing verification concerns.[7]

These shifts in positions revealed the conflicts and confusion in the Eisenhower administration over the merits of this nuclear weapons nonproliferation policy relative to other goals and priorities. The legacy of Atoms for Peace was that preventing nuclear weapons proliferation was less of a priority than enhancing nuclear information and technology sharing within NATO, and sharing the civilian-industrial benefits of nuclear energy with the world. America was undecided about what it could and should do to prevent nuclear weapons proliferation, as could be seen in the cases of France and Israel.

France began seriously to contemplate the acquisition of nuclear weapons after the 1956 Suez campaign. The Eisenhower administration recognized the French policy but could not, or would not, dissuade France from pursuing it.[8]

When EURATOM was founded, with American backing, its statutes were written so as to allow France to acquire nuclear weapons.[9] The United States did not protest France's February 1960 nuclear test, which marked its new status as a nuclear-weapon state. The Eisenhower administration's lack of a response to the Israeli nuclear weapons program, however, was more complex.

LOST IN THE SHUFFLE

Until 10 January 1956 Israel's nuclear activities were of no interest to the American intelligence community. Israel was not categorized as a potential nuclear proliferation threat. In January, however, Israel was added to the Third Category Priority list, the lowest category for intelligence collection purposes.[10] Still, Israel's nuclear activities in 1956—its interest in purchasing a 10-megawatt, natural uranium, heavy water reactor from the United States, in addition to ten tons of heavy water—did not arouse the interest of intelligence analysts and was not taken as an indication of Israel's intention to embark on a major reactor construction program.[11]

In 1957 Israel reversed direction. While in 1956 Israel indicated its interest in skipping the pool-type reactor stage and constructing instead a "real reactor" (10 MW, natural uranium/heavy water), for which it asked to purchase heavy water from the United States, in 1957 this interest was hardly mentioned. Rather, Israel now wanted to utilize the American offer of 1955 to construct a 1-MW, pool-type research reactor, to be designed and manufactured by the firm American Machines and Foundry (AMF) Atomics. In December 1957 the long-awaited project proposal and hazard analysis for the reactor was submitted to AEC by AMF on behalf of Israel for the Nachal Soreq site. This reactor qualified Israel to receive a $350,000 grant from the United States under the terms of the presidential offer. On 19 March 1958 Israel signed its contract with AMF, expecting that the reactor's start-up date would be about fifteen months later.

When an AEC official asked the Israeli science attaché in Washington about the status of the 10-MW, natural uranium, heavy-water reactor, for which in July 1956 Israel had requested ten tons of heavy water from the AEC, the Israeli representative replied that "no firm decision had been taken with regard to this reactor, and that a determination as to whether to proceed with it would be dependent upon the availability of money, manpower, and uranium."[12] Not only was the Israeli flip not registered as a warning flag with the AEC, but the Soreq reactor actually shielded the Dimona reactor. The construction of the Soreq reactor by AMF was an important factor indicating why the United States failed to identify Israel's other, top-secret nuclear project, namely, Dimona.

A series of private and public comments made by chairman Bergmann in 1958–60 about a likely or forthcoming Israeli decision to start building a nuclear power plant added to the American failure to see what was happening. In a public interview given by Bergmann in early 1958, in which he discussed the research reactor to be supplied by the United States (Soreq), Bergmann elaborated on the need for nuclear power in Israel but noted that no formal decision on nuclear power had yet been made by the Israeli government. Two months later, on 15 April, Bergmann said that the decision to build a power reactor had already been taken in principle, but he added that "it would take two and half years to construct the experimental reactor now contemplated, and five to seven years before a large, economically feasible reactor could be put into operation."[13] The United States intelligence assumed that the small experimental reactor that Bergmann mentioned was the small American pool-type reactor which was at the final stage of negotiation with Israel at the time.[14] In that interview Bergmann "stated categorically" that the agreement with France "was limited to the exchange of information on uranium chemistry and the production of heavy water."[15]

A follow-up interview of Bergmann by an officer from the U.S. Embassy in Tel Aviv in July further added to the confusion. In that interview Bergmann stated that "the decision to build a heavy-water plant had been taken, but the capacity of this plant was still undecided." Bergmann added that "he expected to submit a report by the end of July 1958 that would enable the government to decide about the plant." It is unclear whether these statements about nuclear power were part of a deliberate strategy designed to deceive the United States and protect Dimona, a reflection of the discussions about nuclear powers in those days, or the result of Bergmann's tendency for loose talk. In any case, the result was that the United States was blind to the possibility that Israel might be secretly engaging in building a production reactor. Thus Israel was not among the countries the United States was reviewing in connection with the "fourth country" problem. The concern was mostly in regard to France's cooperative relations with other European nuclear energy programs. On the watch list were also West Germany, Italy, China, Poland, and Czechoslovakia.[16]

During 1958–59 there were indications that Israel might have launched a nuclear program, but these indications were not properly interpreted. There were reports relating France's assistance to Israel in the nuclear field, and "a few of these reports indicated that the French would supply, or aid in the development of [Israeli] atomic weapons." On 15 April 1958, however, Bergmann denied that the French-Israeli nuclear cooperation went beyond exchanges of information on uranium chemistry and heavy water, and the United States accepted his explanation (10). In May 1959 the U.S. Embassy learned that the resignation of Dan Tolkovsky as head of the Development Authority in the Israeli Ministry of Defense might be related to his opposition to Peres's attempts to obtain nuclear weapons, but the information was not confirmed and no intelligence action followed (10–11). In June 1959 the Norwegian Foreign Ministry informed a representative of the AEC of its agreement to sell Israel heavy water subjected to "safeguards and inspection," but the AEC representative did not inquire about the quantity of heavy water, and the information was not disseminated to the American intelligence community until mid-December 1960 (11). In April 1960 the Clandestine Service of the CIA (CIA/CS) learned that the Norwegian-Israeli agreement involved twenty tons of heavy water, but the information was not distributed through the intelligence system (11). In early 1960 the CIA/CS "obtained information that specific Israeli observers would be present at the first French nuclear weapons tests," but the information, too, was never passed on "because it could not be confirmed that any observers actually attended" (11).

The most perplexing failure to disseminate intelligence data regarding Israel concerns the early aerial photographs of Dimona. In early 1958 the United States became aware, through U-2 aerial reconnaissance flights, of the construction under way in a Negev site near Beer Sheba.[17] According to Dino A. Brugioni, who served at the CIA Photographic Intelligence Center (CIA/PIC), the first aerial pictures of the "Beer Sheba site" (as the Dimona site was called) were found accidentally, as the United States "was watching periodically" an Israeli practice bombing range in the Negev desert in 1958.[18] The early excavations were determined to be a "probable" nuclear-related site, but U.S. intelligence failed to grasp the meaning of its own findings. It took more than two years for the intelligence agencies to identify Dimona as a nuclear reactor site.[19]

Almost forty years later Brugioni still recalls how the program director, Arthur C. Lundahl, took the first aerial photographs (called "briefing boards") to brief President Eisenhower and other officials in early 1958. Brugioni remembers the episode well because of the appearance of a lack of reaction on the part of Eisenhower and Lewis Strauss, the AEC chairman. Brugioni recalls that Lundahl returned from the White House meeting, noting that Eisenhower "did not say a word."[20] CIA/PIC was not asked for further photographs of the site or for follow-up presentations. For an enthusiastic consumer of intelligence like Eisenhower, this was unusual. Lundahl and Brugioni were left with the feeling that Eisenhower wanted Israel to acquire nuclear weapons.[21]

In itself the 1958 photographic material was inconclusive, and it was difficult to determine the purpose of the excavation. Notwithstanding, Lundahl and his team of interpreters referred to it as a "probable" nuclear-related site.[22] The site stood out: the long security fence erected around the perimeter, the extent of the dig itself and the efforts to conceal the dirt, the extensive road system into the site and around the perimeter, and the power lines that had been constructed.[23]

Those suspicions were fed into the system. As early as 27 March 1958 the CIA Office of Scientific Intelligence (CIA/OSI) requested detailed information about Israel's nuclear activities, particularly Israel's production of heavy water and uranium. The requests were submitted to the American Embassy in Tel Aviv on 13 June 1958, and later "served almost verbatim" to Bergmann. Bergmann "was somewhat perturbed" by the questions, but he answered them "in some detail." He stated that the decision to build a heavy water nuclear plant had been taken, "but the capacity of this plant was still undecided . . . [and] he expected to submit a report later that month which would enable the government to decide about the size." According to the American report, "his [Bergmann's] answers contained no indication of reactor construction."[24]

American intelligence thus failed on the matter of Dimona. In mid-December 1960, shortly after the discovery of Dimona, the United States Intelligence Board (USIB) asked the Joint Atomic Energy Intelligence Committee (JAEIC) "to prepare a detailed postmortem on why the intelligence community did not recognize this development [Dimona] earlier." The study concludes that "information was available to some elements of the intelligence community as early as April 1958 that could have alerted the atomic energy intelligence community to Israeli intentions."[25]

What were the reasons for the failure? On the analytical level, U.S. intelligence failed to identify Israel's intentions and motivations. Israeli secrecy and deception, and Bergmann's confusing references, misled the United States. It was also presumed in those days "that Israel could not achieve this [nuclear weapons] capability without outside aid from the U.S. or its allies, and . . . any such aid would be readily known to the U.S." This assumption "led to a tendency to discount rumors of [the] Israeli reactor and French collaboration in the nuclear weapons area." The other reason for the failure was bureaucratic: important information was available but was not disseminated through the system. Israel may also have had friends in high places in the intelligence and nuclear establishments who might have helped to suppress the early information. Information about Israel was jealously held within the CIA, where James Jesus Angleton was in charge of the Israeli desk. Angleton did not share sensitive information with other agencies, and also withheld much of it from other CIA sections.

The Eisenhower administration had knowledge of the Dimona project as early as 1958–59 but did not act on it, setting the precedent that Israel's nuclear weapons program was treated as a special case. Politicians and intelligence chiefs recognized the need to tread softly around it. The late-1950s might have been the only time the United States could have successfully pressured Israel to give up its nuclear weapons project in exchange for American security guarantees, but the opportunity was not explored.

THE ADMINISTRATION AWAKENS

More than two and a half years after the Eisenhower administration received the initial information about Dimona, the site again became the center of attention. In June 1960 the American Embassy in Tel Aviv became aware of rumors that the "French were collaborating with the Israelis in an atomic energy project near Beer Sheba." Sometime that summer, in response to the embassy's informal inquiries, Israel described the Dimona site as a "textile plant." On 2 August the embassy reported for the first time that a "French-Israeli atomic energy project [is] being built near Beer Sheba." The report was discussed at the 25 August JAEIC and members were requested to report any available information for the next meeting on 8 September 1960.[26] This triggered the chain of events that led to the public disclosure of the Dimona reactor in December.

In September, in response to renewed American inquiries about the Dimona site, Israeli officials referred to the project under construction as a "metallurgical research installation." In mid-September the CIA responded to a State Department probe concerning the 2 August report from Tel Aviv, saying it had "no confirming information" concerning the Dimona construction site and informed the State Department that it had instructed its field officers to obtain answers to specific questions about it. The State Department, too, instructed the U.S. Embassy in Tel Aviv to seek more information on the subject.[27] In late October and early November the United Kingdom informed the United States that it believed a reactor was under construction near Beer Sheba. On 8 November British intelligence provided CIA/PIC with ground photography of the site. The next day, based on a hurried analysis of the photography, a preliminary assessment was made in the CIA—"the site was probably a reactor complex."[28]

The same day, Air Force Intelligence instructed the air attaché in Tel Aviv to obtain additional photographs of the "Beer Sheba site." Once again he was told that the facility under construction was "a metallurgical research laboratory." The attaché took ground photography of the site, but it took a month and a half for the photographs to be disseminated to nuclear intelligence, although a copy of one photograph was received in Washington in early December and made available to JAEIC. It turned out that the Army attaché in Israel had taken many photographs of the site on 9 August, but he had not realized what the installation was. These photographs were processed along with many others by Army Intelligence in October, but only in December was their significance recognized, and they became available to Atomic Energy Intelligence on 8 December.[29]

By late November 1960, in response to a request by the CIA, the U.S. Embassy in Paris reported an interview in which the AEC representative in Paris confronted a CEA official with information that the United States had learned of the "construction of a nuclear power plant in Beer Sheba" and requested information on the French participation. The French CEA official "flatly denied" that the CEA or any French company were collaborating with Israel in the construction of a nuclear power reactor, asserting that the French-Israeli agreement had nothing to do with power reactors, and was limited only to uranium and heavy water production.[30]

Days later came the final confirmation. On 26 November Henry Gomberg, a University of Michigan nuclear scientist who had visited Israel, reported that he had an "urgent and secret" item regarding Israel's nuclear program. He noted that he had already informed Ambassador Reid in Tel Aviv of this information.[31] When Gomberg returned to Washington, D.C., on 1 December, he was debriefed at the State Department by representatives of the AEC, CIA, and State Department. He reported that he was convinced that the large installation Israel had been constructing in the Negev desert, which was referred to as "a large agricultural experimental station," was "a Marcoul-type reactor being constructed with French technical assistance." He said that the construction had been under way for "about two years," and it "was scheduled to be completed in about a year."[32]

He concluded that Israel was pursuing two parallel nuclear paths, one aimed at scientific research at the Nachal Soreq reactor and another aimed toward producing weapon-grade plutonium at Dimona. His suspicions were based primarily on negative evidence. In his visit to the Technion in Haifa, for example, he found no correlation between the institution's program of personnel training and the purpose of the program. "The Israelis had a clear requirement for personnel of specific types which could not be used in any program they would identify. Furthermore, their familiarization program was much more detailed and operational in its nature than was called for by their research activities. A number of trained people had recently been put to work but were not apparent in any known installation."[33] Another reason was the result of his visit at "a facility called Plant or Laboratory No. 4 [Machon 4]":

It was apparent that the people he talked to had been thoroughly briefed to restrict their discussion within security bounds. Nevertheless, it was apparent that work was under way which he was not shown or advised of. One man distressed his guide by mentioning that Plant No. 4 expected to be working with gram quantities of plutonium and curie quantities of polonium in a short time; such material would not come from any existing Israeli facility and presumably would come from either France or the new large reactor.[34]

Israel's particular interest in plutonium was apparent to Gomberg, especially because the Israelis were secretive and reluctant to discuss specific projects or explain personnel needs. Gomberg noted that in his last meeting with Bergmann, he was told that in three weeks Ben Gurion would issue a statement concerning Israel's atomic energy program.[35]

After Ambassador Reid learned of Gomberg's debriefings in Paris and Washington's reactions to it, he acknowledged, on 30 November, that he himself had discussed these issues with Gomberg before the latter's departure. Gomberg reported that he believed "Israel is engaged in a very broad range of activities in this field and is pursuing projects which they were not prepared to discuss with him." In particular, Gomberg called attention to "Israel's strong interest in plutonium"—measured in gram amounts, which he considered significant. In response to Reid's query, Gomberg thought "it was conceivable that Israel could have weapons capability in less than ten years."[36]

Two days later Reid met Bergmann to discuss Israel's nuclear energy program. Bergmann told Reid that Ben Gurion planned to make a policy announcement on nuclear energy the next week while announcing the establishment of a new university in Beer Sheba. Ben Gurion's announcement, according to Bergmann, was to mention a "new 10 to 20 megawatt natural uranium and heavy water nuclear reactor to go critical in about a year and a half." Bergmann also noted that the reactor "is exclusively of Israeli design, with some French equipment." It is "to be used for research in desert plants, drought resistant seeds, short-life isotopes and radio biological research not now possible at present [Soreq] reactor."[37] It was the first time Bergmann acknowledged that a second reactor was being built in Israel.

The first week of December 1960 the American intelligence community finally understood that a new reality was in the making. Gomberg's debriefing, Reid's report, and new information received from Britain revealing that Norway had furnished Israel with twenty tons of heavy water changed the American view of Israel's nuclear activities. Israel's intentions were reinterpreted as directed toward the acquisition of nuclear weapons capability, and Bergmann's comments were now seen as part of Israel's effort to mislead the United States.[38]

On 2 December a technical assessment made by the JAEIC concluded that "a 200 megawatt reactor appeared [to be] under construction near Beer Sheba."[39]

British intelligence reached a similar conclusion.[40] The assessment was inaccurate, but it recognized that this was a major project with implications of nuclear weapons proliferation. The next day, the Joint Atomic Energy Committee in Congress was informed of the new development. On 8 December the CIA issued a Special National Intelligence Report (SNIE) about Dimona, stressing the gravity of the project's repercussions.[41]

The same day, the National Security Council (NSC) was convened, with the Dimona issue high on the agenda. CIA director Allen Dulles informed the NSC that Israel, with French assistance, was constructing a nuclear complex in the Negev desert, which probably included a reactor capable of producing weapon-grade plutonium. Dulles mentioned Ben Gurion's forthcoming announcement, but noted that experts from the CIA and the AEC believed "that the Israeli nuclear complex cannot be solely for peaceful purposes." Dulles reiterated in the CIA estimate that Arab reaction to Dimona would be "particularly severe."[42]

At this point the State Department decided to raise the issue of Dimona with Israel discreetly. On 9 December Secretary of State Christian Herter summoned the Israeli ambassador, Avraham Harman, presented him with the U.S. intelligence findings, including ground photographs, and pointed out that the site seemed to be appropriate for a reactor ten times the declared size. Herter mentioned that in the U.S. estimate such installation, with "this apparent size, would cost on the order of $80 million dollars and has not been mentioned in recent discussions of Israeli economic development plans and possible U.S. financial assistance." Herter referred to the inconsistencies between the American intelligence findings and the Israeli account as conveyed to Ambassador Reid.[43]

Herter talked of the American suspicions that Israel had launched a secret nuclear weapons program, warned of the consequences of this, and asked for an accurate report on Israel's nuclear program. Harman, who "disclaimed any knowledge of facts," told Herter he would request "urgent advice."[44] Herter also called the French charge d'affaires and reported to him what Bergmann had told Reid in Tel Aviv, noting that the United States had ascertained that the reactor was "at least ten times as large as claimed." Herter added that it appeared that the large reactor was not intended to provide power but to produce plutonium, "which in a comparatively short time would give them [Israel] considerable weapons potential." Herter commented that Bergmann's talk about isotope research "does not make any sense since they already have an experimental reactor [Soreq] big enough to take care of that."[45] Within days the story became public.

On 13 December *Time* magazine disclosed that a "small power," which was "neither of the communist nor the NATO bloc," was developing a nuclear weapons capability. Three days later, the London *Daily Express* named Israel as the state, adding that "British and American intelligence authorities believe that the Israelis are well on the way to building their first experimental nuclear bomb."[46] On 18 December the chairman of the AEC, John McCone, appeared on the television program "Meet the Press" to confirm that Israel was secretly building a nuclear reactor and that the United States had asked Israel for information. Without going into details, McCone said that, thus far, the United States had "only informal and unofficial information" concerning Israel's activities in the nuclear field. He pointed out that, while the possession of a reactor did not in itself constitute a weapons capability, it could be used to produce plutonium.[47]

The issue of the Israeli nuclear reactor now became a public issue for the first time. The front-page story in the next day's *New York Times*, written, we now know, with the help of McCone, revealed that "U.S. officials [are] studying with mounting concern recent evidence indicating that Israel, with assistance from France, may be developing the capacity to produce nuclear weapons."[48] The State Department also acknowledged for the first time that Herter had summoned the Israeli ambassador on 9 December to express concern and ask for information, and that "a response has not yet been received."[49] On the same day, 19 December, the Israeli reactor was the topic of a meeting with President Eisenhower at the White House. The minutes indicate that both Herter and Allen Dulles referred to Dimona as a "plutonium production plant." Secretary of Defense Thomas Gates asserted that "our information is that the plant is not for peaceful purposes." In response to Herter's remark that the Israelis "have constructed this plant through diversions from private and public aid to Israel," Eisenhower noted that the cost of the Dimona plant was estimated to be between "100 to 200 million dollars."[50]

Less than six months after Ben Gurion's confrontation with de Gaulle over the future of Dimona, he had a second opportunity to appreciate the limits of the nuclear weapons project, through a confrontation with the United States. Before Israel could fulfill the November 1960 agreement with the French to announce publicly the peaceful nature of Dimona, the secrecy shrouding Dimona was lifted on the other side of the Atlantic.

DOUBLESPEAK

In his first meeting on the subject, it was already possible to discern the president's desire to look the other way with regard to the Israeli case. President Eisenhower suggested that the United States was confident, in view of Israel's adherence to the Vienna agreement on peaceful uses of atomic energy, that the reactor was for peaceful uses, and that Israel should permit inspection visits to the reactor. Later, the president made the point that "there is more of a problem than that involved," and that the United States had now to decide what "we do as further countries become atomic producers." To this, Herter responded that "it may still be possible to head off this production by the Israelis."[51] The next day, 20 December, the political significance of Dimona was highlighted in a follow-up *New York Times* story, which revealed that Israel had led the United States to believe that the nuclear site was a textile plant, and that the issue had been discussed in a high-level presidential briefing at the White House the previous day.[52]

The same day, Ambassador Harman met Secretary Herter and provided, for the first time, the formal Israeli reply to the secretary's queries of 9 December. Harman acknowledged that a 24-MW research reactor had been under construction for a year, not 100 to 300 megawatts as the United States suspected, and that it would "take three to four years to complete."[53] The reactor was described as having no industrial importance; the purposes were the "development of scientific knowledge for eventual industrial, agricultural, medical and other scientific purposes." The project was said to be "part of the general program of development of the Negev." It was acknowledged that the project was assisted by the French and, in a minor way, by several other countries, but it was built under the direction of Israeli scientists. He assured Herter that the project was for peaceful uses only and, once completed, would be open to students from friendly countries. The project cost Israel about five million dollars per year exclusive of local currency costs. He also added that Ben Gurion would issue a public statement on the project in the Knesset the following day. Herter, his doubts not satisfied, posed additional questions to the ambassador.[54]

Now that Dimona's secrecy was lifted, the secrecy itself was fueling speculations about Israel's intentions and capabilities in the nuclear field. The Dimona story became an international crisis, and Israel could no longer delay issuing a public statement explaining the nature of its nuclear project. The first Israeli public responses to McCone's televised statement were unofficial and ambiguous. Bergmann was the first to respond, referring to the reports that Israel was developing nuclear weapons as "very flattering, but untrue," adding that "Israel's industry in the present state is incapable of undertaking such a task."[55] He mentioned nothing about Israel's future intentions. An even more ambiguous message came the next day as the *New York Times* reported that the Israeli Defense Ministry declined to say "whether it was developing the capacity to produce nuclear weapons." The IAEC issued a brief statement, reiterating the chairman's comment of the day before, saying that "Israel is not engaged in the production of atomic weapons."[56] The first official confirmation of French assistance in building a natural uranium reactor in Israel also came on 19 December in separate statements issued by the French Foreign Ministry and the Israeli Embassy. The Israeli Embassy noted that Israel's atomic development was "dedicated exclusively" to the needs of industry, agriculture, medicine, and science. The French statement went beyond that and insisted "that all necessary provisions have been taken by France to assure that the French aid to Israel in the nuclear field would be used only for peaceful purposes."[57]

BEN GURION'S STATEMENT

These statements, however, were not enough to restore calm. The long delay in Israel's response to Herter's official query and the continued absence of any authoritative public statement from Ben Gurion only heightened the crisis. Finally, after three days of speculation, Ben Gurion delivered a circumspect statement on the matter to the Knesset on 21 December. This was the first occasion that the citizens of Israel were told that their country was constructing a nuclear reactor in the Negev, and the only time that an Israeli prime minister issued a statement about Dimona. Since the seeds of the Israeli opaque nuclear posture were planted in this statement, it is worth quoting in full:

> The development of the Negev—which we regard as our principal task for the next decade—requires broad and manifold scientific research. For this purpose we have established at Beer Sheba a scientific institute for research in problems of arid zones and desert flora and fauna. We are also engaged at this time in the construction of a research reactor with a capacity of 24,000 thermal kilowatts, which will serve the needs of industry, agriculture, health and science. This reactor will also be used to train Israeli scientists and technologists for the future construction of an atomic power station within a presumed period of 10 to 15 years.
>
> The research reactor which we are now building in the Negev will not be completed until three or four years from now. This reactor, like the American reactor, is designed exclusively for peaceful purposes, and was constructed under the direction of Israeli experts. When it is finished it will be open to trainees from other countries and will be similar to the reactor which the Canadian Government helped to construct in India, with the difference that our reactor is of smaller capacity.[58]

Ben Gurion dismissed the reports that Israel was manufacturing a nuclear bomb as a "deliberate or unwitting untruth," adding that Israel had proposed "general and total disarmament in Israel and the neighboring Arab states on conditions of mutual rights of inspection." In line with the Couve de Murville-Peres agreement, the statement made no mention of France as the reactor designer, stating only that the reactor was constructed under Israeli direction.[59] By that time the French government was no longer involved in the construction.

Ben Gurion's statement of 21 December held some elements of truth, but it certainly did not tell the whole story. His immediate goal was to allay American suspicions and political pressures. A confrontation with America would jeopardize the project and Israel's relationship with the United States, and Ben Gurion was determined to keep both intact. The strategy seemed to work. The Israeli explanations, especially Ben Gurion's public pronouncements, eased the U.S.-Israeli confrontation, at least in the public sphere, allowing the State Department to issue a statement that "the government of Israel has given assurances that its new reactor . . . is dedicated entirely to peaceful purposes." The State Department noted that the U.S. government welcomed the Israeli statements, and went on to say that "it is gratifying to note that as made public the Israeli atomic energy program does not represent a cause of special concern."[60] It was convenient for the State Department to read Ben Gurion's assurances as going beyond what he actually stated.[61] The Israeli statement created an American expectation "that Israel will make its reactor accessible to the safeguards system of the International Atomic Energy Agency,"[62] even though Ben Gurion did not say anything of the kind. Israel's assurances, however, allowed the United States to defuse the crisis.

Ben Gurion's statement prevented public confrontation, but it was not enough to remove the nuclear weapons issue from the U.S.-Israeli agenda. The United States still insisted on receiving more detailed technical information on the Dimona reactor, but now it decided to pursue the issue less publicly. Ben Gurion's assurances left many aspects of the project unclear. The Eisenhower administration, which only months before had celebrated the opening of Israel's first research reactor at Nachal Soreq, provided by the United States as part of its Atoms for Peace program, had been left in the dark on Dimona and was determined to obtain further clarification and concrete commitments. The Israeli nuclear program thus became a sore point between the two countries.

On 21 December Ambassador Reid was asked to convey to Ben Gurion the message that the U.S. government "is firmly opposed to proliferation of nuclear weapons capabilities and therefore deeply interested in having full and frank account [of] Israeli atomic activities, including plans for disposing of plutonium which will be bred by Israel's new reactor." Furthermore, Reid was asked to tell Ben Gurion that "unless suspicions are firmly laid to rest programs such as those of Israel can have grave repercussions in the Near East area particularly but also outside it."[63] Three days later, on 24 December, Reid met with Ben Gurion to convey the administration's message in person. He told Ben Gurion that the United States welcomed the public and private assurances that Israel provided concerning the "peaceful purposes" of the reactor and Israel's atomic energy program, noting that his government "did not wish to prolong or exaggerate this issue." Reid reiterated Herter's request that safeguards "be applied to any plutonium produced by reactor and referred to Secretary's mention of Israel's affirmative vote on IAEA safeguards at September general conference."[64]

Ben Gurion was "direct and spirited, as always," recalls Reid, but "friendly." At one point, however, he expressed "mild irritation" in reference to the continuing flap in the United States over Israel's reactor. "Why in the States is everything being told everybody," Ben Gurion asked. He added that "he was very sorry that he had not been able to tell President Eisenhower of this project during his recent visit to Washington," and "were it not so close to end of Eisenhower administration, he would wish to give personal account to President, whom he had long known and admired."[65] Reid also raised in that meeting the possibility of having a scientist take a look at the reactor. There is no record of Ben Gurion's reply to his request.[66]

THE FIVE QUESTIONS

The issue of an American or IAEA visit to Dimona continued to preoccupy the State Department and Reid in the last days of December 1960. On 31 December Reid received instructions to raise the nuclear program issue with Ben Gurion or Foreign Minister Meir, despite the domestic cabinet crisis in Israel, since "neither Department nor other interested Washington agencies consider Ben Gurion's statements thus far satisfactory." It appears that Ben Gurion's replies on "plutonium safeguards, reactor's power and production capability, inspection by a visiting scientist" were too vague, if not evasive.[67] Reid was authorized to state that the U.S. government (USG) was "gratified by assurances given thus far," and "would not welcome another round of alarmist publicity," however, this did not signify "cessation legitimate USG interest in this matter," since "USG policy is unequivocally opposed to proliferation of nuclear weapons capabilities." The telegram went on to say that the Israeli government could act to restore confidence in U.S.-Israeli relations "by providing clear and complete answers to such cogent and crucial questions." The five questions were:

(1) What are present GOI [government of Israel] plans for disposing of plutonium which will be bred in new reactor? (2) Will GOI agree to adequate safeguards with respect to plutonium produced? (3) Will GOI permit qualified scientists from the IAEA or other friendly quarters visit new reactor? If so, what would be earliest time? (4) Is a third reactor in either construction

or planning stage? (5) Can Israel state categorically that it has no plans for developing nuclear weapons?[68]

The U.S. documents and Ben Gurion's biographer are in agreement about the content of the five questions, but it is not clear how and when they were presented. According to Bar-Zohar, on 3 January Reid met with Meir and presented her with the five questions as an ultimatum, "requesting that answers be returned to him by that midnight."[69] Meir met with Ben Gurion that day, and the two decided to ignore the American deadline. Ben Gurion was "infuriated by this disrespectful demand" and summoned Reid to Sdeh Boker.[70] He chided him, saying, "you must talk to us as equals, or not talk to us at all," but then responded to the five questions one by one:

As to the first question, he replied: "As far as we know, those who sell uranium do so on condition that the plutonium reverts to them." In reply to the second question, concerning "guarantees," the Old Man replied: "International guarantees—no. We don't want hostile states meddling in our business." At the same time he expressed complete willingness to permit visits by scientists from a friendly state, or from an international organization, but not immediately. "There is anger in Israel over the American action in leaking this matter," he said, and expressed his view that the visit would be conducted in the course of the year. He answered in the negative about the construction of an additional reactor and concluded by declaring that Israel did not intend to manufacture nuclear weapons. "All that I said in the Knesset holds, it was said explicitly, and you must accept it at face value."[71]

The State Department's chronology and Reid's recollections tell a different, less dramatic story. The State Department's record does not show a meeting between Reid and Meir, indicating instead a lengthy meeting between Ben Gurion and Reid on 4 January, in which Reid presented the five questions. According to Reid, the tone of the meeting was friendly and there was no ultimatum—"sovereign states don't act that way"—although it was clear that Ben Gurion was uncomfortable discussing Dimona. For Reid, the questions were designed to elicit "clarifications." As to Ben Gurion's answers, the State Department chronology relates a straightforward exchange: "(a) Plutonium would go to the uranium supplier; (b) Visits by nationals from friendly powers would be permitted; (c) No IAEA safeguards until others agree—"no Russians"; (d) No third reactor is now contemplated; (e) Categoric assurance that no nuclear weapons planned."[72]

The differences between the two versions appears to be a matter of perception and tone. Reid is probably correct that no ultimatum was made, while Bar-Zohar's account probably reflects Ben Gurion's perception of the purpose of the five questions. The State Department's sanitized version of the telegram of 31 December conveys toughness. If Israel wanted "to restore the confidence which should be cornerstone of our relations," it could do so "by providing clear and complete answers to such cogent and crucial questions." There is no formal ultimatum, but the conditioning of restoring relations on the questions is clear. Reid may be right that no formal deadline was set, but the State Department telegram did instruct him of the following: "You should add that the Secretary will welcome a personal report from him at earliest possible opportunity." This is not the last time a U.S.-Israeli exchange on the nuclear program was perceived differently by the two sides, with Israel seeing American actions as on the verge of violating national sovereignty, let alone diplomatic etiquette.

Ben Gurion's assurances to Reid did not end the Eisenhower administration's probe. On 11 January 1961 Herter met Harman for four hours on the issue of the Israeli atomic energy program. Harman reiterated the assurances Ben Gurion had given Reid, noting that Ben Gurion considered the answer to Reid's fifth question—"that Israel has no plans for developing nuclear weapons"—as the "major point." Herter, however, asked for stronger reassurances concerning the issues of international control and ownership of the fissile material that would be produced.[73] On 17 January, two days before the close of the Eisenhower administration, Herter instructed Reid to continue pressing Ben Gurion for an early visit to Dimona by scientists from a friendly power.[74]

PARTING WORDS

The final legacy of the Eisenhower administration on the matter of Dimona was a "secret" report to the Joint Committee on Atomic Energy of the Congress, dated 19 January 1961. The report detailed the American understanding of the Dimona project. It suggested that the U.S. government took Ben Gurion's private and public statements as a solemn pledge not to manufacture nuclear weapons. The first article of the report asserts: "We [the United States] have been assured categorically at the highest level of the Israeli government that Israel has no plans for the production of atomic weapons." The question of a weapons option, as distinguished from actual weapons in stock, was not raised by either the United States or Ben Gurion. As to the question of foreign visits to Dimona, which meant some form of international control, the report states: "We have been assured that Israel will be glad to receive visits by scientists from friendly countries at the Dimona reactor when public interest has quieted down. In particular a scientist from the United States will be welcome as early as possible on this condition."[75]

Israel, however, did not agree to formal IAEA or other international inspections. Although it accepted "the general principle of international safeguards to assure peaceful use of atomic energy," the report noted that Israel also believed in the "principle of equality." Israel would not be willing to open Dimona to international inspections until such procedures applied to "comparable reactors everywhere." These two understandings set the stage for the agreement Ben Gurion and Kennedy would reach in later visits, first in 1961, on provisional visits, and again in 1963, on periodic visits.

Article 6 of the report attributed Israeli secrecy to "fears of participating foreign companies over the prospects of [an] Arab boycott."[76] It is evident from the report that the United States had received "responsible assurances" from the French government concerning the degree of French-Israeli cooperation, and the nature of that cooperation.

> The French-Israeli cooperation program is limited to the 24 MW research reactor, that the French will supply all the uranium for this reactor, that the plutonium produced in the reactor will all be returned to France, that adequate arrangements have been agreed upon to assure the exclusively peaceful use of the reactor, and that resident French inspectors or periodic inspectors visits will be accepted. The French assured us that they do not want to be associated with any Israeli nuclear weapons program, that they have urged public assurances of peaceful intention by the Israelis, and that they support our efforts to this end.[77]

The two-page document also included information Israel provided the United States that went beyond Ben Gurion's public statement. Three items are worth listing:

> b. There is no plutonium now in Israel and plutonium from the reactor will, as a condition attached to purchases of uranium abroad, return to the supplying country. . . .
> g. In addition to the reactor the complex will include a hot laboratory, cold laboratory, waste disposal plant, a facility for rods, offices including a library unit and a medical unit. . . .
> h. The reactor and ancillary facilities are expected to cost $34 million, of which $17.8 million would be foreign exchange. The reactor itself is expected to cost $15.4 million, of which $10 million would be foreign exchange.[78]

The dealings between Ben Gurion and the Eisenhower administration shaped the priorities and policies of both governments. On the Israeli side, Ben Gurion's priority was to lessen American pressures in order to allow for the completion of the physical infrastructure for a nuclear-weapons option.[79] He was willing to say almost anything the United States wanted to hear, giving the impression that his statement in the Knesset was an unequivocal pledge not to produce nuclear weapons. On practical issues, however, Ben Gurion was more cautious. He evaded the question of the ownership of the plutonium and rejected a formal international inspection of Dimona. He accepted a visit by American scientists, but made it clear that it would be carried out under Israeli control.

On the American side, the administration sought to force Ben Gurion to change his original plans. Washington remained skeptical about Ben Gurion's assurances that Dimona was dedicated to peaceful research. American officials were convinced that Dimona's purpose was to produce materials for use in nuclear weapons. In order for the United States to freeze the Israeli nuclear project, it had to insist on verifying Ben Gurion's assurances by placing Dimona under international safeguards or opening it to foreign scientists.

The Eisenhower administration's legacy is mixed and inconsistent. Eisenhower did not act on early intelligence information about Dimona, giving the impression that he might have preferred Israel obtaining nuclear weapons. The lack of action was consistent with Eisenhower's lack of a coherent policy on nuclear proliferation. Once the intelligence about Dimona was shared with other governmental agencies, however, the Eisenhower administration was forceful in drawing the line against proliferation. The determination that the line against nuclear weapons proliferation had to be drawn in Israel evolved during the final weeks of the administration.

No American president was more concerned with the danger of nuclear proliferation than John Fitzgerald Kennedy.[1] He was convinced that the spread of nuclear weapons would make the world more dangerous and undermine U.S. interests. He saw it as his role to place nuclear arms control and nonproliferation at the center of American foreign policy.[2] In the words of Glenn Seaborg, Kennedy's chairman of the AEC, nuclear proliferation was Kennedy's "private nightmare."[3]

Kennedy's global arms control agenda was shaped, to a large extent, by his commitment to nonproliferation. He supported a nuclear test ban agreement—the first arms control issue with which the new administration had to deal—primarily because he saw it as a nonproliferation tool. Even before the presidential election, he had opposed the resumption of nuclear testing because of the pretext it gave to nations wishing to acquire nuclear weapons. Kennedy reminded his advisers that more was at stake than a piece of paper—without an agreement, the arms race would continue and nuclear weapons would proliferate to other countries. The only example Kennedy used to make the point was Israel.[4]

The problem of nuclear weapons proliferation was made more acute in the early 1960s as nuclear technology and knowledge became increasingly available and cheaper.[5] A 1962 study was prepared for Kennedy by the Office of the Secretary of Defense, stating that if there were no basic changes in technology, about sixteen countries, excluding the then four nuclear powers, were capable of acquiring limited nuclear weapons and a crude means of delivery in the next ten years. If the state of technology remained unchanged, the cost to these countries to maintain a modest nuclear weapons program were estimated to be $150–$175 million, and a program aimed at producing one thousand nuclear weapons would cost about a billion dollars. The study warned that "the costs of nuclear weapons can be expected to decline greatly over time through the diffusion of weapon technology, through the wider distribution of research and power reactors, and through advances in technology resulting from continued testing."[6]

The study noted that the lead time from the initial decision to launch a weapon program until the first bomb could vary from three to ten years, depending on the level of technology, industrial capacity, and resources allocated to the task. With the diffusion of nuclear technology, however, "many countries have reduced the lead time and cost of acquiring weapons by getting research reactors and starting nuclear power programs. The technology involved is directly related to [the] weapons program and a decision to initiate a 'peaceful' program provides a lower cost option, later, to have a military program."[7] Regarding proliferation beyond ten years, the study stated that unrestricted testing would significantly lower the cost of acquiring nuclear weapons.

The study saw a linkage between a nuclear test ban and proliferation. Though a test ban would be helpful in stemming proliferation, the study was clear that even a comprehensive ban could only slow a determined proliferator. "It is probably not an exaggeration to say that it is necessary, but not a sufficient, condition for keeping the number of nuclear countries small."[8] One must remember that "even without testing, it is feasible for a country to produce and stockpile nuclear weapons." Clearly a more important factor would be the political pressure that the United States and the Soviet Union would be willing to exert.[9] The study dealt with nuclear proliferation as a global phenomenon, but Israel was regarded as the most likely Nth proliferator state after Communist China. The study referred to China as a country that "most certainly will" acquire nuclear weapons; Israel was defined as the next most likely proliferation case, followed by Sweden and India.[10]

Israel, more than any other nation, impressed the problem of nuclear weapons proliferation on the new president. Israel was the first case of nuclear weapons proliferation in which the United States had political leverage. It was a case of proliferation in a small, friendly state, outside the boundaries of the U.S. policy of containment, and surrounded by larger enemies vowing to destroy it. Unlike China or India, Israel did not aspire to the status of a Great Power. Israel also enjoyed unique domestic support in America. Kennedy was well aware that, without the support of about 80 percent of the Jewish voters, he would not have been elected.

Kennedy was the first American President to have a close political aide who served as a liaison to the Jewish community and as an unofficial adviser on Israel. Myer (Mike) Feldman, a Jewish lawyer from Philadelphia, had been Kennedy's senior legislative aide since 1958. Shortly after Kennedy won reelection to the Senate in 1958, he put Feldman in charge of developing policy issues regarding Israel and the Middle East. During the 1960 presidential campaign, Feldman acted as Kennedy's representative to the Jewish community and handled his contacts with the Israeli government. The day after the election Kennedy appointed Feldman deputy special counsel, with special responsibility for Israel and the Middle East. The Kennedy White House thus had two offices formulating policies on Israel and the Middle East—Robert Komer's section at the National Security Council, and Feldman's.[11] Feldman made secret trips to Israel on behalf of Kennedy on at least two occasions, the one in early 1961 relating to the question of Dimona.[12]

KENNEDY'S PRESSURE ON ISRAEL

Kennedy's interest in the Israeli nuclear program was evident in his meeting with Eisenhower and his national security team on 19 January 1961, on the eve of his inauguration. After forty-five minutes alone, the outgoing and incoming presidents were joined by the secretaries of state, defense, and treasury of both administrations. One of Kennedy's first questions was regarding atomic weapons in other countries. "Israel and India," Herter replied. He told Kennedy that the Israelis had a nuclear reactor capable of generating ninety kilograms of weapon-grade plutonium by 1963, and advised Kennedy to insist on inspection and control before nuclear weapons were introduced in the Middle East.[13]

Kennedy took Herter's advice seriously. Soon after assuming office he asked Dean Rusk, the new secretary of state, for a report about Israel's atomic energy activities. On 30 January Rusk submitted a two-page memo to Kennedy. From the memo and its attached chronology it is evident that the State Department had no knowledge about the Israeli nuclear program before the summer and early fall of 1960, when "rumors reached our Embassy at Tel Aviv." The memo summarizes the diplomatic exchanges that had taken place between the Eisenhower administration and the Israeli government, saying that "categoric assurances" were obtained from Ben Gurion "that Israel does not have plans for developing atomic weaponry." France, too, assured the United States that its assistance to Israel was conditioned on Israel's program being for peaceful purposes. The memo said that Ben Gurion's explanation for the secrecy with which Israel handled the Dimona project—fears that the foreign firms that were assisting Israel would be boycotted by the Arabs—appeared reasonable to the State Department. "There is considerable justification for this Israeli reasoning."[14] The memo also highlighted why the United States should be interested in Israel's nuclear program:

> a) pursuant to congressional legislation and firm executive branch policy the United States is opposed to the proliferation of nuclear weapons capabilities; and b) Israel's acquisition of nuclear weapons would have grave repercussions in the Middle East, not the least of which might be the probable stationing of Soviet nuclear weapons on the soil of Israel's embittered Arab neighbors.[15]

As to Ben Gurion's assurances, Rusk noted that those assurances "appear to be satisfactory, . . . although several minor questions still require clarification."[16] Rusk pointed out, however, that the State Department intended to treat the issue not as a single episode, but as "a continuing subject and it [is] the intention of our intelligence agencies to maintain a continuing watch on Israel as on other countries to assure that nuclear weapons capabilities are not being proliferated." He added that, "at the moment, we are encouraging the Israelis to permit a qualified scientist from the United States or other friendly power to visit the Dimona installation."[17]

The next day Kennedy met former ambassador Reid, who had resigned on 19 January. On Dimona, Reid told Kennedy he thought that "we can accept at face value Ben Gurion's assurances that the reactor is to be devoted to peaceful purposes." He commented that an inspection of the Dimona site could be arranged, "if it is done on a secret basis." Reid suspected that only a few people in Israel knew of the true character of the project, "possibly not even Foreign Minister Meir."[18]

Kennedy was determined to make good on Ben Gurion's pledge for a visit of American scientists to Dimona. Ben Gurion, however, appeared equally determined not to arrange the visit anytime soon. To add to the problem, Ben Gurion's domestic political crisis—the Lavon Affair—intensified (see chapter 8). On 31 December 1960 Ben Gurion resigned in the wake of a ministerial committee's conclusion on the affair, which exonerated Lavon, but he continued to serve as interim prime minister, awaiting the new election. Ben Gurion wanted to avoid a confrontation over Dimona, and continued his search for a solution.[19] During February–April 1961 a pattern emerged in which the United States would press for a date for the visit, while Israel would invoke Ben Gurion's domestic problems or the Jewish holidays as reasons for delaying the visit.

On 3 February, in keeping with Kennedy's interest in Dimona, Assistant Secretary G. Lewis Jones met Ambassador Harman to convey the president's interest in a definite and early date for the Dimona visit. Ben Gurion's resignation made things difficult. Jones expressed his government's annoyance over the continued delay in carrying out Ben Gurion's pledge, to which Harman replied that "in Israel no one is thinking about anything else except the political crisis. . . . Ben Gurion can think of nothing except the reputation of the MAPAI party. I do not see how I could get to him or think that he would be inclined to give an invitation at this time." We may speculate that the domestic crisis was, in part at least, an excuse for Ben Gurion to postpone answering Kennedy's request for visits to Dimona.[20]

Harman assured Jones that there was no reason for the United States to worry about Dimona. It would take two years to complete the reactor, so no plutonium had yet been produced. There was no urgency for the visit. Harman reiterated Ben Gurion's assurances that the plutonium, when produced, would be returned to France. Israel could not understand why there should be a continuing U.S. interest in Dimona. Jones replied that "proliferation of nuclear weapons was absolutely anathema to the United States," and since the suggestion of an American visit "had been volunteered" by Israel itself, he saw no reason why such a visit could not take place "very quietly." In any case, Jones suggested that it would be an "excellent gesture" if he could give a date to the secretary when he met him in the coming days. Harman promised to check on the matter, but stressed that he did not expect quick results from Israel because of the domestic political crisis there.[21]

A week later Harman told Jones that he was authorized to inform the State Department that Ben Gurion did not know whether he would be the next Israeli prime minister, but if he were, one of his first tasks would be to invite U.S. scientists to visit Dimona. Harman passed a similar message to Rusk when he paid a courtesy call to him. Rusk responded that complete candor on this matter would be of "great importance to future relationship."[22] When Teddy Kollek, the director of the prime minister's office, visited Washington two weeks later, he told Jones informally that it would be possible to arrange the visit "during the months of March."[23] President Kennedy was informed of that conversation and about the effort to find qualified American scientists to visit the reactor.

Israel, however, did not rush to set a date for the visit, despite frequent American reminders. On 28 March Jones, impatiently, informed Harman that the United States had been waiting since 4 January for the promised invitation to visit Dimona, and that the White House had inquired the previous day when the visit would take place and had requested a report on the matter by 31 March.

Harman promised to cable Israel, but doubted whether any action would be possible until after Passover.[24]

The State Department's report to Kennedy included a chronology of the American-Israeli exchanges on setting a date for the Dimona visit, which detailed the department's continued effort to "remind" Israel, "at approximately weekly intervals," of the importance of an early, "quiet" visit by Americans to Dimona. The department appeared to believe Ben Gurion's desire to honor his pledge and that the repeated delays were because of his domestic difficulties. After all, he did not want to appear as if he were being pushed by the United States during a time of the "greatest political difficulty of his career." The report stated that an invitation for a visit was not possible before 10 April, after Passover.

By late March Ben Gurion realized he could no longer postpone the visit. He was persuaded by Feldman and Abe Feinberg, a Jewish friend and political ally of Kennedy and also one of the organizers of the fund-raising for Dimona, that a meeting between him and Kennedy, in return for an American visit to Dimona, could save the Dimona project. Ben Gurion determined that the political and technical conditions for the visit would be set in May. He approved the visit to Dimona against the objections of Foreign Minister Meir, who was apparently concerned about the implications of misleading the American scientists.[25]

On 10 April Harman informed the State Department that the American visit to Dimona was scheduled for the week of 15 May. He was ready to discuss the modalities of the visit, and reiterated Israel's request that the visit be kept secret. The State Department responded that it wanted a team of two American reactor experts, "with competence in planning and design of heavy water reactors," to go to Israel for discussions with the technical people in charge of the project. "The discussion would give an opportunity in a most natural way for an incidental visit to the reactor site." The United States agreed to handle the visit "quietly," but said that to consider the visit "secret" and to make an effort to prevent leaks "might be counter-productive." It was also stated that there was "a great deal of Congressional interest."[26]

In the following weeks the preparations for the Dimona visit moved to the working level. The AEC selected two of its scientists to conduct the visit: Ulysses M. Staebler, assistant director of the AEC Reactor Development Division, and Jesse Croach, a heavy-water expert employed by Dupont at the AEC Savannah River facility.[27] In the interest of "avoiding publicity," it was agreed that the AEC scientists would avoid contact with the American embassy in Tel Aviv.[28] After overcoming "scheduling problems," including the State Department's opposition to an official visit by Ben Gurion to the White House, it was arranged that Ben Gurion and Kennedy would meet privately at the Waldorf Astoria Hotel in New York on 30 May, at the end of Ben Gurion's official visit to Canada.[29]

AMERICANS VISIT DIMONA

The two AEC scientists, Staebler and Croach, arrived at Tel Aviv airport on the evening of 17 May. Their official host was Professor Ephraim Katzir-Katchalsky, the head of the Department of Biophysics at the Weizmann Institute. The visit at the Dimona site took place on Saturday, 20 May. (The first two days were devoted to visiting the Soreq reactor, the Weizmann Institute, the Technion, and a tour of the Galilee.)[30]

According to the scientists' notes and memorandum, they were greeted "very cordially" by Dimona director Manes Pratt and informed that they were "the first visitors [to the reactor] from outside the country." The ground rules of the visit were made explicit: "all questions would be answered, no written material would be given, and no pictures would be allowed." The American visitors were told that information at the site was considered classified, since such information could lead the Arabs to "(a) boycott against suppliers, (b) action intended to stop or delay construction, and (c) a better appraisal of their technical capability."[31]

Pratt opened the Americans' visit with a briefing on the rationale and history of the Dimona project. Pratt indicated that Dimona was part of a broad effort by Israel to establish competence in the area of nuclear technology. This included the Soreq swimming pool experimental reactor, the heavy-water pilot plant at the Weizmann Institute, and a uranium recovery pilot plant near Rehovot. In mid-1957 a three-man scientific committee, consisting of Bergmann, Dostrovsky, and Pratt himself, was formed by the prime minister to establish a five-year national nuclear energy program. The committee's objective was to consider Israel's options regarding the use of nuclear power.

The committee first considered "more immediate ventures in power reactors." The initial idea, which was rejected because of its cost, was to build a nuclear station consisting of two 70-MW power reactors of the PWR (pressurized-water reactor) type. The committee next considered acquiring research reactors and decided that "building a research reactor could provide experience in essentially all of the problems posed by power reactor." The Dimona nuclear complex, then, "was conceived as a means for gaining experience in construction of a nuclear facility which would prepare them for nuclear power in the long-run." Pratt also explained that natural uranium was chosen as fuel for reasons of both energy independence and cost, referring to Israel's interest in extracting natural uranium from phosphates in the Negev.[32]

According to Pratt, the committee submitted its report to the prime minister in mid-1958, it was approved by the prime minister in late 1958, and groundbreaking at the Dimona site took place in 1959. It is evident that the chronology was carefully prepared to be consistent with what Israel had told the United States in the past about its nuclear energy plans (such as Bergmann's statements in 1955–58 about nuclear power, the Israeli request for ten tons of heavy water, and so on). It is also apparent that Pratt's strategy was designed to convince his guests that the Dimona project was conceived in 1958, that is, after the decisions about the smaller Soreq reactor had been made.[33]

The Dimona complex was described as a national nuclear research center that would include, in addition to the reactor, various laboratories, including a "pilot plant for Pu [plutonium] separation." As to the reactor, the Israeli hosts said it had a 26-MW power capacity and used heavy water as both a moderator and a coolant. The Israelis acknowledged that the reactor's design calculations were made by the French, and that the design "was very much influenced by the French EL-3."[34] The reactor was expected to be completed in 1964.[35]

Perhaps the most intriguing aspect of the report involved the "pilot plant for plutonium separation." The rationale for having that plant was "to provide experience in fuel processing since they [the Israelis] believe that shipping long distances for processing is impractical for nuclear power in the long run. Also, they want enough plutonium to experiment with as a power fuel." The American scientists were also told that the plant would not have the capacity to process all the fuel from the reactor.[36]

On 25 May, two days after their return, Staebler and Croach discussed their findings with officials at the State Department. Based on these debriefings, a two-page memo was prepared the next day for McGeorge Bundy, the president's national security adviser. The memo described the scientists "as satisfied that nothing was concealed from them and that the reactor is of the scope and peaceful character previously described to the United States."[37] After summarizing what the scientists had been told about the history and rationale of the Dimona project, the memo cited eight "tentative conclusions and opinions" of the scientists that might be "desirable to bring to the President's attention."[38]

First, the scientists felt that a second visit would not be necessary for another year. Second, while "Israel's obsession with secrecy is regrettable," the AEC scientists were persuaded that it was "perhaps understandable in view of Israel's physical and political circumstances." Third, as to plutonium production, while the reactor would eventually produce "small quantities of plutonium suitable for weapons, there is no present evidence that the Israelis have weapons production in mind." Fourth, the Israeli host told the scientists that the reactor would not be completed before 1964, which the scientists thought was "too conservative." Fifth, the scientists saw evidence of close French cooperation. Sixth, the size of the entire complex was estimated to occupy "a 750 square meters to a side," but the surrounded fenced security area was much larger. Seventh, the scientists thought the reactor, when completed, would be a $15 million investment, with the supporting plant costing another $20 million. Eighth, the scientists were impressed by what they saw at Dimona: "Israel's Dimona project is a most creditable accomplishment both in concept and execution."[39]

Israel could not have hoped for a better report. It supported everything Ben Gurion said publicly and privately about the project and its scope. It is striking how uncritically the American technical experts accepted what the Israelis had told them about the project. Did it make sense for a small country to invest in two nuclear projects in a single year—one was admitted to cost $35 million—when it did not yet have a clear idea of its future energy plans? Does it pay for such a small country to invest so heavily in nuclear energy? Why did Israel insist on having access to virtually all aspects of the nuclear fuel cycle, including fuel reprocessing, while its future power program needs were still uncertain? What other motivations could there be for such a program in a small country, surrounded by enemies, whose leaders believed that science and technology would negate some of their adversaries' advantages? These questions could have shed a different light on the nuclear project, especially if Israel's security problems would have been considered.

This, however, was not the scientists' mind-set. Their mission was not to challenge what they were told, but to verify it. They toured the construction site as official guests escorted by their Israeli hosts. In all probability, they were not given access to special intelligence about the Israeli program, in particular the U-2 photographs taken by the American intelligence agencies. They had no indication that a large underground reprocessing plant was under construction. Israel's explanation about the rationale of Dimona made some sense; that is, at that time nuclear energy was widely viewed as the advanced technology solution to provide energy, particularly in countries without indigenous fossil fuels. Seven additional teams of AEC experts visited Dimona in the coming decade, all reaching the same basic conclusions as this team. There was no definitive evidence of a weapons program.

The visit set precedents for both countries. The United States became involved, outside the IAEA framework, in attempting to verify the purpose of a nuclear facility that was built without American help. However, while the United States was prepared to take action to stem the proliferation of nuclear weapons, under the conditions imposed on the visit by the Israelis, it was naive to expect that it would be able to detect any activities embarrassing to Israel (and the United States). The U.S. visit to Dimona thus illustrated the limits of the American's bilateral approach to halting proliferation.

A MEETING AT THE WALDORF-ASTORIA

The Waldorf-Astoria meeting was Ben Gurion's second meeting with Kennedy. Of their first meeting a year earlier, Ben Gurion said, "he looked to me like a twenty-five year old boy . . . at first, I did not take him seriously."[40] This time Kennedy was president. Ben Gurion was "very tense, fearing that Kennedy's stiff position on the matter of the reactor would severely jeopardize the relationship."[41] Although Ben Gurion was anxious, the meeting, which lasted an hour and a half, was anticlimactic. It was friendly, at times even chatty. What set the relaxed and amicable tone was the report on Dimona that Kennedy had received from Rusk a few days earlier. Ambassador Harman took notes for the Israeli side, and Feldman took notes for the American participants. The following account of their meeting is based on official U.S. and Israeli transcripts.[42]

After a brief exchange of amenities, the two leaders "plunged into a discussion of Israel's nuclear reactor."[43] Ben Gurion noted that he had intended to brief the president about the reactor, but this would have been redundant since the U.S. scientists had already visited the site. Kennedy responded that, indeed, he had seen the report and that it was "very helpful." He added that, on the same theory, "a woman should not only be virtuous, but also have the appearance of virtue," it was important not only that Israel's purposes were peaceful, but that other nations were convinced that this was the case.[44] Ben Gurion explained Israel's interest in nuclear energy: Israel lacked fresh water, and development was possible only if a cheap source of energy could be found to allow desalinization of sea water. Israel believed that atomic power, although still expensive, would one day ("in ten or fifteen years") be a source of cheap energy.[45]

After outlining Israel's long-term plan for desalinization, Ben Gurion went on to discuss the present. It is worthwhile to record them as they appear in both transcripts. The text of the Israeli note taker, Harman, reads:

> We are asked whether it is for peace. For the time being the only purposes are for peace. Not now but after three or four years we shall have a pilot plant for separation, which is needed anyway for a power reactor. There is no such intention now, not for 4 or 5 years. But we will see what happens in the

Middle East. It does not depend on us. Maybe Russia won't give bombs to China or Egypt, but maybe Egypt will develop them herself.[46]

The American note taker, Myer Feldman, wrote:

> Israel's main—and for the time being, only—purpose is this [cheap energy, etc.], the Prime Minister said, adding that "we do not know what will happen in the future; in three or four years we might have a need for a plant to process plutonium." Commenting on the political and strategic implications of atomic power and weaponry, the Prime Minister said he does believe that "in ten or fifteen years the Egyptians presumably could achieve it themselves."[47]

Kennedy responded by returning to his earlier point. The United States appreciated Israel's desalinization needs, but it was important for the United States that it did not appear "that Israel is preparing for atomic weapons," especially given the close relationship between the United States and Israel, since Egypt would then try to do the same. "Perhaps in the next five years atomic weapons would proliferate, but we don't want it to happen." At this point the two versions differ slightly. According to the Israeli text, Kennedy said, "The report . . . is a fine report and it would be helpful if we could get this information out." The American summary is more explicit: "The President then asked again whether, as a matter of reassurance, the Arab states might be advised of findings of the American scientists who had viewed the Dimona reactor."[48]

Kennedy asked Ben Gurion to let him share the scientists' findings, and both versions confirmed that Ben Gurion gave Kennedy permission to do whatever he saw fit with the report. Kennedy then asked, "because we [the United States and Israel] are close friends," whether it would be helpful to let "neutral scientists," such as the Scandinavians or Swiss, observe the reactor.[49] Ben Gurion had no objection, and Kennedy expressed his satisfaction with the reply. With this sense of mutual understanding, the nuclear issue was dropped and the conversation shifted to the general issue of Israel's security.

A PATTERN AFFIRMED

In his meeting with Kennedy, Ben Gurion had followed the circumspect path he had taken in his first statement to the Knesset in December 1960. He wanted either to buy time for Dimona's completion, while avoiding a confrontation with the United States or lying outright, without making impossible commitments about the future. It was a juggler's act, and he knew it. His tension before the meeting highlights the point. He must have decided it was too risky to admit Israel's interest in nuclear weapons, and the reactions of both the Eisenhower and Kennedy administrations suggest he was correct.

According to this interpretation, Ben Gurion concealed the real purpose of Dimona behind Israel's professed "need" for cheap nuclear power, especially for desalinization. This explanation was not without foundation. Bergmann convinced Ben Gurion that nuclear energy would be the key to the vision of making the Negev desert bloom. Faith in nuclear energy was a familiar Ben Gurionite theme, and Bergmann often argued that nuclear energy could be used for both peaceful and nonpeaceful purposes.

Ben Gurion emphasized Israel's interest in civilian use of nuclear energy, but during the meeting he never excluded a future interest in developing nuclear weapons. Ben Gurion did not make binding pledges. Both records of the conversation show that he was deliberately ambiguous. By stressing, "for the time being the only purposes are for peace, . . . we will see what happens in the Middle East," he introduced an element of tentativeness and ambiguity to balance his emphasis on peaceful purposes. He did not hide Israel's intention to build "a pilot plant for [plutonium] separation" in four or five years. Kennedy made no comment on the matter.

The briefing papers prepared for Kennedy for the Waldorf-Astoria meeting indicate that U.S. intelligence agencies had reasons to suspect that Israel was moving toward building nuclear weapons,[50] but Kennedy did not ask his guest difficult questions on this issue. He did not ask about Israel's future plans to separate plutonium, nor did he bring up the question of the ownership of the plutonium that might be produced there. Kennedy asked only that the results of the U.S. scientists' visits be released to other nations—meaning the Arabs—to which Ben Gurion gave his approval.[51] Even Kennedy's request to let scientists from a neutral state visit Dimona was not raised as an urgent matter.

Both leaders wanted to avoid a confrontation, and each had a sense of his own political limits. Based on these understandings, the two leaders created the rules of the game as they were muddling through. Kennedy did not raise questions that went beyond what Ben Gurion told him on his own. Kennedy did not question why Israel needed two research reactors, a small American reactor (Nachal Soreq) and a larger one of French design (Dimona), which could produce significant amounts of plutonium. He did not ask why Israel needed a plutonium separation plant, or why Israel would invest so much in a large research reactor whose ostensible purpose was only to serve as an interim step to building a nuclear power plant, or why the French-Israeli nuclear deal had been kept secret. Kennedy did not raise these issues, although they were the ones that had led to the confrontations in December and January. Kennedy did not try to extract a promise that Israel would not develop a nuclear weapons capability in the future. He limited himself to making the U.S. position on nonproliferation clear, pointing out the need to assure others of Israel's intentions.

Ben Gurion respected Kennedy's political needs. He did not question U.S. nonproliferation policy as applied to Israel. Later in the conversation, Ben Gurion expressed his worries about Israel's long-term security and the geopolitical vulnerability of the Jewish state, but he did not use these issues to legitimize Israel's interest in acquiring an independent nuclear deterrent. Only a year earlier France had acquired nuclear weapons. Nonproliferation norms did not yet exist. Ben Gurion, however, did not try to convince Kennedy that Israel was politically or morally justified in pursuing the nuclear-weapons option.

The nuclear issue was the reason for the New York meeting and the cause of Ben Gurion's apprehensions, but it took up no more than ten to fifteen minutes of the conversation. Kennedy exerted no new pressure, and Ben Gurion had no need to use all the arguments he had prepared. As his biographer wrote, "Ben Gurion felt relieved. The reactor was saved, at least for the time being."[52]

MUDDLING THROUGH

The Waldorf-Astoria meeting removed the immediate threat of U.S.-Israeli confrontation over the nuclear issue. It created tacit rules that made it possible for the issue to recede into the background for almost two years, while other topics, such as refugees and water, became central.[53] In June 1962 there was an exchange of letters between Kennedy and Ben Gurion. The exchange involved water issues. Not even a single reference to the Dimona project was made.[54] In mid-August Kennedy secretly sent Myer Feldman to Israel to craft a deal that would tie the U.S. supply of air defense HAWK missiles to Israeli concessions on the Palestinian refugees problem. Again, the nuclear issue was not mentioned even in passing during Feldman's conversations with Ben Gurion and Meir.[55] Thus there is no basis for the rumor that Israel received the HAWK missiles in return for its permission for regular U.S. visits at Dimona.[56]

The Israeli nuclear program, however, was not forgotten. During the first half of 1962 the Kennedy administration tried to persuade Sweden, a neutral Western country, to take over the task of visiting Dimona in light of the Ben Gurion-Kennedy agreement. Sweden was not interested in the job (probably because it had its own nuclear weapons program), and the administration began to negotiate with Israel over another American visit to Dimona sometime during the summer. According to British diplomatic reports from Washington, the administration recognized that the Israelis were "dragging their feet on this," but the administration continued to press.[57] In light of these diplomatic efforts and Israel's persistent effort to delay it, it is even more significant that the administration did not raise the issue at the highest level, either through presidential letters or emissaries.

On 26 September 1962 the second U.S. visit to Dimona took place. It was a brief visit, which Barbour later described as "unduly restricted to no more than forty five minutes."[58] The visit was made to look as a spontaneous Israeli idea during a trip by two U.S. nuclear scientists who arrived to conduct a routine inspection at the Soreq reactor. This "improvisation" had been planned as a way to ease American pressure on Dimona. This time the Israeli escort was Yuval Ne'eman, the scientific director of the Soreq Nuclear Research Center.[59] The visiting scientists found no evidence of weapon-related activity. The positive results allowed the United States to assure Arab governments, for the second time, "that latest observations again confirm Israeli statements that reactor [is] intended for peaceful purposes only," and that no evidence of preparation for nuclear weapons production were found.[60]

American suspicions over the Israeli nuclear program were not dispelled. Israel was a prominent case in American global thinking about nuclear proliferation. In a long Pentagon study on nuclear diffusion, Israel was placed ahead of Sweden and India as the next likely nuclear weapons proliferator.[61] The study also predicted the dates when France, China, and Israel would acquire nuclear weapons. As far as motivation for acquiring nuclear weapons, Israel, along with France and China, was at the top of the list. "The pressures for possession: prestige, coercive and deterrent value and military utility have overridden inhibitions, apart from the two superpowers, only in the cases of the U.K., France, almost certainly China, and probably Israel."[62]

The only occasion in 1962 in which the Israeli nuclear program was raised at the presidential level was probably during a seventy-minute meeting between Kennedy and Foreign Minister Meir on 27 December. The meeting was a friendly exchange of opinions about the situation in the Middle East, during which Kennedy reassured Meir of the U.S. commitment to Israel's security. At the end of the conversation, as Kennedy reiterated the American friendship toward Israel, he noted that "our relationship is a two-way street," and added that "Israel's security in the long term depends in part on what it does with the Arabs, but also on us." This allowed him to allude to the nuclear issue. The American note taker described the brief exchange as follows:

> He [Kennedy] would hope, for example, that Israel could give considerations to our problems on this atomic reactor. We are opposed to nuclear proliferation. Our problem here is not in prying into Israeli affairs but we have to be

concerned because of the overall situation in the Middle East. Mrs. Meir reassured the President that there would not be any difficulty between us on the Israeli nuclear reactor.[63]

It is evident from the transcript that the issue was marginal to the conversation. Kennedy alluded to the subject in passing, and Meir responded in the most general way. Neither was interested in talking more about it.

THE SEARCH FOR A NONPROLIFERATION AGREEMENT

In December 1961 the Kennedy administration endorsed the slightly revised Irish nonproliferation resolution in the UN General Assembly. The language of the Irish resolution made the idea of a nonproliferation agreement compatible with both the legal requirements of the Nuclear Energy Act and with existing NATO nuclear arrangements, as well as with a future collective European nuclear force. The Soviets voted for an alternative Swedish resolution, which did not allow nonnuclear states to receive, deploy, or station nuclear weapons in their territory on behalf of any other country.

The Kennedy administration was the first to recognize that the key to halting nuclear proliferation was an international weapons nonproliferation agreement. Such an agreement should be based on a bargain between the nuclear and nonnuclear states. A prerequisite for such a multilateral agreement must be cooperation with the Soviet Union; both nuclear superpowers must sponsor such an agreement. It was assumed that nonproliferation was one of the few areas in which both nuclear superpowers shared a fundamental common interest. The first U.S.-Soviet talks on a nonproliferation agreement were convened in Geneva in March 1962, but it was soon evident that their opposing interests over the present and future nuclear arrangements in Europe blocked all progress. The United States proposed a nonproliferation agreement based on language similar to the Irish resolution of 1961. This did not satisfy the Soviets, who maintained that it would allow the United States to equip Germany with nuclear weapons under the guise of NATO. The negotiations reached an impasse, setting the stage for the next four years of American-Soviet negotiations on a nonproliferation agreement. The effort to break this stalemate was a major factor in Kennedy's second confrontation with Israel over Dimona in 1963.

The understandings between the United States and Israel, reached at the 1961 Waldorf-Astoria meeting, were ambiguous. The two sides knew that the differences between them on the Dimona matter had not been settled, but only postponed. Kennedy's nonproliferation policies could not be readily implemented in the case of Israel.

Two years later, during the spring and summer of 1963, Kennedy applied the most concerted pressure yet on Israel over Dimona. He urged Ben Gurion to agree to two American visits a year to Dimona in order to verify the Waldorf-Astoria informal understanding that Israel would not build nuclear weapons.

DIMONA SURFACES

There were several developments in late 1962 and the first half of 1963 which pushed Dimona back to the top of the American policy agenda. The Cuban missile crisis of October 1962 highlighted the dangers of the nuclear age and strengthened Kennedy's commitment to prevent the further spread of nuclear weapons.[1] In March 1963 Kennedy gave public expression to his sense of urgency about weapons proliferation:

> Personally I am haunted by the feeling that by 1970, unless we are successful, there may be ten nuclear powers instead of four, and by 1975, fifteen or twenty . . . I see the possibility in the 1970s of the President of the United States having to face a world in which fifteen or twenty or twenty-five

nations may have these weapons. I regard this as the greatest possible danger and hazard.[2]

In February 1963 the Defense Department updated its July 1962 study on nuclear diffusion, pointing to eight states as capable of acquiring nuclear weapons and a crude means of delivery within the coming decade.[3] Again, Israel was at the top of the list as the most likely proliferator after China, with 1965–66 given as the date when Israel could possibly conduct its first nuclear test. The study also concluded that "in some cases we and others would probably have to employ stronger incentives and sanctions than have seriously been considered so far."[4]

By early 1963 the Kennedy administration thus reached the conclusion that Israel was about to make a decision on a nuclear-weapons option, if it had not already done so. The American assessments were based on indications that can now be traced.

In the July 1962 Revolution Day parade, Egypt, for the first time, displayed ballistic missiles, boasting they could cover every point "south of Beirut." Israel knew that Egypt began a missile project by recruiting German rocket scientists in Europe, but the public display of the missiles—they were only early proto-types—alarmed the Israeli defense establishment. Though Israel had launched its own Shavit II missile with great publicity a year earlier, it was merely an experimental meteorological rocket. In July 1962 Israel had no significant bal-listic missile program of its own, and all of a sudden it "discovered" its own "missile gap."[5]

The impact of the Egyptian missile program on the Israeli defense authori-ties was considerable, leading to debates about Israel's future security doctrine. The debates were secret, but their themes appeared in editorials and speeches during the summer of 1962. The debate about nuclear weapons and missiles became part of domestic politics, as Peres and other young MAPAI leaders called for a new security doctrine based on advanced weapons. The American Embassy in Tel Aviv followed these debates (see chapter 8).[6]

In early September 1962, after weeks of consultations at the Ministry of Defense, Peres asked the French company Marcel Dassault to conduct a feasibil-ity study to develop and produce a surface-to-surface ballistic missile for Israel. Negotiations continued through the winter and spring, and on 26 April 1963 an agreement between Israel and Marcel Dassault was signed in Tel Aviv. The mis-sile was referred to as "Jericho," also known by its manufacturer as MD-620.[7]

American intelligence monitored the progress on the construction of Dimona and the secret French-Israeli negotiations over the Jericho missile pro-ject.[8] The United States knew that Dimona was to become critical within a year or so, although it was unsure whether Israel had means to separate plutonium.

The outbreak of the ballistic missile race, and the realization that Israel would catch up to the Egyptians with a sophisticated missile, intensified the concerns in Washington that Israel would act to realize its nuclear weapon option.[9]

On 6 March 1963 the head of the Office of National Estimates at the CIA, Sherman Kent, issued an eight-page memorandum entitled "Consequences of Israeli Acquisition of Nuclear Capability."[10] The memo considered that the consequences of an Israeli nuclear capability were grave. "Israel's policy toward its neighbors would become more rather less tough. . . . it would . . . seek to exploit the psychological advantages of its nuclear capability to intimidate the Arabs and to prevent them from making trouble on the frontiers." In dealing with the United States, Israel "would use all its means at its command to persuade the US to acquiesce in, and even to support, its possession of nuclear capability."[11] The Arab reaction would be "profound dismay and frustration," and "among the principal targets of Arab resentment would be the U.S." The Arabs' recourse would be the Soviets who would "win friends and influence in the Arab world."[12] While it is unknown what specific information triggered writing this report, there is no doubt that the CIA had, early on in the spring of 1963, ample, alarming suspicions about Dimona (see the next section).

America worried that Israel's acquisition of nuclear weapons would have global implications for the United States. In April 1963 the United States submitted to the Soviets its draft for a Non-Transfer Declaration, under which the nuclear powers commit themselves not to transfer nuclear weapons to the control of states currently not possessing such weapons and not to assist such states in the manufacturing of such weapons, while nonnuclear states agree not to manufacture or acquire nuclear weapons.[13] This was an early American formulation of a nonproliferation agreement, written so as not to interfere with existing NATO arrangements and without precluding future formation of multilateral nuclear forces (MLF) in Europe.[14] The Soviets opposed any notion involving Germany's sharing custody of NATO nuclear weapons, and argued that MLF was itself an instance of nuclear weapons proliferation.[15] The negotiations broke down on the issue of Germany's role in the MLF,[16] and, with no signs of progress on a nonproliferation agreement, Kennedy continued to push his nonproliferation agenda on the bilateral level.

NSAM 231

The fear that Israel would soon become a nuclear-weapon state, the Egyptian ballistic missile program, and the consequences of both for U.S. interests led to a new effort to freeze the Israeli nuclear program.[17]

In the second half of March the Israeli nuclear program moved higher on President Kennedy's agenda. On 25 March Kennedy discussed the issue with CIA director John McCone, who handed him the Agency's estimate of the consequences of Israel's nuclearization. After the meeting Kennedy asked Bundy to issue a presidential directive to Rusk, requesting him to look for "some form of international or bilateral U.S. safeguards" to curb the Israeli program.[18] This request was the origin of National Security Action Memorandum (NSAM) 231, entitled "Middle Eastern Nuclear Capabilities," issued the next day.

> The President desires, as a matter of urgency, that we undertake every feasible measure to improve our intelligence on the Israeli nuclear program as well as other Israeli and UAR advanced weapons programs and to arrive at a firmer evaluation of their import. In this connection he wishes the next informal inspection of the Israeli reactor complex to be undertaken promptly and to be as thorough as possible.
>
> In view of his great concern over the destabilizing impact of any Israeli or UAR program looking toward the development of nuclear weapons, the President also wishes the Department of State to develop proposals for forestalling such programs; in particular we should develop plans for seeking clearer assurances from the governments concerned on this point, and means of impressing upon them how seriously such a development would be regarded in this country.[19]

Although NSAM 231 referred to both Israeli and Egyptian nuclear programs, Israel was its main concern. Israel was perceived as being close to making critical nuclear decisions, but U.S. intelligence did not know enough about where the Israeli program was heading. The effect of NSAM 231 soon became apparent.

On 2 April, at the end of a two-hour discussion, Ambassador Barbour presented Ben Gurion with President Kennedy's request for semiannual U.S. visits to Dimona in May and November. Ben Gurion "did not demur," but asked to consider the matter in the next meeting.[20] The same day, when President Kennedy by chance ran into Myer Feldman and Shimon Peres in a White House corridor (Peres was in Washington on HAWK missile-related business), he asked Feldman to have an unscheduled meeting with the Israeli official. In the twenty-minute meeting, Kennedy talked about the Israeli nuclear program:

> Kennedy: You know that we follow very closely the discovery of any nuclear development in the region. This could create a very dangerous situation. For this reason we kept in touch with your nuclear effort. What could you tell me about this?

Peres: I can tell you most clearly that we will not introduce nuclear weapons to the region, and certainly we will not be the first. Our interest is in reducing armament, even in complete disarmament.[21]

Two days later, on 4 April, Israeli ambassador Harman was summoned to the State Department for a similar message. Harman was reminded of Kennedy's comments to Meir in December, and was told that the U.S. interest in Dimona came from the highest level.[22] By that time the State Department had already formed a working group to develop, by early May, a plan of action to obtain an Israeli-Egyptian-American agreement on nuclear technology and missile limitation. In the spring of 1963 the White House was thus seeking arms limitation agreements to prevent the introduction of nuclear weapons and ballistic missiles into the Middle East.

Ben Gurion was expected to respond to Kennedy's request on Dimona in his next meeting with Barbour in mid-April, but new developments in the region allowed him to ignore Kennedy's request. Ben Gurion instead sent letters to Kennedy and fifty other world leaders, discussing new dangers to Israel's security.

BEN GURION'S PERSPECTIVE

In the spring of 1963, as before, Ben Gurion was not ready for a showdown with an American president over Dimona. Nor could he accept Kennedy's terms for semiannual American visits to Dimona. So he stalled. He avoided a confrontation by exploiting the new developments in the region to engage in a lengthy correspondence with Kennedy about Israel's security, while making an effort to diffuse Kennedy's request.

On 17 April 1963 Egypt, Syria, and Iraq signed, in Cairo, an Arab Federation Proclamation, calling for a military union to bring about the liberation of Palestine. Rhetoric about Arab unity was not unusual at such Arab meetings at that time, but Ben Gurion took this one more seriously.[23] The seventy-six-year-old leader saw it as the realization of a nightmare—the formation of a pan-Arabic military coalition against Israel. Other Israeli decision makers, including Foreign Minister Golda Meir and the ministry's senior staff, did not share Ben Gurion's alarm. Ben Gurion, however, launched what his biographer calls an "unprecedented diplomatic campaign," alerting fifty world leaders to the gravity of the new situation in the Middle East.[24] His correspondence with Kennedy was part of this campaign.

On 25 April Ben Gurion wrote a seven-page letter to Kennedy, informing him that "recent events have increased the danger of a serious conflagration in the Middle East" and warning that the Arab proclamation to liberate Palestine meant "the obliteration of Israel."[25] Ben Gurion compared the "liberation of Palestine" to the Holocaust:

> The "liberation of Palestine" is impossible without the total destruction of the people in Israel, but the people of Israel are not in the hapless situation of the six million defenseless Jews who were wiped out by Nazi Germany. . . .
>
> I recall Hitler's declaration to the world about forty years ago that one of his objectives was the destruction of the entire Jewish people. The civilized world, in Europe and America, treated this declaration with indifference and equanimity. A Holocaust unequaled in human history was the result. Six million Jews in all the countries under Nazi occupations (except Bulgaria), men and women, old and young, infants and babies, were burnt, strangled, buried alive.[26]

Ben Gurion proposed a joint U.S.-Soviet declaration to guarantee the territorial integrity and security of all Middle Eastern states. He also suggested cutting off assistance to states threatening their neighbors or refusing to recognize their existence. Ben Gurion acknowledged the unlikelihood of such a superpower joint declaration, but warned that without it the "situation in the Middle East assumes gravity without parallel." He expressed his willingness to fly to Washington "without publicity" to discuss the matter with the president.[27]

Ben Gurion's new campaign upset many of the senior staff at the Foreign Ministry.[28] The substance and tone seemed exaggerated, or in senior diplomat Gideon Rafael's words, "hysterical." Ambassador Harman, and his deputy Mordechai Gazit in Washington, were even more critical of and frustrated with Ben Gurion's actions. They, too, did not see the Arab Federation Proclamation of 17 April as an immediate threat to Israel. From their perspective, Ben Gurion's campaign and his specific proposals were undermining the objectives he himself outlined, which they were pursuing.[29]

As Harman and Gazit expected, the White House dismissed both the alarmist assessment and the specific proposals the letter contained.[30] Kennedy asked the State Department to take another look at the current Arab-Israeli military balance. The assessment he received was that "Israel will probably retain its overall military superiority vis-à-vis the Arab states for the next several years."[31] Two weeks later the White House received a more detailed study by the State Department on the implications for Israel of the Arab Federation Proclamation of 17 April. The study noted no special reason for Israel to be concerned. It predicted that real Arab unity would not be achieved for many years, if ever; that the suggested federation was a loose one, leaving considerable autonomy to the Arab states; and that it would not change the near-term Israeli military superiority. The operational significance of the Arab declaration was "marginal," its legal significance "none," its language "menacing, but vague."[32] The State Department's conclusions were similar to those made by the Israeli military intelligence service.[33]

On 4 May Kennedy replied to Ben Gurion's letter, assuring him that "we are watching closely current developments in Arab world," and that "we have Israel's defense problems very much in mind," but rejecting forthright Ben Gurion's alarm over the Arab Federation Proclamation.[34] While the United States opposed any policies and language, such as "the liberation of Palestine," "the practical significance of these declarations was not that different from that of the many earlier similar declarations put out in other forms and phrases." As to Ben Gurion's idea of a joint superpower declaration, Kennedy confessed to have "real reservations" and questioned Ben Gurion's assessment of the situation.[35] Kennedy also rejected Ben Gurion's request to come to Washington "without publicity": "If such a meeting could really remain private, I think it might be most useful, but experience tells me that at a time like this . . . there is no reasonable prospect that you and I could meet without publicity."[36] While rejecting Ben Gurion's alarm about the near-term situation, Kennedy alluded to other long-term dangers:

> The danger which we foresee is not so much that of an early Arab attack as that of a successful development of advanced offensive systems which, as you say, could not be dealt with by presently available means. I have expressed before my deep personal conviction that reciprocal and competitive development of such weapons would dangerously threaten the stability of the area. I believe that we should consider carefully together how such a trend can be forestalled.[37]

Barbour also delivered an oral message to Ben Gurion regarding the request for two American visits a year to Dimona. Ben Gurion responded that in his 1961 Waldorf-Astoria meeting with Kennedy he was not asked for such a biannual visit arrangement and that he did not agree to it; rather, Kennedy had asked then for a one-time visit of a representative from a neutral state. Barbour replied that he (Barbour) probably misformulated the American request, and that the United States was asking for an Israeli consent to such visits. The problem, Barbour added, was that none of the small neutral states cared about the issue. Ben Gurion responded that he would consult about it with Foreign Minister Meir.[38]

Kennedy's cool response did not deter Ben Gurion. On 7 May he sent a direct message to Myer Feldman at the White House, notifying him of his disappointment with Kennedy's response and that he would continue his dialogue with Kennedy on Israeli security issues.[39] On 8 May the draft of the new Ben Gurion letter was the subject of discussion at the Foreign Ministry. The consensus among the senior Israeli diplomats was that, in the first round of correspondence, Ben Gurion failed to reach his objectives. Gideon Rafael, then deputy director-general of the Foreign Ministry, said that the correspondence must stop immediately and the latest letter should not be sent. He said that Ben Gurion's assessment of the situation "looks sick," and that "the Prime Minister must not speak about something that seems sick." As to Ben Gurion's reference to things that would happen after his death, Rafael commented that, "this would remind Kennedy of the mentality of old men."[40]

Despite the suggestions for substantial and stylistic changes, Ben Gurion accepted only a few changes to the draft. Four days later, on 12 May, he sent another long letter (nine pages) to Kennedy.[41] This letter, too, was pessimistic in tone. Ben Gurion again drew on the memory of the Holocaust, pointing out that "Arab leaders [were] praising Hitler as the liberator of mankind and praying for his success."[42]

Israel's nuclear program was just beneath Ben Gurion's concerns. Without stating it directly, Ben Gurion provided the explanation for Israel's nuclear weapons program: to ensure that another Holocaust would not be inflicted on the Jewish people, Israel must be able to threaten a potential perpetrator with annihilation.

Ben Gurion was still reluctant to connect the Dimona reactor explicitly to Israel's security. His 12 May letter does not contain any reference to Dimona. Ben Gurion simply ignored Kennedy's reference to the development of "advanced offensive systems" and his two recent requests for semiannual visits to Dimona. Instead, Ben Gurion linked the Holocaust to Israel's need for external security guarantees, saying that the best way to prevent another Holocaust was a joint action by the two superpowers. Acknowledging Kennedy's view that such joint action was politically impossible, Ben Gurion asked the United States to conclude a "Bilateral Security Agreement" with Israel, sell more arms to Israel in order to balance the new Soviet supply to the Arabs, and propose a plan for general disarmament in the Middle East.

Ben Gurion was not content with quiet diplomacy. A day after sending this letter to Kennedy, and without waiting for Kennedy's response, Ben Gurion criticized the Kennedy administration in a speech to the Knesset, claiming that its policy of limiting the arms race in the Middle East was "one-sided" and likely "to intensify the danger of war" in the region. He also made public his proposal for a joint action by the United States and the Soviet Union to bring about general disarmament in the region and to guarantee the territorial integrity of all Middle Eastern states. In a reference to Kennedy's policies, Ben Gurion expressed regret that "not all our friends" understood "the vital need to increase the deterrent strength of the Israeli defense forces as the most effective means of preserving peace" in the region.[43]

Ben Gurion had long been attracted to the notion of an American security guarantee for Israel, but by the mid-1950s he realized this was infeasible. As noted earlier, his decision to build the nuclear reactor in Dimona was, to some extent, the result of that realization. In late 1957 Ben Gurion explored the possibility of forming an alliance between Israel and NATO, but these efforts also failed. The Kennedy administration told Israel—the last time in the December 1962 meeting between Meir and Kennedy—that it was committed to Israel's defense in case of an Arab surprise attack and that a formal security arrangement was not necessary for Israel (or useful to the United States).[44] In 1963 Ben Gurion must also have known that a joint superpowers action was impossible. Why, then, was he waging this doomed campaign?

There are no simple answers to this puzzle.[45] Kennedy's continued pressure on Dimona may provide an explanation. Ben Gurion knew how brutal U.S. pressure could be,[46] and he had good reasons to be anxious about an American effort to halt Israel's nuclear program. Ben Gurion's pledge to Kennedy two years earlier and Kennedy's views on nuclear weapons proliferation complicated matters for Ben Gurion. He needed changes in the region to link Israel's nuclear program and its security situation.

In May 1961 he told Kennedy: "For the time being the only purposes are peace . . . but we will see what happens in the Middle East." Two years later Ben Gurion could point to the dangers posed by the Arab Federation Proclamation to justify linking Dimona to Israel's security. If the United States could not give Israel a formal security guarantee, then Israel must rely on its own resources.

This strategy did not work. Ben Gurion did not succeed in softening Kennedy's insistence on Dimona, and he did not obtain security arrangements with the United States.

KENNEDY'S PERSPECTIVE

NSAM 231 instructed the State Department to develop proposals to prevent the spread of advanced weapons technologies to the Middle East. The small interagency working group formed to devise arms control policies met in April–May, at the time of Ben Gurion's correspondence with Kennedy. Ben Gurion's objective was to protect Israel's nuclear program, while the administration's objective was to thwart the program's military potential. Ben Gurion's quest for an American security guarantee shaped the new American plan for regional arms limitation.

In May the Kennedy administration again focused its attention on the problem of advanced weaponry in the Middle East, with the Israeli nuclear and missile programs at the center. On 8 May the CIA issued a new SNIE (30–2–63), entitled "The Advanced Weapons Programs of the UAR and Israel." The fifteen lines dealing with the Israeli nuclear program are still classified, but the estimate's author understood where the Israeli missile program was in early 1963.

> We believe that Israel is undertaking the development of a 250–300 nautical mile (n.m.) surface to surface missile (SSM) system. A wholly independent Israeli effort to develop and produce such a missile with a payload of 2,000 to 3,000 pounds would probably require three to four years and great expense. However, there is evidence that Israel expects to rely on France for substantial assistance. If Israel acquires full access to French technology, components and test facilities, it probably could produce a limited number of missiles with a range of about 250 n.m., a payload of some 400 pounds and an elementary guidance system in about two years (1965).[47]

Days after the SNIE was issued, McCone briefed President Kennedy and Secretary Rusk on the subject.[48] Following the briefings, Kennedy wrote his most direct letter to Ben Gurion on the nuclear issue.

On 10 May Ambassador Barbour received new instructions to press upon Ben Gurion the "intensity of Presidential concern for promptest GOI [government of Israel] reply to our proposals for semi-annual Dimona visits, with first visit this month." The ambassador was told that the State Department suspected that Ben Gurion "may now be attempting [to] throw the question of Dimona into [an] arena of bargaining for things Israel wants from us, such as [a] security guarantee." Barbour was asked to resist such efforts: "this is [a] matter of global responsibility for USG [United States government] transcending what we expect to be reciprocal give and take in our day-to-day bilateral relations." Barbour was also warned that Ben Gurion might use "tactic to delay early affirmative reply," and he should also resist this: Kennedy did not suggest substitution of neutrals for Americans to visit Dimona; rather, Kennedy asked whether it would be helpful to let scientists from neutral countries visit the reactor as well.[49]

On 14 May, the day the White House received Ben Gurion's second letter and Barbour met Ben Gurion, a seven-page document, entitled "Near East Arms Limitations and Control Arrangement—Plan of Action," was submitted by the head of the working group to Rusk. The cover letter said that the proposal, which originated as a response to NSAM 231, was based on lessons learned from previous secret probes with Nasser and Ben Gurion (the 1956 Anderson mission) directed at "a serious exploration with the UAR and Israel of a practicable arrangement to prevent further escalation of unconventional weapons in the Near East." The letter suggested that because of Ben Gurion's renewed interest in obtaining an American security guarantee, a new American initiative to limit arms "would be highly opportune."[50]

The plan of action recommended "that the U.S. seek an unobtrusive, reasonably simple, arrangement in the Near East designed to prevent Israel and the UAR from acquiring, at a minimum, (1) nuclear weapons and (2) surface-to-surface strategic missiles. Given the tremendous stakes involved, there should be an immediate confidential probe of Israeli and UAR willingness to cooperate toward this end."[51] The subject of the plan was "the advanced weapons problem," linking the Egyptian missile program with Israel's nuclear program, but its main concern was clearly the latter.[52] In explaining why the Kennedy administration should seek such an arrangement the memo provided the following reasons:

It is easier to establish control over weapons which are not yet in the possession of either side.

The danger of pre-emptive attack increases as both sides learn of each other's advance in sophisticated weapons development.

As programs developing sophisticated weapons come to fruition, the ability of the U.S. to control any hostilities which might occur between Israel and the UAR will decrease.

The rise in U.S. domestic pressures against arms escalation in the Near East, particularly against the UAR missile efforts make such an approach increasingly urgent.[53]

The plan for action acknowledged that Ben Gurion would be harder to convince than Nasser ("since Israel wishes to rely primarily on its own military capabilities"), but it suggested means under which Ben Gurion might be persuaded to consider such an initiative: exerting pressure on Israel (reminding "that Israel is, ultimately, dependent on the U.S. for security"), and giving a favorable response on American security guarantees.[54] The best means to pursue this would be by designating a secret presidential emissary who could impress both Nasser and Ben Gurion of the risks involved if the arms race were to escalate to the nuclear level. It emphasized that the goal should not be a single formal agreement between the United States, Israel, and the UAR, but bilateral arrangements between the United States and each of the parties. The ultimate objective was to create "an undertaking by both sides not to develop, test, manufacture, or import nuclear weapons or surface-to-surface missiles which would be 'strategic' in terms of the Near East." The initiative should also promote "peaceful nuclear programs and scientific space research programs [that] would be declared and subject to safeguards, with the nuclear programs preferably subject to IAEA safeguards."[55]

Even if it did not succeed, the initiative would be worth trying because it would provide the United States a better sense of the positions of the parties involved. In particular, the memo mentioned three side benefits to the United States, even in case of failure: (1) "if we should undertake another initiative in the future, we will have an important point of reference"; (2) it will generate an "educative effect" among the leaders of both sides by having "a better appreciation of the problems, economic costs, and risks involved if they try to develop unconventional weapons"; (3) the United States will have more freedom of action "to pursue unilateral means to stop nuclear escalation."[56]

Two days later, on 16 May, Rusk forwarded to Kennedy a series of documents prepared by the working group. This was Rusk's response to NSAM 231. These documents included, in addition to the plan of action, a memo on the framework and tactics for negotiations in the coming months, a draft letter from Kennedy to Nasser, and a paper outlining options for possible U.S.-Israeli security assurances. These documents provide us with the best picture of the emerging American arms control initiative.[57]

The new American initiative envisioned two sets of quid pro quo. The first sought to have the UAR and Israel abjure the development of nuclear weapons and ballistic missiles. Nasser's missile program, though, had to be stopped first; thus Cairo was to be the first stop in the emissary's trip. Only a positive Egyptian response would lead the United States to ask Ben Gurion to make a concession on nuclear issues.

Nasser had to be impressed with the gravity of the situation and warned about "Israel's intent and capability to develop nuclear weapons." Nasser should therefore have an incentive to sacrifice his failing missile program for Israel's advancing nuclear weapons project. This, however, was not what the United States had told Nasser since 1961, as it was reassuring him about Dimona's peaceful purpose. Now the United States had to tell Nasser that he may have to face an Israel equipped with nuclear weapons.[58]

The authors of the initiative recognized that such an arrangement would be of little attraction to Ben Gurion. Israel was on its way to producing nuclear weapons, and it had no reason to exchange it for the unproved Egyptian missile program. The only exchange Ben Gurion might entertain was one involving a U.S. security guarantee. In May–July 1963 the White House, for the first time,

started studying what would be involved in such an exchange, concluding that
the only way to dissuade Israel from building nuclear weapons was to meet Ben
Gurion's requests for American security guarantees.

Among the documents that were submitted by Rusk to Kennedy on 16 May
was a five-page memo entitled "Possible United States-Israel Security Assurances," in which the pros and cons of two options for American security assurances were examined. One option was through "executive instruments," either
in the form of a unilateral statement presented in a presidential letter or of a
bilateral agreement; the other was through a formal treaty. The former cannot
go beyond the president's constitutional powers as commander-in-chief, meaning that "any commitment in advance to use U.S. armed forces in event of attack
upon Israel would go beyond powers generally regarded as exercisable participation of Senate or Congress." A treaty, on the other hand, is a legal document
that allows the use of U.S. forces to defend the territory of a foreign state. The
documents noted, however, that "even our most sweeping treaties of alliance
have stopped short of formal commitment to use U.S. forces under specified
circumstances." The memo thus recommended the executive rather than the
treaty approach, and an unclassified presidential letter rather than an unclassified executive agreement.[59]

Komer attached a memo of his own to Kennedy's, noting that the State
Department had difficulties "to adjust to the prospects of a commitment we've
avoided for fifteen years." Komer saw the negotiations over the American initiative as lasting "several months," and ending up "either in a UAR-Israel arms
limitations agreement plus security guarantee, or in a nuclear limitation security arrangement with Israel alone." He noted that the form of guarantee envisioned was "an executive agreement or presidential letter rather than a treaty,
essentially to avoid congressional problems," even though this "falls far short of
demands in BG's latest letter." In a reference to the failed effort to link the
HAWK missile sales to Israeli concessions on the Palestinian refugee issue,
Komer noted that "we want to avoid giving if possible before we've taped down
the quid-pro-quos."[60]

Following the White House meeting on 17 May, and the material the CIA
showed Kennedy on Israel's nuclear program, Kennedy wrote another letter to
Ben Gurion. The letter reflected the objective of Komer's memo: to nail down the
nuclear weapons side of the deal with Israel without yet responding to Ben
Gurion's request for a security guarantee. Kennedy started his letter by saying that
he was giving "careful study" to Ben Gurion's letter of 12 May. Kennedy mentioned
the report he had just received from Barbour on the latter's 14 May conversation
with Ben Gurion concerning the American request to visit the Dimona complex.
It is on this issue, Kennedy noted, that he should add "some personal comments":

I am sure you will agree that there is no more urgent business for the whole world than the control of nuclear weapons. We both recognized this when we talked together two years ago, and I emphasized it again when I met Mrs. Meir just before Christmas. . . .

It is because of our preoccupation with this problem that my Government has sought to arrange with you for periodic visits to Dimona. When we spoke together in May 1961 you said that we might take whatever use we wished of the information resulting from the first visit of American scientists to Dimona and that you would agree to further visits by neutrals as well. I had assumed from Mrs. Meir's comment that there would be no problem between us on this.[61]

In the next paragraph Kennedy pointed out the negative effects on world stability that would be caused by Israel's development of a nuclear weapons capability. Kennedy reiterated the thrust of the CIA memorandum of 6 March:

It is difficult to imagine that the Arabs would refrain from turning to the Soviet Union for assistance if Israel were to develop nuclear weapons capability, what with all the consequences this would hold. But the problem is much larger than its impact on the Middle East. Development of a nuclear weapons capability by Israel would almost certainly lead other larger countries, that have so far refrained from such development, to feel that they must follow suit.[62]

Notably, Kennedy expressed his opposition to an Israeli "nuclear weapons capability," not to "nuclear weapons" per se. This reference to "capability" is politically significant, since it preempted Ben Gurion's ability to make a distinction between having a nuclear weapons capability and having the nuclear weapons themselves. Kennedy signaled his displeasure with any effort leading to the development of nuclear weapons.

After warning Ben Gurion about nuclear weapons, Kennedy reiterated his "deep commitment to the security of Israel," recalling his press conference of 8 May in which he expressed this commitment. He reminded Ben Gurion that the United States "supports Israel in a wide variety of other ways which are well known to both of us." At this point Kennedy continued with a hint of a threat or warning,

This commitment and this support would be seriously jeopardized in the public opinion in this country and in the West, if it should be thought that this Government was unable to obtain reliable information on a subject as vital to peace as the question of Israel's efforts in the nuclear field.[63]

Kennedy went on to say that he saw "no present or imminent nuclear threat to Israel." American intelligence on this matter was good, and he was assured "that the Egyptians do not presently have any installations comparable to Dimona, nor any facilities potentially capable of nuclear weapons production." He ended his letter by reemphasizing "the sense of urgency" he attaches to early assent to the proposal first put to Ben Gurion on 2 April.[64]

The Final Confrontation

In Israel, Kennedy's letter of 18 May was perceived as "harsh," even "brutal," both in substance and form.[65] It was understood that Kennedy's opposition was to Israel's developing a nuclear weapons capability, not just to the production of actual nuclear weapons. The letter showed that Barbour's request of 2 April for biannual American visits to Dimona came from the highest level, and that it was serious. A new showdown over Dimona loomed. In responding to Kennedy, Ben Gurion had to make a choice: either an independent nuclear deterrent without the United States or a U.S. commitment to Israel's security without an independent nuclear deterrent. Ben Gurion wanted both, but this was exactly what Kennedy opposed.

Kennedy's letter caused a "mini-crisis" in Ben Gurion's inner circle.[66] The anxiety was reflected in a draft interim letter to Kennedy, prepared on 22 May for Ben Gurion, in which Ben Gurion asked for more time for consultations. Because "your letter . . . dealt with several problems having momentous significance to my country and its security, . . . [it] must receive a detailed and elaborate answer." The draft also stated that "an urgent and careful reply, with collaboration of several of my colleagues in the government" was being prepared now. Ultimately the interim letter was not sent to Kennedy,[67] and five days later, on 27 May, Ben Gurion sent his substantive reply to Kennedy.

In May 1963, as was the case two years earlier, Ben Gurion was not ready to choose: he wanted to avoid a showdown with Kennedy, but he also did not want to compromise the nuclear project. His 27 May letter to Kennedy focused solely on the nuclear subject. Unlike Ben Gurion's previous two letters to Kennedy, this one was relatively brief, written in a businesslike, even formal, tone:

> Let me assure you, at the outset, that our policy on nuclear research and development has not changed since I had the opportunity of discussing it with you in May 1961. I fully understand the dangers involved in the proliferation of nuclear weapons, and I sympathize with your efforts to avoid such a development. I fear that in the absence of an agreement between the Great

Powers on general disarmament there is little doubt that these weapons will, sooner or later, find their way into the arsenals of China and then of European states and India. In this letter, however, I propose to deal not with the general international aspect on which you express your views so clearly in your letter, but with Israel's own position and attitude on this question.

In our conversations in 1961 I explained to you that we were establishing a nuclear training and reactor in Dimona with French assistance. This assistance has been given on condition that the reactor will be devoted exclusively to peaceful purposes. I regard this condition as absolutely binding, both on general grounds of good faith and because France has extended military assistance of unique value to Israel in her struggle for self-defense, from the Arab invasion of 1948 down to the present day.

In the same sense I informed you in 1961 that we are developing this reactor because we believe, on the strength of expert scientific advice, that within a decade or so the use of nuclear power will be economically viable and of great significance for our country's development. I went on to add that we should have to follow developments in the Middle East. This is still our position today.

Between us and France there exists a bilateral arrangement concerning the Dimona reactor similar to that which we have with the United States in the reactor at Nachal Soreq. While we do not envisage a system of formal United States control at the Dimona reactor which the United States has not helped to establish or construct, as in the case of the reactor in Nachal Soreq, we do agree to further annual visits to Dimona by your representatives, such as have already taken place.

The "start-up" time of the Dimona reactor will not come until the end of this year or early in 1964. At that time, the French companies will hand the reactor over to us. I believe that this will be the most suitable time for your representatives to visit the reactor. At that stage they will be able to see it in an initial stage of operation, whereas now nothing is going on there except building construction.

I hope that this proposal meets the concerns expressed in your letter of May 19.

In 1961, you suggested the possibility that a visit be carried out by a scientist from a neutral country. this idea is acceptable to us, but a visit by an American expert would be equally acceptable from our point of view.

I appreciate what you say in your letters, Mr. President, about the commitment of the United States to Israel's security. While I understand your concern with the prospect of proliferation of nuclear weapons, we in Israel cannot be blind to the more actual danger now confronting us. I refer to the danger arising from destructive "conventional" weapons in the hands of neighboring governments which openly proclaim their intention to attempt the annihilation of Israel. This is our people's major anxiety. It is a well founded anxiety, and I have nothing at this stage to add to my letter of May 12 which is now, as I understand, receiving your active consideration.[68]

A number of points in the letter deserve careful analysis.[69] Ben Gurion did not challenge Kennedy's nonproliferation policy, but he made it clear that he did not share Kennedy's nonproliferation idealism, certainly not the view that Israel's decision would have dire consequences for the future of nuclear proliferation. He argued that without a superpowers disarmament agreement, the spread of nuclear weapons was inevitable, particularly in the cases of China, India, and some European powers. Hence the success or failure of the U.S. nonproliferation policy would not hinge on Israel's choices in the nuclear field.

As to Kennedy's queries and requests concerning Israel's nuclear program, Ben Gurion followed the same strategy he had used successfully in May 1961: he reassured Kennedy in order to avoid a showdown, but did not compromise the project by foreclosing Israel's nuclear-weapons option. Ben Gurion reiterated that Dimona was built with French assistance, given on the condition that its purpose was "exclusively" peaceful, and that that commitment was "absolutely binding." Ben Gurion was less than absolute in his assurance regarding the reactor's purpose, however: "we should have to follow developments in the Middle East."[70]

This strategy dictated Ben Gurion's reply to Kennedy's request for "semiannual visits" to Dimona. Israel would not accept "a system of formal United States control at the Dimona reactor," since the U.S. played no part in building Dimona, but as a gesture of good will it would agree "to further annual visits to Dimona, such as have already taken place." Ben Gurion knew that the United States desired biannual visits, but he explicitly allowed only one visit per year.[71]

Another issue on which Ben Gurion refused to yield was the question of the scheduling of the visits. In April Barbour had asked that the first visit be in May 1963. In his letter Ben Gurion told Kennedy that the "start-up" time of the Dimona reactor would not come before "the end of this year or early 1964," and this should be the appropriate time to begin periodic visits. At this point in time, Ben Gurion wrote, "nothing is going on there except building construction." Ben Gurion knew that a visit by American scientists to the site during the summer would allow them to see more than he wanted them to see, and he was determined to prevent it. Ben Gurion thus responded favorably to the principle of Kennedy's request, but refused to commit himself on the details.

Ben Gurion ended his letter by alluding to his 12 May letter. He could have fashioned a more formal linkage between the two issues, saying he would accept American visits to Dimona in return for American security guarantees; or he could have maintained that, in the absence of security arrangements with the United States, and because of the present Egyptian threats, Israel must maintain an infrastructure for a nuclear-weapons option for the future, and, regretfully, could not accept Kennedy's requests. In his 1961 meeting with Kennedy Ben Gurion hinted at such an eventuality, and his April–May letters laid the moral and political foundations for the possibility that Israel would embark on the nuclear weapons path. Yet Ben Gurion chose not to bring up Dimona or use it as a bargaining chip in the context of Israel's security needs.

On this issue, as noted earlier, Golda Meir sharply disagreed with Ben Gurion. Meir advocated a bolder stand on the nuclear weapons issue, explaining to the United States that Israel was building Dimona in order to provide for the nation's security. States do not make compromises on issues of vital security, and Israel should not be an exception. Hence Meir suggested that Israel should reject Kennedy's demands. The minutes of a Foreign Ministry consultation on 13 June provide evidence of her tough position:

> Regarding Dimona, there is no need to stop the work in Dimona, but we have put ourselves in a situation in which we cannot benefit from the whole thing. The issue is whether we should tell them the truth or not. On this issue I had reservations from the outset of the American intervention. I was always of the opinion that we should tell them the truth and explain why. And it is of no concern to us whether the Americans think, like us, that Nasser is a danger for us. But if we deny that Dimona exists then it cannot be used as a source for bargaining because you cannot bargain over something that does not exist. And I also don't agree that we are such "heroes" to tell Kennedy: "it is none of your business," if we go to him the day before and the day after on different issues and insist that it is his business.[72]

Ben Gurion apparently knew next to nothing about the American plan to send a high-level emissary to the region to explore the American initiative.[73] In late May it was decided that John McCloy, one of Kennedy's "wise men" and his former adviser on disarmament and arms control, would be the ideal candidate for the Middle East mission.[74] Sometime in late May or early June McCloy was offered the secret mission, which he accepted. On 13–15 June he was scheduled for three days of briefings with administration officials, including a private meeting with President Kennedy on the last scheduled day. According to the plan, McCloy was to visit Cairo on 26–29 June, stay on for a two-week vacation, and end with a visit to Israel sometime in mid-July. In a memo to Kennedy before his meeting with McCloy, Rusk noted that the principal issue Kennedy should discuss with McCloy "is the nature of his response to the inevitable request from Ben Gurion for a United States security guarantee accompanied by joint contingency planning and greater access to U.S. military equipment." Rusk noted that Ben Gurion made clear that these were his priorities, and added that "he can be expected to insist on these being met as the price of cooperation on an arms limitation agreement which would mean foregoing the technological advantage Israel has over the Arab states."[75] The link between the security guarantee and the nuclear program was at the heart of the McCloy mission.

In the meantime the administration studied Ben Gurion's reply to Kennedy. On 12 June Bundy was informed by the State Department that all branches of the scientific intelligence community had concluded "that the Prime Minister's terms fail to meet our minimum requirements."[76] The State Department memo went on to spell out why the terms Ben Gurion offered, especially concerning the frequency and the late date for the first visit, would be useless for verification purposes:

A reactor of this size would at the optimum be discharged every two years if devoted to research, but at approximately six months intervals if the object was to produce a maximum of irradiated fuel for separation into weapons grade plutonium. For a reactor of this size, the IAEA minimum inspection system calls for two inspections yearly, with far more complete controls than Israel is prepared to allow us. A visit before the reactor goes critical is essential because a more detailed observation of its structure is then possible than after its operation renders certain portions inaccessible.[77]

Based on these technical considerations, the memo highlighted five specific conditions which would ensure that the visits should be conducted in a manner that would satisfy basic verification requirements. The conditions were the following:

1) There is a June or July 1963 visit.
2) There is a June 1964 visit.
3) Thereafter, visits occur every six months.
4) Our scientists have access to all areas of the site and any part of the complex such as fuel fabrication facilities or plutonium separation plant which might be located elsewhere.
5) Scientists have sufficient time at the site for a truly thorough examination.[78]

The American intelligence community considered these as minimum conditions, without which it could not do its job. This schedule was acceptable "with some reluctance by our scientists, who would prefer a semi-annual schedule from the outset and who are also most insistent on the need for thoroughness covered in points 4 and 5." The schedule was endorsed, however, because it "partially meets Ben Gurion's once-a-year stipulation," and "because we believe that politically it may be found acceptable."[79]

These conditions were accepted by the White House and formed the central part of Kennedy's reply to Ben Gurion. The letter, dated 16 June 1963 and devoted to the Dimona problem, was the toughest and most explicit message from Kennedy to Ben Gurion. Despite Ben Gurion's efforts to avoid a showdown, Kennedy's reply showed a presidential determination to confront a problem, which, in Kennedy's words, "is not easy for you or for your Government, as it is not for mine." The purpose of the letter was to solidify the terms of the American visits in a way that would accord with these minimum conditions on which the intelligence community insisted. To force Ben Gurion to accept the conditions, Kennedy exerted the most useful leverage available to an American president in dealing with Israel: a threat that an unsatisfactory solution would jeopardize the U.S. government's commitment to, and support of, Israel.

Kennedy welcomed the two positive aspects of Ben Gurion's letter: the reaffirmation that Dimona was for peaceful purposes and Ben Gurion's "willingness to permit periodic visits to Dimona." Kennedy continued, "Because of the crucial importance of this problem, . . . I am sure you will agree that such visits should be of a nature and on a schedule which will more nearly be in accord with international standards, thereby resolving all doubts as to the peaceful nature intent of the Dimona project." Kennedy spelled out the five conditions suggested to him by the U.S. intelligence agencies, stressing that the first visit should take place "early this summer." Kennedy again changed the wording concerning the frequency of the visits, referring to Ben Gurion's agreement for "periodic visits," although Ben Gurion's letter referred to "annual visits" (Kennedy's original request was for "semi-annual" visits). The telegram to Barbour also contained instructions for oral comments which he should make to Ben Gurion, particularly that the scheduling request was the result of "the exhaustive examination by the most competent USG [United States government] authorities," and that they were the minimum required "to achieve a purpose we see as vital to Israel and to our mutual interests."[80] The showdown Ben Gurion was trying to avoid now appeared imminent.

BEN GURION RESIGNS

Ben Gurion never read the letter. It was cabled to Barbour on Saturday, 15 June, with instructions to deliver it by hand to Ben Gurion the next day, but on that Sunday, Ben Gurion announced his resignation. Ambassador Barbour, who was prepared to deliver the letter to Ben Gurion that afternoon, notified the State Department and asked for instructions. In his cable Barbour noted that although an early visit to Dimona was of the highest importance to the United States, it was unlikely that the issue could be dealt with until a new prime minister took office. Barbour recommended postponing delivery of the letter until the "cabinet problem is sorted out," and then addressing the letter to the new prime minister.[81]

Did Kennedy's pressure on Dimona play a role in Ben Gurion's resignation? Ben Gurion never provided an explanation for his decision, except in reference to "personal reasons." To his cabinet colleagues Ben Gurion said that he "must" resign and that "no state problem or event caused it."[82]

Ben Gurion's biographer suggested that there was no one specific political reason, but that it was his general mental state—manifested by a series of panicky, even paranoid, actions—of the previous ten weeks that led the seventy-six-year-old leader to resign.[83] Bar-Zohar speculates that domestic politics, not foreign policy, influenced his decision. Yitzhak Navon, Ben Gurion's close aide, also believes that the reason for the resignation might have been personal rather than political, and suggests that concerns over his mental deterioration, particularly his loss of memory, might have played a role. Navon does not think that Kennedy's pressure on Dimona caused Ben Gurion to resign.[84]

Others, however, including ministers in Ben Gurion's cabinet (Pinhas Sapir, for example), believed that Ben Gurion's decision was, in part, connected to Kennedy's pressure on Dimona.[85] Israel Galili, the leader of Achdut Ha'Avodah, was convinced that Ben Gurion's sense of failure and frustration in dealings with Kennedy on the matter of Dimona was among the reasons that led to his resignation.[86] This is also the view of Yuval Ne'eman, who, in 1963, was the director of the Soreq Nuclear Research Center and was involved in the consultations involving the replies to Kennedy's demands.[87] Ambassador Barbour also hints that Kennedy's letters and Ben Gurion's resignation might have been linked. In his telegram on Ben Gurion's resignation, he noted: "while probably not a major cause of dissension, this issue [Dimona] was itself not without controversy when Ben Gurion presented it to his colleagues before dispatching his letter May 27."[88]

Whatever the reasons for his resignation, Ben Gurion's public and private commitments in his last three years in office, particularly the one in his 27 May letter to Kennedy, undermined his long-term objective: to shield the completion of Dimona's infrastructure from international pressure. De Gaulle's reversal on the issue of French aid to Israel and Kennedy's opposition to nuclear weapons proliferation may have persuaded Ben Gurion that Israel would find it difficult to complete the project, especially in the face of American pressure.

Ben Gurion thus concluded that he could not tell the truth about Dimona to American leaders, not even in private.

Ben Gurion, as his critics charged at the time, may have been unnecessarily inhibited. The line he took, however confused and confusing it was toward the end of his reign, presaged much of Israel's future policy. Ben Gurion's legacy was not only the construction of the Israeli nuclear infrastructure, but also Israel's posture of nuclear opacity.

Israel made its first decisions on the nuclear-weapons option in 1957–58. The decisions were met with doubts and opposition, but there was no national debate on the issue. Even the few who were aware of Ben Gurion's decisions and understood their meaning—Foreign Minister Golda Meir, Finance Minister Levi Eshkol, Commerce Minister Pinhas Sapir, Mossad chief Isser Harel, and others—were inhibited from stirring up a debate on whether Israel should take the road Ben Gurion had chosen. Their reservations stemmed from financial, political, and technological reasons, but under the secrecy and opacity Ben Gurion had created, they were reluctant to force Ben Gurion into an open debate in which he would have to reveal his objectives. They were dissenting according to the rules Ben Gurion had set, which they were unwilling to question and be blamed for putting the project at risk.

Only in the early 1960s, after the news about Dimona became public, did Israel witness a semblance of a debate over the nuclear question. It was the only time in Israel's history that an intellectual and political effort was exerted to grapple with the nation's nuclear choices. The debate, which was hidden from the public and conducted in language that few understood, stemmed from Israel's need to make new decisions.

Ben Gurion's decisions in 1962–63 on the nuclear issue were shaped not only in response to Kennedy's pressure but also to the hidden debate in Israel. Consequently, Ben Gurion decided not to restructure the IDF and its military doctrine so as to base it on nuclear weapons. Rather, he would continue to develop a nuclear option without changing the IDF doctrine and basic organization. The decision was critical to the formation of Israel's posture of nuclear opacity. It was Israel's response to its nuclear problem—a response enabling Israel to have it both ways.

THE BACKDROP

In the late 1950s Ben Gurion's authority within MAPAI and the cabinet was unchallenged, and the Dimona project was ranked above all his other projects. His critics recognized that the Dimona project was the old statesman's boldest gamble, and their criticism, in any event, was not of the idea itself but of its feasibility and the people who ran it. The reservations within MAPAI were therefore muted.[1]

The Eisenhower administration's disclosures on Dimona, and its demand for information about the purpose of the project, came at an unfortunate political time for Ben Gurion. In late December 1960 Ben Gurion confronted two challenges—a domestic crisis in his cabinet and party involving the Lavon Affair, and a confrontation with the United States over Dimona. The two issues were unrelated, but their political timing and outcomes reinforced each other. Ben Gurion was a weakened leader, and his domestic political weakness shaped his reactions to the American pressure.

The Lavon Affair was the result of a failed covert operation against U.S. and British installations in Egypt in July 1954. Pinhas Lavon, who had replaced Ben Gurion in late 1953 as minister of defense, blamed the failed operation on Colonel Benjamin Gibly, then head of military intelligence, who, according to Lavon, had initiated the operations without Lavon's knowledge or approval. Lavon was forced to resign as minister of defense in February 1955, and became head of the powerful Histadrut, the labor union federation. In the second half of 1960, as new evidence about Gibly's falsification of documents relevant to the 1954 operation came to light, Lavon demanded exoneration from Ben Gurion. Ben Gurion refused, saying that since he never accused Lavon of initiating the 1954 operations, he was not in a position to exonerate him. He suggested that Lavon take his case to court, but Lavon took it instead to the Knesset's Foreign Affairs and Defense Committee. Lavon's testimony before the committee was conducted behind closed doors, but it was leaked to the press. Lavon used his testimony not only to tell his version of what happened in 1954 but also to level broad accusations against the IDF and the Ministry of Defense, and specifically at Peres and Dayan, Ben Gurion's followers. Lavon, in effect, blamed Peres and Dayan for framing him in order to serve their own political ambitions. As the confrontation between Lavon and Ben Gurion—dubbed the Lavon Affair—

became public, it became increasingly evident that the press overwhelmingly sided with Lavon.

Ben Gurion responded to Lavon's accusations, claiming they were all slanders and falsehoods that undermined public confidence in the Israeli army and civilian control of the military. Ben Gurion was the founder of the defense establishment and had personally promoted Peres and Dayan to their powerful positions. Attacks on the IDF and the Defense Ministry, and on Peres and Dayan, were attacks on him.

In an effort to contain the dispute between the two leaders and prevent further damage to the government and the party, Finance Minister Eshkol arranged for the creation of a committee of seven cabinet members, under the chairmanship of Justice Minister Pinhas Rosen, to look into the Lavon Affair and recommend a course of action to the cabinet. Ben Gurion abstained from voting on Eshkol's motion in the cabinet, even though he had objected earlier to a ministerial committee investigating the affair. The committee debated the case during much of November and December, and, on 21 December, announced its verdict: it exonerated Lavon from any responsibility for the failed operation in July 1954.

The committee's conclusions were submitted to Ben Gurion on 23 December, and two days later they were submitted to the cabinet, which endorsed them. Ben Gurion, who had opposed (though passively) the creation of the committee from the beginning, was furious. He told the cabinet that the committee's procedures were "mistaken and misleading," and that they "led to unfairness, half truths and miscarriage of justice." He refused to accept its findings, insisting that only a judicial inquiry should be looking into the matter. Before leaving the cabinet session, he threatened to resign. Golda Meir then threatened to resign if Ben Gurion pursued the case further, and other MAPAI cabinet ministers indicated that they might follow. The confrontation was damaging the country and the party, and it had to be stopped. Ben Gurion, representing the minority, disagreed.[2]

In late December 1960 Ben Gurion's leadership was at its lowest point. As the Lavon Affair unraveled, Ben Gurion appeared passive, indecisive, and detached. He allowed other politicians, such as Eshkol and Rosen, to make important decisions against his will. His moral and political authority were evaporating, and the MAPAI leadership was more divided than ever before. The Lavon Affair plunged MAPAI into a generational power struggle between the supporters of Ben Gurion (mostly from the younger generation of MAPAI leaders) and those of Lavon (mostly the Old Guard). The struggle was about more than the exoneration of Lavon; it was about the leadership of Israel.

The party elders who rallied behind Lavon's call for justice also wanted to block Ben Gurion's two protégés, Peres and Dayan, whom Ben Gurion had groomed for national leadership when he retired. The opposition of the MAPAI Old Guard to Peres and Dayan went beyond personality differences and competition for leadership and power; it was about the ethos of Israel as a Zionist-Jewish state. The old leadership feared that the pragmatic, can-do style (*bitsuism* in Hebrew) of Peres and Dayan, combined with Ben Gurion's efforts to change Israel's electoral system from proportional to regional-districts representation, would weaken the system of checks and balances in the Israeli political system. "In their eyes," writes Shabtai Teveth, "the military and the defense establishment had proved themselves unworthy of public trust, revealing an uninhibited, unrestrained lust for power, a lust that would stop at nothing, not even the use of lies and deceit to remove a minister who stood in their way."[3]

The discovery in 1960 that Colonel Benjamin Gibly, the commander of military intelligence in 1954, forged documents relating to the initiation of the 1954 "sad mishap" to make it appear that Pinhas Lavon, who was minister of defense in 1954, gave him—Gibly—the go-ahead order to launch the operation, was taken as evidence of the ill-directed regime which developed in the defense establishment under Peres and Dayan. Peres especially was an anathema to the old leaders who feared his raw ambition and what they regarded as opportunistic, manipulative tendencies.

The Dimona project played an important, if implicit, role in this drama. Everybody knew that Peres was the man behind the secret Dimona project. For some it was evidence of Peres's creativity and energy, enhancing his claim to a leadership position; for others it suggested irresponsible adventurism. Peres was accused of creating a state within a state that operated without accountability and supervision outside the normal governmental channels. For critics, the Dimona project epitomized all the ills that surfaced during the Lavon Affair, particularly the danger of a few individuals, acting under the protection of national security, making important decisions on their own.

This was the domestic background against which Ben Gurion worked to protect the Dimona project from the Eisenhower administration's pressure. On 8 December Secretary of State Herter summoned Ambassador Harman to present him with the U.S. findings on Dimona, and requested an explanation. Ben Gurion was forced to make a decision he had wished to postpone for as long as possible: how to present the Dimona project to the United States, and how much of the truth to tell. As the Ben Gurion government continued to vacillate, the United States went ahead on 18 December and made Dimona public. Ben Gurion could wait no longer, and on 21 December he gave his first and last public statement on the subject: Dimona was being built for peaceful purposes.

There are no Israeli documents available to shed light on the decision-making process that led Ben Gurion to adopt that declaratory stance. The pages in Ben Gurion's diary covering the period are missing; the relevant documents in the files of the Foreign Ministry Record Groups at the Israeli State Archives are not available. It is thus difficult to say to what extent Ben Gurion's weakness at home shaped his reply to Eisenhower. It is evident, however, that the timing of his response was slow and defensive—it took three days from the time Dimona became public until Ben Gurion made his statement in the Knesset. The contents of his public response also shows a defensive stance.

By stating that Dimona was being built for peaceful purposes, Ben Gurion must have known that he had created a problem for the future. Such a claim might invite demands to place Dimona under safeguards in order to verify its veracity. It would also make it more difficult for Israel to talk about Dimona in security terms at a later point, depriving Israel of the opportunity to make Dimona an issue relevant to military deterrence in the future. If Ben Gurion wanted Israel to acquire nuclear weapons in order to strengthen Israeli deterrence, why, then, did he take such a defensive stance that left him little room for a future weapons option?

A combination of external and domestic considerations may provide an explanation. Ben Gurion's first priority was to complete the physical infrastructure needed for the project without interruption. Until the infrastructure was in place, a confrontation over the project, either with foreign powers or critics at home, had to be avoided at all costs. It seems reasonable that, for this reason, he approved the "peaceful purposes" formula that Peres had negotiated in Paris a few months earlier—over the objections of Meir, Eshkol, Sapir, Zalman Aranne, and Harel—in return for a continuation of French involvement in the project.[4] In December Ben Gurion decided to make public the peaceful-purposes stand. He was hoping that this would be the least controversial position abroad and at home.

Ben Gurion's domestic difficulties appear to have made things more difficult for him on the nuclear issue as well. That he concealed the truth about the Dimona project from his cabinet, and therefore could not build a consensus behind his nuclear program even among his own party's senior ministers, made the nuclear project vulnerable to external pressure. A weakened Ben Gurion at home was not in a position to stand up to the United States.

Ben Gurion had hoped that his public statement of 21 December and the private message Harman conveyed would reassure the United States. This did not happen. The U.S. government cooled its public rhetoric regarding Dimona, but continued to push for verifiable reassurances of Israel's commitment. It is here that the Lavon Affair and Dimona became intertwined.

As noted, Ben Gurion received the conclusions of the committee of seven on

23 December, which were approved by the cabinet on 25 December, prompting him to threaten his resignation. Simultaneously the American pressure continued to mount, and Ben Gurion, fearing that his resignation would send the wrong signal on Dimona, decided to remain in office (though officially on leave).[5] Subsequently, on 31 January, Ben Gurion did resign over the ministerial committee's exoneration of Lavon. In explaining the reasons for the delay in implementing his resignation, he pointed to "a certain serious matter," a coded reference to Dimona.[6]

Ben Gurion's resignation and the ensuing crisis helped him postpone the American pressure for a visit by about four months. According to Ben Gurion's biographer, there were hints that the MAPAI ministers who led the opposition to Ben Gurion were also ready to surrender to American pressure, which would have meant the abandonment of the Dimona project.[7] This was probably true of Sapir and Education Minister Zalman Aranne, but not of Golda Meir. On the contrary, Meir had questioned from the start Ben Gurion's and Peres's policy of concealing Dimona from the United States, and then presenting it as having only a civilian purpose. She wanted to tell the Americans that Dimona promised a nuclear-weapons option for Israel, believing that honesty with the United States was important in light of Israel's request for American security guarantees.[8]

CLASHING VISIONS

Although Ben Gurion resigned in January 1961, he did not leave office; Dimona was still incomplete, Peres reminded him in a letter in which he urged him to stay on.[9] In this manner Ben Gurion was persuaded that the moment had not yet come to leave. In time, Ben Gurion won the showdown with Lavon, who was expelled from the party and removed from his post as secretary-general of Histadrut. Ben Gurion, unable to put together another governing coalition, continued as the interim prime minister until the new election in the summer. MAPAI won the summer election but lost seats in the Knesset, and Eshkol cobbled a narrow coalition for Ben Gurion. The leaders of the centrist Liberal Party and the leftist MAPAM were now in opposition, which was significant in opening the nuclear issue in the Knesset.

The new Ben Gurion government was presented to the Knesset in November 1961. It survived only twenty months, until Ben Gurion's final resignation in June 1963. During this time Ben Gurion was still prime minister, but he functioned like an old constitutional monarch. It was during this period that a debate on Israel's future military doctrine took place.

In 1957–58 Ben Gurion had the authority, power, and will to initiate, on his own, a secret nuclear project. In 1962–63 he had lost the political authority and will to make major nuclear decisions on his own. Furthermore, decisions on military doctrine, organization, and budget allocation required a national consent. For that, a domestic debate over nuclear issues had to take place.

The primary reason for the public debate in Israel over nuclear issues in 1962–63 was that the nuclear issue was tied to a political agenda. The Dimona reactor was nearing completion, as Egypt tested its first missiles in July 1962. Israel had to decide on the direction and pace of the project: What nuclear posture should Israel be seeking, and how quickly should it do so? Should Israel build nuclear weapons and incorporate them into its military doctrine?

The debate had different degrees of openness in various forums, some public and others closed: academic circles, MAPAI bodies, committees of the Knesset, and political and military organs. The facts and terms of the debate were obscured as military censorship and self-censorship reinforced each other. Those involved adhered to the principle of *kdushat ha'bitachon* (the sacredness of security). The debate was often portrayed as taking place between the proponents and opponents of nuclear weapons,[10] but this is inaccurate. The real debate was hidden, and it was not about nuclear weapons as such.

Dimona was no longer a state secret after December 1960, but Israeli politicians and commentators had no desire to discuss the subject openly. It was possible to raise questions about the scientific and financial soundness of the project as it was officially presented, but few did.[11] The issue of whether Israel should introduce nuclear weapons into the Middle East was also hardly explored.

QUESTIONS IN THE OPEN

Questions regarding the nuclear issue surfaced in early 1962. In an article in *Ha'aretz*, entitled "A Last Moment Warning," Eliezer Livneh, a prominent socialist intellectual and former MAPAI leader, raised the question of Israel's future military doctrine: should Israel change its military doctrine to rely on nuclear weapons and ballistic missiles? Livneh argued that the nuclearization of the Arab-Israeli conflict would be catastrophic to the region, and even more so to Israel. Thus Israel should not introduce nuclear weapons into the region.[12]

Two months later Livneh organized a small group of prominent Israelis to sign a petition urging the Israeli government to take a diplomatic initiative to ban the introduction of nuclear weapons to the region. Among the signers were philosophers and scholars such as Martin Buber, Efraim Auerbach, and Yeshayahu Leibovitz; two former members of the IAEC who resigned in 1958—Gabriel Stein and Franz Ollendorff; religious leaders; and one Knesset member—Shlomo Zalman Abramov of the Liberal Party. The group presented itself as nonpartisan, made of Zionist Jews from both the Left and Right, whose sole interest was in preventing the nuclearization of the region.[13]

There was no direct official response to the petition. Unofficially, however, the Ministry of Defense made efforts to delegitimize the committee, insinuating that its activity was damaging national security.[14] In the wake of Egypt's test of its rockets in July 1962 and its boast that those rockets could reach any targets "south of Tel Aviv," spokesmen for the Israeli defense establishment spoke openly of increasing danger to Israeli security. Peres, Chief of Staff Zvi Zur, and others made oblique references to Israel's need to revise its security doctrine in light of the missile race.[15]

There were plenty of hints that serious discussions were under way. The press reported of discussions in the cabinet and in the Knesset Foreign Affairs and Defense Committee devoted to changes in military capabilities and Israel's need to acquire "weapons of deterrence."[16] In a seven-page report to the State Department, dated 7 October, Ambassador Barbour linked this public campaign to a new concept or doctrine of national security advocated by the "Young MAPAI" group. Barbour's report observed a relationship between the emerging Young MAPAI concept and the Egyptian missile threat.[17]

The government made no official statement on the nuclear issue beyond Ben Gurion's statement to the Knesset, but Peres became, during the summer and fall of 1962, the unofficial spokesman of the new deterrent advocacy group. In interviews, he invoked the idea that a "missile race" had started and that the arms race was now about *pituach technologi* (technological development).[18] Without explicitly advocating the bomb, Peres insinuated the notion that Israel must develop new and powerful "deterrent weapons" not only to win the war but also to warn its Arab enemies of coming to the "wrong conclusions."[19] He hinted that Israel might soon be forced to adopt a new "military doctrine" in view of the new weapons in Arab hands, making this one of the gravest periods in Israel's history.[20] Peres attacked those who called for a ban on nuclear weapons; disarmament, he stressed, must relate to all weapons. As long as the Arabs preached the destruction of Israel, Israel must be prepared.[21]

The Egyptian missile launch in July and the new deterrence rhetoric from the Israeli defense establishment led some of the signers of the denuclearization petition, especially Livneh, Abramov, Stein, and Auerbach, to push their anti-nuclear activities further. In the summer of 1962, with the quiet support of Nahum Goldman, the president of the World Zionist Organization, they founded a new citizen lobby, named the Committee for the Denuclearization of the Middle East. Although only ten to twenty people attended the meetings, which were held in the residence of one of the participants, the group became a loud antinuclear voice in Israel.[22] It lobbied primarily before the leaderships of the nation's political parties, and attempted to educate the intelligentsia of the dangers of nuclear weapons in the region.[23] Given the scientific and political weight of the committee's leaders, they had access to prominent political figures in both the governing coalition and the opposition parties.[24]

The committee's starting point was that the atomic bomb was a distinct type of weapon with the potential to destroy the entire Zionist experiment. Given Israel's geopolitical and demographic situation, it could not, and should not, tolerate the nuclearization of the Arab-Israeli conflict. Israel would never be safe if nuclear weapons were to fall into Arab hands, and the only way to prevent such a danger was to ban nuclear weapons in the region altogether. The presumption was that an Israeli advantage in this field would be short-lived; sooner or later the Arabs would either produce their own weapons or purchase them from a nuclear power. The only way to prevent the nuclearization of the region was through a political agreement among the parties to create a Middle East free of nuclear weapons. It was up to Israel to determine the nuclear future of the region.[25]

Though the committee framed its public opposition to nuclear weapons in regional terms, the context was domestic. Aware that important decisions on the nuclear issue were soon to be made, its leaders wanted to alert the Israeli public, especially parliamentarians, of the significance of the decisions. From the second part of 1962 until 1964, Livneh and his associates were involved in efforts, which were at times politically awkward, to communicate their concerns to leaders of all the mainstream Zionist parties in order to force the issue into parliamentary discussions.

Livneh and his friends saw themselves as the intellectual and moral guard against the nuclear activism of the prime minister's office and the Ministry of Defense. Given the dynamics of technological development, the committee was aware of the short path from a nuclear option to actually producing a bomb once the infrastructure was completed, and was concerned that, under the shroud of secrecy, Ben Gurion could make critical decisions without political consultations.[26]

The public side of the debate of 1962 was inhibited; neither side in the debate was able, or willing, to speak freely. Officially there was no Israeli nuclear weapons program to reinforce either argument, so in order to express their message both sides had to use code words and phrases, such as "new deterrent weapons" and "regional denuclearization." This was particularly difficult on the committee.[27] It could not state its real concerns and fears about the Israeli program, for it would be considered revealing state secrets. Committee members had to be mindful of how far to push their critique without crossing the line, legally and politically. Aware of this, the committee insisted on using only public information, which weakened its critical position. The committee's ostensible objectives—regional efforts for denuclearization—looked hypothetical and unrealistic, while it was inhibited from stating publicly its real worry: that Ben Gurion and Peres would push Israel and the region to nuclearization.[28]

The story of the committee, however, is only a footnote in the political history of Israel's nuclear policy. The committee's warnings of the dangers of nuclearization failed to reach the Israeli public. It also failed to politicize the nuclear issue. The leaders of all the Zionist parties who listened to its arguments were reluctant to politicize its cause.

In the end the committee's advise was ignored. Israel acquired nuclear weapons, and the committee's predictions did not materialize. The committee, however, was not entirely irrelevant. It maintained occasional contacts with cabinet ministers who had reservations about nuclear weapons—Israel Barzilay and Mordechai Bentov of MAPAM, Israel Galili and others of *Achdut Ha'Avodah*, Chaim Moshe Shapira of the National Religious Party, and Pinhas Sapir of MAPAI. The decisions of 1962–63, unlike those of 1956–58, were made through a process of debate in which the Israeli nuclear position was discussed. The committee contributed to this end.

BODY POLITIC

Independently of the committee, distinguished Israeli scientists, including Amos de Shalit of the Weizmann Institute, briefed leading parliamentarians on the nuclear issue. Subsequently, during the spring of 1962, all the major Zionist parties in the Knesset were engaged in closed-door consultations, mostly informal, on the nuclear question. It was the first time that members of the Knesset reflected on the Israeli nuclear program. It was also the first time that the political parties had to make up their own minds on the issue.[29]

The internal discussions took place first among the opposition parties, notably the Liberal Party and MAPAM. The issues were twofold: first, whether Israel should build nuclear weapons or act to denuclearize the region, and, second, what should be the Knesset's role in overseeing the Dimona project. Many felt that, this time, the Knesset should not be bypassed on the issue as it had been five years earlier.[30]

In March, Elimelech Rimalt, the president of the Liberal Party met MAPAM leaders to discuss the issue, noting that his party had reached no official position thus far. In May the Liberal Party discussed the matter in its official political forum, and found itself to be divided. The difficulty was owing to the moral and political consequences of the decision.[31] Ben Gurion responded with silence when the issue was raised by his coalition partners in a cabinet meeting.[32]

Members of the Knesset in all the major parties expressed sympathy for the idea of denuclearizing the Middle East and pressed for further discussions, but it became evident that no party, with the exception of the Israeli Communist Party, felt comfortable politicizing the nuclear issue by either favoring or denouncing it. To take a substantial stand on this issue meant to challenge Ben Gurion's official statements of December 1960, which no mainstream Zionist party was ready to do. Such a challenge to Ben Gurion could damage the national interest. Ben Gurion's absolute refusal to discuss the issue also deterred party leaders. Even those few parliamentarians who had concerns about the nuclear program felt that such a move would not be acceptable to the public.[33] In the wake of those informal party consultations, and in light of Ben Gurion's and Peres's insistence that the issue must not be discussed in public, it became apparent to most parliamentarians that the Israeli nuclear policy was too sensitive to be transformed into a political issue with which to challenge the government.

The reluctance of the major parties to confront the government on the substance of the nuclear issue did not mean that they were ready to accept the government's position on the procedural issue of oversight. Parliamentary leaders, especially of the opposition parties, would not abrogate their right to parliamentary oversight, and Ben Gurion himself was interested in forming a discreet parliamentary mechanism which would allow for secret reporting and budgetary approval that would bypass public discussion of the subject.

Concerned party leaders could raise their questions privately with Ben Gurion, rather than confront him publicly. Sometime in late 1962 or early 1963, the Foreign Affairs and Defense Committee of the Knesset founded an ad-hoc secret subcommittee, first known as the committee of seven (it was composed of seven senior representatives of all the parties, with representation at the full committee) to discuss nuclear affairs.[34] A similar secret subcommittee was established by the Finance Committee to look into the financial aspects of the Dimona project.[35]

This was a convenient solution for both the executive and legislative branches. Like in other Western democracies, the Israeli Knesset did not evince an appetite for meddling in nuclear affairs. Even those MAPAI ministers, who had earlier reservations about the nuclear project, especially Meir and Sapir, were not interested in bringing their case for discussion at party forums. As for other parties, the arrangement allowed them to drop the nuclear issue without betraying their parliamentary duties. The issue was discussed in closed, informal forums, without forming a party line. Israel's parliamentary system was too uncomfortable with making the nuclear question a public issue; thus secrecy had an inhibiting effect on both the public and its politicians.[36]

BEHIND CLOSED DOORS

The real nuclear debate in Israel took place within the government. In 1962, as the Dimona reactor neared its completion, the time had come to decide on the next stage of the project: To what extent should the nuclear option be realized? What kind of military option should Israel develop for the next decade?

These issues related to military doctrine and organization, and to budgetary and political considerations. The choices involved were not of the either-or kind; rather, the choices to be made were arrayed along a proliferation ladder. At its top was full membership in the nuclear club (i.e., testing a bomb, accumulating an arsenal, restructuring the army, developing a nuclear doctrine). At its bottom were the maintenance of the physical and research nuclear infrastructure needed to maintain a nuclear option to be utilized if circumstances changed.

As a sign of Ben Gurion's increasing political weakness, a coalition agreement between MAPAI and Achdut Ha'Avodah of 10 October 1961 imposed formal limits on Ben Gurion's ability to act alone in the area of defense. In an appendix to this agreement, entitled "Ministerial Committee," the two parties agreed that the "development of new weapons systems to be deployed by the IDF" must first be discussed by the Defense Ministerial Committee.[37] This clause was not the result of developments in the nuclear field,[38] but expressed the principle that important strategic decisions could not be made by Ben Gurion alone.

By 1962 two schools of military thought emerged in Israel and engaged in a debate on the nation's future military doctrine and army force structure. I refer to the first school as the "technological-nuclear" approach and to the other as the "conventionalist" school. The immediate question at stake was how the IDF should invest its limited funds.[39] The chief advocates of the technological-nuclear school were Peres and Dayan. Their arguments echoed Ben Gurion's pessimism about the continuation of the arms race and his interest in long-term deterrence that may eventually even bring about peace. They argued that only advanced weapons could provide Israel with the stable deterrence it needed without being caught up in an increasingly hopeless conventional arms race. They made the point that the continuation of the conventional arms race would drain the Israeli economy and tempt the Arabs to prolong the conflict. Israel could not afford to lose even once, and each victory would be increasingly expensive in terms of human lives and materiel; therefore Israel must be in a position effectively to deter the Arabs from waging war.

Peres and Dayan urged "to equip the army for tomorrow," that is, that Israel should invest its limited human and financial resources in technological developments of new deterrent weapons.[40] Nuclear weapons were the most effective deterrent against war, and they would eventually convince the Arabs to come to political terms with the reality of Israel. Moreover, in the absence of a super-power security guarantee to Israel, these weapons would be Israel's independent security guarantee. This was what Peres called "the doctrine of self-reliance."[41]

The chief protagonists of the conventionalist school were the leaders of *Achdut Ha'Avodah*, Minister of Labor Yigal Allon, the former PALMACH commander who was considered one of the military heroes of the War of Independence, and Israel Galili, formerly the chief of staff of the Haganah, whose views on matters of national security were highly regarded. The conventionalist school rejected the two presumptions of the Dayan-Peres analysis, dismissing the pessimism underlying the belief that nuclear weapons were the only solution for Israel's long-term security and, more important, raising doubts about the applicability of nuclear deterrence—the balance of terror—to the Middle East. Conventionalist military doctrine, built on modern mobile armor and a strong tactical air force, should keep Israel secure for many years to come. Furthermore, conventionalists maintained that any Israeli nuclear monopoly would be only a short-term transitional stage, soon to be replaced by a nuclearized Middle East. Even if Egypt were not able to keep up with Israel, it is likely that the Soviets would not allow Israel to maintain a nuclear monopoly. Given the geopolitical and demographic asymmetries of the Arab-Israeli conflict, it would not be in Israel's national interest to nuclearize the conflict; an investment in nuclear weapons would weaken the IDF and might encourage the Arabs to wage another war.[42]

By mid-1962 the debate appears to have reached the moment of decision. According to one account, one forum in which the debate took place was a secret memorial conference for Elyahu Golomb, a former head of the Haganah, with the participation of Ben Gurion, Peres, Allon, Dayan, Galili, and Yigael Yadin. Ben Gurion rejected Allon's doctrine of preventive war, but he did accept Allon's recommendations to purchase more armor and tactical aircraft.[43] In his writings Allon describes a slightly different version of the debate, using vague language. It took place, says Allon, in the Ministerial Committee on Security Affairs when the chief of staff of the IDF, Zvi Zur, requested an additional budget to create a new armored brigade, but "a minister proposed to appropriate the funds [which Zur requested] to accelerate important scientific research." Allon, who supported the army's request, added that the vote between the armor and the "important scientific research" was divided "half-and-half," until Ben Gurion, prime minister and committee chair, added his own vote to the armor camp, saying, "We cannot put all our eggs in one basket."[44]

According to Arnan (Sini) Azaryahu, a close friend and advisor to Israel Galili, sometime in 1962 Ben Gurion arranged a small, informal, high-level conference for which both camps prepared position papers. The conference, which might have been held at Dimona, was attended by Ben Gurion, Dayan, Peres, Eshkol, Allon, and Galili (and possibly a few others). Dayan presented the argument for the technological-nuclearist strategy, pointing out that time and demography worked against Israel, which would soon exhaust its resources in the conventional arms race with the Arabs. The bomb, because of its relatively low cost over time, was the only solution to the Israeli security problem.[45]

Galili then presented the arguments of the conventionalist camp. Referring to the superpowers' seemingly stable balance of terror, Galili pointed out that the geopolitical situation in the Middle East was different from the superpowers' situation, and that a Middle Eastern nuclear balance of terror was likely to be fragile because of the asymmetries among the parties. The incentive to launch a first strike would be high, and it would be difficult, if not impossible, to secure a second strike. Furthermore, Galili and Allon argued that shifting the IDF to a nuclearized force structure would not save funds—the conventional army could not be made much smaller and it would continue to purchase tanks and aircraft—but would weaken the Israeli army, which could, in turn, trigger Arab aggression.

Their final argument was that a nonnuclear Middle East was preferable for Israel. Israel should not build nuclear weapons because this would lead, sooner or later, to Arab nuclearization. Galili and Allon did not propose that Israel should not engage in research and development of nuclear weapons and missiles. Rather, Israel should keep the nuclear option open, always remaining ahead of the Arabs in this field. According to this version, despite his sympathy to Peres's and Dayan's arguments, Ben Gurion sided with the argument of Allon and Galili for continuing to strengthen the conventional army.[46]

Few facts on the debate have been released, and no public record of it exists. The eyewitness accounts are also incomplete. It is not clear whether the Dimona conference was the event to which Allon and Gilboa alluded. All the sources, however, agree that Ben Gurion, in his last year in office, decided to buy more tanks and not to advance the nuclear project further. His decision may have been motivated more by political and technical considerations than by doctrine. His 1962 decision established an important strategic precedent: He decided that Israel would not be the first to introduce nuclear weapons into the Middle East. Ben Gurion apparently used this phrase in a meeting with Israel's newspaper editors.[47]

Peres, in an article published in late 1962 in the IDF monthly publication, *Ma'archot*, in addressing the "time dimension" in the Arab-Israeli conflict, specified five strategic changes in the Arab-Israeli status quo that may lead to another Arab-Israeli war.[48] The first three relate to strategic changes that the

Arabs could introduce, and the last two refer to changes that Israel could introduce or be perceived to introduce. The fifth item on Peres's list is most relevant to our discussion: "If Israel acquires an unpredictable power, real or imagined, the Arabs will react vehemently."

In his visit to the United States earlier that year, Peres was told by his hosts that if the Egyptians became convinced that Israel acquired, or was about to acquire, nuclear weapons, they could launch a preemptive war. By late 1962 Peres appeared to have accepted this view and qualified his pronuclear weapons position: an introduction of Israeli nuclear weapons in the Middle East would be an Arab casus belli. Whether this became Peres's conviction in the wake of Ben Gurion's decision or following his discussion in the United States, is unclear. This is also what he told President Kennedy when he met with him in April 1963.

On 23 June 1963 MAPAI elected Finance Minister Levi Eshkol to succeed Ben Gurion as Israel's third prime minister. In wishing success to the new prime minister, Ben Gurion noted that "this time he [Eshkol] should not always give in and seek compromises." Few among the audience understood to what possible compromises Ben Gurion may have alluded. The prime minister designate replied that there would be "compromises and giving in," because "the movement and the nation now need a somewhat conciliatory spirit."[1]

This comment highlighted the different leadership styles of Ben Gurion and Eshkol. Ben Gurion was Israel's visionary founding father, a decisive and authoritarian leader. Eshkol was a down-to-earth consensus builder, a skillful compromise seeker. This difference was also manifested in the internal changes that had taken place in Israel from 1948 to 1963. In 1963 Israel needed a conciliatory politician who would strengthen the national unity.

The differences between the two leaders were relevant to the nuclear project. Ben Gurion passed the nuclear project to Eshkol at a difficult moment—in the midst of a confrontation with Kennedy's nonproliferation policy. Though most of the financial investment was already made and much of the physical infrastructure was already built, it was still a project without a coherent political or military purpose. Ben Gurion's public and private commitments made it unclear how Israel could gain deterrence or other security benefits from Dimona. Now, in the summer of 1963, as Dimona was soon to become critical, Kennedy was fighting for even stronger assurances that Israel would not develop nuclear weapons.

Eshkol's role was to preserve the Dimona project and determine what its limits and proportions should be. This was a task not for a visionary but for a politician who knew the art of the possible.

KENNEDY'S LETTER

On 5 July, less than ten days after Eshkol became prime minister, Ambassador Walworth Barbour delivered a letter to him from Kennedy. Apart from a brief congratulatory note for Eshkol's election, the letter's wording was almost identical to Kennedy's letter to Ben Gurion of 15 June—the one that was to be delivered to Ben Gurion the day he resigned but was returned to Washington.[2] Kennedy began the letter with a reference to Ben Gurion's 29 May letter concerning his request for American visits to Dimona, "a problem that I know is not easy for your Government, as it is not for mine." Kennedy welcomed "the former Prime Minister's strong reaffirmation that Dimona will be devoted exclusively to peaceful purposes and the reaffirmation also of Israel's willingness to permit periodic visits to Dimona."[3] This formulation was slightly more assertive than what Ben Gurion had agreed to in his 29 May letter, but it allowed Kennedy to move directly to the heart of the matter: "the nature and scheduling" of the periodic visits to Dimona. On this issue Kennedy's letter becomes blunt, even threatening:

> I am sure you will agree that these visits should be as nearly as possible in accord with international standards, thereby resolving all doubts as to the peaceful intent of the Dimona project. As I wrote Mr. Ben Gurion, this government's commitment to and support of Israel could be seriously jeopardized if it should be thought that we were unable to obtain reliable information on a subject as vital to peace as the question of Israel's effort in the nuclear field.
>
> Therefore, I asked our scientists to review the alternative schedules of visits we and you had proposed. If Israel's purposes are to be clear beyond reasonable doubt, I believe that the schedule which would best serve our common purpose would be a visit early this summer, another visit in June 1964, and thereafter at intervals of six months. I am sure that such a schedule should not cause you any more difficulty than that which Mr. Ben Gurion proposed in his May 27 letter. It would be essential, and I understand that Mr. Ben Gurion's letter was in accord with this, that our scientists have access to all areas of the Dimona site and to any related part of the complex, such as

fuel fabrication facilities, or the plutonium separation plant, and that sufficient time be allotted for a thorough examination.[4]

Not since Eisenhower's message to Ben Gurion in the midst of the Suez crisis in
November 1956 had an American president been so blunt with an Israeli prime
minister. Kennedy told Eshkol that the U.S. commitment and support of Israel
"could be seriously jeopardized" if Israel did not let the United States obtain
"reliable information" about its efforts in the nuclear field. Kennedy presented
detailed technical instructions on how his requirements should be executed.
Since the United States had not been involved in the building of Dimona and
no international law or agreement had been violated, Kennedy's demands were
unprecedented. They amounted, in effect, to an ultimatum.

Barbour was instructed to stress to Eshkol "that exhaustive examination by
the most competent USG [U.S. government] authorities has established scheduling embodied in President's letter as minimum to achieve a purpose we see as
vital to Israel and to our mutual interests."[5] The scientific reasons given were the
same as those that appeared in the State Department memo to the White House
on 12 June. In his oral comments to Israeli officials Barbour denied that the timing of Kennedy's letter was related in any way to the internal changes in Israel's
leadership. The letter was prepared for Ben Gurion, and it was Ben Gurion's resignation that forced a brief postponement until a new prime minister took
over.[6] Jerusalem, however, did not believe this explanation. Was it proper for
Kennedy's first correspondence with Israel's new prime minister to focus on the
most sensitive issue between the two countries, without a reference to Ben
Gurion's earlier request in his letter of 12 May? Israel and the United States disagreed on the issue.

KENNEDY'S PERSPECTIVE

For the White House, the letter to Eshkol was the culmination of a five-month
effort to find ways to stop Israel from developing a nuclear weapons infrastructure (for details, see chapter 7). Israel would give up its nuclear ambitions in
return for American security guarantees, while Egypt, in return for an unspecified American technological assistance, would give up its ballistic missiles program. In mid-June John McCloy, the emissary designated to carry out the mission, came to Washington for briefings, including a 15 June meeting with
Kennedy. Kennedy's letter to Ben Gurion was signed that day.

Ben Gurion's resignation did not change the first leg of McCloy's mission,
the trip to Cairo, but it was a factor in the subsequent decision to cancel the trip

to Israel. Nasser did not endorse the American plan, but he did not turn it down either (see chapter 13). In July, however, Washington's attitude toward the McCloy mission changed, and within weeks of McCloy's return to Washington in early July, it became apparent that neither the White House nor McCloy were interested in completing the mission by a trip to Israel (although McCloy was not told of the letter Kennedy had sent to Eshkol).[7]

Why did the White House lose interest in the plan? For one thing, the results of McCloy's talk in Cairo were disappointing. On 3 July Komer reported Nasser's reaction to the American scheme as "negative," but emphasized that Nasser "did not close the door."[8] Komer was clear that there was no point in going to the Israelis before clarifying certain issues with Nasser, while McCloy lost interest in pursuing the initiative. Before his return to Washington, while vacationing in Greece, McCloy met Ambassador Barbour who raised doubts about the desirability of McCloy going to see Eshkol "at this time." Barbour thought that given the "limited results" of the Cairo trip, a visit of a presidential emissary in Israel would be seized by the Israelis "to increase the pressure for a security guarantee."[9]

The change of leadership in Israel was probably also a factor in discontinuing McCloy's mission. Ben Gurion's interest in American security guarantees was known, but in July 1963, Eshkol's was still unknown. Kennedy may have wanted to test how Eshkol operated under pressure.

These setbacks did not change Kennedy's determination to constrain Israel's nuclear program, but he chose a new approach. Rather than trying for a trilateral deal, he now opted for a bilateral arrangement. The threat Kennedy used in his 5 July letter to Eshkol was harsher than the one used in his 15 June letter to Ben Gurion. William Crawford, the State Department official who ran the Israeli desk at the time and who drafted Kennedy's letters, recalls that the strong wording of the letter came directly from President Kennedy, and was without precedent.

Why was Kennedy so keen, in July 1963, to frustrate Israel's nuclear plans? Global considerations were as important as regional ones, and Ambassador Barbour explained that to Eshkol and other Israeli officials. He pleaded with the Israelis not to interpret Kennedy's pressure on Dimona as indicating a change in America's special relationship with Israel. In the spring and summer of 1963 Kennedy was interested in exploring policy ideas on how to bring together nuclear test ban and nonproliferation issues. Dealing with the Israeli nuclear case was an integral part of Kennedy's global nuclear agenda.

In July 1963, in anticipation of Averell Harriman's mission to Moscow to complete the negotiations of the Partial Test Ban Treaty (PTBT), Kennedy was looking for ways to break the stalemate with the Soviets on proliferation. An

Arms Control and Disarmament Agency (ACDA) memo, entitled "Political Implications of a Nuclear Test Ban," pointed out that "although a test ban alone would not offer an answer in the most acute cases, such as that of Communist China, it would increase the leverage the U.S. might exert and would open the way for the development of new combinations of inducements and persuasions, possibly on an international scale, which are difficult to set in motion as long as the U.S. itself continues to test."[10] Harriman's trip to Moscow created a moment of opportunity for the Kennedy administration to engage the Soviets on a number of issues. Pushing for superpower understanding on curbing nuclear proliferation was central.

Harriman's mission to Moscow involved both negotiatory and exploratory aspects. He was asked to explore to what extent the two superpowers could extend their cooperation into the nonproliferation arena.[11] The official National Security Council (NSC) instructions for Harriman, issued on 9 July, adapted the ACDA guidance but made Harriman's mandate more flexible:

> On the exploratory side, you should canvass, in so far as appears practical, the range of issues involving peace and security which divides us from the Soviets.
>
> You should continue to emphasis the relation between the nuclear test ban treaty and our desire to control the diffusion of nuclear weapons. . . . You may indicate that the U.S. will endeavor to secure adherence to or observation of any non-dissemination agreement by those powers associated with it, if the Soviet Union is willing to undertake a parallel responsibility for those powers associated with it.[12]

The minutes provide a better sense of the exploratory aspect of Harriman's mission. Secretary Rusk noted that in his talks with the Russians, they had accepted the American view that the number of nuclear powers should remain four—the United States, the United Kingdom, France, and the USSR.[13] This suggests that Harriman's most sensitive mandate was to check how far the Russians would be willing to go toward a joint effort to ban further proliferation. According to his formal instructions, Harriman was authorized to examine whether the Russians would be ready to work on a nonproliferation agreement that would limit the number of nuclear powers to only four. In particular, if the United States made efforts to bring on board all those powers with which it was associated, would the Soviets do the same? Specifically, would the Russians be ready to make efforts vis-à-vis China as the United States was exerting pressure vis-à-vis Germany and Israel?[14]

Israel or Germany were not mentioned in the NSC document, but there is little doubt that they were the countries for which the United States was willing to "take some responsibility with regards to [nuclear] dissemination." The NSC meeting took place only five days after Kennedy sent his tough letter to Eshkol. Kennedy's most sensitive instructions were conveyed to Harriman orally in a one-on-one meeting on 10 July. There are no minutes of the Kennedy-Harriman meeting, but a later cable from Kennedy to Harriman indicates that Harriman was instructed "to elicit [Khrushchev's] view of means of limiting or preventing Chinese nuclear development and his willingness either to take Soviet action or to accept U.S. action aimed in this direction."[15] Was Harriman also authorized to inform Khrushchev about the ongoing American effort to halt proliferation by its own ally, Israel?[16]

Harriman's discussions with the Soviets concerning a nonproliferation agreement did not provide the breakthrough that some in Washington had hoped for.[17] Even without progress with the Soviets on a nonproliferation agreement, however, Kennedy pushed his aggressive nonproliferation policy, continuing to focus in the summer of 1963 on the Israeli case. From Kennedy's perspective, the Israeli case was a test for the U.S. global nonproliferation policy. If Israel were to detonate a nuclear device in the next two or three years, as the American intelligence community believed it could, this would have devastating effects on the delicate nuclear equation in Europe, especially on Germany.[18] If Kennedy was serious about his commitment to halt nuclear proliferation, he must put pressure on Israel.

In the absence of international nonproliferation norms, the bilateral approach, based on incentives and sanctions, was the only nonproliferation tool Kennedy had. American policy toward Israel's nuclear program had to be crafted in bilateral terms. If the United States could still halt Israeli nuclearization, action would have to be taken immediately. Given the issue at stake, Kennedy was determined not to let Eshkol withdraw from or postpone the agreements Ben Gurion appeared to have already made. Kennedy had to translate Ben Gurion's May agreement-in-principle into a firm and detailed binational arrangement.

Kennedy was determined to slow Israel's progress through American inspection of the Dimona reactor, but he was not sure that the pressure on Eshkol would yield the desired results. In a memo to Kennedy in July, Komer noted that even if Nasser had responded positively to McCloy, Israel was not likely to make concessions on Dimona without obtaining formal American security guarantees. "*Israel will not give us nuclear promises unless we either: (1) literally force them to back down; or (2) pay a price*," he wrote.[19]

Kennedy's concerns about his ability to pressure Israel can be seen by the way he compartmentalized the knowledge about his letter to Eshkol. McCloy was not told about it, and at a meeting Kennedy chaired on 23 July to assess arms control initiative, he did not disclose that he had sent a letter to Eshkol only three weeks earlier.[20] Instead, Kennedy alluded to a "dialogue" that was taking place between the ambassador and Eshkol.

ESHKOL'S PERSPECTIVE

Things looked different from Jerusalem. Eshkol was hardly aware of Kennedy's global nuclear agenda. From his perspective, Kennedy's demands seemed diplomatically inappropriate; they were inconsistent with national sovereignty. There was no legal basis or political precedent for such demands. The original American request of semiannual visits, presented to Ben Gurion in April in general terms, was now introduced to Eshkol with five specific conditions. It was precisely these conditions, which amounted to making visits "as nearly as possible in accord with international standards," that would both compromise the program and violate Israeli sovereignty. Also, by threatening that the U.S. commitment to Israel "could be seriously jeopardized," Kennedy was seen to be testing the new and inexperienced prime minister, forcing him to make immediate concessions. To Eshkol, it seemed that Kennedy was taking advantage of him on a sensitive subject with important national consequences, without even affording him a grace period to get acquainted with his new responsibilities.[21]

Kennedy's letter precipitated a near-crisis situation in the prime minister's office. Even though Eshkol had been informed about the Dimona project almost from its inception, and was generally aware of the Kennedy-Ben Gurion correspondence, it was still Ben Gurion's secret project. Now the Dimona project became Eshkol's responsibility. To compound matters, Kennedy's ultimatum was the first foreign policy challenge the new prime minister had to deal with.

Eshkol might not have been as committed to the nuclear project as Ben Gurion had been; nevertheless it was politically inconceivable for him to alter the direction of the project in a significant way under American political pressure. In June 1963 Ben Gurion endorsed the choice of Eshkol as his successor with the understanding and confidence that Eshkol would find a workable arrangement with the United States that would avoid confrontation without compromising the heart of the project. As Eshkol himself defined his objective in his meeting with the editors of Israel's daily newspapers: "[On the nuclear issue] we should act up to our limits, but we should always make sure that it would not create a rift with the United States."[22]

Given Eshkol's leadership style and his lack of experience on these issues, he needed time and consultations to study the political and technical issues involved in making decisions about the Dimona project before he could respond to Kennedy. He knew that, to find a working compromise that both sides could live with, would be difficult. That Ben Gurion did not leave room to discuss Dimona in the context of Israel's security, and that Ben Gurion had not formed a national political consensus on the project even among his own party's ministers, made Eshkol's job difficult.

Above all, Eshkol needed to make a summer visit at Dimona impossible. His first action was to ask for more time. On 7 July, only two days after Kennedy's letter was received, a draft of an interim reply letter was prepared in Eshkol's office. It was never forwarded, but it is important because it reveals Eshkol's apprehension and strategy. Eshkol noted that "it is only now that I have begun fully to appreciate the range and variety of the security problems that we face." He wrote that he was "studying the correspondence and verbal exchanges which have passed our two governments since 1961." This allowed him to link Kennedy's concerns with nuclear proliferation to "Israel's unique security problems," something Ben Gurion had been reluctant to do: "I fully appreciate your concern on the international plane, just as I am sure that you are aware of Israel's unique security problems." As to Kennedy's concerns, Eshkol only suggested that "the best chance of understanding on the Dimona project and related problems, including the inspection schedule, would be by way of personal contact." To pursue this end, Eshkol proposed that he come to Washington in early August or that Foreign Minister Meir would meet Kennedy at any convenient date. Again, Eshkol explained that he proposed "this method of discussion because there is an inevitable link between scientific development in the nuclear field and various international issues of great complexity." The draft ended by affirming Eshkol's desire "to reach a total understanding between the United States and Israel on all vital issues," including those mentioned in Kennedy's letter.[23]

This draft was not delivered, but on 17 July Eshkol forwarded a revised, somewhat weaker interim reply to Kennedy. Noting Israel's unique security predicament—"we are the only state in the international community whose existence is challenged and indeed the only one threatened by all its neighbors"—Eshkol introduced a vague linkage between Israel's security and nuclear development. As to Kennedy's specific request, Eshkol asked for time for further consultations. He noted that he was giving careful study to Kennedy's letter in the context of becoming familiar "with all the details of the Dimona project," and that he intended to send a substantive reply at an early date. The idea of a special visit by Eshkol or Meir was dropped, apparently owing to the negative reaction of the White House's deputy counsel, Myer Feldman.[24] In his brief conversation with Ambassador Barbour, Eshkol raised his concerns over the question of sovereignty and asked Barbour to check whether the United States had made a similar arrangement with India.[25]

In the meantime, both governments kept secret the contents of the correspondence between Kennedy and Eshkol. In Washington the White House refused to provide details on the exchange, referring to its contents as "private," only noting that Kennedy's initial appeal related to questions of "scientific development in Israel."[26] The Israeli press, under the rules of the military censor, referred to the subject of the exchange as the "sensitive issue" without elaborating on its details.[27] On the diplomatic level, American officials in Washington and Tel Aviv made it clear that Kennedy's interest in Dimona reflected global worries about nuclear proliferation, rather than a particular American-Israeli issue.[28]

As the Israeli consultations continued, the United States continued to pressure Israel, using diplomatic and other means, for an early and positive reply.[29] Israel, for its part, had an opportunity to demonstrate its support for Kennedy's concern for proliferation a month later, when, on 25 July 1963, the PTBT, which banned nuclear-weapons tests in the atmosphere, outer space, and under water, was initialed by its three cosponsors in Moscow. Israel's decision on the treaty was regarded as important, and the United States pressured the Eshkol government to be among the first signers. On 29 July the Eshkol government welcomed the PTBT, noting his government's persistent support of all efforts to ban nuclear tests. The Moscow agreement was considered an important step toward relaxation of international tensions, and Israel declared its intention to sign it as soon as it was open for signature.[30] In a related secret decision, the prime minister and the foreign minister were authorized to make the final decision concerning Israel's participation in the Moscow agreement, without further discussion in the cabinet.[31] On 4 August the Israeli government officially announced its decision to sign. The PTBT was signed by the foreign ministers of its three cosponsors in Moscow on 5 August, and three days later Israel became the twenty-third nation to join.

Throughout July and August Eshkol continued his consultations concerning Dimona. In addition to Ben Gurion, Eshkol consulted with a few senior MAPAI cabinet ministers and with his deputy minister of defense, Peres. On scientific-technical matters, Eshkol consulted with Yuval Ne'eman, then the director of the Nachal Soreq Nuclear Research Center, whom Eshkol had known through family connections for many years.[32] Bergmann, the chair of the Israel Atomic Energy Commission (IAEC), and Manes Pratt, Dimona's director, were also involved in those consultations, but primarily through Peres. The Israeli ambassador in Washington, Avraham Harman, also returned to Jerusalem for consultations.

Kennedy's pressure and the changes in the Israeli leadership created an opportunity for Israel to rethink its nuclear policy. Eshkol could have come up with a new declaratory nuclear policy, as some of his ministers proposed. As noted earlier, a strong voice on this matter was that of Foreign Minister Golda Meir, who advocated since 1961 a bolder and more straightforward stance. She favored a similar position in response to Kennedy's letter of 5 July. In case of a confrontation with Kennedy, Israel should present Dimona in terms of national survival and seek the support of world Jewry. Meir was also concerned with compromising Israel's sovereignty. Ministers Pinhas Sapir and Zalman Aran presented a dovish position. They were ready to accede to Kennedy's demand for biannual U.S. visits to Dimona, in effect relinquishing a future nuclear-weapons option.[33] Their pessimism was supported by Harman, who presented a bleak picture of American-Israeli relations if Eshkol rejected Kennedy's requests.[34]

Peres and Ne'eman proposed a more pragmatic approach that reflected Eshkol's own desire to find a compromise that would permit dropping the issue without compromising the essence of the project. They looked for ways to delay the first visit and accommodate the Americans' concerns while still allowing Israel to carry out its plans. As long as the U.S. visits remained under Israel's control, Eshkol decided, Israel should look the other way on the question of national sovereignty. This approach was also endorsed by Ben Gurion, who had already allowed two such visits in 1961 and 1962, and had agreed to permit annual American visits to Dimona in his 27 May letter.[35]

By mid-August the United States intensified its pressure on Eshkol for a prompt reply. Barbour expressed impatience with the Israeli delays, and the Israeli Embassy in Washington reported that Secretary Rusk, in a private conversation, commented that Dimona was now the "only issue" on the American-Israeli agenda. "Israel must come clean," he was reported to have said, and until this happened, there was nothing else to talk about.[36]

ESHKOL'S REPLY

On 19 August, after six weeks of intensive consultations, including the circulation of at least eight different drafts, Eshkol handed Barbour his reply to Kennedy's letter. The letter began by repeating Ben Gurion's assurances on the peaceful character and purpose of the Dimona reactor, as expressed in the Waldorf-Astoria meeting and Ben Gurion's letter of 27 May. In addition, Eshkol noted that Israel was already committed to the peaceful purposes of the reactor by a specific agreement with France, which was aiding in the reactor's construction.[37] Given "the special intimacy of the relationship between the United States and Israel," Eshkol agreed to visits of U.S. representatives to the Dimona reactor site, even though the assistance for its construction came from another country.

As for the time those visits could begin, here, too, Eshkol followed Ben Gurion's approach, suggesting late 1963 as being appropriate for the first visit. Just as Kennedy's letter was technical, so was Eshkol's reply. He explained that "by that time the French group will have handed the reactor over to us and it will be undertaking general tests and a measurement of its physical parameters at zero power." Eshkol noted that the "start-up stage" would not yet have been reached, so the first visit would set a zero base line.

On the question of the reactor's fuel cycle, Eshkol stated that the uranium to be used was French-owned, "and is fully controlled by the French government, to whom it has to be returned after irradiation, as is the normal practice in such an agreement between sovereign states." Eshkol was explicit in his consent that the first U.S. visit should be held before the start-up stage, but he was less explicit about the frequency of subsequent visits. Responding to Kennedy's request for semiannual U.S. visits to Dimona, Eshkol left this most sensitive issue vague, without directly contesting Kennedy's request: "Having considered this request, I believe that we shall be able to reach agreement on the future schedule of visits."[38]

In addition to the letter, Eshkol drew Ambassador Barbour's attention to three new points in his message that went beyond what Ben Gurion wrote in his letter of 27 May. First, Israel was ready to conduct the initial visit before the start-up stage, hence responding favorably to the ambassador's oral request of 5 July. Second, Israel accepted the ambassador's proposal for regular visits from June 1964 on. Notably, here, too, Eshkol left the question of frequency unresolved. Third, Israel suggested a procedure that would allow the United States to observe fuel control, "the crux of any visiting system designed to verify the purpose of the reactor." While stressing these three concessions, Eshkol made it clear to the ambassador that "for reasons which you will readily understand" the Israeli response must not become public.[39]

Golda Meir also had a separate conversation with Barbour after he received Eshkol's letter. Meir said that serious efforts were put into the preparation of Eshkol's reply to Kennedy, and that she was hoping it would satisfy the president's concerns. To this Barbour replied that Kennedy's concerns were "deep and sincere," and the nuclear issue was the only subject Kennedy had originally raised with him two years earlier on the eve of his departure to Israel. Barbour noted that Kennedy had also raised the issue of Dimona with him in 1962.[40]

Within days, on 27 August, Kennedy replied to Eshkol, thanking him warmly for his letter. The general tone expressed a sense of relief:

> Your letter of August 19 was most welcome here. I appreciate that this was difficult, yet I am convinced that in generously agreeing to invite our scientists to visit the Dimona complex on the regular basis that was proposed you have acted from a deep wisdom regarding Israel's security in the longer term and the awesome realities which the atomic age imposes on the community of men.[41]

Kennedy reiterated Eshkol's proposed arrangement that the initial visit would still take place in 1963 "in the pre-startup stage," and asked the prime minister to keep in touch with Barbour so that the visit could be arranged when the core was being loaded and "before internal radiation hazards have developed." He ended his letter by alluding to the Moscow PTBT agreement, noting his commitment toward "the effective control of the power of the atom so that it may be used only for the welfare of man," adding that "the spirit you have shown in your letter to me is a clear indication that you share that same high purpose."[42]

In addition to the presidential letter, the State Department instructed the charge d'affaires to pass on an oral response to the sensitive points that Eshkol raised orally. As to Eshkol's request that information not be passed on to Nasser, the United States would honor and comply with this request, but urged Eshkol to reconsider his position. The charge d'affaires suggested that the technical arrangements for the first visit be handled by the embassy's scientific attaché. The last point made by the U.S. representative was that, with the resolution of the nuclear issue, Eshkol should expect soon to receive Kennedy's response to Ben Gurion's letter of 12 May. Eshkol thanked him for Kennedy's message and promised to give consideration to the question of assuring Nasser.[43]

The exchange of letters between Kennedy and Eshkol was the most important nuclear correspondence to date between an American president and an Israeli prime minister. Eshkol's decision was decisive for the Israeli nuclear program. Eshkol, like Ben Gurion before him, did not accept Meir's hawkish advice to tell Kennedy "the truth and explain why," and, if necessary, to confront the American president on this matter of survival, nor the dovish advice of Sapir, Aran, and Harman, which would have meant placing limits on Israel's ability to complete its nuclear option.

Why did Ben Gurion and Eshkol feel so uncomfortable with Golda Meir's suggestion to tell "the truth and explain why"? Israel could have insisted, in its private dealings with Kennedy, that it had no less right to develop its independent nuclear deterrent option than Britain or France had. If anything, given

Israel's memory of the Holocaust and its lack of external security guarantees, it had a strong case for developing a nuclear option. Developing an option did not mean that Israel would introduce it later as a weapon. Eshkol could have even taken the position that while Israel insisted on its right to have a nuclear option, it was also committed not to be the first to introduce such weapons into the region, just as Peres told Kennedy in their brief White House meeting four months earlier. In 1963 there was no nonproliferation norm, and a number of European countries—Sweden, Switzerland, and Italy—maintained small nuclear programs directed at military applications.

Meir was also correct on the issue of national sovereignty. There was no precedent for the United States to ask for verification of a friendly state's declaratory policy, threatening that lack of compliance would "seriously jeopardize" their relations. It is more puzzling because at that time the United States hardly provided any military aid to Israel. Meir was probably correct to think that if Kennedy had been told the truth about Israel's nuclear resolve, he would not have gone public to fight Israel and world Jewry on this matter of survival. Had Eshkol or Meir been invited to meet Kennedy in person, as Eshkol had contemplated in July, this path might have been taken.

History, however, took another turn. Facing Kennedy's pressure and Ben Gurion's past commitments, the new prime minister decided not to put Dimona on the table, either by fighting for its legitimacy or by using the nuclear option as a direct bargaining chip. Instead, Eshkol followed the approach Ben Gurion had taken, that is, avoiding a showdown by maintaining that Dimona's purpose was peaceful, agreeing to the principle of U.S. visits to Dimona to confirm its peaceful purposes, and doing so in a manner that would not undermine the nation's commitment to its future nuclear option. This approach required that Israel be less than honest with the United States.

When Eshkol had to decide between Meir's and Ben Gurion's approach, he chose Ben Gurion's. With Ben Gurion's blessing, and under the guidance of Peres, Bergmann, Ne'eman, and Pratt, Eshkol accepted an arrangement that meant both infringement of Israeli sovereignty and being less than honest with the United States. The arrangement that had been imposed led to a less than honest commitment. Israel thus stumbled further into nuclear opacity.

In his desire to avoid a clash with the United States, Eshkol complied with the spirit of Kennedy's letter, but not with its specific terms. Eshkol did not concede on two issues which were left unresolved. On the question of the frequency of visits, Kennedy insisted from the outset on "semi-annual" visits, the minimum number of visits that the U.S. AEC maintained was necessary. Eshkol never agreed to this condition. In his letter he alluded to this request, expressing his hope that a mutually satisfactory agreement could be found, but did not go beyond this vague language. As it turned out, the question of the frequency of U.S. visits to Dimona remained controversial.

The other issue had to do with Kennedy's request to pass on the conclusions of the scientists' reports to third parties, particularly Nasser. From Kennedy's perspective, the idea of passing the information to third parties was at the heart of the visitation arrangement. The United States wanted to use this information to dissuade Nasser from building his own nuclear weapons program, curbing the nuclear race in the Middle East. Kennedy had good reason to expect agreement on this request, since Ben Gurion had already agreed, in their Waldorf-Astoria meeting in 1961, that Kennedy could share these findings with whomever he chose.[44] This issue, too, became central in subsequent exchanges between Eshkol and President Johnson in 1964.

ATOMS VERSUS SECURITY GUARANTEES

The Eshkol-Kennedy exchange of August 1963 prepared the ground for Kennedy's long-awaited response to Ben Gurion's letter of 12 May. It must be remembered that Kennedy's letter of 19 May, in which he raised the issue of Dimona, was not a response to Ben Gurion's letter requesting U.S. security guarantees and arms. That letter had been left on hold, pending a resolution of the nuclear issue. It was handled by both governments as if these were two different issues—global and regional. In reality, however, it was obvious to both sides that the two issues were related. The tacit linkage was conspicuous when Kennedy threatened, in his 5 July letter to Eshkol, that the U.S. commitment to and support of Israel could be "seriously jeopardized" if Israel would not allow the United States to obtain reliable information on Dimona. When Rusk commented in August that Dimona was the "only issue" on the U.S.-Israeli agenda, and that until Israel came clean there was nothing else to talk about, it was also a demonstration of this tacit linkage.[45]

In Israel Ambassador Barbour told senior Israeli officials that it would be "disastrous" if Eshkol's reply on Dimona were linked to Kennedy's response to Ben Gurion's security requests of 12 May. It is not difficult to see why Barbour warned the Israelis against linking the nuclear program with security, as this would have increased Israel's bargaining power in its demand for American security guarantees. The Kennedy administration recognized that the two issues were linked, and this was why Komer saw no point in sending McCloy to Israel until "we've thought through the guarantees problem. *Our dilemma is that the more we talk about inspection, nuclear self-denial . . . the more the Israelis will see leverage to get guarantee, arms and joint planning from us.*"[46]

By July, however, after the stabilization of the situation in Jordan and the lack of results from McCloy's trip to Cairo, the State Department opposed giving Israel formal security guarantees. A commitment to Israel's security already existed, it was argued, and was included in Kennedy's statement of 8 May. The State Department also conceded to the consequences of such a guarantee. To make U.S. commitment to Israel's security more public than it was would only "spook the Arabs," Komer wrote, adding that "State does not see how we can guarantee Israel *without automatically binding ourselves to Israeli position on armistice lines, water, refugees, Jordan, etc.,* unless we negotiated all these issues out in advance."[47] Rusk told Kennedy that given Nasser's negative reaction to McCloy's probe, the administration should pursue separate efforts with Egypt and Israel, keeping apart the effort to slow down Israel's nuclear efforts from the discussion over security guarantees. Otherwise the price the United States would have to pay would be too high.[48]

The United States and Israel, for different reasons, were reluctant, in July 1963, to place Dimona in the context of Israel's security problems. There were benefits for the United States in disassociating the two issues, because it increased the U.S. bargaining power over Israel. Once Kennedy decided against giving Israel formal U.S. security guarantees, he had no interest in linking the two issues. Also, for Kennedy, who was concerned about global proliferation, linking Dimona to Israel's security would have meant that his global policy was tested, and had failed, in the case of a small country most friendly to the United States.

Eshkol, too, hesitated to place Dimona in the forefront and demand a positive security arrangement in return for policy restraints on the nuclear program, as Golda Meir proposed. Why? It appears that Eshkol's reluctance to take Meir's stance was owing to apprehensions of incurring the wrath of both Kennedy and Ben Gurion. Kennedy's threat that the U.S. commitment to Israel "could be seriously jeopardized" if Israel were to reject his request for semiannual U.S. visits to Dimona looked serious. Eshkol was fearful of starting his term as prime minister with a direct confrontation with the president of the United States. It was unthinkable at that time to regard Dimona as a bargaining chip because of the mistaken assessment that the United States would not respond positively to such conditioning.[49]

Equally important in understanding Eshkol's stance were the attitudes of Ben Gurion and Peres. Ben Gurion's past commitments to Kennedy left Eshkol little room for maneuvering on Dimona. Although Ben Gurion did not firmly commit himself at the Waldorf-Astoria meeting not to acquire nuclear weapons, Kennedy understood him to have done so. In 1963 Ben Gurion was not ready to change his position. In his 27 May letter Ben Gurion reiterated his

May 1961 stance: the civilian account of Dimona and his consent for U.S. visits. It was impossible for Eshkol to back off from his predecessor's pledges made less than ten weeks earlier.

There were other factors. Neither Eshkol nor the group of senior ministerial advisers that consulted with him on this matter had a clear idea or consensus on what kind of security guarantees Israel should request from the United States, nor on how Dimona could, or should, be introduced in future political discussions with the United States, or even whether that would be a good move. There was no strategic master plan. From the minutes of their meeting, it is evident that Eshkol did entertain Meir's approach but that he was unclear about how it could be presented and what risks it might involve. Eshkol was also uncomfortable about entering into an arrangement that would force Israel to be less than honest with the president of the United States, but he saw no clear and safe alternative. He was even ready to entertain the notion of telling the Americans that Israel had a separation plant, and was ready to sit tight with merely a nuclear option and without actually developing nuclear weapons, while the United States would provide Israel with conventional forms of deterrence.

Other participants, such as Moshe Dayan, were uncomfortable with the idea of using the option as leverage for other forms of deterrence. Dayan made his point clearly: "At any negotiation or letter that we are engaged, we must be careful not to get into a position in which Dimona is used as a leverage against us or by us. It must not happen that we get some one-hundred million dollars for Israel's security, and we sell out Dimona." In response to a comment by Eshkol that Israel might have to talk openly with the Americans about Dimona, Dayan noted briefly, "I'd rather we would not talk about 'what instead of' Dimona," to which Eshkol replied, "blessed the believer." Eshkol then expressed his own concerns: "What am I afraid of? His [Kennedy's] man will come, and will be told that he can visit anywhere, but when he will go to open something, then Pratt will tell him, this is not. So he will tell it to Barbour or Kennedy. The question is how important it is to us that he [Kennedy] will know that the Prime Minister, or the Foreign Minister, or the whole Government does not lie to him." At the end of the consultation, no specific decision was made; the issue was left to the prime minister's discretion.[50]

Neither side explicitly linked Eshkol's reply to Kennedy on Dimona with the U.S.-Israeli security dialogue, but such a linkage was real, if tacit. As soon as the Dimona issue was settled, Israel rushed to raise security issues with the United States. On 9 September, three days after the ministerial consultations, Eshkol sent a long telegram to Harman and Gazit, instructing them on how to raise Israel's new security requests with the administration. In particular, they were asked to seek "new deterrent weapons, including surface to surface missiles of the kinds that the Egyptians have."[51] Ambassador Barbour in Israel was given the same message: Israel was now seeking in the United States the kind of deterrent weapons that it could not purchase in Europe, and not merely defensive weapons, such as the Hawk surface-to-air missiles. On 30 September Foreign Minister Meir met Secretary of State Rusk in New York and put forward the two types of deterrent weapons Israel was seeking in the United States: surface-to-surface missiles to match those being developed in the Egyptian missile program, and modern tanks.

THE LAST EXCHANGE

On 3 October Kennedy finally replied to Ben Gurion's letter of 12 May. In this six-page letter Kennedy reiterated the American commitment "for the security and independence of Israel," stressing that the United States has "the will and ability to carry out its stated determination to preserve it."[52] Kennedy, however, raised doubts whether formalizing "our known intentions and commitments" could enhance the interests of both nations. Kennedy was not interested in providing formal security arrangements of the kind Ben Gurion had sought in his letter. After a first reading, Eshkol commented to Ambassador Barbour, who hand-delivered the letter to him, "there is not much in it," and added that the letter would not give him anything new with which to reassure the Israeli public. Eshkol informed Barbour that he would show the letter to Ben Gurion.[53] The strategy behind Ben Gurion's 12 May letter thus failed, in that Israel did not obtain any formal security guarantees in return for American visits to Dimona, and Dimona was not recognized as a security asset.

From his perspective, Eshkol was justified in thinking that Kennedy's letter was disappointing. For Eshkol, who six weeks earlier thought he had made painful concessions on Dimona, the letter failed to meet his expectations. He received nothing concrete in return for his earlier concessions, only verbal assurances of the kind that Golda Meir had already received from Kennedy the previous December in Palm Beach. Kennedy behaved as if he did not understand, or did not want to understand, what those concessions meant to Israel. From Kennedy's perspective, however, Ben Gurion's 12 May letter had been a request for a public bilateral security pact between the United States and Israel, to which Kennedy responded. Dimona was never presented by either Ben Gurion or Eshkol as a security issue in their respective letters. Furthermore, the Americans believed that Ben Gurion had given Eisenhower and Kennedy a verbal commitment that Dimona was built for peaceful purposes, a commitment later repeated in his letter of 27 May 1963. Since Israel did not place Dimona on the table as a security issue, it received nothing for its agreement to allow American scientists to verify Dimona's peaceful intent.

Eshkol's disappointment was owing, in part, to the way Ben Gurion had managed the politics of Dimona. Ben Gurion's less than honest separation of the two issues—Dimona and security—meant that the Dimona question was discussed in "deceptive" terms. The two arguments Israel used in its dealings with Kennedy's demands on Dimona—sovereignty and the agreement with France—were not the real issues. The real issues were security, nuclear weapons, and deterrence; but this, because of Ben Gurion's legacy, Eshkol could not say explicitly. From Kennedy's viewpoint, the Dimona arrangement amounted to no more than a confirmation of Ben Gurion's earlier commitment.

Despite the initial Israeli disappointment, Kennedy's letter of 3 October was more positive than Eshkol's view of it. It was the most explicit and comprehensive presidential expression of an American commitment to Israel's security.[54] As Harman and Gazit pointed out in their detailed textual analysis of Kennedy's letter, this was the strongest American pledge to come to Israel's help in times of danger, assuring Israel that whenever "a serious increase in the Arab military threat" were to develop, the United States "will most carefully consider the best ways and means of coping with it." Significantly, Kennedy responded favorably to the Israeli idea to have periodic American-Israeli security dialogues involving senior officials on both sides. In this respect, Kennedy's letter was an open invitation for Israel to initiate a formal security dialogue with the United States.[55] Gazit was even more positive than his ambassador in his assessment of Kennedy's reply. In the fall of 1963 he saw a possibility that the United States would soon become Israel's chief military ally. When he informally raised, with Robert Komer, Israel's request for modern American tanks, the latter's sympathetic response indicated to him that something fundamental was changing in the relations between the two states.[56]

SECURITY DIALOGUE

The idea of a security dialogue between America and Israel was promoted for some time by the Israeli Embassy in Washington, especially by Gazit. It meant the establishment of an institutionalized forum to discuss issues of mutual interest relevant to Israeli security, such as joint contingency military planning in case of a surprise attack against Israel, or intelligence exchanges relating to new threats to Israeli security. Since a formal bilateral pact or treaty was understood to be unrealistic, the Israelis were interested in less formal and more discreet mechanisms that would give substance to the U.S. commitment to Israeli security. Just as U.S. representatives would visit Dimona, Israel asked that Israeli military officers visit the Sixth Fleet and coordinate contingency plans. When Israel conceded to Kennedy's demands on the matter of Dimona, it must have expected that the United States would make good its commitment to Israel's security. Though no formal linkage was made between Dimona and security in the fall 1963 discussions, it is possible to trace its opaque presence.

The first U.S.-Israeli security dialogue had taken place in July 1962. The first exchange was meant to be a one-time meeting, not an institutional discussion. The idea of high-level, regular security dialogues was presented to Eshkol by Gazit in late August 1963.[57] Eshkol liked the idea and presented it days later in his ministerial consultations,[58] authorizing the Israeli Embassy in Washington to give it a prominent place in their coming discussions with U.S. officials.[59] Meir raised the idea, along with a request for tanks and missiles, with Rusk in New York in late September. The secretary agreed to such high-level U.S.-Israeli exchanges within weeks, particularly to discuss missile and other nonconventional weaponry development in Egypt.[60] Deputy Chief of Staff General Yitzhak Rabin and Deputy Chief of Military Intelligence Colonel Aharon Yariv were to represent Israel at that strategic exchange set for mid-November.

On 30 October Eshkol convened another consultation with his ministers, focusing on what Israel should request in the Washington talks. This time concrete requests were discussed and adopted. It was decided that the time was ripe for Israel to ask for direct U.S. military assistance in modernizing the Israeli tank force, specifically replacing the old Sherman M-3s with 200 M-48A3s and 100 M-60s. Furthermore, Israel hoped to purchase M-48s at a low price as military surplus. This emphasis on purchasing hardware at cheaper prices became Eshkol's approach to dealing with America on security issues. Ben Gurion chased after security guarantees, while Eshkol sought deterrent strength at a good price.

To highlight the importance Israel attached to the meeting, Eshkol forwarded another, final letter to Kennedy. After thanking Kennedy for his reassurance of the U.S. commitment to Israel, Eshkol focused on the question of Israeli deterrence in the near future. The primary issue was Egypt's missile development. Eshkol noted that Egypt was advancing toward building an effective missile force. Even if it lacked a great degree of accuracy, such a force would pose a great danger to Israel. "This situation," he wrote, "can be counteracted only by Israel acquiring a balancing deterrent capacity in the same military dimension."[61] As in the past, Dimona was not mentioned in the letter but its opaque presence was there. It was because of the concessions that Eshkol made to Kennedy on Dimona ten weeks earlier that he could now ask for a reward. He told Kennedy that Israel would not possess the necessary deterrent capacity in the near future unless it received considerable help. Specifically, Eshkol wrote, "we need help in obtaining equipment, especially ground to ground missiles, tanks and naval power." In his oral comments to Barbour, Eshkol reiterated that without an effective deterrent capability, Israel would face destruction.[62]

Israel had a broader agenda for the November secret meeting (code-named, *Mifgash*) than the United States was willing to discuss. The American agenda focused on a limited exchange of intelligence assessments on Egypt's missile and other unconventional weapons programs and a discussion on the means to curb such an arms race in the region.[63] Israel wanted more than that. Its agenda was to convince the Americans that in light of the new Egyptian threats, Israel was obliged to enhance its deterrent capability. Two main weapons systems were mentioned as critical to Israel's security: ground-to-ground missiles and medium tanks. The Israeli delegation was authorized to inform the Americans that "Israel was engaging in development of its own missile, but the price was high and the technical difficulties were severe." It was also decided not to tell the Americans that the development of the missiles was taking place in France.[64] As noted earlier, the United States knew about the French-Israeli missile deal almost since its inception in September 1962.[65]

The dialogue took place in two sessions on 13–14 November. On the question of the significance of the Egyptian missile development program, there was a difference of opinion. Both sides agreed that Egypt had made efforts to establish a missile development program, but the United States discounted the military value of the Egyptian effort. The United States rejected the view that there existed any operational Egyptian missile capability, and considered the effort to be in an early research and development stage. It also doubted that Nasser had the technical or financial means to produce a force of one thousand missiles, as Israeli reports suggested, which Americans estimated would cost about half a billion dollars.[66] The Kennedy administration did not share the Israeli view that the Egyptian missile program constituted a real immediate danger to Israel, and opposed providing American surface-to-surface missiles to Israel.[67]

They also differed on the question of the probability of an Egyptian surprise attack against Israel. Ben Gurion was obsessed with Israel's vulnerability to such a possibility, a concern that played an important role in his decision to develop a nuclear option. American officials, however, were less impressed by the danger. If Egypt wanted the maximum strategic surprise, the American analysis went, it must first deploy very large forces in the Sinai. Even a deployment of two divisions, as was the case in the Egyptian deployment in early 1960, would not suffice. If Egypt were to increase its strength in the Sinai permanently, Israel would have time for both diplomacy and military preparations. In addition, the

American analysis argued that Israel too easily dismissed the role of the U.S. military in deterring an Arab surprise attack. "We have done many gaming studies which indicate Sixth fleet capabilities very high for air intervention. Even if Nasser achieves an initial advantage, he must count on losing it rapidly."[68] Such U.S. claims concerning the Sixth fleet, most recently made by Kennedy to Golda Meir less than a year earlier, did not assuage Israeli anxiety. In the absence of a formal commitment or secret military contingency planning, these pledges lacked sufficient credibility for the Israelis.

The only aspect of the dialogue on which Rabin and Komer reached an understanding was the issue of tanks: the IDF needed to modernize its old Sherman fleet. Pentagon officials asked questions and compared numbers. The next day Komer informed the Israelis that he believed they had a case. As Gazit reported earlier, by late 1963 the Kennedy administration was becoming increasingly receptive to the idea of helping Israel modernize its tank force. The United States still did not want to be a major supplier of offensive weaponry to the Middle East, but it was willing to look for avenues for responding favorably to the Israeli request for modern tanks. It took months of negotiations on the tank deal through third and fourth intermediaries (Germany and Italy), but an understanding on the essence of the deal was reached in the meetings of November 1963.

IN CLOSING

Was Dimona, particularly as reflected in Eshkol's 19 August letter, an important factor in making this U.S. policy shift possible? Perhaps it was that letter that made the meeting possible, but Dimona itself was never mentioned in those talks. Both sides behaved as if the Dimona issue did not exist. The United States reacted as if there was no substantial linkage between Israel's new requests for American security arrangements and Eshkol's letter of 19 August. Its three-page "Talking points for Rabin mission" started with the note "talk candidly as de facto allies," yet both sides were authorized not to make any reference to the nuclear issue, and only vague and indirect comments on the matter of missiles. At the same time, the United States noted that it was "a bit surprised Israel wasn't more candid about its own future military intentions," especially in the area of surface-to-surface missiles.[69] On the surface, then, there was a dual-track approach, and this approach seemed to serve the interests and inhibitions of both sides.

Thirty years later, in an extensive series of interviews with the two principal American decision makers, Myer Feldman and Robert Komer, the linkage was presented as a fact, if unstated and tacit. Komer claimed that this tacit linkage was the primary working assumption that led to the creation of new security understandings between the United States and Israel since the end of the Kennedy administration.[70] "There was never really two tracks, security and atom, there was always really only one track."[71] Some of the Israelis who were there saw it differently. Mordechai Gazit still believes that the linkage was invisible and loose, arguing that, even without Dimona, the United States was bound to change its security relationship with Israel.[72]

In any case, in late 1963 Israel and the United States, Kennedy and Eshkol, stumbled further down the path of nuclear opacity. Would the two countries have continued under Kennedy as it did under Johnson? What would Kennedy have done with regard to the Israeli nuclear program had he lived and been reelected, and to what extent would Israel's nuclear history have been different? These questions will never be answered with certainty.

The most sensitive episode in the American-Israeli relationship during the 1960s relating to Israel's nuclear program was the visits by U.S. representatives to Dimona. President John F. Kennedy, who, in the spring of 1963, became concerned with the implications of the Israeli nuclear project for regional and global security, was the author of the arrangement. Kennedy initiated the visits, but they were carried out under President Lyndon B. Johnson.

During the 1960s the visits were a constant reminder that, despite their friendship, the two countries differed in their interests and perspectives on the nuclear issue. As Kennedy explained in his letters to Ben Gurion and Eshkol, the reason for the American visits was to "resolve all doubts as to the peaceful intent of the Dimona project." He was convinced that, without strong American pressure, Israel would develop nuclear weapons, resulting in grave consequences for the region and the world.

In April 1963 President Gamal Abdul Nasser told presidential emissary Robert W. Komer that Israel's acquisition of a nuclear weapons capability would be a cause for war, regardless of the cost to the Arab nations. Thus the purpose of the American visits to Dimona was to curb the Israeli nuclear program and reassure Nasser. The Kennedy administration believed that the preservation of peace in the Middle East depended on its ability to reassure Nasser of the peaceful nature of the Dimona reactor.

The U.S. government believed that only an intrusive inspection system had a chance to thwart the Israeli nuclear effort. This explains the four conditions for the visits that Kennedy demanded in his letter to Prime Minister Levi Eshkol on 5 July 1963. First, the initial visit must take place before the start-up phase—that is, before fuel was loaded into the reactor. Second, American visitors should have "access to all areas of the Dimona site and to any related part of the complex, such as fuel fabrication facilities or a plutonium separation plant." Third, "sufficient time [should] be allotted for a thorough examination." Fourth, the visits should be conducted "at intervals of six months."[1]

These four conditions were meant to assure that an effective protocol would be established after the first visit. The first condition would allow the scientists to establish a historical baseline for verifying the characteristics of the reactor, which is best done before fuel was loaded. It also allowed access to sections of the reactor and related facilities, which would later become radioactive and inaccessible for direct inspection. The second and third conditions would ensure that the visiting team would have sufficient freedom of movement and time in the facility to accomplish its mission. The fourth would ensure effective and continuous monitoring of the facility, especially its fuel cycle. Full compliance with these four conditions meant that the U.S. visits to Dimona would be "as nearly as possible in accord with international standards."[2]

Kennedy, aware of Israel's opposition to IAEA safeguards,[3] sought to shift the safeguards responsibility from the IAEA to the United States. Ben Gurion had already agreed, in 1961, to an American visit to Dimona, even allowing the United States to pass on its results to Nasser. Another American visit to the Dimona site, which was still under construction, had taken place in September 1962. In the summer of 1963 Kennedy pushed to institutionalize that precedent in an arrangement that would operate as a safeguards system but would be politically acceptable to Israel. Such a mechanism would make the United States the watchdog of Israel's nuclear program.

There was a difference, however, between Kennedy's plan to create a system of bilateral inspections of Israel's nuclear program and the way the visitation arrangements were put into practice during the Johnson years. Their authority was not legally, but rather politically based. These visits were the result of a vague political understanding between two heads of state, not the result of compliance with an international agreement. Kennedy wanted the arrangement to "be as nearly as possible in accord with international standards," but Eshkol never saw it that way. For Eshkol, the arrangement was a necessary evil: a way to avoid a confrontation with the president of the United States without simultaneously compromising the project. There was nothing legally binding about the arrangement with Kennedy, and it is not clear to what extent there was even an agreement between Kennedy and Eshkol. Israel never agreed to the four ground rules that Kennedy spelled out in his 5 July letter. In fact, Eshkol responded explicitly only to one, concerning the schedule of the first visit, and politely avoided the others.[4]

Thus, while Kennedy insisted that visits to Dimona take place "at intervals of six months," this never occurred. During the five-year Johnson-Eshkol period, the United States repeatedly reminded Israel that Kennedy's letter asked specifically for "bi-annual visits," but Israel, which never agreed to that, always found reasons to deny such visits,[5] and the intervals between visits were stretched to a year or longer.

The differences in perspectives between the United States and Israel were also manifested in the terminology used. The United States talked of "inspections," referring to those involved as "inspectors." Israel objected to this terminology, referring instead to "scientific visits" and the "invited guests of Israel." In January 1965 Secretary of State Dean Rusk wrote to Ambassador Walworth Barbour about these terminological differences: "We [are] not concerned as to whether team [members are called] 'invited guests of Israel' or 'inspectors' provided they are given right of access to all parts of Dimona site and to all relevant reports."[6] Rusk further wrote Barbour that the "team would normally bring small instruments which could be carried in [a] suit pocket for independent measurements and would hope [this is] acceptable to Israelis."[7] This was unacceptable to the Israelis, and the Johnson administration gave in. The transition from the Kennedy to Johnson administrations changed the character and function of the visits significantly.

THE 1964 VISIT

On 5 December 1963, more than three months after the exchange between Kennedy and Eshkol, Israel invited "U.S. representatives" to visit the Dimona reactor at a convenient date between 10 and 15 January 1964. The invitation letter to Ambassador Barbour, signed by Chaim Yahil, the director-general of the Foreign Ministry, on behalf of Eshkol, explained that "by that date the French group will have turned the reactor over to us."[8] Two days later Barbour informed Yahil of the scientists' names and notified him that "January 14 and 15 have been allocated for inspection of the Dimona site and related facilities." The telegram added that, "should the Israelis ask why three inspectors [were] selected rather than two as on previous inspections," he should tell them that "the United States believes it [is] in [their] joint interest [to] be able [to] assert, should future need arise, that thorough inspection [was] made prior to reactor criticality."[9]

American correspondence used the term "inspection" rather than "visit" and asked for a two-day procedure. Israel was unhappy on both counts. Its reply reminded the ambassador that the correspondence between Kennedy and Eshkol referred to the arrangement as a "visit," not an "inspection," and, more important, it suggested that the visit last one day, and that day should be Saturday.[10] This exchange was the first shot in the ensuing conflict between the United States and Israel over how to translate the understanding between the two heads of states into specific procedures. In the end Israel prevailed on both points, as well as on others. Kennedy's suggested ground rules were never directly challenged by Eshkol, but they were undermined, in form and substance, by the time they were implemented.

The leader of the three-member 1964 team was Ulysses M. Staebler, senior associate director of the Division of Reactor Development at the AEC, who had participated in two previous American visits to Dimona. The other two members were Richard W. Cook, vice president of the American Machine and Foundry Company, which built the Soreq reactor, and an AEC consultant; and Clyde L. McClelland, a nuclear physicist at the U.S. Arms Control and Disarmament Agency (ACDA). In Washington the AEC team was briefed by the CIA, the State Department, and by AEC chairman Glenn T. Seaborg, and its mission was explained to its members. The briefers used terms similar to those Kennedy used in his letters to Ben Gurion and Eshkol, referring to the ground rules as interpreted by the United States.[11] The briefing document made clear that the inspection had two purposes: first, to check that the Israelis were not secretly producing material for nuclear weapons, and, second, to reassure Nasser on this issue. The briefing document was specific on these issues:

1. To prevent escalation of the Arab-Israel arms race and to avoid stimulating a pre-emptive Arab attack, we must be in a position to assure the Arabs that Israel's nuclear activities are strictly peaceful.
2. We continue to be concerned about possible Israeli development of nuclear weapons. Although high Israeli officials have assured us the Dimona reactor is to be used for peaceful purposes only, they have admitted that changing circumstances in the Near East might drive Israel to develop nuclear weapons. Such a decision coupled with Israel's present procurement of missiles from France could be disastrous.
. . .
6. Israeli agreement to periodic inspections was predicated upon our assurances to keep them secret. Public mention of the visit must be avoided and even discussion within the U.S. Government and Embassy Tel Aviv strictly limited. Any breach of security would provide Israeli elements which oppose the inspections with a pretext for terminating them.[12]

The visit lasted two days, 17–18 January, but only the second day was spent at the Dimona site. On the first day the team visited the nuclear physics department at the Weizmann Institute and the Nachal Soreq Nuclear Research Center, thus maintaining the impression, on which the Israeli government had insisted, that it was a scientific visit. The second day was devoted to inspecting the Dimona reactor. According to the official summary report, "The inspection team spent over eleven hours at the Dimona reactor site on January 18 and inspected all significant facilities." It was the first American visit since the reactor was activated. The team learned that the reactor had gone critical on 26 December 1963, and since then had operated at low power. The team determined that the Dimona reactor "was clearly designed as an experimental reactor, capable of operation at 15 to 20 percent above [the] design power of 26 megawatts." Operation at full power was not anticipated "until late 1964."[13]

The team was very interested in the reactor fuel cycle. It was told that the fuel first loaded into the reactor core was French-owned, subject to material controls, and would be returned to France for reprocessing and plutonium recovery. Israel had available to it at least ten tons of natural uranium of its own to fuel the reactor, in addition to the uranium that France had supplied, and discussions were under way with France to obtain eight additional tons of uranium on similar terms. Israel expected that the third and subsequent loadings of metallic uranium fuel would be produced domestically via the recovery of uranium compounds from phosphate ores, followed by production of uranium metal and its fabrication into fuel elements. The team also learned that present and projected facilities would provide Dimona with the capability to produce, in a year and a half to two years, about fifty to sixty tons of uranium metal per year. The capacity of the uranium metal plant, which at the time of the visit was in its initial phase of operation, and the fuel element fabrication facility, which was expected to be in operation by the end of the year, would be sufficient to handle this amount of uranium production.[14]

Israel thus appeared not only to be seeking self-sufficiency with regard to the supply of natural uranium, but its projected production was expected to be five to six times larger than the production rate required to support the Dimona reactor—if the reactor operated according to the stated plans. Why did Israel need such a large amount of natural uranium? The Israeli hosts provided several explanations to the visitors: "desire to conserve the full uranium production potential from phosphates operations"; "the desire to be self-sufficient"; "the equipment installed is the minimum size available commercially for a one-step production process"; and "the belief that uranium price will go up."[15]

On the critical issue of plutonium reprocessing, the team was told that construction of a fuel reprocessing pilot plant, which Ben Gurion had mentioned as a possibility in his conversation with Kennedy in 1961, and which might have been identified by U.S. intelligence photo analysts during the Eisenhower administration, had apparently been delayed indefinitely. Without the construction of complex and expensive plutonium recovery facilities and without a uranium enrichment capability, Israel would lack a nuclear weapons capability. Thus, the report concluded, "Israel, without outside assistance, would not be able to produce its first nuclear device until two to three years after a decision to do so, that is, the time required to construct plutonium separation facilities and fabricate a device."[16]

The team was impressed by the size and plans for the Dimona center, "valued at $60 million," referring to it as "the most diversified and well equipped nuclear installation in Africa or the Middle East." Still, nagging questions remained: Did the Dimona project, as presented to the team, make sense? Was it rational for a small country such as Israel to invest so much of its limited funds in a second research reactor, ostensibly for peaceful research and training? Even if the Israeli statements were true, "the capacity of reactor and of fuel supply and preparation facilities would permit Israelis to redirect program toward achievement of a small nuclear weapons capability should they so decide." The team took note that the reactor was not under safeguards, except those that may have been established by the French and Norwegians. The conclusion of the team's report was that "the plant has no weapons-making capability at present, but continuing periodic inspections are recommended."[17]

THE 1965 VISIT

When Kennedy, in July–August 1963, pushed for American visits to Dimona, he specifically asked that the second visit take place in June 1964. This did not occur. In the fall of 1964 the highest U.S. representative in Tel Aviv, Deputy Chief of Mission N. Spencer Barnes, was instructed to meet with Eshkol to remind him that, in accordance with the agreement of summer 1963, the United States proposed two sets of alternative dates in October for the visit. The mounting tensions between Eshkol and Ben Gurion, however, consumed much of Eshkol's time, and he kept postponing the meeting. On 14 October 1964 the State Department instructed Ambassador Barbour to remind Israel "of high-level USG [U.S. government] interest in semi-annual schedule visits in Dimona." He was also instructed to "insist on need for two-day visit," since "on last visit team spent eleven hours on site, was unable [to] see everything and had to complete inspection by flashlight."[18] When Barbour saw Eshkol a few days later and raised the Dimona issue, Eshkol replied "somewhat wearily that there were 'too many troubles these days', " but that he hoped to provide a date by the end of the month.[19]

It took a direct presidential message to Eshkol, however, to convey effectively the importance Johnson attached to the visits and to have Eshkol set a date for the visit: the weekend of 30 January 1965. By way of explanation, Eshkol again referred to his domestic difficulties as a reason for the delay. Finally, in response to Barbour's insistence for an earlier date, Eshkol responded in jest that in any case "we cannot build a nuclear weapon in two months."[20]

As in the previous visit, the team comprised three government scientists: Staebler, who, as noted above, was senior associate director of the Division of Reactor Development at the AEC, was the team leader; Floyd L. Culler, assistant director of reactor technology at Oak Ridge National Laboratory (ORNL); and McClelland, the nuclear physicist from ACDA. In the absence of de Shalit (the designated liaison with the American teams), Igal Talmi of the Weizmann Institute was designated as the prime minister's liaison with the team. As was the case with de Shalit in the previous visit, the appointment of a well-known scientist as the team liaison accentuated Israel's effort to portray the visit as a scientific exchange between American and Israeli scientists.

The visit began on Thursday, 28 January 1965, with excursions to the Weizmann Institute and the Nachal Soreq reactor. The next day included a morning visit to the Negev Institute for Arid Zone Research at Beer Sheba, and an afternoon visit to the phosphate mine at Oron. As in the previous visit, the inspection of the Dimona reactor was scheduled for Saturday. The official preliminary American report noted that "the team suggested that the trip to Oron be deferred until Sunday to permit the visit to Dimona to begin Friday afternoon. Professor Talmi promised to investigate this possibility, but, on Thursday evening, reported that a visit to Dimona on Friday would require informing many more people about the purpose of the visit." He urged the team to accept the proposed schedule, which it did. The report also stated that "the Israelis made it rather clear that they would not favor an extension of the visit into the late evening." Still, the team wrote that "although the pace was fast and the visit not as detailed as could be desired, it is the consensus of the team that the visit provided a satisfactory basis for determining the status of activity at the Dimona site."[21]

The team's report points to a few interesting changes since the previous visit. The Dimona reactor had begun a three-month "demonstration or acceptance run" at a designated power of 26 megawatts on 7 December 1964, but operation at 32.5 megawatts was said to be within the reactor's design limits. The report stated that "there was little evidence of immediate plans for experimental use of the reactor even though the design power test run should be completed within about one month." This was "at least partially rationalized" by the fact that certain equipment would not be ready for several months. In addition, the team learned that there was "no approval of a research and development program or a budget for the fiscal year starting April 1, 1965." A research and development budget of five million Israeli pounds had been submitted by Director-General Manes Pratt, but he had been advised that he would actually receive less. The report cited Pratt as saying that he "is very pessimistic about future support and even talked of the possibility of having to shut down the reactor. Total cost of running the center would require approximately an additional 26 million Israeli pounds."[22]

There were other indications that the Dimona project was in an organizational crisis. The team was told that the construction of the uranium recovery plant associated with phosphate mining had been discontinued, though discussions on such a plant were still in progress. The plant discussed at the time of the visit would be located at Arad rather than at Oron, with a capacity of producing twelve to thirty tons of uranium a year, although a decision had not yet been made. The fuel fabrication plant in Dimona had been placed on "standby condition" on 1 January 1965, and "operation apparently will not resume for at least one year, based on fuel requirements for reactor." The uranium metal plant, which a year earlier had been said to be "in initial phases of operation," was also being shut down. The first stage of operation had been discontinued in November 1964, the processing of the present stock of material was to be completed by March 1965, at which time the plant would be placed in "standby condition." The report stated that "it was indefinite when or if the plant would be returned to operating condition."[23] The report did not mince words about the disarray in which the project was mired, at least with regard to its declared peaceful mission. In the language of the report: "Major uncertainties exist regarding the future direction of atomic energy in Israel." These were attributed to the possible desalination project (Israel wanted to desalinate sea water in order to irrigate the Negev desert), decreasing interest in developing indigenous natural uranium reactors, and increasing interest in slightly enriched uranium-fueled reactors from abroad.[24]

As to the critical issue of plutonium reprocessing, the report stated unequivocally that "there is no evidence of further activity on Pu [plutonium] extraction from irradiated fuel," apart from some basic work in progress in the extensive plutonium research facilities, using a small portion of the 150 grams of plutonium which France had supplied Israel. Regarding Dimona's potential for weapons manufacturing, the team concluded:

16. While there appears to be no near term possibility of a weapons development program at the Dimona site, the site has excellent development and

production capability that warrants continued surveillance at maximum intervals of one year.

17. Neither the total Israeli capability to produce natural uranium nor to manufacture Pu [Plutonium] at Dimona is now being used. At present, facilities do not exist to produce more than about three tons per year of natural uranium; no capability exists to produce and recover Pu. However the potential to enter into these companion efforts is there and could be implemented by installing additional equipment.[25]

These findings were summarized in a broader policy memorandum, written by the State Department and submitted to National Security Adviser McGeorge Bundy five days later. The memo, like the one of the previous year, was entitled "Dimona Inspection and Need to Implement Initiative to Prevent Nuclear Proliferation in the Near East." It noted that, "although ten hours spent at the site did not permit as detailed a visit as desirable, the team believes there was sufficient time to determine the status of activity at Dimona." On the question of Dimona's weapons potential, the memo reiterated the team's view that nothing presently suggests the existence of an early weapons development program at Dimona. Based on these findings, the memo maintained that "we can afford to accede to Prime Minister Eshkol's request that we postpone the next agreed six-monthly inspection until after the parliamentary elections in November this year."[26]

Still, the policy memo was written in a more cautious and tentative language than the inspectors' report. Unlike the AEC report, the memo raised the possibility that Israel "may have succeeded in concealing a decision to develop nuclear weapons." The memo warned that the benign findings of the team must be weighed against the following facts:

1. Israel concealed the existence of the Dimona reactor from us for about two years.
2. Israeli officials did not allow adequate time for thorough inspection of the Dimona site and arranged no visits to sites of projected related facilities.
3. Israeli officials ruled questions about procurement of uranium from abroad "outside the scope of the visits" and suggested taking them up through normal diplomatic channels.
4. Israel is acquiring missiles from France designed to accommodate either high-explosive or nuclear warhead.
5. Public and private statements by Israeli officials suggest military planning that includes the use of nuclear weapons.[27]

Based on these considerations, the memo urged the White House promptly to approve the State Department's request to initiate negotiations with Israel to extend IAEA safeguards to all Israeli nuclear facilities.

On 14 March 1965 the *New York Times* broke the story of the American-Israeli arrangement concerning visits to Dimona. John Finney's article referred to the visit as an "inspection" aimed at reassuring the United States of Israel's "peaceful intentions" in the nuclear field, and reported that on the basis of two previous inspections American officials came to the tentative conclusion that Israel was not using the Dimona reactor for the production of plutonium for nuclear weapons.[28]

Finney's story grew out of the inadvertent leads given by Deputy Prime Minister Abba Eban on the 7 March "Meet the Press" television program. When Finney questioned Eban about the peaceful nature of the Dimona reactor, Eban replied, "Your people should be satisfied with it." In a response to Finney's question about what that meant, Eban replied, "You should ask your officials in the USG." Finney, who had been the scientific editor at the *New York Times* for some years, ascertained from the AEC team leader, Ulysses Staebler, that he had visited the Dimona facility.[29] Staebler's admission was consistent with his guidance prepared by the State Department in case of questioning. Though the State Department did not initiate the disclosure, it did not deplore its policy impact either. A State Department cable to Barbour made clear that such disclosure would not complicate U.S interests, "and might even offer certain political advantages in terms [of] easing area tensions."[30]

In a damage-control effort, the State Department circulated to its posts background information on Finney's story, aimed to ease Israeli concerns. It stressed that any visits to Dimona were by courtesy of the Israeli government and could not be termed "inspections." Instead, such visits were part of "worldwide US policy of encouraging development of peaceful uses of atomic energy." To stress the routine, politically insignificant aspect of the visits, the statement emphasized that over the years U.S. scientists and students had visited many scientific centers in Israel on the Israeli government's invitation, including the Nachal Soreq reactor, the Weizmann Institute, and the Dimona reactor.[31]

The publication of the story had repercussions. A day after the Finney article was published, Israeli Ambassador Avraham Harman told Assistant Secretary Phillips Talbot that Eshkol and Golda Meir took a dim view of the disclosure. He complained about the American breach of secrecy, and warned that the results of the disclosure would be "unpredictable," since the domestic situation in Israel was "delicate" and that Eshkol was already under fire from Ben Gurion for giving in to American pressure. Talbot said that the United States regretted the leaks, noting that Finney used leads provided by Eban to gather information before American and Israeli officials were aware of the disclosure. He also added that the United States limited its comment to "broad remarks designed to fuzz details," and did not anticipate further disclosures.[32]

THE 1966–67 VISITS

The basic pattern established during the negotiations on the 1964 and 1965 visits repeated itself in subsequent years. There were always a long series of Israeli delays in arranging the visits, attributed to Israeli domestic politics and the need for secrecy. These delays led to a number of persistent presidential interventions in the form of direct messages from Johnson to Eshkol. Eshkol did not openly challenge the American request for biannual visits, based on the August 1963 exchange with Kennedy, but for one reason or another the interval between visits was always a year or more.

Sometime after the January 1965 visit, Eshkol wrote Johnson informing him that the next visit would be after the November elections, owing to domestic political considerations. Johnson agreed, but pressed Eshkol to accept IAEA safeguards for all Israeli nuclear installations or, as a less satisfactory alternative, to permit regularly scheduled semiannual visits by American or neutral third-party teams. Eshkol left these issues unanswered.

Soon after the election Barbour raised the issue of the next Dimona visit with Eshkol, but it took another six months until the visit took place. At first Eshkol claimed that he needed time to put together his new government, then he insisted on obtaining formal guarantees that complete secrecy would be observed "by all agencies of the U.S. government," in the wake of the *New York Times* article of March 1965. In early February Eshkol informed Barbour that he would give the green light for the visit no later than the second part of March, but first he had to consult with his colleagues.[33]

For the United States these delays looked like deliberate stalling. Through a variety of high-level channels, the United States reminded Israel of the quid pro quo between Dimona and other security relations. On 9 February 1966 Secretary Rusk told newly appointed Foreign Minister Eban in unequivocal terms that the "only major question that could have disastrous effect on US-Israeli relations was GOI [government of Israel] attitude on proliferation," adding that Israel must understand that the United States would be "extremely clear and utterly harsh on matter of non-proliferation."[34] After Eban returned to Israel, Barbour was instructed to see him to discuss the long-pending Dimona visit and to press for the March visit to be "as early in the month as possible," stressing that the team should have "full access to facilities and operating records." Once again, Barbour asked for semiannual visits regularly thereafter, during the months of September and March.[35]

The American insistence yielded results, as Barbour's message coincided with the negotiations for the sale of Skyhawks to Israel and the United States reminded Israel of the linkage between the two issues (see chapter 11). Once again, the prime minister's office issued an invitation for American scientists to visit Israeli scientific research institutions, including a one-day visit to Dimona. Saturday, 2 April 1966, was designated as the day of the Dimona visit, fourteen months after the last visit. State Department internal documents noted that the agreement fell short "of what we would have hoped to have achieved with Israelis by now, for example, routine semi-annual visits long enough and with sufficient access to meet our inspection requirements."[36]

Again, John Finney of the *New York Times* disclosed the April visit three months later, and once again his story caused a diplomatic uproar. The story used the term "inspection" to describe the character of the American activity at Dimona, stressing that Israel insisted on calling these annual inspections "visits." It described the inspectors as engineers, not scientists. It also mentioned explicitly only the three visits that took place under Eshkol. No signs of plutonium reprocessing were found, so the team's tentative conclusion was that the facility was not being used for producing plutonium for weapons.[37]

These disclosures embarrassed the Eshkol government, which immediately protested the publicity through diplomatic channels. It so happened that the disclosure coincided with an American decision to take up the issue of the Dimona visits with the Israeli government. After the April visit, the United States was interested in convincing the Israelis to remove the veil of secrecy from their arrangements. Ambassador Barbour decided to respond to Israeli protests by using Finney's leak to strengthen the original points he had been asked to pass on, that is, that such leaks only highlighted that the interest of both governments was to regularize the visits on a six-month basis "once and for all," and to abandon the rigid secrecy. Both governments should "work out agreed public statements announcing facts [of the] visits when they take place." The United States made clear to Israel that in the absence of IAEA safeguards it would continue to press for these visits.

This stratagem did not work. In November 1966 an accident occurred at Dimona (it became public only twenty-eight years later), the cleanup of which ended only in February 1967.[38] The next American visit to Dimona took place about two months later, on 22 April 1967, a few weeks before the 1967 war. The American team again found no evidence of weapon-related activities; the team still continued to believe that Israel lacked a reprocessing plant to extract plutonium.[39]

DUPLICITY AND COMPLICITY

In light of the revelations of Pierre Péan, Francis Perrin, and subsequent sources, it is clear that Israel concealed its reprocessing operations at Dimona from the American visitors.[40] Over the years it became publicly known (though never acknowledged) that a reprocessing plant, used to harvest plutonium from spent reactor fuel, was at the heart of the French-Israeli deal in 1957. Although Charles de Gaulle decided to end French involvement in building that facility in 1960, Israel did not abandon the project. Despite temporary setbacks, it continued the project on its own with some unofficial French assistance. According to Péan, the most intensive period of construction was in 1964–66, the same time as the American visits to Dimona.[41] Israel's cover-up was successful: the American scientists did not find what they were not supposed to find.

Did the American teams fail in their mission? Were they duped by the Israelis? Three of the American visitors to Dimona shed light on these questions—Floyd Culler, the former associate director of ORNL and a reprocessing expert, who visited Dimona four times between 1965 and 1968, the last three times as team leader; George B. Pleat, who was at Dimona three times between 1967 and 1969; and Edwin Kintner, who was at Dimona twice in 1968 and 1969.

Culler was selected for the Dimona mission by Glenn Seaborg, chair of the AEC, for his expertise in the area of reprocessing. Seaborg, along with AEC Director of Intelligence Charles Reichardt, briefed Culler on the sensitivity of the assignment and its importance to the United States. The main purpose of the visit was to determine whether a reprocessing plant and related facilities existed or were planned, based on evidence on the ground.[42]

Culler recalls that before his first trip to Israel in 1965, his team underwent State Department and CIA briefings in which it received background information on Israel and the Dimona nuclear reactor site, including limited design information for a French reactor similar to the Dimona reactor. The team was not given any drawings of the Dimona reactor. The team was then briefed about the Ben Gurion-Kennedy meeting of 1961, in which Ben Gurion laid out the purpose of the Dimona reactor, but no mention was made of Ben Gurion's comment in 1961 that "a pilot separation plant" might be operating within "three to four years." According to Culler, those briefings were preliminary and not very informative. At the time, Culler thought that perhaps it had been decided that the team should not be provided with intelligence data. For example, no aerial photographs of Dimona were shown to the team. Other intelligence, such as ground photographs or drawings or air samples or radiation measurements, were also unavailable. If the CIA had suspected that Israel might be engaged in a clandestine effort to develop a nuclear weapons capability, and it appears that that was its assumption, it chose to protect its information and not to share it with the AEC scientists.[43]

As noted earlier, the ground rules for the Dimona inspections under Johnson were different from what Kennedy had envisioned in 1963. The Israelis managed to limit the visits to Dimona to one day, run by a single team of no more than three AEC scientists. They insisted on always conducting the visit on Saturdays (the Jewish Sabbath) or other national holidays, when almost all the Dimona employees were gone and it was easier to control the visit. The team was also closely escorted by its Israeli hosts.[44] The team asked to bring its own measuring instruments (such as radiation measuring instruments), but the Israelis denied their request. It was also not permitted to collect samples of any kind for later analysis.[45] In addition, none of the team members spoke Hebrew. The record shows that since the first visit in 1961, successive teams repeatedly and pointedly complained that the one-day format was inadequate to conduct even a modest inspection, and that more back-up data were required. They were repeatedly told that these were the Israeli ground rules and that they could not be altered without jeopardizing the entire arrangement.[46]

Equally significant was the Israeli control of the visits' frequency. Fuel from the Dimona reactor could be discharged every six months or less, and subsequently reprocessed to extract plutonium of weapon-grade quality. This was the reason for Kennedy's insistence on semiannual visits. The United States government also pressed this issue with Israel on numerous occasions, but never prevailed.

The arrangements for the visits were secret, both in the United States and in Israel. In the U.S. Embassy in Tel Aviv, dealings with the Dimona visits were separated from all other political and diplomatic matters. Only Ambassador Barbour and his science attaché, Robert Webber, were directly involved in setting the schedule and other arrangements.[47] Limited intelligence briefings were informally given to the AEC team in Tel Aviv, but no debriefing was made in Tel Aviv. For security reasons the teams' reports were not written in Israel. As a matter of routine, the reports (ten to fifteen pages long) were handwritten the next day in Rome, en route from Tel Aviv.[48]

The Israeli host for most of the visits was Amos de Shalit of the Weizmann Institute (as mentioned, Igal Talmi replaced him one time in 1965). He, along with Dimona directors Manes Pratt and Yossef Tulipman, presented the facility to the American visitors and explained its scientific-technological mission. As noted, Ephraim Katzir-Katachalsky had been the host of the first American visit to Dimona in 1961. In 1962 Yuval Ne'eman, director of the Nachal Soreq Nuclear Research Center, improvised a visit of the AEC inspectors who had come to

Soreq and Dimona. De Shalit was apparently asked to be the host for two reasons: first, to highlight the Israeli portrayal of those visits as a scientific exchange, and, second, to add credibility to the explanation that Dimona's purpose was for scientific training and research.[49]

The Israeli desire to portray the visits as scientific exchanges, rather than as inspections, had implications beyond political symbolism. The Israelis insisted on spending a great deal of the time allotted to the Dimona visit discussing scientific projects. This practice resulted in limiting the time available for the team to do its necessary inspections and related activities. Many of these activities had to be delayed into the evening and night hours, and were conducted in a rush.[50]

During each visit, Israeli data about the reactor, its fuel elements, fuel fabrication, and low-level waste plants were gathered and verified by the team to the extent that visual inspection allowed. Culler recalls that on each of his Dimona visits he was shown the spent fuel stored in a standard water-filled cooling basin on site. The team was shown records of irradiation for each fuel rod, which were in Hebrew. The Israeli hosts gave a summary of the operation of the reactor for the period since the last visit, including the hours operated and power levels. On one subsequent visit, the team was told that one shipment of spent fuel had been sent to Marcoule, France, for reprocessing. Subsequently small quantities of plutonium were returned to Israel for experimental purposes. The Israeli statement about the shipment of the spent fuel was confirmed by the French during a visit Culler made at a later date to Marcoule.[51]

The American teams did not find evidence of weapon-related activities, that is, they did not find evidence of the existence of a reprocessing plant at Dimona. Nor were signs of a high-level waste system detected. Israeli claims about the reactor and all experimental programs at the Dimona facility were divulged and verified, and explanations as to the scientific and technological utility of Dimona were given. Israel did not hide the fact that it had an interest in acquiring as much self-sufficiency as possible with regard to the nuclear fuel cycle, including limited experiments in plutonium separation, which were conducted in the small hot cells at Dimona. This, however, was not inconsistent with the explanation given by de Shalit and his colleagues. Such ambitions were consistent with the period's high hopes for the future of peaceful uses of nuclear energy, and was not enough to constitute evidence that Israel was developing nuclear weapons.[52]

Culler and Pleat now confirm, three decades later, that they had many unresolved questions about the Dimona facility and whether its peaceful purpose, as posited by the Israelis, was credible. The research efforts conducted at Dimona were limited in scale and scope for such a facility. Culler was aware of

Science Attaché Webber's questions about Dimona: Would a small country invest so much of its limited resources in a big research reactor just to gain basic nuclear technology?[53] Furthermore, the lack of a clear technological or scientific mission for the Dimona project was obvious to the visiting team as early as 1964–65. Israel did not have a nuclear power program, nor any specific approved plan, yet it made great efforts to establish plutonium fuel cycle self-sufficiency.

For Culler, the official Israeli explanation of the Dimona project did not seem sufficient to justify a facility of its size. Culler and his colleagues, however, recognized at the outset that the political rationale—prestige and posturing—was as important as the technological rationale. It was obvious that beyond any specific power program, Israel was determined to position itself ahead of anybody else in the Middle East as far as nuclear technology was concerned. Peres's and Bergmann's talk of nuclear independence did not seem so different from that in both India and France. This was an era, Culler stresses, when nuclear energy and nuclear reactors were symbols of national prestige. The bottom line was that as long as no indications of plutonium separation beyond the experimental level were found, it was impossible to say that Israel had embarked on the nuclear weapons path.[54]

The American teams were unable to find indications of reprocessing, but to suggest that they were fooled into thinking that Dimona was only a peaceful facility would be inaccurate. As early as the first visit to Dimona in 1961, the Staebler team had recognized both its own technical limitations and the fact that the reactor was providing Israel with a future nuclear-weapons option. This awareness intensified during Culler's years as team leader. The working assumption was that Israel probably lacked a reprocessing facility, but the teams never felt completely confident of their findings. Given the constraining ground rules, especially that no outside instruments or sampling were allowed, the conclusions were always tentative.[55] The steady and visible growth of activities at the Dimona site reinforced the suspicion that the Dimona complex might be of dual use. The teams did not discover the ongoing clandestine activities at Dimona, but they had been equipped with neither the political mandate nor the intelligence and technical means and time required to detect such activity.

THE WEBBER REPORT

Another opportunity to examine the way the United States was grappling with the question of the purpose of the Dimona project may be found in a six-page study, prepared in April 1965 by Robert Webber, the science attaché at the American Embassy in Tel Aviv.[56] The report started with the presumption that

Israel did not have a dedicated nuclear weapons program at the time the report was written ("there is ample independent evidence that Israel has not assembled nuclear weapons and is not now in the process of doing so" [2]) and that Dimona had no capability to separate plutonium. Webber analyzed the issue using methods and arguments from the sociology and economics of science.

One such method is to compare Dimona with true research institutions elsewhere in Israel in terms of capital investment per professional scientist. Such a comparison shows, the study states, that "to bring Dimona into line with the best equipped of these other laboratories would require a staff of professional nuclear scientists about three times as large as the total number of such men now resident in Israel" (3). According to Webber's figures, "the total capital investment in the Dimona establishment is believed to be about $60 million." Even if one allows a generous ratio of capital investment of $100,000 per research scientist (more than the Weizmann Institute) (3),[57] "the operation of Dimona as a research establishment would require a staff of 600 professional scientists and engineers." But the total number of Israeli scientists and engineers doing research in all fields was, in 1965, about twenty-one hundred of which two hundred were estimated to be professional personnel in nuclear science, distributed in the following way: ninety-three at Soreq, fifty-five at the Weizmann Institute, forty at Dimona ("a very rough guess"), ten at the Technion, and five at the Hebrew University (3).

On the basis of this data, Webber drew the following conclusion: "If Israel were to staff Dimona with enough talent to permit a reasonably economical use of the capital investment, it would have to find ways of recruiting three times as many nuclear scientists as now reside in the whole nation." Furthermore, Webber continues:

In studying the impact of Dimona, it must constantly be kept in mind that Israel is a small and not very populous nation. The commendable scientific reputation of the Weizmann Institute, the Hebrew University and the Technion sometimes obscures the fact that these three institutions taken together employ only about 1,000 professional scientists and engineers and that the total capital they have expended on laboratories and research facilities since the establishment of the State amounts to only about $58 million. The $60 million spent on plant and facilities at Dimona looms large in this perspective. It is hardly surprising that the academic scientists sometimes become irritable when they hear Dimona referred to as a research facility. (3–4)

The other perspective in considering the question of Dimona's purpose is in terms of its research equipment and products. Based on the findings of the 1965 American visit to Dimona, Webber noted that "aside from the very modest research activities . . . nearly all of the considerable facilities at Dimona seems to be devoted to the various stages of fueling and operating the reactor and handling the Plutonium which is to be produced." Moreover, Webber questioned Israel's commitment to attain fuel-cycle self-sufficiency since it had no nuclear power program:

> The great expense and considerable talent being devoted to developing this technology are alleged to be justified on the grounds that Israel must prepare itself for the electric power reactors and desalination reactors which will certainly be installed within the next twenty years. Why Israel feels it must be prepared to build its own reactors and produce its own fuel for these commercial enterprises is unclear, particularly since the United States, Canada, Britain and France are all eager to sell reactors and provide fuel on quite favorable terms. In other areas of advanced technology—e.g. jet airplanes, steam turbines, locomotives, oceanliners—Israel seems quite content to let other nations sweat out the development costs and provide the finished product. Autarkic arguments appear to have prevailed with regard to the development of reactor technology. (4)

Webber's conclusion was that it did not make any sense that Dimona was built for scientific research and training, the reasons officially given for it. A country like Israel, which must husband its resources, would not have made such an investment. The Dimona facility, therefore, must be dedicated to national security, that is, the Israelis are positioning themselves "so that they can move to the making of weapons in a relatively short time if the international situation should appear to require it." Webber, like the American visiting teams, did not question the presumption that Israel was committed not to build nuclear weapons, but he was impressed by "how much progress Israel has made along the path to a nuclear weapon." Should the government of Israel make "an early decision to move in this direction," that is, "replace French fuel in [the] reactor with Israeli (uncontrolled) fuel. . . . [and start] construction of chemical separation plant," by 1967 it could "put [the] chemical separation plant into operation," and by 1968 it could "assemble and test [an] explosive device." This timetable led Webber to the conclusion that "in addition to the minor motive of bluff and the somewhat more important one of gaining expertise in nuclear technique, the Israelis have now created a flexible basis of choice regarding the possibility of producing nuclear weapons" (6).

Still, Webber's assumption at the time of writing was that "weapons are not now being made, and there is no evidence that the Israelis have made a decision to move the rest of the way towards producing them" (6). The report was not signed by Barbour but by his deputy chief of mission, William N. Dale. According to Dale, the two of them had initiated the report—it was not the result of a request from Washington or Barbour. The ambassador kept his distance from the document, but he did not discourage his colleagues from writing it.[58]

AFTERTHOUGHTS

The history of the American visits to Dimona was more complex than had been anticipated by Kennedy or the American scientists involved. As early as 1962 or 1963, possibly even earlier, U.S. intelligence agencies assumed that "a reprocessing plant was there [in Dimona] too." This assumption, however, was not shared with Culler's team.[59] There are other indications that the U.S. intelligence community knew more about Dimona than was told to the visiting teams (the CIA station chief in Tel Aviv never met with the teams).[60] Even Ben Gurion's comment to Kennedy in 1961 that a "pilot separation plant" would probably be in operation within "three to four years" was not included in the information the teams received in their Washington briefings.[61]

President Johnson was also more flexible than Kennedy on the rules of the Dimona inspections. The Israelis were able to determine the rules of the visits, and the Johnson administration chose not to confront Israel on the issue, fearing that Israel would end the arrangement. Culler recalls that his assumption at the time was that the restrictions were agreed on at the highest level in both countries.[62] Kennedy threatened both Ben Gurion and Eshkol that noncompliance with his request could "jeopardize American commitment to Israel's security and well being," but Johnson was unwilling to risk an American-Israeli crisis over the issue. Thus it was Johnson's reluctance to press the issue that determined the form and manner of the visits.

Johnson and the CIA likely sensed what Israel was doing. They were probably not fooled by Israel's effort to deceive the American scientists. They must have also concluded that any effort to stop Israel's nuclear weapons project was futile. Unlike Kennedy, Johnson was looking for a compromise that would serve the interests of both nations. The U.S. visiting teams were part of the compromise. They were burdened with an onerous technical task in an awkward political situation. Many years later Culler shrugged off Israel's alleged "cheating" as "perhaps inevitable," given their perception of a threat at the time and their lack of an external security guarantee.[63] It is not that the visiting scientists were incompetent, but that, given Israel's determination and the way Israel controlled the visits, the visitors had little chance to find out what was going on in Dimona.

The American visits to Dimona did not curb the Israeli nuclear weapons program. They succeeded, however, in reinforcing the element of secrecy in Israel's nuclear weapons policy. This was critical to the development of Israel's nuclear opacity.

On 22 November 1963 John F. Kennedy was assassi-
nated and Lyndon B. Johnson became president.
The transition from Kennedy to Johnson reminded
Israelis of the transition from Ben Gurion to Eshkol.[1]
Eshkol and Johnson both pledged to continue their
predecessors' policies, but their style and experience
were different. Both were consensus builders, interested in domestic rather than foreign policies. This
similarity was important for their developing relationship. It also benefited the Israeli nuclear program.

Eshkol was not as anxious as Ben Gurion about
Israel's future and survival, while Johnson was less preoccupied than Kennedy with nuclear weapons proliferation. Like other vice presidents, Johnson was not kept
informed on many foreign-policy issues, Dimona
among them. For Johnson and Eshkol, who seemed to
be more interested in maintaining the good relationship between the two nations, the nuclear issue was a
nuisance to be dealt with but not a reason for a confrontation between Israel and the United States.

Two other factors were relevant to Johnson's policy
toward the Israeli nuclear program. First, Johnson
inherited the Dimona deal that Kennedy had crafted.
He was not in a position to rewrite it, and the bureaucracy expected him to support its implementation.
Second, Johnson became president with only a year
remaining before the next election, and he had to put
together a domestic constituency that would support
him. Johnson already had close ties with prominent
Jews who felt strongly about Israel's security. Furthermore, Johnson had visited the Nazi concentration
camp at Dachau after the end of the Second World

War, and was affected by what he saw.[2] Johnson also lacked Kennedy's interest in nuclear proliferation in addition to his personal and political reasons for supporting Israel. A confrontation with Israel on the nuclear weapons issue was therefore less likely than it had been during Kennedy's years.

The parameters of the compromise on Israel's nuclear program that Eshkol and Johnson cobbled together were these: Israel would not be the first state to introduce nuclear weapons into the Middle East, while the United States would provide Israel with sophisticated conventional armaments so that Israel could defend itself without recourse to nuclear weapons. This compromise was followed by other understandings reached during Johnson's tenure: Eshkol's visit in June 1964 resulted in the supply of hundreds of M-48 tanks to Israel; the Harriman-Komer mission to Israel in March 1965 led to the sale of forty-eight A-4 Skyhawk planes to Israel; and the understandings concerning visits to Dimona.

TANKS AND ATOMS

Israel fulfilled its part of the January 1964 understanding concerning the visit to Dimona—the American visitors found no weapon-related activities there. It now expected the United States to reciprocate, which it did by selling Israel the M-48 tanks. Eshkol requested the tanks in his 4 November 1963 letter to Kennedy, and the request was discussed during the American-Israeli security exchange in Washington later that month.

On 23 December Ambassador Barbour met Eshkol to review "problems of mutual concern that lie ahead." He stressed that Israel must understand "the absolute requirement that the U.S. retain working influence with the Arabs." In this context Barbour referred to Dimona: "Soon Dimona will go critical . . . [and] the fact is not likely to remain long secret." He added that even the *impression* (emphasis in original) that Israel might be developing a weapon may provoke Nasser. Barbour did not say so explicitly, but he subtly reminded Eshkol that the United States wanted to be able to reassure Nasser that the Dimona reactor's purpose was peaceful. Eshkol did not refer to Dimona in his reply, but highlighted Israel's security problem and the need to spend "tens of millions of dollars on tanks and planes." With no formal treaty with the United States, no military contingency arrangements, and no U.S. military assistance, Eshkol noted, "you [the United States] must make a special effort to help us to overcome this impossible burden of security."[3] This was Eshkol's reference to the Americans' obligations in the deal over Dimona.

In mid-January, at the time of the Dimona visit, Israel's request for tanks was studied at the Department of the Army. The issues involved were primarily technical, matters of inventory, scheduling, and financing.[4] The U.S. government decided in favor of the tank sale to Israel, but there were issues involving the impact of the sale on U.S.-Arab relations and the question of Dimona. It took another eight months of negotiations before the deal was completed.

Declassified material available from U.S. and Israeli archives illuminates the linkages among tanks, nuclear weapons, missiles, and "reassuring Nasser." This was evident in a 18 February 1964 memorandum that Robert Komer sent Johnson about differences within the administration on how to reply to Eshkol's 4 November letter. Komer asked Johnson to decide how explicit the linkage should be:

> This reply raises both a major policy issue—how far to link tanks to our concerns over Israel's move toward a missile (and perhaps nuclear) capability—and a tactical question as to whether we should agree right now to sell tanks. Mike [Myer] Feldman favors doing so now. State, Bundy and I are vigorously opposed. We think you should retain flexibility on this matter till the moment of maximum flexibility, and believe we should first attempt to dissuade Israel from taking the highly risky missile road.[5]

The question of linkage emerged in Komer's memo from another angle: reassuring Nasser on Dimona. Kennedy's interest in reassuring Nasser was evident from the beginning, and it was a major reason for his insistence on American inspection of the reactor in 1961. The issue became more important in the spring of 1963, when Kennedy received a private message from Nasser stating that Dimona could trigger another war.[6] In August 1963, however, when Eshkol agreed to American visits to Dimona, he refused to allow information to be passed to Nasser. He agreed to think the issue over, however, leaving the door open for later American appeals.

For American policymakers, persuading Nasser about the peaceful intent of the nuclear research at Dimona was the whole point. Without it, the inspection of Dimona made little sense. McGeorge Bundy said as much in a memo submitted along with the team's findings:

> President Nasser had indicated that acquisition of a nuclear weapons capability by Israel would be cause for war no matter how suicidal for the Arabs. It is vital for the preservation of peace in the Near East, therefore, to reassure Nasser as to the peaceful nature of the 24 megawatt reactor Israel has just activated in Dimona. . . .

With the completion of the first inspection since activation, we should press Prime Minister Eshkol to agree to our discreetly passing our findings to

President Nasser. We regard reassurances to Nasser about Israel's nuclear intentions and capabilities as essential to offset the news of Dimona having gone critical. This is certain to reach Nasser soon. Coming at a time when Israel's building up a sophisticated missile capability that may also become public, we think that passage of such reassurances as we can give is the minimum [needed] to prevent some drastic United Arab Republic move to acquire a new level of Soviet weaponry.

Past experience has shown that direct intervention by the President is the most effective way to obtain Israel's cooperation on the Dimona problem. We believe firm and persistent persuasion by the President will induce Prime Minister Eshkol's compliance. We believe it desirable to continue treating the problem of reassuring Nasser orally. This permits greater flexibility and does not risk hardening either Israel's position or ours.[7]

This memo reflects the dominant thinking among those responsible in Washington for shaping American policy in the Middle East. In early 1964 Dean Rusk and Phillips Talbot (State Department), and Bundy and Komer (White House) believed that reassuring Nasser on the matter of Dimona was a vital aspect of the U.S. strategy to retain its influence with the Arabs. These policy makers impressed upon Israeli diplomats the danger they saw in Dimona: "while Nasser would not see Israeli withdrawal of Jordan basin waters [as a] *casus belli*, he would see Dimona [as a] *casus belli*."[8]

In his 18 February memo to Johnson, Komer asked for presidential pressure on Eshkol to allow the United States to tell Nasser about the Dimona reactor.[9] Two days later Johnson replied to Eshkol's 4 November 1963 letter to Kennedy about the sale of U.S. tanks to Israel. Johnson expressed his personal support for Israel's request to modernize its tank force and his concerns over the missile program and the possibly negative effects of Dimona becoming critical without reassuring the Arab states. Timing was important: the United States wanted to agree on the tank sales before Eshkol's visit to Washington, and it was eager to obtain the Israelis' permission to allow Assistant Secretary of State Talbot to convey a positive message to Nasser during Talbot's planned trip to Egypt in March.

On 28 February Ambassador Walworth Barbour presented the American position to Eshkol, arguing that such an assurance, which Ben Gurion had agreed to in 1961, was important for maintaining stability in the Middle East.[10] On 5 March Barbour received the Israeli reply from Arieh Levavi. He was told that after much "soul searching," Eshkol concluded that he must turn down the American request to reassure Nasser, citing a similar refusal by Ben Gurion in May 1963. Eshkol explained the rejection of the American request by citing two political considerations:

In the first place, it does not appear advisable to release President Nasser from any apprehension he may entertain as to Israel's military capacities. President Nasser loses no opportunity of publicly emphasizing that war with Israel is inevitable, as soon as his military preparations are sufficiently advanced. . . . The Prime Minister is of the view that the removal from President Nasser's mind of uncertainty regarding Israel's deterrent capacity would be contrary to the best interests of both the United States and Israel.

There is a further consideration: it would seem highly imprudent to apprise President Nasser of the nature of the United States-Israel contacts on this as on other matters. In view of past experiences the Prime Minister considers that President Nasser cannot be relied on not to exploit such information either publicly or through diplomatic channels. If such information were to become known harmful consequences and repercussions would ensue.[11]

Levavi, who presented the Israeli reply, told Barbour that Eshkol found it difficult to disagree with Johnson, but that even in August 1963 Eshkol had questioned the wisdom of the U.S. policy. Barbour responded that in case of a negative Israeli response he had been instructed to explain the American point of view in person to the prime minister. A meeting between Barbour and Eshkol was quickly arranged for later that afternoon. Barbour, emphasizing the U.S. concern over Nasser's reaction were he to conclude that Israel was developing nuclear weapons, asked whether Israel would object if the United States, without revealing its sources, told Nasser that, based on its best information, Israel was not producing nuclear weapons. Eshkol said that he had a better idea: Israel was ready to make a public commitment of nonaggression toward any Arab state. Would the United States obtain a similar nonaggression commitment from Egypt? Barbour insisted that this was not what was at stake—the issue was how to prevent Nasser from going to war over Dimona. Eshkol responded that Nasser was repeatedly threatening war against Israel, so that "it is good for Nasser to worry about Israel's military capabilities." When Barbour asserted that the United States would not stand idly by in case of Egyptian aggression against Israel, Eshkol interjected that Israel was still waiting to hear about the sale of American tanks to Israel. Eshkol ended the meeting by repeating that it was difficult for him to reject the American request, but that he saw no other choice.[12]

Israeli diplomats were aware of the unstated linkage between Israel's response to the U.S. request and Israel's chances of obtaining U.S. tanks.[13] Eshkol's negative answer delayed the tank deal; Johnson adopted the recommendations of Bundy and Komer to hold off his final approval on supplying tanks to Israel.[14] On 19 March Bundy issued National Security Action Memorandum (NSAM) 290, entitled "Meeting Israeli Arms Requests," in which the secretaries of state and defense and the director of the CIA were instructed to review all aspects of the problem, recommending a course of action by 1 May 1964. NSAM 290 does not make the linkage explicit, but it is there nonetheless.[15] It relieved Johnson of the need to make an immediate decision on the tank deal and gave him more time to pressure Eshkol about reassuring Nasser on Dimona.

On 19 March 1964 Johnson sent a three-paragraph letter to Eshkol urging him to reconsider his position on the issue, warning him of the consequences:

> We are far from confident that apprehension as to Israel's atomic potential will, as you suggest, help deter Nasser from attacking Israel. Quite the contrary, we believe that Nasser's fear of a developing Israel nuclear power may drive him to a choice between accelerating the UAR military build up or a desperate preemptive attack. Either of these choices would have the greatest effects on the security of Israel. We think it plain that any possible deterrent value that might come from keeping Nasser in the dark is trivial compared to these risks.
>
> It is also hard to see how Nasser could adversely exploit reassurances that Israel's nuclear activities are for peaceful purposes. We certainly do not intend to provide him with details. Nor did he misuse our reassurances when, with the agreement of your government, we last informed him along these lines. Indeed our doing so served to ease Arab-Israeli tensions.[16]

Eshkol replied on 15 April, but his letter is still classified. A week earlier, however, upon Myer Feldman's return from Israel, Eshkol had an occasion to send Johnson another letter in which he set the stage for their discussions at the White House. In the four-page letter he made his case for Israeli deterrence:

> In view of our excessive vulnerability—the paucity of air fields and the density of population within a very small geographical area—the danger of sudden attack is ever present. The U.S. commitment to halt aggression cannot in itself remove this danger. It is our conviction that the only way to prevent war is for President Nasser to know that Israel possesses [an] adequate deterrent capacity.[17]

Dimona was not mentioned, but Eshkol explained why he must refuse the American request to reassure Nasser. To prevent war Nasser must be deterred, not reassured. Eshkol asked Johnson not to link "the specific matter of armor which has passed through all possible stages of study and analysis" to "the clarification of certain security issues on which there may [be] differences of assessments." The tank deal should "find an immediate and affirmative determination," while the latter issue "must await our meeting in June."[18]

In the wake of NSAM 290 and Johnson's 19 March letter to Eshkol, the package—tanks, missiles, and the Dimona reactor—remained on hold. Bundy and Komer recommended delaying the tank deal until Israel clarified its position on missiles and Dimona. In a 23 April conversation with the Israeli diplomat Mordechai Gazit, Bundy and Komer further clarified the linkage: they asked that, in return for the tanks, Israel make an outright commitment not to develop nuclear weapons. When it was made clear that such a commitment could not be made, Bundy noted that, despite all its efforts, the United States still had not reached a completely open relationship with Israel.

On 11 May 1964 Feldman again wrote to Johnson, urging him to approve the sale of tanks to Israel. Feldman did not refer to the Israeli nuclear program, but he mentioned the linkage between supplying tanks to Israel and dissuading Israel from proceeding in its missile program. Although Feldman supported the administration's policy of preventing a missile race in the Middle East, he cautioned against linking the sales of tanks with that objective: "It is difficult to tell a sovereign power what weapons it needs for its defense. The existence of Egyptian missiles and the fact that the Israeli government has already contracted for 25 experimental missiles from France makes it impossible to condition the sale of tanks upon a renunciation of missiles."[19]

By mid-May Israel began to use the linkage between the two issues to advance its own objectives. In a telegram to Rusk on the Eshkol visit, Barbour explained that, without a substantial U.S. contribution to Israeli conventional military capabilities, Israeli leaders would have to adopt an "independent deterrent capability."[20] An Israeli agreement on Dimona depended on Israel's assessment of its security needs.

In April another dispute over nuclear issues erupted between the United States and Israel. On 11 July 1964 the agreement concerning U.S. inspections of the Nachal Soreq reactor was to expire. The United States, as part of a global policy for nuclear facilities built under its Atoms for Peace program, insisted on transferring its inspection responsibilities to the IAEA, making Soreq an IAEA safeguarded facility; if Israel refused, the United States threatened to let the agreement expire. Israel objected, arguing that until Egypt accepted IAEA safeguards on its Soviet reactor, and until Israel was included in the activities of the IAEA in the region, it would not accept IAEA safeguards. Israel asked the United States to extend the agreement for two more years, at which time it would review the situation again.[21]

The tank sale to Israel faced other problems. The Johnson administration recognized that Israel needed to modernize its tank fleet, yet it was not ready to supply Israel directly with offensive weapons, preferring that such sales go through a European country. A small Pentagon team was sent to London and Bonn in early May 1964 to explore ways of selling one hundred to three hundred medium tanks to Israel.[22] On 16 May Johnson sent Feldman to Israel for the second time in two months to urge Israeli leaders to purchase British or German tanks and to caution them against "going for [a] nuclear capability."[23] The Israelis made it clear that they were interested only in American tanks. The tank deal was not resolved and had to await the visits to Washington of Eshkol and German chancellor Ludwig Erhard.

THE FIRST JOHNSON-ESHKOL MEETING

Eshkol's visit to Washington on 1–3 June 1964 was the first official visit by an Israeli prime minister to the White House. In a memorandum to the president on the eve of Eshkol's arrival, Komer spelled out the issues outstanding between the two nations:

> *Tanks.* We appreciate Eshkol's understanding as to why we simply can't afford to sell Israel tanks directly. But we'll do everything we can to help get them elsewhere. . . .
>
> *The UAR Missile Threat and Israel's Own Missile Plans.* We've been over this ground many times unsuccessfully, but Feldman put Eshkol on notice that you'd have a personal try. . . . We can't veto Israel's missile, but as Israel's security guarantor we're entitled to ask it not to buy operational missiles until after it has consulted us.
>
> *Dimona Reactor.* We appreciate Israel's commitment to regular inspection but are disturbed at Eshkol's refusal to let us reassure the Arabs in general terms (you sent two messages on this). We're firmly convinced that Israel's apparent desire to keep the Arabs guessing is highly dangerous. To appear to be going nuclear without really doing so is to invite trouble. It might spark Nasser into a foolish preemptive move. Without in any way implying that Israel is going nuclear, one has to admit that a functioning secret breeder reactor plus an oncoming missile delivery system add up to an inescapable conclusion that Israel is at least putting itself in a position to go nuclear. This could have the gravest repercussions on U.S.-Israeli relations, and the earlier we try to halt it the better chance we have.
>
> *IAEA Controls.* Israel's reluctance to accept IAEA controls also adds to our suspicions. We can't make Israel an exception because we're making sixty or so other clients of ours toe the IAEA line.[24]

Johnson had to decide whether and how to link these issues. The official

American and Israeli minutes of the meeting show that Johnson did not link the sale of tanks to the ballistic missiles and nuclear weapons issues. Instead, he reassured Eshkol of the U.S. commitment to Israel's security ("that he was foursquare behind Israel on all matters that affected their vital security interests"), and said that since the United States could not provide tanks to Israel directly, "we would be glad to help Israel in every possible way to get a sufficient quantity of tanks elsewhere."[25] He could not offer Israel a firm deal, however, and the issue had to wait the Erhard visit.

Johnson highlighted the danger to Israel of ballistic missiles and nuclear weapons competition:

Of course, we know that the Israeli government is worried over the UAR missile threat. But that threat is likely to remain feeble through 1970. Israel should not hasten to counter it and accelerate the arms race. It can always count on the United States in emergency. The President pointed out that the Arabs will inevitably tie Israeli missiles to Israel's nuclear potential. This is why we seek IAEA control and let us reassure Nasser about Dimona. We should like to remind the Prime Minister that we are violently against nuclear proliferation.

If Israel is not going to get into nuclear production, why not accept IAEA controls and let us reassure Nasser about Dimona. It is our firm policy to keep the UAR from getting into nuclear production and we will do everything we can to restrain them.[26]

Eshkol, for his part, elucidated the "do it yourself" approach as the lesson Zionists drew from Jewish history. The Israelis had learned:

that they must work out their own destiny by depending on themselves and doing things for themselves. They could not depend on others. They were now a small nation compressed into 20,000 sq. kilometers and therefore an easy target . . . Nasser would attack Israel if he felt that he could [do] that. Then, in one day or two or three days he could do a great deal of damage. No one could forecast what other problems the United States would have at that time." (5–6)

Eshkol then moved to specific issues. On tanks, he made it clear that Israel needed the American M-48, not the British Centurion (the M-48 can operate twice as long without refueling as the Centurion). On missiles, Eshkol pointed out that Egypt already had two hundred missiles; if Nasser were willing to give up his missiles, Israel would not acquire any. Israel, however, had indications that Nasser was planning to augment his missile force by hundreds of missiles.

He added that "Israel would be prepared to wait a year or two, but Nasser was constantly improving his missiles, and in the next 2 to 3 years Nasser is likely to attack and to use them." If Egypt attacked Israel, other Arab states would join it. Israel could not sit idly by while Nasser continued to add to his arsenal. "In any case, for a year or two there would be no missiles in Israel."

Eshkol then said:

> We cannot afford to lose. This may be our last stand in history. The Jewish people have something to give to the world. I believe that if you look at our history and at all the difficulties we have survived, it means that history wants us to continue. We cannot survive if we experience again what happened to us under Hitler. You may view the situation otherwise and it may be difficult to grasp how we feel. I believe you should understand us. (7–8)

Eshkol again rejected Johnson's proposal that Nasser be given information about Dimona to assuage his suspicions:

> I cannot agree that Nasser should be told the real situation in Dimona because Nasser is an enemy. . . . while the UAR remains an enemy and is committed to the destruction of Israel, it would seem inadvisable to communicate such matters to him. Besides, Nasser has worked for years to become a nuclear power. He will continue to do so. A message that Dimona is not manufacturing nuclear weapons would have no effect. (10)

Eshkol insisted that Israel was not producing nuclear weapons, but posed the question: "Why tell Nasser? Why should we tell Nasser when we don't know from him what he is doing about missiles?" (10–11).[27]

There were differences between the Johnson and Eshkol discussions in 1964 and the talks between Kennedy and Ben Gurion in 1961. Kennedy was concerned about the Israeli nuclear program and its future direction, whereas Johnson did not ask any questions on the purpose of Dimona. Johnson did not comment on U.S. visits to Dimona. Eshkol, except for noting that Israel was not engaged in "nuclear production," said nothing about the peaceful purpose of the Dimona reactor. He also did not refer to or make commitments about what Israel would do in the nuclear field in the future. Eshkol, unlike Ben Gurion, also refused to permit the relaying of information about Dimona to Nasser.

The issue of reassuring Nasser remained a sour point. In a memorandum prepared for Johnson's second meeting with Eshkol, Komer noted that "the issues of whether Israel will *accept IAEA controls* and whether it will permit us to *reassure Nasser on Dimona* are still open," and added "its important that you express your interest in both . . . because Eshkol asked how serious you were about them." Komer recommended that the president continue to push on these issues: "Therefore you urge Eshkol to agree both to *Dimona reassurances*, and to IAEA controls. These two acts would help diminish Nasser's incentive to get exotic weapons help from the USSR. Eshkol's argument 'why reassure an enemy' is short-sighted."[28]

On 2 June, before the second round of discussions between the two delegations, Johnson met Eshkol alone for ten minutes. Johnson urged Eshkol to reconsider Israel's position on reassuring Nasser, referring to his two previous letters on this subject. When they emerged from their meeting, Komer asked Johnson, in front of the two delegations, whether he and Eshkol had settled the issue of reassuring Nasser. Johnson answered, "No, there was no agreement on that." When Komer asked whether they had settled the question of the IAEA, Johnson again replied that there had been no meeting of minds on that either. According to Ambassador Harman's minutes, the American delegation, especially Komer, was disappointed by Johnson's report of no progress on the question of Dimona.[29]

Eshkol did reconsider the issue following a short private meeting with Johnson. Given the successful visit, and the personal way that Johnson had made the request, Eshkol later found it unwise to turn the president down. Shimon Peres, his deputy, was now the problem. The idea of deterrence by uncertainty was his, and he opposed the proposal to reassure Nasser. In any case, Johnson's soft and friendly approach (as Komer called it) paid off. On the most important issue, reported Komer in another memo to Johnson, the Israelis "agreed to let us reassure Nasser on Dimona."[30] The Israelis also offered a compromise on the matter of IAEA safeguards for the Soreq reactor: the agreement would be extended for another nine months, during which time Israel would negotiate with the IAEA on a safeguards agreement for Soreq.[31]

After Eshkol's visit, the United States kept its word and arranged for the sale of American tanks from Germany to Israel,[32] although Johnson had "to twist Erhard's arm" in order to win the chancellor's reluctant consent.[33] Later in the summer the Pentagon agreed to provide Germany 200 new M-48s in return for Germany's delivery to Israel of 150 older M-48s from its inventory.[34]

THE HARRIMAN-KOMER MISSION

In early 1965 the tank sale was leaked to the German press and Chancellor Erhard decided to back out. Of the 150 tanks, 90 remained undelivered. The German decision came while the Johnson administration was considering the sale of tanks to Jordan, leading the administration to consider selling American offensive weapons to both Israel and Jordan. In return for supplying Israel, the administration again linked the sale of conventional arms to the nuclear issue, demanding additional Israeli concessions: the Israelis were asked "to accept full IAEA safeguards on all their nuclear facilities and to provide assurances that they would not develop a nuclear weapons capability."[35]

To explain the sale of tanks to Jordan, and negotiate the terms of the U.S.-Israeli security understandings, Undersecretary of State Averell Harriman and White House aide Robert Komer flew to Israel in late February 1965. In their talks the link between conventional arms and Israel's nuclear program was discussed more explicitly than before. Although Harriman led the mission, it was Komer who handled the more sensitive aspects of the negotiations. Komer knew that negotiating with the Israelis over nuclear issues would be difficult, but he did not realize how difficult it actually would be.[36]

Israel had no objection to the sale of American armor and aircraft to Jordan, as long as Jordan did not deploy the weapons in the West Bank and Israel received compensation. In return, the United States would deliver the remaining ninety M-48A3 tanks of the German-Israeli tank deal of 1964 and an additional hundred or more tanks later. The United States was also ready, for the first time, to consider the sale of jet fighter planes to Israel. Israel asked for a large number of tactical bombers, such as the F-4B (Phantom) or B-66, but the United States was only willing to consider a much smaller number of A-4s (Skyhawk).[37] The real difficulties arose over nuclear issues.

By 1965 the White House and the CIA concluded that the Dimona visits would not accomplish the goal set for them by the Kennedy administration. The visits could not determine the status of nuclear research and development in Israel. The American alternative to the visits was IAEA safeguards on Dimona. Komer's mission was to persuade the Israelis to accept this alternative.[38] Israel objected, pointing out that Egypt had not yet placed its own reactor under IAEA safeguards. Eshkol reiterated that Israel would not be the first country in the region to introduce nuclear weapons, and Peres used a similar phrase when he discussed with Komer the French-Israeli missile project a few months earlier.[39] Bundy and Komer understood, however, that behind the vague pledge a secret development effort was under way.

The negotiations between Komer and the Israelis were described as "rough and tough." According to Yitzhak Rabin, "Komer asked for a personal appointment with me . . . and used tough language, not excluding a veiled threat: 'If Israel embarked in that direction, it might cause the most serious crisis she ever had in her relations with the U.S.'"[40] On 1 March 1965, as the negotiations dragged on, Harriman left for India, leaving Komer in Tel Aviv to continue the talks with the Eshkol government. Komer was instructed to stay in Israel as long as necessary to persuade Israel to accept IAEA safeguards. He stayed ten more days, pressing and pushing, but all to no avail.[41] Finally, the Americans gave up.

The "Memorandum of Understanding," signed on 10 March by Eshkol, Komer, and Barbour, was a landmark in the evolution of Israel's nuclear opacity. In the first article, "the Government of the United States has reaffirmed its concern for the maintenance of Israel's security," and renewed its commitment "to the independence and integrity of Israel." In return, "the Government of Israel has reaffirmed that Israel will not be the first to introduce nuclear weapons into the Arab-Israel area."[42] This is the first time that the Israeli verbal formula became the foundation of U.S.-Israeli understandings.

On 12 March Eshkol wrote to Johnson, thanking him for sending Harriman and Komer and noting the agreements the mission had produced. Eshkol alluded to difficulties in the discussions before the agreements were reached, then added: "For myself, I am custodian of a small state and the representative of a small people. We are surrounded by enemies. I believe we will win our way to peace, but it will be a hard road. We have nowhere to retreat. You can be assured, Mr. President, that we will fulfill the agreement in complete good faith."[43] Ten days later Johnson replied, thanking Eshkol for his "thoughtful" letter, confirming the tacit understandings: "I agree with you entirely that our confidence in each other's understanding, goodwill and friendship is more important than words—though words are important, too."[44]

This exchange was different in content and tone from the exchanges between Kennedy and Ben Gurion and those between Kennedy and Eshkol in the spring and summer of 1963, respectively. In Kennedy's messages the Dimona reactor was the center of discussion, while it was never mentioned in the communications between Johnson and Eshkol on Dimona. Johnson preferred to craft a practical compromise suitable for both sides, while Kennedy was willing to risk a confrontation with Israel over the latter's nuclear program.

Johnson used the Harriman-Komer mission to test how far he could push U.S. nonproliferation policies on the Israelis. Johnson, like Kennedy, wanted Dimona placed under IAEA safeguards, but he took a different approach. He did not exert pressure on Israel through tough presidential letters, but instead relied on an emissary, a government official. When it became evident to Johnson that Eshkol had rejected Komer's pressure regarding IAEA safeguards, he backed off and avoided confrontation. The Israeli rejection of IAEA safeguards did not prevent Israel and the United States from reaching an understanding. Indeed, the United States agreed to supply Israel with conventional armaments, while Eshkol agreed that Israel would not be the first country to introduce nuclear weapons into the region

THE SKYHAWKS DEAL

The 10 March 1965 Komer-Eshkol Memorandum of Understanding was an important turning point in the American-Israeli security dialogue. Much of the dialogue in the following months was about the translation of the American commitment contained in this document into actual practice.

On 19 April 1965 Israel officially submitted to the United States a purchasing request that included 210 M-48A2 tanks, 60 self-propelled 155-mm guns, and 75 combat aircraft.[45] The State Department considered the request as exceeding Israeli security needs; the United States could not afford politically to meet the Israeli request in full, nor was it committed to do so. Instead, the State Department had its own ideas for the May discussions about what kind of military equipment it could provide Israel.[46] The tank issue was relatively easy. The United States was ready to meet the Israeli request for 210 additional M48s, including upgrade kits, to make up for the shortfall in the German delivery (110 tanks) and to offset its tank deal with Jordan (100 tanks).[47] There was bargaining on the technical aspects concerning the upgrading kits, but the deal was finalized on 29 July.[48]

The combat jet issue was a different matter. The language of the March Komer-Eshkol Memorandum of Understanding was general and vague. It stated that the United States agreed to "ensure an opportunity for Israel to purchase a certain number of combat aircraft, if not from Western [European] sources, then from the United States" (article V[c]). What did this commitment mean? This was the first time that the United States was ready to consider a sale of combat aircraft to Israel—for years it maintained that Israel must look to Europe to satisfy all its needs in the air—but such consideration was short of a full commitment to sell. During the May talks the United States maintained that it would sell Israel jet aircraft only after Israel exhausted all possible Western European sources. Furthermore, there were additional American limitations: the United States would not sell supersonic aircraft, the number would not exceed twenty-four planes (one squadron), and delivery would not start before 1967.[49]

Much of the on-going American-Israeli security dialogue in the second half of 1965 and early 1966 was about the meaning of the American commitment. Israel chose to interpret the Komer-Eshkol agreement as a presidential commitment for the sale of American planes. Israel reported to the United States about various European aircraft options it had explored—all were not suitable for one reason or another—but the Americans were left with the impression that Israel was interested in access to American planes regardless of the availability of European aircraft.[50] In June Ambassador Harman officially told the

United States that Israel could not obtain suitable planes in Europe and that the American Phantom was the only long-term solution to IAF needs.[51]

The next phase in the negotiations on the jet sale took place in October 1965, when General Ezer Weizman, the IAF chief, came to Washington to pitch Israel's case for American jets. Weizman delivered "an able and carefully tailored analysis" to a joint DOD/State group, describing the role of the IAF in deterring and winning war with Israel's main Arab adversaries. The crux of Weizman's analysis was the possibility of an all-out confrontation between Israel and the combined forces of Egypt and Syria. To face a larger number of high-performance UAR fighter and strike aircraft, Israel had some two hundred combat aircraft (nearly all of French origin). Almost half the Israeli fleet (Ouragans and Mystères) was already obsolescent and required immediate replacement. The rest of the Israeli fleet was adequate for the next few years, but was not sufficient in number to meet Israel's second-strike requirements to hit the larger number of high performance UAR aircraft and bomb radar sites and airfields in Southern Egypt.[52]

Without revealing the details of the IAF *Moked* plan to destroy the Arab air forces, Weizman hinted at its role in war.[53] The modernization plans of the IAF were derived from this planning and required two types of new aircraft: a small number of supersonic strike aircraft (or fighter bombers) capable of flying to the remote Arab air bases and back on their own, and a large number of subsonic aircraft with short takeoff and landing capabilities, capable of functioning both as interceptors and as ground-support light bombers. Weizman then presented an ambitious shopping list of 210 American combat aircraft, 45 supersonic Phantom or Intruder (A-6) jets (the IAF then had 30), and 165 of the significantly cheaper subsonic Skyhawks (the IAF then had about 120). Weizman placed particular emphasis on the latter, saying that the Israelis had exhausted the European market, particularly France, and found no comparable aircraft which met their range and take-off requirements. In addition, European planes were more expensive than the $630,000 Skyhawk.[54]

The Americans were impressed by Weizman's presentation, but his request exceeded the limits of American policy. They acknowledged the presidential commitment to the integrity and independence of Israel, but argued that Israel had not yet looked at all the possible European sources. In the meantime the American Embassy in Paris made inquiries of its own as to how far the Israelis went to examine the French option, particularly the availability of new models of the Mirages and/or Vautours.[55] Given the uncertainty about the French situation before the presidential election in France, the Americans wanted to postpone their decision until early 1966.[56] Although the Israelis were eager to break the American determination against supplying American combat planes to Israel, that determination was still strong in late 1965.[57]

Was there a linkage between the aircraft negotiation and the nuclear issue, particularly the Dimona visit? Or did the two issues merely run in parallel to each other (as "two distinct operas," using Mordechai Gazit's phrase).[58] On the surface, in 1965 the issues appeared to be unrelated. The record shows that during the early discussions of the aircraft deal, the Dimona issue was never raised. The jet deal was never explicitly mentioned in President Johnson's 1965 correspondence with Eshkol, and related diplomatic exchanges, on the nuclear issue. On 21 May 1965 Johnson wrote to Eshkol asking him to accept IAEA safeguards on all Israeli reactors. Eshkol wrote back asking to defer the issue until after the elections, but without indicating how he would respond then. When Barbour was asked to express Johnson's disappointment with Eshkol's response, he also was instructed, "but without overt linkage," to convey a sense of satisfaction about the conclusion of the tank deal.[59] Evidently the State Department wanted to conceal an explicit linkage between the two issues.

Below the surface, however, there was tacit linkage between the two issues all along. This linkage between atoms and security (as argued in chapter 9) was at the heart of American-Israeli relations since August 1963, when Eshkol reached the agreement with Kennedy about the Dimona visit. This linkage was also at the core of the March 1965 Komer-Eshkol Memorandum of Understanding, even though no explicit linkage was formed between the Israeli nuclear nonintroduction commitment and the American commitment to look after Israel's "deterrent capacity" (Article 3).[60]

In early 1966, as the new Eshkol government was pressing for the aircraft deal while continuing to delay the American visit to Dimona and deferring a response to Johnson's request regarding the IAEA, the Americans were left with no choice but to make the linkage between the two issues visible. If Israel wanted American planes it must put an end to the delaying tactics about Dimona. On 18 January, during his first meeting with Eshkol's new foreign minister, Abba Eban, Barbour made the linkage between Dimona and aircraft apparent. He stated that the "most important matter on the agenda was arranging the next US visit [to] Dimona." Barbour went on in his cable:

> I recalled Eshkol had asked [the] President to forego [the] last regular six-monthly visit until after [the] Israeli elections. Frankly, after [the] elections I was instructed urgently [to] arrange [a] time for [the] visit, but had recommended deferral until after [the] new Government [was] formed. Now we [are] asking GOI [to] invite [an] expert to visit Dimona again ASAP. I noted that [owing to] interruptions [in the] regular schedule we had not visited Dimona in almost a year. [I] [a]lso recalled that despite best efforts, [the] last visit was bobtailed. This has created certain . . . unhappiness in Washington. Now we requested [that the] visit extend through two full days, one of which

[would] be [a] working day with [the] plant in normal operation. I empha-sized again [the] utmost importance attached to these regular visits. This matter transcends others in our relationship.[61]

The linkage became transparent in another cable to Barbour from the depart-ment concerning Eban's upcoming visit to the United States. Barbour was asked to inform Eban that the United States "regard[s] it of great importance [that the] date for [the] Dimona visit be settled prior [to] his Washington visit." The American side was looking forward "to frank and friendly exchanges on [a] broad range of topics." "If [the] question of [a] Dimona inspection is still pend-ing," however, "it may be an inhibiting factor."[62] Once again, the linkage remained implicit but apparent.

Eshkol, however, continued with his delaying tactics concerning the Dimona visit. He told Barbour on 27 January 1966 that while agreeing to undertake arrangements for the Dimona visit, it would take some time. Eshkol made the point that he must consult his new cabinet colleagues, and he did not want Dimona to be the first question he put to his colleagues because it might result in a cabinet crisis. Eshkol indicated that a realistic date for the visit would be in about two months, the second half of March, weeks after Eban's visit.[63]

The linkage became even more apparent (but not yet fully explicit) in the meeting Secretary Rusk had with Eban in Washington on 9 February. After telling Eban that Johnson wanted an early decision on Israel's aircraft request, Rusk said that "the only major question that could have a disastrous effect on U.S.-Israeli relations was Israel['s] attitude on proliferation." Rusk went on: "Israel [is] apparently following a policy designed to create ambiguity in the Arab world. This also created ambiguity in Washington. Israel should expect the U.S. to be extremely clear and utterly harsh on the matter of non-proliferation." Rusk urged Eban "not to underestimate the total involvement of U.S.-Israel[i] relations in this matter."[64]

Eban also passed on Israel's response to Johnson's letter of May 1965 con-cerning IAEA safeguards. Eban stated that Israel preferred a bilateral arrange-ment over IAEA safeguards "because of the increasingly weak position of Israel in the IAEA and the growing strength of the Arabs in that body."[65] Yet he noted that the Israeli government attached "full weight" to the nonintroduction pledge given to Harriman.[66] In response, Rusk observed that this pledge might not prevent the development of a precarious situation somewhat akin to "eight months of pregnancy."[67] The pregnancy metaphor would become Rusk's con-tribution to the growing American-Israeli Talmudic debate about the nonin-troduction pledge that would reach its climax in 1968–69 (see chapters 16–17).

As on previous occasions, it was Robert Komer who made the linkage between the aircraft deal and the nuclear issue not only apparent but also explicit. In a memorandum he prepared for Johnson a day before Johnson met Eban, Komer told Johnson that "McNamara and most of the key State people, as well as Bundy and I, have come reluctantly to conclude that controlled sales best serve the U.S. interest." Among the reasons for this conclusion Komer referred to the nuclear issue in the following way:

> *Can we use the planes as a level to keep Israel from going nuclear?* Desperation is what could most likely drive Israel to this choice. Should it come to feel that the conventional balance was running against it. So judicious US arms supply, aimed at maintaining a deterrent balance, is as good an inhibitor as we've got.[68]

Komer's memo made it clear that when Johnson met Eban on 9 February it had been decided already that the United States would provide jets to Israel. Johnson hinted that to Eban, but without going into details.[69] The details of the deal, including the linkage with the nuclear issue, were left to Secretary of Defense Robert McNamara in his meeting with Eban on 12 February 1966. McNamara, told Eban that the United States could not be Israel's main arms supplier, and it could not sell to any country such sophisticated aircraft as the Intruder, but that the United States was prepared to sell Israel 24 "Skyhawks" (the older A-4Es) and give an option to twenty-four additional planes, "provided Israel meets certain conditions."[70] These conditions were the linkage with the nuclear issue.

A week later Ambassador Harman notified Deputy Assistant Secretary of Defense Townsend Hoopes that Israel accepted the American offer. It was decided that the key aspects of the sale "be consummated" through an exchange of letters between Hoopes and Harman.[71] Article 6 of the American proposed draft for Harman's letter contained the political conditions of the sale, including the two nuclear-related conditions:

> 6. *Other Conditions.* with reference to the discussions between Foreign Minister Eban and the Secretary of Defense on February 12, 1966, the Government of Israel understand[s] that the above described aircraft sale is conditional on the following:
> . . .
> d) The Government of Israel agrees not to use any aircraft supplied by the United States as a nuclear weapons carrier.
> e) The Government of Israel reiterates its undertaking that it will not be the first power in the Middle East to introduce nuclear weapons and it accepts the need for periodic visits by United States scientists to the nuclear facility at Dimona.[72]

Israel did have problems with some aspects of the proposed letter, in particular its nuclear aspects, and it suggested a version of its own. The most important Israeli change was making the nuclear weapons assurance a "prembular positive statement, rather than having it made a condition as in the US draft."[73] The second nuclear-related change concerned the American visits to Dimona. Harman noted that the insertion of that condition "has caused much perturbation." First he denied that it was in the Eban-McNamara talk, and when the minutes were examined he backed off, "acquiescing . . . that we would make this a separate letter."[74]

In a subsequent meeting, however, it was reported that the Israeli government did not approve the ambassador's compromise and insisted on the Israeli original position; that is, placing the reaffirmation of the nuclear nonintroduction pledge as a statement, against an American reaffirmation of its own pledge of commitment to Israel's security (as it appears in the Komer-Eshkol Memorandum of Understanding), not as an explicit condition of the deal, as the issue was put by McNamara in his meeting with Eban on 12 February.[75] In addition, the Israeli representative, Ephraim Evron, was instructed "to have any reference to Dimona taken out . . . and put in a separate memorandum."[76] Evron noted that Eshkol was "adamant" about the reference to the Dimona visit as a condition.[77]

At the end a compromise was worked out that satisfied both sides. There was a classified exchange of letters between Harman and Hoopes of the Pentagon. The Israeli letter carried the Israeli reservations. The opening paragraphs referred to the Komer-Eshkol Memorandum of Understanding of 10 March, in which the security and the undertakings were made one against the other, without formal linkage or conditioning. In addition, there was an agreed Memorandum of Conversation which apparently included reference to the Eban-McNamara conversation and the Dimona visit.[78] The Israelis could have denied the nuclear linkage, saying that this issue was outside the formal agreement on the aircraft deal. Two weeks later the AEC scientists finally had their one-day visit at Dimona (see chapter 10). Two months later the essence of the deal became public; no reference to the nuclear issue was mentioned or hinted at.[79]

The American side understood that both Israeli objections on the nuclear issue turned "on the question of *how* things are stated rather than *what* is stated."[80] At the crux of this dispute was the legalistic question of the linkage between security and atoms: while the linkage was apparent and implicit by way of a statement against a statement, the Israelis, as they had done in the past, were adamant against including it as an explicit condition of the deal. While it was recognized by all players that there was a quid pro quo here, the Israelis refused to make it explicit for political reasons, keeping the veneer of separation ("the two different operas").

WITH A NOD AND A WINK

In the mid-1960s, under Johnson and Eshkol, the United States and Israel reached a number of understandings on the nuclear issue. The unwritten understandings allowed both governments to avoid public confrontation over Israel's nuclear program, without compromising the interests of either. Sometime in the mid-1960s the CIA station in Tel Aviv concluded that the Israelis had a nuclear weapons program, and that it was a fact that could not be reversed. The CIA station felt that the Israelis were engaged in deception, concealing information about the Dimona reactor and leading the American inspectors to the wrong conclusions about the activities there. After the Six-Day War, the CIA station in Israel believed that the visits were becoming an embarrassment for both governments, and, since it was no longer necessary to reassure Nasser, it would be better to bring them to an end. CIA director Richard Helms and Ambassador Barbour probably reached similar conclusions, and possibly conveyed their conclusions to Johnson.[81]

Barbour, who served as U.S. ambassador to Israel from 1961 to 1973, understood the Israeli commitment to acquire nuclear weapons. He also understood that the Dimona reactor was central to Israel's nuclear weapons program, and knew that Israel's leaders would not give it up. He wanted, therefore, to find other ways that would allow the United States to contain the Israeli program. He understood that strengthening Israel through sales of sophisticated conventional arms would be more effective than a public confrontation over keeping the Israeli weapons program under wraps. A central element in the understanding between Israel and the United States would be ambiguity. Barbour, therefore, was not interested in learning too much about Dimona, and he did not instruct the embassy personnel to do much about it. He believed that this attitude would best serve Johnson's interests and wishes.[82]

Barbour interpreted Johnson's interests and wishes correctly. The White House knew something, but also did not want to know too much, just as Barbour knew the essence but did not want to know the details. According to Feldman, neither Kennedy nor Johnson had too many doubts that the Israelis "had to have nuclear weapons, sooner or later. This was a given. They were very advanced and they would have it, if not in one year, it would be in the following year."[83] This was also the view of Seaborg, who now acknowledges that despite the reports of AEC scientists, around the time he visited in Israel in 1966 he knew with "near certainty" that the Israelis had a secret reprocessing facility.[84] Komer, as noted earlier, acknowledged that as early as 1962 or 1963 the CIA assumed that "a reprocessing plant was there, too."[85] As early as December 1964 the speculation among American proliferation experts was that "Israel now has the technical capability to develop the bomb," and could do so within two to three years after the decision was made.[86] Less than two years later, Komer recommended that the president approve the sale of the Skyhawks, "provided that Israel in return: . . . not use our aircraft as nuclear weapons carriers."[87] This language indicates that by 1966 the White House sensed that Israel was getting closer to producing nuclear weapons. The president and his advisers might not have known precisely how far Israel had advanced in the nuclear field, and there was no firm evidence on the status and direction of the Israeli program.

Even without clear indications of the state of the Israeli nuclear weapons program, Israel posed a problem for U.S. nonproliferation policy. According to Feldman, the issue was not stopping Israel's nuclear program, but persuading Israel not openly to become a nuclear-weapon state, engendering a chain of nuclear weapons proliferation as a result.[88] It was thus important to Johnson "to remind the Prime Minister that we are violently against nuclear proliferation," and to receive assurances from the prime minister that he understood the president's position. This was as far as Johnson went.

DIFFERENT PERSPECTIVES

Johnson's dealings with Eshkol should be understood in the context of his administration's nonproliferation policies. For Johnson, the problem of nuclear weapons proliferation was not as central as it was for Kennedy. He also did not believe, at least until late 1966, that the impasse with the Soviets regarding the question of the Multi-lateral Nuclear Force (MLF) could be resolved to allow an agreement on weapons nonproliferation.[89] The Chinese nuclear explosion on 16 October 1964 was a reminder of the dangers of nuclear proliferation,[90] but Johnson was still reluctant to make nonproliferation an important issue in his foreign policy. His administration, like those before, opposed the development of nuclear deterrent forces by other states, but even this assumption was questioned by administration officials. Chief among them was Secretary of State Dean Rusk.[91]

Against the backdrop of this internal debate and weeks after the Chinese explosion, Johnson appointed a special task force, chaired by former undersecretary of defense Roswell Gilpatric, to study the problem of nuclear proliferation. The creation of the Gilpatric Committee was a recognition that after the Chinese explosion, there was a need for a fresh look at the proliferation question, and for greater clarity and coherence in American national nuclear nonproliferation policy.

The Gilpatric report asserted that preventing further proliferation "is clearly in the national interest despite the difficult decisions that will be required," and thus the United States must, "as a matter of great urgency, substantially increase the scope and intensity of its non-proliferation efforts, if it wants to have any hope of success."[92] The report considered nuclear proliferation a threat to the security of the United States, and did not make exceptions or distinctions between friendly or hostile states. Any additional nuclear forces, however primitive and regardless of who developed them, "will add complexity and instability to the deterrent balance between the United States and the Soviet Union, [and] aggregate suspicions and hostility among states neighboring new nuclear powers." Johnson received the Gilpatric report on 21 January 1965, but he was not ready to endorse the committee's conclusions. Rusk opposed the conclusions and the tone of the report, refusing to conceal his views even at the White House ceremony during which the report was given to the president. He claimed that the report was "as explosive as a nuclear weapon" and that a premature disclosure could be damaging. According to Seaborg's memoirs, Rusk added that "we could have an agreement on proliferation by 6 p.m.—it was then about 2 p.m.—if we would abandon the MLF, and that this was an area in which we might have to make a choice."[93] Johnson reminded committee members of the need to guard against leaking the report to the press.[94]

This secrecy was the result of the administration's skepticism about the report's recommendation that the United States give precedence to its commitment to nonproliferation over its commitment to existing and future nuclear arrangements with its European allies. In early 1965 the Johnson administration was not yet ready to abandon the MLF idea in favor of negotiating a nonproliferation agreement with the Soviets. Leaking the contents of the Gilpatric report could politicize the issue and embarrass Johnson.[95]

Johnson's ambivalence toward nonproliferation is relevant to understanding his dealings with Israel. Because Israel was going to develop nuclear weapons anyway, the best way to handle the situation was to get Israel to commit itself not to be the first country to introduce nuclear weapons into the Middle East. The American visits to Dimona provided the administration with the cover needed to claim that Eshkol's assurances regarding nuclear weapons were verified. By June 1964, however, after only one visit to Dimona during Johnson's tenure, the administration became uncomfortable in its role as the witness of Israel's status as a state without a nuclear weapons program. This is why Komer, during the first Eshkol visit, tried to persuade Israel to accept IAEA safeguards on its nuclear installations (as noted, Komer succeeded in the case of Soreq, but Israel refused to accept IAEA safeguards on Dimona). The issue of IAEA control emerged again in 1966,[96] and the pattern of the United States raising the issue and Israel rejecting it became routine.

From the Israeli perspective, the visits were not meant to dispel U.S. suspicions about Israel's nuclear weapons capability. The Eshkol government wanted to convey a dual message: Israel would act responsibly and would do its best to keep the Arab-Israeli conflict conventional; and that it wanted the United States to recognize that Israel had a tangible nuclear-weapons option. Israel, therefore, was not interested in clarity. The question was how far Israel should let the United States in on the details of its capability. The solution was to keep America guessing as to the nature of Israel's nuclear weapons capacity. It was this element of uncertainty that left some U.S. officials, in the mid-1960s, uncomfortable and frustrated as to the Israeli nuclear program.[97] Reliance on nuclear ambiguity resulted in the Israeli posture of opacity. Eshkol and Johnson stumbled further into opacity as they searched and groped for answers that would satisfy their strategic needs, national goals, and political requirements.

Ben Gurion had initiated the Israeli nuclear program, but the challenges Eshkol faced were equally daunting. Eshkol not only had to protect the project from powerful external pressures, but he was also the only Israeli prime minister who had to deal with the nuclear question as part of the political debate at home, something Ben Gurion never quite had to do. Just as Eshkol's approach to the nuclear question evolved in response to the security discussions with the United States, it was also shaped by domestic Israeli politics and strategic and economic concerns.

The antinuclear proponents in the early 1960s, whom Ben Gurion easily shrugged off, were weak and came from the margins of Israeli body politics. In 1965–66 this was no longer the case. This time it was the pronuclear voices, Ben Gurion and his followers, that stirred the debate—people with knowledge of the issue who could and did challenge Eshkol. As the break between Eshkol and Ben Gurion deepened in 1964–66, the nuclear issue emerged as a major, if implied, theme in Ben Gurion's campaign to delegitimize Eshkol as a national leader.

The break with Ben Gurion, and Peres's resignation from his post at the Ministry of Defense, created yet another challenge for Eshkol. When Peres was forced out, Eshkol decided it was time to exert political control over the secret project. He restructured the IAEC, until then not much more than an empty label, and decided that its chair must be the prime minister himself. Subsequent prime ministers followed the same arrangement.

Eshkol had to walk a fine line between resolve and

caution abroad and at home. Under Eshkol's leadership, Israel completed the necessary steps for establishing a rudimentary nuclear option. Eshkol, however, was also the first Israeli prime minister to pledge publicly that Israel would not be the first country to introduce nuclear weapons into the Middle East, thus making nuclear ambivalence a national policy. Succeeding prime ministers have followed this policy.

THE RIFT

When Eshkol became prime minister in June 1963 he declared that his government would continue Ben Gurion's policies. He even referred to himself in private as Ben Gurion's "caretaker prime minister."[1]

This attitude was apparent in the most sensitive topic he inherited from Ben Gurion—President Kennedy's demand for two American visits per year to Dimona. Eshkol knew how important Dimona had been to his predecessor and, in preparing his reply to Kennedy in July–August 1963, he consulted with him. He recognized that his reply to Kennedy would have serious domestic consequences for his leadership, and he made sure to signal that, on this issue at least, he would continue Ben Gurion's policies. He set up a system to pass on sensitive documents to Ben Gurion at Sdeh Boker, especially the correspondence with Kennedy and de Gaulle.[2] Eshkol kept Peres as his deputy minister of defense, as Ben Gurion had urged, and even tried to extend Peres's authority.[3]

In his first year as prime minister, Eshkol made it clear that Ben Gurion's nuclear commitments would be honored. Ben Gurion's commitments to Kennedy—claiming that Dimona was for peaceful purposes, allowing the precedent of U.S. visits to Dimona, and permitting the United States to reassure President Nasser on the nature of Dimona—hamstrung Eshkol when it came to replying to Kennedy's letter. He could have changed Ben Gurion's policy, as Golda Meir had proposed, but he decided to adhere to Ben Gurion's commitments (on Eshkol's 19 August 1963 reply to Kennedy, see chapter 7). He followed this policy in his exchanges with the Johnson administration before and during his first visit to the United States in May 1964 (see chapter 11).

The indications of a rift between Ben Gurion and Eshkol appeared during the first year of Eshkol's government. While publicly pledging to continue Ben Gurion's policies, Eshkol's actions signaled a change. The first shot in the war between the two men was fired in May 1964, when Eshkol and other senior MAPAI members invited Pinhas Lavon and his supporters to return to political activity in the party—in effect, reversing the 1961 MAPAI decision to remove Lavon from his position as head of the Histadrut. Ben Gurion was outraged by what he called the "illegal action" of Eshkol. In October Ben Gurion submitted to the attorney general new evidence on the Lavon Affair and asked Eshkol to appoint a judicial investigative committee to reopen the case. Eshkol decided against that, and the party leadership supported him. The final confrontation took place at the MAPAI convention in February 1965. Ben Gurion's demand to launch a judicial inquiry into the Lavon Affair was rejected in a party central committee vote (60 percent opposed the inquiry). Many of Ben Gurion's supporters considered their loss—by a thin margin—a respectable showing, but Ben Gurion was no longer interested in party politics. He wanted to remove Eshkol altogether and was ready to take his fight to the people.

The break between Eshkol and Ben Gurion in 1964–65 was about more than the Lavon Affair. Since assuming office, Eshkol had become more of a prime minister and a party leader in his own right, and less of a caretaker on behalf of Ben Gurion. Eshkol explored a political alliance with *Achdut Ha'Avodah*, a left-ist movement whose leaders, Israel Galili and Yigal Allon, offered an alternative outlook on national security from that offered by Ben Gurion's protégés, Shimon Peres and Moshe Dayan.

The struggle also symbolized the end of one era and the beginning of another; from a period of laying the foundations and creating new realities to one of maintaining and strengthening the existing edifice. The transition from Ben Gurion's visionary Zionism to Eshkol's more down-to-earth version reflected the changes that had to be made in the nuclear project. For Ben Gurion the nuclear-weapons option was a hope and a dream. Eshkol, on the other hand, had to attend to the financial and bureaucratic needs of an existing organization. The break between Ben Gurion and Eshkol may not have started over the nuclear issue, but it had far-reaching consequences for Israel's nuclear history.

THE 1965 ELECTION CAMPAIGN

A few weeks after the MAPAI convention the *New York Times* reported that the United States had conducted a second visit to Dimona.[4] The article embarrassed Eshkol. It meant that Eshkol agreed to an inspection arrangement that implied a possible violation of Israeli sovereignty, and may have also compromised the central element of the nation's security. The political timing of the leak was particularly inconvenient to Eshkol. It occurred within weeks of the final break with Ben Gurion, and only days after the Harriman-Komer visit. The Israeli public had no clue that Robert Komer had pressed hard but accomplished nothing regarding Dimona, and that it was Eshkol who had conducted the negotiations with mastery and skill. Yet the article gave way to rumors that Eshkol, unlike Ben Gurion, was "soft" on Dimona. It was rumored that the U.S.

visits to Dimona would lead to the slowing down or freezing of the nuclear project and that this was one of the reasons for the deterioration of his relations with Ben Gurion.[5]

The leak was played up in the Israeli press. *Ha'aretz* editorialized that American pressure overwhelmed considerations of national sovereignty, although it did not mean that Israel may have good reasons to allow the visits. Even so, the editorial urged the government to make these reasons public, perhaps through a statement by Eshkol to the Knesset.[6] A day later *Ha'aretz* reported that the decision to allow the American visit was made against the objections of some of Eshkol's "senior advisers," who warned against "surrender" to the U.S. on this issue.[7] The right-wing *Herut* charged that the government deceived and confused the public by playing semantic games with "visits" and "inspections." Whatever the arrangements, they undermined Israeli sovereignty without Israel receiving anything in return. The pro-government papers *Davar* and *La'merhav* argued that there was a real difference between visits and inspections; there was nothing wrong with the visits and the leaks were politically motivated. They, too, urged Eshkol to give a public explanation.[8] Within days Eshkol made a statement to the Knesset that, since 1961, Israel had permitted visits of American scientists to Dimona—not inspections or supervisions, but visits—and that the visits were part of the cooperative scientific relationship between the United States and Israel. The claim that the visits violated Israeli sovereignty was groundless.

Weeks after the leak, in a series of harsh public attacks on Eshkol's character and integrity, Ben Gurion alleged that Eshkol, by his actions, "was no longer qualified to lead the nation."[9] Ben Gurion's charges were interpreted by some to mean that Ben Gurion blamed his heir for compromising Israel's nuclear sovereignty. As the Ben Gurion-Eshkol clash escalated, Eshkol forced Ben Gurion's supporters in his cabinet to make up their mind: either serve as loyal ministers under his leadership or openly support Ben Gurion and quit. Peres recognized that under the circumstances he could no longer serve Eshkol, and resigned. He tried to prevent a split in MAPAI, but to no avail. Ben Gurion also left little choice for his supporters when he founded a new political movement, Israel's Workers List (RAFI), to challenge Eshkol in the upcoming election.[10] Peres found himself in the awkward position of being in a leading position in a new political party born out of whims he did not share, having to fight the man with whom he had served closely the last two years.[11]

The election campaign of 1965 was one of the most bitter in Israel's history. It was dominated by an old man's rage against the successor he himself had chosen. It was also about whether Israel still needed the visionary demands of its aging founder or whether it was secure enough to move to a new kind of leadership. The dramatic story of the rift between the two men notwithstanding, RAFI had to translate Ben Gurion's vengeance into the language of politics and ideology. It was in this way that the nuclear issue became a political theme—the only campaign in Israel's history in which that subject was even mentioned. The use of the nuclear weapons issue was subtle and implied, much of it spoken, not written, but it was an integral part of RAFI's political message.

RAFI portrayed itself as the party of change, the only party advocating technological independence, strong deterrence, and a change in the election system. Science and technology were presented as the new challenges of postindependence Zionism. Its campaign emphasized the commitment and record of its leaders, many with scientific, technocratic, and managerial credentials, particularly in the area of technology-based military industries. References were also made to the role of the party's leaders in the construction of Dimona. RAFI was nicknamed "the atomic party." The MAPAI-*Achdut Ha'Avodah* alliance was presented as the product of the Old Guard, led by a tired, spent leadership lacking in vision and vigor, unqualified to lead Israel into the technological and nuclear age.

Barely concealed in the RAFI campaign was the message that Eshkol had betrayed his role as custodian of the nation's nuclear project. No explicit allegations were made, but although the charges were only insinuated, they came from people who were assumed to be in the know. During the 1962 debate between the conventional warfare school of Galili and Allon, and the nuclear deterrence school of Peres and Dayan, the nuclear theme surfaced here and there, but it remained too obscure to be noticed by the Israeli public. In the 1965 election campaign the debate over nuclear issues came much closer to the surface.

REORGANIZATION

On 2 November 1965 Eshkol won the elections. It was regarded as a national vote of confidence in his showdown with Ben Gurion. Leading the MAPAI-*Achdut Ha'Avodah* alliance, he won a comfortable victory that enabled him to form a new government in which he continued to hold the posts of prime minister and minister of defense. Ben Gurion lost the fight, his RAFI party winning only ten seats in the Knesset. Its leaders, Peres and Dayan, were, for the first time in their public life, outside the center of national decision making. Galili and Allon of *Achdut Ha'Avodah*, after fifteen years of waiting on the sidelines, were now invited by Eshkol to assume lead roles in national decisions.[12]

This change also had profound implications for the nuclear program. Ben Gurion, Peres, and Bergmann, the three men who had initiated the nuclear program a decade earlier, no longer had a say in shaping its future. They were replaced by officials who disagreed with the pro-nuclear position of Peres and

Dayan. Eshkol's close aide from the Treasury Department, Zvi Dinstein, an economist and capable bureaucrat with no experience in strategic, let alone nuclear,
affairs replaced Peres at the Ministry of Defense, first as Eshkol's senior aide and,
after the 1965 elections, as the new deputy minister of defense. In that capacity
Dinstein became the chief administrator of all R&D activities in the ministry.
Already in January 1964 Yitzhak Rabin, a skeptic with regard to technological self-
reliance in general and of "science-based" deterrence in particular, replaced the
pro-technology Zvi Zur as the IDF chief of staff. Rabin, a PALMACH senior officer in the War of Independence, was close to the leaders of *Achdut Ha'Avodah*,
particularly to his former commander, Allon. Eshkol thus surrounded himself
with people who were not enthusiastic about the nuclear project. These individuals were now in charge of making policy decisions concerning the project's
future.

Peres had run the Ministry of Defense as director-general and deputy minister of defense from 1953 to 1965. His management style shaped the organizational and personnel structure of the ministry. He established a decentralized
structure of research, development, and production, based on quasi-
autonomous organizations and government-owned companies, allowing him
to run the ministry on a divide-and-rule approach. After Peres left, Eshkol asked
Dinstein to overhaul the entire R&D structure of the ministry, including the
defense industries (the Israel Aviation Industry and the Military Industries), the
IAEC, and RAFAEL. As Dinstein recalls almost thirty years later, the task Eshkol
gave him was "to bring economic thinking into a bureaucratic structure that
ideologically defied it for so long." The situation he found at the ministry was
contrary to proper management principles: "There was no clear hierarchical
framework, no clear chain of command, no procedures on who was doing what,
no definitive division of labor, no clear-cut procedures about projects.
Everything was small and personal."[13]

The issues at stake were both economic management and political loyalty,
and the distinctions between the two were blurred owing to differences over
R&D matters between Eshkol and Dinstein, on the one hand, and Ben Gurion
and Peres, on the other. Eshkol's and Dinstein's backgrounds were in account-
ing and finance, and for them the problem at the Ministry of Defense was lack
of efficiency and management. The R&D system they inherited seemed wasteful, devoid of any principle of financial accountability, even lacking procedures
for financial oversight and quality control. In 1965 Israel was heading toward an
economic recession, and waste in the Ministry of Defense became especially
glaring to economists such as Eshkol and Dinstein.

By late summer 1965 Dinstein demanded major organizational changes in
RAFAEL, insisting on changing the system by which RAFAEL was operating,

particularly its budgeting procedure. According to the old system, a central budget was allocated for all RAFAEL activities within the Ministry of Defense's overall budget, based on the projects that had been proposed by the management of RAFAEL and approved by the minister and his deputy on the recommendations of the general staff and the minister's scientific adviser. Dinstein, following Rabin's suggestions, insisted instead that each R&D project be sponsored and budgeted either by the IDF or one of the ministry's bureaucracies. It should be up to the sponsoring agency, not the developers at RAFAEL, to specify the technical requirements for the product under development.[14]

In addition, Dinstein wanted to strengthen the office of the scientific adviser as an independent scientific oversight board serving the minister and his deputy. That Ernst Bergmann had three offices—at RAFAEL, the Ministry of Defense, and the IAEC—seemed to Dinstein to be an example of a conflict of interests. Bergmann could not function as the in-house chief scientist at RAFAEL, the chair of the IAEC, and also oversee and evaluate the projects on behalf of the minister of defense.

The nuclear program, because of its sensitivity and cost, was at the center of the storm. Because of the way Peres set up the program—not under one organization, like the Manhattan Project, but divided under a number of organizations, each reporting directly only to his office—major problems arose as the program grew, especially management and communication difficulties among its various elements. There were hardly any channels of communication, for example, between Dimona's boss, Manes Pratt, and other bureaucracies involved in the nuclear weapons program.[15] Pratt particularly refused to accept Bergmann's authority, despite Bergmann's three titles, as the coordinator of all national nuclear activities. At one time Pratt even declared Bergmann a "security risk" and denied him access to the Dimona site.[16] Nor was Pratt prepared to accept instructions from anyone else at the ministry, except Peres and Ben Gurion.[17]

This organizational maze and lack of proper coordination became a major problem for the nuclear project by the mid-1960s. From the time the program was set up, built on a number of interrelated but independent projects, real authority for the program had been closely held in Peres's hands. Accepted as Ben Gurion's long-time and trusted executor, Peres's authority was accepted by all the leaders of the bureaucracies involved. Peres personally selected the leaders of the various organizations and units, assigned them their missions within the program, and oversaw their progress. The unconventional means he used for funding the program, and his tendency to institutionalize redundancy through "friendly competition" among the various organizations involved, increased their dependence on him as the ultimate authority. All major financial and organizational decisions had to be made by him, at times without the knowledge of other program leaders. In the absence of an independent scientific authority to evaluate and assess all aspects of the program—Bergmann was moved to the sidelines as the program progressed—the primary research and development establishment involved saw itself as being in charge of the entire project.[18]

For Eshkol and Dinstein, such Byzantine management was not only financially wasteful, but it also created a problem of political control over the nation's most sensitive program. In 1965 Bergmann was still the official head of the IAEC and R&D at the Ministry of Defense, but without the trust of either the new regime or many of the program's own senior technical leaders; he was seen as a major part of the problem. The idea of creating a new professional administration in charge of all aspects of the nation's nuclear program activities, directly accountable to Eshkol (in his roles as prime minister and minister of defense), was talked about for a long time and even endorsed by Bergmann himself in 1964 (as he realized that somebody else needed to replace him in that job), but it was Peres's resignation and his replacement by Dinstein that made it possible and necessary.[19]

This proposed new administration was thought to function as the technical and financial authority overseeing all aspects of the nuclear program, not merely as a scientific advisory body but also as a body with executive powers. Decisions on all aspects of the program—technical, financial, organizational, and political—would come from one authority directly under the control of the prime minister. Sometime in the spring or summer of 1965, while on a visit to the United States, Dinstein offered the job to Yuval Ne'eman, then a visiting scientist at the U.S. National Laboratory at Brookhaven, who declined. Instead, he recommended Israel Dostrovsky of the Weizmann Institute for the job (rather than General Dan Tolkovski, the former commander of the Israeli Air Force, Dinstein's original candidate).[20] By late 1965, after Eshkol's election victory and his appointment of Dinstein as deputy minister of defense, the search continued apace. In early spring 1966 Dostrovsky, the former head of HEMED GIMMEL, agreed to become the head of IAEC in its enhanced organizational form.

To make the reorganization work, and to be consistent with Dinstein's plan to introduce economic thinking into the Ministry of Defense, other organizational changes in personnel and authority in the R&D structure, some unrelated to the nuclear issue, had to be made. First, Dinstein fired Manes Pratt, the director of Dimona, and replaced him with Yossef Tulipman, a former senior official at Dimona who had been forced out by Pratt. It was felt that Pratt was no longer the right person to run Dimona under the new organization. To build Dimona from scratch was one task, but to run it as a major organization (*Kirya*

Le'mechkar Gariini—Israel's Nuclear Research Center—or KAMAG in its Hebrew acronym) was another. This change in personnel was difficult but politically straightforward.[21]

The real struggle was with Munya Mardor, the director-general of RAFAEL. Mardor was reluctant to accept Dinstein's proposed reorganization. In his autobiography Mardor devoted three long chapters to telling his story of what he called "the battle for the life of RAFAEL."[22] The story is a selective account in two senses—it is Mardor's truth as he saw it and also the unclassified version of that account—but it is still the only available written account of the drama.

According to Mardor, the issues involved in the dispute with Dinstein were two separate and only loosely interrelated ones: first, how RAFAEL, as a research and development authority, should be run: what its philosophy should be, and its appropriate size; second, a dispute over the control and oversight of one specific "leading project," that is, the bomb project.

As to the first issue, Dinstein's proposed changes questioned the very philosophy on which RAFAEL (and earlier EMET), as Israel's central defense R&D authority, was founded and run. This philosophy, based on Ben Gurion's vision, was that Israel must be on the cutting edge of technology, and therefore RAFAEL must maintain its sovereignty in selecting the areas of basic research for future defense projects. This was the idea behind the commitment to a qualitative edge on which RAFAEL was founded in 1958 by Ben Gurion, Peres, Bergmann, and Mardor. It must be up to the RAFAEL leadership, with the approval of the minister and his deputy, to identify new technologies and fields of research for long-term projects. The selection and identification of appropriate projects, especially in the area of basic research, must not be imposed on RAFAEL by army officers. The R&D horizons of RAFAEL must go beyond the military needs of the moment. On this issue, there were frequent clashes in early and mid-1960 between the two philosophies, one that advocated purchasing military hardware off the shelf (Chief of Staff Rabin's view) and the other that highlighted the commitment to technological self-reliance (Peres's view). Dinstein's proposed reforms, especially his strict budgetary procedures, meant (from Mardor's perspective) that RAFAEL would no longer be the supreme policy-making authority on all defense R&D matters, but would be a central R&D agency providing services to the IDF and the Ministry of Defense as a prime contractor. Also, under the proposed reform plan, about a third of RAFAEL employees (approximately 450 people) would be laid off. For Mardor, the changes meant the end of what Peres, Bergmann, and he had built and cherished since the early 1950s.[23]

Dinstein saw things from a different perspective. For him, RAFAEL's excessive sovereignty was at the root of the lack of accountability and coordination

that led to financial waste. He saw RAFAEL as a self-enclosed, elitist R&D organization that operated more like an academic research center than a provider of
services to the military. He noted that many of its projects never came to
fruition. Given Peres's authority, it meant that he (Peres), Bergmann, and
Mardor made all the R&D decisions on their own, whether or not they related
to the actual needs of the IDF. This arrangement gave enormous budgetary
freedom to the RAFAEL leadership to entertain "the whims of its senior scientists," as long as Peres and Bergmann approved. There was a need to introduce
"economic thinking" and "quality control" into a system that fundamentally
lacked "financial accountability."[24]

TURF WARS

Then there was the second dispute about the responsibility for the "leading
development project." According to Mardor, among Dinstein's organizational
proposals was one that transferred "direct control of key technical units
involved in one of the central projects under the responsibility of the
Authority" to another "staff unit" at the Ministry of Defense.[25] These key technical units, in Mardor's account, were engaged in technical coordination and
oversight of a number of related subprojects. The removal of these technical
staff units indicated, Mardor wrote, an intention to deprive RAFAEL of one of
its "leading projects." For Mardor, the removal of that particular project from
the direct responsibility of RAFAEL, given the fact that that "leading project"
was, in the summer of 1965, in a "highly advanced state of development,"[26]
meant a no-confidence vote in RAFAEL. It also meant depriving RAFAEL of the
credit for completing the project. In particular, Mardor was angry that, for
months, there had been secret discussions about such a transfer, of which neither he nor Bergmann had been aware.[27] Mardor never explains what that
"leading project" was, and his wording is vague, but the reader is invited to read
between the lines and make the interpretative leap that would read the "leading
project" to mean the nuclear weapons project.[28]

The battle over the future of RAFAEL lasted for about five months, from late
December 1965 until late April 1966. Mardor saw no other resort but to appeal
to Prime Minister Eshkol, mobilizing a powerful lobby to persuade him to over-
rule Dinstein's demands. That Bergmann no longer functioned as Eshkol's chief
scientist and no longer had the prime minister's ear did not make Mardor's
argument any easier. Dinstein was persistent in his demand that Eshkol, as
prime minister and minister of defense, and he, as his deputy, must gain direct
control over the project.[29] Mardor recognized that Dinstein had a point, and
proposed various ideas to correct the structural problems, but without depriving RAFAEL of its responsibilities. He suggested, for example, the creation of a

scientific board to oversee RAFAEL, manned by some of Israel's distinguished scientists who were familiar with defense issues and headed by Professor Ephraim Katzir—one of the founders of HEMED—of the Weizmann Institute. If Eshkol did not accept his suggestions, Mardor was determined to resign.[30]

Mardor left no stone unturned in his efforts to maintain RAFAEL's control of the project. In his book he maintains that he invited Dinstein and his senior staff to visit that particular "leading project" and meet its chief, Jenka Ratner, and the technical director involved in the supervision of the project, Avraham Hermoni. He also invited the board of scientific advisers associated with the project to review its progress.[31] Mardor's point was simple: RAFAEL had brought that particular project to a very advanced level of development, and it would be unfair and demoralizing to the people and organization who carried out the job to take it from them at that point. Mardor lobbied Eshkol through less formal but even more effective messengers: *Achdut Ha'Avodah*'s leader and Eshkol's close political ally, Israel Galili, and the legendary Haganah figure, Shaul Avigur. Both talked with Eshkol on Mardor's behalf.[32] Ben Gurion, as an opposition leader, considered Dinstein's reform as *bechia le'dorot* (woe for generations), an abandonment of the vision that led him to the establishment of RAFAEL.[33]

On 2 April Eshkol met Mardor and Dinstein to discuss the dispute between them. On the specific issue, Dinstein made a case to remove those "key professional units" relevant to the "leading project" from RAFAEL to the other, newly created scientific bureaucracy. His argument was that because the development phase was completed, it became vital now to switch responsibility to the new body. Mardor made his case to keep the project under the direct responsibility of RAFAEL. Some of his main arguments were about the need to preserve the integrity of RAFAEL as Israel's national defense laboratory.[34]

In the end, and as was so typical of Eshkol, a compromise of sorts was found that allowed Mardor to stay. The compromise was the result of an informal consultation Eshkol had with three trusted men whom he asked to look at the problem: his minister without portfolio, Galili, and the two Katzir brothers (Aharon and Ephraim) of the Weizmann Institute. It appears that the issue was never brought to the cabinet nor even to the Defense Ministerial Committee; it was resolved in an informal, ad hoc forum whose members, except Eshkol, had no formal responsibility for the matter. As often happened in Israel's political past, important decisions were made by an informal "kitchen" forum. Bergmann and Peres were told of the compromise; both endorsed it and promised in return not to politicize the issue further.[35]

Under this compromise, made in a meeting on 19 April, some of Mardor's arguments about the first issue, that is, the need to maintain the integrity and sovereignty of RAFAEL as the supreme policy body in the area of defense R&D, were endorsed. Some aspects of Dinstein's "economic thinking" were accepted as well, stating that for IDF projects the IDF sponsoring body should also fund the project. Other issues were postponed pending further study by the new Office of the Chief Scientist, to be reestablished at the Ministry of Defense under Ephraim Katzir and his deputy, Colonel Amos Horev. RAFAEL did not have to lay off a third of its manpower, as had originally been proposed. On the second issue, the bureaucratic fate of the "leading interdisciplinary project"— the nuclear project—Mardor had to accept Eshkol's and Dinstein's determination that final technical and financial coordination and oversight of the project must be transferred to the new independent scientific administration, though the original demand to transfer immediately those key technical staff units from RAFAEL to the new administration was delayed. Executive responsibility for completing the development phase would temporarily remain with RAFAEL.[36]

The Israeli public knew almost nothing about this power struggle. On 1 April 1966 it was announced that Bergmann had resigned from his three posts at the Ministry of Defense, effective 1 May. It was acknowledged that the resignation was related to the major reorganization effort under way at the Ministry of Defense, and that a new administration would be installed to coordinate the national nuclear activities. In subsequent interviews, Bergmann referred to differences on matters of national science policy between him and the prime minister, on which he was overruled. He was vague and circumspect about speculations in the press that his resignation was tied to policy differences with Eshkol relating to nuclear development. Bergmann and Eshkol did not spell out in public what the policy differences were, though Bergmann laconically suggested that the Eshkol government was less sympathetic to "long-term scientific planning" than the Ben Gurion government had been.[37]

This was only part of the truth. It was easier for Bergmann to present his forced resignation as having been caused by fundamental policy differences with Eshkol. There were differences, but Bergmann did not enjoy the trust and respect of the prime minister any longer. He was actively involved in the 1965 RAFI campaign, which violated the civil-service code. Beyond personal loyalties, Bergmann in 1966 was no longer a contributor to the R&D system that he had helped found fifteen years earlier. Both the Office of the Chief Scientist and the IAEC needed an overhaul, and it was clear that Bergmann had to go. His resignation appeared to be part of the central policy issue to the uninformed public, but it was only a sideshow. The real drama took place elsewhere, between Mardor and Dinstein.

Eshkol accepted Bergmann's resignation, decorated him with the highest

Israeli award for his contributions to the nation's security, and nominated himself, in his capacity as prime minister, to be the new chair of the IAEC, with Israel Dostrovsky as its director-general, transferring the ministerial responsibility for the IAEC from the Ministry of Defense to the prime minister's office. Because the general public knew nothing about the details of the power struggle and the personalities involved, it was easy to suggest in the press that Bergmann's resignation concerned major policy differences with the Eshkol government about nuclear development.[38] Peres, who was informed by Mardor on the talks between Eshkol, Dinstein, and Mardor, kept his promise to Mardor not to politicize the issue as long as Mardor could live with the compromise.[39]

THE FORMULA

Rethinking the nuclear program in 1966 was not limited to its organization. Technological, political, and strategic developments also required the formulation of a long-term policy or commitment. The Eshkol government had to formulate a rationale for what the Israeli nuclear option would be.

Among the questions to be answered was whether the nuclear infrastructure under construction should be an emergency option or whether Israel should actually build nuclear weapons? Should Israel be the first to nuclearize the Middle East or should it keep itself just a step ahead of the Arabs? Should Israel reorient the IDF toward a nuclear strategy? Similar questions were reportedly raised and discussed earlier (see chapter 8), but the nuclear question then was only postponed, not resolved.

In 1966, however, some policy decisions had to be made, by action or by default. The technological, political, and strategic situation in 1966 was different from that in the early 1960s. These differences required the Eshkol government to formulate a strategic rationale for the nuclear project. It was at this time that the formula, "Israel will not be the first to introduce nuclear weapons to the Middle East," became Israel's declaratory policy, and that Eshkol's policy of nuclear ambiguity emerged.

In 1966 the physical infrastructure of the project was completed or about to be completed, including the capability to produce weapon-grade fissile material, weapon design, and the testing of delivery means. According to Pierre Péan, "the first plutonium extraction tests took place during the second half of 1965," and by 1966 Israel had enough plutonium to "manufacture the bomb during 1966, or at the latest early 1967."[40] If the capability to separate plutonium is a primary measure of nuclear weapons capability, then, according to Péan, Israel reached that point around 1966.

Another measure of nuclear weapons capability is knowledge of weapon design. After Mardor details the 1966 struggle for the survival of RAFAEL, particularly maintaining control over that "leading project" whose development "almost reached completion," he writes:

> On November 2, 1966, a test with a special significance was conducted. It meant an end of an era of development, and a step that brought one of our primary weapons-systems to its final phases of development and production in RAFAEL. The test was completely successful, for we received an unequivocal experimental proof of the adequacy of the system that was developed at RAFAEL. We have waited for that result for many years.[41]

According to this interpretation, the test to which Mardor referred as something for which he had been waiting "for many years," was a test of those aspects of the nuclear device that were under the responsibility of RAFAEL (perhaps a test of an entire implosion device, or a zero or near-zero yield test).[42] Regardless of what was actually tested, weeks later the CIA disseminated new intelligence reports suggesting that Israel continued to produce bomb components, and that "assembly of a nuclear weapon could be completed in 6–8 weeks."[43] The American reports highlight Mardor's struggle to maintain the integrity of RAFAEL, especially the integrity of the almost-completed "leading project." By late 1966 Israel had completed the development and testing of all the components of its first nuclear device. This is not, however, equal to possessing a complete nuclear weapon, which needs to be tested in order to be of operational value.

Another element in a nuclear weapons system is the warhead's delivery means—a plane or a surface-to-surface missile. According to French sources, in April 1963 the Israeli Ministry of Defense signed a contract for ballistic missiles with the French manufacturer Marcel Dassault. The contract was for the development of a two-stage, solid propellant ballistic missile capable of carrying a 750-kg warhead. The missile project, known as MD-620, or Jericho, conducted its fire testing in 1965. The first two-stage launch, on 23 December 1965, failed, but the second one, in March 1966, succeeded.[44] In early 1966 the New York Times reported that Israel had purchased the first installment of thirty such missiles from France, and that they were under development.[45] By the time Israel had completed the design work for its first nuclear device, it was still lacking a dedicated delivery system.

By 1966 Israel had thus obtained, or was about to obtain, the three components that constitute a nuclear weapons capability: fissile material production capacity, design knowledge, and access to delivery means. This was as significant as the political developments. In October 1963 Eshkol's inner circle included Peres, Dayan, Meir, Eban, and Chief of Staff Zur. In 1966 Eshkol's inner circle had drastically changed, counting Eban, Galili, Allon, Dinstein, and Chief of Staff Rabin as members. These two groups had different ideologies and worldviews. The new members of Eshkol's close circle of advisers supported a strong conventional IDF and were interested in promoting a U.S.-Israeli security dialogue.

There was also a change in the security relations between the United States and Israel: American military supplies became available to Israel for the first time. Ben Gurion had hoped for this for years, but it was under Eshkol that the United States began to supply Israel with tanks and planes. This was part of the tacit Johnson-Eshkol quid pro quo, that is, American arms to Israel for an Israeli commitment not to introduce nuclear weapons into the region. The "Eshkol-Komer Memorandum of Understanding" of March 1965 sealed this tacit agreement and made it more formal than before (see chapter 11). This memorandum, negotiated and signed when Peres was still Eshkol's deputy, was the first official joint document in which this formula appears.

Another year passed before Eshkol would use this nonintroduction formula publicly for political purposes. In the first half of 1966, following a flurry of rumors in the world press about Israeli advances in its nuclear program, Nasser threatened a "preventive war" against Israel (see chapter 13). Fearing that the Arab's perceptions of Israeli nuclear development might lead to war, Eshkol used the formula to defuse Arab concerns. In an address to the Knesset on 18 May 1966, Eshkol referred to the nuclear issue at great length. Replying to Nasser's threats of preventive war against Israel were it to produce nuclear weapons, Eshkol gave a weapon-by-weapon tally of how Egypt had escalated the qualitative and quantitative arms race in the Middle East during the last fifteen years. Every new class of weapons system, he detailed, was introduced first by Egypt. It was also Egypt that first used chemical weapons in Yemen. In direct response to Nasser's assertion that Egypt was pushed into the development of nuclear weapons because Israel already had done so, Eshkol said:

> Egypt's President was attempting to divert attention from the peril of existing aggressive arms in the region by drawing attention to nuclear weapons, which do not exist in our region and which we do not want to see exist here. I have said before and I repeat that Israel has no atomic weapons and will not be the first to introduce them into our region.[46]

At the same time Eshkol raised some ideas on disarmament and regional arms control. He urged the big powers to draw the line between "the permissible and the impermissible" in establishing a balance of arms in the Middle East. He suggested that the idea of regional limitations on conventional armaments should be explored. "Until general disarmament is attained and the arms race is completely halted, a balance must be ensured by means of reciprocal supervision of agreed arrangements by the states of the region."[47]

Two new factors emerged concerning the nuclear issue in Eshkol's address. First, the prime minister publicly pledged that Israel would not be the first country to introduce nuclear weapons into the Middle East. Eshkol had used this formula in public at least once before in response to a reporter's question,[48] but this time it carried the weight of a national commitment. Eshkol deliberately used the somewhat ambiguous verb "introduce" (as opposed to "develop" or "manufacture"), but he made it clear that Israel did not have such weapons, and that to make them would be against its interest. Second, Eshkol's address was the first to place the nuclear issue in its proper context, that of security and arms control. In particular, Eshkol identified the Arab's superiority in conventional arms as the real problem, implying that Israeli nuclear development was a derivative of asymmetry in the conventional field.

The differences between Ben Gurion's and Eshkol's declaratory stance were important. Ben Gurion, in December 1960, stated that the Dimona reactor was devoted to "peaceful purposes," directed at using atomic energy in industry, agriculture, and science. He denied that Israel had nuclear weapons and was careful not to make future policy commitments. Eshkol, who also denied that Israel had nuclear weapons, made a commitment that "Israel will not be the first state to introduce nuclear weapons into the region." Eshkol, however, no longer talked about Dimona's contribution to industry, agriculture, and science, and, after 1965, no longer used Ben Gurion's references to its "peaceful purposes." Nor did he deny the rumors and speculations in the world press regarding Israel's nuclear capability.

This verbal formula is commonly attributed to Eshkol as its originator, but this is not the case. As documented in chapter 7, Peres is right to claim that he coined it first. In his 2 April 1963 meeting with Kennedy he used a variation on this formula.[49] Later Peres acknowledged that he used the wording without clearing it with anyone, "to get off Kennedy's probing, I tried to say something [positive] without lying." Certainly his answer was not an agreed-on policy. After his return to Israel, Peres recalls, Eshkol criticized him for using this wording.[50] Although Peres may have been the first to use it, Eshkol was the first to make it Israel's declaratory policy. The formula was discussed by Eshkol's advisers, notably Ya'acov Herzog, during preparations for his first official visit to the United States in June 1964.[51] By that time, as the Dimona reactor was operational and Americans were allowed to visit it, Ben Gurion's statement of December 1960 needed updating.

By pledging "not to be the first," Eshkol gave Johnson a commitment to the principle of nonproliferation, but without committing himself to anything in the area of research and development. In 1964 Eshkol started using it informally; in 1965 it was sealed in the Eshkol-Komer secret "Memorandum of Understanding," and in 1966 Eshkol publicly presented it as Israel's policy. According to Dinstein, Eshkol was at first uncomfortable with the formula, but soon "he fell in love with it."[52]

Ironically, in those three years, 1963–66, Eshkol and Peres reversed their roles on this formula. In 1963, according to Peres, Eshkol criticized him for telling Kennedy that Israel would not be the first. In 1966 it was Peres as an opposition leader that criticized Eshkol in the Knesset for publicly using this formula, saying: "It is one thing to reassure friends [i.e., the United States] privately, it is another thing to reassure Nasser in the Knesset."[53]

EARLY STRATEGIC THINKING

Ben Gurion's idea of an Israeli nuclear-weapons option thus moved from an ambitious vision to a national strategic concept during the Eshkol era. Accordingly, the policy issues Ben Gurion had left unexplored now had to be faced.

Until about 1966 there was little systematic effort to define the political and strategic objectives of the nuclear project. To the extent that such thinking did take place, it was left to individuals at the Ministry of Defense who prepared papers for Peres and to the developers themselves, who needed to make certain strategic assumptions about the objectives of the project. Strategic ambiguity also prevailed among the project's developers because the lack of political and strategic guidance was the norm. "Virtually in all the R&D projects with political significance the highest political level tended to avoid giving political guidance concerning technical specifications of the project."[54] Because the political officials were reluctant to provide clear guidance involving the political aspects of the project, the developing establishment itself, sometimes in consultation with individuals from the outside, had to decide on its own how to translate the complex strategic concepts into the technical specifications of the products it was authorized to develop. "We brought the information [about specification options] to the attention of the highest political level, but it often chose not to respond."[55] Left alone to make its own technical decisions, the nuclear development establishment could only assume that it properly understood the strategic intentions of the policy makers, but this may not necessarily have been true. Since the highest political level showed no interest in providing guidance, strategy was made from the bottom up.

The organizational changes that Eshkol and Dinstein introduced into the R&D system in 1966 were accompanied by the development of concepts and strategy at the national level. Eshkol, Dinstein, and Rabin asked a few individuals, among them Yuval Ne'eman, Colonel Avraham (Abrasha) Tamir, and Shalheveth Freier to elucidate Israeli strategic thinking in this area. What Eshkol called the "Samson Option" and Peres described as an "option for a rainy day" became, in these early discussions, the foundation of an original and well-thought-out Israeli rationale for the mission of its nuclear option.[56] It was also during this period that the two functions of the Israeli nuclear program as a national insurance policy were proposed and articulated.[57]

These were two distinct ideas about the role of the nuclear program. In the first case, the specter of Israeli nuclear weapons serves as insurance vis-à-vis the United States, a strong political incentive for America to keep Israel conventionally armed, believing that a sufficiently armed Israel would not have to use its nuclear option. This was not among the primary rationales that had led Ben Gurion to the nuclear project, but, under Eshkol, the insurance component became a central aspect of Israel's national security strategy. This component proved successful, perhaps the single most important cause for the change in the U.S security commitment to Israel.

The nuclear program was also meant as a tool of "last resort" in extreme military and political contingencies. One such case has to do with the possibility that if an Arab state were thought to have produced or purchased a nuclear device of its own, Israel must always be in a position to meet such a threat, especially under rapidly deteriorating political circumstances. Soon after Eshkol came up with the formula "Israel will not be the first country to introduce nuclear weapons into the Middle East," Yigal Allon highlighted this point by adding the caveat that Israel would not be the second country either. Unlike the United States in the Second World War, which feared that Germany was developing its own nuclear weapons, fear of an Arab nuclear capability was not among the original reasons that caused Ben Gurion to initiate the nuclear project. For the Eshkol government, however, the possibility of nuclear weapons in the hands of the Arab states served as a double reminder: first, that nuclearization of the region is against the Israeli national interest; second, that Israel must prudently prepare itself for such a contingency.

Another type of last-resort scenario that haunted those responsible for Israeli security was the possibility of the formation of a pan-Arab war coalition against Israel. Arab rhetoric about the "destruction of the Zionist entity" or "pushing Israel into the sea," defined Israel's worst-case scenario. This fear was the original motive for Ben Gurion to pursue nuclear weapons, and it has remained the strongest incentive for Israel to maintain its nuclear weapons program.

Most political and military leaders did not share Ben Gurion's pessimism in the late 1950s and early 1960s, or Dayan's gloomy conclusions that in the long run Israel would not be able to keep up with the conventional arms race. They did not dispute, however, the notion that Israel must prepare itself for the worst-case scenario—a swift and dramatic deterioration of Israel's basic security. The idea of the nuclear weapons program as a safety net has enjoyed almost total national consensus in Israel.

Around 1966 the Israeli defense establishment for the first time began systematic long-term strategic planning: five-year plans for force-structure and a ten-year plan for R&D. The original Ben-Gurion rationale for acquiring nuclear weapons was conceptualized and defined during these discussions in terms of having an option of "last resort." They also produced the early articulation of "red lines" whose crossing could trigger the use of nuclear weapons. There were four specific scenarios that could lead to nuclear use: (a) a successful Arab military penetration into populated areas within Israel's post-1949 borders; (b) the destruction of the Israeli Air Force; (c) the exposure of Israeli cities to massive and devastating air attacks or to possible chemical or biological attacks; (d) the use of nuclear weapons against Israeli territory. Each of these scenarios was defined, in qualitative terms, as an existential threat to the State of Israel against which the nation could defend itself by no other means than the use of atomic weapons, which would be politically and morally justified. Furthermore, some emphasized, if Israel were to develop a nuclear capability, it must develop the kind of weapon that could be used over its own territory.[58]

There was, however, a strategic counterargument. It was pointed out that any attempt to think of a last-resort nuclear employment in the context of Israel's pre-1967 borders poses a difficult question. To use a nuclear bomb in moments of true last resort, say, when a massive Arab army had already breached the borders of Israel, may be too late, and thus militarily unacceptable. To use nuclear weapons in a preemption of Arab armies, however, would be too early, and therefore politically unacceptable. Israeli strategists discovered the problem with which NATO planners had been struggling throughout the cold war: when is the right moment for nuclear weapons to be used to stop a conventionally superior enemy attack?[59]

One realization that came out in the discussions was that it would be inconceivable for a state like Israel to resort to nuclear weapons in the heat of war without warning. If a state decided to maintain a nuclear-weapons option, its enemies must know something about it, or at least be concerned that the nuclear capability existed. Deterrence works only if the deterrent capability is known and feared by one's adversaries. Israel, however, committed itself not to be the first country to introduce nuclear weapons into the region, and left its nuclear weapons capability ambiguous. How could a state deter if it did not acknowledge that it was in possession of nuclear weapons?

In responding to this problem, Israeli strategists suggested thinking about deterrence and ambiguity in a dynamic way. One may think about deterrence in terms of a spectrum, in which the uncertain end is represented by rumors and speculations, and the other end is represented by full-yield testing and declaration. Israel's nuclear deterrence should rest on the presumption—to be encouraged by sporadic rumors and leaks—that it had a nuclear weapons capability and that, under certain conditions of extreme threat, it might be compelled to use it.

It was understood that leaks and rumors, as long as they were not attributed to identifiable sources, would be in Israel's interest. In case of an actual emergency Israel must be ready to move quickly along the deterrence spectrum. To be able to emphasize the element of nuclear deterrence in a moment of need—during a crisis or even at the outbreak of hostilities—Israel should develop the technical means to demonstrate its nuclear weapons capability on very short notice. These strategic ideas were natural as the project's developers tried to make strategic sense of the notion of an ambiguous and uncertain nuclear deterrence. The political echelon played almost no role in providing guidance to the developers in these discussions. This situation would change somewhat in 1966, when Eshkol reformed the R&D structure, but even these reforms were more about personalities, bureaucratic politics, and economic and financial control than matters of strategic guidance and political oversight.[60]

There was, however, one issue—testing—on which political echelon's guidance was clear. Despite pleas from the project's top leaders that a full test was needed to complete the development stage, Eshkol refused to consider it, or even a "peaceful" nuclear explosion.[61] No matter how much the project's leaders wanted it, they continued to be overruled. Even so, Eshkol allowed the project's leaders to explore the technical side of a nuclear test (apparently such guidance had been given early in the Ben Gurion period, while Eshkol did not challenge it).[62]

It must be stressed that these arguments and counterarguments, to the limited extent they were known to the senior Israeli military establishment in the mid 1960s, were viewed as theoretical and irrelevant to the IDF's mission. Rabin's generals did not believe in any of these gloomy scenarios, which they viewed as utterly unrealistic.[63] These military men were committed to the notion that the IDF mission was to prevent such scenarios from coming to pass. To accomplish this mission Israel must have a strong tactical air force capable of destroying all Arab aircraft on the ground (the *Moked* Plan) and a massive armored force. The meaning of "last resort" was that the military had failed in its mission to defend Israel.

This attitude was also shared by Ne'eman and Tamir who, each under a different institutional arrangement, were asked to elucidate an Israeli nuclear-weapons option. They were in favor of maintaining a national nuclear weapons infrastructure that could materialize quickly if the need arose, but they opposed basing Israel's national security on an open nuclear deterrence posture.[64]

ESHKOL'S LEGACY

As noted earlier (in interpreting Mardor's text), in late 1966 RAFAEL had successfully completed its role in developing the first nuclear explosive device. On 14 December 1966 there was a critical accident in Dimona that caused the death of one employee, forcing operations at the site to stop for almost three months.[65] The accident and its consequences shocked the people in charge of the nuclear project. Dimona was reopened in February. On that occasion Eshkol paid a visit to Dimona, a visit that was even reported in the Israeli press.[66]

Eshkol's February 1967 visit to Dimona signified, in a sense, the completion of his commitment to the development stage of the project. It appears, however, that the completion of this stage, the effects of the accident, as well as Nasser's threats of "preventive war" and renewed American pressure created an opportunity for Eshkol to rethink his nuclear policy: How far should Israel go in pursuing the nuclear project once it has completed the developmental stage? Should Israel maintain or change its policy? Ambassador Walworth Barbour, in his conversations with Eshkol and Eban in late 1966 and early 1967, detected this "lessening in determination to keep Nasser in the dark" with regard to the nuclear project.[67]

It was under Eshkol that Ben Gurion's dream of an Israeli nuclear option became a reality. On the eve of the 1967 war all the components of Israel's nuclear weapons were in place. The challenges that the newly reorganized IAEC, under Eshkol's chairmanship, faced were generally matters of integration and coordination of the various components constituting the nuclear weapons capability. Since 1963 Eshkol had overhauled and completed the technological infrastructure of the project; he opened options for a future nuclear policy; and he placed the project in its proper place in Israel's strategic thinking. Yet, like Ben Gurion before him, in 1966–67 Eshkol was not ready to make decisive long-term decisions on the nuclear issue.

Eshkol was as committed as Ben Gurion to the principle that Israel must have a nuclear weapons program. He was also committed to the principle that financial and strategic priorities must be given to Israel's needs in the conventional field. The IDF must be built and trained so that Israel could defeat its enemies conventionally. The nuclear-weapons option must remain a national insurance policy for an unthinkable eventuality, for a rainy day. Under Eshkol, the strategic objective of the nuclear-weapons option was not to deter the Arabs but to maintain a bargaining chip vis-à-vis the United States and a last-resort nuclear capability.

Eshkol's policies had another implication. No matter how far Israel advanced in the nuclear field, it must not openly be seen as fully acquiring nuclear weapons by testing, declaration, or any other activity which might imply that Israel was moving toward acquiring nuclear weapons and adopting a nuclear strategy. This was the meaning of Eshkol's commitment that Israel would not be the first to introduce nuclear weapons into the Middle East. Eshkol deliberately did not state publicly anything about development, though he did say, in his 1966 Knesset address, that Israel did not possess nuclear weapons and did not want to nuclearize the Arab-Israeli conflict. This was the essence of Eshkol's nuclear strategy in the period before 1967.

Another important domestic aspect of Eshkol's legacy deals with political civilian control. Given the sensitivity of the nuclear project, Eshkol understood that the highest elected official in the land must have firm control over all the nation's nuclear weapons activities. After years during which the IAEC did not function properly, Eshkol reorganized and revitalized the IAEC under his chairmanship and the executive directorship of Dostrovsky as the supervisory and coordinating organ of all aspects of nuclear weapons activities. Eshkol ended the divide-and-rule system by which Peres had managed the nuclear project; he removed Bergmann and Pratt; and, in the face of intense pressure, he modified Mardor's responsibilities. With help from Dinstein, Dostrovsky, Tulipman, Ne'eman, de Shalit, and Freier, Eshkol revamped the nuclear bureaucracy he inherited and declared himself its new boss. These were not small accomplishments for a man who had limited knowledge of nuclear affairs only three years earlier. Eshkol determined the fundamentals of centralized political control over the nation's most secret activities.

Some have suggested that Eshkol's nuclear weapons policy was shaped by his political alliance with the proconventional military thinkers such as Galili and Allon. It is even claimed that under the influence of Galili and Allon, Eshkol slowed down the pace of the nuclear weapons program.[68] This is misleading. More than Galili's and Allon's conventional military doctrine, Eshkol's views were shaped by his senior military advisers, particularly Generals Yitzhak Rabin, Ezer Weizman, Chaim Barlev, Aharon Yariv, and Israel Tal. In 1963–66 these military leaders demanded both longer range tanks (M-48, M-60) and planes (Mirage V, A-4, F-4).[69] They disagreed with one another over the relative importance of each, but they all agreed that Israel should not defy the United States and adopt a strategy based on nuclear deterrence. At the time most generals had only vague knowledge of the state of development of the nuclear project, and almost none were familiar with issues of nuclear strategy.

Eshkol knew that sophisticated conventional weapons from the United States were what his military leaders wanted. A working compromise with the United States on the nuclear weapons issue, which respected American interests and brought tanks and airplanes to Israel without compromising the basic commitment to the nuclear weapons project, was endorsed by both the army and political leaders. Getting sophisticated arms from America in return for a politically ambiguous nuclear pledge, at the small cost of U.S. visits to Dimona, was, for Eshkol, not a concession but a diplomatic achievement.

In reflecting on the relative roles of Ben Gurion and Eshkol, one is struck by the historical irony. Ben Gurion's resolve made the nuclear weapons project possible. The idea of creating long-term stable deterrence for Israel by relying on nuclear weapons was his vision. His caution on the nuclear question, however, undermined his resolve for Israel to acquire nuclear weapons. Ben Gurion managed the politics of the Dimona project, particularly vis-à-vis the United States, in a way that made it difficult to convert it into a vehicle of long-term deterrence for Israel. Because of his caution, Ben Gurion decided, in December 1960, to deny the significance of the Dimona reactor to Israel's security, and later, in 1961 and 1963, to allow U.S. visits to Dimona. The political message of the visits was that Israel was not developing a military nuclear option. Ben Gurion resigned as he and Kennedy came to a showdown on the matter of the Dimona project. The project's founder was unable to find the proper balance between resolve and caution. He left office with a nearly finished physical infrastructure, but with no coherent sense of mission or policy.

That difficult task was left to the inexperienced Eshkol. He inherited the project at its most vulnerable moment, when Kennedy, based on previous commitments from Ben Gurion, brought the question of Israel's nuclear development to the fore. Eshkol skillfully avoided a clash with the United States, closely followed Ben Gurion's path, and still did not create a long-term policy. Yet his resolution of the crisis opened the door for a new U.S.-Israeli security dialogue. Israel was no longer asking for formal security guarantees from the United States; instead, it was asking for arms and a political commitment.

Eshkol was a good custodian of his nation's security interests. He was the first Israeli prime minister to acquire American military hardware. He formed firm, if tacit, understandings with the United States, for which Israel pledged it would not introduce nuclear weapons into the Middle East. In the meantime, Eshkol did not compromise Israel's commitment to a last-resort nuclear weapons capability. He did follow Ben Gurion on the matter of the American visits, but took care that those visits would not compromise Israel's plans.

In the end, however, the legacies of Ben Gurion and Eshkol are not that different from each other. Both directed the nuclear project by muddling through and improvising. The nuclear ambiguity both supported turned out, under Eshkol, to be a virtue for Israel, at least in the short run. Israel seemed to enjoy the best of both worlds.

In the early and mid-1960s many were concerned that Israel's nuclear weapons program would lead to a dangerous regional nuclear arms race. They argued that Egypt (then in a federation with Syria called the United Arab Republic, or UAR), under President Gamal Abdul Nasser's pan-Arabist ideology, would not tolerate it. The Israeli nuclear project could thus undermine Israel's security: instead of creating a stable Israeli deterrent leading to an Arab-Israeli peace, it might destabilize the region and make Israel more vulnerable. Some predicted that Israel's acquisition of nuclear weapons would cause the Soviet Union to become involved in nuclear escalation in the region, either by providing Egypt with nuclear weapons or by including it under the Soviet nuclear umbrella. Others feared that Nasser would launch a preemptive war if he were convinced that Israel was on the verge of obtaining nuclear weapons. It was thus assumed that, one way or another, Egypt would have to react to Israel's nuclear progress.

These predictions did not materialize. Arab governments, lacking information about the project, played down the nuclear issue in Middle Eastern politics as long as Israel and the rest of the world did not talk about it. This was most apparent in the case of Egypt, which was expected to lead the Arab response to Israel's nuclear challenge. Only on two occasions during 1960–67 did Israel's nuclear weapons development become a major issue in Egyptian-Israeli relations, with references to the possibility that it might lead to an Arab-Israeli war. On both occasions the impetus came from outside, as if imposed on Nasser.

The Egyptian reaction to Dimona contributed significantly, if inadvertently, to the creation of the politics of nuclear opacity. Egypt's reaction was not the product of a well-thought-out strategy. Rather, it grew and evolved in response to political, technological, and financial realities. The Israeli nuclear project and the Egyptian reaction to it fed on each other. Israel's policy of ambiguity was designed to allow Nasser to ignore the nuclear issue, and the Arab muted reaction reinforced this ambiguity. The United States, through the American scientists' visits to the Dimona reactor and the reports given to Egypt, contributed to this symbiotic relationship.

EGYPT REACTS

Egyptian scientists had suspected as early as 1959 that Israel had started a nuclear program that would enable Israel to produce nuclear weapons.[1] These suspicions notwithstanding, Egypt was surprised to learn, in December 1960, "that Israel was secretly attempting to develop a capability to produce atomic weapons."[2] Mohammed Heikal, editor of *Al-Aharam*, Cairo's largest newspaper, and one of Nasser's confidants, recognized the centrality of the nuclear issue for the future of the Arab-Israeli conflict. In the first editorial on the subject, he suggested that Israel's acquisition of nuclear weapons was a matter of life and death for the Arabs because such weapons would change the military balance between Israel and its neighbors. If Israel acquired nuclear weapons, the Arabs must get them too, at any price.[3]

On 23 December 1960 President Nasser said as much in a speech, suggesting that Israel's development of nuclear weapons would prompt the Arab states to launch a preventive war.[4] If the UAR discovered that Israel was developing nuclear weapons, it would not wait but would invade Israel first, "to destroy the base of aggression before that base is used against us." Nasser also said that the UAR would arm itself with nuclear weapons of its own. His rhetoric was tantamount to a warning that the development of an atomic bomb by Israel would be an Arab casus belli. The United States took these warnings seriously. That Dimona might provoke an Egyptian military attack was a recurrent theme in discussions among American officials since the early 1960s, and on several occasions such concerns were raised with Israeli diplomats.[5]

Another theme emerged in Nasser's speech: the marginalization of the significance of nuclear weapons. Nasser, referring to the British ultimatum to Egypt in 1956, which Egypt defied, noted that even those who had nuclear weapons could not readily use them against nonnuclear nations. Nuclear weapons were thus irrelevant to the Arab-Israeli conflict, and the Arabs should not feel threatened by them. The Dimona project, then, might be an Israeli bluff, designed to scare and paralyze the Arabs.[6] This line of argument was repeated in Arab rhetoric for many years.

Two weeks after the 30 May 1961 meeting between Kennedy and Ben Gurion in New York, in which Ben Gurion had agreed to share the results of the American scientists' visits to Dimona with other countries, Secretary of State Dean Rusk told Mahmoud Fawzi, Egypt's foreign minister, about the Dimona visit and its findings. Egypt was not impressed by the American assurances. It took the Egyptian foreign minister three months to acknowledge Rusk's letter, noting that Israel's nuclear activity "has been the subject of careful consideration, as well as of consultations with Arab colleagues." Given the Arabs' lack of confidence in Israel, he viewed the Israeli nuclear program "with the utmost concern," regardless of American assurances.[7] This kind of exchange also became a pattern in U.S-Egyptian relations in the early to mid-1960s.

The first surge of Arab public response to the Israeli nuclear project was short-lived. Within weeks the issue dropped from the headlines. The Dimona project was discussed in an Arab foreign ministers meeting in Baghdad in February 1961, where the participants demanded IAEA visits to the reactor, but no action followed. By mid-1961 the issue was no longer addressed in the Arab press.[8] A seven-page State Department memorandum, dated 30 October 1961 and entitled "The Outlook for Nasser," indicated that the Israeli nuclear weapons program was not an issue in Egypt. It did not even mention the topic. With regard to the Arab-Israeli conflict, a war was not expected anytime in the near future.[9]

During 1962–65 Dimona and the idea of preventive war were not publicly discussed in Egypt (or elsewhere in the Arab world).[10] The nuclear weapons issue was hardly raised by the Egyptian foreign ministry in its normal diplomatic dealings with the United States.[11] This did not mean, however, that Nasser forgot about Dimona, since the topic was dealt with through presidential correspondence and American emissaries visiting Nasser. On the few occasions when Egypt did raise the issue, it was in response to American queries.

One such exchange occurred in April 1963, while Kennedy was trying to curb the nuclear and ballistic missile arms race in the region (see chapter 7). The discussion took place in Cairo between Robert Komer and President Nasser. During the meeting Komer mentioned Kennedy's "great concern" with the risks of escalating the arms race in the Middle East, stressing that the president had become concerned before the debacle over the German scientists in Egypt. Nasser responded by noting that Egypt's military buildup was essential to its security vis-à-vis Israel, stating that "on matters vitally affecting UAR security" his country could not rely on American assurances. Nasser went on to describe Egypt's buildup as a response to Israeli moves, pointing out that "Israel started down the path of nuclear development, therefore we had to follow." He also told Komer that the Israelis had conducted the first missile test in the region (the Shavit II missile in 1961) and that the Egyptian missile program was a response to that. Nasser also claimed to have evidence that the Israelis "were planning to use radioactive products in warheads" and that "the UAR knew about the Israeli nuclear installation." Nasser implied, "without saying so directly, that the UAR was moving into military applications of nuclear energy because it was convinced that the Israelis were doing so."[12]

Later in the conversation, after Nasser stated that the UAR and other Arab nations lived in fear of Israeli aggression, the Egyptian president returned to the nuclear issue. Israel's development of nuclear weapons might cause the UAR to go to war: "If it appeared that the Israelis were acquiring a nuclear capability he [Nasser] thought the UAR might have [to] prevent this development in its own self-defense." Nasser told Komer and Ambassador John Badeau that in this case the UAR may be forced to occupy the Negev desert.[13] Nasser stressed that it would be hard for any leader "to trust the vital interest of his nation to others." Nasser then provided another justification for Egypt's missile project: the United States had given surface-to-air HAWK missiles to Israel, which would erode the capability of his bombers, so that the UAR "must go to surface to surface missiles in order to have a deterrent capability against Israel."[14]

In May–June 1963, while corresponding with Ben Gurion, Kennedy also exchanged letters with Nasser. The letters were related to the situation in the Middle East at the time and the shaping of the American arms limitation initiative that grew out of NSAM 231 (see chapter 7). As part of the initiative, John McCloy was sent to the region to discuss arms control ideas with Nasser and Ben Gurion. McCloy began his mission in Cairo.

THE FIRST MCCLOY MISSION

On 15 June 1963, the day Kennedy sent a strongly worded letter to Ben Gurion, he also sent a letter to Nasser. In both letters Kennedy said that "in considering the spectrum of the problems that we both face, I am persuaded that none is more important than that of the continuing arms race in the Middle East." In his letter to Nasser, Kennedy warned of the nuclear danger: "Unless checked, even nuclear weapons may be a possibility in the not too distant future." Kennedy did not inform Nasser that Israel was developing nuclear weapons, but he warned him that without an agreement to limit the arms race, this was a possibility. Kennedy ended his message by saying that in accordance with his earlier readiness to discuss the matter through a presidential envoy, he named John

McCloy to speak on his behalf because of his "unmatched experience in the arms control sphere."[15]

McCloy met Nasser in Cairo on 27 June 1963. He conveyed Kennedy's view to Nasser that a nuclear and missile arms race in the Middle East would be contrary to the interests of the United States and the region's countries, since these weapons were "fantastically expensive" and their continued development would drain the economic resources of both Egypt and Israel. Such an arms race would generate instability "and [would] increase ... tensions with the constant menace of a nuclear catastrophe." This could destroy all that Nasser had sought to accomplish "with consequences no one could accurately appraise."[16]

It was not easy to introduce the subject of nuclear weapons to Nasser, because until then the United States had reassured Egypt that the Dimona reactor was built for peaceful purposes. Now McCloy had to make the point that the reactor had a weapons potential as well. He reminded Nasser that Dimona was a "sizable reactor, which when completed could be used for the purpose of manufacturing material for use in weapons, though we had no information that the reactor was presently being used for such a purpose" (610).

McCloy's statement was inaccurate since the reactor had not yet become critical, which the United States knew. McCloy suggested to Nasser that the United States could offer its services to assist in the inspection and observation of critical sites such as Dimona, so as "to give assurances to both sides that no breach of the commitments was being committed" (610).

McCloy now linked Israel's nuclear program and Egypt's ballistic missile program. He reminded Nasser of the "vigorous reaction" in Israel to the reports of Egypt's employment of German scientists, noting that "if further efforts were made in this direction it could bring about a condition in Israel where the temptation to manufacture material for nuclear weapons would be very great" (610–11). McCloy thus pointed to the Egyptian missile program as the trigger that could change the nature of the Israeli nuclear program. If Nasser was interested in controlling Israel's nuclear program, he had to give up his own missile program.

McCloy noted that he did not come to discuss specific modalities, but to raise important issues and observe the Egyptian reactions to them. McCloy suggested that Nasser meet with him and his aide, Hermann F. Eilts, in two days for further talks. He made it clear that those ideas had not yet been discussed with the Israelis and that the United States would consider an "independent approach along the same lines if the circumstances warranted it." He ended his presentation by stressing that while the matters could not be concluded immediately, they carry a measure of urgency; there were global and regional conditions that require "timely consideration of the problem" (611).

Nasser said that a reply to the American initiative would require careful consideration and consultations that would take more than two days. In the meantime, however, he passed on his immediate reactions. Nasser neither rejected nor endorsed the American initiative. Instead, he raised many questions about it. He was curious as to the timing of the initiative: why did Kennedy choose to deal with this issue now? Nasser's comments during the conversation highlighted his suspicion that the McCloy mission was related to the "Israeli propaganda campaign" about Egypt's missile program. McCloy, in response, cited Kennedy's commitment to arms control, and his own timetable. McCloy did not refer to NSAM 231 or to America's concern that, without action, Israel might soon begin to produce weapon-related materials as the Dimona reactor became active.

Nasser raised a number of "difficulties." He asked why the UAR should be "singled out" from among all the nonnuclear states in the region to make such a commitment. Also, there was the issue of inspection—the UAR had traditionally opposed outside inspection for reasons of national sovereignty. This would put Egypt in a position of a "protectorate" or "satellite state." McCloy pointed out that Israel would be expected to make similar commitments, to which Nasser replied that even if the United States served as an intermediary, it would still appear to be an Israel-UAR arrangement, creating difficulties for Nasser. Nasser suggested that perhaps an exchange of presidential letters between Kennedy and himself would be a better arrangement. In a response to a "written inquiry" from President Kennedy regarding his intentions, Nasser wrote that "(1) he had no intention whatsoever of engaging in nuclear weapons, and (2) he had no intention of attacking Israel" (613). Nasser noted that he might not oppose the publication of such an exchange, stressing that the UAR strategy was "purely defensive" rather than the "attack strategy" he attributed to Israel.

Nasser then elaborated on Egypt's missile program. He said that the missiles were designed for carrying high explosives, noting that he had sought, unsuccessfully, to "find something more powerful than TNT but he could not find anything between TNT and a nuclear warhead." The Egyptian missiles could carry between one and two tons of TNT, but he acknowledged that their guidance system was "a very simple one." As to nuclear facilities, Nasser told McCloy that the Soviet Union had given Egypt a small experimental research reactor, but stressed that Egypt had no nuclear reactors that could produce weapon-grade nuclear materials; therefore there was nothing to inspect in Egypt. McCloy noted that in return for Nasser's renunciation of modern offensive weapons, the United States could assist the UAR in developing peaceful uses of atomic energy, possibly even including space flight experiments. Nasser told

McCloy that he did not expect any major changes in his position, but he welcomed the opportunity to continue the discussion with McCloy and Eilts two days later (612–14).[17]

McCloy met Nasser again on 30 June, accompanied by Ambassador Badeau and Eilts. The conversation was largely a rehash of the issues discussed in their earlier meeting, but Nasser's tone appeared to be considerably more negative than before. Nasser told McCloy that while he appreciated the president's concern, "he could not enter into agreement with the U.S. to renounce those weapons." To do so, Nasser explained, would be tantamount to placing limitations on Egyptian sovereignty. Nasser added that this position would not change if a similar agreement was made between Israel and the United States. Nasser also stressed that "as far as nuclear matters are concerned, there was nothing to inspect."[18] Nasser's negative tone may have resulted because this time, more so than in the earlier meeting, he saw the timing of McCloy's mission as related to Israeli propaganda about the Egyptian missiles. Eilts recalls that Nasser made the point that, in any event, the significance of the project was more for building up national morale and prestige than for military purposes, and thus it would be even more difficult for Nasser to make concessions on the missiles.

Nasser was more negative about the American initiative, but he did not close the door on further discussions, indicating an interest in conducting some kind of inspection of the Dimona reactor. When Badeau asked what he would do if he learned that Israel was using the reactor for the manufacture of weapon-grade nuclear material, Nasser replied, "protective war. We would have no other choice." To this day Eilts recalls this reply as being the most significant and chilling part of that exchange.[19]

When he left Egypt, Eilts recalls, McCloy was no longer interested in going to Israel, and neither was President Kennedy. Nasser had given McCloy too little to justify a trip to Israel. On 3 July Komer wrote a memo to Kennedy on McCloy's mission. Komer was disappointed with McCloy's performance, criticizing him for failing to stress two points: that the American initiative was not a result of Israeli pressure, but an American initiative to restrain Israel in the nuclear field, and that the initiative entailed "real advantages" for the UAR "because of the simple fact that Israel was way ahead in the nuclear field."[20]

There was no point in going to the Israelis, Komer concluded, before the United States received further clarifications from Nasser. The White House, however, lost faith in McCloy and his mission.

On 5 July 1963 Kennedy sent his toughest letter on the matter of Dimona to Israel's new prime minister, Levi Eshkol. McCloy was not informed of the letter. Two days later the State Department cabled Ambassador Badeau, asking him to see Nasser for clarifications of the points on which McCloy had failed to elaborate, that is, the American concern over Dimona. Badeau was asked to tell Nasser that the "Dimona reactor is now in an advanced stage of construction and, while intended for peaceful uses, it does have potential capability of producing fuel for nuclear weapons." He was told to stress to Nasser that it was the American estimate "that Israelis are not and have not decided to start developing such weapons. However, Israelis are approaching [the] stage where their combination of technical skills and physical plant, though developed for peaceful uses, also could give them the capacity for producing a nuclear weapon within a few years if the arms race should expand into highly sophisticated fields."[21]

The cable again linked the UAR missile project and Israel's nuclear development: the Egyptian work on advanced missile development allowed the Israelis to justify "their moving into the nuclear weapons field if they should decide to do so."[22] This was the reason for the U.S. initiative. The cable also criticized the Egyptians for their opposition to inspection and international safeguards for reasons of national sovereignty, even though Egypt had no significant nuclear facilities. This objection-in-principle to inspection only served the Israelis, who already had nuclear facilities at the time, by allowing them to reject international inspections of facilities on similar grounds and argue that Egypt was secretly developing nuclear weapons. It would be in Egypt's interests to accept the external safeguards and allow the United States to press Israel on this matter.

On the missiles, the cable stressed that it was the perception of the utility of the missiles as a means to deliver nuclear weapons that mattered most. Egypt must understand that even if it had no nuclear program, ballistic missiles were viewed as related to nuclear weapons. The United States had reason to be concerned "that Israel is accelerating her own missile effort in response to the UAR's missile developments. We do not know where this would lead." The cable clarified that the United States did not expect "any public abandonment of missile effort," but was looking for ways to "exercise restraints." The cable instructed Badeau to reiterate to Nasser "that [the] U.S. and UAR share a common interest in ensuring that technological development in [the] Near East does not take . . . a disastrous turn." The cable even referred to Nasser's threat of "protective war," stating: "Protective War is not a solution but a last resort and one that would be much more costly to the UAR and far less likely to succeed than [the] approach we are suggesting."[23]

The cable was a plea to Nasser to assist the United States in helping Egypt stop Israel's rush to obtain nuclear weapons. Nasser, however, did not understand the urgency: he did not trust the American effort and was not overly concerned with Israel's nuclear effort. When Ambassador Badeau met him on 11 July to give him the details of the cable, Nasser was still not supportive. He told Badeau that he had consulted with his colleagues, who agreed that inspection would be difficult for the UAR to accept since it would reintroduce "Western control."

The Egyptian response made it clear that Nasser was not willing to cooperate. The American plan for arms control in the Middle East now appeared to be dead. There was no point in sending McCloy to Israel. Secretary Rusk and Ambassador Barbour recommended indefinite postponement of McCloy's mission to Israel, which Kennedy endorsed on 23 July. The first and most serious American effort to curb the introduction into the Middle East of nuclear weapons and their means of delivery came to naught.

ISRAEL IN THE "ICEBOX"

The American initiative faded after McCloy's failure, but Nasser's threat of a preemptive war over Dimona did not. In January 1964, three months before leaving his post, Ambassador Badeau wrote a nine-page memo on the Egyptian situation to President Johnson. The retiring ambassador saw no danger of war between Israel and Egypt in the next several years, with one exception— Dimona. The only trigger that could bring about another Egyptian-Israeli war, Badeau wrote, was "an Egyptian conviction that Israel had started the production of nuclear weapons." If Nasser had proof of this, he might well "attempt a preemptive strike against Israel in the hope of knocking out atomic production centers."[24]

A more detailed assessment is found in another memo, entitled "Various Aspects of U.S.-UAR Relations," which Badeau prepared for the State Department in April, before he had left Cairo. After defining U.S. interest in Arab-Israeli peace as no more than "an interest in preventing large scale hostilities," the memo states the following:

A rather surprising congruence of UAR-U.S. interests emerges. The UAR may not like [it], but is convinced of and has been able to live with U.S. inflexibility on the right of Israel to survive. The UAR has no interest in open and outright aggression against Israel, now or in the foreseeable future. The UAR may have aspirations of a strong and united Arab world bringing Israel to heel militarily while holding the West at bay with Arab political or economic power but few illusions that this is an attainable goal within the next decade. The only circumstances in which the Egyptians would even contemplate a surprise attack on Israel would be if it became clearly apparent that the

Israelis had or were shortly to obtain nuclear weapons. In such a case, the Egyptian objective would be to destroy the Israeli facilities as quickly and effectively as possible and then retire behind the frontier counting on international public opinion and pressure to prevent Israel from retaliating.[25]

Nasser's warnings thus shaped the American concern over Dimona in the mid-1960s.[26] If Israel were to be seen as acquiring nuclear weapons, another war could result. The most dangerous time would be the transition period, when the Egyptians were convinced that Israel was about to acquire nuclear weapons but before Israel had produced them to deter an Egyptian attack.

Despite the failure of the first McCloy mission, the Johnson administration, with Komer as the main instigator, did not abandon the effort to curb the unconventional arms race between Egypt and Israel. Once again, the primary issue was Dimona: if there were a chance that Johnson could convince Israel to accept IAEA safeguards on Dimona, the United States must push Egypt to halt its missile project and subject its own nuclear activities to IAEA safeguards.[27] To achieve this, Johnson wrote Nasser in late May 1964, days before Eshkol's arrival in Washington. The text of the letter is unavailable, but it is clear that it stated that Egypt should accept IAEA safeguards if it wanted Dimona to be under such safeguards. The United States recognized that Nasser was reluctant to discuss such issues directly with Israel, but it was still thinking that "there was ample scope for an arms control arrangement that would avoid points the UAR finds objectionable." The message to Nasser should express the U.S. view that "now is the time to work out something," and its hope that the UAR "will not let slip opportunity to prevent further worsening of situation."[28] The American embassy in Cairo was specifically asked to convey the following to Nasser:

> We have been seeking to persuade Israel, too, not to pursue nuclear and missile development. If UAR continues missile development, we believe this will not only lead other side to obtain or develop matching or better missiles but may also lead them to develop nuclear capability. Therefore we urge Nasser to think this problem through and hope he will consider carefully effects of closing door to our approaches.[29]

The American diplomat was also requested to inquire about Nasser's plans regarding missiles, following reports that the UAR was building a force of one thousand missiles by 1965–66, and, in light of Egypt's use of poisonous gas in Yemen, whether the UAR was planning to install chemical warheads on the missiles. Three days later, on 29 May, the U.S. Embassy in Cairo received more specific instructions, stressing the role of the Egyptian missile program in pushing Israel toward acquiring nuclear weapons. The drafter of the guidelines—most likely Komer[30]—recognized the "thin line between insuring [that] Nasser understands and appreciates [the] nature of this escalation and on the other hand giving him impressions [that] Israel [is] about to go nuclear with our understanding and tacit support." The message should make clear that the United States was not "trying to justify Israeli actions to him"; it was "merely explaining them and his responsibility." Nasser should be convinced that "this [arms race] is a game he cannot win because of Israel's technological development and access to outside financial sources. . . . His periodic opening of [the Palestinian] 'icebox' door has let out blasts of cold air that put great psychological pressure on Israelis to obtain deterrent."[31]

Nasser replied to Johnson's letter on 26 July 1964, addressing Arab concerns and nuclear weapons. Nasser assured Johnson that the UAR "does not think of bringing that terrifying danger (nuclear terror) to the region she [the UAR] lives in," and pointed to Israel as the real threat to peace in the region.[32] The administration, trying to establish a dialogue with Nasser, decided to make another effort to point out the benefits of unconventional arms limitations to Nasser. The specific purpose of the mission was to pursue the possibility of halting or restraining surface-to-surface missile competition between the UAR and Israel.

The emissary was again John McCloy. His objective was "to let Nasser know we believe we can convince Israel to exercise nuclear and missile self-denial if Nasser will limit his acquisition of major offensive missiles either to the number he now has or to a low ceiling."[33] On 28 September 1964 McCloy met Nasser, who promised to consider the U.S. proposals but did not commit himself to them.[34] The talks revealed that much of Nasser's interest in missiles had to do with Egypt's prestige in the Arab world and domestically. Nasser implied that even though he knew he could not win a missile race, it would be difficult to halt the current development project. It also appeared that Nasser did not perceive an Egyptian national interest in closing the Dimona reactor, if the price was losing the Egyptian missile program, or he may have had other reasons for ignoring Dimona. Either way, Dimona was not mentioned in a substantial way in the Nasser-McCloy talks.[35] The threat of Dimona was not strong enough an incentive for Nasser to favor an arms control agreement.

In mid March 1965 John Finney wrote in the *New York Times* about recent American scientists' inspection of Dimona, and two weeks later the Egyptian ambassador in Washington, Mustafa Kamel, on instructions from Cairo, asked the State Department for details of the inspection, "its potential for producing nuclear weapons, and U.S. effort to bring Dimona under IAEA."[36] On 5 April 1965 a State Department officer told Kamel that the department "could not reveal to UARG [UAR government] bilateral U.S.-Israel discussions on so delicate a subject," but added that the United States "had sought to act as mediator between Cairo and Tel Aviv in behalf of regional nuclear safeguards."[37]

Even two weeks later, during a two-and-a-half-hour meeting between Nasser, Assistant Secretary of State Phillips Talbot, and Ambassador Lucius D. Battle, Nasser was alarmed about Dimona. The nuclear issue was raised first by the Americans who commented "about the [inherent] danger . . . [in] any state in the Middle East moving to nuclear armaments." Responding to the U.S. emphasis on the importance of IAEA safeguards, Nasser noted that Egypt had just accepted IAEA safeguards. Egypt opposed American inspections as unilateral operations, but it was in favor of an international effort. Nasser noted that while Egypt had a small reactor "which raised no problem," Israel had a large one: "This in itself was problem of concern in [the] UAR, particularly to the military."[38]

Talbot replied that the issue of unilateral inspection arose only because Israel did not accept IAEA safeguards. He added that the United States, too, "would be concerned if [the] Israeli reactor [was] used for military purposes." Talbot reassured Nasser "that in view of [the] importance of [the] issue we have satisfied our own curiosity on this issue." Answering Nasser's comment that "Israel has influence in the U.S.," Talbot commented that "proliferation is a global problem, and Nasser could have confidence [that the] U.S. is dealing with it in terms of global concerns."[39]

As to the Arab-Israeli conflict, Nasser asserted that "UAR policy was not to have [a] sudden attack on Israel."[40] The message that the UAR was still interested "in putting Israel back in the icebox" was also made in a reply Nasser sent to Johnson on 12 May 1965. The concerns of an Egyptian preventive war aimed at Dimona thus seemed to be remote and theoretical, and appeared to be more of an American concern than an Egyptian military contingency.

Why did Dimona play such a small role in Egyptian policy? There were three primary reasons. First, Egypt was developing its own unconventional weapons, especially missiles.[41] The missiles were central to Egypt's technological prestige, and in the early 1960s the Egyptians thought they were ahead of Israel. Since the early 1960s Egypt also had tried to expand its nuclear program. It said it was interested in nuclear energy for civilian purposes, but it examined the possibility of creating a nuclear weapons program. Salah Hedayat, a former senior military officer with a background in explosives and close ties to Field Marshal Amer, became, in 1961, the leading official in Egypt's nuclear program in his capacities as director-general of the Atomic Energy Establishment and minister of science.[42] To protect these programs, Nasser did not want to draw too much attention to Dimona. Israel followed a similar pattern: to protect its own nuclear program, it did not draw attention to the Egyptian nuclear efforts.

Second, at the time Egypt did not consider Dimona as an immediate military threat. Egypt lacked reliable information about the scope and pace of the project, and about its military potential. Even if the Israeli project were genuine, the Egyptians estimated that Israel was still years away from acquiring and assembling nuclear weapons. To focus on the Israeli nuclear threat then would have lent credibility to the Israeli deterrent. It would also have emphasized Israeli superiority and Egyptian (that is, Arab) inferiority. There was also the view that the United States would not allow Israel to take the final steps to acquire nuclear weapons. In 1961–66 the United States indirectly promoted this view by assuring the Egyptians that American visits to Dimona found no weapon-related activities at the site. This attitude may explain Nasser's grudging responses to McCloy.

The third reason for the lack of visible Egyptian attention to Dimona was that the Arab-Israeli conflict was only of secondary importance to Nasser. The Egyptian president was more interested in his leadership role in the Arab world and the nonaligned movement. The Arab-Israeli conflict played an important role in shaping inter-Arab and the nonaligned movement's politics and rhetoric, but it was not the main issue of the time. Indeed, Nasser was not ready for a military confrontation with Israel, nor was he interested in pushing the Palestinian issue beyond its rhetorical use in inter-Arab politics. The Egyptian attitude toward Israel during this period was captured in a phrase used by both Egyptian and American diplomats: the Palestinian issue and the Arab-Israeli conflict "was in the icebox and could remain there."

RUMORS OF WAR

By the second half of 1965, however, Egyptian perceptions were changing. The issue of Israel's nuclear weapons program resurfaced in Egypt and the Arab world. As was the case in December 1960, the subject came to light not as a result of an Arab initiative, but in response to press reports that Israel had made significant progress in its nuclear program and could acquire the atomic bomb by the late 1960s. Reliable U.S. experts and officials also pointed to this possibility.[43] Leonard Beaton argued that the most volatile period for the Israeli atomic program was, as mentioned above, the transition period, when the Arabs became convinced that nuclear weapons were under production but had not yet been produced.[44] Press reports had circulated in early January 1966 that Israel had purchased from France the first of thirty surface-to-surface ballistic missiles, adding another suspicious element to Israel's nuclear program.[45]

As in 1960 these new stories forced the Arab world, especially Egypt, to rethink the nuclear question. By early 1966 a public debate among journalists, military experts, and academics on the Israeli nuclear issue raged in the Arab press. The questions raised in the debate were the following: What were Israel's intentions regarding nuclear weapons? Could Israel use nuclear weapons in an Arab-Israeli war? What would be the impact of nuclear weapons on the Arab-Israeli conflict? What should the Arabs, specifically Egypt, do? After years of convenient silence, the Israeli nuclear potential imposed itself on the Arab public and leadership.[46]

The most distinct contributor to the new flurry of news and commentary was Mohammed Heikal, who, in August 1965, on his return from discussions in London, concluded that "Israel was about to explode a nuclear device and would be capable of producing an atomic bomb within two or three years." He noted that Israel was financially and scientifically capable of producing atomic weapons. In fact, Heikal expounded that Israel would "find propaganda excuses to pave the way for the detonation of a nuclear device," although Israel had acceded to the Partial Test Ban Treaty in 1963. The Israeli approach, Heikal asserted, would be to propose an agreement with the UAR to ban the production of atomic weapons with mutual inspections. "Naturally, Egypt will refuse to become a party in any agreement with Israel," he said, and Israel could use this as a pretext to produce atomic weapons. He repeated the same theme he had expressed five years earlier: "For more than one reason the United Arab Republic may not want to be the first to introduce nuclear weapons to the Middle East, but it must be able at any moment to catch up for one reason, namely, to survive."[47]

Two months later Heikal returned to the issue, repeating his claim that Israel would attain a nuclear capability within three years and urging the Arab states to work collectively to respond to the Israeli threat: "In confronting the atomic menace the people do not wait until they find themselves facing the critical moment but have to mobilize all resources to be in a position to face it in advance." Heikal called for the creation of a unified Arab air command and for a new and vigorous Egyptian nuclear effort.[48]

There were other views as well. As was the case during the first Arab debate on nuclear weapons, some doubted the value and relevance of nuclear weapons to the Arab-Israeli conflict. Unlike Heikal, who saw the question of nuclear weapons as a matter of life and death to the Arab world, there were those, especially in Syria, who argued that nuclear weapons were not relevant to the "liberation war," a term the Syrians used to describe the Arab struggle against Israel. In their view, nuclear weapons might give Israel a psychological advantage, but they were ultimately not a credible military instrument and the Arabs should not allow Israel to play the nuclear weapons card (see n.46).

By the first half of 1966 the Israeli nuclear program became not only a matter of media interest in Egypt but also an issue in the Arab-Israeli conflict. Egypt had to show that it could face the Israeli challenge, and it responded in several ways. Egypt made it known, but later denied, that the Soviet Union was willing to provide Egypt nuclear protection if Israel developed or obtained nuclear weapons. These rumors, thought to be credible by U.S. diplomats, were spread following the visit of Marshall Andrei Grechko, the Soviet first deputy minister of defense. It was reported that Nasser raised the possibility with the Russians that Moscow would let the UAR buy nuclear weapons, but Grechko offered instead a nuclear guarantee.[49] Egypt also spread the word that it would push its own nuclear research with a view to military applications.[50] In May 1966 Nasser made it known that the UAR was considering the development of nuclear arms because "Israel is working in this field."[51]

After five years of avoiding the nuclear issue, Nasser issued a series of public statements in the first half of 1966, some of them directed at the foreign audience, warning that if Israel were to proceed with the production of atomic weapons, the "only answer" for the Arab states was to launch a "preventive war." "In that event," he continued, the "Arab countries must immediately wipe out all that enables Israel to produce an atomic bomb."[52]

How serious were these threats of preventive war? Were they political posturing or intimations of military plans? How concerned was Nasser with the Israeli nuclear program? Did he share Heikal's view on the gravity of the issue? Were elements in the Egyptian leadership, specifically First Vice President Abdel Hakim Amer and the military, pushing for a preventive war against Israel? These questions may point to a linkage between Nasser's rhetoric on preventive war and the events that led to the Six-Day War in June 1967. To what extent, then, if any, was the May 1967 crisis the enactment of the scenarios painted by Badeau and Komer? These questions are addressed in the next chapter.

Israeli-inspired interpretations of events leading to the June 1967 Six-Day War cite false Soviet intelligence reports of an imminent Israeli attack on Syria as the reason for President Gamal Abdul Nasser's miscalculations that led to war. Arab-inspired interpretations, on the other hand, assert that it was Israel's provocative measures along the Israeli-Syrian border that led to war (this was also Ben Gurion's view at the time). Other accounts divide the responsibility for the miscalculations evenly between the Arabs and Israelis. All accounts agree that the 1967 crisis was the result of miscalculation which led to the failure of conventional deterrence.[1] None of the accounts consider the nuclear issue as having played a role in the outbreak of war.[2]

Issues presented earlier, however, suggest that the nuclear issue ought to be considered in the context of the 1967 crisis. On numerous occasions during the 1961–66 period, Nasser threatened an Egyptian preemptive attack on Dimona. In 1966, as Israel completed its nuclear-weapon infrastructure, it was concerned that Dimona could lead to hostilities with Egypt. Egyptian jets, it was revealed, had made at least two reconnaissance flights over Dimona during the May 1967 crisis. After the war it was discovered that the two Israeli nuclear research centers, at Dimona and Nachal Soreq, were high-priority targets in Egyptian war plans.[3]

These facts indicate that there were nuclear aspects to the background of the 1967 crisis. To what extent was Dimona a factor in the events that led Nasser to challenge the status quo and that led to his decisions during the crisis? To what extent did nuclear considerations shape the Israeli response to and understanding of the crisis? What lessons should Israel draw from the war regarding the nuclear question?[4]

THE EGYPTIAN SETTING

In his book, *The Politics of Miscalculation in the Middle East*, Richard Parker notes that there is a consensus in Egypt today "that Nasser made a terrible miscalculation" when he reacted as he did to the Soviet warning, "but there is little agreement on why he did so."[5] Why did Nasser decide on 13 May 1967 to violate the status quo with Israel? Did he believe Soviet reports about Israeli concentrations on the Syrian border, which Chief of Staff Muhammad Fawzi, two days later, knew were false? Was the Russian report a pretext for another policy objective? Did Field Marshal Abdel Hakim Amer, the vice president and minister of war, or other military leaders have a different policy objective?

Another question is whether Nasser was following a well-planned design throughout the crisis or improvising. Was the 1967 crisis a coincidental series of miscalculations in which Nasser was carried away by his own rhetoric and by Amer's reassurances, or was he pushed into this miscalculation by other objectives? The U.S. Embassy in Cairo and the U.S. intelligence community were divided on these issues. The American intelligence services interpreted the May–June 1967 events on the assumption that Nasser was still interested in keeping the Israeli issue "in the icebox," because he was not ready to face Israel militarily. The U.S. Embassy questioned this assumption. In a telegram dated 27 May 1967, the embassy noted that "over [the] past ten years we have comforted ourselves with [a] number of myths regarding Egypt['s] relative indifference to [the] Palestine problem . . . and have proceeded on [the] assumption [that] Nasser wished [to] keep [the] issue in [the] ice box." This assumption may not be true. "If Nasser's and Heikal's words are to be believed, Egyptians have been prepared for this for some time. . . . Decision to move when opportunity presented itself [was] probably made sometime after . . . last February." Nasser is described as "ready to risk everything" because he "thinks he can win."[6] On this reading, the Russian report might have been a pretext to shatter the status quo and to draw Egypt's Third Army out of Yemen, something Nasser may have planned for some time. Was this planning related to Nasser's warning of "preventive war" against Dimona, which he made a year earlier?[7]

Apart from the few occasions in early 1966 when Nasser invoked the threat of preventive war against Dimona, during 1966–67 the Israeli issue lay dormant. Nasser made it clear that Egypt and the Arab world were not ready to face Israel militarily. The Arab world was divided between "enlightened, forward-looking" states such as the UAR, Algeria, Iraq, and Syria, and "incorrigible reactionaries" such as Jordan, Saudi Arabia, and Tunisia. Nasser's main political and military concern in February 1966 was not Dimona but the situation in Yemen, where seventy thousand Egyptian troops, about a third of the Egyptian army, were still waiting for the implementation of the 1965 political arrangement with King Faisal of Saudi Arabia that would allow Nasser to claim victory and evacuate them. The search for an honorable settlement of the Yemen conflict continued to preoccupy Nasser throughout 1966. By early 1967 Egypt reduced its military deployment there to about forty thousand to fifty-thousand troops. Based on these political and military realities, the State Department prepared a secret memo in mid-August 1966, which stated: "Nasser may well fulminate against Israel but we believe there is practically no possibility that he will attack or provoke the Israelis within the foreseeable future."[8]

Nasser's threats against Dimona were interpreted by senior U.S. diplomats in Cairo at the time as posturing, given the publicity surrounding the Israeli nuclear program. It was thought that the threats were meant for Arab and foreign consumption, talking tough to Israel before the Arab world and pressuring the superpowers, especially the United States, to stop Israel. It was also interpreted as a deterrent signal to Israel. For this reason, Nasser's statements were not taken seriously by diplomats in Cairo and did not change the prevailing view that Nasser had no plans to provoke Israel militarily anytime soon. Supporting this assessment is the fact that soon after Dimona became a hot topic in Cairo in the first half of 1966, it disappeared from public discussion in the following months. Nasser had not repeated his rhetoric on preventive war. Apart from one comment in February 1967 in response to a direct question by a foreign journalist, Nasser was silent on this issue, as he was during 1961–65.[9]

More revealing than the public discussion was the manner in which the issues were handled in diplomatic discussions with the United States. In the second half of 1966 and early 1967 nuclear weapons proliferation was only one of many other topics Egyptian and American officials discussed; it was not a topic of priority. Only two days after Nasser's threats of preventive war were published in the *New York Times*, for example, the third-ranking UAR official, Anwar al-Sadat, then the president of the National Assembly, visited the White House. It was Johnson, not Sadat, who referred to the Israeli nuclear weapons program, saying that the United States was not alarmed by it, as were the Egyptians, and reassuring Sadat that "we were watching the situation closely" and that "the U.S. would be against such a development because of our firm policy against the proliferation of nuclear weapons." Sadat did not follow up on Johnson's comments, allowing the conversation to move to another subject.[10]

Six months later Ambassador Kamel met Johnson and "warned that if any

Middle Eastern country obtained nuclear weapons it would create a very serious situation," to which the president replied: "The US remained adamantly
opposed to the proliferation of nuclear weapons in the Middle East." Again,
ambassador Kamel did not elaborate on the issue beyond his statement.[11] In
another meeting in early 1967 between Kamel and a senior NSC official, the
nuclear issue was not mentioned at all. In the months preceding the May 1967
crisis there was a growing sense that relations between the United States and
Egypt were deteriorating, but the Israeli nuclear issue was not mentioned as a
contributing factor.[12]

Recently declassified intelligence documents also show that the Israeli
nuclear issue was not among the principal topics discussed between the United
States and Egypt, and that it was not central to Nasser's thinking. Lucius Battle,
the U.S. ambassador in Cairo in 1964–67, confirms that the U.S. Embassy did
not consider the Israeli nuclear question among the hottest issues on the
Egyptian agenda at the time. Parker agrees with Battle; the embassy did not consider the Israeli nuclear issue as being central among Egyptian concerns.[13]

Battle and Parker both recall that in early 1967 the U.S. Embassy in Cairo
sensed a storm brewing and even "began quietly to make contingency plans for
an eventual break in relations."[14] Battle recalls that on the eve of his departure
in early March 1967, following his farewell call on Nasser and a dinner conversation that evening (4 March) with Amer, Sadat, and Heikal, he sensed that
Nasser was in political trouble in the Arab world and would have to do something "dramatic" to restore his prestige. A day or two later, Battle expressed his
thoughts in his last cable from Cairo as ambassador. In the cable, which is still
classified, Battle outlined three courses of action he thought Nasser might take:
stirring up trouble with Libya (Egypt had about twenty thousand teachers
there), escalating the Yemen war, or taking the Israeli issue out of the "icebox."
The third option was ranked as the least likely because Nasser had told him earlier that Egypt was not ready to fight with Israel.[15]

Battle's cable supports the hypothesis that the crisis two months later was
planned ahead of time, at least in part. Battle makes it clear, however, that at
the time he did not think of the third option in terms of the scenarios envisioned by Badeau and Komer. Rather, it was in the context of Nasser's status
in the Arab world, not Dimona. When asked about Nasser's statements a year
earlier regarding a preventive war to stop Israel from going nuclear, Battle
recalls that he did not take it seriously for the same reasons: as long as a third
of the Egyptian army was in Yemen, Egypt was not ready to face Israel militarily.[16]

Parker, who interviewed former Egyptian, Russian, and American officials to
explain Nasser's 1967 miscalculation, did not refer to Dimona in his 1993 book

on the crisis. Parker explained the omission by saying that it never occurred to him, at that time and later, when he did research for his book, that the nuclear issue was of relevance to understanding the Egyptian motives in the 1967 crisis.[17] Parker also says that although he was "vaguely aware" of the scenarios drawn up by Badeau and Komer in the mid-1960s, he never thought to follow the nuclear issue in his research on the 1967 crisis because none of the prominent Egyptians with whom he talked in 1989–91 made any reference to Dimona to explain Nasser's miscalculation. As he points out in his book, many prominent Egyptians have written and spoken openly about the events of the 1967 war as they saw them, but none refer to Dimona as a factor in Nasser's decisions.[18]

Despite the differences among the memoirs, an Egyptian version of the 1967 events exists. According to this version, some of the decisions Egypt made in May 1967, particularly the removal of the United Nations Emergency Forces (UNEF) and the deployment of the Egyptian army in the Sinai, had been discussed by Nasser and Marshall Abdel Hakim Amer at various times, long before the Russian intelligence report on Israeli troop concentrations in the north reached Cairo on May 13. According to Heikal, this idea was raised before the third Arab summit at Casablanca in 1964, and again by Amer in 1966 and early 1967. The issue was discussed in response to claims from other Arab states, especially Jordan, that Nasser "was hiding behind the skirts of UNEF." Chief of Staff General Fawzi tells a similar story. He states that "since 1957 the [Egyptian] political and military leadership had wanted to remove UNEF in order to control Egyptian territorial waters." He recalls that both Nasser and Amer made it clear to him before 1967 "that they wanted to seize on any international or regional situation which [would] permit doing away with that force [UNEF]."[19]

Another important theme that recurs in the Egyptian variants is the special relationship between Nasser and Amer—a tacit but tense rivalry—and the role Amer played in heightening the crisis by reassuring Nasser throughout that the army was ready to absorb an Israeli preemption. The accounts, especially Heikal's, stress that from early on in the crisis, the two men pursued different objectives. In some of the accounts, such as those by Fawzi and Heikal, Nasser is portrayed as being interested in a political demonstration of force, hoping to boost his prestige through propaganda and bluffing, whereas Amer was interested in escalating the confrontation, knowing it would lead to an armed clash with Israel but believing that Egypt could prevail.[20] It was noted that the deployment pattern of the Egyptian forces on 4 June revealed a gap between Amer and Nasser: "The troops had been sent forward, readied for attack, but Nasser had stopped them from attacking."[21]

The Egyptian version insists that Nasser was not planning a war against Israel when he made his decision on 13 May, and he did not expect that deploying his forces in the Sinai would bring about a war.[22] This view is consistent with what Nasser had told Battle and others, that Egypt was not ready militarily to face Israel. The developments on the Israeli-Syrian border, however, left him with no choice but to escalate.[23] When Nasser received the Soviet report about an imminent Israeli attack on Syria, he had to take action to deter Israel, given his defense pact with Syria. The Soviet warning raised an issue that Nasser and Amer had entertained for some time, which Amer advocated—the possibility of requesting the withdrawal of UNEF. Nasser knew that such a move would boost his declining prestige at home and in the Arab world without firing a shot.

Still, the Egyptian version of events maintains that Nasser did not intend in mid-May to force the complete removal of UNEF. Rather, he thought first in terms of a partial and temporary withdrawal of UNEF forces along the international border in a way that would keep the credibility of the Egyptian move intact.[24] To avoid opening the question of the UNEF mandate, Nasser decided that the Egyptian request should be made at the military level, between Fawzi and General Indar Jit Rikhye, commander of UNEF.[25] When Rikhye did not comply and referred the issue to Secretary-General U Thant for instructions, the Egyptians were surprised.[26] This blunder was one of Nasser's major miscalculations. Interpreted in this way, the Egyptian move fits well with Battle's sense two months earlier that Nasser would have to do "something dramatic" to restore his prestige and to rally support.

The contemporary Egyptian interpretation places much of the blame for blundering into the 1967 war on Amer. In his memoirs, Muhammad Fawzi portrayed Nasser as a leader who hoped to win a political victory without firing a shot, whereas Amer was looking for a military confrontation from the start. Amer translated Nasser's initial decisions into military orders. According to Heikal and others, Amer assured Nasser during the crisis that Egypt would be able to absorb an Israeli attack, even two waves of an attack, and then counterattack. In 1967 Egypt had two plans for the defense of the Sinai: the first, *al-Qahir*, a position not too far from the Israeli border (the Rafa-Abu Agela line), and the second, *al-Sitar*, in central Sinai. Amer, according to Heikal, reassured Nasser that there was no need even to consider *al-Sitar*, which was prepared "just in case"; Egypt would hold fast at the *al-Qahir* line of defense, and would follow with a counterattack against Israel. Because of Amer's repeated assurances that the Egyptian army was prepared to face Israel militarily, Nasser's gamble became bolder and more provocative.

This Egyptian version of events supports the conclusion that may be derived from U.S. documents, that is, that there is no evidence that Dimona was a significant factor leading Nasser to act as he did. On the contrary, the Egyptian version explains Nasser's miscalculation convincingly: the Soviet warning seemed credible; Nasser could not remain indifferent to the Syrian position; mobilizing troops, deploying them in the Sinai, and asking for the removal of UNEF was the kind of move that would dramatically boost his image among the Arab masses; Amer, who was in charge of the military, advocated such a move and reassured Nasser of the army's readiness; and it was perceived as a low-risk move.

Another indication of Nasser's thinking and intentions during the crisis, and how he believed he could translate it into a diplomatic victory, may be found in the conversation he had with Robert B. Anderson, former secretary of the Treasury, whom Johnson sent to Cairo as a special emissary. In his meeting with Nasser on 31 May or 1 June 1967, Nasser asserted that the Israeli actions along the Syrian border left him "no choice but to mobilize and send troops to Sinai." Although the Syrian issue was at the root of the crisis, Nasser made it clear that he had no intention of compromising on the Egyptian blockade of the straits of Tiran. Nasser said that "he would not begin any fight but would wait until the Israelis had moved," and added that if Israel attacked, "elaborate plans had been made for instant retaliation and that he was confident of the outcome of conflicts between Arabs and Israelis." Nasser recognized that hostilities were likely, but he showed confidence in his army's ability to respond. The Israeli nuclear issue was not mentioned even once in the conversation.[27] This is another indication that Nasser's initial decisions had nothing to do with Dimona.[28]

Based on the evidence, the only conclusion available is that Dimona was not the cause of Nasser's miscalculation. It is still possible, however, that as the crisis evolved and Nasser was reassured by Amer's confidence that the Egyptian army could face Israel, he may have entertained the idea that an Israeli action would provide him an opportunity to attack Dimona. It may well be that derailing the Israeli nuclear program was part of Amer's motives. Nasser, it may be recalled, told Talbot and Battle in April 1965 that Dimona was a matter of concern in Egypt, and "particularly to [the] military." A soon-to-be-built Israeli nuclear weapon would put the Egyptian military in an inferior position, negating Egypt's conventional superiority and reducing the influence of the Egyptian armed forces.

We may speculate that Amer may have been planning to bait Israel into attacking first in the belief that Egypt could absorb the attack and then attack Dimona and other selected targets. There is no way to verify this hypothesis. Amer committed suicide shortly after the war. It may be argued, however, that Dimona was a priority issue to Amer once he set in motion the military steps entailed by Nasser's decision of 13 May, including orders for limited offensive operations. According to Fawzi, as early as 14 May Amer issued orders designed to make the army combat-ready. According to Muhammad Murtagi, the Sinai commander, Amer, in a meeting that day with senior general staff members, already talked about undertaking limited offensive operations against Israel, which had not been considered by the operations planners before.[29]

Whether Dimona figured in Amer's thinking before the crisis, there is evidence that Dimona was high on his and his planners' agenda once the crisis started. The reconnaissance flights that Egyptian planes made over Dimona, the first one on 17 May, highlight this point.[30] Egyptian maps and contingency plans for offensive operations, found in air bases in the Sinai, confirmed that aerial bombing of Dimona was a primary Egyptian objective if hostilities broke.[31] In their memoirs, Fawzi, Murtagi, and Heikal confirmed that the Egyptian Air Force, directed by Amer, had issued orders to attack Israeli targets on 27 May, which Nasser vetoed.[32]

THE ISRAELI SETTING

Even if Dimona were not the cause or a primary motive for the 1967 crisis, nuclear-related events and considerations did play a role in escalating the crisis. Dimona was on the minds of Israeli leaders, especially Prime Minister Eshkol, almost from the beginning of the crisis. Once the crisis began, Dimona became an indicator of the Egyptians' intentions. Dimona also shaped the Israeli assessment of and responses to the crisis. The available evidence is sufficient to conclude that on this account alone, there was a nuclear dimension to the 1967 crisis.

The actions Nasser took in mid-May 1967 did not look at first to be different from a previous episode of brinkmanship in early 1960. On 1 February 1960, following a series of border clashes, Israel launched a military action against Syrian positions in Tawafiq. The operation was limited, but it was the largest one Israel had conducted since the Sinai campaign, creating great anxiety in Syria about further Israeli escalation. Syria was, since 1958, joined with Egypt in the United Arab Republic, and Nasser, the president of the UAR, decided to take action. By 18 February, a force of fifty thousand troops, including five hundred tanks, was deployed in the western Sinai. The move was meant to deter the Israelis.[33] Because of an Israeli intelligence failure, however, the Egyptian deployment was detected only when it was completed, four days after it had begun, by which time the IDF had fewer than thirty tanks to face an Egyptian force twenty times larger. If Egypt were to launch an attack, something Ben Gurion worried about, Israel would have had to rely almost entirely on its air force.[34]

The Egyptian deployment was a direct challenge to one of Israel's "red lines"—a deployment of large forces in the Sinai. Both sides were aware of the gravity of the Egyptian move. Ben Gurion, however, decided to handle the crisis quietly. Since Egypt did not publicize its buildup, Ben Gurion kept the crisis secret; no public statements were issued. The IDF placed its regular forces on alert and moved an additional armored brigade into the Negev, but Ben Gurion insisted on keeping an attitude of business-as-usual. In the meantime, Israel quietly warned Egypt through intermediaries that the status quo must be restored, and if Egypt were to do so, Israel would keep the crisis quiet. On 27 February, five days after the Israeli warning was issued, Egypt began to withdraw its forces. Israel reciprocated with similar moves and the ten-day crisis was over.[35]

This episode, known in Israel as the Operation Rotem, taught both sides a lesson. Nasser concluded that under certain circumstances, he could change the military status quo in the Sinai, defy an Israeli red line, and boost his prestige in the Arab world, all without provoking Israel into a preventive war. He could manage the crisis and keep it under control. Israel learned that an Egyptian military deployment in the Sinai did not necessarily portend war, and that Israel should be cautious so as to avoid an inadvertent escalation that could lead to war. The Israeli military concluded from the episode that Israel must never again be surprised and caught militarily unprepared. Israel must also make its red lines clear to everyone. If a similar crisis occurred again, it must be resolved quickly.

The lessons of 1960, however, were the wrong ones to apply in 1967. Israel and Egypt learned different lessons from the 1960 crisis. In Israel the civilian and military leadership did not even agree on what was learned in 1960. The miscalculations of 1967 were rooted in these different lessons.

For both sides, the 1967 crisis began as a rerun of the 1960 crisis. Nasser estimated that the likelihood of war breaking out was no more than "twenty percent," and that, as a result, his move was a low-risk venture worth taking given its political payoff. For the Israelis, too, the Egyptian deployment appeared to be a replay of Operation Rotem, "but this time without the element of surprise."[36] Interpreted as a repetition of the 1960 experience, the initial assessment of Israeli Military Intelligence (AMAN) was that Nasser would withdraw his forces to the western side of the Suez Canal as soon as the situation on the Syrian-Israeli border calmed down, and would declare a victory for Egyptian deterrence. Based on this assessment, the initial Israeli response, on 14–16 May, was mild and cautious, consistent with the lesson Israeli leadership drew from the events of 1960. The IDF quietly increased the alert status of its regular forces, including preparations to mobilize reserves quickly, but abstained from taking overt escalatory measures. By the evening of 16 May Israel finally decided to call up fifteen thousand reserves, simultaneously attempting to defuse the tension with Syria.[37]

From the outset, however, there were fundamental differences between the two situations. In 1960 the Egyptian deployment was rather small and was made without publicity. In 1967 the initial Egyptian mobilization was significantly larger—three divisions were en route to the Sinai by 16 May—and was widely publicized.[38] The Egyptian army moved through the main streets of Cairo in a paradelike show of force. Such publicity required the Israeli leadership to respond publicly; this publicity made the task of restoring the status quo through quiet diplomacy more difficult. On May 16, however, Israel still did not consider that the situation constituted a crisis; it was still the precrisis period.[39]

FLIGHTS OVER DIMONA

Despite the visibility of the Egyptian deployment, Israel, on the morning of 17 May, was still interpreting it as posturing, not as a demonstration of an intent to launch an attack on Israel. Washington viewed events in the same light, and Johnson, in a message to Eshkol on 17 May, emphasized "in the strongest terms the need to avoid any action on your side which would add further to the violence and tension in the area."[40] The Israeli government, based on the 1960 experience, tried to de-escalate the situation along the Syrian border. The prevailing view was that the aerial battle over Syrian territory on 7 April, in which six Syrians MiGs were shot down by Israel, along with other Israeli warnings to Syria, were at the root of the Egyptian move. When Eshkol appeared before the Ministerial Defense Committee, he told its members what AMAN had told him, that no war was expected, that Nasser was more interested in gaining prestige and deterrence, but that the IDF must be ready. Chief of Staff Rabin said the same to the Knesset's Foreign Affairs and Defense Committee. Moshe Dayan, then an opposition member of the committee, used the opportunity to criticize Rabin for the 7 April operation, adding that given the Israeli provocation, he was not surprised by the Egyptian move. [41]

Two events that took place on 17 May, however, left the Israeli leadership convinced that the situation now was more serious than in 1960.[42] First, the day before, Egypt had requested that UNEF withdraw its forces from its positions in the Sinai, along the Israeli-Egyptian border. Much has been written over the years about this episode, and the role of UN Secretary-General, U Thant, in exacerbating the Egyptian miscalculation by acceding to the Egyptian request, so there is no need to elaborate on it here. This move changed the status quo in the Sinai, highlighting another major difference between the experience of 1960 and that of 1967.[43]

The second event is less known, since it was not announced at the time and was kept quiet for years. On 17 May two Egyptian MiG 21s made a brief high-altitude reconnaissance flight over the Dimona nuclear facility.[44] The Egyptian planes were over Israeli territory less than five minutes and continued into Jordanian air space; Israel failed to intercept them. This was not the first time that Egyptian jets flew over Dimona but the context was different.

Since its inception, Dimona was Israel's most secure installation. The protection of Dimona was the primary reason why Ben Gurion, since 1958, insisted that Israel must purchase a sophisticated air defense system from the United States, against the recommendations of the commander of the Israeli Air Force, General Ezer Weizman, who wanted to buy more planes.[45] In August 1962, after the Israeli request had been pending for more than two years, Kennedy finally agreed to sell the missiles to Israel. The first Israeli HAWK battery was deployed in 1965 around the Dimona nuclear site.[46]

Since Nasser first threatened preventive war to destroy Dimona in December 1960, the protection of Dimona against aerial attack was a major preoccupation of Israeli strategists. Shimon Peres expressed this concern in an article published in late 1962, in which he noted that an Egyptian perception of Israel acquiring a "new powerful weapon" may push Egypt to war.[47] When, in February 1966, Nasser threatened to wage preventive war against Dimona, the Eshkol government made it known that it took all the necessary steps to respond to Nasser's threats.[48]

On the political front, Eshkol delivered a policy speech in the Knesset in May 1966 in which he reformulated his government's position on nuclear weapons (see chapter 12). In a direct response to Nasser's threats, Eshkol asserted that Israel had no nuclear weapons, that it did not want to see them in the region, and that it would not be the first to introduce them into the region.[49] Militarily, Israel also increased its air defense around Dimona, primarily by reinforcing and upgrading the alert status of the HAWK missile batteries in the vicinity. Other cautionary measures were taken, especially in the area of intelligence and physical security. In a 1993 interview, Mordechai Hod, commander of the Israeli Air Force in 1967, confirmed that on the eve of the Six-Day War the Dimona nuclear installation was the most sensitive site in Israel, and there was concern that it was the highest priority target for the Egyptian Air Force.[50]

In May 1967, unlike in 1960, Dimona was an important indicator for both sides. If Egypt intended to provoke hostilities with Israel, Dimona would be a most attractive target. For Israel, an aerial attack against Dimona would be a reason to go to war. Shortly before the Six-Day War, Yigal Allon, then a member of the Defense Ministerial Committee, updated his original list of situations that would constitute an act of war against Israel, justifying Israel launching a preemptive war. The most significant change that he made to his 1959 list was the addition of the following case: "an aerial attack on nuclear reactors and scientific institutions."[51]

On the evening of 17 May, General Aharon Yariv, the head of the Intelligence Branch, altered the basic assessment he had provided during the previous two days: Egypt's intentions were no longer benign, they appeared to be aggressive.[52] That night Eshkol and Rabin decided to call up tens of thousands of additional reserves. By late that evening Eshkol was reported to say to his closest aides, "It is war, I am telling you, it is war."[53]

All the accounts of the 1967 crisis consider 17 May a turning point. The flight over Dimona, no less than the issue of the withdrawal of UNEF, was critical to the change in Israel's assessment of the situation.[54] From that point on, concerns for Dimona's safety became a primary issue for Israeli military and political decision makers, as the crisis began to look as if Nasser were planning to carry out his threat of preventive war.

PRESSURES FOR PREEMPTION

On 21 May the concerns over Dimona were raised in a meeting of the Defense Ministerial Committee. Eshkol expressed his fear that perhaps the Egyptian intent was to attack Dimona: "In my opinion, the Egyptians would act to stop Israeli shipping through the [Tiran] straits, and would bomb the Dimona reactor. A full military assault could follow."[55] Because of Rabin's complaints that he had no clear political guidance from the political echelon, the committee formally approved a set of guidelines for the IDF, proposed in consultations between Rabin and Eshkol.

These guidelines were still meant to de-escalate the crisis—if the Egyptians did not escalate any further, Israel would gradually demobilize its reserves, hoping that the Egyptians would do the same. There was one operational caveat, however: the case of Dimona being bombed. While an all-out Egyptian attack against Israel was still considered unlikely, the Defense Ministerial Committee authorized the IDF, in the event of an Egyptian air attack on Dimona, to respond immediately and without further approval from the committee by attacking all Egyptian airfields in Sinai as well as several airfields on the other side of the Suez Canal.[56] The guidelines confirmed the doctrine that Allon had articulated a few months earlier: an Egyptian attack on Dimona was a reason for Israel to go to war.

The next night, 22 May, Nasser announced the closure of the Straits of Tiran to Israeli shipping. This act breached another Israeli red line. The military pressure on Eshkol to preempt was overwhelming. Israel's military thinking was built on preemption, holding that if war was unavoidable, Israel must strike first, choosing the time and place to destroy the enemy's threat on his own territory. Ben Gurion's principle that Israel must not go to war alone, and certainly not without superpower backing, was shared by a few ministers who urged against going to war. Ben Gurion himself, who blamed Eshkol and Rabin for the crisis, met Rabin and warned him in unequivocal language that Israel should not go to war without the support of at least one international power, and that Israel must dig in for the long haul. A tense cabinet decided to postpone the military decision for another forty-eight hours. In the meantime, the Israeli foreign minister was sent to the United States to meet with President Johnson.

On 25 May the military situation took another dramatic turn. There were strong intelligence reports that the Egyptian deployment was moving from a defensive to an offensive posture. Egyptian airfields were put on the highest alert and the Egyptian Fourth Armored Division began to move into the Sinai. Military intelligence estimated that Nasser was on the verge of launching an attack against Israel, possibly in the coming hours of the night. Dimona, again, was an important factor in heightening Israeli anxiety. If the Egyptians were to attack that night, as many Israelis believed, their priorities would be the airfields and Dimona. That night Israel was under the highest state of alert, waiting for the Egyptian attack.[57]

The same evening, Meir Amit, chief of the Israeli Intelligence Service (Mossad) called the CIA station chief in Tel Aviv, informing him of the disturbing intelligence reports, and asked that the assessment be sent to Richard Helms, director of the CIA, to be forwarded to President Johnson. Johnson received the Israeli estimate by 6:00 P.M., along with a CIA appraisal that threw cold water on the Israeli estimate.[58] In a handwritten cover note attached to both documents, Walt Rostow added: "[unclear] both show how explosive are: Israeli anxieties; Nasser hopes of keeping up posture."[59] Foreign Minister Abba Eban, who had just arrived in Washington, received new instructions to alert Rusk about the new Israeli assessment of the situation and to request a strong American statement that an attack against Israel would be considered an attack against the United States. When Eban met Rusk later that evening, after Rusk had already conferred with Johnson on the situation, he was told that the CIA could not confirm an imminent Egyptian plan to attack, but that the Egyptians would be warned immediately about the grave situation and Moscow would be asked to make a similar demarche.[60]

The Egyptian air force did not attack that night, but on the morning of 26 May the IDF was deployed along the Egyptian frontier expecting to attack the next morning, once a cabinet decision was made. The cabinet was still undecided. Once again, Dimona figured in the considerations. On the morning of 26 May the Ministerial Defense Committee was reconvened for another marathon session. During the session the committee was informed that earlier that morning two Egyptian MiG 21 jets had conducted another high-altitude reconnaissance flight over Dimona. Later that day Rabin informed Eshkol that he had "peculiar and worrisome" intelligence indications that Egypt might intend to bomb "very important sites [Dimona]," even though "their ground forces are still not prepared for offensive operation." Rabin's chief of operations, General Ezer Weizman, was even more pessimistic, warning Eshkol that all indications pointed to an imminent Egyptian attack against air bases and Dimona, and urging him to preempt immediately or at the latest the next morning.[61]

The Israeli and Egyptian armies were poised to strike at each other on 27 May, but their political leadership still did not approve. On the Israeli side, by late afternoon on 26 May, the cabinet decided to wait for Eban's return from Washington; the troops in the field got word that there would be another twenty-four-hour postponement.[62] On the Egyptian side, the air force was ordered to carry out air strikes against Israeli targets on the morning of 27 May; however, Nasser vetoed the orders after receiving the American and Soviet warnings the day before.[63]

When the Israeli cabinet came to its critical vote in a late night meeting on 27 May, it was evenly deadlocked on the question of preemption: nine against nine. Eshkol postponed the decision until the cabinet reconvened the next day, but by that time Johnson's new message to Eshkol changed the situation. Johnson referred to the Soviet message he had received, and warned Eshkol that "Israel . . . must not take any preemptive military action and thereby make itself responsible for the initiation of hostilities."[64] This warning made it impossible for the cabinet to make a decision to go to war. All the ministers except one voted in favor of a waiting period of two to three weeks, until the United States organized an international flotilla to break the Egyptian blockade.[65] In the meantime, Mossad chief Amit was sent to Washington to brief the Americans and to get a feel for the political climate in Washington.[66]

This decision, too, did not hold for long. On 2 June the new national unity cabinet, with Moshe Dayan as the new minister of defense, had its first meeting. This time the prevailing sentiment was different: Israel must act, and soon. It appears that anxieties over Dimona contributed to the change of heart. Veiled references to such anxieties appeared in the military leaders' briefings. General Yariv, military intelligence chief, elaborated on the grave danger of waiting two or three more weeks: Nasser might get carried away by his success and believe that he can initiate military action, such as an effort to bomb Dimona. General Hod, the IAF commander, provided details on four different Egyptian reconnaissance penetrations into Israel, including some over Dimona. Israel was unable to intercept the planes. As a result, the Egyptian air force had become more arrogant and daring. Next time it might be tempted to attack.[67]

The role Dimona played in the 1967 crisis has been suppressed in the Israeli accounts for years. One reason was the perceived sensitivity, enforced by military censorship. Later it became part of the taboo surrounding Dimona. For this reason, neither Rabin nor Israel Lior elaborated on the issue.[68] Apart from Lior's occasional veiled comments, there is still no evidence to assess the depth of the anxiety over Dimona and its impact on the interpretation of the crisis. Recently Yariv and Hod acknowledged the importance of Dimona, but did not provide details.[69] The description of the Dimona factor presented here is partial, but it provides a new dimension to the 1967 crisis.

CRISIS AND MATURITY

In a 24 May 1967 White House meeting of the National Security Council devoted to the Middle East crisis, attended by the president, the vice president, and three cabinet secretaries (McNamara, Rusk, and Fowler), unconventional weapons were discussed. According to the official minutes of the meeting, Helms "was quite positive in stating there were no nuclear weapons in the area."[70]

Helms was apparently wrong. On the eve of the 1967 war, almost all the components of an Israeli nuclear weapon were in place. According to French and American sources (cited in chapters 11 and 12), plutonium began to be separated at Dimona in 1966, design work on the first Israeli nuclear explosive device was successfully completed around the same time, and the French-Israeli missile (designated MD-620) was in the testing stage (reportedly with problems with the guidance systems).

In his autobiography, *Rafael*, Munya Mardor cites the following entry from his diary on 28 May 1967:

> I went to the assembly hall. I met Jenka . . . as he monitored the working teams in the project under his supervision. The teams were assembling and testing the weapon system, the development and production of which was completed prior to the war. The time was after midnight. Engineers and technicians, mostly young, were concentrating on their actions. Their facial expression[s] [were] solemn, inward, as if they fully recognized the enormous, perhaps fateful, value of the weapons system that they [had] brought to operational alert. It was evident that the people of the project were under tension, the utmost tension, physical and spiritual alike.[71]

Mardor does not explain what that unique "weapons system" was or why he called it "fateful." There is no need for further explication or confirmation, however, to interpret what Mardor chose to say vaguely. Some time before the Six-Day War, Israel had achieved a nuclear weapons capability, but it had no weapons as such, and during the tense days of the crisis, that capability was quickly made operational. According to credible reports, on the eve of the war Israel "improvised" two deliverable nuclear explosive devices.[72]

Details are not yet publicly available about the decision-making process that led to readying this fateful weapons system and placing it on an operational alert, but enough is known to make an informed suggestion. During the last week of May, as the crisis reached its climax, Israeli deterrence collapsed. On 25 May the Egyptian forces in Sinai were moving to offensive deployment, and there were indications that the Egyptian Air Force was prepared to strike first. Israel was confronted with an Arab war coalition on three fronts, and was facing it alone. In failing to take prompt action on the closing of the Straits of Tiran, and by Johnson issuing a warning to Israel (on 27 May) against taking unilateral action, the United States appeared to have violated the pledges that Kennedy and Johnson had given regarding Israel's security; further, these actions seemed to have violated a written commitment that John Foster Dulles had given to Abba Eban in 1956, which committed the United States to the use of military force if necessary to keep the Straits of Tiran open. France's behavior seemed even more perfidious and painful. De Gaulle had done nothing to reverse the Egyptian aggression, but on 1 June 1967 he imposed an arms embargo on Israel, an act many in Israel viewed as a cowardly betrayal. At the time France was Israel's primary arms supplier and a partner in a sensitive missile project. In Israel's short history, there never had been greater anxiety over the State's survival.

Domestically Israel was in the grips of a severe political crisis. Eshkol's leadership was challenged in and out of the cabinet during that last week of May. By the end of that week Eshkol was forced to surrender the Defense Ministry to Moshe Dayan and to form a national unity government.[73]

On 26 May war appeared imminent; the only questions were when it would break, and who would start it. Two days later, against the advice of the military, the Israeli cabinet decided to comply with Johnson's request and wait two or three additional weeks before taking military action. Israel entered a phase of strategic vulnerability. There was real concern that Nasser might be tempted to take advantage of the situation and strike first against Israeli air bases and Dimona. If Israel did not attack first, some feared, it could find itself in an extreme national emergency.

Given these uncertainties and pressures, it would have been unthinkable for those in charge not to have placed Israel's most fateful weapons system on operational alert. In a crisis that, for Israelis, evoked memories of the Holocaust, prudence required taking such a step. More significant, Israel had made no deterrent or coercive introduction of its nuclear capability, either directly (vis-à-vis Egypt) or indirectly (vis-à-vis the United States). The United States and Egypt appeared not to have taken the Israeli nuclear potential into their crisis calculations.

There were individuals in Israel, particularly Shimon Peres, who thought, and even proposed, that under the circumstances Israel should make use of its nuclear capability for coercive or deterrent purposes. In his 1995 *Memoirs* he wrote: "My contribution during that dramatic period was something that I still cannot write about openly for reasons of state security. After Dayan was appointed defense minister I submitted to him a certain proposal which . . . would have deterred the Arabs and prevented the war."[74] This remark was interpreted as a suggestion that a demonstrative test of a nuclear device might have deterred war and also established Israel's nuclear status.

Israel could have revealed to the United States that it had a nuclear capability, possibly making an oblique declaration or even conducting a nuclear test. One could argue, as Peres might have done, that the crisis could have been used as the most powerful justification for Israel to introduce its nuclear capability. It might even be consistent with what Ben Gurion had told Kennedy in 1961. (In that conversation Ben Gurion left a caveat, saying that "for the time being" Israel had no intention of building weapons, but circumstances could change.) These ideas, to the extent that some individuals entertained them, apparently never reached discussions at the highest political forum.

If physical possession of nuclear weapons is the criterion by which a state is judged to be a nuclear-weapon state, then, by May 1967, Israel was a nuclear-weapon state. In a political and strategic sense, however, Israel was not a nuclear-weapon state. The Eshkol government did not renege on its pledge not to be the first to introduce nuclear weapons into the region.

Even without access to the actual decision-making process during the crisis, the logic behind the leadership's reluctance to consider the nuclear option is clear: to introduce nuclear weapons in the midst of a crisis would have been a very dangerous gamble. It would have added a huge element of uncertainty without conferring sure political or military benefits on Israel.

An Israeli nuclear demonstration or declaration during the crisis could have been interpreted as a sign of panic which might have invited Nasser to call Israel's hand. It could have triggered further Egyptian defiance of the Israeli deterrence, likely leading to a Soviet nuclear guarantee to the Arab states. In any event, there were allegations that the Soviet Union provided Egypt with a nuclear guarantee during the war and that Soviet nuclear submarines were instructed to target Israel in case Israel used nuclear weapons against Egypt or Syria.[75]

It is also not clear what political benefits Israel would have gained by introducing nuclear weapons in the midst of a crisis. To do so, even in the most discrete way, would have created shock waves with unanticipated consequences. Even if Israel disclosed the existence of its nuclear weapons and induced the United States to act promptly out of fear of nuclear escalation, it would have been interpreted as blackmail and would have damaged U.S.-Israeli relations. Such a disclosure would have been equally dangerous in the Egyptian context. The diplomatic effort to end the crisis would not have eased, but could have become more complicated.

What military benefits such an act would have brought is also unclear. It would most likely have made it more difficult, if not impossible, for Israel to launch a conventional military preemption, while failing to provide the military advantage for such a war. In case of an Egyptian attack on Israel, it is almost impossible to conceive of any last resort in which Israel would use such weapons. In case of a truly desperate military situation, prior disclosure would not make it easier for Israel to use nuclear weapons for self-defense. In any event, Israel's nuclear capability was too small—militarily nonexistent—in 1967 to provide a credible deterrence. Also, disclosure would have forfeited Israel's moral advantage, transforming Israel into the region's aggressive threat.

There is no evidence whether, or to what extent, these issues were discussed among Israeli leaders. The reluctance to contemplate the use of nuclear weapons reinforced the resolve of the handful of Israeli political and military leaders, who were aware of the nuclear issue, to push a preemptive war without delay. In the end Israel launched a preemptive aerial attack, in which most of the Egyptian air force was destroyed on the ground within the first three hours of the war, and in six days the war was over. The Six-Day War had no direct nuclear dimension, but the crisis that preceded the war and the war's legacy must have contained lessons relevant to nuclear weapons.

The most important lesson was the inapplicability of nuclear weapons to almost all military situations for Israel. The situation in May 1967 demonstrated the unsettled nature of the Israeli nuclear dilemma: Israel could not afford not to realize its nuclear option (as a weapon of last resort), but it could also not afford to make any use of it (in circumstances short of last resort). Any attempt to find a military use for nuclear weapons, even in the 1967 context, proved futile. That Israel kept silent on this issue for so long is a strong indication that Israeli decisionmakers understood this point.

The evolution of Israel's nuclear posture was completed after the 1967 war. During 1967–70, first
under Levi Eshkol and, after March 1969, under
Golda Meir, Israel moved from nuclear ambiguity to
nuclear opacity. By 1970 it became publicly known
that the U.S. government considered Israel to be in
possession of an operational nuclear weapons capability.[1]

The post-1967 era brought together a new constel-
lation of political factors—domestic, regional, and
international—all contributing to this move from
ambiguity to opacity. The most important external
change was the advent of the Nuclear Non-Proliferation Treaty (NPT) (chapters 16 and 17). Internal
changes were both technological-bureaucratic and
political.

Domestically, the drift toward opacity was driven
more by technological and bureaucratic pressures
than by political decisions. It was invisible even to
members of Israel's political elite. The change in leadership in Israel and the United States was also important. Under Eshkol, all the components required for a
nuclear-weapons option were developed, but, until
his death in February 1969, he was reluctant to make a
political decision on the matter. The project remained
wrapped in layers of ambiguity and uncertainty as to
its long-term mission, purpose, and future. Golda
Meir succeeded Eshkol at the time that Nixon
replaced Johnson. Under the new administrations,
Israel and the United States cemented the regime of
opacity.

MANAGING THE PROJECT

On 2 June 1967, during the crisis that preceded the Six-Day War, Moshe Dayan replaced Eshkol as minister of defense.[2] The functions of that role were thus separated from those of the prime minister, having been combined for many years.[3] To make the new system work, Eshkol asked former chief of staff Yigael Yadin to work out an informal agreement defining the defense minister's authority and line of command over defense issues. Yadin drafted a two-paragraph document, stipulating the activities for which the minister of defense must have the prime minister's approval and naming the Ministry of Defense and IDF personnel to whom the prime minister should have direct access.[4]

The document did not discuss the chain of command regarding intelligence and nuclear matters, nor did it define the relationship between the two top ministers and the cabinet. After the war Israel Galili and the military secretaries of Eshkol and Dayan drew up a more detailed document—referred to as "the constitution"—which was approved by Eshkol and Dayan. The agreement defined the authorization procedures concerning military activities, including operations the minister of defense could approve on his own, those of which the prime minister must be informed, those requiring the prime minister's approval, and those requiring the approval of the cabinet or its defense committee. The arrangement was informal and not legally binding.[5] Further, it did not alter the tradition of the prime minister being in control of intelligence and nuclear affairs, and the directors of the three organizations involved—Shin Bet (Internal Security Services), Mossad, and IAEC—being subordinate to the prime minister. The control of nuclear matters was less clear though: the prime minister was responsible for policy matters, but the nature of some operational and organizational issues raised the question of who was in charge—Eshkol or Dayan?

It can be said that neither was in charge. After the reorganization of the nuclear project in 1965–66 Eshkol set up a new system to help him oversee the project. Israel Dostrovsky was appointed head of the directorate in charge of coordinating all nuclear-related activities (officially he was the director-general of the reorganized IAEC). In addition, Zvi Dinstein set up a committee whose members were from inside and outside the government—among them Amos de Shalit, Shalheveth Freier, Yuval Ne'eman, and Munya Mardor—to implement government policy. For Eshkol, the existence of such a professional and apolitical body was preferable to discussing these issues in the cabinet or even a ministerial committee. Eshkol believed that only fundamental changes of policy ought to be brought before the cabinet.[6]

Dayan's appointment did not affect these arrangements, except that Eshkol was no longer solely responsible for the nuclear project. On his first day in office

Dayan replaced Dinstein with former chief of staff Zvi Zur as his senior aide (Zur would later become deputy minister of defense). Dayan concentrated on military and political affairs, with special focus on the occupied territories, delegating to Zur the responsibility for the civilian aspects of the defense establishment,[7] including all the military industries.

Zur took charge of the committee overseeing the nuclear project. The post-1967 environment posed new challenges for the project as the need for better coordination with other agencies clashed with the requirements of security. A former IDF chief of staff and an effective bureaucrat with an interest in nuclear issues, Zur was the right man for the task. Eshkol (and later Meir) and Dayan allowed Zur's committee to make decisions on matters of organization, coordination, and security. After 1968 Zur's committee shaped Israel's nuclear policy, with only a few cabinet ministers even aware of its existence.[8]

RECONSIDERATIONS

After the war Dayan, Zur, and Ne'eman sought to change Israel's nuclear posture. On 13 June, only two days after the hostilities ended, the *New York Times* cited "authoritative sources in Tel Aviv" as saying that "Israel's next major military move may be to make the atom bomb."[9] The reason was the crisis before the war: "Israel is said to feel she can no longer accept any guarantee for her security from any of the major powers and therefore must build the bomb as protection mainly against the Arab states."[10] A few weeks later *Newsweek* magazine cited "prominent Tel Aviv civilians" as saying that Israel "has quietly given its scientists the go-ahead to build a nuclear deterrent," and it would be ready "one year from now."[11]

The stories were worded to be consistent with the findings of the American visitors to Dimona. In the last American visit in April 1967 Israel still signaled to the United States that the critical component for a nuclear-weapons option—a plutonium reprocessing facility—was still not built. The news articles gave the impression that the 1967 crisis had forced Israel to change its nuclear policy. Israel could argue that the crisis forced it to face a desperate situation, necessitating a change in policy. It could also state that there was no longer a need to reassure Nasser, as Nasser was no longer in a position to wage a war over Dimona. To informed Americans, the stories meant that Israel was implying that it had decided to acquire the missing link in the nuclear weapons chain— a chemical separation plant. Whether or not the leaks were authorized by Eshkol, they appeared to test the reaction to Israel's changing its nuclear weapons status from where Eshkol left it before the war.

Eshkol apparently considered the proposal but turned it down. A few days later de Shalit acknowledged that Israel had the technical knowledge to produce nuclear bombs and could do so within two to three years if the government so decided, but that the Eshkol cabinet opposed such a move.[12] De Shalit's interview was likely solicited by Eshkol in response to the leaks, which appeared to have originated in Dayan's Ministry of Defense. It is also possible that de Shalit persuaded Eshkol to resist changes in Israel's nuclear status.

De Shalit's interview was important in several ways. It came the closest to an official confirmation that Israel was capable of producing nuclear weapons. The interview also implied that Eshkol's government was still committed to a non-nuclear Middle East and faithful to its political understandings with the United States, but that these commitments were subject to change if necessary. De Shalit's statement also did not challenge the credibility of the American visits to Dimona, in that they implied that Israel had not yet built a separation plant. If there was a debate between Dayan and Eshkol, Eshkol prevailed. In any case, neither of them was interested in bringing their disagreement before the cabinet. Both agreed that the cabinet was not the proper forum for discussion of nuclear policies. These issues should be left to the prime minister in consultations with the minister of defense.

For years Ben Gurion avoided defining the project's objectives. Eshkol continued the practice, contributing to Israel's nuclear ambiguity. This ambiguity explains Israel's responses to the NPT. Until 1968 Israel showed little interest in the NPT, and it was not represented at the Conference on Disarmament (CD). Prime Minister Eshkol, who was in charge of the nuclear issue, was overwhelmed with other political issues after the 1967 war. Only after his visit to Washington in January 1968, when he was asked about the issue (see chapter 16), did Eshkol realize that the new treaty, if entered into effect, could force Israel into a decision on its nuclear policy. Still, he wanted to postpone such a decision as long as possible, waiting to see how the rest of the world would respond to the NPT and how strongly the United States would push the issue on Israel. That 1968 was an election year in the United States also helped to convince Eshkol that he could wait a bit longer.

Eban, still believing that Israel would eventually sign the NPT, apparently held the view that if Israel could live with American visits to Dimona, it could also live with the NPT. Signing the NPT would be consistent with the pledge not to introduce nuclear weapons into the region, without giving up a residual nuclear-weapons option.[13] Eban's views, however, did not count for much, since the Foreign Ministry was kept in the dark about the nuclear project from the start. Those who did count—Dostrovsky's directorate and Zur's committee—

were concerned that the NPT would limit Israel's freedom of action and deterrence capabilities. Dayan supported their position.

The NPT, however, was not brought to a cabinet discussion until the fall of 1968. Then, on 27 October 1968, following Eban's and Allon's briefings to the cabinet about their talks with Rusk on the NPT and missiles, in which Rusk said that Israel joining the NPT was a condition for the sale of U.S. Phantom jets, senior ministers demanded a discussion of the nuclear issue in the cabinet:

Abba Eban (foreign minister): I do not accept the principle that this issue was assigned to some committee. This is a first rate political issue, and it is unacceptable that the cabinet would assign it to some committee. I questioned this. If the cabinet assigned this matter to some committee, it should assign all matters of security and foreign policy to some committee.

Pinhas Sapir (commerce and industry minister): It has never been agreed to appropriate the matter to some committee.

Chaim Moshe Shapira (interior minister): It has been two years since we have been briefed on this matter.[14]

Thus in late 1968 Eshkol's policy of nuclear ambiguity reached its limit. The policy was advantageous for Israel: it allowed it to develop a nuclear weapons capability for desperate, last-resort situations; it prevented a confrontation with the United States; it provided the United States with an incentive to supply Israel with conventional armaments; and it limited the Arab incentives to pursue nuclear weapons. The policy of nuclear ambiguity, however, had its drawbacks as well: it did not allow Israel to translate its investment in nuclear weapons into an open deterrent posture; it forced Israel to deceive the United States; it left the nuclear project lacking in conceptual coherence and organizational clarity. Nonetheless, until 1967–68 it was accepted that the benefits of ambiguity outweighed its disadvantages.

The 1967 war showed that nuclear ambiguity contributed little to Israeli deterrence. It was impossible, however, to extract an additional measure of deterrence from Israel's nuclear capabilities without violating Israel's pledge not to introduce nuclear weapons into the region. In 1967–68 Israel carried its false signaling about Dimona to its limit. It had completed the infrastructure for the construction of its first nuclear devices, but continued to provide American visitors to Dimona with the impression that its nuclear weapons infrastructure was still incomplete. The completion of the NPT in 1968, however, exposed the tensions of ambiguity. The NPT presented Israel with a problem: to join the NPT would compromise the Israeli nuclear project, but to oppose it publicly would mean rejecting the pledges Israel (Eshkol) had made to the United States.

A resolution of Israel's position on the NPT would also have meant a resolution of Israel's nuclear debate. Eshkol, like Ben Gurion, was not interested in making fundamental decisions on the nature and purpose of the project. His priority in 1966–67 was to complete the infrastructure of Israel's nuclear weapons capability without violating his understandings with Johnson. The decisions about that infrastructure had been made many years earlier and, in 1967–68, were nearing completion. The missile project is a good example. Sometime after the Six-Day War, the early excavation of the future missile site began,[15] the result of planning initiated and pursued five years earlier. The commitment to the missile program (MD-620) was made in 1962–63 in response to the Egyptian ballistic missile program. It was modified when the French company, Marcel Dassault, became the prime contractor for developing and testing a surface-to-surface missile for Israel. In 1966 the first missile tests took place at a French test site,[16] but because of the 1967 French embargo, Israel was forced to move the project back to Israel.[17]

The completion of the various project elements and uncertainty about the NPT required a decision on the project's future. Eshkol died in February 1969, leaving that decision to his successor, Israel's fourth prime minister, Golda Meir.

GOLDA'S DECISION

Golda Meir inherited from Eshkol a nuclear project in a state of suspense, similar to what Eshkol had inherited from Ben Gurion in 1963. As Eshkol had faced the need to reply to President Kennedy's demands, Meir also faced the need to reply to President Nixon's demands for Israeli participation in the NPT (see chapter 17).

Almost from the beginning, Meir dissented from Ben Gurion's nuclear policy. She was skeptical about the policy of evasive ambiguity vis-à-vis the United States, and in the summer of 1963, at the height of Kennedy's pressure on Ben Gurion, told her senior staff that she had always held the opinion that "we should tell them the truth and explain why," because "if we deny that Dimona exists then it cannot be used as a source for bargaining because you cannot bargain over something that does not exist."[18] She opposed the American visits to Dimona because they violated Israel's sovereignty and forced Israel to mislead the United States. Deception, she believed, must be avoided in relations between allies.[19]

Meir faced the same problem in 1969 that she had first identified in June 1963—why it would be wrong for Israel not to tell Kennedy the truth about Dimona—this time as prime minister. Should Israel continue to be as a nonnuclear-weapon state, as it was believed to be, or should it change its nuclear status? As long as Americans continued to visit Dimona, however, Israel would not be able to change its nuclear policy.

That the State Department raised the issue of the next American visit to Dimona just weeks after Meir became prime minister highlighted the seriousness of the problem.[20] Meir did not want to confront the Nixon administration on the issue before she had a chance to discuss it in person with President Nixon, so she allowed another American visit in July, a year after the previous visit. She rejected, however, American efforts to expand the terms of the 1969 visit. A few weeks later Undersecretary Elliot Richardson discussed the issue of Israel joining the NPT with Ambassador Yitzhak Rabin, who asked that the matter wait until Meir had a chance to discuss it with Nixon (for details see chapter 17).[21]

Meir's approach in 1969 was similar to the one she had advocated in 1963: "telling the truth and explaining why." Unlike Eshkol, who avoided linking Dimona to Israel's security, Meir maintained that Dimona must be addressed as a genuine security issue. She wanted to modify the understanding Eshkol had reached with Kennedy in 1963. Nixon's more lenient view of nuclear proliferation in friendly states may have convinced Meir that her arguments for Israel's need for a nuclear deterrent and its benefit for American interests would convince Nixon.

The Israeli domestic scene in 1969 was different from that in 1963. Debate in the early 1960s were marked by a division between the nuclear and conventionalist schools, but in 1969 the division had largely disappeared. The nuclear weapons infrastructure was by then a fact, and the political situation in the Middle East was different. In 1969 most senior ministers apparently agreed with Meir that Israel must present the nuclear issue in security terms and that the American visits to Dimona must end. The professionals in the nuclear establishment believed that the July visit had gone sour, and they feared that the American scientists were able to detect Israel's bluff during their eighteen-hour inspection.[22]

The consensus was not complete, however. Yigal Allon and Israel Galili were concerned about American pressure, reportedly suggesting that Meir should follow the same strategy Eshkol had adopted in November 1968 in dealing with the departing Johnson administration.[23] They proposed not to reject the NPT outright and to continue Israeli support for the principle of nonproliferation. Israel should point out its difficulties with the NPT owing to its special situation and, as a condition for joining, should insist on certain requirements—an American guarantee to maintain Israel's military superiority and shield Israel from Soviet aggression. These requirements might be too high a price for the United States to pay, but they were consistent with Israel's past approach. This policy would allow Israel to keep its nuclear capabilities opaque, minimizing the danger of a regional nuclear arms race. Publicly Allon continued to maintain that there were no nuclear weapons in the Middle East; thus the discussion of the issue was, practically speaking, irrelevant.[24]

Dayan appeared to have taken a different approach. He argued that Israel should pursue its nuclear weapons program aggressively and explain to Nixon why it had to reject the NPT in favor of relying on veiled nuclear deterrence. Dayan at times argued for his position in the elliptical manner which came to characterize him. At a ministerial consultation about Dimona, Dayan cited at length intelligence reports about the brutality and torture perpetrated by Arab rulers on their own opponents at home. According to one participant, this was Dayan's way of making his point without mentioning it: he reminded Meir and his colleagues of the standards of behavior of the region in which Israel lived. Meir got the message. She cut off the discussion and announced her decision: Israel could not compromise its nuclear program; it must continue. The decision was backed up by her ministers.

These discussions were important in making Israel's permanent nuclear posture opaque. Since 1967 Israel had an actual bomb in the basement, but no decision had yet been made to incorporate nuclear weapons into Israel's strategic posture. Israel extracted little deterrent benefits from its nuclear weapons, and in fact presented itself as a nonnuclear-weapon state to the United States and the world. The consultations before Meir's trip to the United States were meant to come to a political decision to rewrite the American-Israeli nuclear understanding.

Meir was determined to update the understanding between Johnson and Eshkol, but it was clear to the participants in these consultations that Israel must not publicly adopt a nuclear deterrence posture. Israel should not be the first country to introduce nuclear weapons into the region or to test a nuclear device. For the Nixon administration to look the other way, Israel had to keep its nuclear program opaque. A declared nuclear stance would undermine the American nonproliferation policy and Israel's interest in not introducing nuclear weapons into the Arab-Israeli conflict. Unlike in the early 1960s, it appears that in 1969 no one, not even Dayan, argued for a declared nuclear posture or for changing the IDF doctrine.

THE STRATEGIC ENVIRONMENT

If Israel had a strategic case for adopting a public nuclear deterrence posture, it was weakened after the 1967 war. In that war Israel had gained territorial depth, the lack of which had initially led to Ben Gurion's interest in nuclear deterrence. Nuclear weapons were also not credible in deterring a challenge to the June 1967 cease-fire lines, as demonstrated in the Yom Kippur War six years later. An Egyptian crossing of the Suez Canal would not constitute a last-resort threat to Israel, and thus would not justify the use of nuclear weapons.

The new strategic situation made the argument for an open nuclear deterrence less compelling, but it enhanced the posture of opaque deterrence. The new strategic environment now strengthened of Israel's commitment to a nuclear weapons capability, providing incentives for the adoption of an opaque nuclear stance.

THE THREE NO'S

Immediately after the war Israelis hoped that their decisive victory would engender a solution to the Arab-Israeli conflict through an exchange of land for peace. On 19 June 1967, less than a week after the fighting had ceased, Eshkol's cabinet agreed to offer a complete withdrawal from the Sinai and Golan Heights in return for a comprehensive peace with Egypt and Syria.[25]

These hopes were soon dashed. In late August, in a summit meeting in Khartoum, Arab leaders reaffirmed their opposition to the State of Israel. The summit participants, rejecting Israel's 19 June offer, agreed on three "no's"—no recognition, no negotiations, and no peace agreement. Egypt and Syria, despite their defeat, were not ready for a land-for-peace settlement with Israel.

In Israel, too, new ideas emerged. The military victory moved the nation from despair to euphoria, and it was determined not to allow a repetition of 1956, when Israel was forced to withdraw without realizing the fruits of victory. The idea of a Greater Israel was introduced into the national debate, and new ideological alliances were formed to promote it. Eshkol's National Unity Government could not agree on Israel's long-term strategic objectives, but there was agreement that Israel must resist a withdrawal from the newly acquired territories in exchange for anything short of a stable peace. This agreement kept the National Unity Government in power, with Moshe Dayan emerging as the chief spokesman for that consensus.

In the wake of the Arab defeat, the Soviet Union wasted no time in rearming Egypt and Syria. By the end of the summer the Egyptians had recovered about 70 percent of their material losses. In November Nasser declared that "what was taken by force will be retaken by force, and only by force,"[26] making it clear to Israel's leaders that the military victory was not sufficient to change the Arab-Israeli conflict. To the contrary, with dying hopes for a political breakthrough, they recognized that the stalemate might well lead to another military confrontation.

THE FRENCH EMBARGO

Israel's recognition that the war did not bring the region closer to peace was accompanied by another realization: in the summer of 1967 Israel was cut off from its two main arms suppliers, France and the United States. De Gaulle had imposed an embargo on shipments of new military equipment—ending a decade-old special defense relationship between the two countries—and the Johnson administration had suspended its military shipments to the Middle East.

The French and American decisions endangered the operational plans of the IAF. Before the war Israel had contracted to purchase about one hundred new Mirage Vs and Skyhawks.[27] Since Israel had lost 46 combat aircraft in the war—a quarter of its aerial combat force—the IAF was now committed to purchasing 150 new planes as a minimum near-term objective. The French and American decisions put this plan in question.[28]

The long-term consequences were even more serious. The suspension raised doubts about the prevailing security conception in Israel, and France's embargo highlighted the risks of relying on foreign suppliers for vital needs. The strategic lessons enhanced Israel's commitment to developing a strong, opaque nuclear weapons posture. First, Israel must be as self-sufficient as possible in meeting its national security needs. This was not a new concept. It was the animating spirit of RAFAEL, even if its activities before 1967 were limited mostly to aspects of the nuclear project. Israel remained dependent on foreign suppliers, particularly France, for major weapons. Eshkol's decision in 1963 to sign Marcel Dassault as the primary contractor of the Israeli ballistic missile project, against the pleas of Bergmann, Mardor, and others, showed the limits of self-reliance. Rabin, while chief of staff, was always an advocate of purchasing weapons systems "off the shelf" rather than relying on local development and production.

This attitude changed as a result of the French embargo. De Gaulle's decision marked a turning point in Israel's quest for self-reliance, providing the impetus for restructuring Israel's military industries.[29] Israel launched research and development programs in all fields of military technology, including tanks, jet aircraft, and missiles.[30] In 1968 Israel's capital investment nearly tripled that of the previous year; the average annual growth rate between 1969 and 1973 was almost 10 percent.[31]

Israel soon acknowledged, however, that a small country could not be completely self-sufficient. Thus the French embargo also led to the victory of those who favored the American orientation in Israel's defense procurement. As the United States was to emerge as Israel's major arms supplier, uncertainties surfaced about the reliability of the American commitment, even though the

American decision to suspend deliveries was perceived in a different light from the French embargo.[32] Still, in the summer of 1967 the American decision stirred some apprehension in Israel about the delivery of the Skyhawks and fed the Israeli suspicion that the deal might be used by the administration to press Israel for political and territorial concessions.

The realization that U.S. assistance was not a sure thing and could not be taken for granted proved to be the second lesson of dependence. To hedge against the uncertainties involved in depending on foreign suppliers, Israel had to keep a bargaining chip available for its dealings with the United States. After 1967 this approach became even more important than before, and in November 1968 Israel, as a condition for joining the NPT, insisted on a long-term security agreement with the United States (see chapter 16).[33]

Given the size of Israel's investment in military industries, and the recognition that in some circumstances the United States might suspend its arms shipments to Israel, an opaque nuclear weapons posture, as an insurance against future embargoes, appeared even more attractive than before. A veiled Israeli threat to transform its opaque nuclear arsenal into an open one would provide the United States with an incentive to help Israel maintain its qualitative edge over the Arabs and not to suspend future military assistance to Israel in times of crisis.

THE WAR OF ATTRITION

Another factor introduced into Israeli strategic calculations regarding nuclear weapons in 1967–70 was the change in the Soviet involvement in the Middle East. The Arab defeat brought the Soviet Union deeper than before into the Eastern Mediterranean area. The Soviets replaced Arab war losses, and during the next three years steadily increased their own military presence in the region.[34]

During the final phase of the War of Attrition, in April–August 1970, the Soviet involvement reached its peak.[35] In January 1970 Israel escalated the War of Attrition by initiating air raids deep into Egypt, hoping to break the will of the Egyptian regime. In response, Nasser asked the Soviets to help defend Egypt's air space,[36] and the Soviets sent air force units to Egypt, involving thousands of military personnel, in an effort to set up an air defense system for Egypt. Israel's effort to set up rules of engagement with the Soviets failed, and the first contact between Israeli and Russian pilots took place on 18 April.[37]

Early American reaction to the Soviet deployment was cautious: accepting the Soviet assertion that their purpose was defensive, blaming Israeli miscalculations for the new situation, and forcing Israel to stop the deep-penetration raids by suspending the delivery of the Phantoms. In April–May 1970 Israel became concerned that Soviet objectives might go beyond defending Egypt's air space. The Soviets seemed to be involved in an effort to reverse the Israeli gains in the War of Attrition, perhaps allowing Egypt to start a new war. Israel urged the United States to be more decisive about the Soviet moves, arguing that the Soviet action could threaten American interests as well, but Nixon's response was disappointing: in late April he ordered a reappraisal of the Middle East situation, leaving the issue of supplying Phantom aircraft hanging.

The Soviet involvement raised the issue of American commitment to Israel's basic security. Now, in the face of Soviet encroachment, it was no longer clear what the American commitment entailed.[38] That the United States would not tolerate a direct Soviet attack on Israel was understood; less clear was how Washington would react to a lesser Soviet threat.

In the spring of 1970 these questions were not hypothetical. The United States urged Israeli restraint, but did not clarify how it would react to further Soviet provocations.[39] During June–July the Israeli situation became more acute as the Soviets moved their missile network closer to the canal. The new Soviet missile deployment would give the Egyptians the ability not only to continue the War of Attrition on their terms, but also to cross the canal into the Sinai, protected from the Israeli Air Force by a Soviet missile umbrella. Israeli spokesmen started to equate the "battle of the canal" with the "battle for the security of Israel itself."[40] On 25 July Israeli planes, on their way to bomb Egyptian missile sites, were intercepted by Soviet pilots who pursued the Israeli planes into the Sinai—crossing an Israeli red line. Though a cease-fire agreement was to take effect in a matter of days, Israel decided to meet the Soviet challenge by initiating an aerial ambush of Soviet pilots over the Suez Gulf five days later. Israel shot down five planes in the air battle without suffering any losses.[41] Days later a U.S-sponsored cease-fire was established and the War of Attrition was over.

In these weeks in July Israel, for the first time, was facing the possibility of a confrontation with a nuclear superpower. Israel had to decide whether it was going to maintain its air superiority over the canal and risk a military engagement with the Red Army.[42] Israeli leaders recognized, however, that only the United States could restrain the Soviets.

Nothing is known about the nuclear dimension of the War of Attrition— how nuclear-related considerations might have influenced decisions taken by Israel, the Soviet Union, and the United States. In 1970 Israel already had a working nuclear weapons capability. Even if unacknowledged, the existence of that capability must have exerted an inhibiting influence. There are indications that Dayan was concerned about such an eventuality for some time, perhaps as early as the Sinai campaign of 1956. In his autobiography Dayan talks of his apprehension about Soviet intervention during the 1967 war.[43] After the war Dayan was concerned about circumstances under which the Soviets might intervene in the Arab-Israeli conflict.[44] Dayan could not refer to Israel's nuclear capability, but he had an interest in seeing that both the Soviets and the Americans were aware of Israel's resolve and nuclear capability.[45] A posture of minimum deterrence vis-à-vis the Soviet Union could be an insurance policy against Soviet attack. More important, such a capability would provide an incentive for the United States to prevent an escalation.

There is little doubt that the increasing Soviet involvement in the Middle East was a new factor Israel had to reckon with in its deterrent calculations.[46] Israel raised the possibility of deterring a Soviet attack on Israel in 1968 to explain to the United States why it could not sign the NPT without an American security guarantee in case of Soviet aggression.[47] While the Soviet factor must have reinforced Israel's nuclear commitment, it encouraged doing so in an opaque fashion.

ARAB RETREAT

Finally, the Arabs, too, contributed to the emergence of Israeli nuclear opacity. Before the war, in order to allow Egypt to ignore the issue, the Eshkol government was careful to maintain nuclear ambiguity; it did not use Israel's nuclear capabilities to issue deterrence threats.[48] After the 1967 war this consideration lost much of its force.

The defeat in the Six-Day War shattered Egypt militarily and economically. Egypt now needed its remaining financial resources to restore its conventional army.[49] An Egyptian nuclear weapons program, always hobbled by lack of funds and scientific leadership, was now out of the question,[50] particularly as Egypt's Atomic Energy Establishment (AEE) had its expenditures frozen.[51] Egypt was no longer able to offer a credible military counter to the Israeli nuclear program. Nasser's earlier threats of a preventive war to destroy Israel's nuclear project proved empty. Recovering the occupied territories and restoring the Arab armed forces, not the Israeli bomb, were the most important problems facing the Egyptians.[52]

Opacity allowed Egypt to look the other way on the Israeli nuclear issue. To advertise Israeli advances in the nuclear field would be a loss, not a gain, heightening Egypt's sense of inferiority and defeat. Recognizing Israel as a nuclear-weapon state might have forced the Arabs to recognize reality and negotiate peace with Israel, but this was unacceptable for them in the wake of their humiliating defeat. Thus, as long as Israel did not declare its nuclear weapons status, the Arabs would be better off to ignore the issue.[53]

These circumstances allowed Israel to strengthen its nuclear program without worrying about an Arab reaction. The Arabs, too, were thus a factor in the emergence of the Israeli bomb under the veil of opacity.

DOMESTIC SOURCES OF OPACITY

Domestic factors also contributed to the emergence of opacity. The transition from ambiguity to opacity was possible in the post-1967 era because the nuclear issue vanished from Israeli domestic politics. There are a number of explanations for this.

First, nuclear weapons became a reality. By 1966–67 the project was completed, making debate about it moot. Second, the Six-Day War brought to an end the existence of RAFI, whose leaders showed an interest in using the nuclear issue in order to criticize the Eshkol government. The war brought Dayan back to the government as minister of defense, while Ben Gurion receded even more from the public eye. Six months after the war the RAFI convention decided, against Ben Gurion's wishes, to unite with MAPAI and *Achdut Ha'Avodah* to form the Israeli Labor Party. Dayan and Peres, the nuclear advocates, now joined forces with Galili and Allon, the leaders of the conventionalist school, within the same party and cabinet.

Third, the war changed Israel's domestic agenda in many ways. It created new issues, released new ideological forces dormant since the War of Independence in 1949, stimulated the creation of new political alliances, and consigned old political divisions to oblivion. The future of the new territories became the central issue in Israeli politics, redefining divisions between hawks and doves, Right and Left. These changes marginalized the nuclear debate of the prewar era. Thus the Israeli Committee for Denuclearization of the Middle East, the only public antinuclear lobby in Israel, disappeared quietly after the war. Its founder, Eliezer Livneh, transferred his political energy to a new cause: the Movement for Greater Israel.

Fourth, the nuclear project was removed from politics. The early opposition to the nuclear project, especially within MAPAI, was politically motivated. The MAPAI top echelon combined economic objections with issues of party politics in their opposition to the project. The organizational changes Eshkol initiated in the Ministry of Defense and the IAEC in 1965–66, and the way Dinstein and Dostrovsky managed the secret project, made the project look less political—it was no longer perceived as Peres's vehicle to power—and more professionally managed.

Fifth, Eshkol's policy of ambiguity served to neutralize the doctrinal division over the nuclear project and create a national consensus in its support. The policy of ambiguity blurred doctrinal difference, allowing understandings with the United States and helping to rally bipartisan support at home. All the Zionist parties quietly supported the project as a sacred national insurance policy.

The bomb-in-the-basement posture emerged in the post-1967 era as a synthesis between antagonists in the old nuclear debate. The lack of conceptual clarity allowed the two sides to consider the new situation as satisfying their concerns. The conventionalist school could argue that its antinuclear deterrence stance prevailed, while the nuclear school could maintain that its nuclear preferences won.[54] In a sense, both sides were right.

The sixth factor was the institutional decision-making process. Since 1965, when Eshkol put Dinstein in charge of the project and reorganized the entire nuclear establishment, the executive decision-making responsibility had been delegated to an apolitical professional committee. There was also a secret committee of the Knesset, referred to as the Committee of Seven (including some of the leaders of opposition parties), which was briefed on the government's activities and treated as a mechanism of parliamentary oversight. There have never been political leaks from that secret committee. The arrival of Dayan to the Ministry of Defense in 1967 changed little. Although Dayan replaced Dinstein with Zur, who apparently was already on the secret nuclear committee, the management style remained professional and apolitical.

The nuclear posture as it emerged in the post-1967 period was more than a regime of nuclear secrecy or ambiguity, though it included both. By 1970 it was already recognized that Israel was in possession of nuclear weapons, but the Israeli political system agreed that Israel's nuclear stance should remain opaque.

The senior civil servants and top bureaucrats, particularly Zur, Dostrovsky, and Freier, were the real architects of opacity. They worked under political guidelines, but these were not always clear, so that much of the burden of determining the direction of the nuclear project fell on them. They became the first Israeli nuclear custodians.

The advent of the Nuclear Non-Proliferation Treaty (NPT) in 1968 set the stage for the most direct confrontation between the United States and Israel over the nuclear issue during the Johnson-Eshkol period. The two had crafted the nuclear issue with political ambiguity, and the NPT threatened to shatter that ambiguity. It forced Israel to take a position on an issue on which Israel preferred to be ambiguous.

For U.S. nonproliferation policy, Israel's signature on the NPT was an important objective. It meant that Israel renounced its nuclear-weapons option. Israel, however, could not sign the treaty because of this implication. Because of the public and private assurances Israel had given the United States since 1960, Israel found it difficult to defy the United States. Israel's need to purchase Phantom jets from America set up the context for the confrontation.

The NPT and Israel

The United States fashioned a bilateral arrangement built of sanctions and rewards designed to halt Israel's nuclear weapons development, but the arrangement soon bred uneasiness, even resentment, on both sides. From an American perspective, the visits to Dimona were inadequate (see chapter 10),[1] and by 1965–66 the U.S. intelligence community believed that Israel was working to produce nuclear weapons and was deceiving the United States about it.[2] Almost from the start, therefore, the United States insisted that all Israel's nuclear facilities had to come under IAEA safeguards (see chapter 11).

For Israel, the Dimona arrangement was from the start an imposition: it infringed on Israeli sovereignty, undermined its deterrence vis-à-vis the Arabs, caused domestic embarrassment, created disruptive effects on the mission of Dimona, forced Israel to be less than honest with the United States, and ultimately put both Eshkol and Johnson in a position of being tacit accomplices. By 1966–67 both sides concluded that the visits should be replaced with something else, but each side differed as to what the alternative should be.

For the United States it was the NPT. Until early 1968, however, the fate of the NPT was uncertain. Johnson became committed to the NPT in the summer of 1966, as he endorsed new language that precluded the creation of a European multilateral nuclear force (MLF) after the Soviets dropped their opposition to existing NATO arrangements. These commitments were not sufficient to finalize a treaty. West Germany, which earlier had entertained reservations concerning the NPT because of its ramifications for NATO and the MLF defense arrangements, now became concerned about the possible effects of the treaty safeguards on German industry. A number of European industrial powers insisted on retaining EURATOM safeguards, not IAEA safeguards, and many suspected that the European resistance meant a final hesitation about the NPT bargain: the complete renunciation of nuclear weapons. Only in early 1968, following new American concessions (accepting IAEA safeguards on all its peaceful nuclear activities), the NPT looked to be a realistic hope.

When the NPT was negotiated in the Conference on Disarmament during 1966–68 Israel (which was not a member of the CD) remained outside those consultations. The United States recognized that Israel was a key state for the success or failure of the treaty,[3] but it also understood that Israel's signing was not a sure thing and would require special and laborious negotiations between Israel and the United States. Still, the prevailing view in ACDA was that under the right reward-sanction negotiations Israel probably would be persuaded to sign it, once the treaty was ready and once Israel was promised the appropriate security guarantees.[4] In any case, the question of Israeli signature was absent from the bilateral agenda until early 1968, when the text was almost ready. Both sides appeared interested in avoiding the issue: Israel did not probe the United States about the treaty, nor did the United States offer special briefings to Israel.[5]

The lack of private communication between the United States and Israel regarding the negotiation of the NPT in Geneva was not surprising. For one thing, both governments understood that it would be unwise to discuss the issue until a text existed. Israel was not a member of NATO nor a member of EURATOM and thus was not included among the allies with which the United

States consulted on the NPT. In addition, the timing of the NPT negotiations in Geneva with the events in the Middle East in 1967 did not permit serious discussions between Israel and the United States regarding the NPT before 1968. Until early 1967 the prime issues of contention about the NPT were about present and future nuclear alliances in Europe.

By the spring of 1967 Israel's response to the NPT became more relevant. On 16 May 1967 Harold Saunders, the NSC senior staff member for the Middle East, wrote a memo to National Security Advisor Walt Rostow, urging the United States to pressure Israel to join the NPT.[6] Within days, however, the NPT issue was again irrelevant. The crisis that had started a day earlier, and the Six-Day War that followed, were more pressing. Three months later Israel submitted an emergency request to the United States to purchase fifty Phantom jets (F-4s) and twenty-eight additional Skyhawks (A-4s) to recover the war losses and to replace the French Mirage Vs under embargo. The opportunity for the United States to raise the NPT issue with Israel had arrived, and Eshkol's second visit to the United States in early January 1968 seemed like the right time to broach the subject.[7]

PHANTOMS AND THE NPT

Eshkol's visit to Johnson's Texas ranch on 7–8 January 1968 was devoted to the question of how to start the peace process in the region after the war,[8] but the issue of nuclear weapons and missiles was also of concern to the United States,[9] and it was in this context that the NPT was introduced to the American-Israeli agenda. A few days earlier the NSC Middle East aide, Saunders, set the agenda for the discussions with Eshkol, ranking the nuclear weapons and missile issue as second in importance: "If Israel gets SSM's [surface-to-surface missiles] or decides to build nuclear weapons, we'd have serious second thoughts. We expect Israel to sign the NPT. Will it?"[10] Rostow followed up Saunders's suggestion in his memo to Johnson, saying: "We think we have an acceptable NPT. We believe this will serve Israel's long-range security. We expect Israel to sign. We also believe an Israeli decision to get surface-to-surface missiles would dangerously escalate the arms race."[11] For Eshkol, however, the most important issue was the fifty Phantom jets.[12]

The State Department prepared a briefing book on Eshkol's visit for the President. It included a three-page section on the issue of nuclear weapons and ballistic missiles.[13] Declassified only in June 1997, this section is an extraordinary statement about how the Johnson administration (that is, the State Department, Defense Department, ACDA, but not the CIA) understood and assessed the Israeli nuclear situation in January 1968. As to the factual situation on the ground, the president was told that "on the basis of our irregular visits to Dimona we are reasonably, though not entirely, confident that Israel has not embarked on a program to produce a nuclear weapon" (1). However, a caveat was immediately added: "Our visits to [the] Dimona research facility do not guarantee that production facilities are not being built elsewhere in Israel" (1). As to the administration's assessment of Israeli intentions and policies toward nuclear weapons, the document states: "The Israeli Government is probably determined to preserve its nuclear option as long as there remains a possibility of eventual introduction of nuclear weapons into the area by another nation, or of Israel's losing its relative superiority to the Arabs in conventional military power. We see neither eventuality on the horizon" (1).

Reciting long-held American policy (the document cites Secretary Rusk as saying, "we are as old as Methuselah" on this question), the briefing paper reminded Johnson that his letter to Eshkol of May 1965, which asked Israel to accept IAEA safeguards over all its nuclear facilities, remained unanswered, and urged him to "personally lay out to Eshkol your feelings on the danger of further nuclear proliferation" (2). The authors put the following policy recommendation to the president:

> We therefore *recommend* you make it clear to Eshkol that the United States Government's position on this question has not changed. You wish regular visits to Dimona to continue. You might ruminate out loud on the dangers of nuclear proliferation in general, and your plans for effective NPT. You might also assure Eshkol that the United States will uncompromisingly oppose the introduction of nuclear weapons into the area by any other nation, and cannot visualize any eventuality in the foreseeable future when Israel's self-regenerating military superiority over the Arabs with conventional weapons will disappear. (2)

On the issue of missiles, the briefing paper informs the president that "a French company has nearly completed development for Israel of a surface-to-surface ballistic missile system with a nuclear-carrying capacity. There is also tentative evidence of a similar indigenous Israeli missile development program, perhaps tied into the French effort." On the matter of policy, the paper notes that Eshkol was "equally elusive on these programs, arguing that Israel does not intend to be the first to introduce such missiles into the area but may wish to have them available as a psychological deterrent to the Arabs" (2). The paper urged Johnson to "tell Eshkol that you regard production or acquisition of nuclear-capable ballistic missiles part and parcel of the nuclear question" (3).

The meetings between Eshkol and Johnson went well. Johnson reaffirmed the U.S. interest in Israel's security, and said that the United States would keep

Israel's military defense capability "under active and sympathetic review." He approved the sale of thirty additional Skyhawks to Israel, and promised that a decision on the Phantoms would be made later that year. The Israelis understood that Johnson would most likely approve the request.[14] Johnson asked the Pentagon what the latest date was for him to make a decision on the Phantoms so that, if he approved the sale, Israel would receive the first jets by January 1970.[15] A month later the Pentagon informed him that he would have to make a decision by 31 December 1968.

The United States also raised the question of the NPT during Eshkol's visit. No documents are available on the discussions Johnson had with Eshkol on the NPT, but it appears that Johnson did not link the NPT to the Phantoms. Eshkol, for his part, left the impression that Israel might eventually sign the treaty.[16] At least he did not argue that Israel would never sign it.[17]

AMERICA LEARNS THE TRUTH

A few months after Eshkol's visit the CIA changed its assessment of Israel's nuclear status and notified Johnson about it. The story is still obscure, but apparently it involved physicist Edward Teller, Director of Central Intelligence (DCI) Richard Helms, and President Lyndon B. Johnson.

The measure the NPT used to determine a country's nuclear status was a nuclear test. This criterion was advantageous to Israel, since as long as Israel did not test and the Dimona visits continued, Israel was classified as a nonweapon state. The United States could thus expect Israel to sign the NPT as a nonweapon state.

Edward Teller did not accept this criterion. He knew that a state could build a nuclear weapon without conducting a nuclear test, and, by the late 1960s, he concluded that this was true regarding Israel. By that time he was closely acquainted with Israel's nuclear establishment. In the spring of 1964 Teller met Yuval Ne'eman, and the two became friends. Later that year Teller arranged with Ne'eman to give a seminar at Lawrence Livermore National Laboratory, and they discussed the possibility of using peaceful nuclear explosions to excavate a canal in the Negev desert linking the Mediterranean with the Red Sea.[18] When Ne'eman returned to Israel in October 1965, he told Eshkol of the discussions and suggested inviting Teller as a guest of the IAEC. In late 1965 Teller visited Israel, and Ne'eman introduced him to Eshkol and other IAEC and defense scientists. Teller visited Israel at least one more time in late 1966 or early 1967 as a guest of Tel Aviv University. Teller never concealed his support for an Israeli nuclear deterrent.[19]

Three decades later Teller confirmed that it was during the visits that he con-cluded—he used the words "personal opinion" and "conjecture"—that Israel was in possession of nuclear weapons. "They [the Israelis] have it, and they were clever enough to trust their research and not to test, they knew that to test would get them into trouble." Teller said it was "highly probable" that he con-veyed his "opinion on this matter" to the U.S. government. He did.[20] Teller's views were reported to DCI Richard Helms, and the CIA estimates were revised. A new "Memo to Holders" was issued, asserting that new evidence suggested that Israel already had nuclear weapons. Teller's personal opinion became a fac-tual assertion,[21] when in 1976 Carl Duckett testified before the U.S. Nuclear Regulatory Commission that after receiving information from "American sci-entists" (Teller), he drafted a new National Intelligence Estimate (NIE) on Israel's nuclear capability.[22]

In early 1967 the CIA distributed reports that Israel had produced bomb components and that it would take Israel about six to eight weeks to assemble a bomb.[23] The CIA was not yet ready, however, to change Israel's status as a non-nuclear state. Helms was aware of the sensitivity attached to any CIA determi-nation of Israel's nuclear status ("a real hot potato"). He knew that top policy makers, including the president, were reluctant to accept a change in Israel's nuclear status, and used any indication of uncertainty to make that point.[24] In the spring and summer of 1968, however, it became difficult for Helms to ignore the issue. He passed on several "eyes only" reports on the subject that neither Rostow nor Barbour saw.[25]

Johnson had his own reasons not to act on this information, and it also appears that he concealed the information from Rusk and McNamara. Information contained in an official NIE would have likely leaked, sooner or later, with dire consequences. A public acknowledgment in 1968 that Israel was a nuclear-weapon state would have caused grave damage to the NPT, perhaps even its collapse, as other states might have resisted joining the treaty until Israel did. To admit that Israel acquired nuclear weapons while misleading the United States about it would have also inflicted considerable damage on the relation-ship between the two countries. It would have been tantamount to saying that the Dimona visit arrangement was a farce. It could also have meant that the assurances America had been giving Nasser were false, and U.S. standing in the Arab world would have suffered. Observers might conclude either that Israel had lied to the United States on its nuclear policies or that the United States was an accomplice to Israel's deceit.

Such observations would not have been accurate. Johnson was not deceived by Israel nor was he Israel's accomplice. The U.S.-Israeli nuclear relationship was more subtle and nuanced than that. The subtlety and nuance allowed for the creation of a veneer behind which Israel and the United States did what they felt they had to do. The disclosure that Israel was a nuclear-weapon state would have shattered that veneer.

TO SIGN OR NOT TO SIGN

The expectation in early 1968 that Israel would eventually sign the NPT was not unreasonable or unrealistic. The Eshkol government publicly supported the idea of not introducing nuclear weapons into the Middle East conflict. Israel wanted to enhance its security, and it appeared that a firmer American security commitment would induce Israel to join the treaty.

This thinking appears in a State Department Policy Planning Council research paper entitled "After NPT, What?" and dated 28 May 1968. The paper introduced the concept of "nuclear pregnancy" by pointing out that even after the NPT had been signed and ratified, nations would still be allowed to proceed with peaceful nuclear power programs with implicit military objectives. "It is therefore possible for a nation to proceed a considerable distance toward a bomb capability, to achieve an advanced state of nuclear pregnancy, while remaining within the strictures of the NPT."[26] The paper stresses that uranium enrichment, the stockpiling of separated plutonium 239, or research associated with these activities—all of which could be used in the manufacture of nuclear weapons—would not violate Article 3 of the NPT, as long as those activities were declared to be for peaceful purposes and were under safeguards. The document stated:

> After the NPT, many nations can be expected to take advantage of the terms of the treaty to produce quantities of fissionable material. Plutonium separation plants will be built; fast breeder reactors developed. It is possible that experimentation with conventional explosives that might be relevant to detonating a nuclear bomb core may take place. In this way, various nations will attain a well developed option on a bomb. A number of nations will be able to detonate a bomb within a year following withdrawal from the treaty; others may even shorten this period.[27]

Thus the expectation in 1968 was that Israel would sign the treaty.[28] In late April or early May Rusk sent a message to Eban urging Israel to join the NPT; Eban's response to that message was "encouraging."[29] The positive mood was also evidenced in the Israeli press. On 6 May 1968 Ha'aretz reported that the NPT was under examination by the "appropriate authorities" in Israel, and it was expected that a final, positive decision would be made soon, in time for an announcement later that month at the UN.[30] On 28 May *Ha'aretz* reported that the Israeli cabinet "had decided finally that it is useful for Israel to join those states favoring the treaty." Accordingly, Israel was close "to announcing its intention to join the NPT at the UN, despite its concerns that the extent of its nuclear development would become an 'open secret.' "[31] A day later Israel proclaimed its support for the NPT at the UN, and on 12 June, as the UN General Assembly convened to endorse the NPT, Israel voted in favor of the treaty. General Assembly resolutions are only recommendations, not binding on governments.

Later in June the annual visit to Dimona took place. In anticipation of Israel's signing the NPT, Israeli officials dealing with nuclear matters were concerned about the application of IAEA/NPT safeguard mechanisms to the Israeli case. The American team leader was again Floyd Culler. In instructions from Washington cabled to the Culler team on 27 June, "in connection with [the] discussion of NPT or related subjects that might arise during [the] visit," the visiting team was asked "to avoid possible misinterpretation which might imply US acquiescence in specially-tailored modifications of basic IAEA inspection procedures to meet Israeli sensitivities." The State Department requested that the team "avoid offering any suggestions, even though advanced personally which might be interpreted by Israeli contacts as officially inspired probes of possible Israeli acceptance [of] particular concessions in application [of] IAEA safeguards." Members of the team were instructed to "be alert to and report any conversations which might indicate Israeli thinking on this subject."[32]

In mid-1968 the NPT safeguards mechanism was not yet formed. The existing IAEA safeguards system, as set forth in IAEA Information Circular (INF-CIRC) 66, did not accord in all respects with Article 3 of the NPT, and a new mechanism would have to be created. Still, that Dimona would be subjected to IAEA safeguards was anathema to the project's managers. To have IAEA inspectors roaming around Dimona was inconceivable to them.

Still, by late June the Israeli Foreign Ministry hinted that Israel would eventually sign the NPT. Israel might not rush to sign it, and would certainly look at other countries' behavior, but given the understandings with the United States and the impending Phantoms deal, the message sought to assure the United States. The message probably meant little beyond the interest to avoid confrontation with the United States and the fact that the Foreign Ministry had very little understanding of what the NPT was all about.

On 1 July the NPT was presented for signature in Washington, London, and Moscow, and sixty-five nations signed on that first day. As expected, Israel was not among them. "Authoritative Israeli sources" told the Associated Press on 1 July that although Israel approved the treaty "in principle," it did not sign it because it had "certain reservations" and further action would require new cabinet decisions.[33] *Ha'aretz* reported that Israel would continue to consult on the matter of the NPT with other states "in a similar situation," and that the UN vote did not imply that Israel would be among the first signers. Still, political sources in Jerusalem maintained that Israel would eventually sign, pending another cabinet approval.[34] On 7 August Foreign Minister Eban noted in the Knesset that Israel had voted favorably on the treaty in the UN, and expressed his personal regret that Israel still needed time for final deliberations.[35] Eban's response suggests that there was disagreement among different government agencies about the treaty. By late August it was reported that Israel still had not completed its deliberations on the NPT, and that no decision would be made before the meeting of the nonnuclear-weapon states in Geneva later in September.[36] For the first time Israeli sources made public the point that, unlike other states with a nuclear-weapon potential, Israel had not been consulted during the negotiations in Geneva on the final draft, and it needed more time to examine the treaty.[37] Still, the delay was presented as a tactical move, not a change of heart. This wait-and-see attitude toward the NPT was in keeping with Eshkol's style of governing in any event, and the uncertainties about Israel's strategy following the new regional situation after the Six-Day War added to that.[38]

On the night of 20 August 1968 the Soviet Union invaded Czechoslovakia, bringing an end to the liberal policies of Alexander Dubcek. This invasion had a chilling effect on the East-West relationship, especially in the area of arms control. The United States canceled a joint announcement of a summit that would initiate the Strategic Arms Limitation Talks (SALT). The NPT ratification process in the Senate was slowed down, and on 11 October the Senate decided to postpone action on it. Presidential candidate Richard Nixon made clear that he opposed ratifying the treaty as long as Soviet troops remained on Czech soil.

Other nations followed the American example, signing the treaty and then postponing ratification. Of the three sponsors, only Britain ratified the NPT soon after signing it. By the fall it became evident that the NPT was a long way from entering into effect (the treaty would become effective only when forty-three nations, including the three sponsors, had signed and ratified it). Many of the nonsignatories raised objections to the treaty's provisions, especially regarding security guarantees against nuclear attack or threat of attack.

The Soviet invasion created a climate that helped the forces in Israel who opposed the NPT. By September those voices became public. It became known that Israel had serious issues with the treaty, but was careful in expressing those doubts. Early that month Israeli sources cited substantive security reservations about the applicability of the NPT to the Israeli case, but without rejecting it outright.[39] Unnamed sources made the point that the NPT contained no guarantees against aggression by a nuclear power against a nonnuclear state.[40] Another comment was that the real security threat Israel faced was conventional, not nuclear, and that this issue must be dealt with before Israel could join the NPT.[41]

The lack of evidence on the decision making that led to this conclusion allows only for a logical reconstruction of the dilemma the NPT posed for Israel and the kind of reasoning that might have shaped the new assessment. The NPT forced Israel to make a stand on its nuclear policy: whether to formalize the nonnuclear stance as the act of signing implied or to elevate a posture of ambiguity and uncertainty by not signing, possibly breaking the special understandings with the United States and risking the Phantoms deal. The Israeli decision was shaped by political, legal, and technical considerations. Signing the NPT meant that Israel would renounce its nuclear-weapons option. Under the NPT, a nation would be legally obliged not to carry out any activities directed at the acquisition or manufacturing of nuclear devices (Article 2). Though the treaty is ambiguous as to the exact scope of this prohibition—it contains no definitions of the key terms "manufacture" or "nuclear explosive devices"—its negotiating record suggests that the term "manufacturing" should be meant to encompass all activities that entail the intention to make nuclear weapons. To argue that there was no difference between the American visits to Dimona and the NPT/IAEA safeguards system is to misunderstand the NPT as an international treaty. There is a difference between a secret arrangement between two countries and an obligation a state undertakes not to manufacture nuclear weapons under an international treaty.[42] The legal and political restrictions on a nation's freedom of action under the NPT were greater than the restrictions under the American-Israeli arrangement. Article 3 sets up the terms to verify compliance or noncompliance, requiring a nonweapons signatory state to conclude a full-scope safeguards agreement with the IAEA, "with a view to preventing diversion of nuclear energy from peaceful uses to nuclear weapons." It sets up a safeguards system whose mandate extends to "all source or special fissionable material in all peaceful nuclear activities within the territory of such State."

It could be argued that under the NPT neither uranium enrichment nor stockpiling of separated plutonium nor research associated with these activities—all of which are used in the manufacture of nuclear weapons—would violate Articles 2 or 3, as long as those activities were declared and under safeguards. This is technically true, and yet such reasoning would be grossly mistaken. To manipulate a bilateral arrangement conducted under tight Israeli control of the ground rules is one thing; to do so under an IAEA full-scope safeguards agreement is quite another.

The restrictions embodied in the NPT thus made it inconsistent with a posture of ambiguity, let alone a secret nuclear weapons program. Israel could not have it both ways: NPT and public ambiguity. If Israel had already developed and manufactured nuclear devices, it could not sign the NPT as a nonnuclear state without materially violating it. Joining the NPT would have compromised the Israeli nuclear project, and complying with Articles 2 and 3 would have meant an end to Israel's nuclear option.

These considerations were presumably the topic of discussion among Israeli decisionmakers. If anything, the prevailing sentiment was that Israel should find a way to liberate itself from the confines of the U.S.-Israeli arrangement, which was already imposing limits on Israel's posture of ambiguity. Dayan and other advocates of the nuclear-weapons option could not agree that Israel should commit itself to renounce nuclear weapons, no matter how strongly the United States insisted.

THE RUSK-EBAN ENCOUNTER

The conclusion that Israel could not sign the NPT was reached gradually. In the fall of 1968 the NPT was debated among Israeli decisionmakers, but no cabinet decision was made. Eshkol's health deteriorated, forcing him to cancel his December trip to Latin America and the United States, and he could no longer lead the deliberations. In these debates it appears that Dayan, Zur, and the IAEC director-general Dostrovsky opposed signing the NPT, while Foreign Minister Eban and Deputy Prime Minister Allon were less determined. The consensus was that Israel should wait at least until after the American elections in November 1968.

The main Israeli concern in the fall of 1968 was how to assure the sale of American Phantoms to Israel without making strategic concessions in exchange. The Soviet invasion of Czechoslovakia and the presidential campaign in the United States created an opportunity for Israel to do so. Yigal Allon and Abba Eban visited Washington in September and October, making the case for the Phantoms sale and testing how hard the United States would press Israel on the NPT. Rusk, in a memo to Johnson, characterized the Israeli position on the NPT as "(a) it [Israel] stands on Eshkol's commitment not to be the first to introduce nuclear weapons into the area, (b) it nevertheless sees some advantage in keeping the Arabs in doubt about its capabilities, and (c) it has not decided not to sign the NPT but wants to stay in step with other nations which have doubts about security assurances provided by the NPT."[43]

Allon, in his meetings with President Johnson and Secretary Rusk, urged the United States to supply the fifty Phantoms to Israel "right away," as a means to deter possible Soviet-inspired Arab aggression. He told the president that "the

Czech experience will encourage other actions in the Mid-East to take the spot-light off of Czechoslovakia." He also noted that "the Arabs will not begin to make peace until they know Israel is unassailable."[44] Much of Allon's discus-sions with Rusk, however, focused on the nuclear and missile issue. The secre-tary asked hard, factual questions. First he asked about the status of the MD-620 missile program, to which Allon replied that as far as that program is con-cerned "Israeli dreams had vanished," and that if the Mirage V deal with France was "dead," the MD-620 program was "doubly dead." Asked whether Israel was not itself producing the surface-to-surface missile (SSM), Allon replied, "No, not yet." Both Allon and Rabin told Rusk that they did not attach much impor-tance to SSMs because such missiles equipped with conventional warheads require an extremely high degree of accuracy.

At this point Rusk moved to the issue of nuclear weapons. He asked what kind of assurances Israel could give that the Phantoms would not be used to deliver nuclear weapons and why Israel had not signed the NPT. Allon stated that Israel had no nuclear weapons and reiterated Eshkol's pledge that Israel would not be the first to introduce nuclear weapons, and referred to the American inspections at Dimona as giving additional assurances. On this, Rusk commented that those inspections applied only to Dimona and not to other sites. In moving to the matter of the NPT, Rusk told Allon that Israel's response had been unsatisfactory, vague, and unresponsive. Both Allon and Rabin explained that Israel wanted a degree of uncertainty to persist among the Egyptians as to its nuclear capability "as a form of deterrent." Rusk replied that by leaving such a question unanswered in the Egyptians' minds, Israel also left the United States doubtful as to Israel's true nuclear intentions. Allon responded that he was personally convinced that "sooner or later" Israel would sign the treaty.[45] One cannot escape the impression that Allon confused his own opinions with the facts on the ground—whether this was a deliberate deception or self-deception is hard to say. In any case, Allon took to heart Rusk's interro-gation. In his briefing to his cabinet colleagues on his return, Allon noted that "for Dean Rusk, the NPT is a matter of personal obsession, and I do not exclude that he would link the supply of the planes with our signing the NPT."[46]

Three weeks later, when Rusk met Eban at the UN, most of the discussion was on the NPT issue. Rusk asked if the Israeli cabinet had considered signing the NPT. Eban replied that the NPT was not discussed at the cabinet level but "in a special body established for that purpose." Eban asked Rusk not to inter-pret his June letter as reflecting "any change in the Israeli position. Israel had not gone nuclear and had not decided not to sign [the] NPT. Nuclear activities in Israel were being carried out only at two places known to USG [the U.S. gov-ernment]." Eban noted that "Israel wished to swim in the international cur-

rent," and to work with those states seeking greater security assurances for signing the NPT. "Israel was considering [the] NPT in [a] positive spirit but had to
take [a] long-term view of its security." In addition, Eban added, Israel was concerned about the IAEA inspection system, "given [the] fact that Israel never
enjoyed [a] break in IAEA." Eban evidently ended his comments on a conciliatory note. "Israel was not reneging on its original position but wanted to take
[a] long look at all implications of NPT signature." When the secretary asked
what the Israeli time frame was for such considerations, Eban was noncommit-
tal, saying that the issue would be considered after the Geneva conference of the
nonnuclear nations.[47]

The American effort to link the F-4s sale with the NPT and other Israeli
political concessions intensified and became public in September. As Israel continued to postpone its decision on the NPT, the United States delayed its decision on the F-4s, while quietly approving a less controversial sale of twelve additional A-4s. The administration—with Secretary of State Rusk and Assistant
Secretary of Defense for International Security Affairs Paul Warnke leading the
effort[48]—advocated the use of the F-4s as bargaining chips.[49] In mid-September
"administration sources" leaked to the New York Times that Johnson had
"decided not to sell the Phantoms to Israel in the near future."[50] This was not
the case, however. As Johnson told his advisers at the White House two days
later, "we have made no decision—either to supply them or not to supply
them—although the former is more likely."[51]

The anticipated negotiations on the sale of the F-4s may explain the disclosures in early October by Eshkol and Eban of Israel's nuclear status. In almost
identical language, Eshkol and Eban said that Israel "has now acquired the technical know-how" to produce nuclear weapons, though both emphasized that "it
was a long way from this to producing nuclear weapons."[52] In a speech given at
Kibbutz Deganya Eshkol said he saw no need for Israel to rush into signing the
NPT; he also referred to the heavy Soviet military involvement in Egypt that
might lead to a future Soviet-Israeli confrontation.[53] A day later the Jerusalem
Post openly advocated an Israeli nuclear deterrent.[54] The statements went
beyond the verbal formula that Israel will not be the first country to introduce
nuclear weapons into the region.[55] Others had made similar statements previously, but these words were now uttered by the highest political authority.

The disclosures caught the attention of the Israelis. Some criticized Eshkol
and Eban for their "loose talk," claiming they might have breached national
security.[56] It is inconceivable, however, that the statements were accidental—
there were no casual comments on nuclear matters in Israel. Most likely the disclosures were a coordinated effort to convey the message that Israel had a significant technological lead in nuclear weapons, and signing the NPT would

therefore entail a considerable sacrifice. Israel was thus justified in demanding security guarantees from the United States in return.

On 9 October Johnson announced that the administration would formally negotiate with Israel on the sale of F-4s. This did not mean the end of American pressure on Israel to sign the NPT. On the contrary, a recently declassified "Top-Secret" document prepared for Rusk, dated 18 October and entitled "Structuring the Negotiations with the Israelis," highlights how both the State Department and the Pentagon intended to use the formal negotiations as a tool to get new assurances from Israel on the matter of nuclear weapons and ballistic missiles. The document notes that the F-4 negotiations encompassed very sensitive issues. Those issues were not matters of hardware and financing relating to the sale—those matters required very little discussion—but rather the missile/nuclear issue. The Defense Department did not want to conclude the sale until agreement between the two governments was reached on these sensitive matters. The document states that Secretary of Defense Clifford was interested in obtaining "very firm reassurances from the Israelis in respect to the missile/nuclear issue." It also suggests that "in view of the sensitivity and gravity of this subject it appears desirable for you now to deal directly with Secretary Clifford and the President." The division of labor that was proposed was that both President Johnson and Secretary Rusk would meet Eban on 23 October, but the president would limit his comments and the actual negotiation would be conducted by Rusk, possibly with the participation of Clifford or Nitze.

Rusk and Warnke did not know what Helms had told Johnson earlier that year, namely, that the CIA had now concluded that Israel was already in possession of nuclear weapons. Though Rusk was informed of the 1967 intelligence reports that Israel was weeks away from the bomb, he was also aware of the political utility of the American visits in Dimona, as long as the visitors reported that no hard evidence of weapon-related activities were found there. The State Department's assessment of Israel's nuclear capability was stated clearly in a memo that was submitted to Rusk a day before his meeting with Eban: "According to our best intelligence, Israel is close to, but has not yet crossed the threshold of decision to become a nuclear power in terms of both a nuclear weapon and a delivery system."[57]

As late as 26 November Rusk told Johnson, in a reference to the Israeli nuclear case: "If they are 5-months pregnant, it may not be too late to stop it."[58] Rusk and Warnke thus thought, in late 1968, that the question of whether Israel would become a nuclear-weapon state was still undecided, and that in return for the superior F-4s, Israel should be pressed to abjure nuclear weapons by signing the NPT.[59]

Dean Rusk fired the first salvo in the battle over the NPT in his meeting with

Eban and Rabin on the afternoon of 22 October. During the conversation Rusk pressed Eban hard about Israel's nuclear weapons and missile plans, implying that there was a substantial linkage between the F-4 sale and the nuclear/missile issue. He opened the discussion by referring to their last NPT discussion at the UN in late September, asking whether the Israeli cabinet had completed its review of the matter. Eban replied that the position he had presented in September remained unchanged, and that Israel was studying the issue in light of the Geneva conference. Eban noted that other countries, "in [a] better security position than Israel," were also taking the time to study the problem.[60] Furthermore, Israel had a special problem with the IAEA that other states did not have.

Rusk turned up the heat. He responded by noting that the United States had good reasons to believe that Israel was involved in both nuclear weapons and missiles programs. Such missiles were meant for use with nuclear warheads, not high explosives. These were matters, he continued, "of utmost seriousness affecting our fundamental relationship," and the United States "must have clarification on them." Rusk explained why the United States was so concerned about these issues: "For Israel to develop nuclear weapons would (a) confront us with [the] question of whether we were serious about NPT, which we are, and (b) raise [the] question of what [the Soviets] would do in [the] nuclear field in Arab countries" (3). Rusk noted that he could not see how nuclear weapons would solve Israeli strategic problems, and Israel's problems with the IAEA could be dealt with. Rusk told Eban bluntly that the United States wanted something "more concrete" about Israeli nuclear intentions, and the only way to do so would be for Israel to sign the NPT. In response to Eban's comment that Israel had made no decision to become a nuclear power and had not ruled out signing the NPT, Rusk said that it was that lack of decision to sign that most concerned the United States (3).

On the matter of missiles, Eban asserted that the United States exaggerated the issue. Israel was far from having operational ballistic missiles ready for deployment. Given the strains on Israeli-French relations, that stage could not be reached before 1970. Noting that missile development in the Middle East started in "a non-nuclear context," Eban pointed out that the Israeli missile development program merely followed what the UAR was doing, and it would be difficult for Israel to terminate its program "in [the] absence of similar action by [the] UAR" (4).

At that point Eban changed the subject by thanking the president for his announcement to initiate the negotiations. Eban indicated that he understood the president's announcement to constitute a "decision in principle," while the negotiations themselves would be concerned merely with the technical details. If so, he asked when the negotiations could start and who would represent the secretary? Rusk responded that the negotiations would be handled by an assistant secretary and expressed his hope that by that time Eban would bring new word from the Israeli government on the matter of the NPT. Without saying so explicitly, Rusk made clear to Eban that the issues were linked. When Eban noted that "it would be bad to link these two questions," Rusk asked how the United States could be assured that the F-4s would not carry nuclear weapons. Ambassador Rabin suggested to handle it in the same manner as it was handled in the A-4 Skyhawk sale, to which Rusk replied that the issue should be left to the negotiations with Ambassador Hart. When Rabin noted that in the past, once political agreement was reached, technical negotiations had been conducted by the Pentagon, Rusk insisted that the United States "felt it necessary to have preliminary talks on [the] political side" (4–5).

The dispute over the linkage issue persisted even in subsequent contacts between Rabin and Hart concerning the negotiations. When Rabin asked whether the first negotiation session could be arranged on 23 October, before he left for Israel, Hart replied that such discussions required preparation, but in the meantime he was ready to put Rabin in touch with American disarmament experts to discuss Israeli concerns about IAEA and NPT issues before Rabin left Washington. Rabin declined to discuss those issues, making the point that the NPT and related issues were separate from the F-4 negotiations. Hart referred to Rusk's comment that the political discussion should start first, and suggested that there was not much to talk about before Eban returned with the latest Israeli position on the NPT. It was obvious that linkage was an American presumption for the negotiations (6–7).

President Johnson's role in pressuring Israel on the NPT requires clarification. During the summer of 1968 Johnson saw "several eyes only reports from [Richard] Helms on this subject."[61] They included the CIA determination that Israel was in possession of nuclear weapons or their components, and that Israel would find it difficult to sign the NPT. Johnson kept this information from Rusk, allowing him to insist on linking the sale of Phantom jets to Israel joining the NPT. The linkage originated in the State Department and the Pentagon, but Johnson was aware of Rusk's initiative, and was consulted before the latter pursued this strategy.

On 21 October Rusk sent Johnson a three-page memo for the president's meeting with Eban (before Rusk's own meeting with Eban). The document shows that Johnson's "detailed views" on the question of the Phantoms sale guided Rusk in devising the strategy.[62] In the talking points Rusk prepared for Johnson, it was suggested that Johnson highlight the importance the United States attached to preventing the spread of nuclear weapons and tell Eban that the decision to begin negotiations on the Phantoms should make it possible for

Israel "to make clear its intention not to seek a nuclear option, including signature of the NPT."[63] Also, in a reference to his own meeting with Eban later that day, Rusk informed Johnson that he planned to discuss Israel's F-4 request "in the context of our desire to see rapid progress toward peace and our need to get the Israeli assurance not to go nuclear and not to deploy surface-to-surface missiles."[64] Johnson was asked to make the linkage between the Phantoms and the NPT as explicit as Rusk himself would do in his talks with Eban. It was suggested that Johnson might use the meeting to press Eban as to when Israel would announce its decision on the NPT:

> The decision to begin negotiations was not an easy one, and you trust it will have reassured Israel about our steadfast concern for Israel's security. You also trust it will now be possible for Israel to make clear its intention not to seek a nuclear option, *inter alia* by signing the NPT. Mr. Eban told Secretary Rusk this question would be considered by his Government following the Geneva Non-Nuclear conference. Has it been decided? If not when is a decision expected?[65]

We do not know how closely Johnson followed Rusk's suggested talking points,[66] but after the talks Eban and Rabin flew to Israel for urgent consultations.[67] Even if Israel could not sign the NPT, could it say anything new to ease the American pressure? They brought home the message of an imminent crisis between the United States and Israel over the nuclear issue. Rusk's tough position on the NPT and missiles caused deep concern in Jerusalem. In a cabinet meeting on 27 October, Eban noted soberly: "This was the first time he [Rusk] was telling us 'we do not believe you,' " to which Deputy Prime Minister Yigal Allon added, "He told me that, too."[68] According to Eban, Rusk had told him that "we [the United States] have reasons to believe that you are developing a nuclear weapons program. You are developing Jericho missiles which are fitted to deliver nuclear warheads."[69] These developments would endanger Israel's security because they would make Israel a target for nuclear attack: "The real threat to the security of Israel is if the region becomes nuclear due to Israel's own action . . . Israel will not be the sole nuclear state in the Middle East even for one day."[70] In his memoirs Rusk writes that he warned Eban that if Israel introduced the bomb, "they'd lose the United States and the protection of our nuclear umbrella."[71] Eban's report reinforced the assessment Allon had submitted to the cabinet a few weeks earlier, that the NPT could overshadow all other issues on the American-Israeli agenda:

> The subject of the NPT is the central issue in the relationship with the US. This matter is more important than the Jarring [mission] and the peace. To

the extent that there is a crisis with the US on the horizon, it is on this matter
[NPT].[72]

Yitzhak Rabin, who also attended that cabinet meeting, expressed a similar sentiment: "A confrontation with the United States over the NPT would be most
serious; the entire problem of borders is marginal in relation to this problem.
On this matter, they have a clear position from which I do not think they would
move."[73] Eban proposed a strategy of playing for time until the end of the
Johnson administration, suggesting that, for the time being, Israel's reply to
Rusk should be a reiteration of previous Israeli statements. Rabin seconded the
proposal for stalling until the end of the Johnson administration, but added
that "this matter could not be postponed indefinitely."[74]

In the wake of the cabinet consultations in Jerusalem on 27 October, Prime
Minister Eshkol passed (via Ambassador Barbour) a message to President
Johnson, insisting that the F-4 negotiations and the NPT issue must be delinked.

> The Prime Minister wishes to state that it is his understanding that the nego-
> tiation between our two governments about the sale of Phantom aircraft are
> to commence forthwith without being linked to the question of the non-pro-
> liferation treaty. The Prime Minister assumes and hopes that our negotiating
> team led by Ambassador Rabin will be enabled to start immediately with
> practical discussions relating to the sale of the aircraft.[75]

Along with this message, Barbour was given another paper in response to the
American request for clarifications on the NPT. The paper, however, included
nothing new on the nuclear issue. It simply repeated the familiar Israeli position on nuclear weapons and the NPT and offered no firm assurances on signing. When Barbour noticed that the paper did not advance beyond previous
Israeli positions, he cautioned "not to underestimate the depth of feeling on
NPT at all levels of the United States Government."[76]

Three days later, on 3 November, Rusk met Eban at the UN and raised the
nuclear issue. Rusk told Eban that it would be a mistake to understand the U.S.
concern as an "NPT matter only"; it also involved the entire question of Israel
going nuclear. Eban still insisted that "we [Israel] haven't gone nuclear," but
acknowledged that there were problems of inspection that arise in relation to
the NPT. He told Rusk that the NPT forced Israel to examine "what precisely its
security is based on . . . Can security be based on conventional weapons over
[the] long term? [The] NATO and American security system will be pointed to
and [the] Israeli leadership will be asked questions." Eban concluded that "it [is]
one thing not to go nuclear and another thing to make long-term commitments
which affects security."[77]

THE WARNKE-RABIN ENCOUNTER

For Dean Rusk and Paul Warnke, the negotiations with Israel meant much more than a discussion about the logistics of the aircraft deal. The negotiations were also about Israeli assurances in the area of "advanced weapons," meaning both nuclear weapons and surface-to-surface ballistic missiles. The linkage between the two issues was the underlying premise of the negotiations. Specifically, Rusk's and Warnke's objective was to negotiate a written agreement in which Israel, in return for the Phantoms, would assure the United States that it would "forego nuclear weapons and strategic missiles and adhere to the NPT."[78]

The negotiations started on 30 October in a procedural session at the State Department between Ambassador Rabin, accompanied by IAF commander General Mordechai Hod, and Ambassador Parker Hart. Hart asked Rabin to prepare a proposed Memorandum of Understanding. On 1 November the State Department notified Rabin that Assistant Secretary of Defense Paul Warnke would take over the rest of the negotiations.[79] The next four sessions, on 4, 5, 8, and 12 November, took place in Warnke's office at the Pentagon. Rabin headed the Israeli delegation, which included Deputy Chief of Mission Shlomo Argov, General Hod, and military attaché Brigadier General David Carmon. If Rabin hoped it would be easier for him to negotiate with the Pentagon, he was wrong. Although Warnke was not privy to the CIA assessment of the status of Israel's nuclear program, he had no doubt that Israel had the know-how to make nuclear weapons (and even suspected that it might have done so secretly). Still, Warnke thought there was "an outside chance" that Israel could be pressed to sign the NPT for an immediate delivery of the F-4s.[80] If Israel was honest in its assurances to the United States not to be the first to introduce nuclear weapons, it meant that Israel could be pressed to give the United States firmer assurances not to introduce nuclear weapons than a vague, verbal pledge. Warnke believed that the only chance to obtain such assurances was through a Memorandum of Understanding (MOU) that would firmly link the nuclear issue with the sale of the F-4s. That spring, however, almost all Israeli leaders realized that Israel could not, and must not, sign the NPT, even if this refusal would lead to a confrontation with America.

The result was a confrontation in which the most direct questions about Israel's nuclear program and posture were asked. No American official before Warnke had dared so directly and openly to confront the Israelis on this issue. The 4 November session, a day before the election, was a preliminary session. Rabin summarized the session with Hart on 30 October and noted that Israel had already submitted its proposed MOU to Hart. "We put in it what we thought was necessary, following the precedent of the prior agreement [the

Skyhawk deal] (A-4)," Rabin said. He added that he would like this session "to get an agreement on how to proceed but not go into details." Warnke's response indicated that, for him, the negotiations were substantial political discussions on mutual matters of security. The presidential decision to sell the Phantoms to Israel was a difficult one, he opened, "not because we are not interested in Israel's security, but precisely because we are interested."[81] This decision would be the climax of the process that caused the United States to become Israel's principal arms supplier.

"It is not just 50 Phantoms," Warnke noted, "but 50 Phantoms plus 100 Skyhawks plus the great variety of other equipment that Israel is requesting that makes the policy we are entering upon a distinct change from our prior policy."[82] For years the United States had avoided becoming Israel's primary supplier, which "lessened the risk of U.S.-USSR confrontation in the Middle East." This qualitative change would create "a different set of circumstances concerning our supply relationship to Israel, . . . involving us even more intimately with Israel's security situation and involving more directly the security of the United States." This required discussing sensitive issues that Israel and the United States had hardly discussed before. In Warnke's words: "It is for this reason that we are so concerned with Israel's missile and nuclear plans and intentions and this is why we need to 'up-date' your assurances to us on these matters."[83]

Warnke told Rabin that by the next day his office would prepare a revised MOU that would "incorporate the kinds of assurances we require." Having put the subject of the negotiations in these broad terms, Warnke set the stage to demand from Rabin clarifications and assurances about Israel's nuclear program. This draft MOU, and the linkage it created between the F-4s and assurances over the nuclear issue, was at the center of the third session in the negotiations between Rabin and Warnke.

This draft MOU could not be found in the United States National Archives, but there is now enough information to reconstruct those discussions.[84] Article 3 of this MOU was the most problematic to the Israeli government. Although we do not have the text of this article, it is known that it concerned the means to verify Israel's nonintroduction pledge, apparently extending the American visits to Dimona to other sites. In his *Memoirs* Rabin described his reaction to Warnke's draft in the following way:

At this point the assistant secretary laid his cards on the table while I sat there stupefied, feeling the blood rising to my face. As its conditions for selling the Phantoms, the United States wanted Israel to sign an unprecedented document (never during my five year term in Washington would I encounter anything else like it). We were asked to consent to a U.S. presence in and supervision of every Israeli arms-manufacturing installation and every defense institution engaged in research, development, or manufacture—including civilian research institutions such as the Weizmann Institute of Science and Israel's universities. To say that I was appalled would be a gross understatement, and even though I promised to pass the paper on to Jerusalem for my government's response, I told Vornike [Warnke] that any state that agreed to sign such a shameful document would be forfeiting its very sovereignty.[85]

Warnke, however, has a somewhat different recollection. He recalls that the negotiations were businesslike, conducted in a professional manner, and lacking the drama Rabin's account suggests. The only document discussed was the proposed MOU, which incorporated the kind of assurances he believed the United States should receive. The American minutes of the 8 November session provide a sense of what the issues and the atmosphere were. When Warnke noted that he had not changed his mind concerning the Israeli assurances, Rabin said that his reaction to Article 3 of the MOU might not be diplomatic, and then he read from a prepared statement:

> I am now in a position to confirm that my original personal reaction upon first reading this paragraph—namely, that it is completely unacceptable to us—is indeed my Government's official position. We have come here for the purpose of purchasing 50 Phantoms. We have not come here in order to mortgage the sovereignty of the State of Israel, not even for 50 Phantoms. Furthermore, I wish to state that we consider Article 3 to be in the nature of a very major condition precedent to the sale of aircraft and it is therefore not acceptable to us also as a matter of principle. My Government's position is that the matters raised by Article 3 are extraneous to the question before us.[86]

Rejecting the American linkage, Rabin (reading from his prepared text) reaffirmed the long-standing Israeli pledge not to introduce nuclear weapons. In regard to the "theoretical question" of using the Phantom jets for the delivery of nuclear weapons Israel was reiterating the commitment it had given in 1966 (made into the Skyhawks deal) not to use the planes as a nuclear weapons carrier. Warnke rejected Rabin's first point that the issue was "extraneous," arguing that Israeli strategic missiles and nuclear weapons affect the national security of the United States. "It is the national interest of the United States that I am charged with protecting. By law I am required to consider the impact of the sale on the United States. You . . . do not have to accept my judgments, but I am required to make them." As to the second issue—sovereignty—Warnke insisted that "the assurances we have requested are not, and are not intended to be, an invasion of sovereignty" (2–3).

Warnke continued that "however these negotiations come out," he thought that the dialogue was "useful." It was important for the United States to get across how it feels about Israel's acquisition of strategic weapons. Warnke reminded Rabin that the sales contract contained a provision allowing its cancellation due to "unusual and compelling circumstances." "To me," Warnke said, "if Israel goes ahead with its missile and nuclear programs this would involve that paragraph; and while I cannot speak for the next administration, I feel sure they will feel the same way too" (3).

Rabin responded that he could understand if the American assurances were to apply to how the planes would be used—not as a nuclear weapons carrier—but in Article 3 "you ask for all the rights to know and for us to give agreement for you to inspect in our country. We were very careful not to use the word 'inspect' with respect to Dimona. We see in the two words quite a difference. The word 'visit' means you are a guest in our country—not an inspector." Warnke replied that he would be ready to amend the MOU and to substitute the word "visit" for "inspection." When Rabin responded "we have an agreement today," Warnke said that "that applies only to Dimona, not to the sites where missiles are being produced" (a comment that, according to the minutes, produced "nervous laughter from the Israelis"). At this point Warnke noted that the Phantoms would be part of "Israel's total environment," including protecting missile sites. "It is the totality of Israel's defense that we are involved in; it is not just a question of aircraft" (3–4).

The session ended with the same sharp exchange regarding the legitimacy of the linkage, as it was opened. Rabin protested: "You are only selling arms. How do you feel you have the right to ask all these things?" to which Warnke replied, "I think I do. Otherwise I wouldn't bring it up." Warnke closed the session by saying that he would discuss these things with Secretary Clifford and Nitze, suggesting that the next session would take place the next day (4).

This did not happen. Both sides needed more time to reflect on and rethink their strategy in the wake of this tough exchange. Warnke's strategy, based on his draft MOU, was evidently a nonstarter. The tone of Rabin's *Memoirs* probably fairly reflects the way the Israelis felt about Warnke's pressure. For Rabin, Warnke's zeal in pursuing the nuclear issue seemed to run against the subtle and tacit American-Israeli code of behavior on the nuclear issue that had evolved between Eshkol and Johnson since 1964. Furthermore, from an Israeli perspective, President Johnson had already made his political decision on the Phantoms sale in October. Rusk's and Warnke's effort to link the F-4s negotiations with the nuclear issue seemed to them not only unfair but against the spirit of the president's commitment. Indeed, the Israelis were wondering what the president's intentions really were: were Rusk and Warnke playing the "bad cops" on behalf of the White House or were they doing it outside the authority of the White House?

Shortly after the 8 November session, Israeli representatives petitioned the White House to intervene. Apparently Rabin contacted Abe Feinberg, a friend and strong supporter of the president, and asked him to get Johnson to end the stalemate. Within days Warnke was instructed by Clifford to cancel the MOU at the request of the White House.[87] Warnke was told that President Johnson wished to finalize the Phantoms deal swiftly and without conditions.

JOHNSON'S LETTER TO ESHKOL

Warnke did not know, however, that at the time of his stormy negotiations with Rabin President Johnson had written a letter to Eshkol—a personal plea that Israel would sign the NPT. Johnson started his message by placing the NPT in the context of his presidency and his commitment to nuclear nonproliferation:

> As I look back over my five years in office, I find that one endeavor overshadows all those that have called upon my time and energy. This has been the search for peace. Central to it has been our effort to prevent the spread of nuclear weapons. The United States has assumed a special responsibility for this endeavor. It is at the heart not only of my own nation's security interests but also of the security of every nation in the world. As you know I am personally deeply committed to this task.[88]

Recalling that his concern on this subject was expressed to Eshkol personally in 1964, Johnson wrote: "It would be a tragedy—an irreversible tragedy—if this arms race extended into the field of nuclear weapons or nuclear weapons delivery systems." Johnson also reiterated what Rusk had already told Eban, "that Israel's continued delay in signing the Nuclear Non-Proliferation Treaty will have the effect of increasing, rather than reducing, pressures for other area states to develop or acquire nuclear weapons." For this reason, while welcoming Eshkol's message of 28 October (reaffirming the pledge not to be the first to introduce nuclear weapons), "only Israel's adherence to that Treaty [NPT] can give the world confidence that Israel does not intend to develop nuclear weapons."[89] In reference to the study of the implications of signing the treaty that the Israeli government was engaged, Johnson expressed his "earnest hope" that it would result in a decision to sign the treaty at an early date. Most important, Johnson warned that,

Israel's failure to sign the Non-Proliferation Treaty would be a severe blow to my Government's global efforts to halt the spread of nuclear weapons. The United States would also be deeply troubled if operational strategic missiles were to appear in the Middle East. I hope you can give me an encouraging response on these matters when we talk later this month.[90]

Evidently President Johnson made a strong personal appeal to Eshkol on the matter of the NPT, yet he did not link it with the Phantoms negotiations. Unlike Kennedy's letters to Eshkol in the summer of 1963, Johnson made no threat whatsoever, either direct or veiled. He simply told Eshkol how Israeli signing of the NPT was important to the United States and to him personally. Johnson ended his letter warmly, telling Eshkol, "you are welcome not only as a distinguished and esteemed colleague but as a close personal friend."[91]

WHAT IS A NUCLEAR WEAPON?

The next negotiation session between Warnke and Rabin took place on 12 November. By this time Warnke had received a message from the White House that Johnson wanted the negotiations finalized and was ready to give on the nuclear issue.[92] Warnke now realized that his original MOU was hopeless, but he still wanted to use the negotiations to obtain better assurances and clarifications from the Israelis on the nuclear issue. In particular, he wanted to define operationally what the Israeli "nonintroduction" pledge actually meant. This strategy led the way to an extraordinary Socratic-like (others would say Talmudic-like) discussion about the definition of both "introduction" and "nuclear weapon."

Warnke started the 12 November session by acknowledging the Israeli objections to his wording. Israel proposed instead to add a reaffirmation in the contract of earlier assurances not to use American aircraft to carry nuclear weapons and not to be the first to introduce nuclear weapons into the area. Warnke reminded the Israelis that violations of these assurances would invoke the "unusual and compelling circumstances" clause, which would require the cancellation of the contract. On these bases it would be possible to draft an agreement that would be acceptable to the Israelis, "which will meet your requirements—although not fully meeting mine." The problem is, Warnke continued, that he "could not find in the record any understanding of what Israel means by the provision: 'Israel will not be the first to introduce nuclear weapons into the area.'" So Warnke asked Ambassador Rabin what was meant by this phrase.[93]

Rabin replied in a tautological fashion: "It means what we have said, namely, that we would not be the first to introduce nuclear weapons." So Warnke asked again, what specifically was meant by the word "introduce"? Once again Rabin tried to evade the question by posing the question back to Warnke: "You are more familiar with these things than we are. What is your definition of nuclear weapons?" Warnke replied that there are two aspects to the question: "the definition of what is and what is not a nuclear weapon, and what is and what is not introduction into the area." As to the first issue, Warnke said, "if there are components available that could be assembled to make a nuclear weapon— although part A may be in one room and part B may be in another room—then that is a nuclear weapon." As to the second issue—introduction—"that is your term and you will have to define it." Does nonintroduction mean no physical presence, Rabin asked, and Warnke replied in the affirmative. When Rabin asked whether the United States believed that this was the case, Warnke answered that he was just trying to find the Israeli definition. General Hod asked whether the term "introduction" had an accepted usage in international law and Warnke replied that this was not the case.[94]

At this point Rabin and General Hod raised the issue of testing as the distinguishing mark of an operational weapon system. Rabin asked: "Do you consider a nuclear weapon one that has not been tested, and has been done by a country without previous experience?" "Certainly," Warnke answered. But Rabin insisted: "All nuclear powers—the United States, Russia, the United Kingdom, France, China—have tested nuclear weapons. Do you really believe introduction comes before testing"? Rabin noted that based on his experiences with conventional weapons, he would not consider a weapon that had not been tested to be a weapon.[95]

Rabin's point was, to a large extent, definitional. All weapons systems, conventional and unconventional alike, must be tested before deployment. Without a test it would be impossible to introduce a weapon system to the military. As long as Israel had not conducted a nuclear test it could not by definition be said to have introduced nuclear weapons. Rabin's point was, then, that without a test Israel's pledge not to be the first to introduce nuclear weapons remained intact.[96]

After further exchange Warnke noted that, as he understood it, the Israeli definition of "introduction" contains two essential prerequisites: "notoriety and pretesting." Rabin agreed by saying that he was not sure what Prime Minister Eshkol had said, "but there must be public acknowledgment." Since the purpose of nuclear weapons is to deter, their presence must be known. So Warnke commented, "In your view, an unadvertised, untested nuclear device is not a nuclear weapon," to which Rabin responded, "Yes, that is correct." Warnke remarked that he differed on this, for he would interpret mere physical presence as constituting in itself an introduction.[97]

Warnke concluded the session by acknowledging the two countries' different interpretation of the definition of introduction. Despite the difference, and the fact that no agreement was signed, General Hod was authorized to continue with technical discussions with the air force. The Phantoms deal was by now a "done deal" despite the definitional disagreements.[98]

THE EXCHANGE OF LETTERS

Ultimately, owing to further Israeli objections to the wording of the MOU, it was agreed to scrap the idea of having one political document, an MOU, and to replace it with an official exchange of letters between Rabin and Warnke. In such an exchange neither party has to endorse or condone the other's terms and definitions.

In his letter of 22 November Rabin reaffirmed Israel's "long-standing policy . . . that it will not be the first power in the Middle East to introduce nuclear weapons and agrees not to use any aircraft supplied by the U.S. as a nuclear weapons carrier."[99] As in the past, Rabin left the term "introduction" undefined. The letter also acknowledges the right of the United States, "under unusual and compelling circumstances when the best interest of the U.S. requires it," to cancel the deal. In his reply, dated 27 November, Warnke reiterated the Israeli "non-introduction" pledge, but also inserted his own interpretation as to what would constitute the introduction of nuclear weapons: "In this connection, I have made clear the position of the United States Government that the physical possession and control of nuclear arms by a Middle Eastern power would be deemed to constitute the introduction of nuclear weapons."[100]

Warnke, however, was not ready to concede defeat. Even though the agreement was now in the form of an exchange of letters, not an MOU, Warnke still wanted to have his interpretation to be legally binding. He ended his letter by saying that the two letters "constitute an agreement between our two governments." Once again, Rabin called Warnke on 27 November saying that this wording was unacceptable to Israel, for it "could imply that Israel agreed with the American interpretation of the circumstances which would be deemed to constitute the introduction of nuclear weapons." Warnke asked Rabin if that meant that "he was unable to accept our definition and that this final sentence implied that he did." Rabin confirmed that this was the case. Warnke called Rabin back and suggested to insert some "bland" statement. The final sentence in Warnke's letter now reads: "It is understood that we can proceed to negotiate the technical and financial details of this transaction."[101]

At the end of the negotiations Warnke was clear about one thing: Israel

already had the bomb. Rabin's refusal to accept his physical possession definition of "introduction" said it all. Indeed, when Warnke told Rabin that he
believed that Israel might already possess both weapons components and their
means of delivery, Rabin did not reply.[102] Through these negotiations he realized that the issue was a moot one. The Israeli bomb, whether officially introduced or not, was a fait accompli. By now Warnke understood: Israel would
surely not sign the NPT.[103]

Warnke's tough stand proved to be counterproductive. If anything, it forced
Israel to end its indecision and adopt a firm position on the matter. After
months of hesitancy and delay, it became clear that the presumption that Israel
would eventually sign the NPT was wrong. Israel was spreading the word that
without new and firmer American security assurances, in the form of an
alliance, Israel must remain outside the NPT regime.

On 4 December Prime Minister Eshkol responded to President Johnson's
letter of 14 November. Eshkol's illness (cancer) was now worsening and his visit
had to be canceled. The words of gratitude that Eshkol wanted to convey to
Johnson in person had to be put in writing. "My purpose was to let you know
personally that our people will always remember and cherish the deep understanding which you showed toward it during the Presidency that you have now
chosen to terminate. Israel and the Jewish people have a long historic memory;
and your statesmanlike approach to our problems will long endure in our
hearts."[104]

In the second paragraph, Eshkol replied to Johnson's appeal on the NPT.
Eshkol reiterated the same position he defended in October, namely, that Israel
appreciated the president's interest in the NPT, supported the idea of the treaty,
reaffirmed all that Israel had said before on the nuclear issue, but was still studying "all its implications for long-term security and scientific and technological
development."[105] Behind the polite veneer, Eshkol was essentially saying no to
Johnson's appeal. After Johnson allowed the Phantoms and the NPT issues to
be considered separately, Eshkol was able to thank the president who permitted
him to say no.

By the year's end the White House announced that an agreement had been
reached to sell Israel fifty F-4s, the delivery of which would start in 1969. The
NPT issue was no longer mentioned.[106]

A CHAPTER CLOSES

The encounters between Rusk and Eban and those between Warnke and Rabin
are a landmark in the American-Israeli nuclear dialogue. The battle over the

NPT in the fall of 1968 was a critical juncture in the making of Israeli nuclear opacity. The battle also manifested an important and continuing feature of Israeli nuclear behavior: postponing nuclear decisions as long as possible, and ultimately making them under external pressure.

As we saw earlier, Israeli nuclear restraint was a critical element in the American-Israeli security relationships, at least since 1963, when Kennedy and Eshkol made the Dimona visit arrangement. Since 1963 a tacit, and somewhat vague, quid pro quo evolved: Israel would receive security assistance from the United States in return for an Israeli commitment not to go nuclear. In March 1965 the basic parameters of this vague arrangement were formalized in the Memorandum of Understanding that Eshkol and Komer signed. That document, however, still did not go beyond vague statements: the United States was concerned "for the maintenance of Israel's security" and Israel "will not be the first to introduce nuclear weapons into the Arab-Israeli area." The concrete meaning of both sides' commitments remained unstated and ambiguous. In particular, there was no agreed-on and explicit understanding of what "nonintroduction" of nuclear weapons actually meant. Given the American visits to Dimona, the Department of State understood the Israeli "nonintroduction" commitment as equivalent to "nonphysical possession"; that is, a commitment not to produce or possess nuclear weapons. Under this understanding, Rusk and Warnke were justified in thinking that Israel could sign the NPT and, under political pressure, would do so.

In 1996 Paul Warnke said that he realized at the time that his linkage initiative had only a "long-shot chance" of succeeding—"it was a kind of trial balloon"—but he thought the effort was worthwhile. In looking back, Warnke believes that had he been informed of the way President Johnson had handled the Israeli nuclear issue and aware of what the CIA had told Johnson on this matter, he almost certainly would not have tried that path.[107] Both Rusk and Warnke were victims of Israel's web of nuclear ambiguity and possibly their own fear of the consequences of the reality of a nuclear Israel.

Ultimately even the Israelis became entangled in their own ambiguity. As noted earlier, anxiety dominated the assessment of Ministers Eban and Allon and Ambassador Rabin regarding a confrontation with the United States over the NPT. During the Israeli cabinet meeting on 27 October, Rabin predicted that a direct confrontation with America over this issue "would be most serious" and inevitable.[108] It took only three weeks to realize that those pessimistic assessments were dead wrong. Concerns about the American reaction to an Israeli refusal to sign the NPT were all overdrawn.

In November 1968 it was too late for Rusk and Warnke to exert effective pressure on Israel to sign the NPT. Though at the time Rusk referred to Israel's nuclear status as being "5-months pregnant"; in his autobiographical book, *As I Saw It*, he narrated his last meeting with Eban in October, correcting himself and noting that Israel was "at least eight and three-fourths months pregnant and could produce nuclear weapons on very short notice."[109] Looking back today, one can conclude that the Rusk-Warnke effort to force Israel to sign the NPT was doomed to fail. Not only did they lack firm presidential backing on this sensitive matter (as was the case with President Kennedy in 1963), but late 1968 was not the right time for a departing administration to exert effective pressure on Israel.

In any case, on 5 November 1968 Richard M. Nixon became president elect. His presidency was critical in the making of the last phase of Israel's road to opacity.

On 20 January 1969 Richard M. Nixon succeeded
Lyndon B. Johnson as president of the United
States. A month later, on 26 February 1969, Prime
Minister Levi Eshkol died, and some weeks later Golda
Meir was sworn in as Israel's prime minister. These
changes in leadership brought to an end the understandings initiated in the early 1960s by Kennedy and
Ben Gurion and modified by Johnson and Eshkol. The
new understandings would reflect the political thinking of Nixon and Meir, and the new political and
strategic realities.

Under the new understanding, Israel was assumed,
but not recognized or acknowledged, to be a nuclear-
weapon state. Nixon and Henry Kissinger, if not the
entire State Department, accepted the reality that Israel
was in possession of nuclear weapons, and Nixon conveyed to Meir that the United States would not challenge this reality or try to roll it back if Israel kept its
nuclear profile low. Israel had already won the battle
over the Phantom jets—the sale of the F-4s was not
linked to Israeli signature of the NPT, and the final features of nuclear opacity were now in place.

The most important result of the new understanding was the end of the American visits to Dimona. One
more visit was carried out in 1969, and in 1970 the
United States gave them up. The arrangement Kennedy
and Eshkol had reached in 1963, an arrangement that
brought the United States and Israel to the brink of
confrontation, died quietly at the end of the decade.

By July 1970 the Nixon administration relaxed the
secrecy surrounding the Israeli nuclear program. The
CIA assessment that Israel was a nuclear-weapon state

was no longer a matter of "unconfirmed intelligence reports," but was shared more openly with Congress and even leaked to the media. Israel, without changing its declaratory posture, moved from being an ambiguous nuclear power to an undeclared one.

NIXON AND KISSINGER

The NPT was a product of two Democratic administrations which believed that the spread of nuclear weapons to other countries would undermine U.S. and international security. Thus the United States did not distinguish between proliferation to friendly and hostile states, as all proliferation was considered bad. The best way to combat proliferation was by establishing a nonproliferation norm through an international treaty.

This approach was embodied in the Gilpatric Committee report.[1] The report asserted that nuclear weapons capabilities in the hands of any additional countries, "will add complexity and instability to the deterrent balance between the United States and the Soviet Union, [and] aggregate suspicions and hostility among states neighboring new nuclear powers." In addition, nuclear proliferation would reduce America's role as a world power: "Our diplomatic and military influence would wane, and strong pressures would arise to retreat to isolation to avoid the risk of involvement in nuclear war."[2] The report also called for vigorous measures to discourage further proliferation.[3] Such measures required a coordinated effort at the highest political level, multilateral agreements, and a means of affecting the motivations of specific states.[4]

The Gilpatric Committee urged the United States to conclude a multilateral nonproliferation treaty, to exert American influence on other nations concerning nuclear weapons acquisition, and to use U.S. nuclear policies as examples in arms control and weapons policies. The report suggested that the cause of nonproliferation deserved precedence over NATO nuclear arrangements.[5] It took Johnson two years to adopt the Gilpatric Committee's recommendations. His administration, then, had led the campaign to conclude the NPT.

Nixon's view on nuclear proliferation was different. Republicans tend to be suspicious of universalistic plans and organizations, and the new Republican administration was less than enthusiastic about the effectiveness and desirability of the NPT. The pursuit of a more narrowly defined U.S. interest led the Nixon administration to distinguish between proliferation to hostile or to friendly states. As early as his presidential campaign in 1968, Nixon criticized the NPT for not permitting the transfer of "defensive nuclear weapons."[6] After the

Soviet invasion of Czechoslovakia in 1968, Nixon spoke against the ratification of the NPT as long as Soviet troops were stationed on Czech soil.

The Treaty required that forty-three nations, including the three depositors, must ratify it in order for it to take effect. By late November 1968 about seventy nations had signed the Treaty, but only the United Kingdom, Ireland, Nigeria, and Mexico had ratified it. The momentum for signing the NPT had slowed down because of the Soviet invasion and the American decision to hold off ratification, and because more states were taking a wait-and-see attitude toward ratifying it.

On 5 February 1969, two weeks after his inauguration, Nixon resubmitted the NPT to Congress for ratification. He condemned the Soviet invasion but stressed that it was "time to move forward." He expressed support for the NPT, saying that the United States would urge other nations, including Germany and France, to sign it. The same day, however, National Security Adviser Henry Kissinger circulated a secret National Security Decision Memorandum to the bureaucracy that qualified the administration's public support of the NPT:

> The president directed that, associated with the decision to proceed with the United States' ratification of the Non-Proliferation Treaty, there should be no efforts by the United States government to pressure any other nation, particularly the Federal Republic of Germany, to follow suit. The government in its public posture should reflect a tone of optimism that other countries will sign or ratify, while clearly disassociating itself from any plan to bring pressure on these countries to sign and ratify.[7]

This accorded with Kissinger's view that eventually most regional powers would acquire nuclear weapons. The United States could benefit more by quietly assisting friendly nations than by getting involved in a futile exercise in non-proliferation.[8] Among the states Kissinger apparently had in mind were Japan, India, and Israel, as nuclear weapons were essential to the national security of these states. It would be better for the United States and its allies if the three states had their own nuclear deterrent instead of relying on an American nuclear umbrella. Kissinger appeared to be saying that if he were an Israeli, he would get nuclear weapons, and that the United States should not try to talk Israel out of it.[9]

NEW OBJECTIONS

Israeli leaders were aware that Nixon and Kissinger viewed the NPT, Israel's security, and the Phantoms deal differently than their predecessors did.

Ambassador Yitzhak Rabin sensed that a Republican administration was likely to be more sympathetic to Israel's security needs, including their nuclear capabilities, than the Johnson administration. During Nixon's visit to the Golan Heights in 1967, shortly after the war, Nixon made the point that had he been an Israeli leader he would not have withdrawn from the Heights.

Rabin met Nixon in early August 1968 and received American pledges on the Phantoms and on "the need to keep Israel strong."[10] Weeks later Nixon repeated his pledge publicly in an appearance before a Jewish audience. By then Rabin was convinced that Nixon would be "a good president for our cause, even more than Israel's old friend, Hubert Humphrey."[11] This recognition influenced Rabin's resistance to pressure from Dean Rusk and Paul Warnke on the NPT in September and November. Israel was pushing to finalize negotiations over the Phantoms while continuing to hold off its reply on the NPT.

In mid-November, days after Nixon's electoral victory and after the Johnson White House instructed Warnke to end quickly the negotiations on the F-4s, Israel informed the State Department of its objections to the Treaty. Israel took the formal position that it was still considering and studying the Treaty, but informed the United States that it saw substantial deficiencies in the NPT relating to its security. As long as these problems remained, Israel could not sign the Treaty. The Israeli reservations were leaked to the press with great accuracy.[12] By late November a CIA memorandum on the prospects of the NPT made the assessment that "so long as conditions in the Middle East do not improve, there is little likelihood of a change in [Israel's] position."[13]

Israel raised three requirements with American officials that kept it from signing the NPT at that time: Israel must have an agreement with the United States that would guarantee an American supply of conventional military hardware; Israel must obtain security guarantees from the United States against aggression by a nuclear-weapon state, that is, the Soviet Union; and there must be a link between Israeli withdrawal from the occupied territories and regional peace. Israel also noted that by signing the NPT and renouncing the nuclear option it "would forsake a useful psychological deterrent in keeping the Arab states uncertain about her progress toward becoming a nuclear power."[14] Israel thus conveyed to the United States its determination not to give up acquiring nuclear weapons for anything less than a meaningful security guarantee. Nor would it allow the nuclear weapons question to be isolated from other security issues, and until these issues were addressed satisfactorily, Israel would not sign the NPT. As long as the United States dealt with Israel's armament needs on a case-by-case basis, as was the situation with the F-4s, Israel would have to maintain its nuclear-weapons option.

The novel part of the Israeli position concerned Soviet aggression against

Israel. This was the first time Israeli officials acknowledged that "the hostile Soviet attitude towards Israel" was a factor in Israel's reluctance to sign the NPT. Unlike other advanced states, such as West Germany and Italy, Israel had no formal security commitment from the United States to protect it from nuclear blackmail or attack.[15] Israel was not the only country to raise reservations about the effectiveness of the security assurances attached to the NPT. These assurances were based on the UN Security Council as the implementing mechanism, and a number of nations pointed out that any proposed Security Council action could be thwarted by a permanent member's veto.[16]

The Israeli reply changed the American-Israeli understanding on nuclear issues that had evolved in the 1960s. In effect, Israel acknowledged that the Dimona reactor was related to the nation's security, and should be so considered. This raised Israel's price for signing the NPT considerably, as the three conditions Israel made for joining the treaty were tantamount to a military and political alliance between the United States and Israel.

The breadth and scope of the security issues Israel raised made it doubtful that the Nixon administration, or any other administration, would be willing to pay Israel's price. It is also doubtful that Israel had any real expectation of actually obtaining American security guarantees in exchange for signing the NPT. Rather, it was a way of telling the administration that Israel's interests did not allow it to sign the NPT. Israel had grounds to believe that its objections to the NPT would be acceptable to the new administration.[17]

In mid-December Foreign Minister Abba Eban told the Knesset that the government still had not reached a final decision on the NPT and he could not predict when this would happen.[18] Israel still referred to the matter of the NPT as being "under review," but it was obvious that Israel had no intention of signing it anytime soon, hoping to reach new understandings with the Nixon administration that would remove the issue from their mutual agendas. New information on the increasing Soviet involvement in Egypt added another dimension to the nuclear issue, strengthening the Israeli arguments against signing the NPT.

In late December Rabin met with Kissinger, shortly after he had been named Nixon's national security adviser. According to Rabin, Kissinger avoided making commitments, but some of his phrases eased the ambassador's concerns. For example, he stated that the United States would be receptive to Israeli requests for weapons, and "that the Republican administration would be more relaxed on the nuclear issue."[19]

In early January 1969, days before Nixon took office, the Israeli nuclear program was back in the headlines. NBC News reported that Israel either had a nuclear weapon or would soon have one. According to the report, this was the result of a decision that had been made two years earlier "to embark on a crash program to produce a nuclear weapon."[20] Was this report the first indication that the Eshkol government had decided to leak to the world, and the Nixon administration, new facts about Israel's nuclear program? Was the leak a continuation of the effort Dayan initiated in his meeting with president-elect Nixon? Was it a typical unauthorized effort by Dayan to establish "facts on the ground" in the last days of the Johnson and Eshkol governments? (Eshkol's terminal illness, which had been kept secret from the public, made him incapable of governing in the last six months of his life.)

In any case, the NBC story was dismissed by officials in Jerusalem and Washington. In Jerusalem, "authoritative sources" called the story "speculative and inaccurate," reiterating the old formulas: Israel was not a nuclear-weapon state, was committed "not be the first to introduce nuclear weapons into the region," and was still "studying" the NPT.[21] In a *New York Times* story written by John W. Finney, the reporter who had covered the Dimona visits since 1964, officials of the departing Johnson administration also expressed doubts about the NBC story. They acknowledged that Israel had already acquired a threshold capability of becoming a nuclear power, but added that so far as the United States knew, Israel had not produced a nuclear weapon. They made it clear that they "do not believe that the Israeli government which over the years has emphasized that it would not be the first to introduce nuclear weapons into the Middle East has made a decision to build a nuclear weapon."[22] The administration thus presented the change in Israel as a technological drift, not as a matter of a new political decision, adding:

> It is generally agreed in the United States intelligence community that Israel now stands on the threshold of becoming a nuclear power and needs only a political decision to move in that direction. If such a decision is made, it is estimated that Israel could build in a year or so a crude atomic bomb. Some officials believe that the period might be measured in months. With considerable technical help from France, Israel in the last eight years has acquired most if not all of the ingredients of a nuclear arsenal.[23]

American officials, however, were vague about the missing link in the Israeli nuclear capability: whether Israel had built a reprocessing plant.

Regarding the reprocessing plant, Finney wrote:

> Thus far United States officials have no intelligence information suggesting that Israel has constructed or is constructing such a plant. . . . But Israel misled American intelligence officials once regarding the Dimona reactor by initially passing it off as a textile plant and the possibility is not being excluded that Israel clandestinely is building a small reprocessing plant[24].

By 1969 it became clear that the American visits to Dimona hindered a new American-Israeli nuclear understanding. For Israel to acquire the status of an opaque nuclear power, the Dimona visits must be stopped.

THE LAST DIMONA VISIT

It took nine more months for Nixon and Meir to reach a new nuclear understanding. In the meantime, the State Department bureaucracy continued with a business-as-usual approach. On 7 March 1969 Assistant Secretary of State Joseph Sisco wrote a two-page "action memorandum" for the new secretary of state, William Rogers, briefing him on the history and significance of the American visits to Dimona. Rogers was asked to authorize Ambassador Walworth Barbour to prepare for the next American visit.[25] In 1969 Barbour apparently knew, or at least intuited, what Rogers, Sisco, and the State Department (its Bureau of Intelligence and Research [INR]) did not know, that is, the findings of those visits did not reflect reality. Barbour and the Tel Aviv CIA station chief had already guessed the truth, but the information was too sensitive—it had too many implications—to be accepted by the State Department in Washington.[26]

In his memo Sisco outlined the background of the American visits to Dimona, mentioning that since May 1961 the United States had conducted "seven inspections of the [Dimona] facility"—the memo used the words "inspection" and "visit" interchangeably—the last one taking place in June 1968. "Our understanding with the GOI [Government of Israel] is that the visits will be conducted without publicity, but that we will be free to convey the results of our inspections to other governments of our choice."[27]

Sisco's memo noted that the Israelis had always insisted on maintaining visits at least a year apart, "citing domestic political difficulties." The Israeli ground rules—"one-day visits on the basis of one-year periodicity"—had been "minimally sufficient to give us reasonable confidence that Israel is not engaged in weapons-related activity at this site." The State Department had been concerned that Israel could try to take advantage of its upcoming election in November to postpone the visit, just as it had done in 1965; however, an interval of eighteen months between visits would be "too long a period, in the opinion of our experts."[28] To prevent such a delay, the department proposed that Barbour should start to initiate the visit early.

Notwithstanding the deficiencies of the American visits to Dimona, there were growing suspicions that Israel might have other nuclear weapon–related facilities. Since around 1966 the American intelligence community was of the opinion that the real weapons work might take place not in Dimona but "somewhere else in Israel." Sisco's memorandum expressed this suspicion:

> I would stress that while our inspections in Dimona can give us information about the activities at that site, they cannot exclude the possibility (which we in fact believe to be a likelihood) that the Israelis are engaged in nuclear weapons R&D somewhere else in Israel. Nevertheless, since Dimona is the only installation in Israel to our knowledge that can produce fissionable material in sufficient quantities for a weapons program, we consider it important to check periodically as to whether the operations at this facility are devoted exclusively to peaceful purposes.[29]

Rogers, who had just been briefed about the Dimona arrangement, accepted Sisco's proposal. A day later he signed a telegram sent to Barbour, instructing him to initiate contacts with the Israelis for the next Dimona visit. Among his instructions, Barbour was to request a two-day visit, and he was reminded that on the last visit the visiting team claimed that it was "being rushed to cover everything at [the] site in twelve hours."[30] Barbour needed no such reminder. He had been in Israel since the first visit in May 1961, negotiating the details of the arrangements with both Ben Gurion and Eshkol.

Two weeks later Barbour reported to the State Department that he had started the process of setting up the visit.[31] A few days later he wrote that his Israeli interlocutor was agreeable to a visit in principle, but opposed any changes from the past, insisting on keeping the one-year interval and the one-day duration.[32] Accordingly, he suggested two Saturdays near the end of the one-year period, 29 June or 5 July, assuring Barbour that election considerations would not interfere with scheduling the visit.[33] The State Department's reaction to the Israeli dates did not differ from that of earlier years: the "one-year period" condition was portrayed as a violation of the original 1963 Kennedy-Eshkol agreement. Barbour was instructed to reopen the issue with the Israelis.[34]

The State Department's characterization of the agreement between Kennedy and Eshkol was not accurate. Kennedy had asked for two visits per year to Dimona, but Eshkol's 19 August 1963 response had been deliberately vague. Since 1964 Israel had indicated that it would not permit the visits to be less than one year apart. The Johnson administration had learned to live with the Israeli conditions, and Barbour knew more about this than anybody else. In his reply to the State Department, he was not hopeful about any changes in the terms of the visits and told Washington that "the present assurances are the best we can expect." He reminded Rogers that, despite Eshkol's 1963 letter to Kennedy and his accompanying comments to him, Eshkol never carried out that commitment.[35] In a subsequent cable Barbour told Washington that in his judgment there was no chance Israel would agree to open the question of the frequency of visits.[36] After a few more rounds of correspondence, resolving scheduling problems regarding Amos de Shalit—the official host for the visits—the date was set for Saturday, 12 July 1969.[37]

Setting the date, however, did not end the disagreement between the United States and Israel over the ground rules. To offset the disadvantages of the one-day visit, the State Department proposed having a four-man team that could be divided into two teams, "so as much ground could be covered as thoroughly as possible,"[38] but Israel again told Barbour that it opposed any departure from past practice.[39] Again, the United States had to comply with the Israeli conditions—no more than three members on a team—if it wanted a visit. In addition, the team was not allowed to bring its own measurement instruments or to collect samples of any kind. Barbour, almost as a matter of ritual, was asked to pass on America's irritation with those restrictions.[40]

The one-day visit took place on schedule on Saturday, 12 July 1969. The team consisted of George B. Pleat, AEC assistant director for reactor products, along with Edwin Kintner of the AEC and Edward L. Nicholson of Oak Ridge National Laboratory (ORNL). This was Pleat's third visit to Dimona, for the first time replacing Floyd Culler as team leader, and Kintner's second visit. Both men were familiar with the site and with their hosts, Amos de Shalit of the Weizmann Institute and Yossef Tulipman, Dimona's director-general. As had been the case in previous years, Pleat and his team received background briefings by the State Department and the CIA.[41] The CIA did not share with the AEC scientists its estimates regarding Israeli nuclear weapons—to have done so would have compromised the agency's sources,[42] and would have revealed the procedures of the previous seven years as a sham.[43] The members of the team were disappointed by their CIA briefer's lack of knowledge.[44]

The visit turned out to be a long one—eighteen hours—the longest inspection to be conducted. The American team arrived at the Dimona site early in the morning and left close to midnight. The Israelis spent most of the morning and afternoon hours hosting their guests in their labs, introducing them to their scientific projects. Just as the Israelis seemed eager to talk about their own research, they wanted to hear from their guests about scientific projects and programs undertaken at ORNL and elsewhere in the United States. The Pleat team, however, treated its real job as an inspection, not a scientific exchange. The Israeli approach was a misuse of their limited time. Pleat believed then and now that it might have been a deliberate effort by the Israelis to wear the team down before they started their inspection and to shorten their inspection time.[45] Pleat, like Culler, notes that his team's objective, like that of previous teams, was to inspect the reactor—to count materials and compare logs—and to look for indications of a reprocessing plant or capability. Because of the distractions, the team had to continue its inspection efforts well into the late night hours. The team left the Dimona facility with a sense of frustration and anger.[46]

Again, the secrets of Dimona were not revealed. The Pleat team did not find a reprocessing plant or evidence of its existence. Nor were signs of high-level waste systems found.[47] Kintner, who was as rigorous as possible (under the circumstances) in the conduct of his inspection activities, left the site still believing it was unlikely that a reprocessing plant could be hidden on the site.[48] The American suspicions and frustrations over what was going on in Dimona grew considerably, however.[49] In previous years the Culler team had already expressed its frustration with the circumstances surrounding its visits. The 1969 experience intensified that feeling. Pleat and his team expressed that frustration and sense of futility in the team report, written during a two-night stopover in Rome.[50]

By the end of July Ambassador Barbour officially complained to Prime Minister Meir about the way the visit had been conducted, and in particular the way the Israelis obstructed the team from fulfilling its mission. In a follow-up discussion of the 1969 Dimona visit at the State Department, with Pleat and AEC director of intelligence Charles Reichardt present, the reasons for the fiasco were analyzed. A critical issue was the way the team understood its mandate and the support it had from the U.S. government to fulfill this mandate:

> From a number of sources, the team has drawn the inference that the U.S. government is not prepared to support a "real" inspection effort in which the team members can feel authorized to ask directly pertinent questions and/or insist on being allowed to look at records, logs, materials, and the like. The team has in many subtle ways been cautioned to avoid controversy, "be gentlemen" and not take issue with the obvious will of the hosts. On one occasion it seems that the team was criticized roundly by the Israelis for having "acted like inspectors" and the criticism was passed on rather than refuted.[51]

Given the lack of well-defined and agreed-on mandate and protocol, the mission turned out to be a delicate conflict between the guests and their hosts. As indicated earlier (see chapter 10), this basic tension had always existed, but in 1969 it reached new heights:

> In the absence of a positive mandate to *inspect* with all that word implies, the team has felt constrained to accept the ground rules made evident by their hosts, leading to the present situation in which a "visit" is conducted rather than an "inspection." The team therefore did not make an issue of the fact that the program drawn up by Israel shifted timing and focus in important

ways which limited their access to key facilities. Nor did they take issue with their host's obvious pushing and hurrying past points at which they indicated a desire for a closer look. The fact that the team avoided creating issues can give rise to the semantic interpretation that what went on satisfied them, which is in essence what the Israelis replied to the Embassy. There is no doubt whatever in the mind of the chief of the team but that his hosts effectively tailored the occasion as a "visit" to suit their own purposes: they took great care to emphasize at the outset that it was a visit and nothing more, and obviously relied on the good manners and restraint of the team members to avoid challenges of substance.[52]

The State Department note taker ended the memo by commenting that "visits conducted under these approaches, may even be counter-productive." He also noted that the United States could make the visits more meaningful by instructing the teams "to take a positive approach to inspection, asking for all the access and information they deem required, and leaving it to the Israelis either to accede or make positive denials of what is requested." "At the least," he concluded, "that course would place responsibility where it must rest rather than avoiding the real issues in a manner which prejudices our interests."[53]

THE RICHARDSON-RABIN ENCOUNTER

The contentious exchange between the State Department and the Israeli government regarding the 1969 Dimona visit highlighted the widening gap between the Department of State, on the one hand, and the White House and the CIA, on the other. Both the White House and the CIA recognized that Israel had already crossed the nuclear weapons threshold.[54] Nixon's secretary of state, William Rogers, and his senior Middle East advisers were not told of this recognition.

Days after the Dimona visit, Undersecretary of State Elliot Richardson asked Israel for an answer on the NPT. The response he was given was no different from what Israel had said before—the NPT was still "under study" and the Israeli government could not commit itself as to when that study would be completed or the policy it would adopt once the study was completed.[55] The State Department was not ready to accept the Israeli answer. On 29 July, Acting Secretary Richardson and his counterpart from the Pentagon, Deputy Secretary David Packard, invited Rabin to discuss Israel's nuclear and missile programs. According to the "talking point" memo that Sisco prepared for Richardson, the meeting aimed "to initiate a dialogue on Israel's intentions concerning nuclear weapons and strategic missiles." Given the previous administration's failure eight months earlier to get Israeli signature on the NPT in exchange for the F-4s, Richardson's objectives were ambitious. As stated in Sisco's memo, these objectives were that Israel do the following: (a) sign the NPT by the end of the year; (b) reaffirm to the U.S. in writing that it will not be the first to introduce nuclear weapons into the Near East, specifying that "introduction" shall mean possession of nuclear explosive devices; and (c) give us assurances in writing that it will stop production and will not deploy "Jericho" missiles or any other nuclear-capable missile.[56]

The talking points Sisco prepared for Richardson were similar to the message Rusk and Warnke had given Eban and Rabin in October–November 1968. Both deputy secretaries were to make the case for the importance the United States attached to Israel signature of the NPT. They were asked to tell Rabin straight out that the issue of Israel's nuclear policy "transcends considerations of purely bilateral significance," and with the NPT in existence, "unilateral assurances are no longer sufficient in themselves to give confidence that Israel does not intend to manufacture nuclear weapons." Because of the Israeli nuclear potential the United States was "particularly troubled" by Israel's continued delay in signing the NPT:

> Israel is not just another state that for one reason or another is delaying its adherence to the Treaty. The world knows that unlike most other states Israel has the technical capability to build nuclear weapons. It is also becoming aware that Israel has had developed and is acquiring surface to surface missiles capable of carrying nuclear warheads. Because of this proximity to the nuclear threshold, Israel's attitude toward the NPT is being closely watched by other small and medium-sized states who are waiting to see whether nuclear weapons non-proliferation can be made to prevail as a global principle. We therefore attach utmost importance to Israel's early signature and ratification of the NPT.[57]

Richardson was asked to note Eshkol's letter to President Johnson from December, in which Eshkol stated that Israel was studying the NPT. In case Rabin contended that Israel had not yet completed its deliberations regarding the NPT, Richardson was urged to ask what aspect of the NPT created special problems for Israel, and that the United States would be happy to discuss these issues with Israeli experts.

Sisco's memo to Richardson also referred to the difference that became apparent in the Rabin-Warnke talks in November "over what constitutes introduction of nuclear weapons." Referring to Rabin's point that a state might possess a nuclear explosive device but as long as it was undeclared and untested it could not be considered as having been "introduced," the memo urged

Richardson to reject this definition of introduction. Sisco wrote that the United States must make it clear to Israel that it cannot accept this interpretation of introduction. "We would like to have Israel's assurance that when it says it will not be the first to introduce nuclear weapons into the area it means that it will not possess nuclear weapons." The memo also made a reference to the Jericho missile (MD-620), the missile that was developed and tested by the French government. Those weapons "make sense only as a nuclear weapons carrier." It urged Israel not to produce or deploy these missiles.

The record of that conversation is still unavailable, but Rabin described the meeting in his memoirs. According to Rabin, the two under-secretaries "showed a great deal of curiosity." They insisted on knowing what Israel meant by its nonintroduction commitment. Did Israel have the capacity to produce such weapons, but was avoiding producing them?[58]

Richardson was exploring with Rabin the same issues Warnke had explored with Rabin in November: What was the operational meaning of the Israeli pledge not to introduce nuclear weapons into the region? To what had Israel actually committed itself? These questions were aimed at understanding what the Israeli threshold was—how far would Israel go in its nuclear pursuit? Might the Israeli threshold be based on a distinction between the technical capacity to produce nuclear weapons and the political decision to do so? Richardson probed. From Rabin's description, Richardson clearly wanted him to acknowledge that Israel had the technical capacity to produce nuclear weapons, but had not made the decision to do so, that is, nonintroduction meant nonpossession. This distinction was implicit in de Shalit's comment in June 1967 and in Eshkol's statement of October 1968. The State Department thought that this distinction could still permit Israel to sign the NPT.

Rabin followed the path he had taken in November 1968 during his negotiations with Warnke on the Phantoms: nonintroduction meant nontesting. The United States wanted Israel to commit itself not to produce nuclear weapons, but Rabin was willing to pledge only that Israel would not test such weapons. Rabin also stated that as long as there was no test, there was no complete weapons system. The second interpretation was consistent with the notion that as long as Israel did not turn the last screw to make the device an operational weapon system, it had not introduced nuclear weapons into the region.[59]

Regarding the NPT, Rabin proposed separating the question of the meaning of nonintroduction and Israel signing the NPT. He told Richardson that Meir, who had been on the job for only a few months, was preoccupied with the skirmishes along the Suez Canal and had not had a chance to study this issue. Rabin proposed leaving the question of the NPT for the upcoming discussions with Nixon during her visit to the United States.[60]

THE NEW UNDERSTANDING

In the summer of 1969 the State Department was still treating the Israeli nuclear issue in the same fashion as it had during the Johnson era. The department was now living in the past, out of touch with CIA assessments and the new attitude of the White House to the issue.

Since the mid-1960s some senior CIA officials had concluded that the Israeli nuclear project was unstoppable, and that the Dimona inspectors had been led to false conclusions by the Israelis. By late 1966 the CIA station in Tel Aviv passed on two reports claiming that Israel had completed the development stage of its bomb project and was weeks away from the bomb. The alarmist reports were received with suspicion at the bureau of intelligence and research of the State Department; in the absence of solid confirmation they did not change the assessment of the department. Ambassador Barbour, who was aware of the reports and recognized their credibility, concluded that the AEC Dimona visits were becoming embarrassing for both countries, and that it would be better to end them. While Barbour officially protested to Prime Minister Meir about the Israeli conduct during the 1969 visit, unofficially he lobbied to discontinue the arrangement.[61]

The meeting between Nixon and Meir was the right moment to bring about the needed change. Nixon and Kissinger accepted exceptions to the principle of nonproliferation, and believed that this might be a case where the U.S. national interest permitted a state friendly to the United States to build its own nuclear arsenal.

There was also a change in the Israeli approach to the problem. Golda Meir saw things differently from Ben Gurion and Eshkol, and was not locked into the understandings her predecessors reached with Kennedy and Johnson. In late September 1969 she had her chance to present her view to American leaders.[62] In her memoirs Meir does not discuss the substance of her conversation with Nixon, saying only that "I could not quote him then, and I will not quote him now." In his memoirs Rabin was more forthcoming, saying that the discussions were sensitive. Even in the meetings that included Kissinger, Rogers, and himself, no protocol was taken. The understandings reached were not written and formal.[63]

Some of the understandings were on issues of procedure and communication. Nixon and Meir decided to set up direct channels of communication between their offices, bypassing their foreign policy bureaucracies. The most sensitive, substantive understanding concerned the nuclear issue. Meir followed her old line: "to tell the Americans the truth and to explain why." Nixon and Kissinger understood why.

It was apparently in those discussions that it was agreed to end the American visits to Dimona, putting an end to an affair that had become both embarrassing and not at all useful. From now on the United States would no longer press Israel to sign the NPT, but it would continue to support the principle of the universality of the NPT. The United States would publicly continue to express its interest in Israel signing the NPT and placing all its nuclear installations under safeguards. Israel, for its part, continued to be committed to the Eshkol formula of nonintroduction along the lines Rabin had suggested in his previous meetings: no test, no declaration, hence, no introduction. Rabin referred to these understandings obliquely, "the Nixon Administration no longer pressed on the matter of signing the NPT, and the issue dropped from the [bilateral] agenda."[64] Two decades later an American official searched governmental archives to understand how exactly, and by whose authority, the AEC visits to Dimona came to an end. He found no paper trail showing a formal directive to that extent.[65]

The new understandings of 1969 dealt with the new nuclear reality in the Middle East. During Eshkol's tenure, Israeli commitment appeared to mean that Israel would not produce nuclear weapons. After 1969 Israel committed itself not to reveal its nuclear capability by conducting a test or by declaration.[66] With these new understandings both the United States and Israel moved from the era of nuclear ambiguity to the era of nuclear opacity.

NEW REALITY

On 18 July 1970, when the Soviet military involvement in the War of Attrition reached its peak, the New York Times made public Israel's status as a de facto nuclear-weapon state. The paper's diplomatic correspondent, Hedrick Smith, wrote that "for at least two years the United States Government has been conducting its Middle East policy on the assumption that Israel either possesses an atomic bomb or has component parts available for quick assembly."[67] The story was prompted by the comments of Senator Stuart Symington, a member of the Armed Services and Foreign Relations Committees, made in the wake of "a somber appraisal" of the Israeli nuclear program given to the committee by Richard Helms, director of Central Intelligence, on 7 July.[68] It was apparently the first time the CIA shared its information on Israel's nuclear status with Congress.

The New York Times story made public most of what the U.S. government knew about the Israeli nuclear program. It stressed that while there were disputes within the intelligence community about narrow technical details concerning the Israeli operational status, there was a consensus that "Israel has the capacity to assemble atomic bombs on short notice" if it had not already done so. Without referring to the talks between Nixon and Meir, Smith disclosed that Israel had told American officials that the commitment not to introduce nuclear weapons meant that Israel would not be the first Middle Eastern state to use or test atomic arms. The Nixon administration was convinced that Israel would not use nuclear weapons except in the most dire emergency.[69]

Smith noted that the sensitivity of the information was so great that the CIA had not put it in a "fully coordinated national intelligence estimate." The administration treated the matter separately from other Middle East issues and did not expect to incorporate the nuclear issue into its current diplomacy. American officials were reluctant to discuss the matter because of its explosive implications for the Arab countries and the Soviet Union, as well for the United States and Israel.[70]

We do not know who leaked the information to the New York Times. It is clear, however, that Symington, other senators, and some individuals in the administration wanted the message to be made public. Was the purpose of the disclosure to signal to the Soviet Union that a cease-fire agreement in the War of Attrition must be reached to prevent further Soviet-Israeli escalation? Was it a way to explain to the American public why the United States ought to be concerned about the dangerous situation along the Suez Canal?

The Israeli response to the disclosure was different than in the past. Israel did not deny the story, stating instead that it was "inaccurate, unauthoritative and speculative," repeating the pledge not to be the first country to introduce nuclear weapons into the Middle East.[71] The New York Times noted, however, the nuance in the new Israeli disclaimer: "Responsible Israel officials [in Washington] are said to have told United States officials that this [the disclaimer] means Israel would not be the first Middle Eastern country to test or use atomic weapons."[72] The State Department responded to the story in a similar way, stressing its speculative nature and saying that the United States continued to trust the Israeli commitment not to be the first to introduce nuclear weapons into the region.[73]

The New York Times article signified the beginning of a new era in the public history of the Israeli nuclear weapons program. It revealed what had been known by some for at least two years—Israel was a nuclear-weapon state and should be treated as such. It took a few more years for this recognition to be absorbed into the new thinking about Israel's nuclear capability. The move from nuclear ambiguity to opacity was now complete.

Epilogue

Writing this book was not easy. It required over-coming scholarly and personal difficulties. Some had to do with access to sources, archival and human; some with breaking an Israeli code of silence concerning the discussion of nuclear weapons. The latter was more taxing than the former. I had to abandon acquired habits and practices, and distance myself from modes of thought and speech into which I have been socialized.

Like other Israelis, I had internalized the norms governing the Israeli discourse on nuclear weapons, having learned that Israelis were not supposed to discuss their nation's nuclear weapons program. Israelis avoid uttering the phrase "atomic bomb," using instead phrases such as "nuclear option" and "nuclear capabilities," just as orthodox Jews would never utter God's name, using all kinds of euphemisms instead. I have come to see these circumlocutions for what they were —burdensome and unnecessary evasions—but I still feel a certain unease talking openly about Israel's nuclear arsenal.

Ambivalence toward and inhibition regarding nuclear weapons are not an Israeli invention. They have been present in all nuclear-weapon programs since the Manhattan Project. In Israel, however, these attitudes have been manifested in the extreme. The code of silence over the nuclear issue is a testimony to what Israelis call *kedushat habitachon*—the sacredness of security. As a result, Israel's nuclear status has remained an enigma, referred to both as "the world's worst kept secret" and "the bomb that never is."[1]

Little has been written about Israel's nuclear history, even less about the meaning and interpretation of this history. It is therefore appropriate to close this book with reflections on the subject.

*

Israel was the sixth nation to acquire nuclear weapons, but it had marked differences from the first five nations. The others were powerful countries, large in population and territory, rich in resources (except, perhaps, China), all of them major players on the international scene. Young Israel was small and poor, without an industrial base.

Israel's nuclear project was a distinct product of the Zionist phase in Israel's history. That phase was the age of the grand Zionist projects: the big settlements, economic development, water projects that were initiated in Israel's first decade. The nuclear program was probably the most complex project Israel has ever undertaken—the most sensitive politically, the costliest, the most challenging technologically, and the most secretive.

The nuclear project was, in many ways, the ultimate Zionist project. Its purpose was to ensure the physical existence of the State of Israel, the product of the Zionist movement. At the beginning there were fears, vision, and audacity. The project's managers relied on intuition and opportunities. Action came first, planning came later. With more knowledge and forethought, and a more orderly decision-making process, the project might never have taken off.[2]

Ben Gurion, with his fears, hopes, and authority, was present from the very beginning. What would have happened had it not been for him? I am convinced that without Ben Gurion at the helm, Israel's nuclear project as we know it would not have been launched. No other Israeli leader at the time—Moshe Sharett, Pinhas Lavon, Levi Eshkol, or Golda Meir—had the vision, courage, and authority to make those decisions. In 1955–58, when the important decisions about Dimona were made, the idea of an Israeli nuclear project was beyond the ken of even the most activist and security-minded Israeli leaders. Most members of Israel's small scientific community questioned the viability of the project. But Ben Gurion persisted.

Had the decisions Ben Gurion made in 1955–58 not been taken, Israel might have developed a modest nuclear research program in the late 1950s. It is also possible that, by the late 1960s, it would have had a civilian nuclear power program with some weapon-producing potential. Any Israeli prime minister would have purchased the small research reactor that the United States offered Israel in 1955 because the Israeli scientific establishment firmly supported it. Israel's nuclear program would not have been equal to the Dimona project, however. It would have been different, in purpose and character, from the project Ben Gurion had initiated and Peres executed in 1955–58. What is not in doubt is that without Ben Gurion, Peres, and Bergmann, Israel would not have had an operational nuclear weapons capability on the eve of the Six-Day War.

Had Israel not acted in the mid-1950s as it did, it would have been more difficult for it to do so later. The French assistance was unique. Nowhere else could Israel have expected to receive such a large, unsafeguarded reactor, as well as the accompanying reprocessing technology. It would have been nearly impossible for Israel, technologically and financially, to develop a plutonium-based nuclear infrastructure on its own.

On the domestic front, the secret decisions could have been taken only in the mid- and late 1950s, the period when Ben Gurion's moral authority and bureaucratic control were at their peak. *Kedushat habitachon* was still an absolute value, and Ben Gurion personified it. Had Ben Gurion waited another five or ten years to initiate the project, he would have faced a different Israel, a nation less trusting and gullible, a society that would not have given him the freedom to act as he saw fit. The struggles that split MAPAI in the early 1960s, and brought Ben Gurion down, were early indications of the political transformations that would change Israel.

By the 1960s international attitudes toward nuclear weapons proliferation were changing, and IAEA safeguards were being developed. In 1968 the Nuclear Non-Proliferation Treaty was signed (had it not been for the initiation of the Dimona project a decade earlier, Israel would likely have joined the treaty), and its presence would have changed states' calculations. The opportunities available to Israel in the 1950s would have disappeared. Had Israel tried to develop a nuclear project a decade later, the Arabs and the superpowers would have responded differently than they did a decade earlier.

*

What was the impact of the nuclear project on Israel: on its science and technology, on its national security, on its relations with the Arabs, and on its own self-image? Would Israel without nuclear weapons have been the same Israel as we know it now?

These questions cannot be answered with precision. There are no data available on the effects of the nuclear and related programs on the development of Israeli science, technology, and industry. Part of the difficulty is methodological, having to do with the definition of boundaries of the nuclear project, and with measuring the spillover of the project into other areas. Opacity also makes it difficult to answer the less quantifiable aspects of the puzzle. Since the existence of nuclear weapons is not acknowledged, it is difficult to discern their effects on Israel's foreign and defense relations.

There is no doubt, however, that the nuclear project has had profound consequences for the State of Israel. It has greatly contributed to the rapid development of Israeli science and technology. Virtually all Israeli universities and research institutions benefited from the fruits of the project, in one way or another. The project, and related research and development activities, have also contributed to the advent of Israel's high-tech industries in the 1960s and 1970s, particularly in the areas of computers, aeronautics, and telecommunications.

Even more intriguing are the effects of the bomb on Israel's national security, on Arab-Israeli relations and Arab-Israeli peace. The fact is that Israel has nuclear weapons and the Arabs do not. The 1967 war, related to the nuclear issue but not caused by it, left the Arabs defeated and humiliated. Nasser could no longer respond to the Israeli nuclear challenge, allowing Israel to travel safely through the risky transition to a nuclear-weapon state.

The 1970s and 1980s were the golden era of nuclear opacity. The Arabs were not deterred from waging the 1973 war by the knowledge that Israel was in possession of nuclear weapons (although nuclear weapons might have induced them to limit their war aims), but the war also established that Israel was a prudent nuclear-weapon state. The robustness of opacity was demonstrated in other situations. During the Egyptian-Israeli peace negotiations in 1978–79, Egypt, under American pressure, ignored the nuclear issue, understanding that emphasizing the issue would be counterproductive. Iraq threatened to shatter opacity when it started its own nuclear weapons program, but Israel responded in 1981 by destroying the Iraqi reactor, demonstrating its determination to deny nuclear weapons to Arab states. The Arab reaction was milder than had been anticipated, indicating that the Arabs recognized that it would not be in their interests to confront Israel's nuclear monopoly as long as Israel kept its nuclear profile opaque. The 1986 Vanunu revelations accentuated Israel's nuclear image in the Arab world but were insufficient to undermine opacity.

Opacity has been successful in Israeli eyes, allowing Israel to enjoy a regional nuclear monopoly without incurring the political cost of possessing nuclear weapons. This brought many Arabs to the realization that the conflict could not be settled by military means, but only through negotiation. The peace treaty with Egypt in 1979, the Oslo agreements with the Palestinians in 1993, and the peace treaty with Jordan in 1994 were negotiated in the shadow of opaque nuclear weapons.

Ben Gurion's vision of an Israel secured against existential threats has now been realized. Though nuclear weapons have not been officially acknowledged, they have greatly contributed to Israel's image as the strongest nation in the Middle East. The Jews of Israel will never be like the Jews in the Holocaust. Israel will be able to visit a terrible retribution on those who would attempt its destruction.

Still, some questions persist: Has Israel gone too far in its nuclear pursuit under opacity? Have nuclear weapons made Israel arrogant? Indeed, has Israel's nuclear might led some of its leaders to believe that nothing matters in politics but raw military power?

*

These are intriguing, even disturbing, questions. Unfortunately, opacity has made it difficult, if not impossible, to research and debate them. This leads me to the second, even more fundamental difference between Israel and the first five nuclear-weapon states. Unlike the five declared nuclear powers, Israel has never acknowledged its nuclear-weapon status. If France had invented opacity as a temporary measure to becoming a nuclear power, Israel has made opacity a permanent posture.

Secrecy about the development of nuclear weapons is not unique to Israel. The first five nuclear-weapon states kept their initial development effort secret. Once they acquired nuclear weapons capability, they acknowledged their status while continuing to maintain secrecy with regard to technical matters and doctrine. Israel was the first country that decided to build nuclear weapons but not to declare their possession, first through a policy of denial, later through ambiguity that evolved into opacity. Israel's declaratory policy is still "not to be the first to introduce nuclear weapons to the Middle East." Israel thus chose a schizophrenic path.

Israel's nuclear opacity is by now more than a phenomenon of international politics or strategy—it is a cultural and normative phenomenon as well. Individuals and events determined the way Israel stumbled into opacity in the 1950s and 1960s, but since then opacity has become embedded in Israel's national security culture—in the values, attitudes, and norms passed on to those who are initiated into the culture.

The culture of opacity is rooted in several convictions: that it is vital to Israel's security to possess nuclear weapons; that the Arabs should not be allowed to obtain nuclear weapons, thus maintaining an Israeli nuclear monopoly; that Israel cannot openly make a case for nuclear monopoly and thus must keep its nuclear status unacknowledged; that the nuclear issue must be kept out of public discourse; that the issue should be left to anonymous nuclear professionals; and, finally, that the policy of opacity has served Israel well and has no alternative. Even in today's Israel, when all other security-related organizations and issues, including the Mossad and the *Shin Bet*, have become a matter of public debate and criticism, the nuclear complex is conspicuous in its absence from the public agenda.

There is, however, a price to be paid for this policy. Opacity has stifled public debate on the nuclear issue in Israel.[3] All of Israel's democratic institutions—the Knesset, political parties, the press, academia—have looked the other way when it came to nuclear weapons. They have abdicated their democratic duties—checking, debating, informing, overseeing, critiquing—in the face of the nuclear issue. This code of silence is an anomaly in a political culture characterized now by lively, open debate on virtually every public issue, including other sensitive defense matters. Such a debate is at the heart of Israeli democracy. The culture of opacity thus marks a striking failure of that democracy.

It was this tension between democratic norms and nuclear secrecy that brought me, in the mid-1980s, three years before the Vanunu affair, to reflect on the uniqueness of the Israeli nuclear case. I returned to Israel in 1982, after seven years in the United States. Like many of my generation I was moved by the antinuclear sentiment of the early 1980s. I began to think about nuclear weapons and the philosophical puzzles and paradoxes associated with them. The result was *Nuclear Weapons and the Future of Humanity: The Fundamental Questions*, which Steven Lee and I published in 1986.[4]

Around that time I became aware of the "tragic paradox" (as Robert Dahl called it): the contradiction between nuclear weapons and the principles and values of a liberal democracy. Following Richard Falk, one of the contributors to that volume, I recognized that nuclear weapons create "structural necessities" that contradict the spirit of democratic government. Nuclear weapons corrode and corrupt democratic rule.[5]

The argument that Dahl, Falk, and others articulated is simple but powerful. Decisions about nuclear weapons—development, deployment, doctrine, command and control, safety, and ultimately use—are the most fateful decisions a nation can make. Because of their vast consequences, such decisions require a thorough process of deliberation and discussion. Yet these decisions tend to escape the control of democratic processes. Many of the decisions in all the nuclear weapon states were made in secrecy and under the code of "atomic sovereignty." All nuclear weapons complexes function, in one way or another, as a state within a state, protected by the complexes' own nuclear guardians. But who guards the guardians? In a liberal democracy we know that there are no Platonic guardians who can know, and be motivated only by, the good of the Republic. The guardians have interests of their own that are not necessarily compatible with the common good.

I recognized, then, that Israel's nuclear opacity has elevated the tension between nuclear secrecy and democracy to new heights. It did not occur to me then that a decade later this issue would become, for me, a very personal matter. In April 1994, after months of discussions with the Israeli military censor, he informed me that for "reasons of state" he was banning the publication of a monograph I had written on this subject. I was told that this was the first time in Israel's history that a product of academic research and scholarship, not a journalistic exposé, was suppressed in its entirety by the censor. When all efforts to reach a compromise failed, I petitioned the Israeli Supreme Court of Justice to reverse the censor's decision.[6] I soon realized, however, that the censor's objection had little to do with concerns about information I might have divulged, since during nearly a year of legal correspondence, the censor refused to tell me exactly what he found objectionable or harmful. At issue, I felt, was a violation of a national taboo, breaching the code of Israeli nuclear opacity. The monograph was never published, but it inspired me to write a new and much larger work on the subject.

Israel is the only Western democracy that has a military censor who oversees every publication dealing with security issues. Over the years the impact of the censor has diminished, with the exception of the nuclear issue. The existence of this office reinforces Israel's policy of opacity in two ways. First, it strengthens the code of silence by disallowing serious discussion of nuclear policies. Second, the fact that the office exists makes any published expression seen to carry a message on behalf of the government. If Israeli writers were to start referring to "nuclear bombs" rather than to "nuclear potential," it would be taken as a new governmental policy.

Opacity is thus, in one way, consistent with a deep-rooted Israeli tendency to hold off on important decisions that would determine the country's identity. The nuclear issue has joined a long list of fundamental issues on which Israel conducts itself like an ostrich by avoiding clear-cut, public decisions. Other examples include state versus religion; the Jewish character of Israel; Israel's relationship with the domestic Arab population; its relationship with the Palestinians; and the future of the occupied territories. In the case of nuclear weapons, however, unlike these other issues, the question is hardly discussed; opacity has allowed Israel to make the necessary practical decisions without addressing the fundamental, long-term issues.

*

Can opacity last? Should opacity last? For how long? If not, what should Israel's future nuclear posture be? Israeli leaders assume that the continuation of the current posture of opacity is essential for Israel's security, since only under opacity would Israel be able to keep its nuclear program intact and unchecked. I disagree. The time may have come for Israel to find ways to move beyond opacity. Here are some reasons why (in addition to the democratic argument about the inpact on democratic values discussed above).

In the past Israel's nuclear opacity entailed a significant element of technological and operational uncertainty about the country's nuclear program. This uncertainty has disappeared. In addition to the Vanunu revelations, satellite photos exposed other aspects of Israel's nuclear infrastructure. While many of the details are still unknown, as is the case in all other nuclear nations, the big picture is clear. Opacity has become increasingly anachronistic.

It is true that even after Vanunu, opacity has proved itself impervious to the facts, but this was in an era in which Arab governments were still acquiescing to Israeli opacity. Since the Gulf War this is no longer the case, and opacity has been weakened as a regional regime. The Arabs, especially Egypt, are no longer interested in playing their roles in the game of opacity. They now insist that Israel has nuclear weapons, whether Israel confirms it or not. Indeed, Egypt now publicly considers Israel a nuclear-weapon state, saying that the nuclear issue should be addressed through multilateral bodies, such as the Arms Control and Regional Security (ACRS) working group. Egypt has demanded that ACRS initiate discussions on the establishment of a zone free of all weapons of mass destruction, including nuclear weapons, and has insisted that tangible progress in the nuclear discussions be achieved in parallel to progress in the peace negotiations. The nuclear impasse has put the ACRS process in a deep freeze. It is doubtful that any substantial progress in the arms control track is possible without Israeli readiness to discuss the nuclear issue.

Another consideration is the impact of opacity on Israel's own long-term nuclear policy. Opacity prevents conceptual clarity about Israel's intentions and objectives. This may have been a virtue in the past, when opacity blurred the tension between Israel's commitment to acquire and preserve nuclear weapons capability, and its commitment not to nuclearize the Middle East. In the context of the peace process, however, the intrinsic tension in the Israeli position has become apparent. Israel has projected two contradictory messages. On the one hand, Israel's traditional position on the matter of a Nuclear Weapons Free Zone (NWFZ) sounds as if Israel agrees in principle with the Arab position that once the Middle East is peaceful, no party should have a right to maintain nuclear weapons. On the other hand, Israeli leaders have made it clear that they have no intention of giving up their nation's ultimate deterrent even after signing comprehensive peace agreements. Israeli leaders consider nuclear weapons indispensable to Israeli security and to the architecture of peace.[7]

Under opacity Israel has been able to project contradictory objectives without the need to explain away the contradiction. Opacity about long-term objectives made sense during a time of conflict. The end of the conflict, if it comes, will force Israel to confront its nuclear dilemma. Israel will have to face the moment of truth about its nuclear program.

*

Two kinds of criticism—procedural and substantitive—may be raised against the complaints about opacity I have just made. First, one could argue that my complaints are uninformed and overstated, and that, in reality, despite the unavoidable secrecy, decision making in this area has been rational and has conformed to prudent procedures, with institutionalized mechanisms installed to compensate for the unique character of Israel's nuclear situation.[8] One could argue, for example, that the Knesset has a small subcommittee that hears regular briefings on the nation's nuclear activities.

Second, and more important, many argue that there is no policy alternative to opacity. Any effort to deal more openly with the nuclear issue will generate more costs than benefits. For the sake of strategic stability, nuclear nonproliferation, and Israel's relationship with the United States, Israel cannot and should not change its opaque policy. Despite its flaws, opacity has no alternative, surely not at the current time.

As to the first argument, although it is generally true that the system Israel has institutionalized for its decision making on nuclear issues allows for some outside review and even oversight through classified forums, those discussions tend to be bureaucratic and short-term in nature. They tend to be about procedures, budgets, and tactics, not about long-term policies and strategies. As to the question of parliamentary control, that the Knesset subcommittee has no independent tools and personnel to evaluate what it is being told makes its oversight job not much more than a ritual. The fact remains that no other issue of comparable consequence to Israel's future has been debated so little in public.

The second, more substantive argument, is more difficult to answer. I strongly agree that without adequate preparations, consultations, and assurances, at home and abroad, Israel cannot change its opacity policy, particularly its declaratory posture. Furthermore, I agree that any hasty effort to go beyond opacity could be dangerous, even counterproductive, to the causes of Israeli national security, regional stability, global nonproliferation, and American-Israeli relations. A change of policy without adequate preparation could damage Israel's greatly improved position in the region and the world, and could generate pressure on Israel to give up nuclear weapons entirely. For these reasons I do not advocate any unilateral or abrupt change of policy.

To say one must handle the issue with utmost care, however, is different from saying that there is no alternative to current opacity. First, a post-opacity posture ought not to be confused with complete transparency. No nuclear-weapon state is completely transparent about its nuclear weapons posture, and details about the stockpile, command-and-control procedures, and security issues are not discussed in public. What should be discussed in a post-opacity era are issues relating to strategic-doctrinal concepts, accountability and oversight, and history.

Second, to move beyond opacity in a prudent manner Israel would have to assure itself of political preconditions: (1) an appropriate regional context, perhaps a critical breakthrough in the peace process; (2) careful preparation and coordination with the United States; and (3) progress in the global arms control agenda.

One avenue for a deliberate, cautious move to a post-opacity era could be in the context of the proposed Fissile Material Cutoff Treaty (FMCT). The idea of a treaty prohibiting any future production of fissile material for weapons has been discussed on and off for years. In recent years the proposal was again discussed at the Conference on Disarmament (CD) in Geneva, though at present there are significant problems with that forum. One major political difficulty is the question of how much ground an FMCT should cover, whether it should be linked to a "time-bound" commitment to nuclear disarmament by the weapon states , and to what extent it could make the past transparent.

Notwithstanding these difficulties, a properly constructed FMCT could provide Israel with a number of advantages. First, it could give legitimacy to Israel's possession of weapon-grade fissile material, hence legitimizing Israel's nuclear status. Second, an FMCT puts a halt on the production of weapon-grade fissile material; it does not refer in any way to bombs nor even need it count past production of weapon-grade material.

At the same time, it is hard to believe that a discussion of a fissile material cutoff could be kept to closed forums. What is at stake is too important to be left to a handful of ministers and anonymous bureaucrats. Active discussion of a cutoff would inevitably force Israel to move to a post-opacity stage. It would make Israel's nuclear program more, but not entirely, transparent. Opacity will necessarily diminish, but some ambiguities will long remain.

In the end a formal peace will not alter the fundamentals of Israel's geopolitical situation. The Middle East is still far from reaching the era of democratic peace. Even if peace prevails, it will not be peace among democracies. Furthermore, the trend toward technological competency in the region seems to outpace the trend toward democracy and peace. It is not only the lessons of the past but also the trends of the future that give Israel the right to preserve its nuclear deterrent, in some form or another, as a hedge against the resumption of the Arab-Israeli conflict. Israel should be in a position to say that, and to discuss more openly what such a hedge should look like.

*

I began the epilogue by saying that writing this book was not easy, requiring that I overcome psychological and cultural obstacles. Easing the grip of opacity required a strenuous mental effort.

A similar process should be taking place on the collective level as well. The issues of how Israel should move to post-opacity are complex and sensitive, but the real resistance to change does not lie in this or that specific consideration.

Rather, the opposition comes from the structure of opacity itself, that is, opacity as a self-enclosed culture that does not permit thinking on how to move to a post-opacity era. It is comfortable for those in charge of Israel's nuclear infrastructure to work anonymously, immune from outside criticism. Once the anxiety of silence is eased, it will be easier to deal with the substantive issues. Just as other nuclear-weapon democracies found compromises to ease the tension between nuclear weapons and democratic principles, so too can Israel.

The United States has learned this lesson after the cold war. In recent years Americans have become aware of the mistakes and follies committed under the protection of nuclear secrecy. Nuclear weapons were not used during the four decades of the cold war, but many American citizens were casualties of the secret activities of the nuclear weapons complex. President Bill Clinton recently apologized for these mistakes, but the scope of human and environmental damage caused by these secret nuclear activities done in the name of protecting democracy will probably never be known.

After more than thirty years of possessing nuclear weapons, Israel ought to find better ways to deal with this reality. Just as the end of the cold war allowed the United States to impose better democratic control over its nuclear weapons complex, one hopes that the peace process in the Middle East will allow Israel to place its atomic complex under better democratic rule. The causes of both peace and Israeli democracy require that Israel move to a post-opacity era.

I wrote this book in part with the hope to make these changes easier. Understanding the contingencies and circumstances under which opacity came into being could help to ease its grip.

Notes

Preface

1. The term "opaque proliferation" was coined by Benjamin Frankel in his "Notes on the Nuclear Underworld," *The National Interest*, no. 9 (fall 1987): 122–26. In our joint article (Avner Cohen and Benjamin Frankel, "Opaque Nuclear Proliferation," in *Opaque Nuclear Proliferation: Methodological and Policy Implications*, ed. Benjamin Frankel [London: Frank Cass, 1991], 14–44), we further defined and developed the concept.

2. Munya M. Mondor, *Rafael* (in Hebrew) (Tel Aviv: Misrad Habitachon, 1981).

3. Many of the important political decisions were not properly documented and, for reasons having to do with opacity, many of the decisions were made in discussions among a small number of individuals (Shalheveth Freier [director-general of the IAEC, 1970–76, and Israel's science liaison in Paris, 1956–60], numerous conversations with author, Rehovot, 1991–1994).

Introduction

1. See Yuval Ne'eman, "Israel in the Nuclear Weapons Age" (in Hebrew), *Nativ* 8, no. 5 (September 1995): 38.

2. Hedrick Smith, "U.S. Assumes the Israelis Have A-Bomb or Its Parts," *New York Times*, 18 July 1970, 1.

3. Avner Cohen and Benjamin Frankel, "Opaque Nuclear Proliferation," in *Opaque Nuclear Proliferation: Methodological and Policy Implications*, ed. Benjamin Frankel (London: Frank Cass, 1991), 14–44.

4. Cohen and Frankel, "Opaque Nuclear Proliferation," 19.

5. For a comprehensive history, Richard G. Hewlett and Oscar E. Anderson Jr., *The New World: A History of the United*

States Atomic Energy Commission, 1939–1946; Richard G. Hewlett and Frances Duncan, *Atomic Shield: A History of the United States Atomic Energy Commission, 1947–1952*, vol. 2; Richard G. Hewlett and Jack M. Holl, *Atoms for Peace and War: Eisenhower and the Atomic Energy Commission, 1953–1961* (Berkeley: University of California Press, 1990); Richard Rhodes, *The Making of the Atomic Bomb* (New York: Simon and Schuster, 1986). On the British history, see Margaret Gowing, *Britain and Atomic Energy, 1945–1952* (London: Macmillan, 1964); Margaret Gowing, *Independence and Deterrence: Britain and Atomic Energy, 1945–1952*, 2 vols. (New York: St. Martin's, 1974).

6. See Avner Cohen, "Nuclear Weapons, Opacity and Israeli Democracy," in *National Security and Democracy in Israel*, ed. Avner Yaniv (Boulder, Colo.: Westview, 1992), 197–225.

7. A state could manufacture a yield-producing first-generation fission bomb even without testing it, as the United States did with its Hiroshima bomb. Testing would be required for more sophisticated weapons, such as a small enhanced radiation weapon or an H-bomb (see Theodore B. Taylor, "Nuclear Tests and Nuclear Weapons," in Frankel, *Opaque Nuclear Proliferation*, 175–90).

8. "Eshkol: Israel Knows the Secret of the Production of Atomic Bomb" (in Hebrew), *Ha'aretz*, 4 October 1968; "Eshkol and Eban Comment on Nuclear Knowledge without Prior Discussion" (in Hebrew), *Ha'aretz*, 8 October 1968; Reuters, "Israeli Nuclear Deterrent Urged by Jerusalem Paper," *New York Times*, 5 October 1968.

9. As Shalheveth Freier noted, "There were things I was the only person to know" (Shalheveth Freier, interview by author, Rehovot).

1. MEN AND ETHOS

1. The idea of a triumvirate making the Israeli nuclear project possible is taken from Israel Dostrovsky, "The Establishment of the Israeli Atomic Energy Commission" (in Hebrew), in *David Ben Gurion and the Development of Science in Israel* (in Hebrew) (Jerusalem: Israel National Academy of Science, 1989), 44–49.

2. Tom Segev, *The Seventh Million: The Israelis and the Holocaust* (New York: Hill and Wang, 1993), 82

3. "There is a saying, 'the dead will not praise God'. " he wrote in a letter to a noted Israeli scientist, "and if we face the threat of destruction—and unfortunately we do, and Hitler's Holocaust was only the most extensive and terrible of the attempts to destroy us during our history—to a certain extent this is the most fateful of our existence" (letter, David Ben Gurion to Shmuel Sambursky, 17 March 1963, David Ben Gurion Archive (herafter, DBGA), Letters).

4. David Ben Gurion, *War Diaries, 1948–1949* (in Hebrew), vol. 3 (Tel Aviv: Misrad Habitachon, 1982), 852–53.

5. David Ben Gurion Diaries (hereafter, DBGD), 26 April 1949; DBGD, 23 October 1950. For a detailed analysis of Ben Gurion's view, see Zaki Shalom, *David Ben Gurion: The State of Israel and the Arab World 1949–1956* (in Hebrew) (Sdeh Boker: Ben Gurion University of the Negev Press, 1995).

6. See, for example, Shmuel Sambursky, "Ben Gurion and the Scientific Council" (in Hebrew), and David Mushin, "Ben Gurion's Support for Research, Science, and Technology" (in Hebrew), both in *David Ben Gurion and the Development of Science in Israel*, 12–18, 19–24, respectively.

7. David Ben Gurion, *With What We Will Face the Future* (in Hebrew) (Tel Aviv: Merkaz Mifleget Poalei Eretz Israel, November 1948), 35–36; also cited in Ephraim Katzir, "The Beginning of Defense Research: Ben Gurion and the HEMED" (in Hebrew), in *David Ben Gurion and the Development of Science in Israel*, 26–27; and excerpted in David Ben Gurion, *When Israel Fights* (in Hebrew) (Tel Aviv: Am Oved, 1950), 236. The English translation is the author's.

8. Shimon Peres, *Battling for Peace: A Memoir* (London: Weidenfeld and Nicolson, 1995), 132.

9. See, for example, Ben Gurion's opening speech at the Conference on Science and Developing Countries, the Weizmann Institute of Science, Rehovot, 15 August 1960 (DBGA, Speeches, 1960); and David Ben Gurion, *Vision and Direction* (in Hebrew) (Tel Aviv: Am Oved, 1956), 305–6. French physicist Bertrand Goldschmidt was taken by Bergmann in the mid-1950s to Sdeh Boker to see Ben Gurion. Goldschmidt recalls that after a long conversation with Ben Gurion about the future of atomic energy, Ben Gurion suddenly turned and asked (his favorite question) how long it would take until nuclear desalinization would make the Negev desert blossom. Goldschmidt, surprised by the question, did not know how to answer, and finally said, "fifteen years." Ben Gurion responded that if all the Jewish scientists were brought in, it would take less time (Bertrand Goldschmidt, interview by author, Paris, 15 June 1993). There are numerous testimonies to this sentiment. See, for example, his opening speech at the Conference on Science and Developing Countries, the Weizmann Institute of Science, Rehovot, 15 August 1960, DBGA.

10. Ben Gurion, *With What We Will Face the Future*, 34. Ben Gurion also made it a point to meet with many of the Manhattan Project's physicists, many of whom were Jewish, when they visited Israel. Among them were Robert J. Oppenheimer, Edward Teller, Victor Weisskopf, I. I. Rabi, and others.

11. For expressions of this view, see Ben Gurion's remarks in the opening ceremony of the Institute for Nuclear Physics at the Weizmann Institute of Science on 20 May 1958 (DBGA, Speeches, 1958). See also his opening address to the International Conference on the Nature of the Atom, at the Weizmann Institute (Rehovot, 8 September 1957), quoted in Michael Keren, *Ben Gurion and the Intellectuals* (in Hebrew) (Sdeh Boker: Ben Gurion Research Center with the Bialick Institute, 1988), 30.

12. Katzir, "The Beginning of Defense Research: Ben Gurion and the Hemed," 34; Munya M. Mardor, *Rafael* (in Hebrew) (Tel Aviv: Misrad Habitachon, 1981), 70–73.

13. Mardor, *Rafael*, 72–73.

14. Shlomo Gur, interview by author, Tel Aviv, 20 July 1992.

15. Letter, David Ben Gurion to Ehud Avriel, 4 March 1948 (quoted in Keren, *Ben Gurion and the Intellectuals*, 32).

16. Michael Bar-Zohar, *Ben Gurion* (in Hebrew), 3 vols. (Tel Aviv: Zmora Bitan, 1987), vol. 3, 1365.

17. Bar-Zohar, *Ben Gurion*, vol. 3, 1380, 1384, 1550–53.

18. Shalom, *David Ben Gurion*, 72–79; Uri Bialer, *Between East and West: Israel's Foreign Policy Orientation, 1948–1956* (Cambridge: Cambridge University Press, 1990), 235–75.

19. David Ben Gurion, "The Role of Science in the Building of the State of Israel" (in Hebrew), *Hadoar* 13, no. 1 (Supplement for Young Readers), 2 November 1956.

20. "If the Arabs would know that Israel cannot be destroyed," Ben Gurion told the Foreign Policy Committee of MAPAI on 4 March 1958, weeks after the work at the Dimona site had begun, "then, perhaps, there would be some people among them who would begin thinking that this conflict should be over, that maybe the time has come to make peace with Israel. The prospects of peace with the Arabs depends on strengthening Israel's power and security" (Bar-Zohar, *Ben Gurion*, vol. 3, 1362).

21. Mardor, *Rafael*, 352–54.

22. Cited in Segev, *The Seventh Million*, 369.

23. Letter, Ben Gurion to Kennedy, 12 May 1963, ISA/FMRG, 3377/9.

24. Yuval Ne'eman, correspondence with author, May 1997. In 1953–54 Ne'eman was the head of the Planning Division of the IDF.

25. Dostrovsky, "The Establishment of the Israeli Atomic Energy Commission," 49; Ephraim Katzir, "Introductory Remarks," *In Memory of Ernst David Bergmann* (Address at the Opening Session of the Ninth Jerusalem Symposium on Metal-Ligand Interactions in Organic Chemistry, Jerusalem, 29 March 1976).

26. Chaim Weizmann, *Trial and Deed* (in Hebrew) (Tel Aviv: Schocken, 1964), 349–50.

27. On the rift between Weizmann and Bergmann over the involvement of the Sieff Institute in military research, and on Weizmann's "hatred of these military performances," see Norman Rose, *Chaim Weizmann: A Biography* (New York: Viking, 1986), 453–54. On Weizmann's resentment of the changes in the character of the Sieff Institute, see also Chaim Weizmann, *Mivhar Igrot* (in Hebrew) (Tel Aviv: Am Oved, 1988).

28. Ephraim Katzir, "The Beginning of Defense Research: Ben Gurion and the Hemed" (in Hebrew), in *David Ben Gurion and the Development of Science in Israel* (Jerusalem: Israel National Academy of Science, 1989), 37.

29. Shimon Peres, *From These Men: Seven Founders of the State of Israel* (New York: Wyndham, 1979), 185–201; see also Ephraim Katzir, "The Beginning of Defense Research: Ben Gurion and Hemed," 35–36. References to Bergmann's role in Israel's military R&D are in Mardor, *Rafael*. For a journalistic biography, see James Feron, "Israelis Honor Atom Scientist," *New York Times*, 14 May 1966, 3; also Roni Hadar, "Who Forgot the Father of the Israeli Bomb, and Why" (in Hebrew), *Tel Aviv*, March 1991.

30. "An Israeli Man of Distinction," comments delivered by Shimon Peres at Ernst David Bergmann's funeral, Jerusalem, 7 April 1975, and published as a booklet by the Ministry of Defense (courtesy of Hani Bergmann; the English translation is the author's); cf. Peres, *From These Men*, 186.

31. Zvi Pelah, interview by author, Savyon, 24 August 1992; Avraham Hermoni, interview by author, Savyon, 2 September 1992; and Shalheveth Freier, interview by author, Rehovot, 16 August 1992

32. Peres, *Battling for Peace*, 134.

33. Peres, *From these Men*, 185.

34. Cited in Segev, *The Seventh Million*, 370.

35. Peres, *Battling for Peace*, 134.

36. The reports are included in the Foreign Ministry Files on the Atoms for Peace Conference, 2407/2, ISA. Bergmann generated a large number of official documents, memos, letters, reports, and papers. The impression these documents create may not always correspond to reality. This will complicate the work of future historians who have access to his papers.

37. Quoted in Feron, "Israelis Honor Atomic Scientist," 3.

38. *Ha'aretz*, 13 July 1964; and 20 November 1964; see also Mardor, *Rafael*, 389.

39. Dostrovsky, "The Establishment of the Israeli Atomic Energy Commission," 49.

40. Peres, *Battling for Peace*, 61–84.

41. Yitzhak Greenberg, *Defense Budget and Military Power: The Case of Israel, 1957–1967* (in Hebrew) (Tel Aviv: Misrad Habitachon, 1997), 153.

42. See Michael Keren, *Professionalism Against Populism: The Peres Government and Democracy* (Albany: State University of New York, 1995).

43. Renana Leshem, interview by author, Tel Aviv, 1996.

44. Ephraim Katzir, "The Beginning of Defense Research: Ben Gurion and the Hemed," 25–42; Mardor, *Rafael*, 70–72.

45. Ibid., 198–200.

46. Shimon Peres, "About Shalheveth" (in Hebrew) (talk given in a memorial evening for Shalheveth Freier, Van Leer Institute, Jerusalem, 28 December 1994). A written version of Peres's comments appears in *Shalheveth Freier, 1920–1994* (Tel Aviv: Israel Atomic Energy Commission, 1995), 7–14.

47. Gideon Frank, "Shalheveth's Nuclear Legacy" (talk given in a memorial evening for Shalheveth Freier, Van Leer Institute, Jerusalem, 28 December 1994). A written version of Frank's comments appears in *Shalheveth Freier, 1920–1994*, 30–43. Frank is the present director-general of the IAEC.

48. Peres, *Battling for Peace*, 135–36.

49. Mardor, *Rafael*, 114–17, 120–21, 171–74, 178–82, 198–201.

2. BEFORE THE BEGINNING

1. According to Zvi Pelah, Bergmann's student and colleague, as early as 1949 Bergmann defined Israel's need to become a nuclear state as a high national priority. Zvi Pelah, interview by author, Savyon, 24 August 1992.

2. David Ben Gurion, *War Diaries, 1948–1949* (in Hebrew) (Tel Aviv: Misrad Habitachon, 1982), cited in Alex Doron, "Nuclear reactor: What's the Rush?" (in Hebrew), *Ma'ariv*, 5 December 1986, 19–20, 32.

3. Sylvia K. Crosbie, *A Tacit Alliance: France and Israel from Suez to the Six-Day War* (Princeton, N.J.: Princeton University Press, 1974), 114–15.

4. Shlomo Gur (HEMED commander during the War of Independence), interview by author, Tel Aviv, 20 July 1992.

5. Amos de-Shalit, "The Story of One Group" (in Hebrew), *Rehovot* (special issue) (1962): 3–4. Also, Igal Talmi, interview by author, Rehovot, June 1995; Uri Haber-Schaim, interview by author, Belmont, Massachusetts, 17 July 1995; Gideon Yekutieli, interview by author, Rehovot, September 1995. See also Israel Dostrovsky, "The Establishment of the Israeli Atomic Energy Commission," in Israel Dostrovsky, ed., *David Ben Gurion and the Development of Science in Israel* (in Hebrew) (Jerusalem: Israel National Academy of Science, 1989), 46–47; cf. Munya M. Mardor, *Rafael* (in Hebrew) (Tel Aviv: Misrad Habitachon, 1981), 104–8.

6. Dostrovsky, "The Establishment of the Israeli Atomic Energy Commission," 46–47; cf. Mardor, *Rafael*, 104–8.

7. Mardor, *Rafael*, 104–8.

8. Ibid., 75.

9. Ibid.

10. Norman Rose, *Chaim Weizmann: A Biography* (New York: Viking, 1986), 453–54. On Weizmann's strong resentment of the change of character of the Sieff Institute, see his *Selected Letters* (in Hebrew) (Tel Aviv: Am Oved, 1988); and Mardor, *Rafael*, 75.

11. Letter, Ernst Bergmann to Chaim Weizmann, 15 June 1951, File 2927, the Weizmann Archives, Rehovot, Israel; Mardor, *Rafael*, 75.

12. Letter, Meyer Weisgal to Dewey Stone and Harry Levine, 8 July 1951 (dictated on 4 July), the Weizmann Archives, File 2729, Rehovot, Israel.

13. Letter, Chaim Weizmann to Ernst Bergmann, 2 July 1951, the Weizmann Archives, file 2729, Rehovot, Israel, cited in Barnet Litvinoff, ed., *The Letters and Papers of Chaim Weizmann*, vol. 23, series A, August 1947–June 1952, ed. Aaron Klieman (New York: Rutgers University Press, 1980), 304.

14. Mardor, *Rafael*, 80.

15. Haber-Schaim, interview, 17 July 1995, and other occasions.

16. Mardor, *Rafael*, 53–66, 78–79, 104–6; Shlomo Gur, interview by author, Tel Aviv, June 1993.

17. Letter, Ernst Bergmann to David Ben Gurion, 5 December 1952, cited in Mardor, *Rafael*, 94–95.

18. Mardor, *Rafael*, 66.

19. Mardor, *Rafael*, 104–9.

20. DBGD, 13 March 1952, DBGA.

21. Foreign Ministry, Department of International Organization, 11 June 1954, ISA, FMRG, 2407/2.

22. Israel Dostrovsky, J. Gillis, and D. R. Llewellyn, "Separation of Isotopes by Fractional Distillation," *Research Council Israel Publication*, no. 1 (1952): 62–94; Israel Dostrovsky et al., "Optimal Flow in Fractionating Columns for Isotopes Separation," *Bulletin Research Council Israel*, no. 2 (1952): 68–69; Israel Dostrovsky and F. S. Klein, "On Heavy Water Analysis," *Annals of Chemistry* 24 (1952): 414.

23. Ya'akov Sharett, ed., *Moshe Sharett Diaries*, vol. 2 (Tel Aviv: Ma'ariv, 1978), 400.

24. On France's nuclear history see Lawrence Scheinman, *Atomic Energy Policy in France under the Fourth Republic* (Princeton, N.J.: Princeton University Press, 1965). For a participant's testimony on the French nuclear program in the 1950s, see Bertrand Goldschmidt, "The French Atomic Energy Program," *Bulletin of the Atomic Scientists* 18, no. 7 (September 1962): 39–42; Bertrand Goldschmidt, "The French Atomic Energy Program," *Bulletin of the Atomic Scientists* 18, no. 8 (October 1962): 46–48. On Norway see Astrid Forland, "Norway's Nuclear Odyssey: From Optimistic Proponent to Non-proliferation," *Nonproliferation Review* 4, no. 2 (winter 1997): 1–16.

25. There is disagreement on the date, with Mardor (*Rafael*, 108) citing 1954. Pierre Péan (*Les deux bombes* [Paris: Fayard, 1981], 65–66) also cites 1953 as the year of that agreement. Péan relies on interviews with Bertrand Goldschmidt.

26. Bertrand Goldschmidt, interview by author, Paris, 15 June 1993; Crosbie, *A Tacit Alliance*, 116. Later that year the French ambassador to the United Nations, Jules Moch, surprised the Israelis by making the French-Israeli agreement public in a speech at the General Assembly, following the announcement of Eisenhower's Atoms for Peace plan. He described with enthusiasm his country's intention to use the Israeli method of production of heavy water. This revelation led the Israeli UN ambassador Abba Eban to express pride in the Israeli invention.

27. Sharett, *Moshe Sharett Diaries*, vol. 2, 565.

28. Zvi Lipkin, correspondence with author.

29. Randers, who was involved in defense-related activities in Britain during the war, was, in 1946, appointed director of the Physics Division of the newly established Norwegian Defense Research Establishment. As in Israel under Bergmann, Norway's nuclear activities began in the late 1940s under the auspices of the defense establishment, with interest in both military applications and power. In early 1946 Randers published a book entitled *Atomic Energy: The World's Hope or its Demise* (in Norwegian) (Oslo: J. W. Cappelns Forlag), in which he advocated nuclear energy as the path of the future (cited in Forland, "Norway Nuclear Odyssey," 3).

30. The decision to spend money on this defense project was criticized by a number of Norwegian academic physicists (Forland, "Norway's Nuclear Odyssey," 3).

31. Letter, Ernst Bergmann to Gunnar Randers, 10 May 1954, courtesy of Odd Karsten Tveit.

32. Goldschmidt, interview; Crosbie, *A Tacit Alliance*, 116.

33. Letter, Randers to Bergmann, 9 July 1954, courtesy of Odd Karsten Tveit.

34. Crosbie, *A Tacit Alliance*, 116–17; cf. The State of Israel, *Israel Government Yearbook, 1955* (Jerusalem: State of Israel, 1956), 190.

35. See Sharett, *Moshe Sharett Diaries*, vol. 2, 534.

36. See Sharett, *Moshe Sharett Diaries*, 18 June 1954, vol. 2, 548. There were also questions raised about the direction and management of Israel's nuclear program. See "The Complete and Uncensored Diaries of Moshe Sharett," 17 November 1954, courtesy of Ya'acov Sharett.

37. Sharett, *Moshe Sharett Diaries*, vol. 3, 606.

38. Letter, Amos de Shalit and others to Bergmann, 27 March 1951, courtesy of Uri Haber-Schaim.

39. Memorandum (handwritten draft), Uri Haber-Schaim, 9 December 1952, 1–3; Zvi Lipkin, correspondence with author, January–April 1996; Igal Talmi and Gideon Yekutieli, interviews, Rehovot, June 1995; Uri Haber-Schaim, conversations with author, 1995–97.

40. Memorandum, Haber-Schaim, 1–3.

41. Ibid., 3.

42. See Uri Haber-Schaim, Yehuda Yeivin, and Gideon Yekutieli, "On the Production of *K* Mesons," *Physical Review* 94, no. 1 (April 1954): 184–85. The "Cosmic Ray Section" was Bergmann's invention.

43. Haber-Schaim summarized his frustrations in his four-page memorandum.

44. Talmi and Yekutieli, interviews; Haber-Schaim, conversations.

45. In early 1953 Bergmann asked Haber-Schaim to go on a visit to the French nuclear research center at Saclay for a few months. When he was not given a clear answer as to the purpose of the mission, and when his request to have his wife accompany him was denied, Haber-Schaim told his superiors that he would not go. Bergmann fired him, and threatened that no Israeli science institution would employ him. Haber-Schaim could not find employment, and was told by Dori and Sambursky that, without Bergmann's clearance, he would not find a job in Israel. Haber-Scheim, conversations with author, 1995–97.

46. Zvi Lipkin, correspondence, Weizmann Institute, 24 January 1996.

47. Letter, Amos de Shalit to Uri Haber-Schaim, 12 December 1952, courtesy of Uri Haber-Schaim.

48. De Shalit, "The Story of One Group," 4.

49. Bar-Zohar, *Ben Gurion*, vol. 3, 953–90.

50. That year—1954—is remembered for the Lavon affair: in July 1954 an ill-prepared and ill-executed Israeli intelligence team launched a series of sabotage activities against British and American cultural institutions in Egypt. They were hoping to create the impression that these Western cultural institutions were destroyed by Egyptian nationalists, leading to Britain's cancellation of its plans to withdraw its forces from the Suez Canal zone. The members of the cell were caught, and its leaders executed. It also led to the fall of Pinhas Lavon, Moshe Sharett, and, a decade later, Ben Gurion. See Shabtai Teveth, *Shearing Time* (in Hebrew) (Tel Aviv: Ish Dor, 1992); Bar-Zohar, *Ben Gurion*, vol. 3, 1018–65.

51. Shabtai Teveth writes: "There has never been, either before or since Lavon, a cabinet minister so reckless, so unmindful of and indifferent to international law, the UN, and foreign public opinion. Some of his initiatives—all fortunately aborted by Chiefs of Staffs [Mordechai] Maklef and [Moshe] Dayan—are heavily censored to this day. Had they been carried out, Israel's membership in the family of nations would have been brought into serious question" (Shabtai Teveth, *Ben Gurion's Spy: The Story of the Political Scandal That Shaped Modern Israel* [New York: Columbia University Press, 1996], 271).

52. Letter, Amos de Shalit to Uri Haber-Schaim, 2 March 1954, courtesy of Uri Haber-Schaim; Zvi Lipkin, correspondence.

53. Mardor, *Rafael*, 116.

54. A oblique account of this affair, from this perspective, appears in Mardor, *Rafael*, 113–17.

55. Ibid., 86.

56. Shalheveth Freier, interview by author, Rehovot, June 1992. This is also the recollection of Yuval Ne'eman, then a military liaison at the IAEC (Yuval Ne'eman, interview by author, Austin, Texas, 4 March 1994).

57. Mardor, *Rafael*, 114.

58. Zvi Lipkin, correspondence with author, 21 January 1996, citing his unpublished paper, "Early History of Physics at Weizmann."

59. In handwritten notes written on 9 December 1952, Haber-Schaim ridiculed Bergmann's idea to build Israel's nuclear infrastructure: "It is equivalent to saying: First you build a skyscraper, after that you will train engineers, then, if you have some free time left, you may advance your knowledge in statics, and all that at a time when even cement and steel were unavailable" (3).

60. Shalheveth Freier, numerous conversations with author, 1992–94.

3. THE BEGINNING

1. DBGD, 6 March 1954, 120–21, DBGA, Sdeh Boker, Israel; Michael Bar-Zohar, *Ben Gurion* (in Hebrew), vol. 2 (Tel Aviv: Zmora Bitan, 1987), 1022–23.

2. "Minutes of Meetings," Speech in Ohalo, 16 December 1954, DBGA.

3. Ibid.

4. Ya'acov Sharett, ed., *Moshe Sharett Diaries* (in Hebrew), vol. 4, 958 (this phrase, however, was deleted from the published edition. I am grateful to Yaakov Sharett for making available to me the original manuscript in which this phrase appears).

5. Munya M. Mardor, *Rafael* (in Hebrew) (Tel Aviv: Misrad Habitachon, 1981), 120–21.

6. Ibid.

7. Dror Sadeh, interview by author, Tel Aviv, 29 July 1992; cf. Mardor, *Rafael*, 114; Bertrand Goldschmidt, "The French Atomic Energy Program," *Bulletin of the Atomic Scientists* 18 (1962): 46.

8. Sadeh, interview by author, Tel Aviv, 29 July 1992. Sadeh recalled that in 1954, during his last undergraduate year at Hebrew University, he was secretly invited to EMET offices, where he met Ratner for the first time. At this meeting Ratner told him that the State of Israel had selected him to join its most secret project—the atomic program. Sadeh was not certain whether Ratner used the word "bomb" or "device," but he was confident that one of those words was used.

9. *Public Papers of the Presidents of the United States, 1953: Dwight D. Eisenhower* (Washington, D.C.: Government Printing Office, 1960), 822. On the origins of the Atoms for Peace program, see Richard G. Hewlett and Jack M. Holl, *Atoms for Peace and War, 1953–1961* (Berkeley: University of California Press, 1989), 209–70; McGeorge Bundy,

Danger and Survival: Choices about the Bomb in the First Fifty Years (New York: Random House, 1988), 287–95.

10. Moshe Sharett, *Moshe Sharett Diaries*, 18 May 1955, vol. 4, 1003.

11. *Agreement for Cooperation Between the Government of the United States and the Government of Israel Concerning Civil Uses of Atomic Energy*, signed 12 July 1955 and entered into force 12 July 1955 (State of Israel, *Israel Government Yearbook 1961* [Jerusalem: State of Israel], 38–390). For the text of the agreement see *Atomic Energy: Cooperation for Civil Use, Agreement Between the United States of America and Israel* (Treaties and Other International Acts Series 3311) (Washington, D.C.: Department of State, Publication 5963, n.d.).

12. A Report, "The Geneva Conference on the Peaceful Use of Atomic Energy (8–20 August 1955)," signed by A. D. Bergmann, ISA, FMRG, 2407/2 (the top-secret version).

13. Ibid.

14. Ibid.

15. Department of State, Memorandum of Conversation, 18 August 1955, RG 59, State Lot files, Lot 57D688, Box 417, USNA.

16. This was not completely accurate. The Shippingport reactor, the first American power reactor, did use enriched uranium, but light, not heavy, water was used as the moderator/coolant, and there was no natural uranium blanket.

17. "The Geneva Conference on the Peaceful Use of Atomic Energy (8–20 August 1955)."

18. Ibid.

19. Ibid., 8.

20. Letter, Amos de Shalit to Munya M. Mardor, 28 August 1955, ISA, FMRG 2407/2.

21. Gabriel Sheffer, *Moshe Sharett: Biography of a Political Moderate* (Oxford: Oxford University Press, 1996), 808–859.

22. See Ya'acov Bar-Siman-Tov, "Ben Gurion and Sharett: Conflict Management and Great Power Constraints in Israeli Foreign Policy," *Middle Eastern Studies* 24, no. 3 (July 1988): 330–56; Avi Shlaim, "Conflicting Approaches to Israel's Relations with the Arabs: Ben Gurion and Sharett, 1953–1956," *Middle East Journal* 37, no. 2 (spring 1983): 180–201; Zaki Shalom, *David Ben Gurion: The State of Israel and the Arab World, 1949–1956* (in Hebrew) (Tel Aviv: Ben Gurion University of the Negev Press, 1995), esp. 131–46, 225–44.

23. Bar-Zohar, *Ben Gurion*, vol. 2, 972, 1032.

24. See Shalom, *David Ben Gurion*, 74–79.

25. In its scope and size, the Czech-Egyptian arms deal was unprecedented for that era. The Egyptian air force received 120 Mig 15 jet fighters, 50 IL-28 bombers, 20 IL-14 transports; and its ground forces were given 200 T-34 medium tanks, 500 pieces of artillery, 200 armored vehicles, and more (Yitzhak Greenberg, *Defense Budget and Military Power: The Case of Israel 1957-1967* [in Hebrew] [Tel Aviv: Ministry of Defense, 1997], 31).

26. Mardor, *Rafael*, 127.

27. Ibid.; cf. Mordechai Bar-On, *Challenge and Quarrel: The Road to Sinai–1956* (in

Hebrew) (Sdeh Boker: Ben Gurion Research Center, 1991), 55; Mordechai Bar-On, *The Gates of Gaza: Israel's Road to Suez and Back, 1955–1957* (New York: St. Martin's, 1992).

28. Aluf Benn, "The Project That Preceded the Nuclear Option" (in Hebrew), *Ha'aretz*, 2 March 1995. Benn hints that it was a crash project to develop a chemical option, in response to Ben Gurion's concerns about the use of chemical weapons by the Egyptians. According to Mardor (*Rafael*, 128), Ben Gurion followed the progress of this project, asking detailed questions, "evidently concerned that we would meet the deadline he set, worrying that the enemy would have such capability and we would have nothing to deter or retaliate."

29. According to Bar-On, as early as 1952 the Ministry of Defense had decided to gamble on a French alliance. Before France had even completed the development of its new aircraft (Ouragan, Mystére II) and its new light tanks (AMX 13), Peres had pushed for a defense relationship with France. Peres also acted according to economic considerations, not unrelated to Bergmann's interest in France. The French arms industry, especially its aircraft industry, needed clients outside France to fund its development costs. Among Western countries, France was least dependent on the United States and could fashion its own armaments sale policy. In addition, there was also sympathy toward Israel's struggle within the French military and industrialist circles (Bar-On, *Etgar Vetigrah*, 118–22).

30. Peres, *Battling for Peace: A Memoir* (London: Weidenfeld and Nicolson, 1995), 117. During Lavon's tenure as minister of defense, only one deal was concluded with France. Lavon was not enthusiastic about military research and development, or about Peres. See Mardor, *Rafael*, 113–19; Matti Golan, *Peres* (in Hebrew) (Tel Aviv: Schocken, 1982), 35–39.

31. See Bar-On, *Etgar Vetigrah*, 118–88.

32. Peres, *Battling for Peace*, 120. Through various arms deals with France in 1955–56, Israel received the following military equipment: 30 Ouragans, 60 Mystères IV, 170 Sherman tanks, 175 AMX-13 light tanks, 400 armored vehicles, and more. In the spring and summer of 1956 France also supplied Israel, for free, with 120 Sherman tanks and 200 armored vehicles (figures are cited in Greenberg, *Defense Budget and Military Power*, 170).

33. The relationship between the rebellion in Algeria and the pro-Israeli sentiment in the defense establishment is complex. As Crosbie points out, several issues regarding France's colonial wars created a tense relationship between the military establishment and the Quai d'Orsay, contributing to French sympathy for an activist Israel. Sylvia K. Crosbie, *A Tacit Alliance: France and Israel from Suez to the Six-Day War* (Princeton, N.J.: Princeton University Press, 1974), 47–50.

34. Golan, *Peres*, 40–53, 71–75.

35. Crosbie, *A Tacit Alliance*, 47.

36. Department of State, Memorandum of Conversation, "Subject: Israeli Atomic Energy Program," 11 April 1956, RG 59, State Lot files, Lot 57D688, Box 417, USNA.

37. Peres, *From These Men*, 195–96.

38. Traces of the debate can be found in Peres's essay, "Ernst David Bergmann: Creating a Future out of Naught," in *From These Men*, 185–212; and in the personal diaries

of Ben Gurion (DBGD), though much of it was presumably deleted; also see Mardor, *Rafael*, 195–96.

39. Lipkin, correspondence, January–May 1996. According to Lipkin, the three Weizmann Institute physicists who were knowledgeable about reactors—de Shalit, Pelah, and himself—considered Bergmann grossly uninformed on matters of nuclear reactors and nuclear energy and were concerned that Bergmann could compromise the credibility of Israel on scientific and political grounds. "The situation reached a point where Shalheveth [Freier] intervened by telling us we should stop fighting with Bergmann. He had done great things and all he needed was 'kavod' [respect, in Hebrew]. If we give him the kavod Shalheveth would see to it that Bergmann did no harm. He read all the letters that Bergmann wrote and quietly stopped all the nonsense letters from getting out" (Lipkin, correspondence with author, 29 December 1997).

40. Memorandum of Conversation, "Subject: Presentation of Draft Israeli Power Bilateral," 14 September 1956, RG 59, State Lot files, Lot 57D688, Box 417, USNA.

41. Memorandum, Farley to the Acting Secretary of State, 16 August 1956, RG 59, State Lot files, Lot 57D688, Box 417, USNA.

42. In April 1956 Canada signed a nuclear agreement with India, after two years of negotiations, after which it sold a heavy-water reactor (CANDU type) to India. A month earlier the United States had sold India twenty-one tons of heavy water for the Canadian-Indian reactor, which was named CIRUS.

43. Golan, *Peres*, 63.

44. Ibid.

45. Yuval Ne'eman, then the deputy chief of AMAN, recalls that when he briefed Ben Gurion, with Peres in attendance, in mid-July 1956 on the intelligence contacts with France, Ben Gurion told him straightforwardly that the underlying Israeli interest in the effort was to receive assistance in the nuclear project. "I want a nuclear option," Ben Gurion told Ne'eman (Yuval Ne'eman, interview by author, Austin, Texas, March 1994).

46. Mordechai Bar-On, *The Gates of Gaza: Israel's Defense and Foreign Policy, 1955–1957* (in Hebrew) (Tel Aviv: Am Oved, 1992), 212–39; Peres, *Battling for Peace*, 121–31.

47. Peres, *Battling for Peace*, 122.

48. This is Peres's version of the events. According to Golan (*Peres*, 53), Peres was aware that he had no authority to commit Israel to military action, but he responded as he did, knowing the Israeli government could always withdraw, because of his desire to secure the nuclear reactor deal. Golan writes: "From now on, the small nuclear reactor became an integral part of the process that led [Israel] to the Sinai campaign, perhaps it even became its catalyst. The fact is that the fate of the Sinai campaign was entangled with the fate of the reactor" (Golan, *Peres*, 53–54).

49. Shalheveth Freier, interview by author, Rehovot, 16 August 1992.

50. Pierre Péan, *Les deux bombes* (Paris: Fayard, 1981), 82. According to Peres, the agreement was signed on 21 September. Ben Gurion's cabled response to Peres's news was brief: "Good job. I appreciate very much the agreement on that subject" (Golan, *Peres*, 54). Another unclear issue has to do with the power of the "small" reactor. Peres's biog-

rapher refers to a small reactor of 1MW of power, but Goldschmidt recalls a reactor of about 10MW of power (Bertrand Goldschmidt, interview by author, Paris, 15 June 1993).

51. They added that "the day the Americans see that we are going toward independence in the field of nuclear energy, they will probably give us the guarantees of existence that they have never agreed to give us until now" (Goldschmidt, interview by author, Paris, 15 June 1993).

52. Goldschmidt, interview; Andre Finkelstein (a former senior official at the CEA), interviews by author, Paris, 17 June 1993, and Marburg, 3 July 1997.

53. Peres, *Battling for Peace*, 130.

54. See Peres's interview with Yossi Melman in "Royal Gift" (in Hebrew), *Ha'aretz*, 11 October 1991.

55. Ibid.

56. Mordechai Bar-On, who attended the Sèvres conference as Dayan's military aide, and Ne'eman believe that the nuclear issue was marginal among the factors that led Ben Gurion to the Sinai campaign. For Ben Gurion, the most important issue was to destroy Nasser's military power (Bar-On, *The Gates of Gaza*, 288–93). Bar-On points out that the nuclear aspect of the French-Israeli alliance was so highly classified at that time that even the chief of staff, Moshe Dayan, hardly knew about it. The nuclear dimension of the Israeli-French alliance is hardly mentioned in Bar-On's extensive work on the Suez campaign. The book he wrote in 1958, based on the official records of the Chief of Staff's Office (which Bar-On had directed) makes no reference to the nuclear issue. That book was reissued in 1991, with slight changes, but still with no reference to that issue. Even his later work (Bar-On, *The Gates of Gaza*), written more than thirty years later, makes no reference at all to the nuclear factor.

57. The reference to the Rishon Le-Zion site of the small reactor appears in Péan, *Les deux bombes*, 82. Peres's biographer refers to the fact that construction of the small reactor had already started (Golan, *Peres*, 71).

58. Péan, *Les deux bombes*, 83.

59. "Soviet Protests Canal Blockade," *New York Times*, 5 November 1956.

60. Shimon Peres, *David's Sling* (London: Weidenfeld and Nicolson, 1970), 211; cf. Peres, *Battling for Peace*, 131.

61. Bar-Zohar, *Ben Gurion*, vol. 3, 1271–73.

62. Ibid., 1273–74; cf. Peres, *Battling for Peace*, 131. The American intelligence estimate on likely Soviet actions, especially SNIE 11–9–56 (6 November 1956) concluded it was unlikely that the USSR would employ guided missiles with nuclear warheads in the conflict.

63. Péan, *Les deux bombes*, 83–84.

64. Ibid., 83.

4. THE ROAD TO DIMONA

1. This was the view of many French leaders, including Guy Mollet, after the Suez crisis. See Bertrand Goldschmidt, *The Atomic Complex*, 136–37; Lawrence Scheinman,

Atomic Energy Policy in France under the Fourth Republic (Princeton, N.J.: Princeton University Press, 1965), 171–74; Wilfrid Kohl, *French Nuclear Diplomacy* (Princeton, N.J.: Princeton University Press, 1971), 35–37.

2. Goldschmidt, *The Atomic Complex*, 136–37.

3. Scheinman, *Atomic Energy Policy in France*, 136–41.

4. Details of the EL-3 reactor can be found in International Atomic Energy Agency, *Directory of Nuclear Reactors*, vol 2: *Research, Test, and Experimental Reactors* (IAEA: Vienna, 1959), 295–300.

5. Pierre Péan, *Les deux bombes* (Paris: Fayard, 1981), 96. According to Péan, when members of the French team charged with the building of the extraction plant read the reactor designs, they were surprised that the cooling ducts were three times larger than those needed for a 24-MW reactor.

6. Ibid., 96–97. For a more detailed hypothetical calculation see David Albright, Frans Berkout, and William Walker, *Plutonium and Highly Enriched Uranium 1996: World Inventories, Capabilities, and Policies* (Stockholm: SIPRI/Oxford University Press, 1997), 258–59.

7. Ibid., 111–15.

8. Ibid., 115. The G-1 reactor in Marcoul is graphite moderated; Dimona was moderated by heavy waters.

9. Matti Golan, *Peres* (in Hebrew) (Tel Aviv: Schocken, 1982), 71–72. Ambassador Zur's six-page report about Meir's visit to Paris contains no reference to this discussion. Zur noted, however, that there was a discussion concerning EURATOM and that the foreign minister would report its contents orally to the prime minister (Memo, "Visit and Discussions of the Foreign Minister in Paris," 15 July 1957, ISA, FMRG 3120/23).

10. Bertrand Goldschmidt recalls that, because of Perrin's temporizing, he—Goldschmidt—had to stop him in the parking lot of the Commissariat and, holding the documents in his hand, told him: "Listen, you sign or you don't sign." Perrin said "OK," and signed, but "he always pretended that I had forced him" (Goldschmidt, interview by author, Paris, 15 June 1993).

11. Golan, *Peres*, 72.

12. Ibid.

13. Ibid., 72–74; a slightly different version appears in Shimon Peres, *Battling for Peace: Memoirs* (London: Weidefeld and Nicolson, 1995), 141–42.

14. Péan, *Les deux bombes*, 128.

15. Golan, *Peres*, 73–74.

16. Ibid., 72–73.

17. Ibid., 72–74; French sources, interviewed by author, Paris, June 1993.

18. Péan, *Les deux bombes*, 110. Shalheveth Freier confirmed this in numerous conversations with the author.

19. Péan writes: "When the team in charge of building the plutonium extraction plant read the file on the reactor, it was surprised by its capacity. It appeared to them to be twice to three times more powerful than what had been indicated in the agreement between France and Israel. The cooling ducts, for instance, were three times bigger than

needed for a 24 megawatt reactor" (ibid., 95–96). The power of the Dimona reactor is still a mystery. When Ben Gurion told the Knesset about the reactor in December 1960, he stated its power as 24 MW. This number appeared in all early Israeli official publications, though later official publications referred to 26MW. According to Remi Carle, the chief liaison to the project on behalf of the CEA, Dimona was built with a power of 40MW capacity, with an option to increase it in the future. Remi Carle, interview by author, Paris, 17 June 1993. In his conversation with Gunnar Renders of Norway Bergmann indicated that the reactor power was 40MW (see next section).

20. Ibid., 97; Remi Carle, interview by author, Paris, 17 June 1993.

21. Péan, *Les deux bombes*, 113–21.

22. "The Geneva Conference on the Peaceful Use of Atomic Energy (August 8–20, 1955)," signed by A. D. Bergmann, ISA, FMRG, Box 2407, file 2.

23. Department of State, Memorandum of Conversation, "Subject: Israeli Atomic Energy Program," 11 April 1956, RG 59, State Lot files, Lot 57D688, Box 417, USNA.

24. Memorandum of Conversation, Subject: "Presentation of Draft Israeli Power Bilateral," 14 September 1956, RG 59: State Lot files, Lot 57D688, Box 417, USNA.

25. AEC, Memorandum of Conversation, "Implementation of Atomic Energy Program with Israel," 25 January 1957, RG 59, State Lot files, Lot 57D688, Box 417, USNA.

26. Letter, Randers to Bergmann, 8 December 1956 (courtesy of Odd Karsten Tveit). Odd Karsten Tveit, *Alt for Israel: Oslo-Jerusalem, 1948-1978* (Oslo: J. W. Cappelens Forlag, 1996), 256–62.

27. Letter, Randers to Moller, 9 August 1957 (Courtesy of Odd Karsten Tveit).

28. Randers probably was told in vague and nonexplicit terms about the purpose of the Dimona project, but given his technological background it is inconceivable (to this writer, at least) that he failed to intuit Dimona's true purpose, that is, being the infrastructure of a plutonium-based nuclear weapons program. No other justification of the Dimona 40-MW "production reactor"—e.g., to train personnel for a future power program, to produce plutonium for a civilian power reactor, and so on—makes any economic, technological, or political sense. Furthermore, the fact that in 1958 Israel was involved in initiating two parallel national nuclear projects—one public and cheap, the other super secret and costly—eliminates the possibility that Randers was somewhat deceived by the Israelis. The Dimona project was very different from the multi-MW, heavy-water, power reactors Randers supported in the mid-1960s: in Tunisia, Egypt, Pakistan, and Yugoslavia. Randers must have understood the Dimona project and wanted NORATOM to benefit from it.

29. Letter, Bergmann to Randers, 4 July 1958 (courtesy of Odd Karsten Tveit).

30. Randers made a discrete inquiry with the Americans. Without referring to the sale of Norwegian heavy water, he did inquire of Philip Farley, the special assistant to the secretary of state on nuclear energy, whether the United States would consider the prospect that Israel was building a 40-MW reactor "ominous." Farley had not replied directly, only suggesting that a supply to Israel might present an opportunity for imposing IAEA safeguards. Tveit, *Alt for Israel*, 261–62.

31. Ibid., 262–63; Forland, "Norway's Nuclear Odyssey," 10.

32. Letter, Randers to Bergmann, 12 December 1958 (courtesy of Odd Karsten Tveit).

33. Letter, Yachil to Lange, 25 February 1959, Country File, Norway, Box 2169, USNA.

34. Memorandum of Conversation, 5 June 1959, Olaf Solli (Norwegian Foreign Ministry) and William Fullerton (AEC), USNA (courtesy of Odd Karsten Tveit).

35. Memorandum of Conversation, 6 August 1959, at the Atomic Energy Institute, Kjeller, Norway, Gunnar Randers, director of the Atomic Energy Institute, and Richard J. Kerry, first secretary of the American Embassy in Oslo. RG 59, State Department Central Files, Country File: Norway, 1957–61, Box 2169, USNA.

36. Yuval Ne'eman, interview by author, Austin, Texas, March 1994. According to Peres, in January 1957 a distinguished Israeli physicist cautioned him against being too ambitious, stating that "in our present circumstances it is not within our power to carry this out" (Shimon Peres, *From These Men: Seven Founders of the State of Israel* [New York: Wyndham, 1979], 194). Peres does not name the physicist, but it must be either Racah or, more likely, de Shalit.

37. Peres made brief and cryptic references to this issue in various writings and oral comments. Also, author's interviews with several individuals in a position to know.

38. Zvi Lipkin, correspondence with author. Lipkin was involved with de Shalit in some of those consultations. Cf. Peres, *From These Men*, 193–254.

39. From the sanitized passages in Ben Gurion's diary it is evident that the discussions were about building a small reactor in the Negev desert (DBGD, 11 May 1957; 11 July 1957). Ben Gurion also discussed with two Americans the question of how to set up a national nuclear energy program. These were Philip Sporn, the president of the American Gas and Electric Service Company, and the physicist I. I. Rabi of Columbia University.

40. At least two other IDF senior officers, in addition to Dayan, were involved in discussions with Ben Gurion on the nuclear project: commander of the air force, Dan Tolkovsky, and chief of Central Command, Zvi Zur. Both generals expressed to Ben Gurion an interest in being involved in the nuclear project after their retirement from the military. Both have continued to associate with the project to this day.

41. Ne'eman, interview by author, 11 June 1995. Ne'eman attended the meeting. On Dayan's hesitations concerning the big projects, see Munya M. Mardor, *Rafael* (in Hebrew) (Tel Aviv: Misrad Habitachon, 1981), 149–50.

42. Golan, *Peres*, 72.

43. Peres, *Battling for Peace*, 111–13.

44. Freier, officially the science attaché but in reality Peres's nuclear liaison in Paris, arrived at the embassy with instructions not to discuss his activities with anyone there, including Ambassador Ya'acov Zur. His office operated independently of the diplomatic mission (Shalheveth Freier, correspondence with author).

45. Ibid.

46. Letter, Ben Gurion to Peres, 27 September 1957, in "Letters," DBGA.

47. Golan, *Peres*, 74.

48. Ben Gurion accepted Peres's judgment that "he [Bergmann] is totally committed to the project and I know of no man capable of taking his place as the chairman of the Atomic Energy Commission" (Peres, *From These Men*, 1979), 197.

49. On 17 December 1956, only weeks after the defeat of the Egyptian army in the Sinai, Ben Gurion spoke with his senior commanders of his long-term fears: "It may be that in the next war we shall not be the ones to take the initiative but will face the initiative taken by others; it is extremely likely that we shall be attacked not by one army but by several" (Peres, *From These Men*, 67). In late 1959 Ben Gurion initiated comprehensive discussions in the General Staff on the strategic balance of the conflict, considering the position of the IDF as "too optimistic" (DBGD, 31 December 1959). He proposed an emergency plan for military purchases and armament production (DBGD, 13 January 1960); see also Bar-Zohar, *Ben Gurion*, vol. 3, 1366.

50. Bar-Zohar, *Ben Gurion*, vol. 3, 1316–17.

51. For Ben Gurion the scenarios were not simply hypothetical, worst-case scenarios; these were literally his nightmares. He once said to his aide, Yitzhak Navon, "I could not sleep all night. I had one terror in my heart: a combined attack of all Arab armies" (ibid., 1365, 1368).

52. Ibid., 1379–80, 1384.

53. The quote is from a conversation on 2 April 1963 between Ben Gurion and Barbour, and was reported in a "confidential" State Department cable (Telegram [no 724, pt. 1], Ambassador Barbour to Secretary of State Rusk, 3 April 1963, Box 119, NSF, John F. Kennedy Library [JFKL]).

54. See Bar-Zohar, *Ben Gurion*, vol. 3, 1364–88.

55. DBGD, 28 July 1958; Bar-Zohar, *Ben Gurion*, vol. 3, 1321–32.

56. On the importance of the search for outside security guarantees for Israel's territorial integrity, see Bar-Zohar, *Ben Gurion*, vol. 3, 1316–21. See chaps. 6, 7, in this volume.

57. DBGD, 31 May 1958; cf. Yitzhak Greenberg, *Defense Budgets and Military Power: The Case of Israel 1957–1967* (in Hebrew) (Tel Aviv: Misrad Habitachon, 1997), 188 (Table 15); 194 (Table 21).

58. Ibid.

59. Greenberg, *Defense Budgets and Military Power*, 177–79 (Tables 9, 10).

60. Ibid.

61. DBGD, 31 May 1958, DBGA.

62. "Summary of Additional Recent Information on Israeli Atomic Energy Program," 17 January 1961, NSA; see chapter 6.

63. In 1960 the entire procurement budget was U.S.$26.7 million (in 1961 it was U.S.$27.7) (Greenberg, *Defense Budgets and Military Power*, 184–85 [Table 13]).

64. Peres, *Battling for Peace*, 136–37.

65. This was the figure Eliezer Livneh used in 1962 when he started his anti-Dimona campaign.

66. Because of the unorthodox methods of raising money for the project it is difficult to know whether Ben Gurion was fully informed of the real figures or whether he even wanted to know those figures. According to one story, Peres "missed" one zero in the cost figure given to Ben Gurion, quoting the Dimona project as costing IL30 million (about U.S.$17.5 million in the early 1960s), instead of IL300 million (about U.S.$175 million). When Amos de Shalit, who participated in that meeting, was about to correct Peres's fig-

ures, Peres silenced him by kicking him under the table (Arnon Dar, interview by author, Haifa, 9 September 1992; Dar was a student of de Shalit).

67. Peres, *Battling for Peace*, 135–36.

68. Ibid.

69. Zvi Lipkin, correspondence with author, 15 April 1996.

70. Péan, *Les deux bombes*, 103.

71. Mardor, *Rafael*, 164.

72. Ibid., 166

73. Ibid., 169.

74. Ibid., 173. Also, Yedidyah Shamir and Avraham Hermoni, interviews by author, June–July 1992. Shamir and Hermoni were technical directors at that time.

75. Mardor, *Rafael*, 169.

76. Ibid., 171–74.

77. Ibid., 173.

78. Peres, *Battling for Peace*, 134.

79. This information is based on many interviews and conversations with former senior officials of the various agencies and administrations within the project.

80. Peres, *Battling for Peace*, 136–37.

81. DBGD, 2 June 1958.

82. DBGD, 31 October 1958. According to Seymour Hersh, Abe Feinberg was one of the most important figures in Dimona fund-raising operations. "Feinberg accepted the fact that the expanding and expensive operations at Dimona had to financed outside of the normal Israeli budget process; there were too many critics of the nuclear program inside and outside Israel to raise money any other way" (Seymour Hersh, *The Samson Option*, 93).

83. The seven signatories of that letter were Franz Ollendorff of the Technion; Israel Dostrovsky, Zvi Lipkin, and Igal Talmi of the Weizmann Institute; and Yoel (Giulio) Racah, Shmuel Sambursky, and Solly Cohen of Hebrew University. De Shalit had resigned from the IAEC earlier (Shlomo Aronson with Oded Brosh, *The Politics and Strategy of Nuclear Weapons in the Middle East: Opacity, Theory, and Reality, [1960–1991]* [Albany: State University of New York Press, 1992], 310 n. 7).

84. The letter was never officially made public, but is quoted in Aronson, *The Politics and Strategy of Nuclear Weapons in the Middle East*, 310. We should not, however, read too much into this little-known episode. There is uncertainty about whether all the people mentioned as signatories in fact signed it. Lipkin, one of those said to have signed the letter, wrote to this author on 20 February 1996 that he had no recollection of that episode: "I not only do not recall anything about this resignation story, I also am certain that I had nothing to do with it and that parts of the story if not all of it is completely false." When I checked the matter with another signatory, Igal Talmi, he had a vague recollection of the episode, noting that if he did sign it he probably did so under a sense of obligation and respect to his old teacher, Racah. It appears that the letter was drafted by three commissioners—Ollendorff, Racah, and Sambursky—aimed primarily against Bergmann who kept them out of the loop. Other members of the commission, to the extent that they actually signed the letter, added their names to a vote of nonconfidence

against Bergmann. The resignation had nothing to do with the issue of whether Israel should launch a nuclear weapon project. Nor did the signatories have a collective view on that question, which most of them considered premature and inappropriate for discussion. This point was made by the late Shalheveth Freier in many conversations with the author over the years.

85. DBGD, 15 April 1958, 6 May 1958, DBGA.

86. The major argument was that "the extensive work on defense R&D, and the hiring of massive scientific human power into exciting fields of study in labs with new equipment, could deprive the academic institutions of teaching and research personnel" (Mardor, *Rafael*, 196).

87. Golan, *Peres*, 99.

88. Ibid., 136.

89. Peres, *Battling for Peace: Memoirs*, 137–39.

90. Golan, *Peres*, 99.

91. Charles de Gaulle, *Memoirs of Hope: Renewal and Endeavor* (New York: Simon and Schuster, 1971), 266.

92. Péan, *Les deux bombes*, 126.

93. Ibid., 127.

94. Péan takes up the question of how nuclear cooperation continued for that long. The explanations he proposes do not provide a clear answer. One explanation is a "conspiracy of silence" on the part of French officials who were involved in the project. Another is the secrecy surrounding the project itself. Guillaumat responded to Péan's questions by saying, "The Dimona operation was so secret that nobody knew the entire truth"; yet other sources claim that de Gaulle learned about the Israeli project in mid-1958, at the same time that he learned about the secret Italian-German and French agreement. While he immediately put a halt to the latter, the former continued. Thus, as long as Jacques Soustelle was the minister of energy, the project suffered no interruption (Péan, *Les deux bombes*, 126–28).

95. Ibid.

96. Ibid., 115.

97. Ibid., 134.

98. Golan, *Peres*, 100; cf. Bar-Zohar, *Ben Gurion*, vol. 3, 1373.

99. Ibid., 101.

100. Ibid.

101. Telegram, Walter Eitan, Israel's ambassador to France, to Chaim Yachil, Director-General of Foreign Ministry, 8 June 1960, ISA, FMRG, Box 2350/1.

102. "Minutes of the First Meeting of the Prime Minister with de-Gaulle, June 14, 1960," DBGA.

103. ISA, FMRG, Box 2350/1.

104. Bar-Zohar, *Ben Gurion*, vol. 3, 1383–84. According to Golan's account (*Peres*, 102), de Gaulle leaned toward Ben Gurion intimately and asked him why Israel needed such a nuclear reactor, to which Ben Gurion responded by pledging (as Peres had pledged to Pineau in 1957) that Israel would not build a bomb. The secrecy of the matter is shown

by the fact that the nuclear issue does not appear at all in Eitan's top-secret cable (ISA, FMRG, Box 2350/1).

105. Bar-Zohar, *Ben Gurion*, vol. 3, 1379–80, 1384.

106. Golan, *Peres*, 102.

107. Peres, *Battling for Peace*, 142

108. Ibid.

109. Ibid.; Bar-Zohar, *Ben Gurion*, vol. 3, 1388–89.

110. Péan, *Les deux bombes*, 116–17; also Remi Carle, interview.

111. Péan, *Les deux bombes*, 117.

112. Ibid.

113. Ibid., 118, 120.

114. Richard Rhodes, *The Making of the Atomic Bomb* (New York: Simon and Schuster, 1986), 357–93.

115. Margaret Gowing (assisted by Lorna Arnold), *Independence and Deterrence: Britain and Atomic Energy, 1945–52*, 2 vols. (New York: St. Martin's, 1974).

116. McGeorge Bundy, *Danger and Survival* (New York: Vintage, 1958), 476.

117. Mardor, *Rafael*, 120.

118. Shimon Peres, "About Shalheveth," in *Shalheveth Freier, 1920–1994* (Tel Aviv: IAEC, 1995).

5. DIMONA REVEALED

1. George Bunn, *Arms Control by Committee: Managing Negotiations with the Russians* (Stanford: Stanford University Press, 1992), 64–65.

2. Ibid., 320–21.

3. Ibid., 323.

4. As early as 1953 American tactical nuclear weapons were stationed in Europe for use by NATO ground troops. The United States maintained physical custodianship over its nuclear weapons, and their means of delivery—artillery, aircraft, and missiles—were owned and manned by the NATO allies. This created a "two-key" system of control that required some level of sharing of nuclear defense information with its allies.

5. Department of State, *Documents on Disarmament, 1945–1959* (Washington D.C.: United States Government Printing Office, 1960), 11–86.

6. Ibid., 1520–26; Bunn, *Arms Control by Committee*, 65.

7. Bunn, *Arms Control by Committee*, 64–65.

8. On this issue, see Dean Rusk's remarks on proliferation before the Gilpatric Committee in January 1965 (Department of State, Memorandum of Conversation, "Secretary Meeting with the Gilpatric Committee," 7 January 1965, NSF Committee File, Box 8a, LBJL).

9. Lawrence Scheinman, *Atomic Energy Policy in France under the Fourth Republic* (Princeton, N.J.: Princeton University Press, 1965), 129–65.

10. It is not clear what triggered the addition of Israel to the list, but it was probably

related to the nuclear agreement Israel signed with the United States in 1955. American interest in Israel's nuclear activities was probably also prompted during the Geneva Conference in August 1955, when the Israeli delegation raised the possibility, with AEC Chairman Louis Strauss, that the small experimental reactor which the United States had agreed to supply to Israel would be upgraded to a bigger research reactor that could produce small quantities of plutonium. Strauss's response was negative (Ernst David Bergmann, "Report on the 1955 Geneva Conference, 8–20 August 1955," ISA, FMRG 2407/2).

11. "Post-Mortem on SNIE [Special National Intelligence Estimate] 100–8–60: Implications of the Acquisition by Israel of a Nuclear Weapons Capability," Draft, 31 January 1961, Department of State Lot files, Lot No 57D688, USNA.

12. Memorandum of Conversation, Carl Jones, AEC, and Dr. Ephraim Lahav, Israeli science attaché in Washington, 19 March 1958, Lot 57D688, Box 417, USNA.

13. "Post-Mortem on SNIE 100-8-60," 8–9.

14. Ibid., 10.

15. Ibid.

16. In 1958 the CIA issued a National Intelligence Estimate (NIE 10-2-58), titled "Development of Nuclear Capabilities by Fourth Countries." Post-Mortem, 6–7.

17. The U-2 reconnaissance program started its flights over the Soviet Union in July 1956 from Wiesbaden airfield in West Germany. The focus of the program was on the Soviet Union, but flights over the Middle East began soon after it became operational. The first mission over the Middle East was in late August 1956, when the United States found French-supplied Mystères and Vautours at Israeli air bases. It was reported that Eisenhower was shocked when shown the photos, and "felt that he was betrayed by the Israelis." In a memorandum dated 15 October 1956, Eisenhower added the following note: "Our high-flying reconnaissance planes have shown that Israel had obtained some 60 of the French Mystère pursuit planes, when there had been reported the transfer of only 24." He ordered that the program's activities be stepped up at the time when the U-2s were staged out of Adana, Turkey (Dino A. Brugioni, *Eyeball to Eyeball: The Inside Story of the Cuban Missile Crisis* [New York: Random House, 1991], 32–34).

18. On the history of the CIA U-2 program, see Richard M. Bissell Jr., with Jonathan E. Lewis and Frances T. Pudlo, *Reflections of a Cold War Warrior: From Yalta to the Bay of Pigs* (New Haven: Yale University Press, 1996), 92–140.

19. Dino A Brugioni, interviews by author, 12 March 1996, 9 April 1997, 11 and 25 July 1997. Brugioni recalls that he and others used the adjective "probable" to describe their suspicions that the Beer-Sheba site was nuclear related. See also "Post-Mortem on SNIE 100–8–60," 1–2.

20. Over time Brugioni and Lundahl surmised that Eisenhower might already have known something about Dimona from other intelligence sources, either through American Jews who briefed the administration on that or through intelligence sources inside Israel itself. Brugioni recalls that at one time, probably in the summer or fall of 1958, when he discussed the "Beer-Sheba site" in a conversation with CIA Director Allen Dulles, the latter asked, "Have you seen the Israeli reports?" When Brugioni requested to

see those reports, he was informed by the office of Robert Amory, the deputy director for Intelligence, that he could not see those reports. His assumption was that the reports included very sensitive human intelligence material on Israel's nuclear program (Burgioni, interviews).

21. Ibid.

22. Ibid., 25 July 1997.

23. Brugioni, interviews; cf., Seymour M. Hersh, *The Samson Option: Israel's Nuclear Arsenal and American Foreign Policy* (New York: Random House, 1991), 52–58.

24. "Post-Mortem on SNIE 100–8–60," 9. Bergmann's omissions, half-truths, and contradictory statements added to U.S. confusion. As the postmortem report notes: "[A]t that time, it was assumed wrongly by intelligence that the experimental reactor referred to was the small U.S.-supplied swimming pool research reactor [Soreq]. It was understood that Israel's next project was the nuclear power reactor that Bergmann so often talked about (ibid., 8–9).

25. Ibid., 1–2. This version of the report had a low classification status—"Secret NOFORN"—which explains why it lacked specific references to the U-2 program. The reference to the March–April 1958 intelligence information is likely a reference to the U-2 program (Brugioni, interview, 25 July 1997; Donald Steury [CIA Historian Office], interview by author, Washington, D.C., 24 July 1997).

26. "Post-Mortem on SNIE 100–8–60"; also, "Memorandum for the President: Dimona Reactor in Israel," (an attachment: "History of United States Interest in Israel's Atomic Activities," hereafter cited as "Chronology"), 30 March 1963, RG 59, Central Foreign Policy Decimal files, 250/03/27/04, Box 1297, 611.84a45/3-3061, USNA.

27. "Chronology."

28. "Post-Mortem on SNIE 100–8–60," 12–13.

29. Ibid., 14.

30. Ibid.; "Chronology," 1; Telegram (2612), Amory Houghton to Secretary of State, 26 November 1960, Nonproliferation Collection, NSA.

31. Telegram (2162), Houton to Secretary of State, 26 November 1960; Department of State Despatch (311), Memorandum of Conversation, "Research and Training Program in Field of Atomic Energy," 30 November 1960, Nonproliferation Collection, NSA.

32. Department of State, Memorandum of Conversation, "Subject: Israeli Atomic Energy Program," 1 December 1960, Nonproliferation Collection, NSA; "Post-Mortem on SNIE 110–8–60," 15; "Chronology," 1–2.

33. Department of State, "Subject: Israeli Atomic Energy Program," 1 December 1960.

34. Ibid., 2

35. Ibid.

36. Department of State Despatch (Tel Aviv, 311), Memorandum of Conversation, 30 November 1960, Nonproliferation Collection, NSA.

37. Telegram (486), Ogden Reid to Christian Herter, 3 December 1960, Records of White House Staff Secretary, International File, Box 8: Israel, DDEL.

38. "Post-Mortem on SNIE 100–8–60," 8.

39. "Chronology."

40. Ibid., 1

41. Ibid., 2.

42. "Memorandum of Discussion at the 469th Meeting of the National Security Council, 8 December 1960," in Department of State, *Foreign Relations of the United States, 1958–1960* (hereafter referred to as *FRUS, 1958–60*), vol. 13, *Arab-Israeli Dispute; United Arab Republic; North Africa* (Washington, D.C.: United States Government Printing Office, 1992), 391–92.

43. *FRUS, 1958–60*, vol. 13, 393–94.

44. Ibid., 394.

45. Telephone log of Secretary of State Christian Herter, 9 December 1960, Records of White House Staff Secretary, International File, Box 8: Israel, DDEL.

46. Chapman Pincher, "Israel May Be Making an A-Bomb," *Daily Express*, 16 December 1960, 2.

47. John W. Finney, "U.S. Hears Israel Moves Toward A-Bomb Potential," *New York Times*, 19 December 1960, 1.

48. Ibid. For how McCone helped Finney, see Hersh, *Samson Option*, 71–81.

49. Department of State document, 19 December 1960, International File, Box 8: Israel, DDEL.

50. "Memorandum of Conference with the President, 19 December 1960," 12 January 1961, International File, Box 8, Israel, DDEL.

51. Ibid.

52. John W. Finney, "U.S. Misled at First on Israeli Reactor," *New York Times*, 20 December 1960, 1, 15.

53. Mr. Farley asked whether it meant 24 megawatts thermal or 24 megawatts electrical, "pointing out that in the latter case the size would be in the range of the U.S. estimate." He inquired also whether the reactor would include any "power generating facilities to draw off useful electric power on an experimental basis." Harman did not know the answers to these questions and he would have to inquire (*FRUS, 1958–60*, vol. 13, 398).

54. *FRUS, 1958–60*, vol. 13, 396–99; "Chronology"; cf. Dana Adams Schmidt, "Israel Assured U.S. on Reactor," *New York Times*, 22 December 1960, 5.

55. "Israel Denies Reports," *New York Times*, 19 December 1960, 8.

56. "Defense Ministry Silent," ibid., 20 December 1960, 15.

57. "Peaceful Aims Affirmed," ibid., 15.

58. An English translation of Ben Gurion's statement appeared in the *Jerusalem Post*, 22 December 1960, cited in Department of State compilation of "Political Statements Concerning the Israeli Reactor," 17 January 1961, 3207, NSA. For a summary, see "Ben Gurion Explains Project," *New York Times*, 22 December 1960.

59. Michael Bar-Zohar, *Ben Gurion* (in Hebrew), vol. 3 (Tel Aviv: Zmora Bitan, 1987), 1391.

60. Alvin Shuster, "Israel Satisfies U.S. on Use of Reactor," *New York Times*, 23 December 1960, 6. See also the Department of State Statement of 22 December 1960, USNA.

61. There is evidence, however, that the U.S. media took Ben Gurion's statement to mean more than it actually stated. See, for example, the opening statement in William L. Laurence's column ("Israel's Reactor," *New York Times*, 25 December 1960, 8E): "United States officials were reported last week to be concerned over evidence that Israel was developing the capacity to produce atomic weapons. This officially denied by the Israeli government." This is not accurate. Ben Gurion did deny that Israel was manufacturing nuclear weapons, but he said nothing about the capacity to produce such weapons.

62. Arthur Krock, "In the Nation," *New York Times*, 23 December 1960, 18.

63. Telegram (470), Herter to Embassy Tel Aviv, 21 December 1960, International File, Box 8: Israel, DDEL.

64. Embtel 577 (Tel Aviv), Reid to Herter, 24 December 1960 (section I), International File, Box 8: Israel, DDEL.

65. Ogden Reid, telephone interview by Mike Moore (for the author), New York, 15 December 1994; Embtel 577 (Tel Aviv), Reid to Herter, 24 December 1960 (section I).

66. Embtel 577 (Tel Aviv), Reid to Herter, 24 December 1960 (section II), International File, Box 8: Israel, DDEL.

67. Telegram, Department of State to Amembassy Tel Aviv, 31 December 1960 (Section I), International File, Box 8: Israel, DDEL. The telegram was declassified only in part, and the U.S. complaints about Ben Gurion's replies remain classified.

68. Telegram (502), Acting Secretary Livingstron T. Merchant to Reid, 31 December 1960, International File, Box 8: Israel, DDEL. The telegram also appears in *FRUS, 1958–60*, vol. 13, 399–400. The five questions also appear in Bar-Zohar, *Ben Gurion*, vol. 3, 1391. According to Bar-Zohar, Ben Gurion provided the questions in a press briefing he held on 8 January 1961.

69. Bar-Zohar, *Ben Gurion*, vol. 3, 1391.

70. Ibid., 1391–92.

71. Ibid., 1392. According to another version, Ben Gurion did not pledge not to produce nuclear weapons, but referred to his statement in the Knesset, claiming that his commitment to "peaceful purposes" of the reactor was sufficient. Cf. David Shaham, *Israel: 40 Years* (in Hebrew) (Tel Aviv: Am Oved, 1991), 189.

72. "Chronology," 3.

73. Memorandum of Conversation, "Israel Atomic Energy Program," 11 January 1961, General Records of the Department of State, Box 2057, USNA; Amos Elon, "The Contact with the U.S. on Israel's Nuclear Program Will Continue" (in Hebrew), *Ha'aretz*, 13 January 1961; H. Yustus, "Harman and Herter Discussed the Reactor for Four Hours" (in Hebrew), *Ma'ariv*, 12 January 1961.

74. "Chronology," 4.

75. The report, dated 17 January 1961 and entitled "Summary of Additional Recent Information on Israeli Atomic Energy Program," was enclosed in a letter dated 19 January 1961, from Assistant Secretary of State William B. Macomber to James T. Ramey, the executive director of the Joint Committee on Atomic Energy (the Nonproliferation Collection, NSA).

76. Ibid., 2.

77. Ibid., 1.

78. Ibid., 2.

79. Apparently for this reason, Ben Gurion postponed his resignation for two months. In December 1960 he had been in the midst of a domestic crisis over the Lavon affair, and he was determined not to resign from the government under these circumstances.

6. KENNEDY AND THE ISRAELI PROJECT

1. The characterization of Kennedy as the nonproliferation president repeated itself in all the interviews I conducted with Kennedy's principal advisers: McGeorge Bundy, Carl Kaysen, Myer (Mike) Feldman, and Robert Komer.

2. Glenn T. Seaborg, *Kennedy, Khrushchev, and the Test Ban* (Berkeley: University of California Press, 1981), 30–37.

3. Glenn T. Seaborg with Benjamin S. Loeb, *Stemming the Tide: Arms Control in the Johnson Years* (Lexington: Lexington Books, 1987), 249.

4. Seaborg, *Kennedy, Khrushchev, and the Test Ban*, 48.

5. One example is the introduction of modern gas centrifuges for producing enriched uranium. In the late 1950s research on gas centrifuges had been declassified under pressure from the industry, but in 1960, when the proliferation risks involved were understood, security restrictions and classifications were imposed once again (Seaborg with Loeb, *Stemming the Tide*, 261–66).

6. Office of the Secretary of Defense, Memorandum for the President, "Subject: The Diffusion of Nuclear Weapons with and without a Test Ban Agreement," Office of the Secretary of Defense, 1 July 1962, NSA.

7. Ibid., 1.

8. Ibid.

9. Ibid.

10. Ibid, 2.

11. Feldman recalls that, on the morning after the election, Kennedy told him that he would expect Feldman to do for him the same work he performed before the elections. "I would like you to read all the cables about the Middle East, and be familiar with the CIA information, and to act as my personal representative in these matters," Kennedy told Feldman. Feldman responded: "I am not sure that's a wise choice. I think it ought to be somebody else. As President, it's a lot different than being in the campaign. . . . You just can't take a position that may be opposed by everybody in the administration, and in my case, what you will get is biased advice. I have an emotional attachment to Israel and I will give you advice based on that. I'm not sure that's the right thing to do." Kennedy replied, "That's exactly why I want you to do it" (Myer Feldman, interview by author, Washington, D.C., 10 June 1992). State Department documents do not emphasize Feldman's role in shaping Kennedy's (and later Johnson's) dealings with Israel's nuclear program. This was confirmed by McGeorge Bundy (McGeorge Bundy, interviews by author, New York, 1993; Robert Komer, interview by author, Washington, D.C.,

11 June 1992, and other conversations; and Carl Kaysen, numerous conversations with author, Cambridge, Mass., 1993–96).

12. Feldman, interview.

13. Richard Reeves, *President Kennedy: Profile of Power* (New York: Simon and Schuster, 1994), 32–33.

14. Memorandum, Secretary of State Dean Rusk to President John F. Kennedy, "Subject: Israel's Atomic Nuclear Activities," 30 January 1961 CFSD (Central Files State Department), 884A.1901/1 Box 3061, USNA (also in NSF Box 118, JFKL). The document also appears in Department of State, *Foreign Relations of the United States, 1961–63: Near East, 1962–63* (hereafter referred to as *FRUS, 1961–63*), vol. 17 (Washington, D.C.: U.S. Government Printing Office, 1995), 9–10.

15. Ibid., 9.

16. Ibid.

17. Ibid., 10.

18. The contents of the conversation between Ambassador Reid and President Kennedy appears in *FRUS, 1961–63*, vol. 17, 10–11. An unsigned dictation note, entitled "Conversation with Ogden Reid," in the Israeli file at the JFKL (NSF, Box 118), dated 31 January 1961, reads as follows: "He stated that we had an agreement with the Israelis to send an American scientist through their atomic plant within the next month, in order to make sure that it is for peaceful purposes. He believes that it is."

19. Bar-Zohar, *Ben Gurion*, vol. 3, 1393.

20. *FRUS, 1961–63*, vol. 17, 13–14.

21. Ibid., 14.

22. "Chronology," 4.

23. Ibid.

24. Ibid., 5.

25. *David Ben Gurion Diaries* (DBGD), 29 March 1961, DBGA.

26. Memorandum of Conversation, 10 April 1961, in *FRUS, 1961–63*, vol. 17, 79–80. On 12 April Harman also informed Secretary of State Dean Rusk on the matter (Memorandum, Assistant Secretary Lewis Jones to Secretary Rusk, "Your Appointment with Israeli Ambassador Harman," RG 59, NEA/NE, Records of Dimona Reactor, 1960–63, Box 453–7, USNA).

27. Memorandum of Conversation, 10 April 1961, 79 n. 1.

28. Memorandum, Philip Farley (State Department) to John Hall (AEC), "Visit to Israel," 5 May 1961, RG 59, NEA/NE, Records of Dimona Reactor, 1960–63, Box 453-7, USNA.

29. DBGD, 29 March 1961, and 21, 22, and 24 April 1961, DBGA; Feldman, interview, 10 June 1992; Bar-Zohar, Ben Gurion, vol. 3, 1993.

30. The only people on site were the security guards and the eight senior Dimona officials led by the site director, Manes Pratt. Professor Efraim Katzir-Katchalsky was also present "at the request of the Prime Minister" ("Notes on Visit to Israel, U.M. Staebler–J. W. Croach Jr.," DRAFT 5/23/61 [including attachments], RG 59, NEA/NE, Records of Dimona Reactor, 1960–63, Box 453-7, USNA). The official inspection report has not been found, see *FRUS, 1961–63*, vol. 17, 126 n. 1.

31. "Memorandum of Discussions with Mr. Pratt and Staff," attached to "Notes on Visit to Israel, U.M. Staebler–J. W. Croach Jr.," DRAFT 5/23/61.

32. Ibid., 2–3.

33. Ibid., 3–4. This might explain how Israel became involved in the construction of two research reactors, one smaller and the other larger, at the same time. Otherwise, it made no sense for Israel to construct the two research reactors.

34. Ibid.

35. The American inspectors considered this date to be "unduly late" given the state of the construction. However, they were told that because of difficulties in welding, some components were not expected to be delivered for about a year (ibid.).

36. "Highlights on Other Technical Facilities," attached to "Notes on Visit to Israel, U.M. Staebler–J. W. Croach Jr.," DRAFT 5/23/61.

37. Memorandum, Special Assistant to the Secretary of State Lucius Battle to National Security Adviser McGeorge Bundy, "U.S. Scientists' Visit to Israel's Dimona Reactor," 26 May 1961, in *FRUS*, 1961–63, vol. 17, 125–27.

38. Ibid.

39. Ibid., 126–27.

40. Bar-Zohar, *Ben Gurion*, vol. 3, 1393.

41. Ibid. Before Ben Gurion's departure he wrote a personal letter to President de Gaulle, outlining the explanations that he would present the U.S. president. De Gaulle responded in a friendly letter in which he gave his consent.

42. "Meeting of President Kennedy and Prime Minister Ben Gurion, Tuesday, May 30th, Waldorf-Astoria Hotel, Suite 284, 4:45–6:16pm," ISA, FMRG, 3294/7 (referred to hereafter as Harman's notes); Memorandum of Conversation, "Subject: Conversation between President Kennedy and Prime Minister Ben Gurion," 30 May 1961, 033.84a11/5–3061 (referred to hereafter as Feldman's notes).

43. Feldman's notes, 1.

44. Ibid.

45. Harman's notes, the Atomic Reactor, 1.

46. Ibid.

47. Feldman's notes, 2.

48. Ibid.

49. Ibid.

50. "Franco-Israeli Nuclear Collaboration," n.d., NSF, Country File: Israel, Box 119, JFKL.

51. With Ben Gurion's consent, the United States passed the findings of the visit to Arab governments, including Egypt, Iraq, Jordan, Lebanon, and Saudi Arabia. These governments were advised that "the observations of U.S. scientists tended [to] support public and private [Israeli] assurances regarding the peaceful intent [of the] Dimona project" (Airgram [CA-4726], Department of State, "Israel's Dimona Activity," 24 October 1962, NSF, Country File: Israel, Box 119, JFKL).

52. Bar-Zohar, *Ben Gurion*, vol. 3, 1393.

53. This was evident, for example, in the discussions Peres had during his visit in

Washington in late May 1962. In his meetings with Walt Rostow, Paul Nitze, William Bundy, McGeorge Bundy, and Myer Feldman, the focus was on the political and military situation in the Middle East, and Israel's request for defensive weapons systems (in particular the HAWK missiles). The nuclear issue was mentioned in passing on two brief occasions, once in response to William Bundy's question of what Israel thought about the introduction of nuclear weapons to the region, to which Peres obliquely responded that "for the next four years surely one cannot talk about nuclear weapons in the Middle East, and in general Israel would not want to see nuclear weapons in the region at all" (Colonel Yehuda Prihar [Israeli military attaché in Washington], "Report on the Visit of Deputy Minister of Defense in Washington," 24 May 1962, Appendix V, ISA, FMRG, 4317/1).

54. Letter, Prime Minister David Ben Gurion to President John F. Kennedy, 24 June 1962, NSF, Box 118 (also Box 119a), JFKL.

55. The conversation between Ben Gurion and Feldman is recorded in an outgoing Foreign Ministry cable to the embassy in Washington, dated 20 August 1962 (ISA, FMRG, 3377/7). Also, Myer Feldman, interview by author, 10 June 1992, 14 October 1994 and 14 July 1997.

56. This claim appears in many American and Israeli sources. See McGeorge Bundy, *Danger and Survival: Choices about the Bomb in the First Fifty years* (New York: Random House, 1988), 510.

57. Zaki Shalom, "From 'Low Profile' to 'Smashing Strategy': The Kennedy Administration and Its Response to Israel's Nuclear Activity, 1962–1963" (in Hebrew), *Iyunim Be'Tkumat Israel* 4 (1995): 126–64.

58. Telegram (721), Walworth Barbour, U.S. Ambassador to Israel, to Secretary of State Dean Rusk, 3 April 1963, RG 59, Box 3727, USNA.

59. Yuval Ne'eman, interview by author, Austin, Texas, 27 February 1994.

60. Airgram (CA-4726), Department of State, "Israel's Dimona Activity," 24 October 1962; Ne'eman, interview. Ne'eman was then the director of the Nachal Soreq facility and arranged the U.S. visit at Dimona. A reference to this visit appears in *FRUS, 1961–63*, vol. 17, 197, ff.3

61. "Subject: The Diffusion of Nuclear Weapons with and Without a Test Ban Agreement," (2d cite in chapter—n.6).

62. Ibid., 2.

63. U.S. Department of State, "Memorandum of Conversation: Conversation with Israel's Foreign Minister," 27 December 1962, NSF Box 118, JFKL.

7. THE BATTLE OF DIMONA

1. Glenn T. Seaborg with Benjamin S. Loeb, *Kennedy, Khrushchev, and the Test Ban* (Berkeley: University of California Press, 1981), 171.

2. *Public Papers of the Presidents of the United States: John F. Kennedy, 1963* (Washington, D.C.: U.S. Government Printing Office, 1964), 280.

3. Memorandum to the President, "The Diffusion of Nuclear Weapons with and without a Test Ban Agreement," 12 February 1963, Nonproliferation Collection, NSA.

4. Ibid., 5.

5. On the Shavit II episode, see Munya M. Mardor, *Rafael* (in Hebrew) (Tel Aviv: Misrad Habitachon, 1981), 319–47; former senior RAFAEL official, numerous conversations with author, April–May 1995.

6. On the hidden debate in Israel, see chapter 8; cf. Airgram (A-232), Walworth Barbour, U.S. Ambassador to Israel, to Department of State, "Israel's Security: The Concept of Preventive War and Definitive Victory," 5 October 1962, NSF, Box 119, JFKL.

7. Only in 1996 was Dassault allowed to tell the story of the Jericho project (Claude Carlier and Luc Berger, *Dassault: 50 ans d'aventure aeronatique* [Paris: Editions du Chene, 1996]). The Israeli specifications refer to a two-stage missile, capable of delivering a 750-kg warhead a distance of 235–500 km within a circular error probable of less than 1 km. Israel requested an all-weather missile, "launchable at a firing rate of 4 to 8 missiles per hour, from fixed or mobile bases, within a maximum preparatory time of two hours." A reference to the Jericho chapter appeared in Pierre Landereux, "Dassault Lifts Veil over Jericho Missile. The Ground-to-Ground Tactical Missile Was the Base of Israel's Ballistic Armament" (in French), *Air and Cosmos/Aviation International*, 6 December 1996, English translation provided in "FRANCE: Dassault Publication Reveals Secret Israeli Missile Program," FBIS Report, FBIS-EST-97–008.

8. On 8 May 1963 the CIA issued SNIE (30–2–63), entitled "The Advanced Weapons Programs of the UAR and Israel," in *FRUS, 1961–63*, vol. 18, 517–18.

9. The publication of an editorial in the London weekly *Jewish Observer and Middle East Review* (a publication known to have close connections with Israel's defense establishment) of 28 December 1962, entitled "An Independent Deterrent for Israel," intensified those concerns. While using veiled language, the editorial hinted that Israel might already have made fateful decisions toward an "independent deterrent." The editorial was circulated in the NSC, and a reference to it appeared in a memorandum by Komer to President Kennedy ("Memorandum from Robert W. Komer of the National Security Council Staff to President Kennedy," 22 March 1963, in *FRUS, 1961–63*, vol. 18, 432.

10. CIA, Office of National Estimate, Memorandum for the Director, Sherman Kent, "Consequences of Israeli Acquisition of Nuclear Capability," 6 March 1963, 1, NSF Box 118, JFKL. The memo says:

> For the purposes of this Memorandum, Israeli "acquisition of a nuclear capability" may mean either (a) Israeli detonation of a nuclear device, with or without possession of actual nuclear weapons, or (b) an announcement by Israel that it possessed nuclear weapons even though it had not detonated a nuclear device. (It is conceivable that Israel might manufacture a weapon according to acquired designs, without testing, through its access to nuclear technology in the international scientific community and possibly its special relationship with the French.)

11. Ibid., 2–3.

12. Ibid., 3–6.

13. "Briefing for Gilpatric Committee on Nuclear Non-Proliferation," 1 December 1964, NSF, Box 4, LBJL.

14. On the idea of MLF during the Kennedy era, see Glenn T. Seaborg, *Stemming the Tide: Arms Control in the Johnson Years* (Lexington, Mass.: Lexington Books, 1987), 83–93.

15. Ibid., 83–118.

16. Seaborg, *Kennedy, Khrushchev, and the Test Ban*, 172–232.

17. In a note attached to Kennedy's reading material for the weekend of 23 March, Deputy National Security Adviser Carl Kaysen wrote that these documents amount to "what we know at this moment on nuclear and missile capabilities in the UAR and Israel. It is clearly not enough and we are pushing ahead on arranging for another inspection of the Israeli activities" (Memorandum, Carl Kaysen to President Kennedy, 23 March 1963, NSF, Box 318, JFKL).

18. *FRUS, 1961–63*, vol. 18, 432–33, 435.

19. Ibid., 435; also in NSF, Box 340, JFKL.

20. Telegram (721), Barbour to Secretary of State Dean Rusk, 3 April 1963, Box 3727, USNA. The Dimona issue was handled with such sensitivity that Ambassador Barbour made no reference to it in his regular State Department report on the meeting with Ben Gurion. It was classified "Confidential" and sent to all U.S. posts in the Middle East (Telegram [774], Barbour to Rusk, 3 April 1963 [2 sections], NSF, Box 119a, JFKL).

21. "Protocol of Conversation with President Kennedy on 2 April 1963," ISA, FMRG 4326/16. It turned out that Peres's reply to Kennedy would become Israel's declaratory line on nuclear weapons. Treasury Minister Levi Eshkol, who criticized Peres on his return to Israel for telling Kennedy too much, incorporated his words into Israel's official stance. Peres has said that this formula was the result of an improvisation: "I did not want to lie to the president, but I could not answer his question straight either. So I came up with what became Israel's policy for years to come" (Shimon Peres, interview by author, Tel Aviv, 31 March 1991). For the American record of the meeting, taken by Myer Feldman, see *FRUS, 1961–63*, vol. 18, 450–51; cf. Shimon Peres, *Battling for Peace: Memoirs* (London: Weidenfeld and Nicolson, 1995), 258; Matti Golan, *Peres* (in Hebrew) (Tel Aviv: Schocken, 1982), 125; Avner Cohen, "Peres: Peacemaker, Nuclear Pioneer," *Bulletin of the Atomic Scientists* 52, no. 3 (May–June 1996): 16–17.

22. Cable, Avraham Harman, Israeli Ambassador to the United States, to Foreign Ministry, 4 April 1963, ISA, FMRG, 3377/11.

23. "The anxiety the Cairo Tripartite proclamation triggered in Ben Gurion exceeded even situations in which Ben Gurion had faced much more real and serious dangers" (Michael Bar-Zohar, *Ben Gurion* [in Hebrew], vol. 3 [Tel Aviv: Zmora Bitan, 1987], 1550).

24. For a detailed account of Ben Gurion's letters, see Bar-Zohar, *Ben Gurion*, vol. 3, 1550–52. Bar-Zohar quotes Meir as saying: "We knew about Ben Gurion's appeals. We treated Ben Gurion with respect. We said nothing, but we were amazed." Bar-Zohar makes the point that Ben Gurion "lost his sense of proportion" and acted under extreme anxiety.

25. The text of the letter appears in a telegram (172), Shimshon Arad, Alternate Israeli Representative to the UN, to Harman, 25 April 1963, ISA, FMRG, 3377/9. Also, the intent

of the letter appears in a diplomatic telegram (751), State Department to Amembassy Tel Aviv (NSF, Box 119a, JFKL), which includes the essential elements of the prime minister's message to the president. See also Bar-Zohar, *Ben Gurion*, vol. 3, 1551–52.

26. Telegram (172), 3–4.

27. Ibid., 7.

28. Shimshon Arad (then head of the U.S. Department at the Foreign Ministry), and Gideon Rafael (then deputy director of the Foreign Ministry), interviews by author, Jerusalem, summer 1994.

29. Ambassador Harman expressed his growing frustration and criticism over the way Ben Gurion handled the dialogue with Kennedy in a number of telegrams to Jerusalem (mostly addressed to Director-General Yahil): Telegram (183), Harman to Foreign Ministry, 25 April 1963, ISA, FMRG 3377/9; Telegram (145), Harman to Yahil, 30 April 1963, ISA, FMRG, 3377/6; Telegram (146), Harman to Yahil, 7 May 1963, ISA, FMRG, 3377/9.

30. In a telegram ([806], 27 April 1963, NSF, Box 119, JFKL) from Ambassador Barbour to the State Department, he noted that Ben Gurion was "not disposed [to] get hysterical," and, therefore, his use of the phrase "gravity without parallel" should be taken seriously. The ambassador questioned the desirability of a joint declaration, noting that it would be "particularly untimely at [the] moment." He also questioned the possibility of arranging a meeting with the president "without publicity."

31. On 2 May Komer provided Kennedy with a memo on the Arab-Israeli military balance. The cover letter to the memo states its conclusion (NSF, Box 119a, JFKL).

32. Memorandum, State Department to National Security Advisor McGeorge Bundy, "The Implications for Israel of the Arab Unity Proclamation of 17 April," 9 May 1963, NSF, Box 119a, JFKL.

33. Bar-Zohar, *Ben Gurion*, vol. 3, 1550–54; Yoel Ben Porat, interview by author, Glilot, August 1992.

34. Letter, Kennedy to Ben Gurion, in State Department Deptel 780 (Tel Aviv), 4 May 1963, NSF, Box 119a, JFKL. The text can also be found in an outgoing telegram (50) to the Israeli Embassy in Washington (5 May 1963, ISA, FMRG, Box 3379/9).

35. State Department Deptel 780, 3.

36. Ibid., 5.

37. Ibid., 4.

38. The conversation between Ben Gurion and Barbour is recorded in an outgoing Foreign Ministry cable to the embassy in Washington, dated 5 May 1963 (ISA, FMRG, 3377/9). It is also recorded in a sanitized form in Barbour's Deptel (833) to Secretary of State Rusk, dated 5 May 1963 (NSF Box 119a, JFKL).

39. Message from Ben Gurion to Feldman, 7 May 1963, ISA, FMRG, 3377/6. The text is also included in a telegram (75) from Yahil to Harman (7 May 1963, ISA, FMRG, Box 3377/9).

40. "Consultation Regarding the Letter of the Prime Minister to President Kennedy on 8 May," ISA, FMRG 3377/9.

41. Letter, Ben Gurion to Kennedy, 12 May 1963, ISA, FMRG, 3377/9.

42. Ibid.

43. W. Granger Blair, "Ben Gurion Sees War Peril in U.S. Curb on Arms," *New York Times*, 14 May 1963.

44. Department of State, Memorandum of Conversation between Governor Averell Harriman and Jewish Leaders, "Subject: U.S. Security Guarantee to Israel," 8 May 1963, NSF, Box 119a, JFKL.

45. His biographer hints that the explanation might have to do with the mind of an aging man, not with the changing circumstances of international politics (Bar-Zohar, *Ben Gurion*, vol. 3, 1552).

46. In January 1949, when victory was within reach in the Sinai, Israel was forced to withdraw under American threat. In 1956 Eisenhower's threats forced Israel again to leave the Sinai without a political settlement.

47. "SNIE 30–2–63," in *FRUS, 1961–63*, vol. 18, 517. Israel signed the contract with Marcel Dassault in Tel Aviv on 24 April 1963; the estimate was prepared before the signing but hinted that it was likely.

48. *FRUS, 1961–63*, vol. 18, 528.

49. Telegram (800), Department of State to Barbour, 10 May 1963, in *FRUS, 1961–63*, vol. 18, 525.

50. Department of State, Memorandum, "Arms Limitations in the Middle East," 14 May 1963, in *FRUS, 1961–63*, vol. 18, 529–35.

51. Ibid, 530–31.

52. Robert Komer, interview by author, Washington, D.C., June 1994.

53. *FRUS, 1961–63*, vol. 18, 531.

54. Ibid., 534.

55. Ibid.

56. Ibid., 535.

57. Memorandum, Secretary of State to President Kennedy, "Israel Security Assurances: Near East Arms Limitations," 16 May 1963, NSF, Box 119. JFKL.

58. The working group proposed that the most appropriate way to put Nasser on notice on the new American initiative, including the gravity of the Israeli nuclear program, was through a presidential letter from Kennedy to Nasser. A proposal for such a letter, drafted by the State Department, was submitted to the White House for the 17 May meeting. The draft letter deals with three main issues: the escalating arms race, the Arab unity proclamation, and the situation in Jordan. On the matter of the arms race, it elaborates on the Egyptian missile program as a cause for Israel's missiles and nuclear weapons program. It tells Nasser that "Israel is extremely nervous over your rocket program." As to the Israeli nuclear weapons program, it states that, "while Israel has not yet undertaken development of nuclear weapons, and we will continue to counsel against such a policy, Israel could have the capability to do so in the next several years if it were to divert its efforts in that direction." It also informs Nasser that Kennedy was studying ways "by which Israel's nervousness can be reduced, the Arab can be reassured against Israeli expansionism, and the escalation of weaponry in the Near East can be halted" (Draft letter to President Nasser, n.d., POF, Israel, Box 119a, JFKL).

59. "Possible U.S.-Israel Security Assurances," POF, Israel, Box 119a, JFKL.

60. Memorandum, Robert Komer to President Kennedy, 16 May 1963, in *FRUS, 1961–63*, vol. 18, 540–41.

61. Deptel 835 (Tel Aviv), Rusk to Barbour, 18 May 1963, POF, Israel, Box 119a, JFKL; cf. *FRUS, 1961–63*, vol. 18, 543–44.

62. Ibid.

63. These four lines are still "classified" on the American side and they do not appear in the *FRUS, 1961–63* version of the letter. The letter can be found in full at ISA 7233/5/A.

64. *FRUS, 1961–63*, vol. 18, 544.

65. Yuval Ne'eman, interview by author, Austin, Texas, 27 February 1994. Ne'eman was the director of the Research Nuclear Center at Soreq that was involved in Ben Gurion's consultations on the nuclear issue in 1963.

66. Bar-Zohar, *Ben Gurion*, vol. 3, 1554.

67. Draft letter, Ben Gurion to President Kennedy (unsigned), 22 May 1963, ISA, FMRG 3377/11.

68. The text as found in Foreign Ministry outgoing telegram to Harman, 27 May 1963, ISA, FMRG 3377/9.

69. In ISA there is at least one draft of this letter, which is substantially different from this version on at least three points (ISA, FMRG, 3377/14).

70. The first draft of the letter expressed this point in even stronger terms: "I said to you then [in 1961] that for the time being our only purpose was for peace but that we shall have to follow developments in the Middle East" (ibid.).

71. On this issue the text in the first draft was more ambiguous. It reads as follows: "You will appreciate, Mr. President, that this arrangement with France does not allow me to accept a permanent system of United States control at Dimona since the United States has not participated in the establishment or construction of this reactor, as she has in the case of Nachal Soreq. On the other hand I have considered the proposal for periodic visits to the Dimona reactor by your representatives, such as have already taken place. I now reiterate our agreement to such future visits as well" (ibid.)

72. Foreign Ministry minutes, "A Discussion on Israeli-U.S. Relationship," 13 June 1963, ISA, FMRG 3377/6 (translation by author).

73. In a meeting between Komer and Gazit on 15 May, the idea of a diplomatic dialogue between the two countries to discuss the Ben Gurion-Kennedy correspondence was raised by Komer as a "private idea," and endorsed by Gazit. In Komer's memorandum of that conversation he said nothing about a presidential emissary to discuss the American initiative for arms control in the region (Memorandum for the Record, Robert Komer, 15 May 1963, POF, Israel, Box 119a, JFKL). In Gazit's report of his conversation "with a credible source who knows all the players on our matters," however, there is a reference to the possibility of a special presidential emissary (outside the regular channels of the State Department) to discuss questions related to Ben Gurion's requests (Telegram, Mordechai Gazit to Foreign Ministry, 15 May 1963, ISA, FMRG, 3377/9).

74. Memorandum, Komer to Bundy, 28 May 1963, POF, Israel, Box 119a, JFKL.

75. Memorandum, Rusk to President Kennedy, "Meeting with Mr. McCloy on His Near East Mission," n.d., POF, Israel, Box 119a, JFKL; "Memorandum for Presidential

Emissary," n.d., and "Scenario with Ben Gurion," 29 May 1963, POF, Israel, Box 119a, JFKL.

76. Memorandum, Department of State to Bundy, 12 June 1963, in *FRUS, 1961–63*, vol. 18, 575–76.

77. Ibid., 576.

78. Ibid.

79. Ibid.

80. Deptel 938 (Tel Aviv), 15 June 1963, POF, Israel, Box 119a, JFKL.

81. Embtel 1043 (Tel Aviv), 16 June 1963, NSF, Box 119, JFKL. Barbour told Israeli diplomats that he received the cable with Kennedy's letter on Sunday morning. He had planned to play golf in Cesarea, so he arranged to deliver the presidential message to the prime minister's office in the afternoon. When he reached his residence after returning from the golf course, he learned of Ben Gurion's resignation. He called the Department of State and asked to postpone the letter's delivery until a successor was sworn in. His suggestion was accepted, and the letter was sent back (ISA, FMRG, 3377/6, 3377/11).

82. DBGD, 16 June 1963, DBGA.

83. Bar-Zohar, *Ben Gurion*, vol. 3, 1546–48, 1550–55, 1557.

84. Yitzhak Navon, interview by author, Jerusalem, 19 August 1992. Navon acknowledged that he had almost no access to the Dimona consultations.

85. Moshe A. Gilboa, *Six Days, Six Years* (in Hebrew) (Tel Aviv: Am Oved, 1968), 33.

86. Arnan Azaryahu, interview by author, Kibbutz Yiron, 2 September 1993.

87. Yuval Ne'eman, many conversations with author, 1994–96; cf. Yuval Ne'eman, "Israel in the Nuclear Age" (in Hebrew), *Nativ*, September 1995, 38.

88. Embtel 1043 (Tel Aviv), 16 June 1963, NSF, Box 119, JFKL.

8. Debate at Home

1. One of the senior ministers who questioned the financial cost of the project, Minister of Finance Eshkol, asked Ben Gurion in January 1960 to discuss the nuclear project before the party leadership rather than the cabinet, but Ben Gurion refused. Instead, he proposed to discuss it in a forum of four party leaders—David Ben Gurion, Levi Eshkol, Golda Meir, and Shimon Peres (Matti Golan, *Peres* [in Hebrew] [Tel Aviv: Schocken, 1982], 99).

2. There is a voluminous literature in Hebrew on Ben Gurion and the Lavon Affair. For a recent comprehensive history, see Shabtai Teveth, *Shearing Time* (in Hebrew) (Tel Aviv: Ish Dor, 1992); an abridged version of the book appeared in English (*Ben Gurion's Spy* [New York: Columbia University Press, 1996]). See also Bar-Zohar, *Ben Gurion*, vol. 3, 1471–1518.

3. Teveth, *Ben Gurion's Spy*, 269–70.

4. Bar-Zohar, *Ben Gurion*, vol. 3, 1388–89. Bar-Zohar does not say precisely what they opposed in Peres's compromise agreement.

5. Bar-Zohar, *Ben Gurion*, vol. 3, 1505–6.

6. Ibid., 1506; Tevet, *Shearing Time*, 452.

7. Bar-Zohar, *Ben Gurion*, vol. 3, 1393, 1506.

8. Golda Meir's dissent was not made public, but it was known among the people who dealt with the Dimona issue. A hint of Meir's attitude toward Dimona appears in a Foreign Ministry consultation held on 13 June 1963 (ISA, FMRG, 3377/6). See also, Yuval Ne'eman, interview by author, Austin, Texas, 4 March 1994; and Shimshon Arad, interview by author, Jerusalem, August 1994. Meir had reservations about the U.S. visit to Dimona in 1961. See DBGD, 29 March 1961, DBGA.

9. Golan, *Peres*, 115–16.

10. For example, Uri Bar Joseph, "The Hidden Debate: The Formation of Nuclear Doctrines in the Middle East," *Journal of Strategic Studies* 5, no. 2 (June 1982): 205–25; Shlomo Aronson with Oded Brosh, *The Politics and Strategy of Nuclear Weapons in the Middle East: Opacity, Theory, and Reality, 1960–1991: An Israeli Perspective* (Albany: State University of New York Press, 1992); Avner Yaniv, *Deterrence without the Bomb* (Lexington, Mass.: Lexington Books, 1987).

11. There were a few exceptions. Eliezer Livneh, "The Nuclear Reactor Affair" (in Hebrew), *PiHa'aton*, 31 January 1961.

12. Eliezer Livneh, "Warning in the Last Moment" (in Hebrew), *Ha'aretz*, 12 January 1962.

13. "Professors Against Nuclear Armament in the Middle East" (in Hebrew), *Ha'aretz*, 13 March 1962.

14. One such intervention received some publicity. In late March 1962, shortly after the issuance of the Committee's statement, "senior officials" from the Defense Ministry exerted pressure on the Israeli press association to cancel a briefing by Livneh on "nuclear weapons in the Middle East," because of considerations of national security. The talk was canceled, but the episode was critically discussed in the press and was brought to the attention of the Knesset Foreign Affairs and Defense Committee. See "Unacceptable Intervention" (in Hebrew), *Ha'aretz*, 27 March 1962; "Peculiar Decision" (in Hebrew), *Ha'aretz*, 5 April 1962. See also Eliezer Livneh, "Nuclear Interim Review" (in Hebrew), *Ha'aretz*, 12 October 1962.

15. Interview with Shimon Peres (in Hebrew) published in *Davar*, 24 August 1962; interview with Shimon Peres in *Ma'ariv*, 27 July 1962. Among the unofficial spokesmen, see Elkana Gali, "How Israel Would Respond to Nasser's Missiles" (in Hebrew), *Yediot Achronot*, 10 August 1962; Poles, "Defense Outlook in the Missile Age" (in Hebrew), *Ha'aretz*, 28 September 1962.

16. "Stress in Acquisition of Deterrence Weapons" (in Hebrew), *Yediot Achronot*, 13 August 1962.

17. Airgram (A-232), Barbour to State Department, 9 October 1962, NSF, Box 118, JFKL.

18. Rafael Bashan, "Interview of the Week with Shimon Peres" (in Hebrew), *Ma'ariv*, 27 July 1962.

19. Interview with Shimon Peres (in Hebrew) in *Davar*, 24 August 1962; Bashan, "Interview of the Week with Shimon Peres."

20. "Shimon Peres Criticizes Public Figures and Scientists Who Demanded Denuclearization" (in Hebrew), *Kol Ha'am*, 17 September 1962; see also *Ha'aretz*, 16 September 1962; and *Davar*, 16 September 1962.

21. Bashan, "Interview of the Week with Shimon Peres."

22. Twenty-five years later, in the wake of the Vanunu Affair, the secretary of the Committee published his memoirs about the group's activities (Yehuda Ben Moshe, "25 Years Before Vanunu" [in Hebrew], *Koteret Rashit*, 26 November 1986).

23. "Scientists Call for Regional Denuclearization" (in Hebrew), *Ha'aretz*, 25 July 1962.

24. Ben Moshe, "25 Years Before Vanunu"; Amos Korchin (Korchin was a member of the Committee), interview by author, Tel Aviv, 18 August 1992; Yoram Nimrod (Nimrod was a member of the Committee), interview by author, Ein Hahoresh, 4 September 1992.

25. The views of the Committee members were published in late 1963, after lengthy bickering with the military censor (*Israel-Arab: Nuclearization or Denuclearization* (in Hebrew) [Tel Aviv: Amikam Press, 1963]).

26. Korchin, interview; Nimrod, interview.

27. In 1961 the Ministry of Defense asked daily newspapers not to publish Livneh's articles on the subject for reasons of national security (letter, Gavriel Ziforni [editor of *Haboker*] to Eliezer Livneh, 5 January 1961, Box 29, Livneh Archive, Efal, Israel).

28. Shlomo Zalman Abramov (former Liberal Party member of Knesset), interview by author, Jerusalem, 26 August 1992; Korchin, interview; Nimrod, interview.

29. "Discussions among the Parties on Nuclear Armament in the Middle East" (in Hebrew), *Ha'aretz*, 15 March 1962; "Party Heads Discuss Nuclear Armament" (in Hebrew), *Ha'aretz*, 6 May 1962; "The Liberal Party on the Issue of Denuclearization: Voices in the Party in Favor of Israeli Initiative" (in Hebrew), *Ha'aretz*, 29 May 1962; "Discussion in MAPAM on Nuclear Free Zone in the Region" (in Hebrew), *Ha'aretz*, 17 June 1962; "Appeal to MAPAI to Discuss Denuclearization" (in Hebrew), *Ha'aretz*, 7 July 1962.

30. Abramov, interview; Yossef Tamir (former Liberal Party member of Knesset), interview by author, Tel Aviv, 20 August 1992.

31. "The Liberal Party on the Issue of Denuclearization."

32. Party Heads Discuss Nuclear Armament" (in Hebrew), *Ha'aretz*, 6 May 1962.

33. Abramov, interview; Tamir, interview.

34. Zeev Zur (former *Achdut Ha'Avodah* member of Knesset), interview by author, Ramat Efal, 7 July 1992.

35. "Difficult Discussion on the Nuclear Issues at Subcommittees" (in Hebrew), *Ha'aretz*, 24 January 1963.

36. Yizhar Smilansky (former MAPAI and RAFI member of Knesset; also a leading Israeli novelist), interview by author, Meishar, 20 August 1992.

37. The appendix to the coalition agreement, entitled "Ministerial Committee," was signed by Israel Galili for *Achdut Ha'Avodah* and Levi Eshkol for MAPAI (Galili collection, Box 2, 49–1, Hakibbutz Hameuchad Archive, Yad Tabenkin, Israel).

38. The incident that directly prompted this clause was the launching of the small meteorological rocket, Shavit II, in early July 1961. Ben Gurion authorized the highly publicized event on his own without informing the cabinet. The event looked to the

leaders of *Achdut Ha'avodah* like a campaign gimmick. Their strong protest led to a cabinet decision, made on 16 July 1961, stating that all "tests [of military funded systems] with international ramifications" must be preapproved by the government.

39. Moshe A. Gilboa, *Six Years, Six Days: Origins and History of the Six Day War* (in Hebrew) (Tel Aviv: Am Oved, 1968), 29–30; Yigal Allon, *Contriving Warfare* (in Hebrew) (Tel Aviv: Hakibbutz Hameuchad, 1990), 200, 205, 207, 305; Yair Evron, *Israel's Nuclear Dilemma* (Ithaca: Cornell University Press, 1994), 6–7.

40. Gilboa, *Six Years, Six Days*, 30.

41. Peres never argued publicly in Israel for nuclear weapons; he always used code phrases like "technological edge" or "independent deterrent." Outside Israel, however, he allowed his views to be echoed by others close to him. See editorial in the *Jewish Observer*, "An Independent Deterrent to Israel," 28 December 1962. The editor of the *Observer*, John Kimche, was known to have close contacts with Peres.

42. Yigal Allon, *Curtain of Sand* (in Hebrew) (Tel Aviv: Hakibbutz Hameuchad, 1968), esp. 400–402; see also Allon, *Contriving Warfare*, 195–209.

43. Gilboa, *Six Years, Six Days*, 29–30.

44. Allon, *Contriving Warfare*, 305; cf. Gilboa, *Six Years, Six Days*, 30.

45. Arnan Azaryahu, many conversations with author, Kibbutz Yiron and Tel Aviv. Azaryahu wrote the position paper for Galili for that meeting. The episode also appears in Evron, *Israel's Nuclear Dilemma*, 6–7.

46. Arnan Azaryahu, interview by author, Kibbutz Yiron, 22 August 1992; Evron, *Israel's Nuclear Dilemma*, 17–18.

47. Moshe Zak (former senior editor of *Ma'ariv*), interview by author, Tel Aviv, June 1996.

48. Shimon Peres, "The Time Dimension" (in Hebrew), *Ma'arachot* 146 (1962): 3–5.

9. Kennedy and Eshkol Strike a Deal

1. W. Granger Blair, "Israel Looks to a New Leader," *New York Times*, 23 June 1963, 1.

2. Letter, President John F. Kennedy to Prime Minister Levi Eshkol, 5 July 1963, ISA, FMRG, 3377/14. The letter, including instructions to Ambassador Walworth Barbour, is contained in Deptel 19 (Tel Aviv), 3 July 1963, POF Box 119a, JFKL.

3. Ibid.

4. Ibid.

5. Deptel 19 (Tel Aviv), 3 July 1963.

6. After Barbour handed Kennedy's letter to Eshkol, he assured Gideon Rafael and Chaim Yahil, the senior members of the Foreign Ministry, that there was no special meaning to the delivery of the letter to Eshkol so soon after he assumed office. The original letter was to be delivered to Ben Gurion on the afternoon of 16 June, but when he heard about Ben Gurion's resignation that day, he asked the State Department to wait in order to deliver the letter to the new prime minister (Memorandum, Gideon Rafael to Levi Eshkol, 7 July 1963, ISA, FMRG, Box 3377/6).

7. Hermann Eilts, telephone interview by author, 22 June 1997.

8. Memorandum, Robert Komer to President John F. Kennedy, 3 July 1963, in *FRUS, 1961–63*, vol. 18, 623.

9. Memorandum, Secretary of State Dean Rusk to President John F. Kennedy, 23 July 1963, in *FRUS, 1961–63*, vol. 18, 653–55; Hermann Eilts, interviews by author, 19 January 1996 and 29 May 1997.

10. Memorandum, William C. Foster to President Kennedy, "Political Implications of a Nuclear Test Ban," 12 July 1963, 2, National Security Files (NSF), Box 255–65 (ACDA), JFKL.

11. This point was elaborated in the ACDA guidance prepared for Harriman's mission in the following way:

> One of the principal interests of the United States in a test ban agreement is an interest in it as one of a series of steps designed to prevent the proliferation of nuclear weapons throughout the world. It is probable that the U.S.S.R. has a similar interest. It might be advisable to discuss this interest with the Soviet Union with relation to the interests of the U.S. and U.S.S.R. in a test ban. In the first instance the U.S. should point out that the signing of a test ban treaty would mean that there would be no additional nuclear powers in our camp. We should point out that we would attempt to obtain adherence by the French and as a result a reduction of the intensity of the French nuclear development program. ("Points to Be Covered in Preparation of Forthcoming July 15 Mission of Governor Harriman to Moscow," 20 June 1963, unsigned, prepared in ACDA, NSF, Box 255–65, JFKL)

12. "Instructions Proposed for Honorable W. Averell Harriman," 9 July 1963, prepared for 515th NSC Meeting, NSF, Box 255–65, JFKL.

13. "Summary Record of the National Security Council Meeting, 9 July 1963: Harriman Instructions for Mission to Moscow," 3, NSF, Box 255–65, JFKL.

14. According to Glenn Seaborg, before Harriman's mission to Moscow Kennedy considered abandoning the idea of MLF in order to advance the cause of a nonproliferation agreement with the Soviets. Because of opposition from both Rusk and Bundy, however, he gave up the idea (Glenn T. Seaborg, *Stemming the Tide: Arms Control in the Johnson Years* [Lexington, Mass.: Lexington, 1987], 92).

15. Cited in Seaborg, *Stemming the Tide*, 111.

16. There is no way to know whether, and to what extent, the pressure on Israel was discussed between Kennedy and Harriman, or whether Harriman was authorized to say anything on this matter to the Russian leader. Carl Kaysen, Harriman's deputy on this trip to Moscow, was not informed about the Israeli developments. The Israeli issue was limited to three senior staff members at the White House: McGeorge Bundy, Robert Komer, and Myer Feldman (Carl Kaysen, interviews by author, Cambridge, Mass., 3 August and 6 December 1995).

17. Kaysen, interviews, 3 August and 6 December 1995.

18. In such a case, warned Adrian Fisher, ACDA acting director, the Germans would

not remain content with MLF participation, "for under such circumstances there would be strong forces to argue that Germany would remain a second class nation so long as she had less independent nuclear capability than Israel or Sweden or India, however small that capability might be (Memorandum for the Secretary of State, "Nonproliferation of Nuclear Weapons and the MLF," 15 June 1964, Nonproliferation Collection, NSA).

19. Memorandum, Robert Komer to President Kennedy, 23 July 1963, in *FRUS, 1961–63*, vol. 18, 651 (emphasis in original).

20. Memorandum of Conversation, "McCloy's Near East Arms Limitations Probe; Security Guarantees for Israel," 23 July 1963, in *FRUS, 1961–63*, vol. 18, 658–61. Apparently four of the ten participants had no idea about the letter, including Badeau, McCloy, Nitze, and Eilts (Eilts interview, 22 June 1997).

21. Miriam Eshkol, interview by author, Jerusalem, 27 May 1995.

22. "Prime Minister: Ten Minutes Compared to Four Years" (in Hebrew), *Ha'olam Hazeh*, 17 July 1963.

23. "Draft Reply to President Kennedy's Letter of 5 July 1963," 7 July 1963, ISA, FMRG, Box 3377/14.

24. Ibid.

25. Telegram (86), Shimshon Arad to Avraham Harman, 13 August 1963, ISA, FMRG 3377/10.

26. Elyahu Salpeter, "Israeli Scientific Development—the Subject of Correspondence between Kennedy and Israel's Prime Minister: The Background—U.S. President's Fears about Nuclear Production Proliferation" (in Hebrew), *Ha'aretz*, 14 July 1963.

27. "Disagreements among Cabinet Members Regarding 'A Sensitive Political-Security Matter' " (in Hebrew), *Kol Ha'am*, 9 August 1963.

28. Telegram (45), Arad to Harman, 8 July 1963, ISA, FMRG 3377/9; cf. Telegram (77), Arad to Gazit, 14 July 1963, ISA, FMRG 3377/9.

29. On 21 July three U.S. unarmed reconnaissance planes were forced to land at Lod Airport while flying over or around Dimona. Though both Israel and the United States made efforts to keep the incident secret, it was interpreted in the Israeli press as an espionage mission conducted by the same U.S. organization that ran the reconnaissance flights over the Soviet Union (*Ha'aretz*, 21 July 1963, as cited in Telegram [123] from the Foreign Ministry to the Israeli Embassy in Washington, D.C., 21 July 1963, ISA, FMRG, 3378/1). The flight characteristics (it was conducted not by a lone U-2 but by three slower planes on an allegedly administrative-training mission) led to the thought that it was meant more as an effort to exert pressure on Israel than a genuine intelligence operation.

30. "The Cabinet Announced Israeli Readiness to Join the Moscow Agreement" (in Hebrew), *Ha'aretz*, 1 August 1963.

31. The secret resolution appears in a memo from the cabinet secretary to the prime minister and the foreign minister, ISA, FMRG, Box 3044/77.

32. Yuval Ne'eman, interview by author, Austin, Texas, March 1994.

33. Ibid.

34. Mordechai Gazit, interview by author, Jerusalem, 14 June 1995; also, Gazit, correspondence with author, 26 November 1995.

35. Michael Bar-Zohar, *Ben Gurion* (in Hebrew), 3 vols. (Tel Aviv: Zmora Bitan, 1987), vol. 3, 1560.

36. Telegram (79), Israeli Embassy in Washington to Foreign Ministry, 15 August 1963, ISA, FMRG 3377/10.

37. The text of Eshkol's letter appears in Telegram (117), Shimshon Arad to Ambassador Avraham Harman, 19 August 1963, ISA, FMRG, 3377/10.

38. Ibid.

39. Telegram (121), Arad to Harman, 19 August 1963, ISA, FMRG 3377/10.

40. Ibid.

41. Deptel 193 (Tel Aviv) (contains text of Kennedy's letter to Eshkol), 26 August 1963, POF, Box 119a, JFKL. The text of Kennedy's letter is also cited in full in a telegram (227) from Arad to Harman, 27 August 1963, ISA, FMRG, 3377/10.

42. Deptel 193 (Tel Aviv), 26 August 1963; Telegram (227), Arad to Harman, 27 August 1963.

43. Ibid.

44. This point was at the core of the oral message that the U.S. representative was requested to convey to Eshkol on behalf of Kennedy. The first draft of these instructions was the most elaborate on this issue:

> President Kennedy is troubled by [the] fact that you (Primin) should wish to place too rigid a restriction on the use to which we might put information attesting the peaceful purpose of Israel's nuclear program. We would, of course, observe your wishes in this matter, but the President is anxious that you understand our purpose in this matter. It is not to reveal any specific arrangements with you but in a general sense to allay apprehension which could have great dangers both worldwide and particularly in the Near East. The President is convinced that the utility of setting to rest fears which otherwise could lead to a nuclear weapons efforts by others in the area far outweighs the deterrent effect of uncertainty.... If at any time this uncertainty was accidentally accentuated, it would also create the greatest threat of disastrous military adventure. This must be prevented. The President and Mr. Ben Gurion agreed on this in May 1961. So the President asks that the agreement then reached be continued with respect to the future visits to which you have assented. (Draft Deptel 193 [Tel Aviv], 23 August 1963)

45. Telegram (79), Israeli Embassy in Washington to Foreign Ministry, 15 August 1963.

46. *FRUS, 1961–63*, vol. 18, 650–51 (emphasis in original).

47. Ibid. (emphasis in original).

48. Memorandum, Rusk to Kennedy, 23 July 1963, in *FRUS, 1961–63*, vol. 18, 653–55.

49. There was another school of thought at the Israeli Embassy in Washington. Ambassador Harman's deputy, Mordechai Gazit, did not share the pessimistic views of his ambassador and thought that proper verbal commitments would resolve the issue. He saw the issue as a trigger for increasing U.S. involvement in Israel's security (Mordechai Gazit, interview by author, Jerusalem, 6 June 1995; Minutes, "Meeting of

Prime Minister Levi Eshkol and Mr. Mordechai Gazit," 30 August 1963, ISA, FMRG, 3379/4).

50. "Consultations on the Matter of the Exchange with the President of the United States," 6 September 1963, ISA, FMRG 3377/10, pp. 20–21.

51. Telegram (61), Levi Eshkol to Avraham Harman and Mordechai Gazit, 10 September 1963, ISA, FMRG 3377/10.

52. Letter, Kennedy to Eshkol, 3 October 1963, ISA, FMRG, 3377/10.

53. Telegram (571), Arad to Harman, 4 October 1963, ISA, FMRG 3377/10.

54. Telegram (103), Mordechai Gazit to Chaim Yahil, 18 October 1963, ISA, FMRG, 3377/10.

55. The point was made to Ambassador Harman by Myer Feldman (Memorandum, Avraham Harman to Chaim Yahil, "Conversation with M. Feldman," 14 October 1963, ISA, FMRG, 3377/10).

56. Komer presented a lengthy argument to Gazit that the IDF should be interested in purchasing attack helicopters, the weapons of the future battlefield, not tanks (Mordechai Gazit, interview by author, Jerusalem, 6 June 1995).

57. Minutes, "Meeting of Prime Minister Levi Eshkol and Mr. Mordechai Gazit," 30 August 1963; Mordechai Gazit, *President Kennedy's Policy Towards the Arab States and Israel: Analysis and Documents* (Ramat Aviv: Shiloah Center for Middle Eastern and African Studies, Tel Aviv University, 1983), 44–45.

58. "Consultations on the Matter of the Exchange with the President of the United States," 6 September 1963, ISA, FMRG 3377/10.

59. Telegram (61), Levi Eshkol to Avraham Harman and Mordechai Gazit, 10 September 1963, ISA, FMRG 3377/10. See also Robert Komer, "Memorandum for Record: Luncheon with Israeli Minister Gazit, 23 September 1963," 24 September 1963, NSF, Box 119, JFKL.

60. Telegram (10), Harman to Yahil, 2 October 1963, ISA, FMRG 3377/10; Telegram (18) Harman to Yahil, 2 October 1963, ISA, FMRG, 3379/4; Telegram (34), Harman to Yahil, 3 October 1963, ISA, FMRG 3377/10.

61. The text of Eshkol's letter appears in an outgoing telegram (797), Arad to Harman, 4 November 1963, ISA, FMRG 3377/10.

62. Ibid.

63. Telegram (858), Foreign Ministry to Harman, 11 November 1963, ISA, FMRG 3379/4.

64. Telegram (10), Arad to Harman, 3 November 1963, ISA, FMRG 3379/4.

65. Special National Intelligence Estimate (SNIE) 30–2–63, "The Advanced Weapons Programs of the AR and Israel," 8 May 1963, in *FRUS, 1961–63*, vol. 18, 517–18.

66. "Talking Points for Rabin Session," 14 November 1963, 002948–94, Library of Congress, Washington, D.C.; Robert Komer, interview by author, Washington, D.C., 17 May 1995.

67. Telegram (63), Harman to Ben Gurion, 13 November 1963, ISA, FMRG, 3379/4.

68. "Talking Points for Rabin Session"; Komer, interview.

69. "Talking Points for Rabin Session"; Komer, interview.

70. Robert Komer, conversations with author, Washington, D.C., 1992–1995.

71. Komer stated this in a Center for National Security Negotiations (CNSN) workshop, "Lessons and Legacies of Nuclear History," Washington, D.C., 24 May 1995.

72. Mordechai Gazit, interview by author, Jerusalem, 9 June 1995.

10. THE DIMONA VISITS (1964–1967)

1. Letter, President John F. Kennedy to Prime Minister Levi Eshkol, 5 July 1963, ISA, FMRG 3377/9; cf. "Telegram from the Department of State to the Embassy in Israel," 4 July 1963, in *FRUS, 1961–1963*, vol. 18, 624–26.

2. *FRUS, 1961–63*, vol. 18, 625.

3. Israel's opposition to placing Dimona under IAEA safeguards was argued differently at different times. An early argument, first made by Ben Gurion and Peres, was that a system of international safeguards must be equally applied to all states, otherwise it would contradict the principles of national sovereignty (what Peres, following the French, called "atomic sovereignty"). Later, when Israel still opposed placing its smaller American reactor under IAEA safeguards, it argued against the Agency's refusal to include Israel as a Middle Eastern country. After the Eshkol government agreed to accept IAEA safeguards for the Soreq reactor, Israel argued, privately, that even though it had pledged to the United States that it would not develop nuclear weapons, it had no interest in reassuring Nasser on the point, and preferred "letting him guess" (see "Atom Control View Explained in Israel," *New York Times*, 20 April 1964, 6; "Israel Will Accept Atom Control Shift," *New York Times*, 9 June 1964, 6).

4. The State Department was aware of the differences between the two countries in interpreting the ground rules for the visits, but decided to interpret Eshkol's letter to mean that he had accepted Kennedy's rules ("Memorandum from Acting Secretary of State George Ball to President Kennedy," 23 August 1963, in *FRUS, 1961–63*, vol. 18, 685–87).

5. William N. Dale (deputy chief of mission at the U.S. Embassy in Tel Aviv, 1964–68), telephone interview by author, 24 April 1995; Michael Sterner (former State Department official who was involved in the visits), interview by author, Washington, D.C., April 1995.

6. Telegram (568), Secretary of State Dean Rusk to U.S. Ambassador to Israel Walworth Barbour, 5 January 1965, RG 59, Central Foreign Policy Files (CFPF), 1964–66, Box 3068, USNA.

7. Ibid. Barbour responded to the terminological issue in this way: "While status of team as 'guests of Israel' or 'inspectors' not of concern to U.S., it is of major concern to prime minister in light [of] domestic political considerations involved, and I am sure that recognition [of] this fact by team will considerably enhance value and atmosphere [of] visit" (Embtel [771], Barbour to Rusk, 6 January 1965, RG 59, CFPF, 1964–66, Box 3068, USNA; Culler, numerous letters and telephone conversations with author, May–June 1996.

8. Letter, Foreign Ministry Director-General Chaim Yahil to Barbour, 5 December 1963, ISA, FMRG 3377/11.

9. Letter, Barbour to Yahil, 7 January 1964, ISA, FMRG 3377/14; Telegram (599), Rusk to Barbour, 6 January 1964, RG 59, CFPF, 1964–66, Box 3068, USNA; cf. Embtel 706 (Tel Aviv), Rusk to Barbour, 6 January 1964, RG 59, CFPF, 1964–66, USNA.

10. Telegram (758), Barbour to Rusk, 8 January 1964, RG 59, CFPF, 1964–66, Box 3068, USNA; Draft Letter, "DRAFT 1," n.d., ISA, FMRG 3377/14.

11. For the American interpretation of Eshkol's letter to Kennedy, see "Memorandum, from Acting Secretary of State Ball to President Kennedy," 23 August 1963, in *FRUS, 1961–63*, vol. 18, 685–87.

12. Memorandum, Director of the Office of Near Eastern Affairs Roger P. Davies, Department of State, to Assistant Secretary of State for Near Eastern and South Asian Affairs Phillips Talbot, "Briefing of Dimona Inspection Team," 11 January 1964, RG 59, CFPF, 1964–66, Box 3068, USNA.

13. "Summary of Findings of Dimona Inspection Team," 7 February 1964, RG 59, CFPF, 1964–66, Box 3068, USNA.

14. Ibid; Telegram (7058), Rusk to London Embassy, 29 April 1964, RG 59, CFPF, 1964–66, Box 3068, USNA.

15. Ibid., 1.

16. Ibid., 2.

17. Ibid.

18. Telegram (301), Rusk to Barbour, 14 October 1964, RG 59, CFPF, 1964–66, Box 3068, USNA.

19. Embtel (407), Barbour to Rusk, 21 October 1964, RG 59, CFPF, 1964–66, Box 3068, USNA.

20. Telegram (660), Barbour to Rusk, 7 December 1964, RG 59, CFPF, 1964–66, Box 3068, USNA.

21. "Preliminary Draft Report of Dimona Inspection Team," n.d. (attached to memo dated 4 February 1965), RG 59, CFPF, 1964–66, Box 3068, USNA.

22. Ibid., 3.

23. Ibid., 2.

24. Memorandum, State Department to National Security Adviser McGeorge Bundy, "Dimona Inspection and Need to Implement Initiative to Prevent Nuclear Proliferation in the Near East," 4 February 1965, RG 59, CFPF, 1964–66, Box 3068, USNA.

25. "Preliminary Draft Report of Dimona Inspection Team," 4.

26. "Dimona Inspection and Need to Implement Initiative to Prevent Nuclear Proliferation in the Near East," 1.

27. Ibid., 2.

28. John W. Finney, "Israel Permits U.S. to Inspect Atomic Reactor," *New York Times*, 14 March 1965, 1, 8.

29. John W. Finney, interview by author, summer 1996.

30. Telegram (922), Rusk to Barbour, 11 March 1965, RG 59, CFPF, 1964–66, Box 3068, USNA.

31. Telegram (1691), circular, 14 March 1965, RG 59, CFPF, 1964–66, Box 3068, USNA.

32. Telegram (941), Rusk to Barbour, 16 March 1965, RG 59, CFPF, 1964–66, Box 3068, USNA.

33. "Background Paper: Dimona Visits," n.d., RG 59, CFPF, 1964–66, Box 3068, USNA; Memorandum of Conversation with Foreign Minister Abba Eban, "Subject: Dimona Visits," 7 February 1966, RG 59, CFPF, 1964–66, Box 3068, USNA.

34. Telegram (652), U.S. Ambassador to Turkey Raymond A. Hare to Barbour, 10 February 1966, RG 59, CFPF, 1964–66, Box 3068, USNA.

35. Telegram (698), Rusk to Barbour, 1 March 1966, RG 59, CFPF, 1964–66, Box 3068, USNA.

36. Telegram (761), Rusk to Barbour, 19 March 1966, RG 59, CFPF, 1964–66, Box 3068, USNA.

37. John W. Finney, "U.S. Again Assured on Negev Reactor," *New York Times*, 28 June 1966, 8.

38. In 1994 the IAEC confirmed that, on 14 December 1966, an accident, in which a technician was killed and three others were injured, occurred in one of the labs at the Dimona facility (Alex Doron and Liat Ron, "A Mysterious Accident in the Nuclear Reactor in Dimona" [in Hebrew], *Ma'ariv*, Special Supplement, 14 September 1994, 4–7).

39. John W. Finney, "Israel Could Make Atom Arms in 3 or 4 Years, U.S. Aides Say," *New York Times*, 6 July 1967.

40. Pierre Péan, *Les deux bombes* (Paris: Fayard, 1981), 111–15, 118–20; interview with Frances Perrin, *Sunday Times*, 6 October 1986.

41. Péan, *Les deux bombes*, 111–15, 118–20.

42. Floyd Culler, letter to author, 9 May 1996; Culler, numerous letters and telephone conversations with author, May–June 1996.

43. Ibid. Former Director of Central Intelligence (DCI) Richard Helms confirms Culler's assumption that it was decided that intelligence data not be shared with the Dimona inspection team. Helms suggests that they were not properly briefed by the CIA because the CIA briefers were probably told not to tell them anything. The dominant urge at the time was to contain any firm American acknowledgment of an Israeli nuclear capability (Richard Helms, interview by author, Washington, D.C., 2 October 1997).

44. These details are mentioned in the recently declassified correspondence between Secretary of State Rogers and Ambassador Barbour in 1969.

45. Culler, letters and conversations.

46. Ibid.

47. Dale, telephone interview; former senior U.S. intelligence officer, interview by author, 17 April 1995; Culler, letters and conversations.

48. Culler, letters and conversations.

49. Ibid.

50. Ibid.; George B. Pleat, letter to author, 26 July 1996.

51. Culler, letters and conversations.

52. Ibid.

53. Airgram (A-742), "Current Status of the Dimona Reactor," 9 April 1965, RG 59, CFPF, 1964–66, Box 3068, USNA.

54. Ibid.

55. Finney, "Israel Permits U.S. to Inspect Atomic Reactor," 1, 8; Finney, "U.S. Again Assured on Negev Reactor," 8.

56. Airgram (A-742), "Current Status of the Dimona Reactor," 9 April 1965.

57. According to the figures Webber presents in his study, the average cost of a scientist at the Weizmann Institute ("with facilities as good as any in the world") is slightly under $100,000 per scientist; at the Hebrew University the cost is about $80,000; at the Technion that cost is about $69,000; at the Standards Institution of Israel it is about $58,000; while at Soreq nuclear establishment the average cost is about $75,000.

58. Dale, interview. Dale recalls that Barbour's comment was that the "time has come for the embassy to write such a report." He added that they could not have sent such a sensitive document without the ambassador's consent.

59. Robert W. Komer, interviews by author, Washington, D.C., 22 June 1992, and 13 April 1995.

60. Former senior U.S. intelligence officer, interview by author, 26 August 1996.

61. Ibid. Chief of Counter-Intelligence Staff, James Jesus Angleton, a controversial cold warrior who was a close friend of Israel, had overall responsibility for the Israeli desk at the CIA. For more on Angleton, see David C. Martin, *Wilderness of Mirrors* (New York: Harper and Row, 1980); and Tom Mangold, *Cold Warrior, James Jesus Angleton: The CIA's Master Spy Hunter* (New York: Simon and Schuster, 1991). Again, it is important to note Helms's conviction that the CIA briefers were probably instructed not to divulge special intelligence information to the inspection teams (Helms, interview).

62. Culler, letters and conversations.

63. Ibid.

11. AMBIGUITY BORN

1. Arel Ginai, "What Lyndon Johnson Was Ready to Promise to Levi Eshkol" (in Hebrew), *Yediot Achronot*, Weekend Supplement, 29 May 1964.

2. Seymour M. Hersh, *The Samson Option: Israel's Nuclear Arsenal and American Foreign Policy* (New York: Random House, 1991), 126–28.

3. Memorandum, Shimshon Arad to Ambassador Avraham Harman, 25 December 1963, ISA, FMRG 3378/1.

4. Memorandum for the Assistant Secretary of Defense, "Possible Sale of Medium Tanks," 13 January 1964, NSF-NSAM, Box 3, LBJL; Memorandum for the Secretary of Defense, "Arms for Israel," 18 January 1964, NSF, Box 144–45, LBJL.

5. Memorandum, National Security Council Senior Staffer Robert Komer to President Johnson, 18 February 1964, Office Files of Robert Komer, Box 6, LBJL.

6. Nasser's threat was made during his conversation with Robert Komer in Cairo on

15 April 1963) (Airgram [A-767], "Memorandum of Conversation with President Nasser," 18 April 1963), courtesy of Jim Walsh.

7. Memorandum for McGeorge Bundy, "Subject: Need to Reassure President Nasser on the Peaceful Nature of the Dimona Reactor," n.d., Department of State, Center for Foreign Policy Files, RG 59, CFPF, 1964–66, Box 3068, USNA.

8. Telegram (75), Shimshon Arad to Simcha Dinitz (for Foreign Minister Golda Meir), 29 February 1964, ISA, FMRG, 4320/6.

9. Memorandum, Komer to Johnson, 18 February 1964, Office Files of Robert Komer, Box 6, LBJL; Robert Komer, interview by author, Washington, D.C., October 1994.

10. Telegram (904), Ambassador Walworth Barbour to Assistant Secretary of State Philip Talbot, 29 February 1964, RG 59, CFPF, 1964–66, Box 3068, USNA.

11. Telegram (766), Arieh Levavi to Ambassador Avraham Harman, 3 March 1964, ISA, FMRG, 4320/6; also Telegram (11), Arieh Levavi to Simcha Dinitz, 3 March 1964, ISA, FMRG, 4320/6; Telegram(916), Barbour to Rusk, 3 March 1964, RG 59, CFPF, 1964–66, Box 3068, USNA.

12. There are separate but not discordant Israeli and American versions of these conversations. For the Israeli version, see Telegram (770), Arad to Harman, 3 March 1964, ISA, FMRG 4320/6; Telegram (776), Arad to Harman, 3 March 1964, ISA, FMRG 4320/6. For the American version, see Telegram (916), Barbour to Rusk, 3 March 1964; Telegram (919), Barbour to Rusk (three parts), 4 March 1964, RG 59, CFPF, 1964–66, Box 3068, USNA.

13. Telegram (75), Arad to Dinitz (for Foreign Minister Meir), 29 February 1964.

14. Memorandum, Bundy to Johnson, 13 March 1964, NSF, NSAM Box 3, LBJL.

15. National Security Action Memorandum No. 290, "Meeting Israel's Arms Requests," 19 March 1964, NSF, NSAM Box 3, LBJL.

16. Letter, Johnson to Prime Minister Levi Eshkol, 19 March 1964, ISA, FMRG 3377/14.

17. Letter, Eshkol to Johnson, 7 April 1964, ISA, FMRG 3377/14.

18. Ibid.

19. Memorandum, Deputy Special Counsel Myer Feldman to Johnson, 11 May 1964 (enclosed three-page memo, entitled "Tanks for Israel" dated 14 March 1964), NSF, Country File—Israel, Box 144–45, LBJL.

20. Telegram (1140), Barbour to Rusk, 15 May 1964, NSF, Country File—Israel, Box 139, LBJL.

21. "Atom Control View Explained in Israel," New York Times, 20 April 1964, 6; "The U.S. Was Not Convinced by Israeli Objections to International Control on Soreq" (in Hebrew), Ha'aretz, 21 April 1964; Elyahu Salpeter, "Israel Wants to Extend the Agreement for Two Years" (in Hebrew), Ha'aretz, 22 April 1964; Ze'ev Schiff, "The Danger in Control over the Atomic Reactor" (in Hebrew), Ha'aretz, 24 April 1964; Yossef Harish, "Israel Demands of the United States to Renew the Nuclear Agreement for Two Additional Years" (in Hebrew), Ma'ariv, 20 April 1964; Eliezer Wiesel, "Despite the American Pressure, Israel Rejects Supervision of Nuclear Research," Yediot Achronot, 19 April 1964, 1.

22. Telegram (967099), Secretary of Defense Robert McNamara to Ambassador in Bonn, 5 May 1964, NSF, NSAM, Box 3, LBJL.

23. Memorandum of Conversation, 18 May 1964, NSF McGeorge Bundy Files, Box 19, LBJL.

24. Memorandum, Komer to Johnson, 28 May 1964, NSF, Country File—Israel, Eshkol Visit, Box 143, LBJL; cf. Memorandum, Acting Secretary of State George Ball to Johnson, n.d., NSF, Country File—Israel, Box 142–43, LBJL. In this State Department briefing memo for the same occasion the U.S. policy is defined in the following way:

> We are concerned about the escalation of the Near East arms race *and firmly oppose proliferation of nuclear weapons and missile acquisition* by either side. *We consider acquisition of missiles, even with conventional warhead, a significant step toward the acquisition of nuclear capability.* We have discussed restraint in this field with both Israel and the U.A.R. and *intend to pursue it further.* We are not unhopeful of positive results. (Emphasis added.)

25. Memorandum of Conversation, Johnson, Feldman, Eshkol, Harman, 1 June 1964, NSF, Country File—Israel, Box 143, LBJL (hereafter referred to as EJAV); Memorandum of Conversation, Johnson, Feldman, Eshkol, and Harman—First Meeting, 1 June 1964, ISA, FMRG 3504/17 (hereafter referred to as EJIV).

26. EJIV.

27. EJAV, 5.

28. Memorandum, Komer to Johnson, 2 June 1964, NSF, Country File—Israel, Box 143, LBJL (emphasis in original).

29. "Second Meeting of Prime Minister Eshkol with President Johnson, June 2," n.d., ISA, FMRG, 3504/17; note for file by Mordechai Gazit, 9 June 1964; Mordechai Gazit, interview by author, Jerusalem, 28 May 1995.

30. Memorandum, Komer to Johnson, 3 June 1964, NSF, Country File—Israel, Box 143, LBJL.

31. Memorandum, Gazit to Levavi, 3 June 1964, ISA, FMRG, 3504/17.

32. Telegram (3457), Rusk to Embassy (Bonn), 3 June 1964, NSF, NSAM, Box 3, LBJL; Telegram (3638), Rusk to Embassy (Bonn), 17 June 1964, NSF, NSAM, Box 3, LBJL

33. Memorandum, Bundy to Johnson, 12 June 1964, NSF, Memos to the President File, Box 2, "Bundy, vol. 5," LBJL.

34. Letter, Assistant Secretary of Defense John McNaughton to Komer, 15 July 1964, NSF, Country File—Israel, Box 144–45, LBJL.

35. Memorandum, Ball (for Rusk) to Johnson, "Near East Arms," 19 February 1965, NSF, Country File—Israel, Box 144–45, LBJL.

36. Robert W. Komer, interview by author, Washington, D.C., 22 June 1992.

37. Memorandum (and Attachments), Deputy Assistant Secretary Peter Solbert to Bundy, 8 March 1965, NSF, Country File—Israel, Box 144–45, LBJL.

38. Komer, interviews by author, Washington, D.C., 22 June 1992; 13 April 1995.

39. "Memorandum of Conversation Between Shimon Peres and Robert Komer," 2 October 1964, ISA, FMRG, 3504/17.

40. Yitzhak Rabin, *A Service Record* (in Hebrew), vol. 2 (Tel Aviv: Ma'ariv, 1979),

129–30; Yitzhak Rabin, *The Rabin Memoir* (Berkeley: University of California Press, 1996), 65.

41. Komer, interviews, 22 June 1992; 13 April 1995.

42. Memorandum of Understanding, Eshkol, Komer, Barbour, 10 March 1965, ISA, FMRG 3501/17.

43. Letter, Eshkol to Johnson, 12 March 1965, NSF, Country File—Israel, Box 144–45, LBJL.

44. Letter, Johnson to Eshkol, 22 March 1965, NSF, Country File—Israel, Box 144–45, LBJL.

45. Briefing Memorandum, Handle to Averell W. Harriman, "Your Meeting with Israeli Ambassador," 13 May 1965, RG 59, CFPF, 1964–66, Box 2356, USNA; State Department, Memorandum of Conversation, 15 June 1965, RG 59, CFPF, 1964-66, Box 1644, USNA.

46. Memorandum, Secretary of State Dean Rusk to President Lyndon B. Johnson, 7 May 1965, RG 59, CFPF, 1964–66, Box 1644, USNA.

47. Telegram (1254), Rusk to Ambassador Walworth Barbour, 5 June 1965, RG 59, CFPF, 1964–66, Box 1644, USNA; State Department, Memorandum of Conversation, 15 June 1965.

48. Telegram (83), Rusk to Barbour, 27 July 1965, RG 59, CFPF, 1964–66, Box 1644, USNA.

49. Telegram, George Ball to Barbour, 12 May 1965, RG 59, CFPF, 1964–66, Box 1644, USNA; Memorandum of Conversation, "Israeli Arms Procurement Request," 3 June 1965, RG 59, CFPF, 1964–66, Box 1644, USNA; Telegram (1254), Rusk to Barbour, 5 June 1965.

50. Memorandum, Handley to Rusk, "The Israeli Aircraft Request: General Weizman's Visit," RG 59, CFPF, 1964–66, Box 1644, USNA.

51. Letter, Ambassador Avraham Harman to Phillips Talbot, 10 June 1965, NSF Files, Box 139, LBJL; Telegram, Rusk to Barbour, 11 June 1965, RG 59, CFPF, 1964–66, Box 1644, USNA. Harman's letter was sent to National Security Adviser McGeorge Bundy with the following note:

> As the President knows, this request for Phantoms is completely outside the agreement reached in Israel in March. We have made Israeli officials aware informally of the impossibility of supplying Phantoms and intend to inform the Israeli Government officially of our position. We propose to continue to explore with the Israelis the meeting of their requirements within the context of the Memorandum of Understanding and agreed minutes of March 10, i.e., to ensure Israel an opportunity to purchase a certain number of mutually agreed combat aircraft. (Memorandum, Benjamin Read to Bundy, NSF, Box 139, LBJL)

52. Memorandum, Jeffrey C. Kitchen to Thompson, "Israel-US Discussions on Aircraft Procurement," n.d., RG 59, CFPF, 1964–66, Box 1644, USNA.

53. *Moked* was the code name for the IAF plan to obtain aerial superiority by destroying Arab air forces on the ground in the first hours of war. Ezer Weizman was the "father-

founder" of this concept, and operational plans were continuously updated since 1962 (Eitan Haber, "The Man That Downed 376 Enemy Planes" [in Hebrew], *Yediot Ahronot*, 5 June 1992, 8).

54. Memorandum, Jeffrey C. Kitchen to Thompson, "Israel-US Discussions on Aircraft Procurement."

55. Deptel (Paris), Bohlen to Rusk, 29 October 1965, RG 59, CFPF, 1964–66, Box 1644, USNA; Memorandum, Robert W. Komer to Johnson, 28 October 1965, NSF, Box 139, LBJL; Telegram (416), Rusk to Barbour, 10 November 1965, NSF, Box 139, LBJL.

56. Memorandum, Hare to Alexis Johnson, "Your Appointment with Ambassador Harman at 11:30 Today," RG 59, CFPF, 1964–66, Box 2356, USNA.

57. Ibid.

58. Correspondence between the author and Mordechai Gazit, 1996–97.

59. Embtel, Rusk to Barbour, 30 July 1965, RG 59, CFPF, 1964–66, Box 1644, USNA.

60. On 25 January 1966 Ambassador Harman clarified that Weizman's request was based on two separate articles in the 10 March Komer-Eshkol MOU, Articles III and V(c). The former article refers to the long-term effective Israeli deterrent; it was in this broad context that Weizman made his request for 210 new planes. Article V(c) refers to near-term needs and it was in this context that Weizman requested forty-five Phantoms (Memorandum of Conversation, "Aircraft for Israel and Jordan," 25 January 1966, RG 59, CFPF, 1964–66, Box 1644, USNA).

61. Embtel (939), Barbour to Rusk, 19 January 1965, RG 59, CFPF, 1964–66, Box 1644, USNA.

62. Deptel (606), Rusk to Barbour, 26 January 1966, RG 59, CFPF, 1964–66, Box 1644, USNA.

63. Embtel (3747), Barbour to Rusk, 27 January 1966, RG 59, CFPF, 1964–66, Box 1644, USNA.

64. Memorandum of Conversation, "Nuclear Proliferation" (part 2 of 2), 9 February 1966, RG 59, CFPF, 1964–66, Box 2356, USNA; cf. Deptel (652), Rusk to Barbour, 10 February 1966, RG 59, CFPF, 1964–66, Box 2356, USNA.

65. Ibid.

66. Ibid.

67. Ibid.

68. Memorandum, Komer to Johnson, 8 February 1966, NSF, Box 6 (Komer files), LBJL. Emphasis in original.

69. Memorandum for the Record, "President Talk with Israeli Foreign Minister Eban," 9 February 1966, RG 59, CFPF, 1964–66, Box 2356, USNA.

70. Deptel (691), Rusk to Barbour, 26 February 1966, NSF, Box 139, LBJL.

71. Ibid.

72. The proposed draft of the letter, prepared by the State Department, was located, along with a cover letter from Davies to Hoopes dated 21 February 1966, in RG 59, CFPF, 1964–66, Box 1644, USNA.

73. Memorandum of Conversation, "Letter on Aircraft Sale to Israel," 4 March 1966, RG 59, CFPF, 1964–66, Box 1644, USNA.

74. Ibid.

75. Memorandum of Conversation, "Letter Request for Modification Aircraft Agreement Arrangements," 14 March 1966, RG 59, CFPF, 1964–66, Box 1644, USNA.

76. Ibid.

77. Ibid.

78. Action Memorandum, Hare to Rusk, 16 March 1966, RG 59, CFPF, 1964–66, Box 1644, USNA.

79. Deptel (2250), Rusk to Barbour, 17 May 1966, RG 59, CFPF, 1964–66, Box 1644, USNA.

80. Ibid. (emphasis in original).

81. Former senior U.S. intelligence official, interview by author, 2 August 1996.

82. William N. Dale, telephone interview by author, 24 April 1995. Also, former senior U.S. intelligence official, interview, 2 August 1996. The official was familiar with Barbour's views on this matter. Cf. Hersh, *The Samson Option*, 159–69.

83. Myer Feldman, interview by author, Washington, D.C., 10 June 1992.

84. Glenn T. Seaborg, telephone interview by author, 15 July 1996. It is not yet confirmed whether the CIA based its assumption that the Israelis possessed a reprocessing plant on hard evidence. Seaborg indicated his uncertainty on the matter.

85. Komer, interview, 22 June 1992.

86. The quote is taken from a U.S. government document entitled, "Background Paper on Factors Which Could Influence National Decisions Concerning Acquisition of Nuclear Weapons," NSF, Committee on Nuclear Proliferation, LBJL.

87. Memorandum, Komer to Johnson, 8 February 1966, NSF, "Komer Memos, vol. 2," Box 6, LBJL.

88. Feldman, interview, 10 June 1992.

89. Glenn T. Seaborg, *Stemming the Tide: Arms Control in the Johnson Years* (Lexington, Mass.: Lexington Books, 1987), 105–7.

90. In a speech to the nation, Johnson noted that in recent years Khrushchev had shown himself "aware of the need for sanity in the nuclear age," but Communist China had no "long experience as major powers in the modern world," and

> its nuclear pretensions are both expensive and cruel to its people. . . . Communist China's expensive and demanding effort tempts other states to equal folly. Nuclear spread is dangerous to all mankind. What if there should come to be 10 nuclear powers, or maybe 20 nuclear powers? What if we must learn to look everywhere for the restraint which our own example now sets for a few? . . . The lesson of Lop Nor is that we are right to recognize the danger of nuclear spread; that we must continue to work against it, and we will. . . . We continue to believe that the struggle against nuclear spread is as much in the Soviet interest as in our own. We will be ready to join with them and all the world in working to avoid it. (Address of the President, 18 October 1964, Office of the White House Press Secretary)

91. Rusk raised the question of whether the United States would not be better off if

India and Japan were able to respond to Chinese threats with nuclear weapons of their own. In late 1964 and early 1965 Rusk invoked the possibility of having an Asian group of nuclear weapons countries, explaining that the nuclear rivalry was among Asian countries, not between northern countries and Asians. He argued that "it is easier for the U.S. to speak against proliferation, but the Prime Minister of India or Japan must look at the question quite differently." It was natural for the United States to be against nuclear proliferation in areas where American defense alliances already existed, such as in Europe, but preaching nonproliferation was more difficult in cases in which such alliances did not exist, as in the case of India:

> De Gaulle doubts the US commitment even in Europe—it is much easier to have such doubt in distant areas not traditionally bound to us. Moreover, do we want to give guarantees which would guarantee that we will be involved at the risk of 100 to 150 million lives ten years from now in the face of possible Sino-Soviet alliance? An Asian nuclear defense community, perhaps with the US nuclear stockpile available for it to draw upon, may be one solution. (Department of State, Memorandum of Conversation, "Secretary Meeting with the Gilpatric Committee," 7 January 1965, NSF Committee File, Box 8a, LBJ)

92. "A Report to the President by the Committee on Nuclear Proliferation," 21 January 1965, NSF, Box 5, LBJL.

93. Seaborg, *Stemming the Tide*, 145.

94. Ibid.

95. The report was politicized a few months later when Robert Kennedy used the report's recommendation in his maiden speech in the Senate, urging a stronger American commitment to nonproliferation. He attacked the Johnson administration's position on the MLF issue, claiming that India and Israel "could fabricate an atomic device within a few months" ("The Bomb: A Special Report," *Newsweek*, 9 August 1965, 54).

96. Hedrick Smith, "U.S. Studies a Plan to Bar Israeli-U.A.R. Atom Race," *New York Times*, 28 February 1966.

97. Komer, interview, 22 June 1992.

12. GROWING PAINS

1. Miriam Eshkol, interview by author, Jerusalem, 5 June 1995. Ms. Eshkol used the words "caretaker prime minister" to describe the way her husband initially saw his job. The American Embassy, in its first report on Eshkol's new government, asserted "the return of Ben Gurion seems quite probable" (Airgram [842], 25 June 1963, RG 3948, State Department Central Files (SDCF), 1963, USNA.

2. Michael Bar-Zohar, *Ben Gurion* (in Hebrew), vol. 3 (Tel Aviv: Zmora Bitan, 1987), 1560.

3. Matti Golan, *Peres* (in Hebrew) (Tel Aviv: Schocken, 1982), 123–24.

4. John W. Finney, "Israel Permits U.S. to Inspect Atomic Reactor," *New York Times*, 14 March 1965, 1, 8.

5. Avner Yaniv, *Politics and Strategy in Israel* (in Hebrew) (Tel Aviv: Sifriat Ha'Poalim, 1994), 199.

6. Editorial, *Ha'aretz* (in Hebrew), 16 March 1965.

7. *Ha'aretz* (in Hebrew), 17 March 1965.

8. *Lamerhav* (in Hebrew), 17 March 1965. Summary of the press commentary on this issue was forwarded to the Israeli embassy in the United States by the Foreign Ministry. See also Telegrams (161), 16 March 1965, (175), 17 March 1965, (197), 18 March 1965, (199), 18 March 1965, ISA, FMRG 3504/17.

9. *Davar* (in Hebrew), 13 May 1965.

10. Golan, *Peres*, 136.

11. Shimon Peres, *Battling for Peace: A Memoir* (New York: Random House, 1995), 98–99; Golan, *Peres*, 138–39.

12. Galili used to say, "only in 1965 did we become real partners in national decisions" (Arnan [Sini] Azaryahu, interview by author, Efal, June 1995).

13. Zvi Dinstein, interviews by author, Tel Aviv, 6 and 19 July 1992.

14. Ibid.; Avraham Hermoni, interview by author, Savyon, 24 August 1992; Munya M. Mardor, *Rafael* (in Hebrew) (Tel Aviv: Misrad Habitachon, 1981), 379–409.

15. Dinstein, interviews, 6 and 19 July 1992.

16. Ibid.; Hani Bergmann, interview by author, Jerusalem, 19 August 1992.

17. According to Dinstein, Pratt used to say that he reported only to Peres and Ben Gurion. When Eshkol became prime minister, Pratt hardly agreed to talk with him, asking, "Who should be coming to whom?" (Dinstein, interviews, 6 and 19 July 1992).

18. Former senior Ministry of Defense executives and scientists, interviews by author, 1994–95.

19. Yuval Ne'eman, interviews by author, Austin, Texas, 16 and 19 February 1994; 25 May 1995.

20. Ibid.

21. Dinstein (interviews, 6 and 19 July 1992) recalls his own discomfort about asking Pratt to leave. He remembers telling him, "Pratt, we have to part. You created something that will be remembered forever in our history, and I don't know if it could have been done without you, but just as Moses did not reach the Promised Land, so Manes must go." Pratt, the former official recalls, was stunned. "Do you tell me that I have to go? You must be joking," he responded. Dinstein interpreted that to mean, "What does he *really* want from me?"

22. Mardor, *Rafael*, 382.

23. Ibid., 382–83.

24. Dinstein, interview, 19 July 1992.

25. Mardor, *Rafael*, 383.

26. Ibid., 389.

27. Ibid., 383.

28. The interpretative gap between this "leading project" and the nuclear project was

first suggested by Aluf Benn, "The Age of Big Projects" (in Hebrew), *Ha'aretz*, 15 November 1991, B3.

29. Mardor, *Rafael*, 387–89.

30. Ibid., 390–98.

31. Ibid., 388–89.

32. Ibid., 391–98.

33. Elkana Gali (then editor of *Mabat Hadash*, a RAFI biweekly magazine), interview by author, Tel Aviv, 23 July 1992.

34. Mardor, *Rafael*, 400.

35. Ibid., 402–7.

36. Ibid., 405–9.

37. James Feron, "Israelis Honor Atom Scientist," *New York Times*, 14 May 1966, 3. On the occasion of his departure, Bergmann was the most explicit about Israel's nuclear capability, pointing out that "it's very important to understand that by developing atomic energy for peaceful purposes, you reach the nuclear option; there are no two atomic energies."

38. "The Resignation of the Professor" (in Hebrew), *Yediot Achronot*, 22 April 1966, 4; see also the exchange between Amos Elon and Shimon Peres (in Hebrew), *Ha'aretz*, 20 and 21 April 1966.

39. Mardor, *Rafael*, 404–5. The reforms Eshkol and Dinstein suggested did not ease concerns over the democratic control of the secret nuclear program, although Eshkol's style of governing was less autocratic than Ben Gurion's. The combination of a classified research program and an ambivalent political leadership may be hospitable to unauthorized activities.

40. Pierre Péan, *Les deux bombes* (Paris: Fayard, 1981), 120.

41. Mardor, *Rafael*, 409.

42. In February 1967 the Lebanese newspaper *Al-Hayat*, reported that "Israeli scientists trained in the United States exploded an underground atomic device in the Negev desert late last year" (sometime between 26 September and 3 October 1966). The newspaper said that "the blast occurred in a chamber 2,600 feet underground." Associated Press (AP) cited that report, and it appeared in various American newspapers (see, for example, *Las Vegas Review Journal*, 27 February 1967). The AP story was also cited in *Ha'aretz*, 26 February 1967. Prime Minister Eshkol denied the story with three words: "It is untrue" (*Ha'aretz*, 4 April 1967). See also a commentary on this issue in Thomas B. Cochran and Christopher E. Paine, *The Role of Hydronuclear Tests* (Washington, D.C.: NRDC, April 1995), 29. The author is grateful to Aluf Benn and Christopher Paine for bringing this information to his attention.

43. Memorandum, Ambassador Bunker to Rodger P. Davies, "NEA Views on the Israeli Desalting Project," 17 February 1967, RG 59, CFPF, 1967–69, E 11-3 ISR 1-1-67, Box 603A, USNA.

44. Pierre Langereux, "Dassault Lifts Veil over Jericho Missile," *Air & Cosmos/Aviation International*, 6 December 1996, cf. English translation in *FBIS Report*, FBIS-EST-97–1008.

45. John W. Finney, "Israel Said to Buy French Missiles," *New York Times*, 7 January 1966, 1, 8.

46. James Feron, "Mideast Atom Curb Is Urged by Eshkol," *New York Times*, 19 May 1966, 1, 11; "Eshkol: We Will Not be the First to Introduce Nuclear Weapons to the Middle East," (in Hebrew), *Ha'aretz*, 19 May 1966.

47. Ibid.

48. To the best I can determine, Eshkol's earliest public use of the phrase was on 1 July 1964, during his visit to Paris. In a press conference he stated: "I hope there are no nuclear weapons in the region, and I can promise that we will never be the first to introduce such a weapon. First, because that would be very expensive; second, because it negates our spiritual principles; and, third, because the accumulation of conventional weaponry is bad enough" (Amos Elon, "Eshkol on the Chances of Improving Arab-Israeli Relations: Willing to Meet with Khruschev—'We Will Not Be the First to Introduce Nuclear Weapons'" [in Hebrew], *Ha'aretz*, 2 July 1964).

49. "Protocol of Conversation with President Kennedy on April 2, 1963," ISA, FMRG 4326/16; Peres, *Battling for Peace*, 258; Peres, interview by author, Tel Aviv, 31 March 1991; also Golan, *Peres*, 125. See chapter 7, n. 22.

50. Peres, interview; Peres, *Battling for Peace*, 258.

51. Dinstein, interview, 19 July 1992. According to Dinstein, he and Ya'acov Herzog, anticipating the way Johnson might raise the nuclear issue, first proposed the formula. Moshe Zak, former editor of *Ma'ariv*, recalls that Ben Gurion used this formula in a 1962 meeting with newspaper editors (conversation with author, 1995).

52. Former senior official in Israel's Ministry of Defense, interview by author, Tel Aviv.

53. "Leaking, Leaking" (in Hebrew), *Ha'aretz*, 6 July 1966.

54. A former senior Israeli Ministry of Defense official, interview by author, Tel Aviv.

55. Ibid.

56. Yuval Ne'eman, interviews by author, 16 and 19 February 1994; 25 May 1995.

57. Avraham Tamir, interviews by author, Tel Aviv, 16 September 1992; July 1993.

58. Former senior civilian and military Ministry of Defense officials, interviews by author, 1992–94.

59. This argument was made by Yuval Ne'eman. Ne'eman supported Israel's advanced nuclear R&D, but he maintained that "nuclear weapons are not the answer to Israel's real security needs." In the early 1960s he opposed the adoption of a nuclear doctrine by the IDF. Years later, as a leader of Tehiya, a small right-wing party, he argued against the dovish advocates of an Israeli shift to reliance on nuclear weapons (those who argued that Israel could substitute the territories occupied in 1967 for an open nuclear deterrence posture). See Yuval Ne'eman, "Israel and Nuclear Deterrence" (in Hebrew), *Ma'archot* 308, 19–21.

60. Interviews with former senior officials who played a role in these matters in the 1960s, 1993–97.

61. Dinstein, interview, 19 July 1992. Dinstein recalled that Eshkol used to ask Bergmann, who always pushed for a way to conduct a test, "Do you think that the world would sit and applaud us for our achievement?"

62. Former senior civilian and military officials in Israel's Ministry of Defense, interviews.

63. Matti Peled (Chief of Logistics from 1966 to 1968), interviews by author, Tel Aviv, 9 and 16 July 1992.

64. Years later, now retired, both Ne'eman and Tamir expressed views about the dangers of legitimizing nuclear deterrence in the Middle East, and Israel's commitment to do its utmost to prevent the nuclearization of the region (Ne'eman, "Israel and Nuclear Deterrence"; also Ne'eman, interviews, 16 and 19 February 1994; 25 May 1995; Avraham Tamir, *A Soldier in Search of Peace* [in Hebrew] [Tel Aviv: Edanim, 1988], 232–33; also Tamir, interviews, 16 September 1992; July 1993).

65. Only in 1994, following a report on Israeli television, the IAEC confirmed that on 14 December 1966 an accident occurred in one of the labs at the Dimona facility. A technician was killed and three others injured. The accident, interpreted as a critical accident, required three months to dlean up, which ended in February 1967 (Alex Doron, "A Mysterious Accident in the Nuclear Reactor in Dimona" [in Hebrew], *Ma'ariv*, Special Supplement, 4–7).

66. *Jerusalem Post*, 3 February 1967. The publicity of the visit led Ambassador Barbout to "suggest that the Israeli Government is moving toward a more open attitude towards the Dimona nuclear complex vis-à-vis the public" (Airgram [A-494], "Dimona Nuclear Research Center," 10 February 1967, Box 141, LBJL).

67. In a letter dated 9 March 1967, marked "official-informal," to a State Department colleague concerning the desalting project, Barbour writes:

> I must confess that up until six months or so ago I was certain that the Israelis could not be persuaded to surrender their nuclear weapons option in return for the desalting project. A quid pro quo of this kind would be impossible for the GOI [government of Israel] to keep quiet and its revelation would arouse a storm of protest in many important political quarters here . . . But I believe that some new hopeful elements have recently entered into the picture. It is possible now to detect a lessening in determination to keep Nasser in the dark about what Israel's nuclear intentions are. Israeli awareness of the dangers of this course of action has been manifest in several of my recent conversations with the Prime Minister and the Foreign Minister . . . Moreover, my own impression . . . is that Dimona is not running at full blast.
>
> . . . The most promising device at present on the horizon is the possibility that Israel will open Dimona to an appreciable number of non-Israeli research scientists. As I have reported, Eban is thinking along that line and significantly (more significantly, I think, than the two "intelligence" reports which seem to be scaring everybody to death) at least one trial balloon has recently been lofted in that direction. (Letter, Ambassador Barbour to Rodger Davies, 9 March 1967, RG 59, CFPF, 1967–69, E 11-3 ISR 1-1-67, Box, 603A, USNA)

68. Avner Yaniv, *Politics and Strategy in Israel*, 199–200; Shlomo Aronson with Oded Brosh, *The Politics and Strategy of Nuclear Weapons in the Middle East: Opacity, Theory*

and Reality. 1960–1991: An Israeli Perspective (Albany: State University of New York Press, 1992), 83–111.

69. Eitan Haber, *Today War Will Break Out: The Reminiscences of Brig. Gen. Israel Lior* (in Hebrew) (Tel Aviv: Edanim, 1987), 54–57, 67–70, 97–99.

13. THE ARABS AND DIMONA

1. An Egyptian physicist, studying at the Argonne National Laboratory in Illinois, noticed that two Israeli scientists, also working at Argonne, were interested in plutonium processing, and he reported his suspicions to the Egyptian government (Shyam Bhatia, *Nuclear Rivals in the Middle East* [London: Routledge, 1988], 54, 108–9). In 1992 Mohammed Heikal said that in 1957 Egypt first recognized that Israel had started a nuclear weapons program (Mohammed Heikal, *Illusions of Triumph: An Arab View of the Gulf War* [London: Harper and Collins, 1992], 72).

2. John W. Finney, "U.S. Misled at First on Israeli Reactor," *New York Times*, 20 December 1960, 1, 15.

3. Ariel E. Levite and Emily B. Landau, *Israel's Nuclear Image: Arab Perceptions of Israel's Nuclear Posture* (in Hebrew) (Tel Aviv: Papyrus, 1994), 73.

4. "Nasser Threatens Israel on A-Bomb," *New York Times*, 24 December 1960, 6.

5. For example, the issue was raised in a conversation between Robert Strong of the State Department and Shimon Peres during the latter's visit to Washington in May 1962 (ISA, FMRG, 4317/1; Ambassador William Crawford [then in charge of Lebanon-Israel affairs in the State Department], interview by author, Washington, D.C., July 1997).

6. Levite and Landau, *Israel's Nuclear Image*, 73.

7. Letter, Foreign Minister Mahmoud Fawzi to Secretary of State Dean Rusk, 16 September 1961, Department of State, Central Files (CF), 1960–63, Box 2057, USNA.

8. Levite and Landau, *Israel's Nuclear Image*, 39, 64, 73–74.

9. "While Nasser from time to time will try to use the Israeli issue to distract attention from internal difficulties, it is highly unlikely that he would intentionally embark on a course that would lead to large-scale hostilities" (Research Memorandum, U.S. Department of State, Bureau of Intelligence and Research, "The Outlook for Nasser," 30 October 1961, Department of State, CF, 1960–63, Box 2057, USNA).

10. Levite and Landau, *Israel's Nuclear Image*, 73.

11. It was not discussed even at the level of the UAR ambassador in Washington. For example, twice when Ambassador Mustafa Kamel discussed U.S.-UAR relations with Johnson on 25 May and 10 August 1964, the nuclear issue was not raised (Memorandum of Conversation, Ambassador Mustafa Kamel with President Lyndon B. Johnson; National Security Files [NSF], Box 158, LBJL).

12. Telegram (A-767), Ambassador John Badeau to Rusk, 18 April 1963, RG 59, CFPF, February–December 1963, POL UAR, USNA.

13. Ibid.

14. Ibid.

15. Telegram (3479), Rusk to Badeau, 15 June 1963, in *FRUS, 1961–63*, vol. 18, 594.

16. Telegram (2470), Badeau to Rusk, 28 June 1963, in *FRUS, 1961–63*, vol. 18, 610.

17. Also, Hermann F. Eilts, telephone interview by author, 23 May 1997.

18. Telegram (2491), Badeau to Rusk, 30 June 1963, in *FRUS, 1961–63*, vol. 18, 616.

19. Ibid., 618; Eilts, interview, 23 May 1997.

20. Memorandum, Robert W. Komer, National Security Council, to President John F. Kennedy, 3 July 1963, in *FRUS, 1961–63*, vol. 18, 623; Eilts, interview, 23 May 1997.

21. Telegram (121), Rusk to Badeau, 7 July 1963, in *FRUS, 1961–63*, vol. 18, 635.

22. Ibid., 636.

23. Ibid., 637.

24. Ibid.

25. Telegram (A-737), Badeau to the Department of State, "Various Aspects of U.S.-UAR Relations," 11 April 1964, NSF, Country File—UAR, Box 158, LBJL.

26. In a memo to Johnson on the eve of Eshkol's visit, Komer wrote the following on the matter of reassuring Nasser:

> We appreciate Israel's commitment to regular inspection but are disturbed at Eshkol's refusal to let us reassure the Arabs in general terms (you sent Eshkol two messages on this). We're firmly convinced that Israel's apparent desire to keep the Arabs guessing is highly dangerous. To appear to be going nuclear without really doing so is to invite trouble. It might park Nasser into a foolish preemptive move. (Memorandum, Komer to Johnson, 29 May 1964, NSF, Country File—Israel, Box 143, LBJL)

27. Robert W. Komer, interviews by author, Washington, D.C., 22 June 1992; 11 January 1995.

28. Embtel (5567), George W. Ball to American Embassy, Cairo, 26 May 1964, NSF, Country File—UAR, Box 158, LBJL.

29. Ibid.

30. Komer, interview, 11 January 1995.

31. Embtel (5592), Ball to American Embassy, Cairo, 29 May 1964, NSF, Country File—UAR, Box 158, LBJL.

32. Memorandum, McGeorge Bundy to Johnson, 3 August 1964, NSF, Box 159, LBJL. At about that time the U.S. Embassy in Cairo reported that Egypt was interested in acquiring a nuclear power reactor, but that it had no interest in concluding an IAEA safeguard agreement nor any other bilateral agreement that the United States would require (Embtel [363], Boswell to Rusk, 29 July 1964, NSF, Box 159, LBJL).

33. Memorandum, Rusk to Johnson, n.d., National Security Files, Box 159, LBJL.

34. The minutes of the McCloy-Nasser meeting are still classified. The two-page memorandum of the meeting McCloy gave Dean Rusk is available at the LBJL (Memorandum of Conversation, John McCloy with Rusk, NSF, Box 159, LBJL).

35. This attitude was evident in Nasser's public statements. In an interview he gave the British *Observer* on 4 July 1964, the Egyptian leader said that although the Dimona reactor was capable of producing nuclear weapons, according to the information Egypt had,

it was not used for that purpose (Mordechai Oren, "Israel as a Nuclear Factor" [in Hebrew], *Al-Hamishmar*, 18 November 1966).

36. John W. Finney, "Israel Permits U.S. to Inspect Atomic Reactor," *New York Times*, 14 March 1965, 1, 8; Telegram, Ball to Battle, 6 April 1965, RG 59, CFPF, 1964–66, POL UAR, USNA.

37. Telegram, Ball to Battle, 6 April 1965, RG 59, CFPF, 1964–66, POL UAR, USNA.

38. Embtel (3653), Battle to Rusk, 18 April 1965 (section 1 of 4), NSF, Box 159, LBJL.

39. Ibid.

40. Ibid.

41. The program did not bear fruit because its scientists were unable to overcome technical problems involving the missiles' guidance system and the weight of the warhead. According to Robert Komer, the German scientists were "leftovers" from the few Second World War German scientists who, in the 1950s, worked for the French rocket program. The number of scientists who went to Egypt was small, perhaps fewer than half a dozen. The CIA, which kept tabs on these scientists, knew from the start that they had difficulties with developing guidance systems and that the Egyptian project would not be of value militarily as long as those problems remained unsolved (Komer, interview, 11 January 1995).

42. The military interest behind the Egyptian effort to develop a national nuclear program was apparent in the interviews Jim Walsh conducted in Egypt in 1994–95 on the history of the Egyptian nuclear program (Jim Walsh, "Nuclear Threats, Resources Constraints and State Behavior: Egypt's Nuclear-Decision Making, 1955–1992" [paper presented at the Western Political Science Association Meeting, 10 March 1994]; Jim Walsh, "Why States Don't 'Go Nuclear'" [paper presented at the American Political Science Association Meeting, San Francisco, 31 August 1995]). For more on the Egyptian nuclear weapons program in the 1960s and the pro-bomb advocacy of Salah Heydayat, see Bhatia, *Nuclear Rivals in the Middle East*, 51–56; Tayser N. Nashif, *Nuclear Warfare in the Middle East: Dimensions and Responsibilities* (Princeton, N.J.: Kingston, 1984).

43. William Foster wrote in *Foreign Affairs* that both India and Israel could develop nuclear weapons shortly; Elyahu Salpeter, "Israel Has the Knowledge to Produce Nuclear Weapons" (in Hebrew), *Ha'aretz*, 18 July 1965; Elyahu Salpeter, "Increased Worry in Washington about Proliferation of Nuclear Possession" (in Hebrew), *Ha'aretz*, 26 June 1965; Senator Robert Kennedy made a similar point in a speech in Congress in June. Glenn Seaborg, in a press interview, also made the point that Israel had the knowledge and capability to produce nuclear weapons (see Salpeter, "Israel Has the Knowledge to Produce Nuclear Weapons").

44. Leonard Beaton, *Must the Bomb Spread?* (London: Penguin, 1966).

45. John W. Finney, "Israel Said to Buy French Missiles," *New York Times*, 7 January 1966, 1, 18.

46. This debate was monitored in Israel. The Israeli intelligence services' translation unit, *Chatzav*, the equivalent to the U.S. Foreign Broadcast Information Service (FBIS), translated the Arab debate into Hebrew and made it available to Israeli journalists. For Israeli summaries of this debate, see Ze'ev Schiff, "Arab Pretexts for Preventive War Against Israel" (in Hebrew), *Ha'aretz*, 28 January 1966; Eliezer Ben Moshe, "Israeli Atom

in the Eyes of the Arab" (in Hebrew), *La'merhav*, 11 February 1966. For a historical retrospective, see Ariel E. Levite and Emily B. Landau, "Arab Perceptions of Israel's Nuclear Posture, 1960–67," *Israel Studies* 1, no. 1 (spring 1996): 34–59.

47. "Cairo Editor Says Israel Plans to Test Nuclear Device Soon," *New York Times*, 21 August 1965, 2; Hedrick Smith, "Soviet Said to Offer Cairo Atom Defense," *New York Times*, 4 February 1966, 1, 12; Mohammed Heikal's article was also translated into Hebrew and was published in a shortened version in "Is Israel Capable of Producing an Atomic Bomb?" *Ha'aretz*, 25 August 1965.

48. Smith, "Soviet Said to Offer Cairo Atom Defense," 1, 12; Mohammed Heikal, "Israel Will Reach Nuclear Weapons Production Capability Within Three Years" (in Hebrew), *Ma'ariv*, 15 October 1965.

49. Smith, "Soviet Said to Offer Cairo Atom Defense," 1, 12.

50. *Daily Telegraph*, 26 January 1966, cited in Yossef Lapid, "*Daily Telegraph*: Egypt Informed Arab Representatives That It Is Engaged in Nuclear Research Capable of Being Adopted to Military Needs" (in Hebrew), *Ma'ariv*, 27 January 1966.

51. "Nasser Cites Need for Nuclear Arms," *New York Times*, 9 May 1966, 8. 19.

52. Hedrick Smith, "Warning on Bomb Given by Nasser," *New York Times*, 21 February 1966, 8; Hedrick Smith, "Nasser Says U.S. and Britain Back His Rightest Foes," *New York Times*, 23 February 1966, 1, 2, "Nasser Threatens to War on a Nuclear Armed Israel," *New York Times*, 18 April 1966, 6; "Nasser Cites Need for Nuclear Arms," *New York Times*, 9 May 1966, 8.

14. THE SIX-DAY WAR

1. Donald Neff, *Warriors for Jerusalem: The Six Days That Changed the Middle East* (New York: Simon and Schuster, 1984); Avner Yaniv, *Deterrence Without the Bomb: The Politics of Israeli Strategy* (Lexington, Mass.: Lexington Books, 1987), 109–25; Michael Brecher, with Benjamin Geist, *Decisions in Crisis: Israel 1967 and 1973* (Berkeley: University of California Press, 1980); Janice Gross Stein and Raymond Tanter, *Rational Decision-Making: Israel's Security Choices, 1967* (Columbus: Ohio State University Press, 1980); Michael Bar-Zohar, *Embassies in Crisis: Diplomats and Demagogues Behind the Six Day War* (Englewood Cliffs, N.J.: Prentice Hall, 1970); Richard B. Parker, *The Politics of Miscalculation in the Middle East* (Bloomington: Indiana University Press, 1993); Eitan Haber, *Today War Will Break Out:: The Reminiscences of Brig. General Israel Lior, Aide-de-Camp to Prime Ministers Levi Eshkol and Golda Meir* (in Hebrew) (Tel Aviv: Edanim, 1987); Moshe Gilboa, *Shesh Shanim, Shisha Yamim: Mekoroteiah Ve'koroteiah shel Milchemet Sheshet Hayamim* (Six years, six days: Origins and history of the Six-Day War) (Tel Aviv: Am Oved, 1968); Yitzhak Rabin, *The Rabin Memoirs* (Boston: Little, Brown, 1979), 67–99; Indar Jit Rikhye, *The Sinai Blunder* (London: Frank Cass, 1980).

2. The decisions relating to nuclear weapons were suppressed for years. As part of its opaque nuclear posture, Israel has had an interest in belittling or even ignoring these decisions. Israeli publications on the crisis, especially the memoirs of principal deci-

sionmakers, are vague about nuclear issues. The Israeli military censor has only recently become more lenient about the issue. U.S. documents referring to the nuclear dimensions of the crisis had also been classified for years, and some of them have only recently been declassified.

3. Aluf Benn, "The First Nuclear War" (in Hebrew), *Ha'aretz*, 11 June 1993, B1. Oblique confirmation of these flights, without mentioning Dimona specifically, appeared in the longer, Hebrew version of *The Rabin Memoirs* (Yitzhak Rabin, *Pinkas Sherut* [Tel Aviv: Ma'ariv, 1979], 136–37, 163–66); also Haber, *Today War Will Break Out*, 161–63, 187–86, 208.

4. These questions have hardly been explored. Two recent publications, both by Israeli researchers, discuss the nuclear issue in the context of that war. Shlomo Aronson was the first to suggest that Israeli nuclear ambiguity over Dimona "might have generated" the 1967 war, and that Nasser's initial moves and subsequent escalation aimed to prevent Israel from acquiring nuclear weapons (Shlomo Aronson with Oded Brosh, *The Politics and Strategy of Nuclear Weapons in the Middle East: Opacity, Theory, and Reality, 1960–1991: An Israeli Perspective* [Albany: State University of New York Press, 1992], 109–18). Aronson, however, does not rely on concrete historical evidence concerning Nasser's intentions or strategy. He admits that "we do not know which was the primary motive" for Nasser's action (109). More recently Ariel Levite and Emily Landau, in a study on Arab perceptions of the Israeli nuclear posture, raised the question of the role of nuclear weapons in the Six-Day War. However, they do not reach a firm conclusion: "This historical issue remains for now still a mystery" (Ariel E. Levite and Emily B. Landau, *Israel's Nuclear Image: Arab Perceptions of Israel's Nuclear Posture* [in Hebrew] [Tel Aviv: Papyrus, 1994], 41–42).

5. Parker, *The Politics of Miscalculation in the Middle East*, 37.

6. Embtel 8080 (Cairo), Richard H. Nolte to Secretary of State Dean Rusk, 27 May 1967, cited in Parker, *The Politics of Miscalculation in the Middle East*, 242.

7. These questions cannot be answered with certainty. Most of the Egyptian material is not available for research, and Nasser and Amer died shortly after the war before writing their memoirs. Materials of this kind in any case would likely have been self-serving. In addition to the open literature, my answer is based on recently declassified U.S. archival material, oral testimonies, and my understanding of earlier Egyptian patterns of dealing with the Israeli nuclear issue.

8. Department of State, "Current Status of US-UAR Relations," n.d. (but prepared for the meeting between President Johnson and Egyptian Ambassador Kamel on 12 August 1966), NSF, Box 159, LBJL.

9. In their study of the way the Arab press dealt with the Israeli nuclear program, Levite and Landau found almost no references to Dimona in the Egyptian press during early 1967 (Levite and Landau, *Israel's Nuclear Image*, 41).

10. "Memorandum of Conversation," the White House, 23 February 1966, NSF: UAR, Box 159, LBJL.

11. Ibid., 12 August 1966.

12. Memorandum, Walt W. Rostow to President Johnson, "Our Latest Brush with Nasser," NSF: UAR, Box 159, LBJL.

13. Lucius Battle, interview by author, Washington, D.C., 27 December 1994; Richard Parker, interviews by author, Washington, D.C., 23 and 26 December 1994. In January 1969 the Historical Studies Division of the State Department completed a comprehensive and authoritative study entitled "United States Policy and Diplomacy in the Middle East Crisis," based on all the material related to the crisis in the files of the U.S. Department of State. This study was recently declassified almost in its entirety. It does not include even a single reference that could suggest that the 1967 war was a replay of the Badeau-Komer scenarios of 1964. From this study, too, one gets the impression that from the American perspective, the Israeli nuclear issue played no role in the 1967 crisis (NSF, NSC-History, Box 20 [Middle East Crisis], LBJL).

14. Battle, interview, 27 December 1994; Parker, interviews, 23 and 26 December 1994. See also Parker, *The Politics of Miscalculation in the Middle East*, 92, 104–7.

15. Battle, interview, 27 December 1994. Also Parker, *The Politics of Miscalculation*, 92.

16. Battle, interview, 27 December 1994.

17. His interviewees never raised the issue of Dimona, but Parker made it clear that he did not ask them about it either. He acknowledged that when he researched his book, he was unaware of the Egyptian reconnaissance flights over Dimona in May 1967 (though he knew from Egyptian sources that a reconnaissance flight took place over Beer Sheba), and he was not aware of the prominence of Dimona in Egyptian contingency air strikes on Israel. Had he been aware of those issues, he would have explored the question more thoroughly (Parker, interviews, 23 and 26 December 1994).

18. Among the Egyptians to whom Parker is referring are Anwar Sadat, Hassanein Heikal, Mahmoud Riad (foreign minister in 1967), General Muhammad Fawzi (chief of staff), Sayeed Marei (Sadat's deputy in the National Assembly), General Murtagi (commander of the Sinai front). Heikal, editor of *Al-Ahram* and Nasser's closest confidant, provided the most detailed apologetic account of Nasser's actions and decisions in his (Heikal's) thousand-page volume *1967—The Explosion* (in Arabic), published in Arabic in 1990 by *Al-Ahram*.

19. In his memoirs Fawzi accounts for two occasions on which the idea was entertained. The first was in 1965, when the First Division returned from Yemen; "another time this hope was mentioned [was] when Marshal Amer went to Pakistan in 1966. From there he sent a telegram to Nasser proposing to send troops to Sharm Al Shaykh, and to threaten Israel with closure of the straits. Until now no one knows the reason for that message. Nothing was done about it" (cited in Parker, *The Politics of Miscalculation in the Middle East*, 91).

20. Parker, *The Politics of Miscalculation in the Middle East*, 75–82.

21. Rikhye, *The Sinai Blunder*, 168.

22. Ehud Ya'ari, "June 1967: How Nasser Was Lured into War," *Jerusalem Report*, 4 June 1992, 14–18. According to Ya'ari, new historical material, including "material from newly opened archives, as well as the memoirs of Egyptian generals and civilian leaders," indicates that,

> none of the leaders of Middle East countries wanted all-out war in 1967. It
> shows that the real culprit of 1967 was Abd al-Hakim Amer, Egypt's vice pres-

ident and commander in chief, an overconfident blunderer who recklessly pushed his country into the fateful confrontation with Israel. . . . He was certain Israel would not attack even after Eilat was blockaded; he failed to prepare defenses, and he did not respond to Nasser's own warnings of an impending Israeli attack. (Ibid., 14)

23. On 7 April 1967 Israel engaged Syrian planes in an air battle deep inside Syria and shot down six Syrian MiGs, demonstrating Syrian vulnerability. A month later Rabin publicly warned the Syrian regime.

24. According to Heikal, Nasser's miscalculation started in a meeting with Amer on the evening of 13 May at Nasser's home, prompted by the Soviet warning. Both took the Soviet warning seriously and felt that this time, given the Egyptian-Syrian defense pact, Egypt must take military action. The two agreed, according to this version, that supporting Syria required a demonstration of force by deploying troops into the Sinai. They also recognized that something would have to be done with regard to UNEF, but they were divided on what exactly should be done. Amer thought that Egypt should use the moment to ask for the total withdrawal of UNEF, as he had suggested in the past. Nasser, however, was more cautious, deciding that Egypt's request should be limited to the withdrawal of UNEF from the 1948 lines in the Sinai. This was also General Rikhye's view: "It seemed clear, therefore, that Nasser never wanted or even approved complete withdrawal of UNEF at this stage, and his subsequent statements to this effect would, therefore, appear to be valid" (*The Sinai Blunder*, 160).

25. According to Rikhye, the commander of UNEF, the primary reason for the Egyptian request was tactical, not political, to allow them to dominate the hills near the international border (ibid., 160, 168).

26. Rikhye makes the point that the Egyptians may have had reasons for expecting that their request be complied with at the military level (ibid., 161).

27. Embtel 1517 (Lisbon), Robert Anderson to President Johnson, 2 June 1967, NSF, NSC History, Box 18, LBJL.

28. This judgment is based on viewing the absence of evidence as evidence. This absence of evidence may be an indication of deception, perhaps indicating that the nuclear issue did play a significant role in Nasser's thinking, but this is unlikely. If the Israeli nuclear issue played a critical role in Nasser's decision to initiate the 1967 crisis, it is likely that some support for this notion would have emerged by now. The reality is, however, that thirty years after the event, there is still no shred of evidence to support the claim. Human nature and political realities would have seen to it that the role of nuclear weapons, if any, would have become public knowledge by now.

While there is no evidence that nuclear weapons played a role in initiating the 1967 crisis, there is plenty of circumstantial evidence—the kind of evidence historians rely on—to support the contrary claim. In 1967 Nasser did not talk about the nuclear question openly as he did a year earlier. He also did not raise the issue in diplomatic contacts with the two superpowers in order to pressure Israel to open its nuclear facilities to outside inspections. Nasser also did not share his concerns about nuclear weapons with his associates, among them Heikal, Sadat, Riad, and Fawzi.

29. Parker, *The Politics of Miscalculation in the Middle East*, 43.

30. Benn, "The First Nuclear War," B1. Oblique confirmation of these flights, without mentioning Dimona specifically, appeared in Rabin, *Pinkas Sherut*, 136–37, 163–66; also Haber, *Today War Will Break Out*, 161–63, 187–86, 208.

31. Levite and Landau, *Israel's Nuclear Image*, 41, 65.

32. William B. Quandt, *Decade of Decisions: American Policy Towards the Arab-Israeli Conflict, 1967–1976* (Berkeley: University of California Press, 1977), 512; Ehud Ya'ari, "June 1967," 17–18.

33. Yaniv, *Deterrence Without the Bomb*, 84.

34. Rabin, *The Rabin Memoirs*, 56–57.

35. Avner Yaniv, *Politics and Strategy in Israel* (in Hebrew) (Tel Aviv: Sifriat Ha'Poalim, 1994), 154–56; also Rabin, *The Rabin Memoirs*, 56–57.

36. Rabin, *The Rabin Memoirs*, 68; Bar-Zohar, *Embassies in Crisis*, 21.

37. Rabin, *The Rabin Memoirs*, 68–69; Haber, *Today War Will Break Out*, 147–51; Dov Goldstein, "Interview with Ezer Weizman" (in Hebrew), *Ma'ariv*, 5 June 1973.

38. Parker, *The Politics of Miscalculation in the Middle East*, 43, 89–90.

39. See Brecher, *Decisions in Crisis*, 35–50.

40. Letter, Johnson to Prime Minister Levi Eshkol, 17 May 1967, Box 17, NSF, LBJL; also, Memorandum, Rostow to President Johnson, "Urgent Message to Eshkol," 17 May 1967, NSF, NSC History, Box 17, LBJL.

41. Haber, *Today War Will Break Out*, 152.

42. Brecher, *Decisions in Crisis*, 230–34.

43. Rikhye, *The Sinai Blunder*, 14–62.

44. Rabin, *Pinkas Sherut*, 137; also Bar-Zohar, *Embassies in Crisis*, 36–37.

45. Ezer Weizman, *On Eagle's Wings* (New York: Macmillan, 1976), 183–87.

46. This was recently acknowledged by Mordechai Hod, former commander of the Israeli Air Force (IAF), in Aluf Benn, "The First Nuclear War," B1.

47. Shimon Peres, "The Time Dimension" (in Hebrew), *Ma'arachot* 146 (1962): 3–5.

48. "Israel Is Ready to Thwart Egyptian Action" (in Hebrew), *Ha'aretz*, 22 February 1966.

49. James Feron, "Mideast Atom Curb Is Urged by Eshkol," *New York Times*, 19 May 1966, 1, 14; also "Eshkol: We Will Not Be the First to Introduce Nuclear Weapons to the Middle East" (in Hebrew), *Ha'aretz*, 19 May 1966.

50. For Hod's comment, see Benn, "The First Nuclear War," B1; also former senior IDF officers (active in 1966–67), interviews by author.

51. Yigal Allon, "The Last Stage of the War of Independence" (in Hebrew), *Ot* (November 1967): 5–13.

52. Rabin, *The Rabin Memoirs*, 70.

53. Haber, *Today War Will Break Out*, 153; Bar-Zohar, *Embassies in Crisis*, 35–41; Rabin, *The Rabin Memoirs*, 69–70.

54. Egypt's demand for the withdrawal of UNEF from the international border was broadcast by Cairo radio at 6:00 A.M. The Israeli Defense Ministerial Committee, which convened at 11:00 A.M., already knew about this move. In the meeting, however, Eshkol

still considered the Egyptian move to be primarily political posturing, not an indication of plans for war. Rabin's statement before the Knesset committee was also that morning.

55. Haber, *Today War Will Break Out*, 161.

56. Ibid., 62–63.

57. Rabin, *The Rabin Memoirs*, 85–86.

58. Former senior U.S. intelligence official, numerous interviews by the author, summer 1996.

59. Memorandum, Rostow to Johnson, 25 May 1967, 6:00 P.M., NSF, NSC History, Box 17, LBJL.

60. Quandt, *Decade of Decisions*, 36–37; also Bar-Zohar, *Embassies in Crisis*, 114–15.

61. Haber, *Today War Will Break Out*, 186; Benn, "The First Nuclear War," B1.

62. Rabin, *The Rabin Memoirs*, 89–90; cf. Moshe Dayan, *Story of My Life* (London: Weidenfeld and Nicolson, 1976), 259.

63. Quandt, *Decade of Decisions*, 51 n. 38. According to another version, after the blockade was imposed there was mounting pressure on Nasser by his general staff to attack first. At a meeting of the Egyptian general staff on 25 May Nasser was told that Egypt should be prepared for some hard blows from the air, and then to retaliate. Despite pleas from his air force chief to attack first, Nasser said, "We have a political decision not to start a war" (Ehud Ya'ari, "How Nasser Was Lured into War," 14–18).

64. Telegram (203943), Johnson to Eshkol, 27 May 1967, NSF History, Box 17, LBJL.

65. Rabin, *The Rabin Memoirs*, 91–92; Haber, *Today War Will Break Out*, 191–93; Bar-Zohar, *Embassies in Crisis*, 137–43; Brecher, *Decisions in Crisis*, 144–48.

66. Yossi Melman, "They Did Not Sit Shivah" (in Hebrew), *Ha'aretz*, 30 May, 1997, 16.

67. Haber, *Today War Will Break Out*, 205, 207.

68. In the 1979 Hebrew version of his memoirs, *A Service Record*, which is longer than the English version, Rabin only hints at the issue (136–37, 163–66). In Israel Lior's memoirs, written by Haber (*Today War Will Break Out*), the issue appears in various ways, but always in code ("sensitive strategic site").

69. General Yariv, who died in 1994, acknowledged the issue in passing at private occasions in recent years. General Hod's comments were cited in Aluf Benn, "The First Nuclear War," B1.

70. Memorandum for the Record, "Record of National Security Council Meeting Held on May 24, 1967, at 12 Noon—Discussion of Middle East Crisis," NSF, NSC History, Box 17, LBJL. Thirty years later Helms confirmed that he knew at the time that this statement needed qualifications. He was aware of the reports that Israel probably had a chemical separation plant, and that Israel might have been six to eight weeks from producing a nuclear weapon. There was no official National Intelligence Estimate that accepted these reports, however. The last AEC visit took place only six weeks earlier and revealed no weapon-related activities. Under the circumstances, he thought it would be a mistake to raise the possibility and unconfirmed reports (Helms, interview, February 1996). As another senior American intelligence officer recalls, the Operational side of the CIA, those "in the know," would have *never* either contributed to or commented on NIEs referring to Israel (interview, 1998).

71. Munya M. Mardor, *Rafael* (Tel Aviv: Misrad Habitachon, 1981), 499.

72. Myer Feldman recalls that, early on, elements within the U.S. government knew or estimated that the Israelis had two nuclear bombs: "I remember very well the number two" (Myer Feldman, interview by author, Washington, D.C., 22 June 1992). Other credible sources have confirmed Feldman's comments.

73. Shlomo Nakdimon, *Toward the Zero Hour: The Drama That Preceded the Six-Day War* (in Hebrew) (Tel Aviv: Ramdor, 1968); Gilboa, *Shesh Shanim, Shisha Yamim* (Six years, six days); Haber, *Today War Will Break Out*, 177–89.

74. Shimon Peres, *Battling for Peace: Memoirs* (London: Weidenfeld and Nicolson, 1995), 166–67.

75. In 1992 the Israeli newspaper *Yediot Achronot* published the story of a Soviet immigrant who had served on a Soviet submarine in the Middle East during the 1967 war. According to him, the submarine was prepared to hit Israeli targets on orders (Yehudit Yechezkelli, "We Were to Order the Launch of a Nuclear Missile on Israel" [in Hebrew], *Yediot Achronot Magazine—Shivah Yamim*, 8 May 1992).

15. TOWARD OPACITY

1. Hedrick Smith, "U.S Assumes the Israelis Have A-Bomb or Its Parts," *New York Times*, 18 July 1970.

2. When Dayan took office he was briefed on the state of the project, including the contingency plans that had been prepared. He commented to his briefer that "this time, there was no need for any of that."

3. The 1954–55 period, during which the two functions were divided between Moshe Sharett and Pinhas Lavon, was too brief to set a precedent.

4. Eitan Haber, *Today War Will Break Out: The Reminiscences of Brig. Gen. Israel Lior* (in Hebrew) (Tel Aviv: Edanim, 1987), 184; Moshe Dayan, *Story of My Life* (New York: Morrow, 1976), 422–23; Yoram Peri, *Between Battles and Ballots* (New York: Cambridge University Press, 1983), 136–37; Yehudah Ben Meir, *Civil-Military Relations in Israel* (New York: Columbia University Press, 1995), 101.

5. Peri, *Between Battles and Ballots*, 137–38; Ben Meir, *Civil-Military Relations in Israel*, 102.

6. Joseph Burg, interview by author, Jerusalem, 19 August 1992. Burg was a leader of the National Religious Party and a cabinet member during that period.

7. Dayan, *Story of My Life*, 338–39.

8. Personal communication with a former senior Israeli official.

9. "Israel Said to Plan to Make Atom Bomb," *New York Times*, 14 June 1967. Whether the story was a deliberate leak is not clear. The military censor did not clear the dispatch, and the Canadian Press was unable to report the story from Tel Aviv. According to the dispatch, "sources in Tel Aviv say it is likely that the Israeli government will make a formal decision to join the nuclear 'club' as soon as a Middle Eastern peace agreement is worked out." On the same day officials at the U.S. State Department denied that the Israeli government was intent on acquiring nuclear weapons.

10. Ibid.

11. "An A-Bomb for Israel," *Newsweek*, 17 July 1967.

12. *Ha'aretz* (in Hebrew), 21 July 1967.

13. "Motions to Discuss the NPT Were Removed" (in Hebrew), *Ha'aretz*, 8 August 1968.

14. Minutes from the meeting of the Israeli cabinet, 27 October 1968

15. Seymour M. Hersh, *The Samson Option: Israel's Nuclear Arsenal and American Foreign Policy* (New York: Random House, 1991), 173–74.

16. Smith, "U.S. Assumes"; Hersh, *The Samson Option*, 173–81.

17. Smith, "U.S. Assumes."

18. Foreign Ministry minutes, "A Discussion on Israeli-U.S. Relationship," 13 June 1963, ISA, FMRG 3377/6 (author's translation).

19. Mordechai Gazit, interview by author, August 1996.

20. Telegram (1093), Walworth Barbour to the Secretary of State, 24 March 1969.

21. Yitzhak Rabin, *A Service Record* (in Hebrew), vol. 2 (Tel Aviv: Sifriat Ma'ariv, 1979), 251–52.

22. Former senior Israeli official, interview by author.

23. John W. Finney, "Israelis Reported to Be Reluctant at This Time to Sign Treaty Barring Spread of Nuclear Arms," *New York Times*, 20 November 1968.

24. Yigal Allon reformulated his opposition to nuclear deterrence:

> A discussion of the problem of nuclear weapons is, practically speaking, irrel-evant to the situation in the Middle East in the conceivable future because it [nuclear weapons] does not exist in any of the region's states. However, it can be said theoretically that if it [were] possible to achieve nuclear balance this would not have been a guarantee against war. Nuclear balance would deny Israel the advantage of conventional weapons, in which the character of the regime, its social structure and the quality of the soldier are decisive aspects of the balance of power. At the same time we must not allow the enemy to reach any advantage in the nuclear area. We must continue maintaining a high level of nuclear research and technology for peaceful and developmental purposes, that will not allow the enemy to catch us. I accept the public statement of Prime Minister Levi Eshkol, that "Israel will not be the first to introduce nuclear weapons to the Middle East." But I will permit myself to add that we should never allow the enemy to be the first one either. If we had, hypotheti-cally speaking, the choice between nuclear weapons for both sides, or to none, we should prefer conventional over nuclear balance. (*Curtain of Sand* [in Hebrew] [Tel Aviv: Hakibbutz Hameuchad, 1968], 2nd ed., 401–2)

This statement captures one of the points of view in the debate of the early 1960s. In 1968 Allon knew of Israel's nuclear-weapon capabilities, but he argued that his position was the policy of Israel.

25. Dayan, *Story of My Life*, 490–92; Haber, *Today War Will Break Out*, 271.

26. President Gamal Abdul Nasser, Cairo radio on 23 November 1967, and the BBC,

on 25 November 1967, quoted in Ya'acov Bar-Siman-Tov, *The Israeli-Egyptian War of Attrition, 1969–70* (New York: Columbia University Press, 1980), 213–14.

27. Before the war the entire combat force of the IAF (about 180 jets on the eve of the war) consisted of French aircraft; two-thirds of them were older jets scheduled to be phased out in the coming years. The prewar plans of the IAF aimed at a force of about 250 modern combat aircraft by the end of 1968 by adding 48 American Skyhawks (A-4H) and 50 French Mirages (with an option for another 50) (see Eliezer Cohen, *Israel's Best Defense* [New York: Crown, 1993], 252–53).

28. Ibid., 269–71; Haber, *Today War Will Break Out*, 195–96. The situation of the IAF was a matter of discussion between Ambassador Harman and Vice President Humphrey on 30 November 1967 (see Memorandum, Humphrey to Johnson, 12 December 1967, White House Central Files [WHCF], Confidential File (CF), Box 34, National Archives).

29. Peter Grose, "Israeli Industry Easing Dependence on Foreign Arms," *New York Times*, 23 April 1971.

30. Dayan, *Story of My Life*, 437–38; William Beecher, "Israel Building Prototype for a Jet Fighter-Bomber," *New York Times*, 15 September 1971; Grose, "Israeli Industry Easing Dependence on Foreign Arms."

31. Aharon Klienman and Reuven Pedatzur, *Rearming Israel: Defense Procurement through the 1990s* (Jerusalem: Jaffe Center for Strategic Studies, 1991), 75–77.

32. The United States did not retract its contractual obligations. Its suspension decision had no effect—in early August the administration had already exempted $3 million worth of military items that Israel urgently needed—and it was assumed that the suspension would be lifted altogether before the December 1967 delivery of the Skyhawks.

33. Finney, "Israelis Reported to Be Reluctant."

34. By late 1970, when the Russian presence in Egypt reached its peak, there were about fourteen thousand Russian military personnel in Egypt (Drew Middleton, "14,000 Russians Play Big Role in Egypt," *New York Times*, 3 October 1970).

35. Ze'ev Schiff, *Phantom Over the Nile: The Story of the Israeli Air Corps* (in Hebrew) (Haifa: Shikmona, 1970); Bar-Siman-Tov, *The Israeli-Egyptian War of Attrition*; Dan Schueftan, *Attrition: Egypt Post-War Political Strategy, 1967–1970* (in Hebrew) (Tel Aviv: Misrad Habitachon, 1989); David A. Korn, *Stalemate: The War of Attrition and Great Power Diplomacy in the Middle East, 1967–1970* (Boulder, Colo.: Westview, 1992); Avi Shlaim and Raymond Tanter, "Decision Process, Choice and Consequences: Israel's Deep Penetration Bombing in Egypt, 1970," *World Politics* 30, no. 4 (July 1978): 483–516.

36. Mohammed Heikal, *The Road to Ramadan* (New York: Ballantine, 1975), 78–85; Schueftan, *Attrition*, 253–59.

37. Bar-Siman-Tov, *The Israeli-Egyptian War of Attrition*, 152–54.

38. Yitzhak Rabin, then the Israeli ambassador in Washington, expressed his sense of uncertainty in the following way:

> The United States is under no formal obligation to come to the aid of Israel, even if the latter is attacked by the USSR. Without going into the causes, the state of Israel has no prospect today, in the present state of affairs in America, of receiving any American support or pledge of this kind. There is no prospect

of the United States issuing a warning that a blow directed against Israel will be seen as blow at the United States. (*Ma'ariv*, 5 June 1970, quoted in Bar-Siman-Tov, *The Israeli-Egyptian War of Attrition*, 158)

39. Bar-Siman-Tov, *The Israeli-Egyptian War of Attrition*, 158–59.

40. Ibid., 166–69.

41. In his autobiography Dayan writes that during the debriefing he had with the pilots, he said: "Israel was not Czechoslovakia, and our generation was not the generation of Massada, where the defenders of the last Jewish outpost in the war against the Romans in the first century B.C. held out to the end and then committed suicide. We would continue to fight and live" (Dayan, *Story of My Life*, 450).

42. Central Intelligence Agency, SNIE 30–70, "The USSR and the Egyptian-Israeli Confrontation," 14 May 1970.

43. Moshe Dayan, *Milestones* (in Hebrew) (Tel Aviv: Edanim, 1976), 475, 485.

44. Moshe Dayan, *New Map: Different Attitudes* (in Hebrew) (Haifa: Shikmona, 1969), 64, 68.

45. In May–July 1970 Dayan repeatedly alluded to the linkage between Israeli resolve and American preparedness to take a bold line:

We have to be ready to fight physically on the cease-fire lines, even in conditions of Soviet involvement in Egypt, since no other force will fight our war for us. If we possess the readiness to fight, then maybe other nations—including perhaps the United States—will be likely to help us. (*Ma'ariv*, 5 May 1970, quoted in Bar-Siman-Tov, *The Israeli-Egyptian War of Attrition*, 156)

Ten days later Dayan issued another deterrent signal:

If we do not fight, no one will come to our help, we shall not get the Phantoms, and tomorrow the Russians will already be installing SA-3 missile sites on the canal, if they discover that this does not involve their pilots clashing with ours. We are not going to rush to meet the Russian pilots, but if there is a line we shall fight on that line. We cannot allow ourselves anything else than this, and on this basis alone can we have any prospect of getting support from others as well and hope that the Russians will calm down and be deterred and not press things to the point where we shall have to fire at them and also bring down their planes. (*Ma'ariv*, 15 May 1970, quoted in Bar-Siman-Tov, *The Israeli-Egyptian War of Attrition*, 156)

46. Hersh, *The Samson Option*, 176–77.

47. Finney, "Israelis Reported to Be Reluctant"; also Smith, "U.S. Assumes."

48. James Feron, "Mideast Atom Curb Is Urged by Eshkol," *New York Times*, 19 May 1966.

49. *New York Times*, 22 July 1967. The article referred to the Egyptian economic situation as "desperate." Lost revenue from the Suez Canal was estimated at about $230 million a year, and the balance of payments deficit was believed to exceed half a billion dollars.

50. Ibid., 56.

51. Before the 1967 war the AEE negotiated with three American firms to expand the nuclear research center at Inchas, but the contracts were now suspended. The other plans of the AEE, to build a dual-purpose nuclear power station and desalination plant at Burg El Arab with other supporting fuel cycle facilities, were also postponed (and then died) in the wake of the war (ibid., 55–59).

52. Shyam Bhatia, *Nuclear Rivals in the Middle East* (London: Routledge, 1988), 55–59.

53. Even Heikal, who was the most open about the significance of the nuclear issue to the conflict, evaluated the issue in July 1970. In response to the *New York Times* story of 16 July 1970, Heikal conceded that Israel had the ability to produce nuclear weapons, "but he said that the bombs could not be used within the context of the present world balance of nuclear power" (*New York Times*, 22 July 1970).

54. Yigal Allon exemplified this point in his public writings and speeches (cf. Allon, *Curtain of Sand*, 401–2).

16. The Battle Over the NPT

1. When Secretary of State Dean Rusk met French Prime Minister Georges Pompidou on 15 December 1964, they briefly discussed Israel's nuclear activities. Rusk noted that the United States was not sure that Israel had abandoned the idea of producing nuclear weapons. Pompidou replied that France was not sure either (cited in Glenn T. Seaborg, *Stemming the Tide: Arms Control in the Johnson Years* [Lexington, Mass.: Lexington, 1987], 154); Myron Kratzer (AEC), interviews by and correspondence with author, 1992–97; Michael Sterner, interview by author, Washington, D.C., 3 April 1995; Joseph Sisco (State Department), interview by author; Robert Komer, interviews by author, Washington, D.C., 1992–97; and Spurgeon Keeny (NSC), interviews by author, Washington, D.C., 1994–97.

2. Former senior U.S. intelligence official, interview by author; Komer, interviews, 1992–97.

3. In their discussions with the Germans, American officials often referred to India and Israel as the "real targets" of the treaty (Telegram [Bonn, 7342], Ambassador George C. McGhee to Secretary of State Dean Rusk, 20 December 1966, NSF, Box 26, LBJL).

4. George Bunn, interviews by author, 1991–97; Culver Gleysteen (former ACDA senior official), interview by author, March 1996, and correspondence with author, 3 June 1996.

5. Bunn, interviews. Bunn also said the following: "What it comes down to is that there were many countries we talked to but none (that I know of) that was handled in the way Israel was handled: At a very high level leaving most officials working on the treaty completely in the dark. I knew almost nothing about the discussions with Israel . . . maybe my boss Bill Foster knew about the discussions with Israel, but if he did, he didn't tell me. Some of the discussions with India about security assurances in return for accession for the NPT were quiet, but I knew about them—perhaps because India

was a member of the Geneva disarmament conference but more likely because the discussions were handled quite differently" (Bunn, letter to author, 19 July 1996). It is
unlikely that there were no American-Israeli discussions on this issue, but I found no
trace for such discussions. Also Keeny, conversations.

6. Memorandum, Harold Saunders to Walt W. Rostow, "The President's Stake in the
Middle East," 16 May 1967, NSF, Box 7, LBJL.

7. For example, the question of the NPT was not mentioned in the eight-page talking
points prepared for the visit of Foreign Minister Abba Eban to the United States on 23–24
October 1967 (NSF, Box 140–41, LBJL).

8. In his "talking points" for President Johnson prepared for Eshkol's visit, National
Security Advisor Rostow made it clear that the "main [American] issue" for the meeting
is movement for peace:

> The real issue between us is that the Israelis think the Arabs will come around
> if they just sit tight and we think the Israelis may have to go more than half way
> to get the Arabs to negotiate. We can't dictate Israeli tactics, . . . But we must be
> assured that the Israelis aren't going to sit themselves tight right into a "fortress
> Israel" that we would not want to be tied to. (Memorandum, W. W. Rostow to
> President Johnson, "Talking Points for Prime Minister Eshkol," 5 January 1968,
> NSF, Country File—Israel, Box 144–45, LBJL)

9. Ibid.

10. Memorandum, Saunders to Rostow, "Rough Sketch of Package for Eshkol," 29
December 1967, NSF, Country File—Israel, Box 144–45, LBJL.

11. Memorandum, "Talking Points for Prime Minister Eshkol," 5 January 1968.

12. On 30 November departing Israeli ambassador Avraham Harman put forward the
Israeli argument in his farewell meeting with Vice President Hubert Humphrey. Given
the Israeli losses during the war and the likelihood that the French embargo would continue, Harman pointed out that even if Israel were to receive an additional 78 planes
Weizman asked for, it was still short of its goal of a fleet of 250 modern aircraft by the
end of 1968. Taking into account the long lead time for aircraft supply, Israel made the
case that it was essential that decisions be made immediately to ensure Israel's ability to
deter a renewal of hostilities. On 12 December Humphrey passed on the Israeli request
in a five-page memorandum to President Johnson.

13. "Visit of Levi Eshkol, January 7–8, 1968: The Nuclear Issue and Sophisticated
Weaponry," NSF, Country file, Israel, Eshkol Visit Briefing Book, 1/7–8/68, Box 144, POL
7 ISR 1-1-68, LBJL.

14. Mordechai Hod, interview by author, Tel Aviv, 27 May 1996. General Hod was the
commander of the Israeli Air Force, and he attended the meeting.

15. "Notes on Meeting Between President Johnson and Prime Minister Eshkol," 7–8
January 1968, NSF, Country File—Israel, Box 142–43, LBJL.

16. For example, in Rostow's four-page memorandum to President Johnson the issue
of the Phantoms is discussed without reference to the NPT. The reason for holding off
the Phantoms decision is explained by the need "to have a clearer picture of Soviet and

French policy and Jarring's progress" (Memorandum, "Talking Points for Prime Minister Eshkol," 5 January 1968; see also note 17 below).

17. Another indication of this attitude appeared in an interview with Foreign Minister Eban that appeared a few weeks later in *Ha'aretz*. In the interview Eban was asked directly, "Will Israel join the NPT?" to which he replied:

> Israel's position is that it will first study the draft and views of countries simi-lar to itself, that is without military atomic power but with a marked interest in maximum freedom of atomic development. If such countries want the draft amended, it will only be reasonable to join them. Ultimately, when the best possible draft has been written, Israel will not be the exception. In this respect, Israel is not a separate problem but part of the general international problem. (*Ha'aretz* interview with Eban, quoted in Embtel 2438, 7 February 1968, NSF, Country File—Israel, Box 142–43, LBJL; the English translation of the inter-view appears in Airgram [Tel Aviv] A-576, 12 February 1968, NSF, Box 142–43, LBJL)

18. The "Plowshare" Project originated in November 1956 during the Suez campaign as a proposal to consider the use of nuclear explosions to build a sea-level canal across Israel as an alternative to the Suez Canal. In the mid-1960s there was talk about replac-ing the Panama Canal with a new one, through Nicaragua, using Plowshare. On the ori-gins of the Plowshare Project, see Richard G. Hewlett and Jack M. Holl, *Atoms for Peace and War, 1953–1961* (Berkeley: University of California Press, 1989), 528–30; see also Seaborg, *Stemming the Tide*, 309–52.

19. Yuval Ne'eman, correspondence with author, 28 April 1996.

20. Edward Teller, telephone interview by author, 27 April 1996. Carl Duckett, a for-mer deputy director for Science and Technology, told Seymour Hersh that in 1968 Teller said he "was convinced that Israel now had several weapons ready to go." If the CIA was waiting for an Israeli test before it would make a determination on Israel's nuclear sta-tus, it was wrong. "The Israelis have it and they aren't going to test it" (Seymour M. Hersh, *The Samson Option: Israel's Nuclear Arsenal and American Foreign Policy* [New York: Random House, 1991], 186–87). In addition to Teller's more general stand for open-ness in nuclear matters, he might have believed that convincing American decision mak-ers about Israel's true status as a nuclear-weapon state would ease American pressure on Israel to sign the NPT. Teller did not believe that Israel should give up its nuclear weapons in order to join the NPT. If Israel was inhibited about telling the United States what it had, Teller would do so. Teller did not confirm or deny this reading.

21. In his 1991 interview with Seymour Hersh, Duckett acknowledged that without Teller's "opinion," and other circumstantial evidence regarding diversion of nuclear material, the CIA had little to support this finding.

22. According to Duckett's testimony (released in 1978):

> He showed it to Mr. Helms. Helms told him not to publish and he would take it up to President Johnson. Mr. Helms later related that he had spoken to the President, that the President was concerned, and that he said "Don't tell any-

one else, even Dean Rusk and Robert McNamara." (Inquiry into the Testimony of the Executive Director for Operations, vol. 3, Interviews, Office of the General Counsel, U.S. Nuclear Regulatory Commission, National Security Archive Collection on Non-Proliferation, # 26090)

Richard Helms said he had no recollection of Johnson asking him to keep information from Rusk and McNamara. Helms says that since Teller was a consultant of the Agency, it makes sense that he passed information on to Duckett. Helms says it is less likely that such sensitive information was drafted as an NIE in 1968. To do so would have required approval by the Board of National Estimates. Helms does not recall how the issue got to his attention, but thinks it likely that Duckett passed the information on to him and he conveyed it to Johnson (Richard Helms, interview by author, Washington, D.C., 9 September 1996).

23. Memorandum, from Davies to Bunker, NEA Views on the Israeli Desalting Project, 17 February 1967, 3, USNA

24. Richard Helms, interview by author, Washington, D.C., 13 August 1997.

25. Cover note, Saunders to Bromley Smith, n.d., NSF, Box 142–43, LBJL.

26. Department of State, Policy Planning Council, "After NPT, What?" 28 May 1968, NSF, Box 26, LBJL.

27. Ibid.

28. Memorandum, Rostow to Johnson, 22 April 1968, NSF, Country File—Israel, Box 142–43, LBJL.

29. Note, Keeny to Rostow, 3 May 1968, NSF, Country File—Israel, Box 142–43, LBJL.

30. "Israel's Position on the Treaty under Review" (in Hebrew), *Ha'aretz*, 6 May 1968.

31. "Israel: We Will Join the Nuclear Treaty" (in Hebrew), *Ha'aretz*, 28 May 1968.

32. Telegram (5181), Department of State to Tel Aviv Embassy, 27 June 1968.

33. " 'Reservations' Said to Keep Israel from Signing Treaty," *New York Times* , 2 July 1968.

34. "Israel Conducts Consultations on the Nuclear Treaty" (in Hebrew), *Ha'aretz*, 2 July 1968.

35. "Motions to Discuss the NPT Were Removed" (in Hebrew), *Ha'aretz*, 8 August 1968.

36. This month-long ninety-eight-nation conference of nonnuclear-weapon states, chaired by the foreign minister of Pakistan, in which the nuclear-weapon states were given only observer status, produced a number of criticisms of the NPT, including its lack of adequate security assurances. Nevertheless, nearly all the participating countries eventually joined the treaty. I owe this note to Charles N. Van Doren who was an American observer in that conference.

37. Many of the advanced states in the nuclear field, such as Italy, India, Brazil, and Sweden, were members of the Eighteen Nation Disarmament Conference (ENDC) and were consulted. Germany sought information and got it. Israel, not a member of the ENDC, showed no interest in the treaty. Had Israel shown interest, the United States would have provided information about it (Gleysteen, correspondence).

38. In August 1968 Ambassador Rabin met with Richard Nixon, the Republican can-

didate for president. Rabin formed the impression that Nixon understood Israel's security needs and that "Nixon might be proved an even better president for Israel than Hubert Humphrey might be" (Yitzhak Rabin, *A Service Record* [in Hebrew] [Tel Aviv: Ma'ariv, 1979], vol. 1, 222–23).

39. Amos Ben Vered, "Israel's Nuclear Option" (in Hebrew), *Ha'aretz*, 5 September 1968; *Ha'aretz*, 11 September 1968.

40. "Israel Will Set Its Policy after the Non-Nuclear State Conference" (in Hebrew), *Ha'aretz*, 30 August 1968.

41. *Ha'aretz*, 11 September 1968.

42. George Bunn and Roland M. Timerbaev, *Nuclear Verification under the NPT: What Should It Cover—How Far May It Go?* PPNN Study, No. 5 (The Mountbatten Center for International Studies, University of Southampton, April 1994), 3–8. According to Bunn and Timerbaev, during the negotiations on the NPT the United States gave its own criteria for defining "manufacture" to potential signatories who asked for clarification. In his testimony before Congress, William C. Foster, the U.S. chief negotiator, characterized the criteria, developed in consultations with the Soviet Union and Sweden, as the following:

> Facts indicating that the *purpose* of a particular activity was the acquisition of a nuclear explosive device would tend to show non-compliance. (Thus the construction of an *experimental* or prototype nuclear explosive device would be covered by the term "manufacture" as would be the *production of components which could only have relevance to a nuclear explosive device*.) Again, while the *placing of a particular activity under safeguards* would not, in and of itself, settle the question of whether the activity was in compliance with the treaty, it would be helpful in allaying any suspicion of non-compliance. (Ibid., 5)

The Foster criteria, the authors stress, put the prohibition on manufacture in terms of activities much earlier than "the final assembly of an explosive device," as Sweden suggested. Nevertheless it did not list what these activities were, but rather defined them by their purpose.

43. Memorandum, Dean Rusk to President Johnson, "Your Meeting with Israeli Foreign Minister Abba Eban," 21 October 1968, NSF, Box 144, LBJL.

44. The reference to Rusk's meeting with Allon appears in "Notes on President's Meeting with House Leadership on 9 September 1968," Tom Johnson's notes of Meetings, Box 4, LBJL.

45. Telegram, Rusk to Barbour, 11 September 1968, RG 59, CFPF 1967–69, Box 2055, USNA.

46. The quote, taken from a cabinet session, appears in Reuven Pedatzur, "Shamir May Consider a New Nuclear Policy" (in Hebrew), *Ha'aretz*, 11 November 1991. As noted earlier, Rusk was not an NPT proponent until President Johnson began supporting it in the summer of 1966.

47. Telegram (765), Rusk to Barbour, 1 October 1968, RG 59, CFPF 1967–69, Box 1486, DEF 12-5 ISR, USNA.

48. Memorandum, Rusk to the President, "Your Meeting with Israeli Foreign Minister Abba Eban," 21 October 1968; also Paul C. Warnke, interview by author, Washington, D.C., 11 January 1994.

49. William B. Quandt, *The Peace Process* (Washington, D.C.: Brookings, 1993), 56.

50. Neil Sheehan, "Johnson Barring Jets for Israelis," *New York Times*, 15 September 1968.

51. "Notes of the President's Meeting with the Tuesday Luncheon Group, 17 September 1968," Tom Johnson Notes of Meetings, Box 4, LBJL.

52. "Eshkol: Israel Knows the Secret of the Production of Atomic Bomb" (in Hebrew), *Ha'aretz*, 4 October 1968; "Eshkol and Eban Comment on Nuclear Knowledge without Prior Discussion" (in Hebrew), *Ha'aretz*, 8 October 1968; "Israeli Nuclear Deterrent Urged by Jerusalem Paper," *New York Times*, 5 October 1968.

53. "Eshkol: Israel Knows the Secret of the Production of Atomic Bomb," 4 October 1968.

54. "Israeli Nuclear Deterrent Urged by Jerusalem Paper," *New York Times*, 5 October 1968.

55. This was noticed by Schweitzer, "A Bomb, by the Way" (in Hebrew), *Ha'aretz*, 13 October 1968.

56. Ibid.

57. Memorandum, Hart to Rusk, 21 October 1968, RG 59, CFPF 1967–69, Box 2060, USNA.

58. "Notes on Foreign Policy Meeting, Tuesday, November 26, 1968," in Tom Johnson Notes of Meetings, Box 4, LBJL.

59. See note 16, above. This was confirmed by Warnke (Warnke, interview, 11 January 1994).

60. Telegram (261146), Rusk to Barbour, 22 October 1968, RG 59, CFPF 1967–69, Box 2060 POL ISR 1968, USNA.

61. Cover note, Saunders to Bromley Smith, undated, NSF, Box 142, LBJL. Helms, interview by author, 9 September 1996.

62. Memorandum, "Suggested Talking Points for President's Meeting with Foreign Minister Eban," n.d., 1968, NSF, Box 144, LBJL; Memorandum, W. W. Rostow to President Johnson, "Your Meeting with Abba Eban, NSF, Box 142–43, LBJL.

63. Memorandum, Dean Rusk to the President, "Your Meeting with Israeli Foreign Minister Abba Eban," 21 October 1968, NSF, Box 144, LBJL.

64. Ibid.

65. Memorandum, "Suggested Talking Points for President's Meeting with Foreign Minister Eban."

66. According to Eban's memoirs, the tone of the discussion was more that of a friendly farewell than pressure. Johnson wanted Eban to pass on to Eshkol that "Lyndon B. Johnson has kept his word," and expressed his intention to sign the agreement for the supply of the Phantoms (Abba Eban, *Personal Witness* [New York: Putnam's, 1992], 474). Eban hardly mentioned the nuclear issue in his memoirs. Johnson most likely did mention his expectation that in the context of the negotiations to provide the Phantoms,

Israel would be able to strengthen its nonproliferation stance by signing the NPT, but he probably left the tough business of pressing Israel on the NPT to Rusk and Warnke. If it succeeded, which he must have doubted, he would get the credit; if it did not, he could call off the effort. He did not ask Rusk and Warnke to stop them from pressuring Israel.

67. Before his departure to Israel, Eban told the press that the negotiations would proceed "urgently and swiftly," but American sources were not so certain. They noted that the talks may be "prolonged." There was a press reference that "one problem to be ironed out" is the Israeli attitude toward the NPT. Eban continued to say publicly that Israel was still "studying" the text of the treaty, and refused to indicate when or if it would sign it ("U.S., Israel Open Talks on Purchase of Jets," *Evening Star*, 23 October 1968).

68. These statements were made by Yigal Allon and Abba Eban in a cabinet meeting on 27 October 1968.

69. Abba Eban's comments at a cabinet meeting on 27 October 1968; and Pedatzur, "Shamir May Reconsider a New Nuclear Policy."

70. Ibid.

71. Dean Rusk, *As I Saw It: Dean Rusk as Told to Richard Rusk* (New York: Viking, 1990), 343.

72. Ibid. See Pedatzur, "Shamir May Consider a New Nuclear Policy."

73. Ibid.

74. From minutes of the Israeli cabinet, 27 October 1968.

75. Telegram (5862), Barbour to Rusk, 28 October 1968, RG 59, CFPF, 1967–69, Box 1484 POL ISR 1968, USNA.

76. Ibid.

77. Telegram (253), UN to Rusk, 5 November 1968, RG 59, CFPF, 1967–69, Box 1486, POL ISR 1968, USNA.

78. "Talking Points for the Secretary's Meeting with Israel's Foreign Minister Eban, October 22," NSF, Box 142–43, LBJL.

79. Memorandum of Conversation, "Subject: Negotiations with Israel—F-4 and Advanced Weapons," 4 November 1968, NSF, Box 142–43, LBJL, 1.

80. Paul C. Warnke, telephone interview and conversations with author, 2 November 1993, 21 May 1996, and 11 November 1997.

81. Ibid.

82. Ibid.

83. Ibid.

84. By 1997 the minutes of those sessions have been declassified almost in full. Rabin's version of the climax of these negotiations was told in his *Rabin Memoirs*. Paul Warnke was kind to sit with me, a number of times, in order to recount those negotiations.

85. Rabin, *The Rabin Memoirs*, 141–42; for the Hebrew version of the meeting—there are small differences of wording between the two accounts—see Rabin, *A Service Record*, vol. 2, 236. In his brief author's note Rabin touches the objectivity issue. He notes that the book is his own personal memoir, describing events from his point of view, but he also stresses that, in writing it, he was assisted by official documents written at the time, "papers and cables . . . including cables and summaries dating from my period of service

as Israel's ambassador to Washington." Rabin stressed that "at all times my first interest has been to preserve the accuracy of events and exchanges as reflected in these sources."

86. Office of the Assstant of Secretary of Defense, Memorandum of Conversation, "Subject: Negotiations with Israel—F-4 and Advanced Weapons," 8 November 1968, 1–2, attached to memorandum, Joseph J. Sisco to the Acting Secretary, "Subject: Talking Points for Initial Meeting with Israelis on Nuclear and SSM Issue July 29—Briefing Memorandum," 28 July 1969, RG 59, CFPF 1967-69, Box 2060, POL ISR-US 1969, USNA.

87. Warnke, telephone conversations. For a similar version of that encounter, including the cite from Harry H. Schwartz, see Hersh, *The Samson Option*, 189–91.

88. Telegram (269999), Rusk to Tel Aviv Embassy, 8 November 1968, attached to memorandum, Hart to Rusk, "Subject: Response to Israeli Government's Paper of October 28," 8 November 1968, RG 59, CFPF, 1967-69, Box 2060, POL ISR-US 1968, USNA.

89. Ibid., 2.

90. Ibid., 2–3.

91. Ibid., 3.

92. If earlier Johnson had seemed to endorse Rusk's efforts to press Israel, he now decided to back off when he realized the extent of the Jewish community's opposition. Warnke speculates that Rusk was informed shortly after his mid-October meeting with Eban of the CIA's conclusion that Israel already had nuclear weapons. The speculation is based on Warnke's observation that Rusk and Parker Hart played no part in nor showed any interest in the negotiations with Rabin and his team in November. Warnke today can think of no other explanation for Rusk's abandonment of the effort to get Israel to sign the NPT (Warnke, letter to author, 27 June 1996).

93. Memorandum of Conversation, "Subject: Negotiations with Israel—F-4 and Advanced Weapons," 12 November 1968, 1, attached to memorandum, Joseph J. Sisco to the Acting Secretary, "Subject: Talking Points for Initial Meeting with Israelis on Nuclear and SSM Issue July 29—Briefing Memorandum," 28 July 1969, RG 59, CFPF, 1967-69, Box 2060, POL ISR-US 1969, USNA.

94. Ibid., 1–2.

95. Ibid., 2.

96. General Hod noted that this was the first time he heard the argument, and he was quite impressed by the conceptual point Rabin made (Mordechai Hod, interview by author, Tel Aviv, 27 May 1996).

97. Memorandum of Conversation, "Subject: Negotiations with Israel—F-4 and Advanced Weapons," 12 November 1968, 3–4.

98. Memorandum of Conversation, 18 November 1968, RG 59, CFPF, 1967–69, Box 2060, POL ISR-US 1968, USNA.

99. Letter, Rabin to Warnke, 22 November 1968, 1, attached to memorandum, Joseph J. Sisco to the Acting Secretary, "Subject: Talking Points for Initial Meeting with Israelis on Nuclear and SSM Issue July 29—Briefing Memorandum," 28 July 1969.

100. Ibid.

101. Memorandum of Conversation, "Subject: F-4 Negotiations with Government of

Israel," 27 November 1968, attached to memorandum, Joseph J. Sisco to the Acting Secretary, "Subject: Talking Points for Initial Meeting with Israelis on Nuclear and SSM Issue July 29—Briefing Memorandum," 28 July 1969.

102. Warnke, interview; telephone conversations. Warnke's version of the exchange appears in his "Nuclear Israel," a book review of Seymour M. Hersh's *The Samson Option* (*Bulletin of Atomic Scientists* 48, no. 3 [March 1992]: 41–42). A different account of the meeting appears in Hersh, *The Samson Option*, 189–90. According to Hersh, citing Warnke's aide Harry Schwartz, the meeting ended with an acrimonious tone when Warnke said: "Mr. Ambassador, we are shocked at the manner in which you are dealing with us. You, our close ally, are building nuclear weapons in Israel behind our back." Warnke stated categorically in 1994 that he has no recollection of the exchange as it appears in Hersh's book, and he believes that such words were never said (Warnke, interview).

103. Warnke, interview; telephone conversations.

104. Letter, Eshkol to Johnson, 4 December 1968, attached to memorandum, Joseph J. Sisco to the Acting Secretary, "Subject: Talking Points for Initial Meeting with Israelis on Nuclear and SSM Issue July 29—Briefing Memorandum," 28 July 1969.

105. Ibid.

106. Hedrick Smith, "US Will Start Delivering F-4s Jets to Israel in 1969," *New York Times*, 28 December 1968.

107. Warnke, telephone conversation, 21 May 1996.

108. From minutes of the Israeli cabinet, 27 October 1968.

109. Rusk, *As I Saw It*, 343.

17. Opacity Takes Hold

1. "A Report to the President by the Committee on Nuclear Proliferation," 21 January 1965, NSF, Box 5, LBJL.

2. Ibid., 1–2.

3. Ibid., 3–4.

4. Ibid., 4–5.

5. Glenn T. Seaborg, with Benjamin S. Loeb, *Stemming the Tide: Arms Control in the Johnson Years* (Lexington, Mass.: Lexington, 1987), 136–48.

6. Seymour M. Hersh, *The Samson Option: Israel's Nuclear Arsenal and American Foreign Policy* (New York: Random House, 1991), 209.

7. Seymour Hersh, *The Price of Power: Kissinger in the Nixon White House* (New York: Summit, 1983), 148; cf. Hersh, *The Samson Option*, 210.

8. Hersh, *The Price of Power*, 140.

9. Ibid. According to Hersh, citing Shlomo Aronson, Kissinger was frank about his views during his visit to Israel in February 1968. In a meeting with a group of Israeli academics, Kissinger told the audience that the United States would not "lift a finger for Israel" if the Soviets were to intervene directly in a conflict with Israel. The implication

was that for the sake of Israel and the United States, Israel should take care of its own security (ibid., 177). Aronson gives the date of the informal meeting as sometime in the mid-1960s (Shlomo Aronson with Oded Brosh, *The Politics and Strategy of Nuclear Weapons in the Middle East: Opacity, Theory, and Reality (1960–1991)* [Albany: State University of New York Press, 1992], 328).

10. Yitzhak Rabin, *Pinkas Sherut* (in Hebrew), vol. 2 (Tel Aviv: Ma'ariv, 1979), 222.

11. Ibid., 223.

12. John W. Finney, "Israelis Reported to be Reluctant at This Time to Sign Treaty Barring Spread of Nuclear Arms," *New York Times*, 20 November 1968, 11.

13. CIA, Directorate of Intelligence, "Prospects for the Non-Proliferation Treaty," NSF, NPT files, Box 26, LBJL.

14. Finney, "Israelis Reported," 11; Elyahu Salpeter, "The Nuclear Treaty vis-à-vis Israel's Security: Conventional and Nuclear Guarantees are Needed Prior to Signature" (in Hebrew), *Ha'aretz*, 24 November 1968.

15. *Ha'aretz*, 11 September 1968; "Change of Government Could Lead to Cancellation of Eshkol's Visit" (in Hebrew), *Ha'aretz*, 26 November 1968.

16. India, having also raised the issue, asked whether the United States or Britain would use their nuclear weapons to defend India. Other nations demanded stronger international agreements that would eliminate the UN as the implementing mechanism.

17. In these consultations Israel came closest to saying that its nuclear program was a compensation for its material inferiority relative to Arab conventional military power. This argument is still at the heart of the Israeli position, and is central to its position to the Nuclear Weapons Free Zone (NWFZ) in any arms control forum.

18. "Israel and the NPT" (in Hebrew), *Ha'aretz*, 18 December 1968.

19. Rabin, *Pinkas Sherut*, vol. 2, 226.

20. "TV Report of an Israeli A-bomb Draws a Denial in Washington," *New York Times*, 9 January 1969, 2.

21. "Responses in Jerusalem" (in Hebrew), *Ha'aretz*, 10 January 1969; "Israeli Bomb Is Doubted," *New York Times*, 10 January 1969.

22. John W. Finney, "U.S. Aides Doubt That Israel Has Decided to Build A-Bomb," *New York Times*, 11 January 1969, 3. According to former ambassador James Leonard, who was in 1966–68 a senior analyst at the State Department's Bureau of Intelligence and Research (INR), this was his own view at the time, which he believes was also shared by INR and the State Department.

23. Ibid., 3

24. Ibid.

25. Department of State, Action Memorandum to the Secretary of State, "Subject: Visit by US Team to Israeli Nuclear Reactor at Dimona," 7 March 1969, RG 59, CFPF, 1967–69, AE11–2 ISR, USNA.

26. Former senior CIA officer, interview by author, 2 August 1996.

27. Department of State, Action Memorandum to the Secretary of State, "Subject: Visit by US Team to Israeli Nuclear Reactor at Dimona," 7 March 1969.

28. Ibid.

29. Ibid.

30. Telegram (36436), Secretary of State William Rogers to Ambassador Walworth Barbour, 8 March 1969, CFPF, 1967–69, RG 59, AE11–2 ISR, USNA.

31. Telegram (1093), Walworth Barbour to Secretary of State William Rogers, 24 March 1969, RG 59, CFPF, 1967–69, AE11–2 ISR, USNA.

32. Telegram (1246), Barbour to Rogers, 10 April 1969, RG 59, CFPF, 1967–69, AE11–2 ISR, USNA. The document was only partially declassified in 1992.

33. Ibid., 1.

34. The telegram to Barbour read:

> We are disappointed in PM's [Golda Meir's] request that [the] visit be postponed until late June. Our experts have always felt [that the] lapse of [a] year between visits [is] too great to give us complete confidence concerning activities at Dimona. This was [the] reason we pressed for semi-annual visits in 1963 and we have always considered Eshkol's August 19, 1963, letter to President Kennedy together with his accompanying comments to you as constituting GOI [Government of Israel] commitment to visits on [a] semi-annual basis. Accordingly, you should reopen [the] question with GOI, asking that PM be reminded of our 1963 understanding with Eshkol, and that she reconsiders [the] response cited [by] reftel. We would strongly prefer [that the] visit take place May 3. (Telegram [54653], Rogers to Barbour, 10 April 1969, RG 59, CFPF, 1967–69, AE11–2 ISR, USNA)

The document was only partially declassified in 1992.

35. Telegram (1246), Barbour to Rogers, 10 April 1969.

36. Telegram (1308), Barbour to Rogers, 12 April 1969, RG 59, CFPF, 1967–69, AE11–2 ISR, USNA.

37. Telegram (97540), Rogers to Barbour, 14 June 1969, RG 59, CFPF, 1967–69, AE11–2 ISR, USNA.

38. Ibid.

39. Telegram (2378), Barbour to Rogers, 23 June 1969, CFPF, RG 59, 1967–69, AE11–2 ISR, USNA.

40. The passage is as follows:

> [The] Dimona facility has steadily grown in size and complexity in recent years and our experts have increasingly felt [that a] one-day visit by [a] team of only three members is inadequate to cover [the] entire facility. This inadequacy [was] inevitably reflected in [the] team's report in [the] form of reservation to conclusions of report which can only have [the] effect [of] feeding already existing uncertainties concerning Israel's nuclear intentions. You should make [the] further point that [the] attempt to limit [the] size of [the] team, duration of visit, or periodicity of visits is contrary to assurances conveyed by Eshkol to you in 1963 that visits would be conducted QUOTE as we desire. UNQUOTE Refusal to allow [the] team to be made up of four members is particularly puzzling and disappointing since this change could not

possibly be embarrassing to GOI. (Telegram [105618], Rogers to Barbour, 29 June 1969, RG 59, CFPF, 1967–69, AE11–2 ISR, USNA)

41. George B. Pleat, telephone interview by author, 14 July 1996; Pleat, correspondence with author, 26 July 1996.

42. A former senior CIA officer who was familiar with the issue characterized the Agency's attitude in a letter to the author in the following way: "In the Agency view, there was no need for the team to be given any information. They were supposed to gather information, not assess it. Once you get scientists talking to each other, there would be no control at all over information made available to them" (former senior CIA officer, correspondence with author, 9 November 1996).

43. Ibid.

44. Edwin Kintner, interviews by author, June 1996. Pleat, interview, 14 July 1996. Kintner recalls returning from the CIA briefing so disappointed that he told his wife that if the United States needed to rely exclusively on CIA collection and analysis, it would be in bad shape.

45. Pleat, interview, 14 July 1996.

46. Pleat, correspondence with author, 26 July 1996. Pleat adds: "I do recall vividly the experience as I descended alone thirty or so feet to inspect the facility which I recall was there in conjunction with the waste system. At that time I asked myself what am I doing—thirty feet from the surface, in a foreign facility, in the middle of the Negev desert at midnight? I still get a chuckle thinking about it."

47. Pleat, interview, 14 July 1996; Floyd Culler, correspondence with author, 9 May 1996; Kintner, interviews, June 1996.

48. In spite of revelations about Dimona by Péan, Perrin, and Vanunu, Kintner still believes that a reprocessing plant probably did not exist in Dimona at the time of his visits there (Kintner, interview, June 1996).

49. Glenn Seaborg, a former AEC chairman, voiced these suspicions in his diary: "We had difficulty and were not given permission to make the necessary inspections to assure ourselves that such a nuclear weapons program was not under way" (Glenn T. Seaborg, personal diaries, 25 September 1966. The entry was made available to the author by Seaborg).

50. Pleat, interview, 14 July 1996; Culler, correspondence, 9 May 1966; Kintner, interviews, June 1996. According to the *New York Times*, the 1969 team "complained in writing about the limitations on its inspections and reportedly stated that, for this reason, it could not guarantee that there was no weapons-related work at Dimona" (Hedrick Smith, "U.S. Assumes the Israelis Have A-Bomb or Its Parts," *New York Times*, 18 July 1970, 1, 8).

51. Department of State, Memorandum of Conversation, "1969 Dimona Visit," 13 August 1969, RG 59, CFPF, 1967–69, Box 2649, AE11-2 ISR, USNA.

52. Ibid.

53. Ibid.

54. Smith, "U.S. Assumes," 1, 8; Hersh, *The Samson Option*, 209–15.

55. Rabin, *A Service Record*, vol. 2, 251.

56. Memorandum, Joseph S. Sisco to the Acting Secretary, n.d., RG 59, CFPF 1967–69, Box 1486, USNA.

57. Ibid.

58. Rabin, *A Service Record*, vol. 2, 251–52 (translation by author).

59. Richardson may have wanted a factual acknowledgment from Rabin about Israel's nuclear program (that is, that Israel was not manufacturing nuclear weapons or weapon-grade material), but instead he received an analytical pledge. Rabin evaded the factual question of whether Israel was producing nuclear weapons, saying only that as long as Israel did not conduct a nuclear test, no one should assert that Israel had nuclear weapons.

60. Rabin, *A Service Record*, vol. 2, 251–52 (translation by author).

61. Former senior CIA officer, interviews by the author, 1995–97; correspondence with author, 9 November 1996.

62. Peter Grose, "Mrs. Meir Greeted Warmly by Nixon; Seeks U.S. Pledge," *New York Times*, 26 September 1969, 1, 3.

63. Yitzhak Rabin, *The Rabin Memoir* (Boston: Little, Brown, 1979), 155.

64. Rabin, *A Service Record*, vol. 2, 257 (translation by author).

65. Gary Samore, conversation with author, Washington D.C., 26 November 1997.

66. The American intelligence community believed at the time that the Israeli nuclear arsenal was composed of devices that were not fully assembled (former senior CIA officer, interview, 2 August 1996).

67. Smith, "U.S. Assumes," 1.

68. Ibid., 8.

69. Ibid.

70. Ibid.

71. "Israelis Criticize Article in the *Times*," *New York Times*, 19 July 1970; "Jerusalem Response: Israel Will not Be the First to Use Nuclear Weapons" (in Hebrew), *Ha'aretz*, 19 July 1970.

72. Smith, "U.S. Assumes," 1.

73. "Washington Responds: Facts on Israeli Atom Speculative" (in Hebrew), *Ha'aretz*, 19 July 1970.

EPILOGUE

1. These headlines appeared in the *Economist* (26 October 1991; 19 October 1996).

2. Shimon Peres, in *From These Men: Seven Founders of the State of Israel* (New York: Wyndham, 1979), 196, says: "It is possible that if we had foreseen all the difficulties on the way, we might have decided that the odds were against us." Israeli journalist Dan Margalit has recently noted the following: "The Israel in which I started as a journalist had built the atomic reactor in Dimona in ways which, in 1997, would have resulted in the imprisonment of David Ben Gurion and his lieutenants. In the 1990s—with exposure, investigative journalism, and criticism—the nuclear reactor would have never been built" (Dan Margalit, *I Saw Them* [in Hebrew] [Tel Aviv: Zmora Bitan, 1997], 7).

3. One can even argue that the price Israel paid for opacity is expressed not only in democratic terms but even in terms of its security. It has been pointed out recently that "Israel's defense doctrine has never been updated to take into account the major changes that have swept the Middle East over the past few decades ... The [military] doctrine is now obsolete, unsuited to present realities" (Ze'ev Schiff, "Facing Up to Reality," *Ha'aretz*, 9 January 1998; Amnon Barzilai, "Seminar to Examine Military's Strategies" [in Hebrew], *Ha'aretz*, 18 January 1998). One can argue that one prominent reason for the stifling of military doctrine is the culture of nuclear opacity that has not allowed coherent and thorough conceptualization of Israel's security and military doctrine that systematically includes the nuclear issue.

4. Avner Cohen and Steven Lee, eds., *Nuclear Weapons and the Future of Humanity: The Fundamental Questions* (Totowa, N.J.: Rowman and Allenheld, 1986).

5. Robert Dahl, *Controlling Nuclear Weapons: Democracy versus Guardianship* (Syracuse: Syracuse University Press, 1985), 5; Richard Falk, "Nuclear Weapons and the Renewal of Democracy," in Cohen and Lee, *Nuclear Weapons and the Future of Humanity*, 437–56.

6. Little has been written in the Israeli press about the petition, in part because the censor issued a gag order. See Ethan Bronner, "MIT Scholar Fights Israel Censor on Nuclear Article," *Boston Globe*, 28 April 1994; Mike Moore, "Avner Cohen, Meet Franz Kafka," *Bulletin of the Atomic Scientists* (September/October 1994): 5–6; Ethan Bronner, "Taking on the Censor," *Boston Globe*, 23 February 1995.

7. When Shimon Peres, in 1995, sounded as if he might give up nuclear weapons for peace, he was harshly attacked by many as ready to compromise Israel's vital interests. Within hours he corrected himself by simply saying that he was only reiterating Israel's official view about NWFZ. The episode was a firsthand demonstration of the tension I describe. Under opacity, of course, the issue was brushed aside as if it did not exist.

8. The late Shalheveth Freier, the director general of the IAEC (1971–1976) and the "unofficial" foreign minister of the IAEC until his death in 1994, told me that when he was in charge he made it known that every senior employee in the system could have an open door with the prime minister (Golda Meir) without his presence. He was heavily criticized for installing that policy, but he thought it would be one form of institutionalizing a "watchdog" into the system. In reality, rarely did anyone use that opportunity.

Glossary

Individuals

Allon, Yigal (1918–80). Israeli general and statesman; Palmach's commander-in-chief (1945–48); commander of the southern front during the War of Independence (1948–49); *Achdut Ha'Avodah* leader and member of Knesset; minister of labor (1961–68); deputy prime minister (1968); minister of education (1969–74); foreign minister (1974–77); leader of the "conventionalist" school that advocated reliance on conventional deterrence.

Amer, Abdul Hakim (1919–67). Egyptian general; member of the Free Officers' group that toppled King Farouk in 1952; chief of Egypt's armed forces and vice president during the 1967 war; after the war was accused of conspiring against Nasser, was arrested, and committed suicide.

Angleton, James Jesus (1917–87). Long-time CIA operative; director of CIA counterespionage (1954–74); handled the CIA Israel account; was forced to resign from the CIA after questions were raised concerning his search for a Soviet "mole" inside the agency.

Badeau, John S. (1903–). U.S. ambassador to Egypt (1961–64).

Ball, George W. (1909–94). Undersecretary of state during the Kennedy and Johnson administrations (1961–68); early opponent of U.S. involvement in Vietnam; developed a name as a critic of Israel.

Barbour, Walworth (1908–82). U.S. ambassador to Israel (1961–73).

Ben Gurion, David (1886–1973). Considered the founding-father of the state of Israel; founder of the Histadrut Labor Federation (1920); MAPAI preeminent leader; chairman of the Jewish Agency Executive (1935–48); Israel's first prime minister and minister of defense (1948–53, 1955–63); in 1965 left MAPAI and founded the RAFI party; also the founding father of Israel's nuclear program.

Bergmann, Ernst David (1903–75). German born; organic chemist; Chaim Weizmann's protégé and scientific director of the Sieff Institute and subsequently the Weizmann Institute of Science (1934–51); member and head of the scientific department of the Haganah and IDF, first chair of the IAEC (1952–66); head of research in the Ministry of Defense (1950–66); recognized as the scientific inspiration for Israel's nuclear program.

Bourgès-Maunoury, Maurice (1914–93). French minister of defense under the Fourth Republic (1956–57); major supporter of the French-Israeli nuclear cooperation.

Bundy, McGeorge (1919–96). National security adviser to Presidents John F. Kennedy and Lyndon B. Johnson (1961–66).

Clifford, Clark M. (1906–1998). Lawyer, government official, special assistant to President Harry S. Truman (1946–50); secretary of defense (1968–69).

Couve de Murville, Maurice (1907–). French prime minister (1968–69) and foreign minister (1959–68) under President Charles de Gaulle.

Croach, Jesse W. (1918–). Scientist employed by Dupont at the Savannah River Laboratory; member of the first U.S. inspection team at Dimona.

Culler, Floyd L. (1923–). Chemical engineer; expert on chemical reprocessing of nuclear fuels; assistant, associate, and acting director of Oak Ridge National Laboratory; visited Dimona four times as a member and leader of the American inspection team (1965–68).

Dassault, Marcel (1892–1986). French industrialist; founder of Marcel Dassault Aviation Industries, which was Israel's primary supplier of aviation equipment in the 1950s and 1960s.

Dayan, Moshe (1915–81). Israeli general and statesman; the fourth IDF chief of staff (1953–58); minister of agriculture (1959–64); minister of defense (1967–74); foreign minister (1977–79). Credited with developing the IDF aggressive, mobile war-fighting doctrine; supporter of the nuclear program.

De Gaulle, Charles (1890–1970). French general; leader of the anti-Nazi Free France forces; led the liberation army into Paris in 1944; prime minister (1946–48); founder of the Fifth Republic (1958) and president of France (1958–69).

De Shalit, Amos (1926–69). Prominent Israeli scientist (nuclear physicist); among the HEMED physicists who were sent in 1949 to study nuclear physics overseas; created (1954) and headed (1954–64) the Department of Nuclear Physics at the Weizmann Institute; scientific director of the Weizmann Institute; served as the official escort to most of the American AEC teams to Dimona.

Dinstein, Zvi (1925–). Palestinian-born; Ph.D. (Law); an economist; Eshkol's senior assistant at the Ministry of Defense (1965–66); after the 1966 election became Knesset member and deputy minister of defense (1966–67).

Dostrovsky, Israel (1918–). Prominent Israeli scientist (nuclear chemist); joined the Weizmann Institute in 1948 and founded the Department of Isotope Research; commander of HEMED Gimmel (1948–51); director of research at the IAEC (1953–57); director-general of the IAEC under Prime Ministers Levi Eshkol and Golda Meir (1965–71); vice president and later president of the Weizmann Institute (1971–75).

Dulles, John Foster (1888–1959). Secretary of state under President Dwight D. Eisenhower (1953–59).

Eban, Abba (1915–). South-African-born; Israeli ambassador to the United States and the United Nations (1950–59); minister of education (1959–63); deputy prime minister (1963–66); foreign minister (1966–74).

Eisenhower, Dwight D. (1890–1969). Supreme Allied commander during the Second World War; thirty-fourth president of the United States (1953–61).

Eshkol, Levi (1895–1969). Russian-born; among the founders of kibbutz Degania; MAPAI leader; minister of finance (1952–63); third prime minister of Israel (1963–69); minister of defense (1963–67). The first to use publicly the formula "Israel will not be the first to introduce nuclear weapons into the Middle East" (1964).

Feinberg, Abraham (Abe) (1908–1998). American Jewish leader; fund-raiser for the Democratic Party in the 1950s–1960s.

Feldman, Myer (Mike). Deputy counsel in the White House under Presidents John F. Kennedy and Lyndon B. Johnson (1961–64); counsel under Johnson (1964–65).

Finney, John W. (1923–). *New York Times* reporter in the 1960s who followed the story of Dimona.

Freier, Shalheveth (1920–94). German-born; Israel's science attaché in Paris (1956–60); IAEC director-general under Prime Ministers Golda Meir and Yitzhak Rabin (1971–76).

Gaillard, Felix (1919–70). Last prime minister of the French Fourth Republic (1957–58).

Galili, Israel (1911–86). Russian-born; chief of staff of the Haganah (1947–48); leader of *Achdut Ha'Avodah*; senior cabinet minister under Prime Ministers Levi Eshkol, Golda Meir, and Yitzhak Rabin (1965–77); supporter of the "conventionalist" school, which advocated reliance on conventional deterrence.

Gazit, Mordechai (1922–). Israeli diplomat; minister at the Israeli embassy in Washington, D.C. (1960–65); director-general of the prime minister's office under Golda Meir and ambassador to France.

Gilpatric, Roswell (1906–). Deputy secretary of defense in the Kennedy administration; chairman of the committee that looked at American nonproliferation policies in 1964.

Goldschmidt, Bertrand Leopold (1912–). French physical chemist; participated in the French contingent to the Manhattan Project; among the major contributors to the French CEA as head of the Chemistry Division (1946–59) and head of External Relations and Planning.

Haber-Schaim, Uri (1926–). German-born, came to Israel as a child; physicist and educator; among the HEMED physicists who were sent overseas in 1949 to study nuclear physics; left Israel in 1953; taught physics in the United States; devoted his professional life to science education.

Harel, Isser (1912–). Latvian-born; second head of the Mossad (1952–63); led the campaign against the German scientists in Egypt (1961–63).

Harman, Avraham (Abe) (1914–1992). British-born; diplomat, Israeli ambassador to the United States (1960–67) and subsequently president of the Hebrew University.

Harriman, Averell W. (1891–1986). U.S. ambassador to the United Kingdom and the Soviet Union; governor of New York (1955–59); undersecretary of state in the Kennedy and Johnson administrations.

Heikal, Mohammed Hassanein (1923–). Egyptian journalist; editor of *Al Ahram* (1957–70); confidant of President Gamal Abdul Nasser; minister of national guidance (1970).

Helms, Richard (1913–). Among the founders of the CIA; spent most of his career in covert operations, deputy director (1965–66) and director of the CIA (1966–73).

Hermoni, Avraham (1926–). Palestinian-born; chemist; senior official in RAFAEL.

Herter, Christian A. (1895–1966). U.S. undersecretary of state (1957–59); secretary of state (1959–61).

Jones, Lewis G. Assistant secretary of state for Near Eastern and South Asian Affairs (1959–61).

Johnson, Lyndon B. (1908–73). U.S. vice president under John F. Kennedy (1961–63); thirty-sixth president of the United States (1963–69).

Katzir-Katachalsky, Aharon (1913–72). Polish-born, came to Israel as a child, Israeli-trained; among HEMED founders; pioneer in polymer research; professor at the Weizmann Institute; oversaw defense research at RAFAEL and other agencies; died in a terrorist attack at Ben Gurion airport.

Katzir-Katachalsky, Ephraim (1916–). Ukrainian-born, came to Israel as a child, Israeli-trained; among HEMED founders; pioneer in biophysics research; professor at the Weizmann Institute; founded the Department of Biotechnology at Tel Aviv University; fourth president of Israel (1973–78); in 1966 was directly involved in the reorganization of defense research.

Kennedy, John F. (1917–63). U.S. congressman (1946–50) and senator (1950–61) from Massachusetts; thirty-fifth president of the United States (1961–63).

Kintner, Edwin (1920–). Member and team leader of the AEC visits to Dimona (1968–69).

Kissinger, Henry A. (1923–). National security adviser (1969–74); secretary of state (1973–77) in the Nixon and Ford administrations.

Kollek, Teddy (1911–). Hungarian-born; Haganah operative in the United States (1947–52); director-general of the prime minister's office under David Ben Gurion (1954–63); mayor of Jerusalem (1965–96).

Komer, Robert W. (1922–). Staff member at the National Security Council in the Kennedy and Johnson administrations (1961–65); deputy and acting national security adviser to President Lyndon B. Johnson (1965–66).

Lavon, Pinhas (1904–76). Polish-born; MAPAI leader; minister of defense (1953–55); chairman of the Histadrut (1955–61); known for his role in the Lavon Affair.

Leibovitz, Yeshayahu (1903–94). Latvian-born; scientist, philosopher, and social critic; professor at the Hebrew University; among the first to voice opposition to the Dimona project.

Lie, Haakon (1905–). Secretary-general of Norway's Labor Party (*Arbeiderpartiet*, with a social-democratic orientation) in the 1950s and 1960s; a friend of Israel; instrumental in promoting the Norwegian-Israeli heavy-water deal.

Lior, Israel (1921–81). Polish-born; brigadier general, IDF; military assistant to Levi Eshkol and Golda Meir (1966–74).

Lipkin, Harry J. (Zvi) (1921–). American-born, immigrated to Israel in 1950; nuclear physicist; was recruited in 1952 to work for the IAEC; trained in reactor physics in Saclay, France (1953–54); consultant to the IAEC (1956–58); involved in the early discussions about Dimona; professor at the Weizmann Institute (1954–).

Livneh, Eliezer. Writer, editor, commentator; leading MAPAI member (1940s); Knesset member (1950s); expelled from MAPAI (1956); founder of the Committee for the Denuclearization of the Middle East (1962–66); among the founders of the Greater Israel movement (1967).

Mardor, Munya M. (1913–84). Haganah operative; director of EMET (1952–58); founding director of RAFAEL (1958–70).

McCloy, John J. (1895–1989). Lawyer and diplomat; assistant secretary of war (1942–45); president of the World Bank (1946–49); military governor and high commissioner for Germany (1949–52); instrumental in the creation of the Arms Control and Disarmament Agency (ACDA) (1961); sent to Egypt twice to discuss arms control with Nasser (1963–64).

McCone, John A. (1902–91). Businessman, government official; founded the Bechtel-McCone construction company (1937); assistant secretary of defense (1948–50); undersecretary of the air force (1950–53); chairman of the AEC (1958–60); director of the CIA (1961–65).

McNamara, Robert S. (1916–). Secretary of defense under Presidents John F. Kennedy and Lyndon B. Johnson (1961–67); president of the World Bank (1968–81).

Meir, Golda (1898–1978). Russian-born, American-educated; MAPAI leader, minister of labor (1949–56); foreign minister (1956–65); MAPAI secretary general (1965–68); fourth prime minister of Israel (1969–74).

Mollet, Guy (1905–75). Socialist prime minister of France under the Fourth Republic (1956–57).

Nasser, Gamal Abdul (1918–70). Leader in the Free Officers movement that toppled King Farouk (22 July 1952); president of Egypt (1954–70); among the organizers of the Bandung Conference (18–25 April 1955), which created the nonaligned movement.

Ne'eman, Yuval (1925–). Palestinian-born; distinguished theoretical physicist; colonel, IDF (1948–60); Ph.D. in theoretical physics (1962); director of Nachal Soreq (1961–63); founder of the Department of Physics at Tel Aviv University; president of Tel Aviv University (1971–75); member and acting chairman of IAEC (1966–92); minister of science (1982–84, 1988–92); discovered classification of elementary particles (1961) and conceived quarks as constituents of protons, neutrons, and so on (1962).

Nixon, Richard M. (1913–94). U.S. congressman (1946–50) and senator (1951–53) from California; U.S. vice president (1953–61); thirty-seventh president of the United States (1969–74).

Pelah, Israel (1923–82). Polish-born, came to Israel as a child; educated in Israel and Holland; nuclear physicist (experimental); was in the first group of Israelis sent overseas in 1949 to study nuclear physics; built the Nachal Soreq reactor; appointed director of the Soreq Nuclear Research Center (1971).

Peres, Shimon (1923–). Polish-born, came to Israel as a child; Ben Gurion's protégé; director-general of the Ministry of Defense (1953–59); deputy minister of defense and MAPAI Knesset member (1959–65); RAFI secretary general (1965–69); minister of communication (1969–74); minister of defense (1974–77, 1995–96); minister of finance (1986–88); foreign minister (1988–90; 1992–95); prime minister (1984–86; 1995–96); played a central role in the Israeli nuclear project during its first decade (1955–65).

Perrin, Francis (1901–1992). French nuclear physicist; professor of nuclear physics at the University of Paris (1946–51); high commissioner of the French Atomic Energy Commission (1951–70).

Pineau, Christian (1904–). French minister of foreign affairs (1956–58).

Pleat, George B. (1922–). Chemist and industrial engineer; deputy director AEC Division of Intelligence (1960–65); assistant director for reactor products, AEC; member and team leader in three AEC visits to Dimona (1967–69).

Pratt, Emanuel (Manes) (1911–1988). Polish-born; engineer; colonel, IDF; headed IDF Engineering Corps (1948) and the Ordnance Corps (1951); military attaché in Burma (1955–57); in charge of building the Dimona reactor (1958–66).

Rabin, Yitzhak (1922–95). Palestinian-born; lieutenant general, IDF; seventh chief-of-staff (1964–68); ambassador to the United States (1968–72); prime minister (1974–77; 1992–95); minister of defense (1984–90, 1992–95).

Racah, Giulio (Yoel) (1909–65). Italian-born; founder of the Department of Theoretical Physics at the Hebrew University and its first professor in that subject; member of the IAEC (1952–58).

Randers, Gunnar (1914–92). Norwegian physicist; joined the Norwegian military forces in exile in the United Kingdom, working mostly on radar research; later involved in the Alsos operation; after the war founded and directed the Norwegian Institute for Atomic Energy Research; known worldwide as a champion of the peaceful use of nuclear energy.

Ratner, Jenka (Yevgeni) (1909–77). Engineer; weapons designer; among the founders of HEMED, EMET, and RAFAEL; the first head of the Israeli nuclear project.

Reid, Ogden R. (1925–). U.S. ambassador to Israel (1959–61).

Richardson, Elliot L. (1920–). Lawyer and government official; undersecretary of state (1969–70); secretary of health, education, and welfare (1970–73); secretary of defense (1973); attorney general (1973); secretary of commerce (1976–77).

Rogers, William P. (1913–). Secretary of state in the Nixon administration (1969–73)

Rostow, Walt W. (1916–). Economist; deputy national security adviser to Presidents John F. Kennedy and Lyndon B. Johnson (1961–66); national security adviser to President Johnson (1966–69).

Rusk, Dean (1909–94). Secretary of state under Presidents John F. Kennedy and Lyndon B. Johnson (1961–69).

Sambursky, Shmuel (1900–90). German-born; the Hebrew University's first physics lecturer; later chairman of the scientific council; among the founding members of the IAEC (1952–58).

Sapir, Pinhas (1909–1975). Polish-born; MAPAI leader; minister of trade and industry (1955–63); minister of finance (1963–68, 1969–74); the only cabinet minister to oppose the Dimona project.

Saunders, Harold (Hal) (1930–). National Security Council staff member for the Middle East under Presidents Lyndon B. Johnson, Richard M. Nixon, and Gerald Ford (1968–75).

Seaborg, Glenn T. (1912–1999). Nuclear chemist and a Noble Laureate (1951); chairman of the AEC under Presidents John F. Kennedy, Lyndon B. Johnson, and Richard M. Nixon (1961–71).

Sharett, Moshe (1894–1965). Russian-born; MAPAI leader; Israel's first foreign minister (1948–56) and second prime minister (1953–55).

Sisco, Joseph (1919–). Assistant secretary of state for Near Eastern Affairs (1969–74).

Smith, Hedrick (1933—). Journalist, author, commentator, and documentary creator. A veteran *New York Times* correspondent who reported from Saigon, Paris, Cairo, Moscow, and Washington. Smith broke the story "U.S. Assumes Israelis Have A-Bomb or Its Parts" on 18 July 1970.

Soustelle, Jacques (1912–90). Anthropologist specializing in the Aztec and Mayan cultures; French politician; member or the Free France forces during the Second World War; governor-general of Algeria (1955–56); minister of information (1958); minister of nuclear energy (1959–60); broke with de Gaulle over the issue of Algerian independence.

Staebler, Ulysses M. (1920–?) Senior scientist, AEC; participated in the first four American visits to Dimona (1961–65).

Strauss, Lewis (1896–1974). Investment banker; architect of American nuclear policies in the 1950s; commissioner and chairman of the AEC (1948–50, 1953–58).

Symington, Stuart (1901–88). U.S. senator from Missouri (1952–75); dealt extensively with nuclear proliferation.

Talbot, Phillips. (1915–) Assistant secretary of state for Near Eastern and South Asian affairs under President John F. Kennedy.

Talmi, Igal (1925–). Palestinian-born; in the first group of Israelis who went overseas in 1949 to study physics; one of the founders of the Department of Nuclear Physics at the Weizmann Institute; official escort of one of the American visits to Dimona (1965).

Teller, Edward (1908–). Hungarian-born; theoretical physicist, known as the father of the Hydrogen Bomb; founder of Lawrence Livermore National Laboratory (LLNL); associate director and director of LLNL (1954–75).

Tolkovsky, Dan (1921–). Palestinian-born; major general, IDF; commander of the Israeli Air Force (1955–58); since 1958 served in various posts related to the Israeli nuclear project; member of the IAEC.

U Thant (1909–74). Burmese diplomat; secretary-general of the United Nations (1962–71).

Warnke, Paul C. (1920–). Lawyer and government official; assistant secretary of defense for international security (1967–69); ACDA director (1977–78).

Webber, Robert T. (1921–?). Science attaché in the American Embassy in Tel Aviv in the early to mid-1960s.

Weisgal, Meyer (1894–1977). Chaim Weizmann's aide; chairman of the Executive Committee of the Weizmann Institute (1949–66); president of the Weizmann Institute (1966–70); chancellor of the Weizmann Institute (1976–77).

Weizman, Ezer (1924–). Palestinian-born; major general, IDF; commander of the Israeli Air Force (1958–65); chief of operations (1965–70); minister of defense (1977–80); seventh President of Israel (1993–).

Weizmann, Chaim (1874–1952). Russian-born; chemist; prominent Zionist leader; founder of the Daniel Sieff (later renamed Weizmann) Institute (1934); first president of Israel (1948–52).

Yekutieli, Gideon (1926–1999). Palestinian-born; physicist; in the first group of Israelis who were sent overseas in 1949 to study physics; one of the founders of the Department of Nuclear Physics at the Weizmann Institute.

Zur, Zvi (1923–). Russia-born; lieutenant general in the IDF; sixth chief-of-staff of the IDF (1961–63); special assistant to the minister of defense (1967–74); served in various posts related to nuclear matters; member of the IAEC.

ORGANIZATIONS AND CONCEPTS

Achdut Ha'Avodah (Unity of Labor). A Zionist political party; founded by Berl Katzenelson and David Ben Gurion in 1919; in 1930 merged with *Ha'Poel Ha'Tzair* to form MAPAI; revived in 1944 as an opposition to Ben Gurion within MAPAI; in 1949 joined with *Ha'Shomer Ha'Tzair* to form the left-wing party MAPAM; in 1954 split from MAPAM to become an independent party. The party combined a leftist economic philosophy with an activist, defense-oriented foreign policy. Since 1955 *Achdut Ha'Avodah* was a junior partner in MAPAI-led coalition. In 1965 it merged with MAPAI to form the *Ma'arach* (Alignment); in 1968 RAFI (see below) joined the Alignment to form Israel's Labor Party.

Al Ahram. The most influential newspaper in Egypt; achieved its preeminent position in the 1950s and 1960s, under the editorship of Mohammed Heikal.

Atoms for Peace. An initiative by President Dwight D. Eisenhower, announced in December 1953, to promote the peaceful uses of atomic energy.

Committee for the Denuclearization of the Middle East (1962–66). A committee created by intellectuals and public figures in Israel to promote the idea of a Middle East free of nuclear weapons.

Committee of Seven. Ministerial inquiry committee, composed of seven cabinet members, established by David Ben Gurion in October 1960 to look into the Lavon Affair.

EMET (*Agaf Mechkar Ve'tichun*). The organization in charge of defense research at the

Ministry of Defense (1952–58), headed by Professor Ernst David Bergmann as head of research and Munya M. Mardor as chief administrator.

Haganah (Defense). The underground militia of the Yishuv, the Jewish community in Palestine. In 1948, after the state of Israel was established, the Haganah was renamed the Israeli Defense Forces (IDF), Israel's national army.

HEMED GIMMEL. The HEMED unit in charge of exploration of precious minerals and energy; some of its personnel and resources were transferred to the IAEC when the latter was established in 1952 within the Ministry of Defense (EMET).

Histadrut. Israel's General Federation of Labor, founded in 1920.

Knesset. The parliament of Israel, composed of 120 members.

Lavon Affair. This political affair originated when Pinhas Lavon demanded that David Ben Gurion exonerate him of the charge that he was responsible for the "mishap" in Egypt in 1954, when Lavon was minister of defense, and Ben Gurion refused. The subsequent controversy continued until the mid 1960s, weakening both the ruling party MAPAI and Ben Gurion's regime. The disclosure of the Dimona reactor, and the domestic debate that followed it, were overshadowed by the affair.

Machon (Institute) 3. EMET's main facility of research and development in the Haifa area; renamed Machon David after Ernst David Bergmann.

Machon (Institute) 4. EMET's facility related to atomic energy, formerly HEMED GIMMEL; subsequently known as the IAEC laboratories. In 1960 it merged with the Soreq Nuclear Establishment (MAMAG).

MAPAI (Hebrew acronym for *Mifleget Poalei Eretz Yisrael*, or Israel's Workers Party). MAPAI was the ruling party in the State of Israel's early history (1948–65). Founded in 1930 as a result of the merger between *Achdut Ha'Avodah* and *Ha'Poel Ha'Tzair*, for thirty-five years it dominated Israel's public life. In 1965 it became the Alignment (*Ma'arach*), and in 1968 it merged with two other factions—*Achdut Ha'Avodah* and RAFI—to form Israel's Labor Party.

MAPAI Youth. A group of Ben Gurion's younger supporters in MAPAI whose leaders were Shimon Peres and Moshe Dayan. The group challenged the Old Guard of MAPAI leadership and was recognized as the core of political support for the Dimona project.

MAPAM (Hebrew acronym for *Mifleget Ha'Poalim Ha'Meuchedet*, or the United Workers Party). A small socialist-Zionist party established in 1948 by the union of *Achdut Ha'Avodah* and *Ha'Shomer Ha'Tzair* as a left-wing opposition to MAPAI. In 1954 Achdut Ha'Avodah split, and the *Ha'Shomer Ha'Tzair* element retained the name MAPAM.

Nachal Soreq Nuclear Center (*Merkaz Le'mechkar Gari'ini*, MAMAG). Israel's smaller nuclear center, about fifteen miles south of Tel Aviv. It includes a swimming-pool 5-MW reactor purchased from the United States as part of the Atoms for Peace program. It was opened in 1960 and, until the mid-1960s, was safeguarded by the AEC, then by the IAEA.

NORATOM. A Norwegian company established in 1957 with the aim of becoming a leading national producer and exporter of nuclear technology.

RAFAEL (Hebrew acronym for *Rashut Le'pituach Emtzaei Lechima,* or Armament Development Authority). Israel's central organization in charge of research, development, and production of high-tech weapon systems. Successor of EMET, it was founded 1958.

RAFI. (Hebrew acronym for *Reshimat Poalei Yisrael,* or Israel's Workers List). The party Ben Gurion founded in 1965 after his split with Eshkol. Among its other leaders were Shimon Peres and Moshe Dayan. The party advocated reliance on science and technology, particularly nuclear energy.

Saint Gobain Nucleire. The French company that built the Israeli reactor at Dimona.

Weizmann Institute of Science (Rehovot, Israel). Israel's main science research center. It was founded by Chaim Weizmann in 1934 as the Sieff Institute, and in 1949 was renamed after its founder.

Yishuv (Settlement). The Jewish community in Palestine during the British mandate period (1918–48).

Sources and Bibliography

Interviews and Communications*

Abramov, Shneor Zalman. Jerusalem, 26 August 1992.

Arad, Shimshon. Jerusalem, August 1994.

Arnan, Azaryahau (Sini). Numerous interviews and correspondence, 1992–97.

Austin, Granville. Washington, D.C., 15 September 1997.

Bar-On, Mordechai. Jerusalem, 1 July 1992.

Bar Zohar, Michael. Tel Aviv, 7 September 1992.

Battle, Lucious D. Washington, D.C., 27 December 1994, 3 February 1995.

Ben Porat, Yoel. Glilot, 1994.

Ben Porat, Yeshayahu. Tel Aviv, 4 September 1992.

Bergmann, Hani. Jerusalem, 19 August 1992.

Brugioni, Dino A. Numerous telephone interviews, 1996–97.

Bundy, McGeorge. Numerous interviews, 1992–95.

Bunn, George. Numerous interviews, 1991–97.

Burg, Yossef. Jerusalem, 19 August 1992.

Carle, Remi. Paris, 17 June 1993.

Cohen, Haim. Jerusalem, 3 September 1992.

Crawford, William. Numerous interviews, correspondence, and conversations, 1994–97.

Culler, Floyd. Numerous telephone interviews and correspondence, 1995–97.

Dale, William N. Telephone interview, 24 April 1995.

Dar, Arnon. Haifa, 1 and 10 September 1992.

Dinstein, Zvi. Tel Aviv, 19 July and 6 August 1992.

Dvoretzky, Arie. Rehovot, August 1992.

*This is a partial list. Some interviewees have asked that their names not be listed.

Eilts, Hermann F. Numerous interviews, telephone interviews, and correspondence, 1994–97.

Eshkol, Miriam. Jerusalem, 5 June 1995.

Feldman, Myer (Mike). Numerous interviews and conversations, 1992–97.

Finkelstein, Andre. Paris, 17 June 1993; Marburg, Germany, 4 July 1997.

Finney, John W. Numerous telephone interviews, 1995–97.

Freier, Shalheveth. Rehovot, numerous interviews and conversations, 1991–94.

Gali, Ealkana. Tel Aviv, 23 July 1992.

Gazit, Mordechai. Numerous interviews and correspondence, 1992–97.

Gleysteen, Culver. Numerous interviews and correspondence, 1996–97.

Goldschmidt, Bertrand. Paris, 15 June 1993.

Gur, Shlomo. Tel Aviv, 20 July 1992.

Haber-Schaim, Uri. Numerous interviews and corresopndence, 1994–97.

Hadden, John. Numerous interviews, telephone interviews, and conversations, 1994–97.

Harkavy, Yehoshafat. Jerusalem, 24 September 1992.

Helms, Richard. Numerous telephone interviews, 1996–97.

Hermoni, Avraham. Numerous interviews, 1992–97.

Hod, Mordechai. Tel Aviv, 27 May 1996.

Kaysen, Carl. Cambridge, Mass., numerous interviews and conversations, 1991–97.

Keeny, Spurgeon. Numerous interviews and conversations, 1994–97.

Kintner, Edwin. Numerous telephone interviews, 1995–96.

Komer, Robert W. Numerous interviews and telephone interviews, 1992–97.

Korchin, Amos. Tel Aviv, 18 August 1992.

Kratzer, Myron. Numerous interviews and correspondence, 1992–97.

Leonard, James. Numerous interviews, correspondence, and conversations, 1991–97.

Lipkin, Zvi. Numerous correspondence and conversations, 1994–97.

Lipson, Shneor. Rehovot, 23 December 1992.

Maor, Uri. Numerous interviews and letters, 1992–96.

Mushin, David. Rehovot, 8 July 1992.

Navon, Yitzhak. Jerusalem, 19 August 1992.

Ne'eman, Yuval. Numerous interviews, correspondence and conversations, 1994–97.

Nimrod, Yoran. Ein Hachoresh, 4 September 1992.

Parker, Richard B. Numerous interviews, correspondence, and conversations, 1995–97.

Pelah, Zvi. Savion, 24 August 1992.

Peled, Matti. Tel Aviv, 9 and 16 July 1992.

Peres, Shimon. Tel Aviv, 31 March 1991.

Pleat, George. Telephone interviews and correspondence, 1996–97.

Quandt, William B. Numerous interviews and conversations, 1993–97.

Rafael, Gideon. Telephone interview, summer 1994.

Rechav, Uri. Numerous conversations, 1995–97.

Reid, Ogden. Numerous interviews and telephone interviews, 1995.

Rosenfeld, Shalom. Tel Aviv, 13 August 1992.

Sadeh, Dror. Numerous interviews and correspondence, 1992–94.

Samore, Gary. Washington, D.C., 26 November 1997.

Saunders, Harold. Numerous interviews and conversations, 1995–96.

Schiff, Ze'ev. Tel Aviv, numerous conversations, 1992–97.

Seaborg, Glenn T. Numerous interviews, telephone interviews, and correspondence, 1995–96.

Shamir, Yedidyah. Ramat Gam, 21 December 1992.

Sisco, Joseph J. Washington, D.C., 1995–97.

Smilansky, Yizahar. Maishar, 20 August 1992.

Sterner, Michael. Washington, D.C., 3 April 1995.

Steury, Donald. Telephone interview, 24 July 1997.

Talmi, Igal. Rehovot, June 1995.

Tamir, Avraham (Abrasha). Numerous interviews and conversations, 1992–94.

Tamir, Yossef. Tel Aviv, 20 August 1992.

Teller, Edward. Telephone conversation, 27 April 1996.

Van-Doren, Charles. Numerous telephone conversations and correspondence, 1994–96.

Warnke, Paul C.. Numerous interviews and correspondence, 1993–97.

Ya'akobi, Gad. Tel Aviv, 16 July 1992.

Yekutieli, Gideon. Rehovot, September 1995.

Zak, Moshe. Tel Aviv, June 1996.

Zur, Ze'ev. Ramat Efal, 7 July 1992.

ARCHIVES

AMERICAN ARCHIVES AND DOCUMENT DEPOSITORIES

Dwight D. Eisenhower Library (DDEL), Abilene Kans.

White House Central Files (WHCF).

John F. Kennedy Library (JFKL), Boston, Mass.

National Security Files (NSF).

Lyndon B. Johnson Library (LBJL), Austin, Tex.

National Security Files (NSF).

National Security Archive (NSA), George Washington University, Washington, D.C.

United States National Archives (USNA), College Park, Md.

Record Group (RG).

Central Foreign Policy Files (CFPF).

ISRAELI ARCHIVES AND DOCUMENT DEPOSITORIES

David Ben Gurion Archive (DBGA), at Ben Gurion Research Center, Sdeh Boker.
David Ben Gurion Diaries (DBGD).
Israel State Archives (ISA), Jerusalem, Israel.
Foreign Ministry Record Group (FMRG).

PERSONAL COLLECTIONS

Odd Karsten Tveit Collection, Oslo, Norway.
Ya'acov Sharett Collection, Tel Aviv, Israel.
Uri Haber-Schaim Collection, Belmont, Mass.
Eliezer Livneh Collection, Yad Tabenkin Archives, Ramat Efal, Israel.

GOVERNMENT DOCUMENTS

UNITED STATES GOVERNMENT

Department of State. *Documents on Disarmament, 1945–1959*. Washington, D.C.:
United States Government Printing Office, 1960.
————. *Foreign Relations of the United States, 1958–1960*, vol. 13, *Arab-Israeli
Dispute; United Arab Republic; North Africa*. Washington, D.C.: United States
Government Printing Office, 1992.
————. *Foreign Relations of the United States, 1958–1960*, vol. 17, *Near East, 1961–
1962*. Washington, D.C.: United States Government Printing Office, 1994.
————. *Foreign Relations of the United States, 1958–1960*, vol. 18, *Near East,
1962–1963*. Washington, D.C.: United States Government Printing Office, 1995.
Dwight D. Eisenhower. *Public Papers of the Presidents*; 1953, Washington, D.C.:
United States Printing Office and the Office of the Federal Register, National
Archives and Record Service, General Services Administration, 1960.
John F. Kennedy. *Public Papers of the Presidents; 1961–1963*, 3 vols. Washington,
D.C.: United States Government Printing Office and the Office of the Federal
Register, National Archives and Records Service, General Services Administration,
1962–64.

GOVERNMENT OF ISRAEL

Israel Atomic Energy Commission. *Shalheveth Freier, 1920–1994* (in Hebrew). Tel
Aviv: Israel Atomic Energy Commission, 1995.
State of Israel. Israel Government Yearbook, 1955 (in Hebrew). Jerusalem: State
of Israel, 1956.
————. *Documents on the Foreign Policy of Israel*, vol. 14, *1960*. Edited by Baruch
Gilead. Jerusalem: Israel State Archives, 1997.

NEWSPAPERS

ENGLISH LANGUAGE NEWSPAPERS

Boston Globe
Daily Express
Economist
Evening Star
Jerusalem Post
Jerusalem Report
Jewish Observer and Middle East Review
Las Vegas Review Journal
New York Times
Newsweek
Sunday Times (London)
Time

FOREIGN LANGUAGE NEWSPAPERS

Al'Ahram
Al Hamishmar
Air and Cosmos/Aviation International (French)
Davar
Ha'aretz
Ha'Boker
Ha'Doar
Ha'Yom
Ha'Olam Ha'Zeh
Kol Ha'Am
Koteret Rashit
La'Merchav
Ma'archot
Ma'ariv
Nativ
Pi Ha'Aton
Rehovot
Tel Aviv
Yediot Achronot
Yediot Achronot-Shivah Yamim

UNPUBLISHED MATERIALS

Lipkin, Zvi. "Early History of Physics in Weizmaim."

Katzir, Ephraim. "Introductory Remarks." In *In Memory of Ernst David Bergmann* (in Hebrew). Address at the Opening Session of the Ninth Jerusalem Symposium on Metal-Ligand Interactions in Organic Chemistry and Biochemistry, Jerusalem, 29 March 1976.

Walsh, Jim. "Why States Don't 'Go Nuclear.'" Paper presented at the American Political Science Association Meeting, San Francisco, 31 August 1995.

————. "Nuclear Threats, Resources Constraints, and State Behavior: Egypt's Nuclear Decision Making, 1955–1992." Paper presented at the Western Political Science Association Meeting, 10 March 1994.

JOURNAL ARTICLES, ESSAYS, AND BOOK CHAPTERS

FOREIGN LANGUAGE ARTICLES AND ESSAYS

Allon, Yigal. "The Last Stage of the War of Independence" (in Hebrew). *Ot* (November 1967): 5–13.

Dostrovsky, Israel. "The Establishment of the Israel Atomic Energy Commission." In *David Ben Gurion and the Development of Science in Israel* (in Hebrew), 44–49. Jerusalem: Israel National Academy of Science, 1989.

Frank, Gideon. "Shalheveth's Nuclear Legacy" (in Hebrew). In *Shalheveth Freier, 1920–1994*, 30–43. Tel Aviv: Israel Atomic Energy Commission, 1995.

Katzir, Ephraim. "The Beginning of Defense Research: Ben Gurion and the Hemed." In *David Ben Gurion and the Development of Science in Israeli* (in Hebrew), 25–42. Jerusalem: Israel National Academy of Science, 1989.

Mushin, David. "Ben Gurion's Support for Research, Science, and Technology." In *David Ben Gurion and the Development of Science in Israel* (in Hebrew), 19–24. Jerusalem: Israel National Academy of Science, 1989.

Peres, Shimon. "About Shalheveth" (in Hebrew). In *Shalheveth Freier, 1920–1994*, 7–14. Tel Aviv: Israel Atomic Energy Commission, 1995.

Sambursky, Shmuel. "Ben Gurion and the Scientific Council." In *David Ben Gurion and the Development of Science in Israel* (in Hebrew), 12–18. Jerusalem: Israel National Academy of Science, 1989.

Shalom, Zaki. "Ben Gurion's and Sharett's Opposition to Territorial Demands on Israel, 1949–1956" (in Hebrew). *Iyunim Be'Tkumat Israel* 2 (1992): 197–213.

————. "The Reaction of the Western Powers to the Disclosure of the Dimona Reactor in the Early 1960s" (in Hebrew). *Iyunim Be'Tkumat Israel* 4 (1994): 136–74.

ENGLISH LANGUAGE JOURNAL ARTICLES AND ESSAYS

Bar Joseph, Uri. "The Hidden Debate: The Formation of Nuclear Doctrines in the Middle East." *Journal of Strategic Studies* 5, no. 2 (June 1982): 205–25.

Bar-Siman-Tov, Ya'acov. "Ben Gurion and Sharett: Conflict Management and Great Power Constraints in Israeli Foreign Policy." *Middle Eastern Studies* 24, no. 3 (July 1988): 330–56.

Cohen, Avner. "Nuclear Weapons, Opacity, and Israeli Democracy." In Avner Yaniv, ed., *National Security and Democracy in Israel*, 197–225. Boulder: Lynne Rienner, 1993.

———. "Toward a New Middle East: Rethinking the Nuclear Question." Cambridge: Center for International Studies, Massachusetts Institute of Technology, Defense and Arms Control Studies (DACS) Working Paper, November 1994.

———. "The Nuclear Equation in the Middle East." *Nonproliferation Review* 2, no. 2 (winter 1995): 12–30.

———. "Peres: Peacemaker, Nuclear Pioneer." *Bulletin of the Atomic Scientists* 52, no. 3 (May 1996): 16–17.

Cohen, Avner, and Benjamin Frankel. "Opaque Nuclear Proliferation." In Benjamin Frankel, ed., *Opaque Nuclear Proliferation: Methodological and Policy Implications*, 14–44. London: Frank Cass, 1991.

Dostrovsky, Israel, and F. S. Klein. "On Heavy Water Analysis." *Annals of Chemistry* 24 (1952).

Dostrovsky, Israel, et. al. "Optimal Flow in Fractionating Columns for Isotopes Separation." *Bulletin Research Council Israel*, no. 2 (1952).

Falk, Richard. "Nuclear Weapons and the Renewal of Democracy." In Avner Cohen and Steven Lee, eds., *Nuclear Weapons and the Future of Humanity: The Fundamental Questions*, 437–56. Totowa, N.J.: Rowman and Allenheld, 1986.

Forland, Astrid. "Norway's Nuclear Odyssey: From Optimistic Proponent to Nonproliferator." *Nonproliferation Review* 4, no. 2 (winter 1997): 1–16.

Frankel, Benjamin. "Notes on the Nuclear Underworld." *The National Interest*, no. 9 (fall 1987): 122–126.

Goldschmidt, Bertrand. "The French Atomic Energy Program." *Bulletin of the Atomic Scientists* 18, no. 7 (September 1962): 39–42.

———. "The French Atomic Energy Program." *Bulletin of the Atomic Scientists* 18, no. 8 (October 1962): 46–48.

Haber-Schaim, Uri, Yehuda Yeivan, and Gideon Yekutieli. "Production of *K* Mesons." *Physical Review* 94, no. 1 (1954): 184–88.

Levite, Ariel E., and Emily B. Landau. "Arab Perceptions of Israel's Nuclear Posture, 1960–1967." *Israel Studies* 1, no. 1 (spring 1996): 34–51.

Shlaim, Avi. "Conflicting Approaches to Israel's Relations with the Arabs: Ben Gurion and Sharett, 1953–1956." *Middle East Journal* 37, no. 2 (spring 1983): 180–201.

Shlaim, Avi, and Raymond Tanter. "Decisions Process, Choices, and Consequences: Israel's Deep-Penetration Bombing in Egypt, 1970." *World Politics* 30, no. 4 (June 1978): 483–516.

Taylor, Theodore G. "Nuclear Tests and Nuclear Weapons." In Benjamin Frankel, ed., *Opaque Nuclear Proliferation: Methodology and Policy Implications*, 175–90. London: Frank Cass, 1991.

Warnke, Paul C. "Book Review: *The Samson Option*." *Bulletin of the Atomic Scientists* 48 (March 1992): 41–42.

BOOKS

FOREIGN LANGUAGE BOOKS

Allon, Yigal. *A Curtain of Sand* (in Hebrew). Tel Aviv: Ha'kibbutz Ha'meuchad, 1968.

———. *Contriving Warfare* (in Hebrew). Tel Aviv: Ha'kibbutz Ha'meuchad, 1990.

Bar-Zohar, Michael. *Ben Gurion* (in Hebrew), 3 vols. Tel Aviv: Zmora Bitan, 1987.

Bar-On, Mordechai. *Challenge and Quarrel: The Road to Sinai, 1956* (in Hebrew). Sdeh Boker: The Ben Gurion Research Center, 1991.

———. *The Gates of Gaza: Israel's Defense and Foreign Policy, 1955–1957* (in Hebrew). Tel Aviv: Am Oved, 1992.

Ben Gurion, David. *With What Will We Face the Future* (in Hebrew). Tel Aviv: Merkaz Mifleget Po'alei Eretz Israel, November 1948.

———. *When Israel Fights* (in Hebrew). Tel Aviv: Am Oved, 1950.

———. *Vision and Direction* (in Hebrew). Tel Aviv: Am Oved, 1956.

———. *War Diaries, 1948–1949* (in Hebrew), vol. 3. Tel Aviv: Misrad Habitachon, 1982.

Carlier, Claude, and Luc Berger. *Dassault: 50 ans d'aventure aeronatique*. Paris: Editions du chene, 1996.

Committee for Denuclearization of the Middle East. *Israel-Arab: Nuclearization or Denuclearization* (in Hebrew). Tel Aviv: Amikam, 1962.

Dayan, Moshe. *New Map: Different Attitudes* (in Hebrew). Haifa: Shikmona, 1969.

———. *Milestones* (in Hebrew). Tel Aviv: Edanim, 1976.

Evron, Yair. *Israel's Nuclear Dilemma* (in Hebrew). Tel Aviv: Ha'kibbutz Ha'meuchad, 1987.

Gilboa, Moshe A. *Six Days, Six Years* (in Hebrew). Tel Aviv: Am Oved, 1968.

Golan, Matti. *Peres* (in Hebrew). Tel Aviv: Schocken, 1982.

Greenberg, Yitzhak. *Defense Budget and Military Power: The Case of Israel* (in Hebrew). Tel Aviv: Misrad Ha'bitachon, 1977.

Haber, Eitan. *Today War Will Break Out: The Reminiscences of Brig. Gen. Israel Lior, Aide-de-Camp to Prime Ministers Levi Eshkol and Golda Meir* (in Hebrew). Tel Aviv: Edanim, 1987.

Keren, Michael. *Ben Gurion and the Intellectuals*. Sdeh Boker: The Ben Gurion Research Center with the Bialick Institute, 1988.

Klienman, Aharon, and Reuven Pedatzur. *Rearming Israel: Defense Procurement Through the 1990s* (in Hebrew). Jerusalem: Jaffe Center for Strategic Studies and Westview, 1991.

Levite, Ariel E., and Emily B. Landau. *Israel's Nuclear Image: Arab Perceptions of Israel's Nuclear Posture* (in Hebrew). Tel Aviv: Papyrus, 1994.

Mardor, Munya M. *Rafael* (in Hebrew). Tel Aviv: Misrad Habitachon, 1981.

Margalit, Dan. *I Saw Them* (in Hebrew). Tel Aviv: Zmora Bitan, 1997.

Nakdimon, Shlomo. *Toward the Zero Hour: The Drama That Preceded the Six-Day War* (in Hebrew). Tel Aviv: Ramdor, 1968.

Péan, Pierre. *Les deux bombes*. Paris: Fayard, 1981.

Rabin, Yitzhak. *A Service Record* (in Hebrew), 2 vols. Tel Aviv: Ma'ariv, 1979.

Randers, Gunnar. *The World's Hope or Its Demise* (in Norwegian). Oslo: J. W. Cappeles forlag, 1947.

Schiff, Ze'ev. *Phantom over the Nile: The Story of the Israeli Air Corps* (in Hebrew). Haifa: Shikmona, 1970.

Schueftan, Daniel. *Attrition: Egypt's Post-War Political Strategy* (in Hebrew). Tel Aviv: Misrad Habitachon, 1989.

Shaham, David. *Israel: 40 Years* (in Hebrew). Tel Aviv: Am Oved, 1991.

Shalom, Zaki. *David Ben Gurion: The State of Israel and the Arab World, 1949–1956* (in Hebrew). Sdeh Boker: Ben Gurion University of the Negev Press, 1995.

Sharett, Ya'akov, ed. *Moshe Sharett Diaries* (in Hebrew). Tel Aviv: Ma'ariv, 1978.

Tamir, Avraham. *A Soldier in Search of Peace* (in Hebrew). Tel Aviv: Edanim, 1988.

Teveth, Shabtai. *Calaban* (in Hebrew). Tel Aviv: Ish Dor, 1992.

Tveit, Odd Karsten. *All for Israel: Oslo-Jerusalem, 1948–1978* (in Norwegian). Oslo: J.W. Cappelens Forlag, 1977.

Weizmann, Chaim. *Trial and Deed* (in Hebrew). Tel Aviv: Schocken, 1964.

———. *Selected Letters* (in Hebrew). Tel Aviv: Am Oved, 1988.

Yaniv, Avner. *Politics and Strategy in Israel* (in Hebrew). Tel Aviv: Sifriat Ha'Poalim, 1994.

ENGLISH LANGUAGE BOOKS

Albright, David, et al. *Plutonium and Highly Enriched Uranium, 1996: World Inventories, Capabilities, and Policies*. Stockholm: SIPRI/Oxford University Press, 1977.

Aron, Raymond. *The Great Debate: Theories of Nuclear Strategy*. Garden City, N.Y.: Doubleday, 1965.

Aronson, Shlomo, with Oded Brosh. *The Politics and Strategy of Nuclear Weapons in the Middle East: Opacity, Theory, and Reality, 1960–1991: An Israeli Perspective*. Albany: State University of New York Press, 1992.

Bar-Siman-Tov, Ya'acov. *The Israeli-Egyptian War of Attrition, 1969–1970: A Case Study of Limited Local War*. New York: Columbia University Press, 1980.

Bar-Zohar, Michael. *Embassies in Crisis: Diplomats and Demagogues Behind the Six Day War*. Englewood Cliffs, N.Y.: Prentice-Hall, 1970.

Beaton, Leonard. *Must the Bomb Spread?* Harmondsworth, England: Penguin, 1966.

Ben Meir, Yehudah. *Civil-Military Relations in Israel.* New York: Columbia University Press, 1995.

Bhatia, Shyam. *Nuclear Rivals in the Middle East.* London: Routledge, 1988.

Bialer, Uri. *Between East and West: Israel's Foreign Policy Orientation, 1948–1956.* Cambridge: Cambridge University Press, 1990.

Bissel, Richard M, Jr., with Jonathon E. Lewis and Frances T. Pudlo. *Reflections of a Cold War Warrior: From Yalta to the Bay of Pigs.* New Haven: Yale University Press, 1996.

Brecher, Michael, with Benjamin Geist. *Decisions in Crisis: Israel, 1967 and 1973.* Berkeley: University of California Press, 1980.

Brugioni, Dino A. *Eyeball to Eyeball: The Inside Story of the Cuban Missile Crisis.* Edited by Robert F. McCort. New York: Random House, 1991.

Bundy, McGeorge. *Danger and Survival: Choices about the Bomb in the First Fifty Years.* New York: Random House, 1988.

Bunn, George. *Arms Control by Committee: Managing Negotiations with the Russians.* Stanford: Stanford University Press, 1992.

Bunn, George, and Roland M. Timerbaev. *Nuclear Verification Under the NPT: What Should It Cover—How Far May It Go?* PPN Study, no. 5. The Mountbatten Center for International Studies, University of South Hampton, April 1994.

Cohen, Eliezer. *Israel's Best Defense: The First Full Story of the Israeli Air Force.* New York: Orion, 1993.

Crosbie, Sylvia K. *A Tacit Alliance: France and Israel from Suez to the Six Day War.* Princeton, N.J.: Princeton University Press, 1974.

Dahl, Robert. *Controlling Nuclear Weapons: Democracy versus Guardianship.* Syracuse: Syracuse University Press, 1985.

Dayan, Moshe. *Moshe Dayan: Story of My Life.* New York: William Morrow, 1976.

De Gaulle, Charles. *Memoirs of Hope: Renewal and Endeavor.* New York: Simon and Schuster, 1971.

Eban, Abba. *Personal Witness: Israel Through My Eyes.* New York: Putnam's, 1992.

Evron, Yair. *Israel's Nuclear Dilemma.* Ithaca: Cornell University Press, 1994.

Gazit, Mordechai. *President Kennedy's Policy Toward the Arab States and Israel: Analysis and Documents.* Tel Aviv: Shiloah Center for Middle Eastern and African Studies, Tel Aviv University, 1983.

Golan, Matti. *Shimon Peres: A Biography.* New York: St. Martin's, 1982.

Goldschmidt, Bertrand. *The Atomic Adventure: Its Political and Technical Aspects.* New York: Pergamon, 1964.

———. *Atomic Rivals.* New Brunswick, N.J.: Rutgers University Press, 1990.

Gowing, Margaret, assisted by Lorna Arnold. *Independence and Deterrence: Britain and Atomic Energy, 1945–1952,* 2 vols. New York: St. Martin's, 1974.

Heikal, Mohammed. *The Road to Ramadan*. New York: Quadrangle/New York Times, 1975.

———. *Illusions of Triumph: An Arab View of the Gulf War*. London: Harper and Collins, 1992.

Hersh, Seymour M. *The Samson Option: Israel's Nuclear Arsenal and American Foreign Policy*. New York: Random House, 1991.

———. *The Price of Power: Kissinger in the Nixon White House*. New York: Summit, 1983.

Hewlett, Richard G., and Jack M. Holl. *Atoms for Peace and War, 1953–1961: Eisenhower and the Atomic Energy Commission*. Berkeley: University of California Press, 1989.

Jabber, Fuad. *Israel and Nuclear Weapons*. London: Catto and Windus, 1971.

Keren, Michael. *Professionalism Against Populism: The Peres Government and Democracy*. Albany: State University of New York Press, 1995.

Kohl, Wilfrid L. *French Nuclear Diplomacy*. Princeton, N.J.: Princeton University Press, 1971.

Korn, David A. *Stalemate: The War of Attrition and Great Power Diplomacy in the Middle East, 1967–1970*. Boulder, Colo.: Westview, 1992.

Mangold, Tom. *Cold Warrior, James Jesus Angleton: The CIA's Master Spy Hunter*. New York: Simon and Schuster, 1991.

Martin, David C. *Wilderness of Mirrors*. New York: Harper and Row, 1980.

Nashif, Taysir N. *Nuclear Warfare in the Middle East: Dimensions and Responsibilities*. Princeton, N.J.: Kingston Press, 1984.

Neff, Donald. *Warriors for Jerusalem: The Six Days That Changed the Middle East*. New York: Simon and Schuster, 1984.

Parker, Richard B. *The Politics of Miscalculation in the Middle East*. Bloomington: Indiana University Press, 1993.

Peres, Shimon. *David's Sling*. London: Weidenfeld and Nicolson, 1970.

———. *From These Men: Seven Founders of the State of Israel*. New York: Wyndham, 1979.

———. *Battling for Peace: Memoirs*. Edited by David Landau. London: Weidenfeld and Nicolson, 1995.

Peres, Shimon, with Arye Naor. *The New Middle East*. New York: Henry Holt, 1993.

Peri, Yoram. *Between Battles and Ballots: Israeli Military in Politics*. New York: Cambridge University Press, 1982.

Quandt, William B. *Decade of Decisions: American Policy Towards the Arab-Israeli Conflict, 1967–1976*. Berkeley: University of California Press, 1977.

Rabin, Yitzhak. *The Rabin Memoirs*. Boston: Little, Brown, 1979.

Reeves, Richard. *President Kennedy: Profile of Power*. New York: Simon and Schuster, 1993.

Rhodes, Richard. *The Making of the Atomic Bomb*. New York: Simon and Schuster, 1986.

Rikhye, Indar Jit. *The Sinai Blunder: Withdrawal of the United Nations Emergency Force Leading to the Six Day War of June 1967.* London: Frank Cass, 1980.

Rose, Norman. *Chaim Weizmann: A Biography.* New York: Viking, 1986.

Rusk, Dean. *As I Saw It: Dean Rusk as Told to Richard Rusk.* Edited by Daniel S. Papp. New York: W. W. Norton, 1990.

Scheinman, Lawrence. *Atomic Energy Policy in France Under the Fourth Republic.* Princeton, N.J.: Princeton University Press, 1965.

———. *The International Atomic Energy Agency and World Nuclear Order.* Washington, D.C.: Resources for the Future, 1987.

Seaborg, Glenn T., with Benjamin S. Loeb. *Kennedy, Khrushchev, and the Test Ban.* Berkeley: University of California Press, 1981.

———. *Stemming the Tide: Arms Control in the Johnson Years.* Lexington, Mass.: Lexington, 1987.

———. *The Atomic Energy Commission Under Nixon: Adjusting to Troubled Times.* New York: St. Martin's, 1993.

Segev, Tom. *The Seventh Million: The Israelis and the Holocaust.* New York: Hill and Wang, 1993.

Sheffer, Gabriel. *Moshe Sharett: Biography of a Political Moderate.* Oxford: Oxford University Press, 1996.

Shils, Edward A. *The Torment of Secrecy.* Chicago: Elephant Paperback, 1996.

Stein, Janice Gross, and Raymond Tanter. *Rational Decision-Making: Israel's Security Choices, 1967.* Columbus: Ohio State University Press, 1980.

Teveth, Shabtai. *Ben Gurion's Spy: The Story of the Political Scandal That Shaped Modern Israel.* New York: Columbia University Press, 1996.

Weismann, Steve, and Herbert Krosney. *The Islamic Bomb: The Nuclear Threat to Israel and the Middle East.* New York: Times Books, 1981.

Weizman, Ezer. *On Eagle's Wing.* New York: Macmillan, 1976.

Yaniv, Avner. *Deterrence Without the Bomb: The Politics of Israeli Strategy.* Lexington, Mass.: Lexington, 1987.

———. *National Security and Democracy in Israel.* Boulder, Colo.: Lynne Rienner, 1993.

Index